The Ideology Behind ISLAMIC *Terrorism*

By

Brother Rachid

ISBN: 978-1-935577-66-9
Brother Rachid
The Ideology Behind Islamic Terrorism

Translated, edited, and amended by Waterlife Publishing.

Table of Contents

A necessary Introduction 5

1 In the beginning, there was hatred.... 11

2 Permanent hatred fuels eternal enmity toward Jews and Christians 37

3 We and the others are the "angels" and the "demons" 53

4 We are "the best nation ever brought forth...." 75

5 From the Prophet to the caliphs, Christians are at the mercy of Islam 95

6 Declaring a person an infidel (*kāfir*) is an Islamic disease 135

7 "Nullifiers of Islam" can transform a Muslim into an infidel 163

8 Inception and rise of Islamic State mirrors Islam 203

9 Raiders and criminal gangs are a past and present part of Islam 237

10 The Islamic legacy of captivity, murder, expulsion, and destruction is revived 277

11 For Islamic terrorists, jihad is an Islamic decree 313

12 The Islamic caliphate dream has become a nightmare 343

13 Decapitating and burning infidels is lawful (*halāl*) 379

14 *Je suis* Charlie ("I am Charlie") | *Je suis Muḥammad* ("I am *Muḥammad*") 423

15 Dābiq is our appointed destination at the end of time 455

16 Is it lawful (*halāl*) to carry out suicide attack operations? 475

17 Islam is at a crossroads in Muslim countries 507

Works Cited 535

Name Index 543

Subject Index 557

A necessary Introduction

Islamic terrorism became a global threat with the manifestation of Al Qaeda and its multipronged attack on the United States on September 11, 2001. In the nearly two decades since that horrific event, the world has been fighting this new kind of terrorism. But this terrorism has continued with little pause, renewed and revived by individuals and groups that have consumed and applied a cursed ideology.

Today Islamic State, the most successful and savage of these groups, is on the verge of an absolute military defeat, and Al Qaeda has lost most of its leaders. Though the immediate future may doom the relevance and power of these two major jihadist terrorist groups, does that mean that this Islamic terrorism has really been defeated when this terrorism remains an ongoing part of breaking news bulletins? What nurtures its regeneration and what generates its ideology?

We will never defeat this terrorism without first defeating the ideology and mind-set that motivates these terrorists to kill others and willingly sacrifice their own lives in killing others. US President Donald Trump has spoken about America's determination to defeat Islamic State and its evil ideology.[1] But what is its ideology? How do we define it without being labeled as fanatics or racists? How do we explore this minefield, which is full of hidden and visible explosives, without any of them blowing up in our faces?

I began writing this book since the day I saw Iraqi Christians, barefoot and naked, heading towards Kurdistan after being deported by Muslim militant groups. I cried bitterly over this unjust, barbaric treatment and decided then to write a book explaining this human tragedy from all aspects.

For I was born into a conservative Muslim family, educated as a Muslim and lived thirty-two years of my life in a Muslim country. I began studying Islam and the Qur'ān from a young age, and I am extremely familiar with the teachings, practices, beliefs, and history of this religion. Since 2007 I have hosted a television program where I debate Muslims about different Islamic topics.

But I have paid the price for criticizing Islam and I still pay now. I was forced to leave my native country, Morocco, because I had decided to leave Islam and to criticize it publicly. At that point it was impossible for me to continue living in Morocco without endangering my wife and me.

I now live in a Western country. I cannot visit any Arab Muslim country because I am well-known in all these countries, and that "celebrity" puts me at great risk. I am not exaggerating if I say that I am the most famous apostate from Islam in the Arab Muslim world. That classification is a death sentence in many Muslim countries. Consequently, I receive dozens of threats on a weekly basis, and I am targeted by extremists—even though I live in a non-Muslim country. I am obliged to employ bodyguards for my protection at venues where I lecture on Islam.

[1] David, Javier E. "Trump Applauds Defeat of ISIS in Raqqa, Promises to Promote 'Lasting Peace' in Syria and 'Justice' for Terrorists." *CNBC.com*. NBCUniversal News Group, 21 Oct. 2017. Web (https://www.cnbc.com/2017/10/21/trump-applauds-defeat-of-isis-in-raqqa-promises-to-promote-lasting-peace-in-syria-and-justice-for-terrorists.html). In his remarks, US President Trump stated that the US-supported Syrian resistance had resulted in "a critical breakthrough in our worldwide campaign to defeat ISIS and its wicked ideology."

My family and I cannot live a normal life because of this subject: Islamic terrorism. It has become entangled in my life, and I am threatened by it every day.

We cannot defeat Islamic terrorism without understanding the reasons behind it. We cannot understand those reasons if we draw red lines around religion. Religion is an essential component in the Middle East. In fact, it is the most important component of its social, political, and spiritual life, and religion plays a central role in all the major global conflicts that are taking place today.

The culmination of my life experiences living as a Muslim in a Muslim country imbues this book with a distinctive perspective, an "inside look" if you will, at Islam and the psychology of these Islamic terrorists. Many of these fighters were born or lived in the same environment that I lived in, and they were taught the same ideas that I was taught and heard the same sermons that I heard. In short, we experienced and shared the same issues and concerns.

And who knows? I could have been one of them today if I had not questioned these teachings and ultimately made the decision not to follow them, a decision that changed the course of my life. I write this comment to point out that my deep understanding of these terrorists and their mind-set stems from my own similar experiences and living reality and not solely from academic studies, though they have an important role and are also a part of my personal education.

In this book, I will focus most extensively on Islamic State (and precursors, ISIL and ISIS),[2] because it is the most visible and successful model for Islamic terrorist groups in recent history. It has also received the largest media coverage compared to any of the other Islamic terrorist organizations. However, this focus does not mean that it is unique in its doctrine or beliefs. Islamic State is just one of the many names of these Islamic groups, like Al Qaeda and Boko Haram, that all share the same ideology. They all dream the same dreams, they all yearn for the same goals, and they all follow the same applications even if they differ in some small details. The ideology behind Islamic terrorism is the same regardless of the many names and regardless of the different circumstances. There are many names, but the ideology is one.

[2] **Note:** The acronym ISIL is the abbreviation of "Islamic State of Iraq and the Levant," and the acronym ISIS is the abbreviation of "Islamic State of Iraq and Syria." Both ISIL and ISIS are names for the same Salafi jihadist terrorist organization that eventually declared itself Islamic State on June 29, 2014.

The terrorism that we read about in the newspapers or see on television is nothing but the last stage of a complicated and combined series of events, doctrines, and illusions. The terrorist who detonates an explosive belt or a hand grenade is only an executioner who has behind him a history that must be studied. No action comes from nothing—many people are involved in the formation of that terrorist, either directly or indirectly. For behind that terrorist stands a dense, tangled, and widespread forest of ideas that we must fearlessly enter to find the clearing that supports and protects the factory producing these terrorists. This book is the map for navigating through that forest to reach the clearing.

No one can accuse me of being hostile against Muslims because my blood is from a Muslim father and a Muslim mother, and I myself have lived as a Muslim for a long time. Most of my family and extended family are still Muslim. I continue to hold great love for them and for other Muslims, even though I choose not to be a Muslim anymore.

My Muslim father and mother cannot be terrorists just because they are Muslims. And we cannot exonerate Islam because they and many good Muslims are not terrorists. The last word about Islamic terrorism should not rest on emotions or accusations but on facts, texts, and related reality. This book firmly and courageously, without bias or prejudice, documents the roots of Islamic terrorism and the ideology that has generated it.

ONE

In the beginning, there was hatred....

People will not be able to understand Islamic State or any other Islamic terrorist group, if they do not understand the hatred that is planted in the souls of those who were born and live as Muslims: the hatred towards traditional infidels. When I write "traditional infidels," I mean Christians and Jews, the "People of the Book," because they have been the main enemies of Islam since its inception. Islam's prophet Muḥammad (c. AD 570-632) considered them in this way, and this enmity or negative judgment has persisted since the beginning of Islam to this day, for 1400 years. We Muslims and those of us from Muslim backgrounds have been raised to consider Jews and Christians our main enemies, though every now and then other enemies have been categorized by us as infidels or apostates. But Jews and Christians have always been considered the foremost enemies of Islam. This hostile view has been instilled within us through our religious texts and from public opinions repeatedly mentioned in our societies and religious communities.

And even, sometimes, when evidence points to enemies who are clearly not one of these two groups, we will still suspect that Jews and Christians are responsible for certain crimes or human disasters. For instance, the evidence is clear and indisputable that the perpetrators of the September 11, 2001 attacks on American soil were associated with Al Qaeda. Yet even today there are some Muslims who claim that Jews were behind these attacks and that this truth was suppressed by Christian America in order to find an excuse to attack Islam through the Muslim countries.[1] As their "proof," these skeptics state that not a single Jew was in the two towers of the World Trade Center when they were brought down.[2]

According to many Muslims, "the enemy" is always Jews and Christians who continually weave plans to attack them by attacking Islam. Furthermore, amid all the killing and slaughtering that Islamic State (and its precursors, ISIL and ISIS) carries out against other Muslims as well as non-Muslims, the Arab media circulates rumors that Israel created ISIS, and that Abū Bakr al-Baghdādī is an Israeli agent named Elliot Shimon[3] who was trained by the Mossad, where he learned the art of public speaking and the essentials of the Islamic religion. These media outlets also declare that America's Central Intelligence Agency (CIA) supports him with the help of the Mossad in order for them to execute the so-called "Hornet's Nest" strategy.[4] The plan of this alleged strategy is to gather all the terrorists into one organization so they can hit many targets in order to blacken the image and reputation of Islam and spread chaos in the Middle East. The goal is to ensure that Israel maintains its strength and power. The resulting instability will also provide an excuse for America to intervene to exploit the oil resources (wealth) of Iraq and

---

[1] **Note:** For the purposes of this book, the term *Muslim countries* refers to those countries with Muslim-majority populations.

[2] Although this claim is not true, some Arab Muslim Web sites still repeat this lie, using a variety of different wordings. The most widespread claim is that "4,000 Jews" were absent from their work in the World Trade Center the day of the attacks. (See these URLs: http://www.nationalreview.com/article/222127/jews-knew-anne-morse; http://www.nowtheendbegins.com/pages/israel/were-4000-jews-told-to-stay-home-on-911.htm; https://robertlindsay.wordpress.com/2010/04/12/not-one-jew-was-killed-in-the-9-11-attacks-and-the-wtc-is-full-of-jewish-workers)

[3] Many Arab newspapers have written about this rumor and others. Examples: Habib, Anas. "American Site: ISIS Amir Is an Agent for the Israeli Mossad Named 'Elliott Shimon.'" *Alyaum.com.* Al Yaum, 7 Aug. 2014. Web (http://preview.tinyurl.com/zctn22h); Mabrouk, Nadia. "[Top Five] Rumors of September 11 on Its 13th Anniversary...." *Vetogate.com.* Vetogate, 10 Sept. 2014. Web (http://www.vetogate.com/1216813); Sabri, Jalal. "Confirming That [September 11] a Scapegoat for Bush...A New Book: September 11...15 Mysteries...." *Alyaum.com.* Al Yaum, 12 Sep. 2003. Web (http://www.alyaum.com/article/1109936).

[4] "Saudi Minister: ISIS Accomplishes 'Hornet's Nest Plan'; Al-Khawārij Is Not 'A Companion Plant.'" *MBC.net.* Middle East Broadcasting Center, 9 Feb. 2015. Web (http://preview.tinyurl.com/jq3274a). **Note:** This official statement is from Sheikh Saleh al-Sheikh, Minister of Islamic Affairs, Da'wah, and Guidance.

the geostrategic significance of Syria and eventually divide them into small states, where they will no longer be a threat to Israel in the future.

Similar secret foreign schemes to destroy Islam through ISIS have been attributed to American individuals, particularly Hillary Clinton. Some Arab media have circulated reports that she "confessed" in her memoir *Hard Choices* that America created ISIS. However, the supposed excerpts (if given) provided by these Arab news sources cannot be found in her book.[5]

All these supposed foreign conspiracies are like a kind of stew, a swirling mixture full of contradictions. However, these alleged conspiracies only reflect the fact that in our culture, we Muslims (or those of us of Muslim background) are not brought up to believe what our eyes see and our ears hear, if what we see or hear results in having to face our own truth. Our Muslim culture conditions us to blame others for everything. When it concerns Islamic State, we do not want to acknowledge that its rise and spread through its earlier forms, ISIL and ISIS, and related groups is the result of both education and family combined with the Islamic texts, Muslim media, and Saudi oil money; all these factors have revived the original radical form of Islam in the hearts of many Muslims.

This form of Islam has produced terrorists who are prepared to go to any place where there is tension, where they have the opportunity to unload those shipments of hatred against the enemy. It is even better if this enemy is Christian or Jewish or any country that has a relationship with them or helps them or has mutual interests. If the terrorists conclude that any of these relationships are collaborative, they seize upon these cooperative relationships as religious justification to express their disapproval and hatred through violence, because that hatred was established within them since childhood. To them, removing the enemy will remove this hatred, or in the Qur'ān's words, *"...heal the breasts of a people who believe."*[6]

This early and deeply instilled hatred also means that we Muslims are quick to blame others for our miseries instead of searching for the truth,

[5] Mansour, Samir. "What Is the Secret of the Sudden Invasion of the Town of Arsal? Hillary Clinton: 'We Are the Founders of ISIS!'" *Annahar.com*. An Nahar, 6 Aug. 2014. Web (http://preview.tinyurl.com/jb5bmdm); Goodenough, Patrick. "Speech on Khamenei Website: Hillary Clinton 'Confessed' That US Created ISIS." *CNSNews.com*. Conservative News Service, 2 Aug. 2015. Web (http://preview.tinyurl.com/pau8529).

[6] Q 9.14 (Palmer trans.): *"kill them! God will torment them by your hands, and disgrace them, and aid you against them, and heal the breasts of a people who believe."*

and the best candidate for this blame is obviously the two traditional arch foes. We are convinced that Jews and Christians want to destroy our countries and our religion, so naturally (miraculously) Abū Bakr al-Baghdādī becomes a Zionist agent. Despite the fact that he is a genuine Arab, this outlandish belief then becomes accepted by Muslims. Once such a belief gets established, it becomes difficult to convince people otherwise, even if or when presented with solid but opposing evidence.

One example that illustrates this mind-set concerns the massacre of twelve people at the Paris headquarters of the French satirical weekly magazine *Charlie Hebdo* by two Islamic terrorists on January 7, 2015. The vast majority of the Arabic-speaking commentators on social media and newspapers claimed that this horrific event was arranged by French intelligence[7] in order to distort Islam's image and halt the spread of Islam, because Europeans have been embracing Islam in huge numbers. This unsubstantiated claim persists, despite the presence of documentation from cameras and the terrorists' own shouted words "*Allahu Akbar*" and "We have avenged the Prophet Muḥammad. We have killed *Charlie Hebdo*!" Yet all of this recorded evidence is dismissed in the eyes of the majority of Muslim youth, who view this event as just a silly play concocted by the French intelligence.

Why all this animosity and where did it come from? And why do we Muslims believe in this theory of conspiracy regarding the infidel West and the Zionist Jews?

Religious texts and their inculcation

The development of this Muslim mind-set and world view began with the Islamic texts, because it is Islam that has shaped our cultural and historical identity, our upbringing at home, and our studies in the traditional and public schools. Islam dominates our media and our books and the subjects that we read. Nothing is untouched or out of reach from Islamic influence in our Muslim countries. Thus, our way of thinking is inextricably linked to Islam's religious texts. These sacred works have been an inseparable part of our culture for over fourteen centuries. Islam, through its religious texts, has become such an integral

[7] Wadi'i, Abdel 'Ali. "The World's Online Activists Are Skeptical about the Truth of the Massacre of France." *Hespress.com*. Hespress, 10 Jan. 2015. Web (http://www.hespress.com/facebook/251690.html).

part of our existence that it has become like the air we breathe and the water we drink.

Muslims believe that a human is born a Muslim by nature and that all newborns in the world are Muslims, but some parents convert them to another religion—especially Jewish and Christian parents who convert their newborns to their own religious beliefs.[8] Being born into a Muslim family—not only Muslim but also a conservative one—I was told by my mother that the moment I was born, my father took me in his arms and said the *adhān* (Islamic call to prayer) in my ear as if he was about to pray. My father wished to follow the example of the prophet Muḥammad with his grandson al-Ḥasan.[9] Through the *adhān*, the Muslim declares al-Shahāda (the Testimony), which is the first Pillar of Islam. It is the Muslim's testimony that there is no God but Allah and that Muḥammad is the Messenger of Allah. In stating this Islamic creed, Muslims dissociate themselves from any religion other than Islam and any god other than Allah.

My mother told me that when I was a toddler, I would try to imitate my father during his prayers by standing next to him and mimicking his actions and words. Like most children, I was proud of my father and considered him my role model. I wanted to do everything like he did, including praying.

When I was four years old, my father gave me my first lesson in religion: he wanted to teach me how to pray. I still vividly remember that incident although it happened to me at a young age. My father told me to take off my pants to teach me how to clean myself, but I felt shy and refused. So he hit me, and then he began to teach me how to pray in spite of the fact that Islam commands fathers to teach their children to pray at the age of seven and to hit them if they refuse at the age of ten.[10] But being the imam of the mosque and one of the religious symbols of piety in the village, my father was eager to teach me, and so he began his instruction with me at such a very early age.

[8] *Sahih Bukhari*, Book of Funerals 311; *Ṣaḥīḥ al-Bukhārī*, Kītāb al-Janā'iz 1: 454. According to this *ḥadīth* (as narrated by Abū Hurayra), Muḥammad says, "Every child is born with a true faith of Islam (i.e, to worship none but Allah Alone) but his parents convert him to Judaism, Christianity or Magainism [polytheism]...."

[9] *Musnad Ahmad* 7: 537. According to a *ḥadīth* narrated by 'Abd Allah Ibn Abū Rāfi' (quoting his father) "...the Prophet said the *adhān* in the ear of al-Ḥasan Ibn 'Alī when Fatima gave birth to him."

[10] Ibid. 2: 376. According to a *ḥadīth*, "Teach your children to pray when they are seven years old, and smack them if they do not pray when they are 10 years old, and separate them in their beds."

Al-Fatiha (Q 1.1-7) is the first sura, or chapter, in the Qur'ān that we learn as children. It is as important and universal as the Lord's Prayer for Christians. Muslims cannot perform their prayers without reciting Sura al-Fatiha, and the prayers are unacceptable to Allah without it. It is the sura that acts as the Qur'ān's "opener," a kind of introduction, and adults as well as children in the Muslim world memorize this sura by heart:

> *In the name of the merciful and compassionate God.*
> *Praise belongs to God, the Lord of the worlds,*
> *the merciful, the compassionate,*
> *the ruler of the day of judgment!*
> *Thee we serve and Thee we ask for aid.*
> *Guide us in the right path,*
> *the path of those Thou art gracious to; not of* ***those Thou art wroth with; nor of those who err.***
> (Palmer trans.; emphasis added)

When I grew older my father explained to me that the phrase *"those Thou art wroth with"* in this sura refers to Jews because Allah is angry with them and curses them. The intended party in the phrase *"those who err"* are Christians, because they "err" by following Jesus. According to Islam, Christians made Jesus a god instead of a prophet and thus corrupted the true Gospel (Injīl).[11] They follow a path other than the straight path.

I wish my father was the only one with this view of Jews and Christians, but I heard it also from my grandfather, who has memorized the Qur'ān by heart, and I heard it from my mother. I even heard it from my friends and my teachers, who taught it to us in our school. When I grew older and began reading the *ḥadīths*[12] and the interpretations of the Qur'ān, I found the same view written there.[13]

---

[11] According to Islam, the Injīl is the book that Allah revealed directly to Jesus and supposedly contains a prophesy about Muḥammad's birth and coming. Muslims assert that the Injīl is a singular book and that the four Christian gospels are corruptions of this original gospel of Jesus, or Injīl, a book that is supposedly lost or no longer exists. The Arabic word *Injīl* is a translation of the Greek word Ευαγγέλιο, which means "Gospel."

[12] **Note:** During the early centuries of Islam, a *ḥadīth* was used to relate Muḥammad's verbal utterances, and a *sunna* was used to describe his sayings, actions, and approvals. This book refers to the organized collections of these *ḥadīths* and *sunnas* as the Hadith literature or Sunna, respectively. (See *The Qur'an: An Encyclopedia* 606.)

[13] *Musnad Ahmad* 6: 76. Excerpt: A man asked Muḥammad, "O Messenger of Allah, who are *'those Thou art wroth with'*? So he [Muḥammad] pointed at the Jews. The man said, "Who are these?" He said, "*'Those who err'* means Christians." See the commentary on Q 1.6, *Tafsīr al-Ṭabarī* 1: 67: "[The phrases] *'those Thou art wroth with'* are the Jews and *'those who err'* are the Christians."

Recently, I wanted to find out if this view still exists in school curricula in Morocco. I discovered it does exist in one of the school courses, but that Morocco has now decided to change the entire curriculum, and these references will be removed at the beginning of the 2016-2017 school year.

However, these negative views about Christians and Jews continue to be taught in other parts of the Muslim world. By way of example, Peace TV aired a sermon by the Malaysian sheikh Hussein Ye, which was later translated by the MEMRI (Middle East Media Research Institute) Web site. Sheikh Ye states in the sermon that when Allah says *"those Thou art wroth with"* or mentions anger, Allah means the Jews. He also states that when Allah uses the phrase *"those who err"* or speaks about erring, Allah is referring to Christians. Then the sheikh wonders aloud as to why the Qur'ān does not mention the Hindus or Buddhists. He suggests that Muslims should know the reason because they recite these verses in the Qur'ān every day:[14]

> ...Because the Jews—they have gone so far against Allah's commands. They like to do a lot of things that are very extreme. The most extremist nation in this world is the Jews. So if they used "extremists," it doesn't apply to Muslims. It applies to Jews....

According to this Muslim sheikh's interpretation, the Jews (*"those Thou art wroth with"*) are "the extremists of the world," and Allah called Christians *"those who err"* because they always manipulate the world.[15]

The Muslim world, from Morocco to Malaysia, believes that Jews are *"those Thou art wroth with"* and Christians are *"those who err."* So, every day when pious Muslims pray Sura al-Fatiha five times, they repeat these phrases at least seventeen times in a day,[16] reminding (and reinforcing) themselves every day that Jews are *"those Thou art wroth with"* and Christians are *"those who err."*

What is a little Muslim child going to think when he or she is taught that Allah is angry with Jews and that they deserve his wrath, and that

---

[14] "Malaysian Cleric Hussein Ye Explains Why the Jews 'Have Incurred the Wrath of Allah,' and Why 'The Christians Have Gone Astray.'" Peace TV (India). Lords Production Ltd., 17 Oct. 2006. Television. (See MEMRI transcript clip #1302: http://www.memritv.org/clip_transcript/en/1302.htm)

[15] Ibid.

[16] Sura al-Fatiha is recited 17 times a day: *ṣalāt al-fajr* (sunrise prayer) 2 times; *ṣalāt al-zuhr* (noon prayer) 4 times; *ṣalāt al-'asr* (midafternoon prayer) 4 times; *ṣalāt al-maghrib* (sunset prayer) 3 times; *ṣalāt al-'isha* (evening prayer) 4 times.

Christians are no better than the Jews because they have taken the wrong religious path?

This perception became embedded during my childhood into my thoughts. I imagined Jews and Christians as two fearsome, dangerous enemies in my mind. Not one single day passed by without me forgetting that they were my enemies. I was reminded of this belief seventeen times a day during my daily prayers. Isn't this kind of repetition a form of brainwashing?

There is not a single official Islamic institution in the Muslim world that does not know that this sura refers to Jews and Christians. Al Azhar, one of Sunni Islam's most important mosques and the most prestigious Muslim university, knows this, as well as the schools and universities in Saudi Arabia and the Web sites and the videos of sheikhs on YouTube.

Hatred in the dominant culture

This antagonism toward Jews and Christians, instilled and nurtured by Islamic text and teachings, is always present in our daily conversations. We endlessly imagine that the West is planning intrigues against us in order to control or overthrow our countries and our Islam.

Yet, one day, when I was twelve, I heard about a different ideology and a different religion. I had tuned in to Radio Monte Carlo (Trans World Radio), and I heard the story of Christ as it is stated in the Bible. I was facing—for the first time in my life—ideas that were completely different and even contrary to what I thought I knew about Christianity from the Qur'ān.

I was angry because even though the program was in Arabic it was broadcasting from a foreign, non-Arabic country. Surely this program, with its startling ideas, is coming from France, a Christian country (especially since Morocco, my homeland, was occupied by France for decades). France wants to invade our minds, I thought, after we have thrown it out of our country because it was unable to maintain its military domination over us. So France taught some of its children the Arabic language and directed its radio stations toward us to convert us from our religion. Christian France envies us for our beautiful religion, which has no parallel, and for our Qur'ān and for our Prophet, because we are the best nation on earth....

Or so I thought and how I looked at things back then. This wasn't only my view. I had heard the same view expressed by my friends at school and repeated by my family members at home, as well as by all the other people who had had an active role in my upbringing or were a major influence in my life.

I realized later my incorrect assumptions about this radio program. Apparently, the broadcasters were Christians from the Middle East (from Lebanon and Egypt), and they believed that it was their duty to preach to the Arab world. They purchased air time each day from Trans World Radio, and they used it to broadcast programs for North Africa.

But of course, the "conspiracy" theory was easier for me to believe, given my cultural and religious environment.

Who established this "conspiracy" theory? Why do we always feel that we are being targeted because we are a Muslim nation? Why do we believe that Christians and Jews (and by extension, Europe, United States, Israel, i.e., the West) are our enemies, who are continually plotting against us?

The answer is found in Islam's roots, the sacred Qur'ānic texts, which have been melded into our culture and formed our consciousness.

Perpetuation of Muḥammad's experiences

In the beginning of Muḥammad's call, according to the Hadith literature, Muḥammad faced great resistance from his own people, the Quraysh. In the beginning of his ministry, he was tolerant of and kind to Jews and Christians, considering them natural allies, especially because he believed that his call was from the same God, and he had similar beliefs concerning the prophets and messengers of the Children of Israel. Biographical books about Muḥammad state that the first person Muḥammad consulted about his first revelation and prophethood was a Christian, Waraqa Ibn Nawfal.[17] When Muḥammad's early followers experienced persecution from the pagan Meccans, Muḥammad advised them to migrate to the country of a Christian ruler, the Negus of Abyssinia, who was reputed to be just and kindhearted. Muḥammad said to them, "If you were to go to Abyssinia (it would be better for you), for the king will not tolerate injustice and it is a friendly country, until such time as Allah shall relieve you from your distress."[18]

---

[17] Ibn Hishām (Ibn Isḥāq), *The Life of Muḥammad* 83; Ibn Hishām (Ibn Isḥāq), *Al-Sīra al-Nabawīya* 1: 407. Khadīja, Muḥammad's first wife, tells Waraqa Ibn Nawfal, her paternal first cousin, about a monk's prophecy that Muḥammad is the Messenger of Allah.

[18] Ibn Hishām (Ibn Isḥāq), *The Life of Muḥammad* 146; Ibn Hishām (Ibn Isḥāq), *Al-Sīra al-Nabawīya* 2: 90. First migration to Abyssinia is mentioned.

And when Muḥammad eventually went to Medina, he hoped that the Jews and Christians there would support him, but they refused. So he changed his position from conciliation to enmity with the People of the Book and began to act hostilely against their books, beliefs, and their presence near him. Once he attained political and military supremacy in the region, Muḥammad expelled or killed as many Jews and Christians from the neighboring tribes as he could. Those he spared became subjects under his control.

Many of Muḥammad's battles were waged against his Jewish and Christian neighbors, in his stated belief that they, out of envy, did not want to convert to Islam even when they knew Islam is the truth. (See Q 3.71; Palmer trans.: *"O people of the Book! why do ye clothe the truth with falsehood and hide the truth the while ye know?"*) Islamic sources report that the Jews and Christians were always scheming to attack the Muslims.

This characterization of this conflict between Muḥammad and his non-Muslim neighbors has been circulated so widely and repeatedly throughout Islamic history that it has become a permanently defining description of Jews and Christians.

Why must Muḥammad's experiences with and aggression toward small tribes of Jewish or Christian communities that were living in his vicinity become the standard measure for Muslims' treatment of all Jews and all Christians through all times and places? Unfortunately, some Muslim sheikhs, when speaking out on satellite television or through their books to describe Jews and Christians based on Qur'ānic text, will use the article *the* in their speech or text, as in *the* Jews and *the* Christians. By using this article, they are generalizing their accusations and negative assessments to *all* Jews and *all* Christians—essentially, they gather all Jews and Christians together in one basket and speak about them with no differentiation.

Conspiracy theory in religious texts

Among the Qur'ānic texts that implicate Jews and Christians behind this conspiracy theory is Sura al-Baqara (Q 2), which is the sura Muslims believe was revealed to Muḥammad when he moved to Medina at the beginning of the Medinan period:

> *Many of those who have the Book would fain turn you back into misbelievers after ye have once believed, through envy from themselves, after the truth has been made manifest to them....* (Q 2.109; Palmer trans.)

One of the earliest commentators of the Qur'ān, Persian scholar al-Ṭabarī (AD 838-923), states that the meaning of this verse is that "the People of the Book envy you [Muḥammad and Muslims] for what Allah has given you of success."[19] Highly influential Sunni scholar Ibn Kathīr (AD 1301-1373) also confirms the same meaning:[20]

> After it had become clear that Muḥammad was the Messenger of Allah, they [Jews and Christians] found it mentioned in the Torah and the Bible, but they disbelieved him out of envy and rebellion, because he was not one of them.

These statements do not remain buried inside these commentaries, forgotten over time, but have been continually repeated over the centuries through daily conversations, mosque lessons, Friday sermons, school instruction, television programs, and radio broadcasts. All of these communications cite this verse (and similar ones) and these interpretations, teaching each successive generation that this interpretation is an absolute truth—that out of envy only, Jews and Christians have not accepted Islam and would like Muslims to become infidels. As long as Allah has made this statement in his book, the Qur'ān—which can never be wrong—then this perception will remain in effect through all times.

In upholding the validity of this verse and others like it, today's Muslim scholars and leaders mention the Western colonization of Muslim countries, the Crusades, America's invasion of Afghanistan and Iraq, Israel's occupation of Palestine, and America's intervention in Middle Eastern affairs. When the question is raised, "Why would they do that?" the Muslim answer is "they will never be satisfied with the Muslim world until it becomes an infidel world."

This Islamic logic teaches us that these historical occurrences of Western aggression confirm the validity of the Qur'ān and the validity of its text concerning the tribes of Jews and Christians neighboring Muḥammad and his fellow Muslims, and that this perception—that Jews and Christians are the enemy—shall continue in effect against all

---

[19] See the commentary on Q 2.109, *Tafsīr al-Ṭabarī* 1: 385.
[20] See the commentary on Q 2.109, *Tafsīr Ibn Kathīr* 2: 19.

Jews and all Christians until the Day of Resurrection. This perception is continually emphasized every time we recite and hear these types of verses from the Qur'ān at home and in prayer and in every part of daily life.

Imagine if you are a Muslim and you are hearing all around you on a daily basis that Jews and Christians are planning to force you to change your religion because they envy you for the blessing of Islam. How would you feel? How would this belief affect the development of your personality, if you are constantly imagining that Jews and Christians have nothing else to do but weave plots against you, because they want you to be an infidel? Such a belief leads to the impression that America, along with Israel, hates Islam and plots against it. Political factors for us are secondary factors; religion is the main factor. Thus, we believe America (and Israel) does not intervene in Muslim countries for its own political and geostrategic interests only, but because it hates Islam.

This belief persists, even when America does intervene on behalf of our own interests, such as the time it defended Muslim countries from the aggression of Iraq's Saddam Hussein in the first Persian Gulf War (AD 1991) or participated in the multistate North Atlantic Treaty Organization (NATO) coalition to protect the Libyans from the oppression of its dictator Muammar el-Qaddafi during Libya's civil war (AD 2011), or when it intervened with other nations to end the Bosnian War (AD 1992-1995), an international conflict infamous for shameful acts by mainly Serb forces of ethnic cleansing, systematic mass rapes, and indiscriminate shelling of civilians in Muslim communities.

All these positive humanitarian and military interventions by America and its Western allies are soon forgotten. We hardly give them any value, because we believe that America hides its hatred for our Islam and for us. It does not help us out of compassion, love, mercy, or for the sake of Allah but only if such help benefits its own interests. Therefore, its interventions do not earn America praise or thanks, because the "fact" that it hates us is well established within us; it will always hate us because Allah says so in the Qur'ān and Allah is more truthful than America and its foreign policy. Similarly, another verse, Q 2.120 (Arberry trans.), in the same sura reiterates the same meaning:

> *Never will the Jews be satisfied with thee* [Muḥammad], *neither the Christians, not till thou followest their religion. Say: 'God's guidance is the true guidance.' If thou followest their caprices, after the knowledge that has come to thee, thou shalt have against God neither protector nor helper.*

Prominent Muslim commentators uniformly interpret this verse to mean that "the Jews or the Christians will never be satisfied with you, O Muḥammad, so turn away from seeking to suit and satisfy them."[21]

Unfortunately, Muslims do not relegate this conflict between Muḥammad and his opponents as just a point in time in Islam's history. Because this conflict is heavily discussed in the Qur'ān, a sacred text, Muslims see this conflict as a universal truth about all Jews and Christians that applies in all times and places—that Jews and Christians will not be pleased with Muslims until Muslims follow their own religion (Judaism or Christianity).

Impact of religious texts on discussions and in media

I have personally heard again and again a particular stock response from Muslims after debates or discussions following televised news, comments, or statements on a war involving the United States. There is always someone who will recite the Qur'ānic verse Q 2.120 (*"Never will the Jews be satisfied with thee, neither the Christians, not till thou followest their religion..."*). Its use as evidence silences everyone. No one can counter or dispute it because it would mean that he or she doubts the validity of the Qur'ān and thus opposes Allah—and Allah speaks the truth. So if Allah describes Jews and Americans as infidels and schemers, it must be so. As an example, if someone should state that Israel and the Palestinians have reached an agreement, someone else would respond that the Jews will just breach the agreement and not honor it. According to these doubters, no concessions will satisfy the Jews unless Muslims give up their religion; there is no point of negotiations or anything else, because nothing really works for dealing with Israel except jihad.

So, when some Western analysts attempt to explain our religion to us, speaking about their travels in the Muslim world and sharing their personal experiences that Muslims love the West, I laugh at their naiveté. These people have not sat down with me and heard my father argue with my uncle and cite this verse (Q 2.120), nor have they listened to the imams when they meet to discuss current matters and corroborate their point of view with Qur'ānic verses and Hadith literature. These people did not attend my school or university where students and professors demonstrated with posters of dead children and other victims from

[21] See the commentary on Q 2.120, *Tafsīr al-Ṭabarī* 1: 411.

America's war in Iraq and Israel's war against Palestinians, accompanied with the same aforementioned verses (e.g., Q 2.109, Q 2.120). Do these Westerners not realize the influence of repeated denigration of Jews and Christians has on the thousands of these students across the entire Muslim world from Morocco to Malaysia?

This verse, Q 2.120, is also featured in religious edicts, or fatāwa,[22] found on the Internet. For example, the *Journal of Islamic Research* (which is published on the official Web site of the Kingdom of Saudi Arabia) has posted the following disquieting commentary on this verse by Muḥammad Ibn Sa'd al-Shwaī'ir, who holds a doctorate from Al Azhar University in Egypt and served as an adviser to the Grand Mufti of Saudi Arabia, Sheikh 'Abd al-'Azīz Ibn Bāz (AD 1910-1999), and his successor, the Grand Mufti Abdul-'Azīz Ibn 'Abdullah al-Sheikh:[23]

> For this reason [because Allah said it in Q 2.120], the Jews will continue to be in first place, then comes the Christians, [both] striving to fight against this religion [Islam], scheming for its children in many ways and different purposes. They are fanatics for their beliefs and very keen to attract people to it, and for this sake, they are spending money and effort. They do not shy away from shedding blood and sabotaging families and homes to achieve their ultimate goal, which is to repel people from the religion of Allah.

Muḥammad Ibn Sa'ad al-Shwaī'ir is of great importance, let alone those who follow him. As an advisor to the Grand Mufti, he is also the editor-in-chief of the main Islamic magazine in Saudi Arabia, the *Journal of Islamic Research* (*Mijalat al-Buḥūth al-Islāmīya*).

But this opinion is not exclusive to Saudi Arabia, so no one can blame this opinion on Wahhabism, an ultraconservative branch of Sunni Islam centered in Saudi Arabia. Even moderate Morocco, which follows the Mālikī and not the Ḥanbalī school, has posted on its official Web site, *Ministry of Endowments and Islamic Affairs*, the same Qur'ānic verse (Q 2.120) with similar commentary:[24]

[22] Definition of *fatwa* (plural, *fatāwa*): The legal opinion or learned interpretation an authoritative Islamic jurist gives on a particular issue in Islamic law.

[23] al-Shwaī'ir, Muḥammad Ibn Sa'd. "Never Will the Jews or the Christians Be Satisfied with Thee." *Journal of Islamic Research* 23 (June-Sept. 1988): 202. *General Presidency of Scholarly Research and Iftā'*. Kingdom of Saudi Arabia. Web (http://preview.tinyurl.com/h82po74).

[24] "The Future of Islam in Morocco." *Da'ūat al-Haq* (*Call for Truth*). No. 47. N.d. Ministry of Endowments and Islamic Affairs. Kingdom of Morocco. Web (http://www.habous.gov.ma/daouat-alhaq/item/1088).

> Contemporary life is not the only episode of this dangerous conflict between truth and falsehood, light and darkness, and the reason [Islam] and the idolatry [other religions], although present global conditions have introduced to the field of intellectual and cultural conflict, new and fast factors in the resources of publication and radio, converging time and space to [such] the extent that parts of the globe are closer and more connected to each other than ever.

So our conflict with Jews and Christians is being portrayed as a struggle between right and wrong and between light and darkness—even if the circumstances and the means change.

Islam's enemies in religious texts

Another Medinan verse with similar content to Q 2.109 and Q 2.120 is found in Sura al-Mā'ida (Q 5). Muḥammad first recited this verse at a later stage in his life, when his followers had become a powerful army: *"Thou wilt surely find that the strongest in enmity against those who believe are the Jews and the idolaters..."* (Q 5.82; Palmer trans.). (I will address the rest of the verse later in this chapter, because it contains a textual subterfuge that masks its true meaning and intent and thus requires its own discussion. See page 27.)

The first part of this verse acknowledges that the Jews are the most hostile to those who believe. (The phrase *"those who believe"* refers to Muslims.) Notice that the Qur'ān does not state "some Jews" or "the Jewish neighboring tribes," the local Jewish tribes in conflict with Muḥammad. Instead, the Qur'ān clearly states "the Jews," using the article *the*, which means it is referring to *all* the Jews, any time and any place.

This meaning in this verse is definitive. I wish that I could say that my conclusion—that this Qur'ānic declaration about Jews means all Jews—is incorrect or that I am treating this text unfairly. For if my wish was true, then we would have been able to remove centuries-long Muslim intolerance towards Jews. This intolerance toward Jews has exhausted us and consumed the energies of successive generations.

Unfortunately, my conclusion regarding this text is not wrong; it is an established interpretation in reputable Islamic commentaries. Ibn Kathīr, who was schooled by Ibn Taymīya (AD 1263-1328 and considered the "father" of Salafism), writes this comment on Q 5.82:[25]

[25] See the commentary on Q 5.82, *Tafsīr Ibn Kathīr* 5: 311.

> ...that [reason for the strong enmity] is because the disbelief of the Jews is only stubbornness, ingratitude and a slander against the truth, and looking down on people and dismissing the [Muslim] exegetes. This is why they killed many of the prophets. They even tried to kill the Messenger of Allah more than once and used sorcery against him. They conspired against him with the other polytheists who are just like them, those who shall be constantly cursed by Allah until the Day of Resurrection.

Ibn Kathīr thinks that misbelief and ingratitude are two main traits ingrained in the Jewish race. These inherent qualities are the reasons they killed the prophets who preceded the coming of Muḥammad and tried to kill Muḥammad himself. (Muslims believe that a Jewish woman from Khaybar poisoned Muḥammad's food.[26] Another story from Islamic sources reports that a group of Jews of Banū al-Naḍīr planned to assassinate Muḥammad by throwing a rock down upon him from a rooftop.[27]) So these two traits are indelibly part of Jews until the Day of Resurrection. Thus, they are to be cursed until the Day of Resurrection.

This stereotype about Jews prevails in all Muslim countries, found and promoted in the official media of these countries as well as in the national school curricula and Web sites. This virulent characterization is heard repeatedly in daily conversations and among Muslim clerics in their sermons and platform speeches. It has formed our consciousness, even our subconsciousness, programming us to look at all Jews with caution, fear, and contempt—all at the same time.

This indoctrination is so overpowering and long lasting, that even years after I left Islam and became a Christian, I could not suppress my nervous response when I encountered a Jewish man at a meeting. I experienced an inner fear of him the moment I reached out my hand to greet him.

I realize that this response is some kind of an irrational phobia, the result of the "education" I received as a child. Today I understand it and

---

[26] *Sahih Bukhari*, Book of Gifts (pp. 595-6); *Ṣaḥīḥ al-Bukhārī*, Kitāb al-Hiba wa Faḍluhā 2: 922-923. This *ḥadīth* (as narrated by Anas Ibn Mālik) reports that a "Jewess brought a poisoned (cooked) sheep for the Prophet who ate from it. She was brought to the Prophet and he was asked, 'Shall we kill her?' He said, 'No.' I [Anas Ibn Mālik] continued to see the effect of the poison on the palate of the mouth of Allah's Apostle." See *Sahih Muslim*, Book on Salutations and Greetings: Poison (pp. 1348, 1349); *Ṣaḥīḥ Muslim*, Kitāb al-Salām 2: 1044.

[27] See Ibn Hishām (Ibn Isḥāq), *Life of Muḥammad* 437-438; Ibn Hishām (Ibn Isḥāq), *Al-Sīra al-Nabawīya* 3: 387.

can control it, but the deep psychological residue of this education still remains in me.

My involuntary reaction is not a coincidence or an anomaly but representative of the entire Islamic heritage without exception. For example, the journal *Da'ūat al-Haq* (*Call to Truth*) of the Ministry of Endowments and Islamic Affairs in Morocco has published the following text concerning the Muslim-Jewish relationship:[28]

> The fierce war between Israel and the Arab states is only a result of the mean religious Jewish hatred [towards Muslims], which is inherited from [Jewish] fathers and grandfathers. As evidence we would like to show in brevity the brief hostile stance of the Jews against the Holy Prophet, and against Islam, the Qur'ān, and the Muslims since the noble mission until the day when a malicious Jewish woman poisoned the great Prophet with a sheep's arm containing poison.

The Arab-Israeli conflict is not primarily a conflict over land, as some people think. It's an eternal struggle over religion. This is the view of Muslims, because it exists not only in their books and their media today, but since the time of Muḥammad. It has continued to this day because in the eyes of Muslims, all Jews have been and will forever be imbued with hostility toward Islam. Our hatred towards Jews is part of Islam's doctrine before it even became political as well.

Deception in Q 5.82 (last part)

As mentioned earlier, the last part of Q 5.82 (Palmer trans.) requires a full discussion because it appears as if the text praises Christians: "*...and thou wilt find the nearest in love to those who believe to be those who say, 'We are Christians;' that is because there are amongst them priests and monks, and because they are not proud.*"

Many people are fooled by this verse. Yes, the meaning of the verse appears to be commending Christians, but the context is really praising a special kind of Christian. I have heard and read text by both Christians and Muslims citing this verse to initiate respectful dialogue between these two religions or to claim that the Qur'ān praises Christians.

Actually, this positive interpretation of this part of the verse means that its supporters are either unknowingly being deceived by the text or they

[28] "The Hostile Stance of the Jews towards the Holy Prophet." *Da'ūat al-Haq* (*Call for Truth*). No. 153. N.d. Ministry of Endowments and Islamic Affairs. Kingdom of Morocco. Web (http://www.habous.gov.ma/daouat-alhaq/item/3917).

are deliberately separating this part from its context without referring to the accredited commentary on this verse by highly respected Muslim scholars. According to these Islamic commentaries and the Muslim world, this text praises only those Christians who believe in Islam, Christians who are on their way to conversion. This text is not about those Christians who are still—and determined to remain—Christians. By reading the following, complementary verse (Q 5.83; Palmer trans.), the complete, uncensored meaning becomes evident and aligns with the Islamic commentaries:

> *And when they* [Christians] *hear what has been revealed to the prophet* [Muḥammad], *you will see their eyes gush with tears at what they recognise as truth therein; and they will say, 'O our Lord! we believe, so write us down amongst the witnesses.'*

The full context shows that when these Christians hear the Qur'ān, the divine revelations as given to Muḥammad, their eyes will overflow with tears and they will acknowledge its truth by stating *"we believe"* it. With this declaration of faith in Islam, they seek to be written down with the Muslims and be rewarded with paradise.

So how can Q 5.82, when read within its entire context, be a verse that praises Christians? The Christians described in Q 5.83 are those Christians who abandoned their Christian faith. No other conclusion is possible because we cannot claim that these Christians were combining the two religions, Islam and Christianity, as their faith, or, in other words, that they were infidels and believers at the same time.

Dangerous pattern of overgeneralization

One of the most dangerous causes of intellectual corruption in the Muslim world is simplistic overgeneralization. We do not study logic in schools and we never learn about logical fallacies. In fact, I did not study critical thinking on a regular basis until I enrolled in a Western university. Throughout my schooling, there was no lesson that focused on the use and application of critical thinking. Our education system is based on memorization and rote recall and not on the study of critical analysis. Our students are encouraged to memorize their lessons from childhood. The purpose of exams is to evaluate the student's ability to memorize the subject under study.

Islam fosters this kind of educational system, because Muslim scholars are exalted for their ability to memorize texts and not for their skills of analysis, using research and review to scientifically and logically reach their conclusions. Muslims believe the power is in the text. Therefore, all that the student has to do is to memorize the text. Over time this type of education, based on repetition and memorization that is rarely challenged or questioned, becomes the norm, the standard model for instruction.

One of the most perilous fallacies is the overgeneralization of one certain characteristic to stereotype an entire race. One such harmful overgeneralization, where we have stereotyped all Jews and Christians as evil enemies of Islam, has become an indelible notion in our communities. This widespread belief will never disappear, unless we reconsider everything we study and learn from our families and our schools. This change should begin with our educational system, the media, and influential, respected writers.

Without respected institutions, such as schools or the press, to identify and challenge questionable stereotypes, the generalizations that instigated these stereotypes can last for centuries. For example, in Q 2.105 (*"Those unbelievers of the People of the Book and the idolaters wish not that any good should be sent down upon you from your Lord..."*; Arberry trans.), the text indicates that the infidel People of the Book (Jews and Christians) and the polytheists do not want Allah to bring goodwill to Muslims. Al-Ṭabarī comments on this verse:[29]

> ...there's significant evidence in this verse that Allah Almighty has prohibited the believers from relying on their enemies, the People of the Book and the polytheists, and from listening to their words or from accepting anything that they bring to them as an advice. The Almighty is showing them [Muslims] the hatred and envy, which the People of the Book and the polytheists hide in their hearts for them, even though they show and say otherwise.

Even though al-Ṭabarī wrote this comment more than eleven centuries ago, his opinion is the same as that of a twenty-first century Muslim: Allah is urging Muslims not to trust the advice of infidels—Christians, Jews, and polytheists—no matter how much it seems to serve the interests of Muslims, because it really hides evil and wickedness.

[29] See the commentary on Q 2.105, *Tafsīr al-Ṭabarī* 1: 375.

Why this extremely negative characterization of infidels? According to the Qur'ān and its interpretation by Muslim scholars, Allah knows the mysteries of the souls of all people and knows that the infidels want only evil for Muslims, even if they overtly show otherwise. This characterization does not only apply to the Jews, Christians, and pagans of Muḥammad's era, but it also applies to the Jews, Christians, and pagans of al-Ṭabarī's era, too (which is almost three centuries after the death of Muḥammad), and also applies to the Jews, Christians, and pagans of the present time.

To verify that this Islamic stereotype of Jews and Christians as evil and deceitful has continued from the seventh century AD until now, I searched the Internet and quickly discovered many sites where this stereotype is clearly accepted and promulgated. The Web site of Safar al-Ḥawālī, a contemporary Saudi sheikh, is representative of this view about Jews and Christians. In a posted lecture, al-Ḥawālī discusses this characterization and mentions many Qur'ānic verses to support this view, including Q 2.105. His conclusion echoes the same opinion as al-Ṭabarī and his Muslim contemporaries:[30]

> The verses are too many, and perhaps we will need a lot of time if we are to discuss and interpret them all, and they all indicate that the Western world is resentful towards this [Muslim] nation.

Some may refuse to accept this linkage and may claim that al-Ḥawālī is just a Wahhabi Saudi sheikh and that he is obviously going to adopt such an interpretation because of his fundamentalist leanings. However, the problem is that such critics of this view have not undertaken a comprehensive survey of the Muslim countries, their books, and schools to learn the truth of the matter.

Compounding this problem are offbeat Muslim voices (unrepresentative of most Muslims) who claim that Islam does not see the West as envious and evil. Western media gives these voices undeserved attention and credence, forgetting or ignoring that these voices only represent personal beliefs and are exceptions to the majority of opinions. These atypical voices promote a beautifully compassionate version of Islam that is unknown or unfamiliar to the vast majority of Muslims who have grown up with and have been immersed in its religious texts for centuries.

[30] al-Ḥawālī, Safar. "This Religion." *Alhawali.com*. Web site of Safar al-Ḥawālī, n.d. Web. (To hear audio recording, see URL: http://audio.islamweb.net/audio/index.php?page=FullContent&audioid=110470)

The Muslim voices who do represent the majority view (the West is envious, deceitful, and evil) use current events and political conflicts to establish some kind of incriminating pattern to support their negative view. Dhū al-Fiqār Bil'ūdī, a Moroccan writer and devout Muslim, discusses in a newspaper article the military intervention of a "Christian" France in "Muslim" Mali in January 2013 during the Northern Mali Conflict. He writes that in the eyes of Muslims, this intervention is considered a confirmation of Qur'ānic teaching as given by Allah and cites Q 2.105 (Arberry trans.): *"Those unbelievers of the People of the Book and the idolaters wish not that any good should be sent down upon you from your Lord...."* He further states in his article that it was "Christian" France that decided with "Christian" Spain to divide the Western Sahara (Moroccan Sahara) in 1900, with France taking control of an area that would become Mauritania and Spain keeping control of the remaining area, Spanish Sahara (Moroccan Sahara). Then in 1904 "Christian" France signed an agreement (Entente Cordiale) with "Christian" Great Britain, where each party was granted freedom of action—France in Morocco, Great Britain in Egypt.[31] By sequencing and analyzing these historical events in this way, Bil'ūdī characterizes these Western nations as Christian countries whose Christian citizens, or "People of the Book," are still conspiring against Muslims even during the twentieth century.[32]

Bil'ūdī's article is not published in a Muslim electronic newspaper but an open publication that publishes articles on a variety of subjects, secular as well as religious. However, articles such as his would not be published if the readers of this online publication did not want to read them. It should also be noted that Dhū al-Fiqār Bil'ūdī, a Moroccan moderate but conservative Muslim, shares the same logic as the fundamentalist Saudi sheikh, Safar al-Ḥawālī, by using similarly superficial analyses to describe these modern political conflicts in Qur'ānic terms.

Unfortunately, these dubious charges (based on our hatred toward the "People of the Book") that accuse Jews and Christians of plotting to destroy Muslims through these political conflicts are found in

[31] Bil'ūdī, Dhū al-Fiqār. "The Intervention of France in Mali between the Return of the Colonizer and the Humiliation of the Help Seeker." *Hespress.com*. Hespress, 5 Mar. 2013. Web (http://www.hespress.com/opinions/73948.html).

[32] Interesting note: One detailed analysis of this conflict reports that a majority (97%) of southern Malians welcomed the French intervention as determined in a February 2013 poll. See Bergamaschi, Isaline. "French Military Intervention in Mali: Inevitable, Consensual yet Insufficient." *Stability: International Journal of Security and Development*. 12 June 2013. Print and Web (http://www.stabilityjournal.org/articles/10.5334/sta.bb/).

many current publications available in both very conservative Muslim countries, e.g., Saudi Arabia, to more open-minded Muslim countries, e.g., Morocco. When I began my work on this book, I chose to focus more on those texts that contain in them the "conspiracy" theory, because it is one of the ideas that has established this doctrine of hatred and made it an integral part of our thinking and the way we analyze our politics, economy, foreign relations, and everything else that revolves around us. We see the world through the eyes of our religion. No political analyst should overlook the role of religion in the formation of our peoples or ignore its impact on our view of the world and our relationship with other nations.

Influence of religious texts on perception of America

On September 11, 2001, I was a guest at the house of one of my American friends, who was living in Casablanca with his family at that time. While we were talking, he received a phone call informing him about the attack. We turned on the TV to watch the news, and I noted that it had a greater impact on him than me. He turned to me with questions in his eyes. (We were as yet unaware that a second plane had crashed into the south tower of the World Trade Center.) I said to him, almost automatically, that this attack wasn't an accident but the work of Muslim terrorists.

We tried to follow the news on the Internet because local television stations did not give sufficient details. After the crash of the second plane, my speculations were confirmed. At this point my friend fearfully asked me what he should do. He wondered if he could safely go out that day or if he should remain in the house. I tried to reassure him, telling him that he would be fine—Morocco was one of the safest countries (then).

I did not make this statement because I could guarantee only peaceful actions of Muslims towards an infidel American; I said these words because I knew the tight security in Morocco. There would be no unrest, because the police and security services controlled the state and would not want any problems with the United States of America. If security was lost in Morocco, then I wouldn't be able to guarantee my friend's safety—and I wouldn't be able to guarantee my own life (because I am a Christian, an "infidel") either.

Intense animosity toward "the others" (non-Muslims) is always there, generation after generation, century after century, because of Islamic teachings on this matter. When it does not openly show itself, it only means it is submerged, ready to appear whenever the opportunity presents itself.

One such illustration is Libya, when America helped the Libyans get rid of their dictator, Muammar el-Qaddafi. Despite America's critical support during the Libyan civil war, the first foreigners killed in Libya, after the establishment of its new government, were Americans. During this transitory and somewhat unstable period, four people, including US Ambassador Christopher Stevens, were killed during a domestic attack on the US embassy. As reported by the British *Daily Mail* newspaper, Stevens sent a message before his death, stating that the US embassy in Benghazi was in danger because two Libyan militias providing security threatened to withdraw because of a disagreement over America policy.[33]

Initially, the assault and resulting deaths were attributed by US President Obama to a violent, spontaneous reaction against an anti-Muslim video about Muḥammad. However, further investigation verified that this video was not the main catalyst; the military-style attack appeared to have been planned far in advance. Accusatory fingers pointed at Anṣār al-Sharīʿa, a Salafist Islamic militia, with Libyan leader Aḥmed Abū Khattala considered the main leader—and suspect—behind the attack. (He was later captured in June 2014.)

Yet even if one presumes that an offensive video of Muḥammad instigated protests that triggered the deadly attack, why would Libyans attack the US embassy, which represents America, after all of America's helpful support during the Libyan civil war? In this instance, the United States of America is being blamed for the actions of one person, "Sam Bacile" (a.k.a. Nakoula Basseley Nakoula), an Egyptian-born US resident who actually wrote, produced, and promoted the anti-Muslim video, *Innocence of Muslims*.

On the same day, September 11, 2012, Muslim protesters, supposedly enraged by this same video, attacked the US embassy in Cairo, Egypt. Yet no one was killed, possibly because of the protective presence of US marines within and Egyptian security forces outside the embassy.[34]

---

[33] Gye, Hugh. "Revealed: Ambassador to Libya Told Officials of Security Worries on Day He Died in Consulate Raid as Special Forces Chief Says He Asked for 'More Not Less' Backup Month before Attack." *Dailymail.co.uk*. Telegraph Media Group, 8 Oct. 2012. Web (http://www.dailymail.co.uk/news/article-2214665/Libya-consulate-attack-Ambassador-Chris-Stevens-told-officials-security-worries-day-died.html).

[34] Khalil, Ashraf. "Cairo and Benghazi Attacks: Two Sets of Fundamentalisms Unleash Havoc." *Time.com*. Time Inc., 11 Sept. 2012. Web (http://world.time.com/2012/09/11/cairos-u-s-embassy-incident-two-sets-of-fundamentalisms-unleash-havoc/).

These two events highlight important issues: Why are Muslims attacking US embassies, i.e., America, when America had acted as a good friend in helping to eliminate tyranny in Libya and did not produce the anti-Muslim video? Why didn't any sheikhs or Arab media clarify that America itself should not be blamed for the actions of one person?

None of these Muslim representatives will exonerate America, because they and their people are determined to negatively stereotype America despite such specific events to the contrary: No matter where we are—Libya, Egypt, or other Muslim countries—we will not change our preconceived stereotype of "the others" in our minds.

US Ambassador Christopher Stevens was not the only American foreigner who was killed in Libya. In December 2013 American Ronnie Smith was killed by unknown assailants. Ronnie was a chemistry teacher who came to Libya with his family to help Libyans build a better future after the collapse of el-Qaddafi's dictatorship.

As I followed comments on Twitter regarding his tragic killing, I saw some comments from Muslims who claimed that he did not teach the Libyans because of his love for them, but because he was a Christian missionary sent by his church in Texas. They justified his murder, claiming that he was proselytizing to Muslims under the pretext of teaching them. Ronnie Smith was treacherously gunned down by drive-by shooters while he was jogging in al-Fuwayhat, a district in Benghazi, leaving behind his little child and his wife Anita Smith, who appeared on Arab media and said in Arabic, "I want the Libyan people to know that I love you and I miss you. And to those who killed my husband I forgive you through the forgiveness of Jesus Christ, who taught us to love all people, even our enemies."[35] She said these words, while fighting back her tears and swallowing her pain.

Great is the difference between what Anita was taught in her childhood, encouraging her to control her anger and forgive people even if they are the killers of her husband and made her son fatherless, and what we are taught in our countries since childhood—that even if

[35] Smith, Anita. Interview. *Alarabiya.net*. Al Arabiya Hadath, Washington DC. 20 Dec. 2013. Television. (To view YouTube video, see URL: https://youtu.be/s6vl_O_IX5Y). **Note:** Anita Smith's Arabic words occur approximately 1:35-2:15 minutes in the video. See Martinez, Michael. "Widow of American Teacher Forgives Attackers Who Killed Her Husband in Libya." *CNN.com*. Cable News Network, 20 Dec. 2013. Web (http://www.cnn.com/2013/12/20/us/libya-widow-teacher-forgives-attackers/); Johnson, Eric M. "Slain Benghazi Teacher Ronnie Smith's Widow: I 'Love' and 'Forgive' His Killers." *NBCNews.com*. National Broadcasting Corporation, 21 Dec. 2013. Web (http://www.nbcnews.com/news/other/slain-benghazi-teacher-ronnie-smiths-widow-i-love-forgive-his-f2D11787726).

the Crusader West helps us outwardly, they still hate us inwardly. We grew up with these beliefs poisoning our minds, which make us unable to accept or forgive others, assuming always that their motives are evil, even when they are not.

Although those who have joined or supported Islamic State and similar jihadist groups are from different Muslim countries, they did not come from a vacuum. They have been subjected to the same beliefs and the same brainwashing that I and the millions like me have endured since childhood!

The difference is that I decided to resist and ultimately rid myself of these beliefs, whereas millions of other Muslims have given themselves up to these Islamic beliefs and consider them as the absolute truth.

TWO

Permanent hatred fuels eternal enmity toward Jews and Christians

The conspiracy theory exists in all countries, including Western countries, but it runs in our blood in the Muslim world. It is so entwined in our everyday lives that I joke with my friends that I wouldn't be surprised if a Muslim woke up one morning to find his toilet seat broken and blame America or Israel for it. Because of this unreasonable distrust of the West (especially America and Israel), Muslim people doubt everything. This doubt is not based on a general mistrust of the West's foreign policies (and specifically the foreign policies of America and Israel) but rather as the result. In our view, all the Western nations envy us. But colonialism and foreign interventions are not the reasons for our world view—they are used only as examples to reinforce it, to prove that what our culture has taught us all these centuries is true. Foremost, we argue that the West envies the superiority and legitimacy of our culture!

If one of my Muslim friends asks me about Israel's actions toward the Palestinians and if we should condemn Israel's occupation and the killing of innocent people, I ask him if our hatred towards the Jews was before or after the founding of the state of Israel. Did we start hating the Jews after 1948? Of course not. No Muslim can make that claim because our own Islamic books and religious teachings testify against us. We learned hatred towards Jews from our most authoritative reference books long before the statehood of Israel. Enmity toward Israel existed before its statehood, but we use the Palestinian situation to feed this enmity and to consecrate or justify it. All Muslim nations unite in this enmity toward Jews.

What relates the Moroccan Muslim to the Palestinian one? Is it Israel's occupation? In northern Morocco, Ceuta and sister city Melilla are considered political enclaves by Spain but occupied territories by Morocco. However, we Muslim Moroccans do not hate the Spanish like we hate the Jews. We do not justify any reasons for any bombing in Ceuta and Melilla, and I do not see any Muslim nation denouncing the occupation by Spain of Ceuta and Melilla with demonstrations or other political protest. Why? It is because the enmity toward Jews in our books is more venerated and irrevocable than toward any nation—as a kind and not as a state, as a race and not as a political entity. We grew up believing that a Jewish person is treacherous and deceitful; in fact, we call any deceiver by the term "Jew." The characteristic of deceit is attributed to all Jews.

One of our local Moroccan proverbs professes that "you can eat with a Jew but do not sleep in his house, and do not eat with a Christian, but you can sleep in his house." The explanation is that Jewish food is lawful (*ḥalāl*), because both Islam and Judaism prohibit, for example, the eating of pork and blood, but Christians do not prohibit it. So we can trust the Jew's food but not trust the Christian's food because it might include prohibited (*harām*) ingredients or processing in its preparation. However, in regards to sleeping, it is preferable to be with the Christian because a Christian will not betray us or kill us in the night, while it is expected behavior of the Jew.

Islam has established a culture of enmity toward all that is Christian and all that is Jewish, especially the Jewish. Islam even forbids us to befriend Jews or Christians. Of course, there are many Muslims who disregard these texts and have Jewish and Christian friends. These friendships only mean that they have been able to overcome their cultural bias and programming because of self-interest or philanthropy.

However, the bitter truth is that for generations many Muslim people have remained under the strong influence of this "enmity" culture and they have not been able to overcome it. They stand prepared, waiting for the right conditions and leaders to unleash this internalized enmity and translate it into the overt destruction and killing of "the others."

Forbidden befriendment of Jews and Christians

Let us start with some clear Qur'ānic text from Sura al-Mā'ida (Q 5) that constitutes one of the cornerstones of enmity towards Jews and Christians:

> *O believers, take not Jews and Christians as friends; they are friends of each other. Whoso of you makes them his friends is one of them. God guides not the people of the evildoers.* (Q 5.51; Arberry trans.)

This verse constitutes an important part of a core Muslim belief called *al-walā' wa al-barā'* ("loyalty and disavowal").[1] This belief prohibits the Muslim from taking Jewish and Christian friends; whoever extends friendship to either group will be considered a Jew or a Christian. Such conduct is one of the most despicable acts to commit in the eyes of a Muslim.

This concept has been in effect since the early days of Islam. Al-Ṭabarī explains it in his commentary on this verse:[2]

> Allah Almighty has prohibited all believers to take Jews and Christians as intimates [close friends] and allies for the people of faith [Muslims] in Allah and His Messenger. He [Allah] has told that whoever takes them [Jews and Christians] as supporters, allies, or intimates other than Allah, His Messenger, and the believers, then this person becomes one of them [Jews and Christians] in taking partner against Allah, his Messenger, and the believers. Allah and His Messenger will disavow him.

---

[1] The phrase *al-walā' wa al-barā'* is generally referred to as the Islamic concept of friendship toward fellow Muslims, but this concept of friendship is never complimentary or loving of non-Muslims. The first part, or *al-walā'*, means "loyalty and friendship," and the second part, or *al-barā'*, means "disavowal and enmity." Muslims are to hold fast to what is pleasing to Allah and oppose what is displeasing to Allah, i.e., nonbelievers.

[2] See the commentary on Q 5.51, *Tafsīr al-Ṭabarī* 6: 180.

Ibn Kathīr, who lived five centuries after al-Ṭabarī, does not differ much from his predecessor's commentary. He also confirms the same understanding of the text:[3]

> Allah Almighty prohibits his believing servants [Muslims] from befriending Jews and Christians, as they are the enemies of Islam and its people. Allah fights them [Jews and Christians] and says that some of them are friends of each other. He then threatens whoever [Muslim] would do that [befriend them] and vows, "... *Whoso of you makes them his friends is one of them. God guides not the people of the evildoers* [Q 5.51]."

According to this verse and the interpretations by highly respected Muslim commentators, Jews and Christians have been friends and allies of each other since the time of Muḥammad and will continue to be friends and allies of each other until the Day of Resurrection. They—Jews and Christians—agree with and support each other and are united against Muslims. The generally positive, close relationship between America and Israel is only confirmation of this belief.

As Muslim individuals, we are not to favor Christian and Jewish friends over Muslims, either individually or as political states. Therefore, when Islamic groups accuse Arab governments of working favorably with the West because of their inaction in applying this principle (disavowal and enmity toward Jews and Christians), the sheikhs who defend their governments' foreign policy state that this cooperation with the West is only a matter of political interest. In reality, this response means that the cooperation or alliance is not a real friendship, that stems from the heart, but a fake friendship based on practical expediency. The enmity toward these Western nations continues to exist, hidden in the heart, only to be revealed and applied when circumstances are appropriate and the interests of Muslims are not threatened.

Whenever my mother wanted to insult me (or anyone else, for that matter), she would call me "Jew" or "Christian" to offend me. Using these two names for insulting and offending others is a part of Moroccan tradition (and the rest of the Muslim world). Even when the word *Jew* is mentioned in a conversation, an apology must be extended as if it is obscene. We say, for example, "There is a Jew... 'be it far from you'...," as if mentioning "Jew" is not appropriate. It is impossible for such enmity to

[3] See the commentary on Q 5.51, *Tafsīr Ibn Kathīr* 5: 253.

be just a coincidence or not religiously rooted, because Islam dominates and shapes our lives and culture, creating this permanent enmity for everyone who is non-Muslim, especially Jews and Christians.

Let us reverse the situation and imagine that Q 5.51 (Arberry trans.) has been published in a Western newspaper but with some crucial substitutions:

> *O **ye Christians**, take not the **Sunnis** and **Shiites** as friends; they are friends of each other. Whoso of you makes them his friends is one of them. God guides not the people of the evildoers.* (Emphasis added to substitutions)

If this imaginary newspaper or I was to state these words publicly, the newspaper owner or I would be immediately accused of bigotry and Islamophobia and perhaps put on trial.

On the other hand, Muslims read and recite this Qur'ānic verse (Q 5.51) where it can be heard by Jews and Christians all over the world. Muslims consider this verse as divinely given; no one dares to criticize this verse because whoever does so in an Arab country would go on trial for religious defamation (if not killed by mobs!).

Yet if a Western country published and promoted this verse with Muslims as the target, its government would be lambasted for being religiously intolerant, racist, or anti-Muslim. This political correctness dulls people's sense of critical thinking in favor of this ideology of generalized enmity and hatred.

Hatred and cursing of Jews and Christians in Qur'ānic texts

Some Qur'ānic text provides this reason to curse Jews and Christians:

> *The Jews say Ezra is the son of God; and the Christians say that the Messiah is the son of God; that is what they say with their mouths, imitating the sayings of those who misbelieved before.—God fight them! How they lie!"* (Q 9.30; Palmer trans.)

The expression *"God fight them"* means Allah curses them—all Jews and all Christians in every time and place because of their beliefs (regardless of whether the Qur'ān has correctly summed up these beliefs).

Imagine if this verse was altered to read, *"The **Sunnis** say **Muḥammad** is the **apostle** of God; and the **Shiites** say that **'Alī** is the **friend** of God; ...God fight them! How they lie!"* (emphasis added to substitutions). If

Christians used this text during services in their churches or Jews in their synagogues, would this text go unnoticed?

Today European, American, and Asian Saudi-funded mosques are disseminating and publicly reading speeches and verses that curse Jews and Christians, e.g., Q 9.30, on the basis that these verses contain divinely given words. While the West faces charges of Islamophobia if it criticizes Islam or Muslims, Muslims are not severely rebuked for chanting verses and cursing non-Muslim people based on their religious beliefs that are full of racism and bigotry. Christian children in Egypt must listen, day and night, to Islamic verses that curse them through loudspeakers. They cannot open their mouth to complain, or else they would be tried for "defaming religions," but in actuality only religious "offenses" against Islam are prosecuted. In similar fashion, Christians in Iraq and Jordan hear the same insulting, offensive verses but must accept them passively, saying to the media that they live in love and harmony with their Muslim brothers. They are not safe to publicly express their pain over these insults.

Another tragedy is that these hate-filled Qur'ānic texts are taught in some countries to Muslim and Christian children alike, and the Christian children have to memorize these verses even though these texts curse them and their religion. Imagine a Muslim child reciting Q 9.30 to a Christian child, insulting him, and the Christian child, crying, does not know how to respond. His father has no right to protest because all verses are sacred texts for the Muslim—unless he is willing to face charges of blasphemy or defamation (or both) of Islam and possible imprisonment.

The Qur'ān explicitly prohibits making friends with infidels. So it is difficult for Muslims, who would like to practice their religion in Western countries, to fraternize or assimilate with Westerners because their religion discourages these interactions and relationships. Instead, the Qur'ānic texts not only encourage Muslims not to integrate with non-Muslims, they also urge them to hate infidels.

At the behest of Allah, this hatred, which is central to the doctrine of *al-walā' wa al-barā'* ("loyalty and disavowal"), means loyalty to Muslims but repudiation of infidels. As defined by the former Grand Mufti of

Saudi Arabia Ibn Bāz (AD 1910-1999), "it means to love and be loyal to believers, and to hate and be enemies with the nonbelievers."[4]

The well-known influential Saudi sheikh Muḥammad Ibn Ṣāliḥ al-'Uthaymīn (AD 1925-2001) states that "the infidel is an enemy of Allah, His Prophet, and the believers, and we must hate the infidel with all our hearts."[5] This command for hatred includes every type of infidel: anyone who is not a Muslim. So then Islam commands that one and a half billion Muslims (if they really wish to submit to Allah) must become enemies with the six billion non-Muslims, even if these infidels are family members or other relatives, and they must only take other Muslims as friends.

Sura al-Tawba (Q 9), considered by most Muslim scholars to be one of the last revealed suras of the Qur'ān (after Muḥammad had firmly established Islam with his conquest of Mecca), declares in one of its verses, *"O believers, take not your fathers and brothers to be your friends, if they prefer unbelief to belief; whosoever of you takes them for friends, those—they are the evildoers"* (Q 9.23; Arberry trans.).

This verse and others have been used to justify the killing in battle of infidel relatives and friends by the early Muslims and Companions of Muḥammad. While Q 9.23 only mentions two classifications, *"fathers and brothers,"* Q 58.22 (Palmer trans.) is more expansive in its scope:

> *Thou shalt not find a people who believe in God and the last day loving him who opposes God and His Apostle, even though it be their fathers, or their sons, or their brethren, or their clansmen. He has written faith in their hearts, and He aids them with a spirit from Him....*

Ibn Kathīr states that the phrase *"even though it be their fathers"* was revealed to Muḥammad regarding Companion Abū 'Ubayda, who killed his infidel father during the Day (Battle) of Badr,[6] and the phrase *"or their sons"* refers to Abū Bakr (one of Muḥammad's earliest and closest Companions), who intended on that day to kill his son 'Abdul Raḥmān. The phrase *"or their brethren"* concerns Companion Muṣ'ab Ibn 'Umayr,

---

[4] Ibn Baz, Abd al-Aziz. "The Meaning of Loyalty and Disavowal." *Binbaz.org*. Official Web site of al-Imam Abd al-Aziz Ibn Baz, n.d. Web (http://www.binbaz.org.sa/fatawa/1757).

[5] al-'Uthaymīn, Muḥammad Ibn Ṣāliḥ. "Fatwa no. 8340: What is Loyalty and Disavowal?" *Islamway.net*. 1 Dec. 2006. Web (http://preview.tinyurl.com/gs7rjnf).

[6] Battle of Badr (AD 624) was a turning point for early Muslims in establishing Islam in their region. Unlike earlier skirmishes, this battle was the first large-scale engagement between Muḥammad's military force and its main adversary, the Quraysh (tribes of Mecca). It is one of the few battles specifically mentioned in the Qur'ān.

who killed his infidel brother ‘Ubayd Ibn ‘Umayr on the same day. The phrase *"or their clansmen"* refers to Companions ‘Umar Ibn al-Khaṭṭāb, who killed one of his infidel relatives, and Ḥamza Ibn ‘Abd al-Muṭṭalib (Muḥammad's uncle), ‘Alī Ibn Abī Ṭālib (Muḥammad's cousin and son-in-law), and ‘Ubayda Ibn al-Ḥārith, who killed that day infidel Quraysh tribesmen ‘Ataba, Shība and al-Walīd Ibn ‘Ataba.[7]

If the early Muslims confronted their family members over religious differences and killed them because they were infidels, then it is not surprising that we, today's Muslims, have kept alive the same great enmity towards infidels. The Qur'ān gives me the right—actually, the command—to hate even my closest relatives, because blood kinship must never be preferred or protected over the faith brotherhood. The Islamic brotherhood is stronger than any kinship. This thinking allows no other ties to be stronger than religion—neither family ties nor patriotic ties. The tie above all ties is the faith tie; it is the tie that rules all other relationships.

In Islam, it is permissible to be kind to your parents even if they are infidels. However, being kind to Christians and infidels does not mean that you must love them in your heart. In fact, you should hate them, and this hatred is for the sake of Allah. The Hadith literature addresses this point, where Muḥammad states that the "strongest bond of faith is love for the sake of Allah and enmity for His sake."[8] True faith consists of loving Muslims for the sake of Allah and hating infidels for the sake of Allah, or else we cannot be considered true Muslims.

An exception to this rule is when we Muslims are defeated and vulnerable, and we want to win the sympathy of non-Muslims. Then we can pretend to love infidels, but we must hide our hatred inside of us. This deception is a Qur'ānic principle: *"The believers never ally themselves with the disbelievers, instead of the believers. Whoever does this is exiled from GOD. Exempted are those who are forced to do this to avoid persecution…"* (Q 3.28; Khalifa trans.).

---

[7] See the commentary on Q 58.22, *Tafsīr Ibn Kathīr* 13: 468.
[8] *Musnad Ahmad* 5: 362.

The term *taqīya*[9] derives from this verse. However, some believe that the principle of *taqīya* is followed by Shiites more than the Sunnis. Even if this distinction is true, the application of *taqīya* is a principle that exists in the Qur'ān, regardless of which Muslim sect has adopted it more as a result of its own experiences with persecution. The Sunnis did not need to practice it as often because they have always been the majority Muslim sect, whereas the Shiites have always been the minority. As Islamic history shows, the Shiites' minority status and persecution, especially by Sunnis since the death of Muḥammad, easily explains their greater propensity to apply this principle.

Al-Ṭabarī, the highly regarded Sunni commentator, defends and explains its appropriate application. He comments that the phrase *"Exempted are those who are forced to do this* [ally with disbelievers] *to avoid persecution"* in Q 3.28 means that Muslims will not be banished from Allah in this situation. He states that if Muslims fear for themselves while under the control of disbelievers, then they can "manifest allegiance in front of them by your speech while concealing your enmity from them."[10]

Some of my Muslim friends have told me that they apply this principle while living in the West. They smile to others but curse them in their minds or within their inner circle. They act this way in order to preserve their interests and their social status. This principle is very dangerous because it isolates Muslims living in multicultural societies by making them hate it and pretending to assimilate with it—all the while harboring within themselves extremely conflicted feelings.

Fortunately, not all Muslims apply this Islamic principle; otherwise, it would create a real catastrophe in every society that has Muslims. The fact that this doctrine exists in the Islamic texts does not necessarily mean that every Muslim will apply it, but it does exist. Still, for those Muslims who do decide to repent and fully embrace Islamic rules, then they will be obliged to adopt this dangerous principle, hiding hatred when necessary, towards all non-Muslims, especially Jews and Christians.

---

[9] The pretext for the principle of *taqīya* is found primarily in two Qur'ānic verses: Q 3.28 and Q 16.106. The term *taqīya* means to say or act differently from what one believes to ward off harm to one's wealth, honor, and self. Famed lexicographer Ibn Manẓūr states in his comprehensive *Lisān al-'Arab* that "those who practice *taqīya*...fear each other but outwardly show peace and agreement; yet, inwardly, they harbor opposite feelings" (4902-4903). However, it should be noted that *taqīya* is permissible for Muslims not just for life-threatening situations but for living in communities that do not follow Islam.

[10] See the commentary on Q 3.28, *Tafsīr al-Ṭabarī* 3: 154.

Hatred toward non-Muslims, particularly Jews and Christians, is a permanent enmity because it has become a sacred enmity. Its source is the Qur'ān and other Islamic texts. It is not an enmity that can fade away under different circumstances. Islam forms my identity as a Muslim and teaches me that I am better than non-Muslims, and that we as Muslims ought to love Muslims but not love others.

In our prayers we pray for Muslims but pray against the infidels, asking that they get hit by disasters. Allah takes on our revenge by sending epidemics, diseases, earthquakes, and hurricanes upon our enemies. Yet when these misfortunes happen to us, we consider them as a test for us from Allah. Sometimes we consider these misfortunes as a punishment from Allah because we did not abide by or follow the teachings of Islam as much as we should; we did not apply it wholeheartedly but allowed unlawfulness, evil and immorality to be part of our lives. However, if we but repent and follow Islam as we should, then Allah will take away those tribulations from us.

Effect of Qur'ānic texts on Islamic terrorism

The terrorists who are members of Islamic State and other Islamic militant groups today have absorbed these hate-filled doctrines since childhood, when it was implanted there by the Islamic educational system, a mixed study of Western subjects with an overdose of Islamic subjects. Thanks to Saudi funds that support the Arab Muslim countries, Islamic-based books have flooded the large-scale "book fair" exhibitions in those countries until these materials have become the largest selling genre in book exhibitions held in Cairo, Casablanca, Beirut, and Riyadh. Since the 1970s, these exhibitions now sell mostly Islamic religious books repeatedly published on a limited number of topics. Most of these materials are related to misbelief and faith and the relationship between the infidel and the Muslim. Reading these materials has influenced the Muslim youth to separate themselves from their society and dream of living instead in some kind of Islamic utopia.

Any Muslim youth who lives geographically in Europe and America must live historically in the seventh century AD if he wants to be a committed Muslim. Under this religious commitment, he would relive the war between the Prophet and the infidels, a war between faith and misbelief. Though he is physically on, and perhaps born on, Western soil, his mind would become Islamic, stuffed with the doctrines of loyalty and disavowal by loving Muslims but hating infidels for the sake of Allah. His mind is also stuffed with the necessity of staying away from infidels and their festivals, customs, and traditions, because they are blasphemous and against the Islamic faith.

What drives a young man from London, leaving the United Kingdom, to join the ISIS *mujāhidīn* (Islamic guerilla fighters) in Raqqa, Syria? Who convinced him that this is the right decision, and that the advantages of it exceed the disadvantages? There is no logical explanation, except that this person is convinced to join the believers in their war against the infidels, because for him this is the right and righteous decision in life. This eternal battle is between faith and misbelief about an eternal enmity that exists between the Prophet and the Muslims on one side and the infidels (Christians, Jews, and polytheists) on the other. A person who leaves to join the *mujāhidīn* has lived immersed in this kind of ideology for a long time. This ideology becomes his identity and his cause.

Unfortunately, when the ideology is this deeply embedded and embraced, the believer becomes a captive of it. Sadly, many Muslim parents living in Western countries, who have provided their children with an Islamic education or enabled them to seek out information and teachings about Islam on their own in an effort to preserve their Muslim identity in their children, discover to their shock and dismay that they have created terrorists who then leave their families to join ISIS, Al Qaeda, or a similar Islamic jihadist group.

British citizen Ahmed Muthana (originally a Yemeni) experienced firsthand the shock, heartache, and dismay that occurs when children replace family and home with an Islamic terrorist group. Two of his four sons left the family and the United Kingdom to fight overseas with ISIS. His first son, Nasser Ahmed Muthana (age 20), disappeared suddenly before starting studies at a medical school. Eventually he appeared in a video produced by ISIS, calling young people to join its ranks. Several months after Nasser left the UK for Syria, younger brother Aseel (age 17) left home to presumably join him. Some British officials state that Aseel may be one of the youngest Britons to join an Islamic terrorist network.[11]

---

[11] Morris, Steven, and Matthew Taylor. "Father of ISIS Volunteer: 'My Son Has Betrayed Britain.'" *The Guardian.com*. The Guardian, 22 June 2014. Web (https://www.theguardian.com/world/2014/jun/22/father-isis-video-son-betrayed-britain); Mendick, Robert, Patrick Sawer, and Tim Ross. "The Brilliant Brothers Who Left British Suburb for Jihad in Syria." *Telegraph.co.uk*. Telegraph Media Group, 21 June 2014. Web (http://www.telegraph.co.uk/news/worldnews/middleeast/syria/10917357/The-brilliant-brothers-who-left-British-suburb-for-jihad-in-Syria.html).

Their father Ahmed commented that "my son [Nasser] was brought up to love and respect my country, which is Britain."[12] Even if this father's statement is true, at some point Nasser certainly did not love or respect the UK. Otherwise, why would he leave to fight in the ranks of its enemies?

Ahmed Muthana said that his son Nasser was "brainwashed" when he began to go to different mosques in Britain.[13] Now it is possible that his son became radicalized over a certain period of time because of his frequent visits to different mosques that were possibly sympathetic toward militant jihadism. However, some sort of seed of this violent ideology had to have been instilled in him prior to his conversion. This seed would have made him receptive to receiving and adopting this ideology with little argument, analysis, or criticism.

Islamic teachings and love-hate relationship toward the West

I can recall a personal experience with this very issue, concerning my cousin, who was once a close friend of mine. He knew about my criticism of Islam before he left Morocco to settle in Belgium. Initially, he was not an Islamic extremist or fanatic but was a very open-minded thinker; in fact, his closest friends were Belgians, and they helped him to get a visa so he could remain in Brussels. There, he married a non-Muslim woman. But gradually he became more extreme in his views. He began to teach his children more about Islam, insisting that they criticize the "infidel" West and "racist" Belgium and listen to audio recordings issued by certain sheikhs of Saudi Arabia.

Recently, I decided to visit him, but he refused to see me because I continue to criticize Islam. He said that he did not want to see me, and that he did not want me to attend his funeral when he dies. He justified his position by saying that he could tolerate anything at all except the insult of his Prophet and his religion (because of my public criticism of Islam on television and the Internet). Religion had become his main identity.

---

[12] Marsden, Sam. "'You Don't Keep the Devil in Your House': Furious Father Says He Has B[a]nned Family Pictures of British Medical Student, 20, Who Went to Fight Jihad and Appeared in Chilling ISIS Recruitment Video." *Dailymail.co.uk*. Telegraph Media Group, 20-21 June 2014. Web (http://www.dailymail.co.uk/news/article-2663558/ISIS-releases-chilling-recruitment-video-featuring-young-British-men.html).

[13] Mendick, Robert, Patrick Sawer, and Tim Ross. "The Brilliant Brothers Who Left British Suburb for Jihad in Syria." *Telegraph.co.uk*. Telegraph Media Group, 21 June 2014. Web (http://www.telegraph.co.uk/news/worldnews/middleeast/syria/10917357/The-brilliant-brothers-who-left-British-suburb-for-jihad-in-Syria.html).

Most Muslims, especially young people, who leave their home countries for strange foreign countries experience difficulties in trying to integrate with the new country because of language and cultural differences. In these situations, they feel a loss of identity. Some may then seek out the local mosque and become more religious, finding comfort in the familiar language and customs. It is also a way to renew and preserve their past identity from their native land. But their religion, Islam, with its exclusion of non-Muslims, isolates them even more from their new surroundings. Therefore, it should not be surprising to see how the hatred of non-Muslims can be planted and nurtured, and, over the years, surface and show its fruit.

Other young people leave their Muslim countries to find better economical, educational, and political opportunities in Western countries. But after they arrive, they decide that they want to make their new countries resemble their Muslim homelands, the very ones from which they made their escape. Perhaps they think that the economical, technological, and political prosperity of Western countries progressed this far without the personal freedoms provided and protected by democracy. They don't seem to realize that if these countries were converted to Islam, it would mean the loss of all those personal rights and freedoms, because there is no freedom in Islam and there is no progress without freedom.

This desire by immigrants to "Islamize" the West reminds me of a tweet that one of my friends shared with me, a comment attributed to the late Iraqi writer 'Alī Alwardi: "If Arabs were given a choice between two countries, a secular and a religious, they would vote for the religious state, and then move to live in the secular state." In other words, the secular state preserves the rights of its citizens more than the religious state that they long for.

Therefore, those of us who grew up as Muslims want to have the bounties of the West, its money and its technology, but, at the same time, we curse this West, its morals, and the nakedness of its daughters. We accuse the West of immorality. We inhabit a kind of dual personality, because although we know that we cannot live without the infidel, we hate the infidel.

We know that modern, "technology-related" products, e.g., smartphones, cars, high-definition televisions, etc., in the Muslim world come from the non-Muslim infidel West. We do not say a word when we consume these products, but then we publicly insult the West and advise our children not to be swept behind this Western product (and cultural) invasion. In this way, we exhibit a schizophrenic state of mind: a love for the civilized world of infidels, mixed with hatred of that world and its principles.

We consider the principles and doctrines of Islam higher than the principles of the infidel West—higher than their freedoms, their democracy, and their constitutions. We are taught that the law of hand amputation is divinely given, and the law of stoning is divinely given, and the law of flagellation is divinely given; Western political systems are the ones that have tarnished our divinely given laws.

For example, Morocco is governed by an interbreeding of Islamic and French law. The family and inheritance laws are Islamic, but many articles regarding the penal system in criminal law are French. Therefore, we consider that the West has corrupted our laws because our Moroccan laws are a blend of both Islamic and French (Western) laws. For us, it is only a matter of time until we completely install Islamic law (*sharīʿa*) and supplant current Western-based principles and laws.

Until now, Muslim countries have been living with this contradiction. They teach their children that the Islamic law and the system of *ḥudūd* (Islamic limits or restrictions) are the highest laws because they are divinely given, but, in fact, they are not entirely applied in reality. This reality creates internal conflict in the Muslim youth who yearn for a pure Islamic theocracy. Thus, they become attracted to Islamic groups that promise to apply the "forgotten" *sharīʿa*. For this reason, no one should be surprised when these impressionable, idealistic young people from Arab countries—whether from Morocco or Tunisia or Jordan or Egypt or Saudi Arabia—join Islamic State. We have foolishly fueled this attraction by first filling up our youth with stories from Islamic tradition of an ideal Islamic state, governed by Islamic law, but then failing to realize these dreams in reality. This failure creates in them an emptiness that can be exploited by groups offering them tantalizing promises of a Muslim country free of "infidel" Western laws. Can it be any wonder, then, that huge numbers of young Muslims in the West and East, seduced by these promises of an Islamic-ruled state, are attracted to Islamic State?

Dual governing standards in Muslim countries

In the Muslim world, mosques constantly pray for the doom and destruction of infidels, the children orphaned, the women widowed, their blood frozen in their veins (especially if the infidels live in America and Israel). Many such speeches are given in the public glare of Muslim governments without recrimination. Even though Morocco is an ally of America, it allows these mosque speakers the freedom to broadcast their ideology of hate against the infidels, especially of America and Israel. Saudi Arabia is also an ally of America, but it too disregards the Web sites, videos, audio recordings, radio programs, public speeches and religious lessons in which sheikhs incite hatred against America, describing it as the biggest enemy of Muslims.

The problem is that these mosques are often funded by their respective government, and so we may live in a country seemingly pro-American in its official foreign policy but anti-American regarding its internal or domestic policy. Because of this contradiction, young jihadists consider Arab governments as traitors and hypocrites because they appear pro-Western and especially favorable toward America. Their feelings stem from the mixed message they have received during their lives: As children, they are told that Islamic religious thinking is true and right and America is an aggressor, but as young adults, they are told that America is their country's ally and they see their country supporting American (infidel) policy. Thus, to reconcile this apparent contradiction, they conclude that their government is a traitor to Muslims because it does not oppose or hate infidels but actively supports them. Supporting infidels is one of ten ways that can nullify a person's Islam—making that person an infidel; any person who (or state that) supports infidels becomes a non-Muslim because that person (or state) becomes one of them (an infidel).

All of these supplications of hatred against the infidels do not arise from some unknown void. For an entire month, the prophet Muḥammad himself prayed to Allah in a special kind of prayer (*qunut*) to curse certain Arab tribes and infidels—by their names: "…'O Allah! curse the tribe of Lihyan, curse Ri'l, and Dhakwan,' and then fell in prostration. It is after that the cursing of the unbelievers got a sanction [explicit approval]."[14] Furthermore, when Muḥammad was on his deathbed during his last

[14] *Sahih Muslim*, Book of Prayers: The excellence of *qunut* in all prayers when any calamity befalls the Muslims (p. 392); *Ṣaḥīḥ Muslim*, Kītāb al-Masājid wa Mawāḍi' al-Ṣalāt 1: 303.

illness, one of his final statements was a curse: "Allah cursed the Jews and the Christians that they took the graves of their prophets as mosques...."[15]

His actions are viewed by Muslims as evidence that it is not only permissible but a necessary example (because it is a *sunna*, or a saying or action by Muḥammad) to curse Jews and Christians. As a result, this cursing of Jews and Christians happens in all Muslim countries, even ones where Jews and Christians live. These minorities are continually inundated with these curses and supplications against them during the Friday sermons from the *minbar* (pulpit inside a mosque). Regrettably, they must silently accept this humiliating treatment because any criticism by them is considered a criticism of Islam, which can lead to imprisonment or even death in some cases.

Imagine if Muslims must daily pass by churches in America and be subjected to blaring loudspeakers cursing them with such declarations as "May God curse Muslims because they have converted the grave of their prophet into a mosque!" How would the world react to such derogatory treatment? Yet, the world seems to ignore or take little notice when it sees and hears Muslim animosity towards Jews and Christians as well as those who do not believe in Islam.

[15] *Sahih Muslim*, Book of Prayers: Forbiddance to build mosques on the graves and decorating them with pictures and forbiddance to use the graves as mosques (p. 318); *Ṣaḥīḥ Muslim*, Kītāb al-Masājid wa Mawāḍi' al-Ṣalāt 1: 239.

THREE

We and the others are the "angels" and the "demons"

I grew up in a culture that fears "the others" and assumes that they are evil. We believe in envy and the evil eye, and so we attribute unpleasant consequences of our own wrong actions or decisions to envy, magic, or the evil eye instead of our own laziness or poor judgment. This attitude or belief allows us to shirk our responsibility.

I remember my mother advising me not to tell the neighbors about my school grades and family secrets because they might envy us. This envy might cause my grades to drop and for something bad to happen to our properties and livestock. She asked me to use caution because the evil eye is real and it happens to people, telling me stories that "proved" it.

The source for this Muslim belief is the Islamic religion, which has inherited many customs, traditions, and superstitions of the medieval Arabs, including belief in the evil eye (*'ayn al-ḥasūd*, or "eye of the envious"). This belief has become enshrined as doctrine, spreading wherever Islam proliferates. Prophet Muḥammad himself claimed that the evil eye is real.[1] In fact, Muḥammad asserted that most Muslims will die because of the evil eye.[2]

The Qur'ān itself mentions magic, its origin and its insinuation into people's lives: *"And they* [disbelievers] *follow that which the devils recited against Solomon's kingdom;—it was not Solomon who misbelieved, but the devils who misbelieved, teaching men sorcery..."* (Q 2.102; Palmer trans.). In Islam, magic is real. A girl who fails to get married will believe, for instance, that she's been enchanted by her neighbor or one of her acquaintances. If a young man fails in a project or his marriage or cannot find a job or suffers depression, he might go to special imams (*fuqahā'*) and Islamic exorcists (people who practice *ruqya*, or magic spells). He might call certain television channels hosted by sheikhs who interpret dreams and will practice a magic spell over the phone to remove his ill luck, or the evil eye.

Moreover, Saudi Arabia has a special police force unit with the sole purpose of finding and prosecuting magicians. Islamic State's legislation is more brutal: Anyone convicted of practicing witchcraft is sentenced to death, and a few of the executions have resulted in the beheading of the offenders in public squares.

While it is true that all societies have members who believe in witchcraft and the occult, including Western societies, there is a difference when the belief in witchcraft concerns only an individual or a group's practice of trying to harness magical powers to perform impossible actions and when it is considered an integral part of a formalized religion, established by that religion's sacred texts as an absolute reality and as a belief enforced by the state.

---

[1] *Sahih Bukhari*, Book of Medicine (p. 1282); *Ṣaḥīḥ al-Bukhārī*, Kitāb al-Ṭib 5: 2167. In one *ḥadīth* (narrated by 'Ā'isha), Muḥammad would order an exorcism (*ruqya*) if there was danger "from an evil eye." In another *ḥadīth* (narrated by Um Salama), Muḥammad concludes that a girl with a black facial spot was "under the effect of an evil eye" and to treat her "with a *ruqya*." A third *ḥadīth* (narrated by Abū Hurayra) reports that Muḥammad says, "The effect of an evil eye is a fact."

[2] al-Albānī, *Silsilat al-Aḥādīth al-Ṣaḥīḥa* 2: 372. In a *ḥadīth*, Muḥammad states, "Most of those who will die from my nation after what Allah has decreed will be from the Evil Eye."

We learn from Islamic sources, that the prophet Muḥammad was considered bewitched. One *ḥadīth* reports that he imagined himself having sexual relations with his wives.[3] Other *ḥadīths* report other incidents where Muḥammad confused reality with imaginary occurrences and pronounced it bewitchment by the Jews. Several *ḥadīths* mention a Jew named Labīd Ibn al-Aʿṣam from the tribe of Banū Zurayq, who "worked magic on Allah's Apostle till Allah's Apostle started imagining that he had done a thing that he had not really done."[4]

As exemplified here in the Hadith literature, the Islamic heritage continually demonizes all Jews, associating them even in the evil work of witchcraft. This belief has shaped our view of "the others," thinking that "the others" are responsible for our failures and calamities. It is a view that has become sacred in Islam, ensuring that "the others" are evil and we must fear them, especially if these "others" are infidels.

Placement of blame in Muslim culture

Blaming others and placing the responsibility for our failures on others for every setback or calamity has become an integral part of our language and our culture. For example, in the West if someone arrives late for an appointment or engagement, he would say, "I'm sorry I am late," apologizing using the first-person *subject* pronoun (i.e., I) and thus accepting responsibility for the tardy arrival. However, in our everyday conversations, we make statements, such as "the time passed me by," "the train left me behind," "sleep fell on me," "the cup fell from me," "my memory betrayed me," "the airplane took off without me," and the like. In other words, in using first-person *object* pronoun (i.e., me), we avoid stating (and accepting) any personal responsibility for our failures. In these particular examples, it's *time* that is to blame for me being late because it passed me by and it's the *train* that is guilty of leaving me behind. The *airplane* is at fault for my missed flight (instead of perhaps my carelessness in not minding the flight departure time)...and so on. By framing language in this way in our everyday conversations, we learn how not to voice and thus not take responsibility for our actions.

---

[3] *Sahih Bukhari*, Book of Medicine (p. 1287); *Ṣaḥīḥ al-Bukhārī*, Kitāb al-Ṭib 5: 2175. This *ḥadīth* (as narrated by ʿĀʾisha) reports that "magic was worked on Allah's Apostle so that he used to think that he had sexual relations with his wives while he actually had not...."

[4] *Sahih Bukhari*, Book of Medicine (pp. 1287, 1288); *Sahih Muslim*, Book of Salutations and Greetings: Magic and spell (p. 1348); *Ṣaḥīḥ Muslim*, Kitāb al-Salām 2: 1044.

From these personal, cultural examples, it is then natural to generalize about international situations using these same language structures, always blaming our defeats on Western colonialism and the infidel West and the Jews, or, in general, "our enemies" who are ready to pounce on our countries and religion. We accuse the infidel West of plundering our wealth and stealing our best thinkers, while exporting to us its culture of immorality and social sicknesses. We are convinced that the infidel West and Jews want to corrupt us because we are dangerous to them, especially now after the collapse of communism.

Our own governments encourage this kind of thinking because it exempts them from any accountability for social or political problems within our own countries or responsibility for natural or human-created disasters, such as floods, diseases, bombings, etc. Rarely do we hold our officials accountable for any negligence or malfeasance on their parts, because in all cases, the deaths of the victims are considered fate, predetermined by Allah.

This mind-set—of blaming "the others" for our own misfortunes—resonates widely in our media and publicized discussions as well as on the street. Yet no one wants to address this infantile mind-set and teach people the wisdom and maturity of taking responsibility—ownership—of personal behavior! In fact, it is we and our governmental and educational institutions that have failed our people.

Those who have fled from their Muslim homelands in search of a better future have tried to settle in communities where they will be able to develop unimpeded their abilities, fully express their talents, and enjoy a better standard of living. However, in their migration and resettlement the danger of bringing along this long-enculturated "blame" mind-set is not necessarily removed. Even as these new immigrants enjoy greater personal and economic freedom in their new communities, they may still maintain internal enmity and hatred towards "the others," especially the infidel West. The continuation of this "blame" mind-set affects then the young people, consuming their energy and fomenting a desire for revenge, a desire to punish the infidel West that is responsible for all our misfortunes. Not surprisingly, videos produced by Al Qaeda and Islamic State emphasize and encourage this mind-set of blame upon "the others."

While it is true that this type of hateful, blame-filled speech is highlighted in these videos, similar kinds of statements and speeches can easily be found throughout the Muslim world, from mosques, newspapers, and Web sites, with encouragement from the respective governments and noticeable reinforcement from religious and educational institutions. Even now, none of the Muslim countries seem to care about this inflammatory rhetoric or take serious measures to curb its access or influence upon the youth, allowing them to read or listen to this kind of speech without filters or reasoned objections. Thus the blame and the enmity toward the infidel West, the Crusaders, and the Christians and Jews is allowed to flourish, because the governmental institutions implicitly know that such enmity is an integral part of Islam and that anyone—person or state—that stands up against this sanctioned hate speech would have to face the Islamic religious leaders.

Demonization of Jews in religious texts

Islam demonizes infidels, Christians, and non-Muslims, but it especially demonizes Jews. Their image is distorted in the popular imagination of Muslims. In films, particularly religious films, Jews are always depicted as people full of fraud, cunning, deception and intrigue against the Prophet and Muslims. This unsavory representation is the result of the ideology that we received from Islamic tradition about Jews: Jews are the brothers of apes and pigs anytime and anywhere.

Muḥammad himself cursed the Jews of his time, calling them, "brothers of apes and pigs." The Hadith literature reports that, during his siege of the Jewish tribe Banū Qurayẓa, Muḥammad addressed them as "brothers of apes and pigs!" to which they replied, "O Abū al-Qāsim [another name for Muḥammad], you did not use to be obscene."[5] Muḥammad and his warriors continued to besiege Banū Qurayẓa until they agreed to accept a judgment from Sa'd Ibn Mu'ādh, leader of the Medinan Arab tribe, Aws. (Though he was by then a Muslim, he and his tribe had once been an ally with the Jewish Banū Qurayẓa in conflicts with another Medinan Arab tribe.) Sa'd decreed that the men should be beheaded, the women and children enslaved, and their property taken by the Muslims.[6] (Apparently, the Jewish tribe's former ally was unmoved by its appeal for a merciful judgment despite their prior mutually beneficial partnership.)

This representation—Jews as apes and pigs—is found in the Qur'ān. In several verses (see Q 2.65, Q 5.60, and Q 7.166), Allah curses and

---

[5] Ibn Kathīr, *Al-Bidāya* 6: 74-75; al-Nīsābūrī, *Al-Mustadrak* 3: 37. See Ibn Hishām (Ibn Isḥāq), *The Life of Muhammad* 461.

[6] al-Nīsābūrī, *Al-Mustadrak* 3: 37.

punishes a Jewish tribe that did not obey him or his Sabbath, turning them into *"apes, despised and spurned!"* In another passage (Q 5.59-60; Palmer trans.), the Qur'ān seeks to humiliate Jews by "reminding" them of these disobedient ancestors:

> *Say, 'O people of the Book* [Christians and Jews]*! Do ye disavow us, for aught but that we believe in God, and what was revealed to us before, and for that most of you are evildoers?' / Say, 'Can I declare unto you something worse than retribution from God?' Whomsoever God has cursed and been wroth with—**and he has made of them apes and swine**—and who worship Tâghût* [idolatry], *they are in a worse plight and are more erring from the level path.* (Emphasis added)

Al-Qurṭubī (AD 1214-1273), the esteemed and important Muslim intellectual and scholar, states in his commentary that when this verse Q 5.60 was revealed, Muslims would then call Jews the "brothers of apes and pigs," and the Jews would respond by bowing their heads in shame. Al-Qurṭubī adds that regarding the Jews, "the poet says, 'Allah's curse on the Jews / The Jews are brethren of apes.'"[7]

Imagine if Jews or Christians were to recite these words about Muslims in their synagogues and churches and force Muslims to hear these derogatory terms in publicly broadcasted sermons via loudspeakers. Imagine if an article was published in an American newspaper stating that Muslims are apes and pigs. Imagine if news hosts on an American television program were to claim that Muslims are brothers of apes and pigs. The whole world would condemn this bigotry, and the first condemners would be the Muslims! Yet Muslims in return accept these dehumanizing descriptions about Jews. They consecrate it and prohibit the criticism of these terms by anyone. They will allege that anyone who does criticize the Islamic text insulting Jews and Christians is only trying to stir up hatred against Muslims and Islam.

Unfortunately, this Muslim characterization of Jews as "brothers of apes and pigs" is not the only hateful slur used to denigrate Jews. Muḥammad even called Jews "rats." (In Islam, the rat is called *al-fuwaysiqa*, or "the trivial evildoer.") In the Hadith literature, Muḥammad states that Jews as evildoers were cursed and transformed by Allah into rats:[8]

---

[7] See the commentary on Q 5.60, *Tafsīr al-Qurṭubī* 6: 236.

[8] *Sahih Bukhari*, Book of the Beginning of Creation (p. 766); *Ṣaḥīḥ al-Bukhārī*, Kītāb Bad' al-Khalq 3: 1203. See *Sahih Muslim*, Book Pertaining to Piety and Softening of Hearts: Miscellaneous Ahadith (pp. 1778-9).

> The Prophet said, "A group of Israelites were lost. Nobody knows what they did. But I do not see them except that they were cursed and changed into rats, for if you put the milk of a she-camel in front of a rat, it will not drink it, but if the milk of a sheep is put in front of it, it will drink it…."

As confirmation of his assertion that Jews have been transformed into rats, Muḥammad states here that one only needs to test the rats' milk preferences. According to Muḥammad, rats will shun camel's milk and drink only sheep's milk, which means the rats—the cursed and transformed Jews—are obeying the Torah's prohibitions regarding the eating (and drinking the milk) of "unclean" animals, e.g., the camel. (See Lev. 11.4; Deut. 14.7). Since the meat and milk of sheep are not prohibited for consumption by Jews, Muḥammad is suggesting that even as devolved creatures, the Jews continue to keep the teachings of the Torah as "religious" rats.

Jews, the eternal enemies, in religious texts

The religious texts concerned with the hostility towards and demonization of Jews are diverse and rooted. Islam portrays Jews as the sworn enemy who will remain an enemy for Muslims until the Day of Resurrection. As reported in the Hadith literature, Muḥammad states that even the stones and trees will assist Muslims in destroying the Jews in the Last Hour:[9]

> The last hour would not come unless the Muslims will fight against the Jews and the Muslims would kill them until the Jews would hide themselves behind a stone or a tree and a stone or a tree would say: Muslim, or the servant of Allah, there is a Jew behind me; come and kill him; but the tree of al-Gharqad would not say, for it is the tree of the Jews.

Now imagine a Muslim child, listening to these types of texts being recited in his presence. He must learn about them in school and have his knowledge of them tested and evaluated. During his elementary and secondary schooling, he must research and write about these texts. All the while, he will hear these texts in weekly sermons and many Muslim television programs and channels that discuss the correct behavior for Muslim daily living. As an adult, he then passes on this education to

[9] *Sahih Muslim*, Book Pertaining to the Turmoil and Portents of the Last Hour: The last hour would not come until a person would pass by a grave and wish that he should have been the occupant of that grave because of this calamity (p. 1740); *Ṣaḥīḥ Muslim*, Kitāb al-Fitan wa Ashrāṭ al-Sā'a 2: 1335.

the following generations. In this environment, wouldn't he grow up to hate Jews and be prepared to fight the decisive "Last Hour" battle against them?

The hatred found in these religious texts did not derive from the current hatred toward today's state of Israel, because these texts were written twelve centuries before the statehood of Israel in 1948. We all have been brought up hearing these texts since childhood, with the understanding that one day we will face all the Jews and kill them (and with nature's help, except for the Jews' support from the tree of al-Gharqad).

With the use of oil money, these texts have been translated into all the world's main languages, including English and French books. These texts are even a part of the curriculum in the Islamic Studies departments in Muslim universities across the world, including Al Azhar and major Saudi universities, without supervision or control.

Unbelievably, Muslims do not consider these teachings as texts that incite hatred against a particular group of people. As illustration, read the following excerpt published in the electronic newspaper *Aafāq* concerning comments made by an imam, Muḥammad al-Arīfī, when he was interviewed on the Palestinian television channel Al-Aqsa TV on September 12, 2008:[10]

> Now the reports of those who visited there [Israel]...say that many of the Jews are growing trees of al-Gharqad around their houses...to be able to hide when the fight takes place...because they're not man enough to stand in front of the Muslims to fight them.

From where did the imam al-Arīfī get this perspective, references (final battle with Jews) and vocabulary ("trees of al-Gharqad")? By evoking this terminology to an audience who knows this *ḥadīth*, this imam is trying to prove that Muḥammad's statements about the final days were true then and now—even as this imam distorts the reality of the Israeli landscape, where the majority of its Jewish citizens live in cities and do not grow any trees of this kind in front of their homes. It is disturbing that the imam will say falsities to manipulate the feelings of Muslims in his effort to assure to them that Muḥammad's words are true and that Muslims will enjoy a final victory over the Jews with the help of stones and trees.

---

[10] "Saudi Iman Muḥammad al-Arīfī: Jews Are Planting al-Gharqad Trees around Their Homes to Protect Them from Muslims."*Aafāq*. Aafaq Foundation, 29 Sept. 2008. Web (http://aafaq.org/news.aspx?id_news=7082).

Despite his outlandish claims, the imam's overall perception of the final days is clearly reiterated in seemingly more reputable sources, such as the following fatwa, published on a Web site sponsored by the Ministry of Endowments and Islamic Affairs of Qatar:[11]

> ...[T]he war that the Prophet mentioned, where Muslims will fight the Jews and they will overcome them in the end of days, will apparently happen at the time of the coming of the Anti-Christ, the descent of Jesus, son of Mary, and the appearance of the Mahdī.[12] In al-Ṣaḥīḥayn [*Ṣaḥīḥ al-Bukhārī* and *Ṣaḥīḥ Muslim*], Abū Hurayra narrates that the Messenger of Allah said, "The last hour would not come unless you will fight against the Jews until the stone would say: come Muslim, there is a Jew behind me; come and kill him!"...**It must be noted that Muslims must not stop themselves from jihad against the Jews until that hour comes**.... (Emphasis added)

This fatwa is but one representation of the accumulated Islamic texts that primarily teach hostility towards Jews (and Christians). This hostility toward Jews (and Christians) is kept continually simmering in the minds of Muslims in the course of their learning, memorizing, and acceptance of these texts. Therefore, it should come as no surprise that average Muslims might be drawn to any Muslim imam, sheikh, group, or nation that reaches out to them, using these highly familiar and sanctioned texts and related terms to win support for a particular opinion or agenda.

In 1998, Osama Bin Laden of Al Qaeda and Ayman al-Ẓawāhirī of Egyptian Islamic Jihad, along with four other radical Islamic groups, formed a coalition they named "World Islamic Front for Combat against the Jews and Crusaders."[13] They knew that choosing such a title for this coalition, with its obvious connotations, would resonate deeply with Muslims and Muslim nations, because the word *Jews* would arouse strong negative feelings among Muslims, and the word *Crusaders* could be generalized to mean all "Christian warriors," i.e., Westerners, and not just the medieval Christian soldiers during the religious wars of the Middle Ages. In declaring jihad against the infidel West, the front used

[11] See Fatwa no. 16494. "The Messenger's Prophecy about the Muslims' Fight with the Jews." *Islamweb.net*. Ministry of Endowments and Islamic Affairs of Qatar. 13 May 2002. Web (http://fatwa.islamweb.net/ fatwa/ index.php?page=showfatwa&Option=FatwaId&Id=16494).

[12] In Islamic eschatology the Mahdī is the prophesied deliverer in Hadith literature who will come to fill the world with justice and restore true religion before the final days. The Mahdī, however, is not explicitly mentioned in the Qur'ān.

[13] "Profile: Ayman al-Zawahiri." *BBC.com*. British Broadcasting Corporation, 13 Aug. 2015. Web (http:// www.bbc.com/news/world-middle-east-13789286).

Islamic text and terms to capitalize on and stoke the carefully taught, deeply held feelings of hatred in Muslims toward Jews and Christians after centuries of this Islamic instruction.

From the very beginning of its establishment in 1988, Al Qaeda enjoyed wide popularity among a large segment of Muslims. Its message and mission was a powerful magnet for many jihadists in the Arab and Muslim world...before the organization of Islamic State (and precursors, ISIL and ISIS) snatched the spotlight from Al Qaeda and became the new direction, a new Mecca, for the jihadists.

Qur'ān's ugly descriptions of Jews and Christians

The dehumanization of Jews and Christians is centuries old and begins with the Qur'ān, which uses language considered some of the ugliest verbal insults in the Arab culture to describe nonbelievers. For example, Qur'ānic text (e.g., Q 7.175-176; Arberry trans.) has compared evildoers, liars, or nonbelievers as dogs:

> *And recite to them the tiding of him to whom We gave Our signs, but he cast them off; and Satan followed after him, and he became one of the perverts. / And had We willed, We would have raised him up thereby; but he inclined towards the earth and followed his lust. So the likeness of him is as the likeness of a dog; if thou attackest it it lolls its tongue out, or if thou leavest it, it lolls its tongue out. That is that people's likeness who cried lies to Our signs. So relate the story; haply they will reflect.*

Unlike the West, where human comparisons to dogs can connote positive associations, i.e., loyalty, friendliness, or unconditional love, in the Arab culture, the dog is considered by many to be unclean and that Islam forbids dog ownership unless it is used for hunting or guarding livestock and farms.[14]

What if this verse was revised to read *"So the likeness of him is as the likeness of a dog.... That is the likeness of* ***the Muslim people****...*" (emphasis added to substitution). If Muslims would never tolerate this comparison to describe themselves, how then can this likeness become sacred text, recited by people in their prayers, to describe more than six billion humans around the world who are non-Muslims?

The word *ass* is another derogatory term used in the Arab culture to insult a person. For Arabs the ass is always a symbol of stupidity and

[14] *Sahih Bukhari*, Book of Agriculture (p. 525); *Ṣaḥīḥ al-Bukhārī*, Kītāb al-Muzāra'a 2: 818.

to verbally use this term against another person is considered a grave insult. The Qur'ān uses this term against Jews, and Muslims read it today without qualm, as in Q 62.5 (Palmer trans.):

> *The likeness of those who were charged with the law* [Torah] *and then bore it not is as the likeness of an ass bearing books: sorry is the likeness of the people who say God's signs are lies! but God guides not an unjust people.*

In other words, this verse is comparing an ass—considered here a stupid animal—to Jews, stating that both do not understand the books that they carry. The word "books" in this verse refers to the Torah, the first five books of the Old Testament and the source of Jewish written laws.

Imagine if someone read aloud, *"The likeness of those who were charged with* ***the Qur'ān*** *and then bore it not is as the likeness of an ass bearing books…"* (emphasis added to substitution). If this version was published in newspapers and people read it in churches and Jewish synagogues, how would Muslims across the world react?

Muslims have reacted with violent demonstrations and riots just because of cartoon drawings of the prophet Muḥammad, claiming that the world has insulted, offended, and disrespected them. Yet they continuously insult Jews and use the words *ass* and *dog* to disparage and degrade Jews and other non-Muslims. They consider these terms sacred words appropriate for use during their worship. They even recite these words in their prayers, read them in the Friday sermons, and cite them on religious programs when talking about the "stupidity" of Jews and the "animality" of non-Muslims. They do all these things without paying any attention to the feelings of anyone who is not a Muslim, as if Muslims are the only ones in the world who have feelings. Muslims believe they have the right to verbally abuse all the rest of the world with these kinds of descriptions and comparisons—and no one has the right to object.

The dehumanization of "the others" is clearly reflected in another description we use about infidels. Infidels are "unclean," intrinsically unclean; their essential inner nature is impure. Only Muslims are pure and clean, according to the Qur'ān: *"O ye who believe! it is only the idolaters who are unclean; they shall not then approach the Sacred Mosque after this year…"* (Q 9.28; Palmer trans.). As interpreted by the significant Muslim commentators, "the idolaters [mentioned in this verse] are only the abomination of swine and dogs."[15] Indeed, one of the Muslim scholars, al-Ḥasan al-Baṣrī (AD 642-728) states, "the idolaters are unclean...do not shake hands with them, and whoever does, let him perform *wuḍū'* [ablution to remove impurities]."[16]

Christians and Jews are considered "idolaters" because they associate other gods with Allah, according to Islam. For this reason, the Umayyad caliph 'Umar Ibn 'Abd al-'Azīz (AD 682-720) made it administrative policy to forbid Jews and Christians entrance into the mosques, basing his prohibition on the belief that the idolaters are unclean.[17]

What we learn as Muslims about non-Muslims, or "infidels," is that they are intrinsically unclean, just as the infidel polytheist is unclean, while the Muslim is pure in himself. The Qur'ān and Muḥammad's words as reported in the Hadith literature have taught us this differentiation. In one *ḥadīth*, Muḥammad tells Companion Abū Hurayra, "The Muslim never becomes impure."[18]

We look at "unclean" infidels with contempt and prejudicial discrimination. Undoubtedly, this attitude toward infidels prompted Muḥammad (while on his deathbed) to command his followers to "expel the pagans [Jews and Christians] from the Arabian Peninsula...."[19] In another *ḥadīth*, he declares, "I will expel the Jews and Christians from the Arabian Peninsula and will not leave any but Muslim."[20]

Muḥammad's attitude and declarations underlie the real reason behind the prohibition of non-Muslims entering Mecca, because according to the Kingdom of Saudi Arabia non-Muslims are impure and will defile this sacred place. Non-Muslims are the most despicable creatures and if they enter this place, it will be like a pig entering into a mosque. Fatāwa confirm this rationale, like this fatwa found on the Qatar Web site: "It is not permissible for a non-Muslim to enter Mecca because of the words of Allah: *"O ye who believe! it is only the idolaters who are unclean; they shall*

[15] See the commentary on Q 9.28, *Tafsīr al-Ṭabarī* 10: 77.

[16] Ibid.

[17] Ibid.

[18] *Sahih Bukhari*, Book of Bathing (pp. 78, 79); *Ṣaḥīḥ al-Bukhārī*, Kītāb al-Ghusl 1: 109. **Note:** Original Arabic text states, "The Muslim never becomes impure," whereas the English (mis)translation reads, "A believer never becomes impure."

[19] *Sahih Bukhari*, Book of Fighting for the Cause of Allah (Jihad)(pp. 702-703); *Ṣaḥīḥ al-Bukhārī*, Kītāb al-Jizya wa al-Muwāda'a 3: 1156.

[20] *Sahih Muslim*, Book of Jihad and Expedition: Evacuation of the Jews from the Hijaz (p. 1091); *Ṣaḥīḥ Muslim*, Kītāb al-Jihād wa al-Sīyar 2: 846.

not then approach the Sacred Mosque [Q 9.28; Palmer trans.]...."[21] Notice that the same verse (Q 9.28) that declares "Jews and Christians" impure is the same verse that prohibits them from entering Mecca.

Imagine if Italy deported all Muslims from Rome by an executive order titled, "Italy will deport all Muslims, leaving none except Christians" or under the title "It is only the Muslims who are unclean; they shall not be allowed to approach Italian cities." By reversing the targeted groups, these fictional Italian edicts bluntly expose the bigotry of the Muslim fatāwa.

Even so, Muslims have a difficult time looking outside or beyond their own perspective. Muslims have been taught to memorize and repeat these bigoted texts to such an extent that they believe them factual and indisputable. Their education normalizes this view that Jews and Christians—and non-Muslims in general—are contemptible human beings. For them, this attitude is necessary and proper because the texts are sacred—they came to Muslims from Allah. It is Allah who has decreed that non-Muslims are unclean. It is Allah who has decreed through his prophet Muḥammad to expel non-Muslims from sanctified cities and other religious Muslim places.

Responsibility for Muslim catastrophes

The Islamic ideology that accepts and encourages the contemptibility of Jews and Christians does not question the use of them as scapegoats for Muslims on the Day of Resurrection, as Muḥammad states in this *ḥadīth*: "...There would come people amongst the Muslims on the Day of Resurrection with as heavy sins as a mountain, and Allah would forgive them and He would place in their stead the Jews and the Christians."[22]

This sanctioned hatred for Jews and Christians has made them, in the Islamic imagination, acceptable and deserving scapegoats to bear the sins of Muslims. So, it's no wonder that today in the Muslim world we subject all our own failures and sins, even if they are abhorrently bad (like mountains), on the shoulders of Jews and Christians, "the others,"

[21] See Fatwa no. 91221. "Forbidding Non-Muslims from Entering Makka [Mecca]. *Islamweb.net*. Ministry of Endowments and Islamic Affairs of Qatar. 27 Feb. 2006. Web (http://preview.tinyurl.com/zjq7eul). For the Arabic Web page, see Fatwa no. 3225: "It Is Not Permissible for a Non-Muslim to Enter Mecca." *Islamweb.net*. Ministry of Endowments and Islamic Affairs of Qatar. 18 Feb. 2000. Web (http://preview.tinyurl.com/j62vqtm).

[22] *Sahih Muslim*, Book Pertaining to Repentance and Exhortation to Repentance: Throwing of nonbelievers in hellfire for believers as divine grace and mercy (p. 1652); *Ṣaḥīḥ Muslim*, Kītāb al-Tawba 2: 1269.

because this belief has been carefully planted and nurtured in our hearts by the indoctrination we have received from our Islamic religious texts. These texts have instilled in us the teaching to carry this hidden hatred toward "the others," demonizing in particular Jews and Christians, whom we have even made into human sacrifices for our mistakes.

Because of our extreme hatred towards Jews and Christians, we blame them for all the catastrophes of the Islamic nation. We even blame the death of Muḥammad on the Jews, because the Hadith literature reports several narrations claiming that a Jewish woman from Khaybar gave Muḥammad poisoned meat to eat and that he died three or more years later because of that incident. In one *ḥadīth*, Muḥammad, on his deathbed, alludes to this incident to a favored wife: "O 'Ā'isha! I still feel the pain caused by the food I ate at Khaybar, and at this time, I feel as if my aorta is being cut from that poison."[23] Therefore, based on the Hadith literature and Islamic tradition, Jews are magicians and murderers. They are the ones who bewitched the prophet and are responsible for his death.

We understand from these religious texts that Jews will continuously plot until the Day of Resurrection against Muslims. These warnings of constant Jewish intrigues against Muslims are often repeated by the traditional or fundamentalist sheikhs and even those who claim to be modern, such as Sheikh Adnan Ibrahim, who preaches in the Shura mosque (located in the Leopoldstadt district of Vienna, the capital city of Austria) and promotes himself as a reformer, a "Martin Luther" of Islam.[24] Yet he too adopts the same traditional Islamic ideology. In one of his video recorded speeches about Jews, he makes these comments:[25]

---

[23] *Sahih al-Bukhārī*, Kītāb al-Maghāzī 4: 1611. For English translation, see *Sunnah.com*: Book of Military Expeditions Led by Prophet. Web (https://sunnah.com/bukhari/64/450).

[24] Ibrahim, Adnan. Interview by 'Abd Allah al-Mudayfir. *Fī al-Ṣamīm*. (Episode 14). Rotana TV. Rotana Group, Riyadh. 23 July 2013. Television. (For video footage, see URL: https://www.youtube.com/watch?v=ps7bdeKDwjU)

[25] Ibrahim, Adnan. "Take Revenge for Muḥammad." 16 Sept. 2012. Sermon. (For video footage, see URL: https://vimeo.com/129147313).

> If we have a memory, then we would want to take revenge for Muḥammad. If we have an intellect, then we should re-employ the historical facts in order to teach these bastard dwarfs [Jews] a lesson. Muḥammad died a martyr at the hands of the Jews...he died at the hands of the Jews. I say to you also that your Messenger (Peace be upon him) faced fifteen assassination attempts—fifteen attempts. Three of them were by the polytheists and twelve attempts were by... do you know who? The Jews! May Allah curse the Jews! All they can do is vile[ness], villainy, murder, assassination and treachery.

If such speech is not challenged but is repeated in Western mosques, then we should not be surprised if Jews are being targeted in these countries.

Culpability of religious texts, culture, and hostility toward Jews

Our hatred toward Jews dates prior to the statehood of Israel. It has been ingrained from the beginning into our consciousness and our subconsciousness from the massive accumulation and indoctrination of our religious Islamic texts. These texts have directly and systematically encouraged us to become a hostile culture, particularly toward Jews and Christians. Therefore, it should not be surprising to witness Islamic groups today targeting Christian churches, Jewish synagogues, and cemeteries.

For example, Libya has been a site for this type of religious antagonism. During the Libyan Civil War (which erupted soon after the Arab Spring in 2011) the embattled Libyan dictator Muammar el-Qaddafi vowed to find all the rebels by tracking them down in every corner, "*zanga zanga*" (alley to alley). However, the rebel forces of the National Transitional Council (de facto government of the revolution) soon received the support and assistance of the United Nations and NATO, enabling the NTC to score a decisive victory against el-Qaddafi's Libyan Army when it tried to attack Benghazi. This Western intervention saved Benghazi, protecting thousands of civilians, and enabled the revolution to eventually overthrow el-Qaddafi.

But in the eyes of many Muslims, Western nations are considered the enemy "Crusaders." About a year after the city was liberated, some thirty armed Muslim residents entered the British Commonwealth War Graves Commission cemetery and calmly desecrated the grave headstones of over 200 British soldiers and airmen who died and were buried there during World War II. The vandals also used mallets to damage the cross on the cemetery's cenotaph (main remembrance monument), with one onlooker yelling, "Break the cross of the dogs." When video footage of the desecration (taken by the perpetrators themselves) was circulated on YouTube, the NTC expressed its regrets, apologies, and condemnation.[26] BBC correspondent Gabriel Gatehouse in Tripoli reported that "the attackers [in the video footage] referred to 'Christian dogs' and a Jewish memorial was also targeted."[27] (Notice the use of the word *dogs* by these attackers, a slur that is well known and widespread in the Muslim culture to demean Christians. Doesn't its use here indicate that those who carried out this destruction were acting on this cultural mind-set? And while it is true that the NTC apologized for this desecration—whether from political or humanitarian motivations—they cannot deny the proliferation of this hostility culture toward "the others" in Libyan society, which is no different than other Muslim societies.)

The city of Casablanca in Morocco has also been the scene of hostile attacks against "the others." On May 16, 2003, a Spanish restaurant as well as the Belgian consulate, a Jewish community center, a Jewish cemetery, and the five-star Hotel Farah, were the targets of suicide bombers.[28] Presumably these targets were selected because the Spanish restaurant serves a large number of Western foreigners or Moroccans influenced by Westerners or Christians. The Jewish community center and cemetery are obvious gathering sites for Jews, whether living or dead. The five-star hotel assuredly catered to foreign (and most likely Christian) guests, and, of course, the Belgian consulate is a consulate of a Western, "Christian" country. All these targets show that the attackers intended to harm Jews and Christians—perhaps because they are perceived as a corruptive influence in Muslim societies, e.g., the Spanish restaurant and five-star hotel offer alcohol to their customers. Consumption of alcohol by Christians, Jews, and other non-Muslims in a Muslim country is viewed by devout Muslims as immoral behavior that must be purged from their country. To justify their view, Muslims need only look at similar actions undertaken by their prophet Muḥammad, who first

[26] Jones, Sam, Chris Stephen, and agencies. "Libya Apologises for Desecration of British War Graves." *TheGuardian.com*. The Guardian, 4 Mar. 2012. Web (https://www.theguardian.com/world/2012/mar/04/libya-apologises-british-graves-desecration). **Note:** Link to the video footage of the desecration available in this article. Notice the camera close-up of the Jewish star on one of the headstones before it is uprooted by one of the men.

[27] "Fury over Attack on British War Graves in Benghazi." *BBC.com*. British Broadcasting Corporation, 4 Mar. 2012. Web (http://www.bbc.com/news/uk-17244211).

[28] "Terror Blasts Rock Casablanca." *BBC.co.uk*. British Broadcasting Corporation. 17 May 2003. Web (http://news.bbc.co.uk/2/hi/africa/3035803.stm).

expelled Banū Qaynuqā‘ and then Banū al-Naḍīr, Jewish tribes living near Medina, when they refused to embrace Islam.[29]

On January 9, 2015, two days after the horrific massacre at the *Charlie Hebdo* newspaper offices in Paris, France, Amedy Coulibaly, a close friend of the Charlie Hebdo shooters and a French Muslim of Malian-born immigrant parents, seized a Jewish supermarket and then killed four Jews he had taken hostage before he was killed by police. After his death, the police learned that he had shot and killed the day before a policewoman who was investigating a traffic accident near a Jewish school. Later, the police discovered maps of Jewish schools in Coulibaly's car and have concluded that his original target destination that day was the Jewish school. When the traffic accident prevented his access to the school, he shot the policewoman instead.[30]

On February 14, 2015, a young Danish Muslim of Jordanian-Palestinian descent named Omar Abdel Hamid El-Ḥussein attempted to enter a small public event at a cultural center in Copenhagen, Denmark. He shot and killed one attendee who tried to stop him and then opened fire through the window of the center, wounding three police officers at the event, before he escaped. One of the keynote speakers at this event—and likely the gunman's primary target—was Swedish artist Lars Vilks, an artist whose provocative caricatures of the prophet Muḥammad in 2007 led to condemnation of Vilks and his work by the governments of several Muslim countries and death threats from Al Qaeda and other Islamic terrorist groups.[31] (See Chapter 14, page 427.)

Just after midnight, El-Ḥussein showed up outside the Great Synagogue, which is the main house of worship for Jews in Copenhagen.

---

[29] For the Banū Qaynuqā‘ account, see al-Wāqidī, *Kitāb al-Maghāzī* 177. For the Banū al-Naḍīr account, see Ibn Kathīr, *Al-Bidayah* 5: 533-549. Ibn Kathīr states that only one pack animal was allowed per three Jews to carry all their personal belongings during this forced expulsion.

[30] Collins, David. "Paris Terror Attack: Jewish Schools and Police on High Alert Amid Terror Target Fears." *Mirror.co.uk*. Mirror Online, 11 Jan. 2015. Web (http://www.mirror.co.uk/news/world-news/paris-terror-attack-jewish-schools-4961800); Penketh, Anne. "Paris's Jewish Community Retreats in Shock after Deadly End to Siege." *TheGuardian.com*. The Guardian, 10 Jan. 2015. Web (https://www.theguardian.com/world/2015/jan/10/paris-jewish-community-shock-terror-attacks-amedy-coulibaya); Bisserbe, Noemie, and Inti Landauro. "Wall Street Journal: French Prosecutors Investigate Whether Gunman Targeted Jewish School." *WSJ.com*. Wall Street Journal, 12 Jan. 2015. Web (http://www.wsj.com/articles/french-prosecutors-investigate-whether-gunman-targeted-jewish-school-1421064200). See Weitzmann, Marc. "Kosher Supermarket Gunman Caught on Tape Casing Jewish School in August [2014]." *Tabletmag.com*. Tablet Magazine, 23 Jan. 2015. Web (http://www.tabletmag.com/scroll/188518/kosher-supermarket-gunman-caught-on-tape-casing-jewish-school-in-august).

[31] "Denmark Attacks: Large Crowds Mourn Shooting Victims." *BBC.com*. British Broadcasting Corporation, 16 Feb. 2015. Web (http://www.bbc.com/news/world-europe-31493764).

There he killed a Jewish community member providing security protection for a bat mitzvah celebration taking place inside the building. El-Hussein wounded two policemen before fleeing the site without entering the synagogue. Several hours later, El-Hussein was tracked to another building, where he died in an exchange of gunfire with Danish police forces.[32]

Religious and cultural reasons for hatred toward Jews

What drives these young Muslims to target these non-Muslims, especially Jewish people and in Jewish places? The attempt to limit the basis of this violent hatred to the rather recent Israeli-Palestinian conflict, which began during the last century, is a deliberate disregard of the influence of the Islamic heritage on the psychological and ideological composition of the Muslim mind-set toward non-Muslims, especially Jews and Christians, since the time of Muḥammad. This religiously and culturally cultivated mind-set, developed and sustained for nearly fourteen centuries, is the most important reason undergirding this hostility. This continuously held Muslim hatred toward Jews helps to explain the exodus of Jews throughout history from Muslim countries in the Middle East because of the systematic persecutions, massacres, forced conversions, and limited economic and political rights and opportunities. By the 1970s most of the remaining Jews in Arab and Muslim countries have voluntarily left or been forcibly expelled.[33]

Today Morocco, once considered the best place for Jews in the Muslim world in comparison with the rest of the Muslim countries, has experienced a decrease in its Jewish population because of more overt manifestations of the hostility inherent in the predominantly Muslim society towards them. If it were not for the ruling power (the constitutional monarch of Morocco, King Mohammed VI, who wields

[32] "Copenhagen Shootings: Police Kill 'Gunman' after Two Attacks." *BBC.com*. British Broadcasting Corporation, 15 Feb. 2015. Web (http://www.bbc.com/news/world-europe-31475803); Green, Chris, and Richard Orange. "Copenhagen Shootings: Suspected Gunman Omar Abdel Hamid El-Hussein Was a Danish National with a History of Gang Violence." *Independent.co.uk*. The Independent, 15 Feb. 2015. Web (http://www.independent.co.uk/news/world/europe/copenhagen-shootings-suspected-gunman-omar-abdel-hamid-el-hussein-was-a-danish-national-with-a-10047741.html). See Smith-Spark, Laura, and Nic Robertson. "Who Was Copenhagen Gunman Omar Abdel Hamid l-Hussein?" *CNN.com*. Cable News Network, 27 Feb. 2015. Web (http://www.cnn.com/2015/02/17/europe/denmark-copenhagen-gunman).

[33] Trigano, Shmuel. "The Expulsion of the Jews from Muslim Countries, 1920-1970: A History of Ongoing Cruelty and Discrimination." *Jerusalem Center for Public Affairs: Israeli Security, Regional Diplomacy, and International Law*. 2 Nov. 2010. Web (http://jcpa.org/article/the-expulsion-of-the-jews-from-muslim-countries-1920-1970-a-history-of-ongoing-cruelty-and-discrimination/).

considerable authority over military, foreign, and religious affairs), then there would likely be a formalized expulsion of the Jews in Morocco, and they would become the first target for attacks should there be any security lapses.

Even though the current ruling authority in Morocco is restrained by world political considerations, the local Muslim population is more influenced and controlled by its religious and cultural inculcation and thus more willing to express its anger at and hatred toward its "eternal enemies," the Jews and Christians. Whether in Morocco or any other Muslim country, Jews and Christians will always be the primary targets by extremists in all these countries. People must realize and acknowledge that this focused objective—to attack Jews and Christians—is not the result of political differences but a religious culture that sanctifies and promotes this irrational hatred toward non-Muslims.

Tangible evidence—that this Muslim hatred toward non-Muslims is religiously and not politically based—can be found on the Arabic (but not necessarily the English) Web site of the Muslim Brotherhood. It posts content that discusses and acknowledges Islam's religious conflict with Jews. Even though this viewpoint is very well known and aligns with other Islamic groups, Western media chooses to explain this Muslim-Jewish hostility in political terms and shies away from the religion link because its reality is too frightening.

On one Web page on the Muslim Brotherhood site, Palestinian sheikh 'Abdul Qādir al-Shaṭlī, a graduate of the Islamic University in Gaza with a bachelor's degree in Islamic law (*sharī'a*), makes this comment:[34]

> The conflict between us and the Jews is a conflict of fate and is a constant conflict that will not end until Allah authorizes us to triumph over them. The evidence for this [nonending conflict] is when Allah Almighty talks about the conflict between us and the Children of Israel, both Jews and Christians...Allah Almighty says [in Q 2.120; Arberry trans.], *"Never will the Jews be satisfied with thee, neither the Christians, not till thou followest their religion...."* It is clear from this verse and the abovementioned verses [al-Shaṭlī mentions Q 3.137-141, Q 7.167] that the truth about the conflict is that it is a religious conflict.

[34] al-Shaṭlī, 'Abdul Qādir. "Our Conflict with the Jews: When Did It Begin? What Are Its Motives and Causes? What Is Its Nature and Reality? And When Will It End?" *Ikhwanwiki.com*. Muslim Brotherhood, n.d. Web (http://preview.tinyurl.com/hjw9ydc).

According to Islam, Muslims believe there is a neverending conflict between them and non-Muslims—particularly Jews and Christians—and, as described here by this sheikh, this conflict is primarily religious and not territorial. And framing this conflict in religious terms is the predominant method used by Islamic groups to manipulate the feelings of Muslims, who are receptive to this rationale because of their Muslim upbringing and environment. (In fact, Muḥammad himself originated this position by basing his own conflict with the Jews and Christians and other infidels on religious grounds, as mentioned earlier in this chapter.)

For centuries, Muslims have absorbed Islamic teachings and been immersed in a culture that continuously demonizes Jews and Christians as devious schemers. The Qur'ān and Hadith literature degrade Jews and Christians, likening them to "apes and swine" and "dogs," respectively, and other dehumanizing characterizations. This Islamic heritage also demeans Jews and Christians—in fact, all non-Muslims—by asserting they are essentially "unclean" and will never be treated by Allah as a Muslim. Needless to say, such constant negative representation of Jews and Christians (and non-Muslims in general) and their presumed evil intentions toward Muslims and Islam will naturally produce conflict—a religious conflict—between Muslims and their "eternal enemies." This ongoing religious hatred, instigated in the seventh century AD, precedes and envelops any political conflict and endures after it.

Yet this religious conflict has paradoxical qualities, for we view non-Muslims with a schizophrenic eye: we consider them inferior beings, because our texts regard them as despicable and inferior, but we are dazzled by their scientific advancements. And so we live in a state of internal as well as religious conflict. We love these Western countries and we curse them. We want their smartphones and computers and machines, but we insult and revile their creators. We wish to get a visa to visit (and stay in!) their countries, and we want to marry their daughters in order to convert them to Islam. But—at the same time—we hate and despise them.

When all is said and done, our Islamic texts have succeeded in manipulating our feelings and distorting our psyche and our humanity, turning us into psychologically sick people who require treatment. Without treatment or intervention, those of us (especially Muslim teenagers) who have succumbed to these religious teachings and a culture promoting hatred toward "the others," too frequently become the susceptible recruits of Islamic State, Al Qaeda, and other Islamic jihadist organizations that, in turn, only exploit our religious hatred and gullibility to serve their own brutal religious agendas.

FOUR

We are *"the best nation ever brought forth...."*

Religiosity can create a conceited pride in people, making them believe that others not as "religious" are inferior or less worthy. The "religious" people may believe that they are better than other people because they pray, fast, and perform daily and detailed rituals while the less or nonreligious others do not. Therefore, the "religious" people might consider themselves superior beings. The Qur'ān uses this belief as a foundational rule: *"O ye folk! verily, we have created you of male and female, and made you races and tribes that ye may know each other. Verily, the most honourable of you in the sight of God is the most pious of you; verily, God is knowing, aware!"* (Q 49.13; Palmer trans.).

According to the Qur'ān, our dignity doesn't derive from our humanity but from our righteousness. Our depth of piety has a direct relationship with our "religiosity," because piety in the Islamic understanding is associated with the strength of a Muslim's commitment to Islam. In his commentary on Q 49.13, al-Ṭabarī states,"The Almighty says: the most honorable among you, O people, in the sight of your Lord are the most righteous, those who perform divinely decreed duties and abstain from what God has forbidden."[1]

Based on this measure, the devout Muslim is better and more honorable than the uncommitted Muslim, and a Muslim in general is better than a non-Muslim. Thus, every non-Muslim, even if he or she is righteous, is inferior to any Muslim just for being a non-Muslim. This hierarchy, which is based on a person's Islamic religiosity, has guided us Muslims to believe that we are always better than other peoples and other nations. We believe in particular that we are better than Jews and Christians and certainly better than the rest of the "infidels."

This Muslim perception of superiority towards others derives from the Qur'ān. Islam's holiest book describes Muslims in Q 3.110 (Arberry trans.) in this way: *"You are the best nation ever brought forth to men, bidding to honour, and forbidding dishonour, and believing in God. Had the People of the Book believed, it were better for them; some of them are believers, but the most of them are ungodly."* This verse declares that Muslims are the best nation ever in the history of humankind because Muslims command right conduct and prohibit wrong. Jews and Christians ("People of the Book") are admonished for not believing in Islam; though some are believers in Islam, the majority of them are wicked sinners.

Regrettably, this belief has proved calamitous for the Muslim world, for by believing themselves superior to non-Muslims they do not feel there is any need for improvement and their extreme self-pride only justifies and nurtures their hatred toward "the others."

Religious arrogance toward the West

This religious arrogance formed me and many young people like me. This belief in our religious superiority has convinced us that we Muslims are the best morally. In contrast, the West has no morals, and this immorality is the cause of diseases, misfortunes, and social disintegration, e.g.,

[1] See the commentary on Q 49.13, *Tafsīr al-Ṭabarī* 26: 89.

dysfunctional families, elder abuse, homosexuality, same-sex marriage, public indecency, promiscuity, female sexual objectification, etc. We thank Allah that our women are well covered with the *ḥijāb* (head veil). Our Muslim countries report low percentages of AIDS cases (Praise be to Allah!), and even claim that these cases are caused by visiting foreign tourists.

And so we repeat these statements and "findings" to convince ourselves that they are true—even though we know that in our countries many serious offenses are being committed secretly (and sometimes in public). Adultery and corruption certainly exist in our countries, but we cover it up. Homosexuality also exists in our countries. Yet we blame the West for all these social "evils," ignoring or disclaiming that we too have incest, rape (both of male and female persons), pregnant but unwed women, abortion, and abandoned children, as well as bribery and corruption.

However, the West openly discusses these problems and enacts laws to address social problems by protecting fragile populations, e.g., children and the elderly, and prosecuting those who commit sexual assaults. Acts of financial corruption are also punishable by law, and those responsible are held accountable through fines, imprisonment, or both.

We, on the other hand, prefer to deny that such problems exist, pretending that there is no corruption in our countries. Instead, we blame our corruptions on "the others" and so our diseases continue, our suffering continues, and our hypocrisy continues. Over time, these problems all worsen, deepening our crisis.

Some Western leaders believe that they well understand the Muslim world, acting in ways that only reinforces the opinion of our youth that we Muslims are the preferred and premier nation. For example, in April 2009 at the G-20[2] London Summit, US President Obama bowed while greeting the Saudi king.[3] (At that time ʿAbd Allāh Ibn ʿAbd al-ʿAzīz al-Saʿud was the reigning monarch.) Perhaps Obama thought his bow showed respect to the king of one of the most influential and powerful Muslim countries. Perhaps he thought that his behavior would create sympathy for his country, by attempting to change the negative stereotype

[2] G-20 refers to the "Group of Twenty," a consortium of finance ministers and central bank governors from nineteen of the world's largest economies as well as the European Union. Key issues related to the global economy are discussed during these summits with the purpose of promoting global growth and economic development.

[3] "Obama Bows to Saudi King." *YouTube.com*. YouTube. Uploaded 2 April 2009. Web (https://www.youtube.com/watch?v=9WlqW6UCeaY).

many Muslims have for America. (The White House, however, denied that President Obama bowed to the Saudi monarch after public criticism erupted following the publicized video of his meeting with him.)

But how did Muslims interpret this incident? For me, born a Muslim and growing up in an Islamic environment and absorbing its culture from all those around me, I viewed Obama's bow as an act of submission or subservience. To many Muslims, President Obama was "speaking" nonverbally to the Muslim world, saying, "Yes, you are the *'best of nations brought forth unto man,'* and the president of the greatest country in the world bows to you and kisses the hand of one of your kings." So they think, Allah even makes the kings and presidents of the West bow to Muslims and be humiliated in front of them!

Many Muslims wrote public comments about this incident, including this one: "Almighty Allah is the one who has subjected him [Obama] to do what he has done, and this is a reminder for us that there's no pride for us except in Islam."[4] A commentator writes on *Elfagr*, "Allah decrees the affairs of His creations...and this is a prestige from Allah Almighty...O Allah, exalt the status of Islam and Muslims...."[5] In fact, a forum opened a debate concerning this occasion titled, "Look How Allah Has Humiliated the Infidels and Their End Is Approaching."[6]

This view concerning this event represents how we interpret similar events. We see the world through different eyes, which the West does not understand but perpetrates it by its irresponsible and ill-considered actions rather than help us abandon it.

Abū Hurayra (AD 603-681), a Companion of Muḥammad, narrated a huge number of *ḥadīths* (sayings) reportedly spoken by the prophet. He presents this interpretation of Q 3.110 in one *ḥadīth* concerning the superiority of the Muslim nation (*"You are the best nation ever brought forth to men..."*): "[This verse] *'You* [true Muslims] *are the best nation ever brought forth by men'* means, the best of peoples for the [benefit of the] people, as you bring them [non-Muslims] with chains on their necks

[4] Many Muslim Web sites are full of reader comments about this incident. On April 12, 2009, reader Abū Muḥammad's comment (quoted above) was in response to this article: "Obama Bows to the King Abdullah on April 3, 2009." *Abunawaf.com*. Abū Nawāf Network, 3 Apr. 2009. Web (http://preview.tinyurl.com/jj7eqg2).

[5] al-Bīshī, Omar. "Why Does the US President Bow in Front of the Kings of Saudi Arabia?" *Elfagr.org*. Elfagr Electronic Gate, 28 Jan. 2015. Web (http://www.elfagr.org/1637969).

[6] This discussion opened on April 4, 2009, on Al-Mu'ashir Net Web site (*Indexsignal.com*) in its global and Arabic stock market forum. Web (http://indexsignal.com/community/threads/160345).

till they embrace Islam."[7] This interpretation means that the Muslim superiority over non-Muslims rests in their military power, which is supported by Allah, to force others to embrace Islam.

So, according to this Companion and *ḥadīth* narrator, Muslims' forcefulness (which he describes in harsh, oppressive terms) in making people accept Islam is a factor in their designation as *"the best nation brought forth"* by using their power from their victory over "the others" to humiliate and force "the others" to embrace Islam are the signs of this superiority.

Muslims' justification of their substandard quality of life

Muslim youth today are aware that Muslim countries are far from the top of global rankings that measure the wealth and success of countries, the so-called "best" countries.[8] At the same time, we insist that the Muslim nation is the best nation *"ever brought forth"* just because the Qur'ān makes this declaration. Therefore, it must be true because the Qur'ān is the word of Allah. So how can we explain this contradiction?

We fault our substandard quality of life, as compared to non-Muslim countries, to our weak religiosity, or as the second caliph 'Umar Ibn al-Khaṭṭāb (AD 584-644; Companion and a father-in-law of Muḥammad) states, "We were a people who lived in humiliation and then Allah gave us honor through Islam. Accordingly, if we were to seek honor through anything other than Islam, Allah would humiliate us once again."[9] And so, if our honor is in Islam, then we conclude that our low global rankings reflect our alienation from the true religion. This predicament confuses and discourages us, but it also motivates us to become more religious in the hope we can restore our historical glory.

We are a nation that lives in its past. We do not live in the present nor plan for the future. We only look at the past, recalling the glorious battles and victories of the Prophet, the battles of his Companions and his successors and the time of the large-scale conquests. Because of our successful military

[7] *Sahih Bukhari,* Book of Prophetic Commentary on the Qur'ān (p. 992); *Ṣaḥīḥ al-Bukhārī*, Kītāb al-Tafsīr 4: 1660.

[8] For an example, see the 2016 "Overall Best Countries Ranking." *USNews.com.* US New and World Report (partnered with BAV Consulting and Wharton). Web (http://www.usnews.com/news/best-countries/overall-full-list). **Note:** Out of sixty countries listed and analyzed, thirteen Muslim countries made the list: Malaysia (#28) Saudi Arabia (#29), Turkey (#30), Morocco (#35), Egypt (#39), Indonesia (#42), Tunisia (#47), Jordan (#51), Azerbaijan (#53), Kazakhstan (#55), Pakistan (#56), Iran (#58), and Algeria (#60). Top five countries: Germany (#1), Canada (#2), United Kingdom (#3), United States (#4), Sweden (#5).

[9] al-Nīsābūrī, *Al-Mustadrak* 1: 130.

conquests, territorial expansion, and religious domination, we believe we are the best nation, and our victory came from Allah, who duly rewarded those early Muslims for their religious piety *("...bidding to honour, and forbidding dishonour, and believing in God...")*.

Today we attribute our low global position in the world to a decrease in our religiosity. Many of us do not routinely pray the five daily prayers. Many of us do not practice Islam as stipulated to us from the prophet Muḥammad. Therefore, we consider that whatever bad happens to us must be a kind of divine punishment for neglecting our religion. But if we renew our religious ways, then we will be able to recover our stolen lands, especially Palestine and al-Andalus (Muslim Spain/Islamic Iberia), and we'll be able to restore our lost glories.

This view dominates the minds of young Muslims and the doctrines and agendas of Islamic groups, both jihadist and proselytistic groups. They all believe that the total return to Islam is the main path to honor, and that honor will return one day. Once honor returns, the Islamic world will regain leadership of the world. It will overcome all the other nations of the world—Christian, Jewish, and those of disbelief—and the words of the Qur'ān will again be fulfilled: *"When there comes God's help and victory, / And thou shalt see men enter into God's religion by troops, / Then celebrate the praises of thy Lord, and ask forgiveness of Him, verily, He is relentant!"* (Q 110.1-3; Palmer trans.).

Young Muslims dream of this victory, a victory that they believe will only be achieved through greater religiosity and the strict application of Islamic law (*sharīʿa*). Therefore we shouldn't be surprised when groups, such as Al Qaeda or Islamic State or Al-Nuṣra Front, call for the strict application of Islamic law. Even after the so-called Arab revolutions during the 2011 Arab Spring, Islamic groups continue to flourish in Morocco, Tunisia, Egypt, and Libya, and these groups are at the forefront in Syria and Yemen. These groups thrive because youth in the Muslim world have been saturated in this theory that links their miserable standard of life with the abandonment of religion and the corruption of rulers with the negligence of religion. Even Islamic groups consider Saudi Arabia a political system that uses religion only to tighten its grip and not a truly Islamic regime, because it befriends infidels and applies Western political agendas subject to Western desires and policies.

This view is shared by young people in all Arab Muslim countries. They believe that the demise of their political systems is not just occurring because of the suppression and domination of citizens by the ruling governments but also the negligence of religion. So with this view, it becomes easy for Islamic groups to steal the revolutions in these Muslim countries after the people have ousted the ruling governments, because the people are ready to give power to whoever restores for them Islam's lost glory by honoring and emphasizing the religion and instituting the full application of *sharī'a*.

Of course, the majority of these people do not understand exactly what the full application of *sharī'a* would entail, because they see the application of *sharī'a* from a highly fanciful point of view, as depicted from the podium sermons and on Islamic satellite TV, where justice will always prevail, thefts will disappear (for fear of the harsh penalties), and adultery will subside (for fear of stoning). People will be able to leave their shops unlocked, so they can go to prayers, and no one will dare steal any goods because (1) everyone will be forced to participate in the prayers, and (2) anyone who tries to steal will have his or her hand amputated. Banks will be closed and the practice of usury (lending money with interest) will be abolished, yet funds will exist in abundance, ensuring prosperity for everyone. Liquor and cigarettes will no longer be available, and the state will become a nation of prayer and piety. Mandatory wearing of the *hijāb* will be re-established, and all tempting evils will be removed, such as immodest attire, public nudity, dance, and songs.

This simplistic and overly optimistic view makes people gravitate toward the Islamic groups that promise to bring back for them the idealized reign of the second caliph 'Umar Ibn al-Khaṭṭāb. Islamic sources describe him as a principled ruler known for his piety and simple living. In one story, the Persian Hormuzan discovered 'Umar sleeping under a tree instead of his residence and marveled at the sight. How can a caliph be sleeping so peacefully without fear and with no bodyguards? He then said: "O 'Umar! You ruled. You were just. Thus, you were safe. And thus you slept."[10]

Best nation in religion and reality

Are we really the *"best nation ever brought forth to man"*? Is the Muslim world the "best nation"? If yes, in what way? Are we the "best nation" in manufacturing? Are we the "best nation" in science and technology?

[10] al-Manāwī, *Fayḍ al-Qadīr* 4: 497.

Are we the "best nation" in human rights? Are we the "best nation" in controlling political and economic corruption?

Actually, the opposite is true. Global statistics should make us feel ashamed of our position relative to the rest of the world. For example, Muslim nations occupy the bottom or near the bottom of the 2015 index list compiled and posted by *Transparency International: The Global Coalition against Corruption*. The index ranks 168 nations on a scale from 0 to 100 points. A score of 100 indicates no corruption; a score of 50 or lower indicates serious corruption. Any score 25 or lower indicates high corruption. According to this index, Muslim country Somalia ties North Korea at the bottom of the list with a score of 8 points. Of the fifty-seven Muslim countries listed in this index, over 67% (thirty-nine) score 50 points or lower. None of the first twenty countries listed in the index is a Muslim country. (Denmark topped the list with a score of 91 points.) The highest-ranking Muslim country listed is Qatar (71 points), which still is less than the much larger United States (76 points). Only one other Muslim country receives a score within the more acceptable "clean" range: United Arab Emirates (70 points).[11] Don't these low scores indicate that political and economic corruption is rampant throughout the Muslim countries?

What about higher education, an important factor for improving literacy in a nation? According to the British newspaper, *The Guardian*, only one university in the Muslim world is ranked in the top hundred universities in the world (Turkey's Middle East Technical University). One university in a non-Muslim Middle Eastern country is found on this list—Israel, a country with resources far less than many of its Muslim neighbors, especially the Persian Gulf countries.[12] In another academic global index, only ten Muslim universities are listed among the top 500 universities in the world.[13] How disillusioning to realize that the Muslim world has produced so few outstanding academic institutions, despite the fact that almost one-fifth of the world's population is Muslim.

---

[11] "Corruption Perception Index 2015." 27 Jan. 2016. 4-7. *Transparency.org*. Transparency International. Web (http://preview.tinyurl.com/z6swbau).

[12] Sedghi, Ami. "World's Top 100 Universities 2014: Their Reputations Ranked by Times Higher Education." *TheGuardian.com*. The Guardian, 6 Mar. 2014. Web (https://www.theguardian.com/news/datablog/2014/mar/06/worlds-top-100-universities-2014-reputations-ranked-times-higher-education).

[13] "Academic Ranking of World Universities 2016." *Shanghairanking.com*. Shanghai Ranking Consultancy. Web (http://www.shanghairanking.com/ARWU2016.html).

In tandem with our poor university rankings are our lower adult literacy rates. The Organization of Islamic Cooperation (formerly Organization of the Islamic Conference and includes fifty-seven Muslim countries) has published that the world adult literacy rate is 79.6% (male=85.6%, female=73.7%) while the OIC countries have an adult literacy rate of 70.2% (male=77.9%; female=62.5%). Compare these OIC literacy rates with the much higher rates for developed countries (primarily the Western nations): 97.8% (male=98.5%; female=97.0%).[14]

The Legatum Prosperity index studies 149 nations and ranks their prosperity based on 104 variables. According to its most recent report (2016), the highest ranking Muslim country is Malaysia (#38). The majority of the Muslim countries rank in the bottom 50% (or lower) on the list, such as Saudi Arabia (#85), Morocco (#101), Egypt (#117), Iran (#118), Pakistan (#139), Iraq (#143), Sudan (#146), Afghanistan (#148), and Yemen (#149), the absolute bottom of the list.[15]

Not only do the Western "infidel" nations monopolize the higher rankings on this list (see rankings #1-18),[16] these countries publish a far greater number of journal articles, an indicator of a country's intellectual and academic scholarship, research, and scientific contributions. According to the Statistical Economic and Social Research and Training Centre for Islamic Countries (SESRIC), the OIC member countries have markedly increased their publication output, from 18,391 to 63,342 articles (in 2000 and 2009, respectively). However, "more than half of the articles...originate from only two member countries": Turkey (31.6%) and Iran (21.1%). In contrast, two "infidel" nations—United States and China—*each* published more than 100,000 articles in 2009. This output by either country far surpasses the entire total of the IOC member countries for that year. Even small Japan's publication output of approximately 66,000 articles exceeds the total sum of the fifty-seven members of the OIC.[17]

---

[14] Organisation of the Islamic Conference (OIC)/Statistical Economic and Social Research and Training Centre for Islamic Countries (SESRIC). "Education and Scientific Development in OIC Member Countries." 2010. Print and Web (http://www.sesric.org/files/article/416.pdf). See Figure 1, page 3.

[15] "The Legatum Prosperity Index 2016." *Prosperity.com*. Legatum Institute Foundation. Web (http://www.prosperity.com/rankings).

[16] Ibid.

[17] Organisation of the Islamic Conference (OIC)/Statistical Economic and Social Research and Training Centre for Islamic Countries (SESRIC). "Education and Scientific Development in OIC Member Countries." 2010. Print and Web (http://www.sesric.org/files/article/416.pdf). See Figure 48, page 43.

Gross Domestic Expenditures on Research and Development (GERD) by OIC countries lags far behind the amount spent by developed countries. The United States (33.5%), the European Union (23.5%), and Japan (13.4%) account for most of these expenditures, with the OIC countries accounting for a measly 1.8% of the world's total.[18]

Despite the fact that the OIC countries "are well-endowed with potential economic resources" in many areas, e.g., agriculture, energy, mining, and human resources, and constitute "a large strategic trade region," they are unable to attain "reasonable levels of economic and human development." In 2014, fifty-five OIC member countries produced just 15.0% of the world total Gross Domestic Product (GDP) even though this group accounts for 23.1% of the world total population.[19]

The Global Firepower Index is a listing that judges and ranks the military strength of 126 nations against a perfect but unattainable value of 0.000. The power index score for each country reflects the balance of "a large, strong fighting force across land, sea and air backed by a resilient economy and defensible territory along with an efficient infrastructure...." Its most current index places United States first (0.0897), followed by Russia (0.0964) and China (0.0988). Only two Muslim countries are listed in the top 10% of this index: #8 Turkey (0.2623) and #12 Egypt (.3056). The majority of the other Muslim countries rank in the bottom 50% of the index. These poor index scores definitely indicate that the overall military strength of the Muslim countries is weak in comparison to most Western nations, despite the current unrest and warfare in the Middle East.[20]

These figures are just a cursory glance at our low standards and rankings in the world, but any young Muslim who knows how to search the Internet will be able to reach the same conclusion that is already visible in his or her surroundings. Not only will the Internet be able to confirm these findings by supplying concrete, verifiable numbers, proving that we are not *"the best nation brought forth"* according to all the objective global standards, it will also show that we are among the worst

[18] Organisation of the Islamic Conference (OIC)/Statistical Economic and Social Research and Training Centre for Islamic Countries (SESRIC). "Education and Scientific Development in OIC Member Countries." 2010. Print and Web (http://www.sesric.org/files/article/416.pdf). See Figure 39, page 34.

[19] Organisation of the Islamic Cooperation (OIC)/Statistical Economic and Social Research and Training Centre for Islamic Countries (SESRIC). OIC Economic Outlook 2015. Print and Web (http://www.sesric.org/files/article/517.pdf). See Figure 1.1, page 14.

[20] "Countries Ranked by Military Strength (2016)." *Globalfirepower.com*. Global Firepower. Web (http://www.globalfirepower.com/countries-listing.asp).

countries, succeeding in nothing except in claiming that we are the best nation. Only in this false publicity do I think we succeed over all other nations.

Contradictions and the Islamic caliphate dream

Despite all these less than superlative statistics and related information, there is still a feeling among Muslims of superiority over "the others," which is the result of the religious texts that have been deeply ingrained within us since childhood. We are so bound to our religion's past, we cannot be easily set free of it, and so we consider ourselves *"the best nation brought forth."* We have the best prophet, the best book, the best religion and the most eloquent language. We will invade the world and subdue it until the whole world becomes subject to the rule of Allah, under the feet of the Islamic nation.

This Muslim view, fed by our religious texts and accumulated heritage, assumes that the power and authority of all the countries and the organizations of countries, i.e., NATO, United Nations, etc., are just temporary entities. We eagerly await our destiny to rule the infidels and subject them to the banner of Islam! This feeling produces a constant state of alertness in Muslims, especially if they are totally immersed in—perhaps even obsessed by—the religious texts, inevitably turning these expectant Muslims into people living in the moment. They place little value on where and how they live, believing these things are temporary, for they are on the edge of waiting, waiting for the promised day when the Islamic nation triumphs over its enemies—where Muslims become the masters and the infidels their slaves to serve and obey, and to pay the tribute, or until the infidels surrender and embrace Islam.

This feeling is what drives all the Islamic groups to adopt the dream of an Islamic caliphate. In general, the Muslim does not see the West as a standard for comparison, because the Muslim world must be different from the West; the Muslim world must reject all the ways of the West, from the smallest and most ridiculous thing to the biggest and most important thing. Therefore, Islamic groups denounce democracy, with its rule by the people (and not Allah) through a system of elected representatives, and castigate members of Muslim groups that favor democratic reform as infidels. Everything that comes from the West is infidel in their view. They pressure instead for the restoration of the historical *majlis al-shūrā*, the religious consultative council that advised the caliphs, and the political power models that existed in the first century of the Hijra (migration of Muḥammad and his followers from Mecca to Medina in AD 622; see Chapter 12, page 343.) They dismiss the successful political models of the West, which acknowledge and respect human rights and individual freedoms, as only negative forms of government.

In general, Islam rejects anything that comes from the infidels, believing that even if it looks good on the outside its core is still bad.

Disapproval of Christian and Jewish religious practices

Muḥammad warned his followers repeatedly of their emulation of the Christians and Jews, indicating that the early Muslims were following the Christians and trying to imitate their religious practices or learn from them.[21] Many Islamic texts include prohibitions concerning Christians and Jews as religious role models. In the Hadith literature, Abū Sa'īd al-Khudrī, one of Muḥammad's Companions, narrates Muḥammad's view on this matter:[22]

> [Muḥammad said:] "You would tread the same path as was trodden by those before you inch by inch and step by step so much so that if they entered into the hole of the lizard, you would follow them in this also." We said: "Allah's Messenger, do you mean Jews and Christians (by your words) *'those before you'*? He said: "Who else (than those two religious groups)?"

Even as Muḥammad warned the early Muslims not to follow the Jews and the Christians, he knew they were already doing so because the influence of the Christians was evident in all the nations surrounding them, such as Syria, Iraq, and Egypt, and the rest of North Africa. Perhaps Muḥammad was worried that this non-Muslim influence would negatively affect, distort, or dilute his followers' belief in Islam.

But this possible fear of adopting Jewish and Christian beliefs or practices was unfounded. When the Muslims became strong enough to invade and subdue the surrounding nations, the resulting cultural and social assimilation seemed to most benefit the Muslims, who exploited

[21] *Sahih Bukhari*, Book of Prayer (*Adhaan*) (p. 148); *Sahīh al-Bukhārī*, Kitāb al-Adhān 1: 219. In this *ḥadīth*, the early Muslims discuss different ways to call for prayers, mentioning the Christian practice of a bell and the Jewish practice of a trumpet or horn. But 'Umar suggested a man to call the prayers and Muḥammad agreed. See *Sunan Abū Dawūd*, Book of Ṣalāt (The Prayer) 1: 392. This *ḥadīth* reports that Muḥammad said, "Be different than the Jews, for they do not pray in their sandals or their *khuff* [thin leather shoes]."

[22] *Sahih Muslim*, Book of Knowledge: Following the footsteps of the Jews and Christians (p. 1597); *Ṣaḥīḥ Muslim*, Kitāb al-'Ilm 2: 1230.

the natural resources, enslaved parts of the populations, and instituted the *jizya* (head tax) on non-Muslims to generate revenue. The Muslims learned the languages of these nations and gained access to their libraries of translated works on such topics as medicine, philosophy, and even engineering.

But in integrating these aspects of the civilizations they encountered and conquered, the Muslims attributed the achievements of these civilizations to themselves and discredited or disregarded the Christian and Jewish contributions in those countries. This intentional propaganda was designed to ignore or dismiss the work of Syriac Christian translators, Christian doctors and scholars and their works, and all the Christian and Jewish contributions, because Muslims must not glorify the infidel.

In hindsight, it appears that the Christians and Jews did not realize the impact of this policy on the future, perhaps believing that history would eventually deliver the truth. But history is primarily written by the victorious. During those beginning centuries of Islam, Muslims ruled by the sword, and Christians and Jews could do little except to submit to their rule and live for generations trying to please their Muslim rulers. Through this domination, these Muslim rulers were able to take full advantage of these civilizations, including major contributions by Christians and Jews, and claim credit for these achievements.

Today we only hear about the wonderful achievements of the Islamic Umayyad and 'Abbāsid dynasties but hear nothing about the early Syriac Christians or Copts, as if they had accomplished nothing memorable. The Islamic media machine never praises the infidel but only praises the Muslim and polishes the image of the Muslim on the account of the infidel. No matter what an infidel does, his works should never be preferred over the works of a Muslim.

Pre-Islam, era of ignorance

Islam teaches us that anything other than or anything before Islam is ignorance. But then the "best of mankind" (Muḥammad) came to enlighten the way. Consequently, the pre-Islam world is depicted with only ugly images in order to embellish the image of Islam, as if humankind was sinking into darkness until Muḥammad came, as if there was no worthy civilization until Muḥammad and Islam came.

References about this era of ignorance (*jāhilīya*) are sprinkled throughout the Qur'ān. In one example, the Qur'ān admonishes the wives of the Prophet to *"stay still in your houses and show not yourselves with the ostentation of the ignorance of yore..."* (Q 33.33; Palmer trans.). This verse suggests that the wearing of showy or pretentious finery was widespread during the era of ignorance, but Islam brought decent or modest attire.

More important than the wearing of proper apparel is the application of proper rulings. Even though early Islam actually retained some *jāhilīya* rulings, e.g., pilgrimage rituals, hand amputation as punishment, inheritance laws, etc., it still generally disparaged those earlier rulings, praising instead the rulings of Islam: *"Is it the judgment of the Ignorance they crave? but who is better than God to judge for people who are sure?"* (Q 5.50; Palmer trans.). According to this verse, Allah has decided that Islamic rulings are better than the rulings of ignorance.

Today even the laws of Western nations are considered laws of ignorance. Sovereignty belongs to Allah alone (*ḥākimīya*) while any other kind of governance falls under the rule of "ignorance." The Qur'ān considers that all those who do not govern by Islamic law are evildoers and misbelievers, the unjust: *"...but he whoso will not judge by what God has revealed, these be the unjust"* (Q 5.45; Palmer trans.).[23]

Muslim scholars try to further darken the perception of the era of ignorance by reporting that females were routinely killed during this time. They claim that pre-Islam Arabs preferred male to female children and felt ashamed of female infants. They base this claim on their interpretations of selected Qur'ānic verses:

> *And when the child who was buried alive shall be asked / for what sin she was slain* (Q 81.8-9; Palmer trans.)
>
> *When any one of them has tidings of a female child, his face is overclouded and black, and he has to keep back his wrath. / He skulks away from the people, for the evil tidings he has heard;—is he to keep it with its disgrace, or to bury it in the dust?—aye! evil is it that they judge!* (Q 16.58-59; Palmer trans.)

Additionally, during *jāhilīya* women were inherited like heirlooms because they had no value. But when Islam came, it gave women value and forbade female infanticide.

However, this Islamic propaganda does not stand up to simple questions: (1) If female infants were routinely buried alive, where did

[23] See Q 5.44 (*"...for whoso will not judge by what God has revealed, these be the misbelievers"*; Palmer trans.) and Q 5.47 (*"...for whoso will not judge by what God has revealed, these be the evildoers"*; Palmer trans.).

Muḥammad and the rest of the Arab men find Arab wives to marry? (2) If women were given as inheritance and were of no value, why then was Khadīja (Muḥammad's first wife) a successful merchant with servants who could not only hire Muḥammad as an employee but later propose marriage to him—and not the opposite? Of course, there may have been some exceptional cases in which a father killed his daughter, but historical records indicate that this kind of killing was no more prevalent than in today's world.

The Islamic negative view to anything that is non-Islamic makes it despise the cultural customs, traditions, and behavior of non-Muslims. It considers everything that is not Islamic invalid and evil, and that Islam alone brings goodness to humanity. This belief is the reason why there is always Muslim resistance to the traditions and customs of the West and everything that it represents, because Islam is supposed to contain all the elements of progress and excellence and any positive recognition of rulings or accomplishments of "the others" is like a tacit admission that these non-Muslims have outperformed Islam.

Superior people, language, and prophet

Islam teaches us that the Arabic language is the most eloquent of all the languages, that Arabs are the best of all people groups, and that the Qur'ān is the best book ever to come down. Our prophet Muḥammad is the best prophet, because he came from the best tribe and best lineage, as he himself once expressed to one of his followers:[24]

> I am Muḥammad Ibn 'Abd Allah Ibn 'Abd al-Muṭṭalib. The day Allah created the creation, He placed me among the best of them. Then He divided them. He placed me again among the best of them. Subsequently, as He divided them into tribes, He placed me among the best of tribes. Finally, when He made families, He placed me among the best of families. So, I am the best of them in lineage, and the best of them among the families, and I am the best soul.

His speech, with its arrogant and discriminatory overtones, is perceived as religious text and thus sacred to Muslims. Since the prophet Muḥammad spoke these words, then Muslims should consider his words truthful without objection, even if his words would be considered discriminatory today.

---

[24] *Musnad Aḥmad* 1: 345.

Sunni theologian, jurisconsult, and reformer Ibn Taymīya makes this comment about Muḥammad's pedigree:[25]

> And the majority of Sunni scholars are of the opinion that the Arab race is better than the non-Arab races (Hebrews, Assyrians, Romans, Persians, and others), and Quraysh is the best of all Arabs, and the tribe of Banū Hāshim is the best of Quraysh, and the Messenger of Allah is the best of Banū Hāshim. Therefore he [Muḥammad] is the best created soul and the best in lineage.

Now that we believe that we are the best nation ever, how then will we look at other nations? With pride and arrogance about ourselves and a sense of contempt toward others. Those are the feelings I felt as a Muslim while reading these texts, believing them true and sacred texts. I never doubted or questioned them as they in turn nourished my interior hollow pride.

This egotistical mind-set generates many derogatory statements and insults against Westerners and anyone who is not a Muslim. We call such infidels, "*al-'ulūj*"[26] just like Iraq's Prime Minister al-Ṣaḥḥāf in his daily press conferences before the fall of Baghdad during the 2003 invasion of Iraq.[27] We feel free to call non-Muslims "dogs," and we call Jews "pigs" without any feeling of guilt. This offensive treatment toward non-Muslims does not arise independently from ordinary and simple Muslims but is initiated and supported by well-respected Muslim scholars, such as Ibn Taymīya, who comments that the Arabs are superior in their intellectual and linguistic abilities, the Persians are superior in their propensity for a volatile temperament, and the Romans are superior in their physical appetite for food and sex. For this reason, "the Arabs are the best nation, followed by the Persians...and then followed by the Romans."[28]

Therefore, with the support and confirmation of our religious scholars, we believe that Arabs are superior to the rest of the nations in terms of our intellectual powers. Through the eyes of Ibn Taymīya and, more importantly, Muḥammad, we believe that we are the masters of science,

---

[25] Ibn Taymīya, *Iqtiḍā' al-Ṣirāṭ* 1: 419-420; see al-Manāwī, *Fayḍ al-Qadīr* 4: 676.

[26] Ibn Manṣūr, *Lisān al-'Arab* 3065. In this comprehensive and highly respected dictionary, the word '*ulūj* in plural form (or '*ulj in* singular form) means "the misbeliever," and it also describes the huge and strong man from the infidels.

[27] Iraqi Prime Minister al-Ṣaḥḥāf used the term '*ulūj* to insult the invading American forces in Iraq. At the time, some Arab media sources defined this rather obscure word to mean "bloodsucking insect." See the article "Muhammad Saeed al-Sahhaf." *Wikipedia.org*. Wikipedia, 2016. Web (https://en.wikipedia.org/wiki/Muḥammad_Saeed_al-Sahhaf).

[28] Ibn Taymīya, *Majmū' Fatāwā* 15: 428.

the masters of technology, and the masters of progress; only the world is blind to our clear progress.

Not only are the Arab Muslim people elevated as the best of nations, a specific group of Arabs is singled out as the best of the best Muslim leaders. Muḥammad himself has said that the infidels of the Quraysh are the leaders of the world's infidels, but the Muslims of Quraysh are the leaders of the world's Muslims. This delineation as given by Muḥammad means that the rightful succession in leadership should be a Muslim member from the Quraysh; it would not be right for a caliph to be of any other people group. The Hadith literature includes Muḥammad's view on this matter: "People are subservient to the Quraysh: the Muslims among them being subservient to the Muslims among them, and the disbelievers among the people being subservient to the disbelievers among them."[29]

This belief concerning legitimate Muslim succession explains why the leader of Islamic State, Abū Bakr al-Baghdādī (born Ibrahīm al-Badrī in AD 1971 in Samarra, Iraq), claimed he is a descendant of Muḥammad when he declared ISIS-captured territory spanning Syria and Iraq a caliphate and appointed himself Caliph Ibrahim in late June 2014.[30] After his proclamation, his supporters "circulated the genealogy of his tribe, which traced its lineage back to Muḥammad's descendants." [31] (Al-Baghdādī also knows that he needs this qualification in order to "fulfill" Islamic prophesies concerning the end times, when supposedly a descendant of Muḥammad will one day rule as caliph—an office that has been unoccupied since the fall of the Ottoman Empire after World War I.[32] (See Chapter 12, page 343.)

Muslim scholars know about the legitimate Arab-Muslim succession and the prophesized caliph from the sacred texts that they have studied. But do other non-Arab Muslims know about this preference? How do they explain that the succession must be a Quraysh tribesman because he is the best—even if only two Muslims, Quraysh and non-Quraysh, were left in the whole world.[33] Muḥammad himself urged Muslims to love the

[29] *Sahih Muslim*, Book on Government: The people are subservient to the Qura[y]sh and the caliphate is the right of the Qura[y]sh (p. 1136); *Ṣaḥīḥ Muslim*, Kītāb al-'Imāra 2: 882.

[30] McCants, William. "Who Exactly Is Abū Bakr al-Baghdādī, the Leader of ISIS?" *Newsweek.com*. Newsweek, 6 Sept. 2015. Web (http://www.newsweek.com/who-exactly-abu-bakr-al-Baghdādī-leader-isis-368907).

[31] Ibid.

[32] Ibid.

[33] *Sahih Muslim*, Book on Government: The people are subservient to the Qura[y]sh and the caliphate is the right of the Qura[y]sh (p. 1137); *Ṣaḥīḥ Muslim*, Kītāb al-'Imāra 2: 882. The *ḥadīth* states that "the caliphate will remain among the Qura[y]sh even if only two persons are left (on the earth)."

Arabs more than other people groups: "Loving the Arabs is a belief, and hating them is hypocrisy."[34]

But what about loving the rest of the non-Arab people groups? Why advocate preferential love to the Arabs and make it a belief? Don't such texts promote discrimination?

These texts are publicized even in universities and are being taught to students. One example can be found posted on the Web site of Umm Al-Qura University in Saudi Arabia. Muḥammad Ibn Yūsuf Fajāl, a professor of Arabic language for more than twenty years, works as a consultant in the Ministry of Awqaf and Islamic Affairs in Riyadh. He published the article, "The Preference of the Arabic Language to All Other Languages Is Like the Superiority of a Full Moon Night to the Planets," on the university Web site. He quotes text from Ibn Taymīya, who describes the Messenger of Allah as the best of Banū Hāshīm, which is the best of the Quraysh, which is the best Arab nation. Fajāl concludes his article with this comment:[35]

> This is what I wanted to state, in order for anyone with a mind, a heart, and knowledge to clearly know that the Arab race is better than the Persian race, and the Arabic language is the most perfect in eloquence among other languages. The majority of scholars are of the same opinion.

Imagine if this opinion was published by any professor in any Western university, talking about the preferences of one particular European nation over the rest of the world or the preference of a specific language, claiming that it is the best of all, over the rest of the world's languages. Would such a professor remain in his job? But in our countries, a person can say whatever he or she chooses if a religious text is used to support that opinion. What can be expected from young people graduating from these universities? Do we expect them to call for equal rights between human beings?

It is true that I am an Arab, and, as an Arab, I could have confined myself to these religious texts and my Islamic heritage and brag about my ethnicity and language, but I do not accept these teachings and their preferential view of a selected group of people or consider myself superior

[34] al-Nīsābūrī, *Al-Mustadrak* 4: 97.

[35] Fajāl, Muḥammad Ibn Yūsuf. "The Preference of the Arabic Language to All Other Languages Is Like the Preference of the Full Moon to the Planets." *Uqu.edu.sa*. Umm al-Qura University, 29 Mar. 2007. Web (http://units.imamu.edu.sa/rcentres/Arabic_Literatures/ScientificMaterials/Pages/a3.aspx).

to the rest of humankind. My love for myself and my people does not give me the right to consider myself better than non-Arabs.

The scourge of Islamic groups is that their origins and purpose are based on these religious texts to establish some kind of religious superiority. It is a kind of sacred "Nazism," which will only lead to despotism and the brutal tyranny over others. Didn't Nazism claim the superiority of Germanic groups over all others? For Islamic State and similar Islamic groups, they operate on the belief that Muslims are better than non-Muslims, and so Muslims should and will govern the world. Furthermore, Muslim Arabs are the best of the best Muslims. Therefore, the leadership of Muslims must come from this select group of Arabs—in fact, the best, most authentic caliph must come from the prophet Muḥammad's own clan and tribe, the Banū Hāshīm, the "mother of all tribes." The rest of the world should be under the feet of Muslims and subservient to them.

FIVE

From the Prophet to the caliphs, Christians are at the mercy of Islam

In June 2014, published images of displaced Christians fleeing their homes in Mosul (Iraq's second largest city), which was attacked and captured by ISIS, shocked the world. On Thursday, July 17, ISIS—now renamed Islamic State—issued an ultimatum, addressed to the remaining Christians, which presented three choices. The first two choices were to convert to Islam or abide by the Islamic *dhimmi*[1] contract, where the Christians would have to pay a head tax (*jizya*) to receive protection. If they refused the first two choices, "the sword" would be the third choice.[2] This ultimatum was publicized during the Muslim Friday prayers on July 18 and broadcasted through mosque loudspeakers and distributed in the streets through printed leaflets.

---

[1] The term *dhimmi*, coined by Muḥammad and the early Muslims, refers to non-Muslim people, particularly Jews and Christians, living permanently in Muslim lands under Islamic law. Historically, *dhimmi* had certain protected rights if they paid the *jizya* but not the full citizenship or political rights of Muslims.

[2] "The Organization of Islamic State…[Gives]…Mosul's Christians [Choice] to Convert to Islam… Tribute…[or] Killing." *BBC.com/arabic*. British Broadcasting Corporation (Arabic), 19 July 2014. Web (http://www.bbc.com/arabic/middleeast/2014/07/140718_iraq_isis_mosul_christians). See "Iraqi Christians Flee after ISIS Issue Mosul Ultimatum." *BBC.com*. British Broadcasting Corporation, 18 July 2014. Web (http://www.bbc.com/news/world-middle-east-28381455); Evans, Dominic, and Isra' al-Rube'i. "Convert, Pay Tax, or Die, Islamic State Warns Christians." *Reuters.com*. Reuters, 18 July 2014. Web (http://www.reuters.com/article/us-iraq-security-christians-idUSKBN0FN29J20140718).

By the time Islamic State had overwhelmed the city, only a few hundred of Mosul's Christian population were left to receive the ultimatum. A decade ago, Mosul was the home of many different faiths and 100,000 Christians, but years of persecution of and attacks on Christians by Iraqi Muslims since the Iraqi War of 2003 had pressured most of the city's Christians to emigrate to other countries or flee to neighboring regions, especially Kurdistan.

After the ultimatum was issued, the Christians were given a grace period of less than two days, or until noon on Saturday, July 19. During that short time-period, the "Caliph" of Islamic State, Abū Bakr al-Baghdādī, agreed to allow those Christians who did not want to convert to Islam or pay the tax to leave the borders of his "Caliphate"—but only by themselves.[3]

With the exodus of Mosul's remaining Christians following Islamic State's ultimatum, Chaldean Catholic Patriarch of Babylon and head of the Chaldean Catholic Church in Iraq Louis Raphaël I Sako declared that for "the first time in the history of Iraq, Mosul is now empty of Christians." Sako also stated that Mosul Christians were leaving behind about thirty churches, some dating back 1500 years.[4]

Western political and religious leaders, the United Nations Security Council,[5] and Muslim groups, e.g., Organization of Islamic Cooperation (OIC) and International Union of Muslim Scholars (IUMS),[6] condemned the criminal acts of Islamic State/ISIS toward Mosul's Christians. Even Al Azhar, the world's chief center of Islamic and Arabic learning, expressed deep alarm about the reports of forced displacement of the Mosul Christians because it "totally contradicts the principles and the tolerant teachings of Islam, which calls for coexistence and communication

[3] "Deadline Expires Saturday: Daesh [ISIS] [Gives] the Christians in Mosul [Choice] between Islam or Tribute or Murder." *Arabic.CNN.com*. Cable News Network (Arabic), 18 July 2014. Web (http://arabic.cnn.com/middleeast/2014/07/18/isis-mawsil-christians-mesaage).

[4] "Christians Are Leaving Mosul Ahead of the Deadline Set by...Islamic State...." *France24.com/ar*. France 24 (Arabic), 20 July 2014. Web (http://preview.tinyurl.com/jfnm65d). See "Convert, Pay, or Die: Iraqi Christians Flee Mosul after Islamic State Ultimatum." *RT.com*. RT (formerly Russia Today), 19 July 2014; updated 20 July 2014. Web (https://www.rt.com/news/174104-iraqi-christians-isis-ultimatum/).

[5] "Security Council Adopts Resolution 2170 (2014) Condemning Gross, Widespread Abuse of Human Rights by Extremist Groups in Iraq, Syria." *UN.org*. United Nations, 15 Aug. 2014. Web (https://www.un.org/press/en/2014/sc11520.doc.htm).

[6] "Muslims against ISIS Part 1: Clerics and Scholars." *Wilsoncenter.org*. Woodrow Wilson International Center for Scholars. 24 Sept. 2014; updated 17 Mar. 2015. Web (https://www.wilsoncenter.org/article/muslims-against-isis-part-1-clerics-scholars).

between all people...."[7] Many of these Muslim critics of Islamic State denounced its declaration as the new caliphate as a "big mistake" that "damages the reputation of Islam." Its expulsion of the Mosul Christians was an unjustified "affront to the innocent."[8]

Yet this criticism of Islamic State, coupled with assertions that Islam "is a merciful religion and a peaceful one among all people,"[9] is rather disingenuous, because these same critics cannot deny the fact that Islamic State is applying the Qur'ān and Islamic texts in its decrees concerning its treatment and expulsion of the Christians living in Mosul. They cannot deny the similarity between the actions of Muḥammad and his Companions toward the Christians and Jews in the Arabian Peninsula and the actions of Islamic State toward the Christians in Mosul.

Exiled Chaldean Catholic Archbishop of Mosul, Emil Shimoun Nona, submitted in an interview that Christians in the Middle East are now "incapacitated" as if caught between the jaws of a plier. On one hand are the extremist groups, with their language of weapons, and, on the other hand, the Muslim communities that are going backwards instead of opening up to the world and respecting the differences of others.[10] The Archbishop even spoke about collusion between the Mosul Muslims and ISIS forces before the fall of the city. "The complicity of Mosul's [Muslim] population is not surprising. It was evident even before it fell. There is a great sympathy among some [Muslim] residents of Mosul and this extremist group...."[11]

Many of these emigrating Christian families spoke to me during my televised and recorded program *Daring Question* in November 2014 about this collusion.[12] Some of the callers told me that they were mocked

---

[7] Fayez, Wael. "Al-Azhar Condemns the Forced Displacement of Christians in Mosul: Incompatible with Islam." *Elwatannews.com*. El Watan News, 27 July 2014. Web (http://www.elwatannews.com/news/details/528175).

[8] "Muslims against ISIS Part 1: Clerics and Scholars." *Wilsoncenter.org*. Woodrow Wilson International Center for Scholars. 24 Sept. 2014; updated 17 Mar. 2015. Web (https://www.wilsoncenter.org/article/muslims-against-isis-part-1-clerics-scholars).

[9] Ibid.

[10] Bishāra, Layāl. "Archbishop of Mosul Surprised by the Arrogant Position of Al-Azhar." *Elaph.com*. Elaph Publishing, 20 Dec. 2014; updated 3 Jan. 2015. Web (http://elaph.com/Web/News/2014/12/967365.html).

[11] "Archbishop of Mosul Is Surprised by the Arrogant Position of Al-Azhar." *Elfagr.org*. Elfagr Electronic Gate, 20 Dec. 2014. Web (http://www.elfagr.org/757836).

[12] "Christian Persecution in Iraq" (Episode 386). Narr. Brother Rachid. *Daring Question*. Al Hayat TV. 27 Nov. 2014. Television. (To view YouTube video, see URL: https://www.youtube.com/watch?v=raS7o0zWVjc); "Persecution of Minorities in the Middle East" (Episode 387). Narr. Brother Rachid. *Daring Question*. Al Hayat TV. 4 Dec. 2014. Television. (To view YouTube video, see URL: https://youtu.be/kIat_ZrbXII)

and threatened by their closest Muslim neighbors, who told them, "We will slaughter you, you worshippers of the cross, you dogs" and "We will take your property when Islamic State enters." One of these Christians expressed astonishment over how the Muslim friends of yesterday turned into today's enemies, seemingly emboldened by the news that ISIS had arrived into the region. He was shocked because he had no idea that the Islamic culture had contributed in shaping these Muslims' feelings, and that these "friends" did not suddenly turn into enemies but had harbored hostility rooted deeply in their soul, waiting only for a favorable opportunity for these feelings to safely emerge. Even the few Muslims who did defend the Christians couched their support by classifying the Christians as inferior, second-class citizens, saying, "These people are *dhimmi*. We have to treat them with kindness."

The harsh treatment of the Mosul Christians by Islamic State reflects similar treatment of the *dhimmi* by Muḥammad and his Companions. However, these modern-day Christians rejected the ultimatum, preferring instead to leave Mosul rather than live in a state of humiliation, paying an unwarranted tax and submissively accepting likely persecution or worse.

Religious backing of Islamic State decision to expel Christians

Where did Islamic State get the idea of expelling the Christians and seizing their property and valuables? Where did it get the idea of giving the Christians these particular three choices in its ultimatum? Did these ideas originate with Islamic State or were they generated by the Qur'ān and Hadith literature? These direct questions require clear, honest answers, because deflection from and distortion of the truth is the reason behind the horrific death and destruction in the Middle East.

Historical study indicates that Christians reluctantly accepted humiliating and degrading conditions at the hands of Muslim rulers in order to protect themselves and their people. Unfortunately, their acceptance of these conditions did not necessarily protect them, and their populations in many regions were greatly reduced through forced conversion or execution. Those Christians who were permitted to practice their faith by paying the *jizya* (as *dhimmi*) still greatly suffered, living under these conditions. The continual, underlying threat of persecution and the constant societal pressure to renounce their faith pressured many of these Christians to give up their Christian belief and join the religion of the Muslim majority in order to remove these daily stressful and inequitable conditions from their lives and families.

In fact, the use of these demeaning conditions to help force conversion to Islam is one of the purposes for their enactment among the *dhimmi*. However, some of these Christians emigrated from their Muslim-controlled homelands, especially those with sufficient financial means. Others were killed because of their intransigence and their insistence to maintain their beliefs and rights.

Even with this history of ill treatment of non-Muslims, Muslims have always defended their religion, manipulating their interpretation of the Qur'ān and other Islamic religious texts to support their defense. When one group of Muslims commits atrocities in the name of Islam ("*Allahu Akbar!*"), another group will rush in to separate and exonerate Islam from these horrific deeds, claiming that Islam is "a religion of peace." The victims of these atrocities, such as Christians or Jews, are then lost in the middle between those Muslims who apply the religious teachings to guide and validate their brutal actions and those who uncritically exonerate their religion and seek only to embellish Islam's image in the media.

Sadly, those who choose to exonerate their religion do nothing to rescue the victims of Islam's ardent but violent followers. Instead, these "exonerators" steadfastly continue to polish a strictly positive image of their religion. Those Muslims who believe in the religious texts that promote and support the killing of non-Muslims are not influenced by the exonerators and remain resolute in their views.

As a result, Christians pay the price as they fall between both groups. Thus, Islam escapes from the cage of condemnation, but the truth is that this religion is not innocent as it is the primary cause of the tragedies suffered by Christians, since the dawn of Islam till now.

The Qur'ānic text is crystal clear about how Muslims should treat Jews and Christians:

> *Fight those who do not believe in Allah, nor in the latter day, nor do they prohibit what Allah and His Apostle have prohibited, nor follow the religion of truth* [Islam], *out of those who have been given the Book, until they pay the tax in acknowledgment of superiority and they are in a state of subjection.* (Q 9.29; Shakir trans.)

According to renowned Muslim commentator al-Ṭabarī, the Qur'anic text *"in a state of subjection"* has several possible meanings:[13]

> ...it means to be humiliated and oppressed, because a despicable and humiliated person is "in a state of subjection"...but some commentators state that it means that the taker is sitting while the giver is standing...[while] others state that *"until they pay the tax in acknowledgment of superiority"* means to abase themselves.

This command in this text is strictly applied by Islamic groups toward Christians, which means here the nonresistant Christians. However, if any Christian resists, refuses, protests or criticizes Islam and these unfair treatments, then such a person will no longer remain protected as a *dhimmi*; instead, that person will be considered an infidel warrior and should be killed on the basis that he or she is fighting against the Islamic state. Thus, if the Mosul Christians were to argue with members of Islamic State and accuse them of being unreasonable or unjust, they too would be subject to extermination because then they would be considered infidel warriors and not *dhimmi* and should be killed accordingly.

Requiring the *jizya*, or head tax, is another humiliation for Christians. Even so, some Muslims defend the imposition of this tribute because it is a Qur'ānic decree, saying that it is just a simple tax or that it is a reasonable price for protection. Christians pay it in order for Muslims to protect them, since Christians do not serve in the Muslim military; the tribute affords them this exemption.

Of course, these justifications are all excuses because the tribute is a tax that is to be accompanied with humiliation, according to this Qur'ānic verse. A Muslim does not pay it even if he does not serve in the military. Additionally, it is a tax Christians pay to avoid beheading; in other words, Christians must pay this financial extortion to save their necks.

The *jizya*, or tribute, can be an expensive tax. Historically, it was levied for each adult non-Muslim male. For example, a *dhimmi* father with three adult children must pay a dinar[14] or two or even four (depending

---

[13] See the commentary on Q 9.29, *Tafsīr al-Ṭabarī* 10: 78.

[14] According to Islamic law, the Islamic dinar is a 22-carat gold coin weighing 4.25 grams. The Islamic dirham is a pure silver coin weighing 3.0 grams. (See URL: https://www.e-dinar.com/cgi/index.cgi?page=dinardirham&a=_1). In early Islam, the ratio of the dinar to the dirham was 10: 1, but during the caliphate of 'Umar Ibn al-Khaṭṭāb, the value of one dinar equaled 13 dirhams because of an increased silver supply, which increased its cost and affected the relative cost of gold. (URL: https://www.researchgate.net/publication/235761489_A_Brief_History_of_Money _in_Islam_and_Estimating_the_Value_of_Dirham_and_Dinar; see page 63.)

on the ruling Muslim governor) for himself and for each of his three adult sons. The Hadith literature reports that the Prophet set the tax as one dinar to those living in Yemen.[15] The second caliph 'Umar Ibn al-Khaṭṭāb imposed "four dinars on those living where gold was the currency and forty dirhams where silver was the currency."[16] During Muḥammad's time, a middle-class person might annually earn fifty dirhams or its equivalent in gold.[17] Since the *jizya* was an inflexible, flat tax and not proportional to an individual family's income level, the tax burden for a low-income family was much greater than for an affluent family.

In contrast, the Muslim single or head of a family household pays an annual *zakāt* (obligatory religious tax for charitable purposes) of only 2.5 percent—of his (or her, in today's time) annual net worth, which means the percentage is based on the income total after the subtraction of all necessary expenses, i.e., food, clothes, housing, etc. The *zakāt* is levied per family, regardless of the number of adults or total family members.

How can this kind of taxation be considered just? Imagine a country that imposes two types of taxes based on the religion of each citizen: The Muslim citizen proudly pays a lenient tax of 2.5 percent, based on annual income minus expenses, while the Christian citizen pays a flat tax not proportional to his or her annual gross income for each adult child in the family with no deductions for expenses. And the Christian citizen must grovel when paying it and be humiliated and despised by Muslims. Is this type of taxation system to be considered part of the ideal Islamic state that Muslims hope and call for the whole world?

Muslim sheikhs who condemn Islamic State do not declare that the systemized application of *jizya* is defective, nor do they state that it is unfair to non-Muslims, especially Jews and Christians. They only state that Islamic State's method and timing of its application is inappropriate. But they all agree that it is a divine legislation, and eventually it must be applied to all Christians and Jews. Herein lies the catastrophe for non-Muslims. For all practical purposes, the moderate Muslim and the radical Muslim do not differ on the concept of *jizya* and its imposition on the *dhimmi*; they only differ in how and when it is administered to them.

Demanding tribute (*jizya*), a relic from the early centuries of Islam, from Christians by Islamic State is not unprecedented in modern times.

[15] *Sunan Abū Dawūd*, Book of Kharāj, Fai' and Imārah (Leadership) 3: 520.
[16] Mālik Ibn Anas, *Muwatta'* 1: 279; see Kitāb al-Zakāt.
[17] *Sunan Abū Dawūd*, Book of Zakāt 2: 282.

In 2004, Islamic jihadist groups, such as Al Qaeda, "asked" the Christians in Dora ("Vatican of Iraq"), the southern district of Baghdad, Iraq, to pay money to help support the *mujāhidīn*, or Al Qaeda fighters, as compensation for guaranteeing their protection.[18] (In general, Muslims have used this same logic to defend and justify the idea of the *jizya*.) This imposition of a tribute on Christians, accompanied by death threats, car and church bombings, assassinations, and kidnappings by Sunni jihadist groups, has led to the emptying of Christians in entire regions.[19] Dora, once home to one of the largest concentrations of Christians in Iraq with 150,000 in 2004, numbered just 1500 a decade later.[20]

Whether or not the *jizya* or tribute is being levied against *dhimmi* today or centuries ago, the Qur'ānic text (Q 9.29) concerning its administration is considered—like the rest of the Qur'ān—divine, incorruptible, and everlasting; in short, the Qur'ān's text has always been in effect, both now and since its revelation. Therefore, the directives given in this verse, Q 9.29, cannot be viewed as an isolated, historical text that only concerned the Christians and Jews of Muḥammad's time. Indeed, the Muslims of the first generation of Islam understood its enduring perpetuity and applied it during their time. Correspondingly, all the successive caliphs following Muḥammad also believed that this text and this tax were still in effect for their own times. Not one of these rulers deemed the commands in this text obsolete or defunct.

Not only does this verse command Muslims to exact the *jizya* from Christians and Jews, they are ordered to fight these non-Muslims if they do not pay it. Islamic State, in its ultimatum to Christians, is only carrying out Qur'ānic text when it decrees that Christians must pay this tax or perish. The third option—convert to Islam to avoid fighting or death—is also supported in the Qur'ānic text. If an infidel converts to Islam, this change in belief is sufficient to exempt him from paying the tribute to and facing attack from Muslims:

---

[18] Salloum, Saad. "Christians in Iraq: The Last Signs of Disappearing." *Studies.alarabiya.net*. Al Arabiya Institute for Studies, 10 Aug. 2014. Web (http://preview.tinyurl.com/zpntweq). See "Iraqi Christians Flee Baghdad." *AINA.org*. AINA Syndicated News and Assyrian International News Agency, 9 May 2007. Web (http://www.aina.org/news/20070508233923.htm).

[19] Salloum, Saad. "Christians in Iraq: The Last Signs of Disappearing." *Studies.alarabiya.net*. Al Arabiya Institute for Studies. 10 Aug. 2014. Web (http://preview.tinyurl.com/zpntweq).

[20] Spencer, Richard. "Iraq Crisis: The Last Christians of Dora." *Telegraph.co.uk*. Telegraph Media Group, 22 Dec. 2014. Web (http://www.telegraph.co.uk/news/worldnews/middleeast/iraq/11307515/Iraq-crisis-The-last-Christians-of-Dora.html).

> *But when the sacred months are passed away, kill the idolaters wherever ye may find them; and take them, and besiege them, and lie in wait for them in every place of observation; but if they repent, and are steadfast in prayer, and give alms, then let them go their way; verily, God is forgiving and merciful.* (Q 9.5; Palmer trans.)

According to this verse, known as the Sword verse, infidels are safe from attack and free to go *if* they repent, pray, and give alms. By doing these three actions, these infidels become Muslims and are now safe from harm, because it is religiously unlawful (*ḥarām*) for a Muslim to kill another Muslim.

Christian expulsion by Muslims, past and present

Photographs document the expulsion of Christians from their homes after Islamic groups wrote the Arabic letter *nūn* (ن) on their property.[21] (The letter *nūn* represents the word *Nasārā*, a derivative and derogatory form of the word *Nazarenes*, and refers to Christians. Muslims prefer to attribute the name of Christ's hometown city Nazareth and not Christ himself when referring to Christians, because Muslims believe Christians do not properly honor Christ. The Qur'ān itself uses the term *Naṣārā*. Consequently, the most extreme Salafists and sheikhs, who preach on satellite television or during Friday sermons in the mosques, never use the term *Christians*—only the Qur'ānic term *Naṣārā* to further insult Christians.)

The expulsion of these Christians and the confiscation or destruction of their property are similar to the narratives concerning the expulsion of Jewish tribes from the Arabian Peninsula mentioned in the traditional Islamic sources. One chapter in the Qur'ān, Sura al-Hashr ("The Banishment"), describes the subjugation and expulsion of the Jewish tribe Banū al-Nadīr with palpable feelings of righteous satisfaction:

[21] Sisto, Christine. "A Christian Genocide Symbolized by One Letter." *NationalReview.com*. National Review, 23 July 2014. Web (http://www.nationalreview.com/article/383493/christian-genocide-symbolized-one-letter-christine-sisto).

> *He it was who drove those of the people of the Book who misbelieved forth from their houses, at the first emigration; ye did not think that they would go forth, and they thought that their fortresses would defend them against God; but God came upon them from whence they did not reckon, and cast dread into their hearts! They ruined their houses with their own hands and the hands of the believers; wherefore take example, O ye who are endowed with sight! / Had it not been that God had prescribed for them banishment, He would have tormented them in this world; but for them in the next shall be the torment of the Fire! / That is because they opposed God and His Apostle: and whoso opposes God, verily, God is keen to punish!* (Q 59.2-4; Palmer trans.)

According to Islamic sources, Muḥammad and his army besieged the Banū al-Nadīr, who had retreated to their fortress outside Medina. (The early Muslims claimed that the tribe had plotted to assassinate Muḥammad.[22] However, Orientalists suggest that the Jewish tribe was targeted because of their vociferous criticism and mockery of Muḥammad, raising doubts about his prophethood and the authenticity of the Qur'ān among his followers.[23]) After two weeks, the Banū al-Nadīr surrendered when promised reinforcements did not arrive, and the Muslims began to cut down and burn their surrounding orchards of palm trees. Under the terms of the surrender, Muḥammad ordered the deportation of the tribe but allowed members to take what they could carry on their camels. Their lands were divided between Muḥammad and those Companions who emigrated with him from Mecca.[24]

The Islamic sources also detail that prior to the evacuation the men of the Banū al-Nadīr destroyed "their houses down to the lintel of the door which they put upon the back of the camels and went off with it."[25] In all likelihood, these Jews were trying to remove their *mezuzah*[26] from their door frames. To the uninformed Muslims, the Jews were ruining their homes with their own hands. Seemingly pleased by this

---

[22] Ibn Hishām (Ibn Isḥāq), *The Life of Muhammad* 437; Ibn Hishām (Ibn Isḥāq), *Al-Sīra al-Nabawīya* 3: 387.

[23] *History of al-Tabarī* (Introduction) xxxv; Nöldeke et al., *The History of the Qur'ān* 138-139.

[24] Ibn Hishām (Ibn Isḥāq), *The Life of Muhammad* 437-438; Ibn Hishām (Ibn Isḥāq), *Al-Sīra al-Nabawīya* 3: 389.

[25] Ibn Hishām (Ibn Isḥāq), *The Life of Muhammad* 437; Ibn Hishām (Ibn Isḥāq), *Al-Sīra al-Nabawīya* 3: 387.

[26] The Hebrew word *mezuzah* means "doorpost" and refers to a skillfully made parchment on which is handwritten the most famous Jewish prayer, Shema. The lines of this prayer come from the Torah (see Deut. 6.4-9, 11.13-21) and express the oneness of God and his connection to his people, the Children of Israel. The *mezuzah* is usually housed in some container and then affixed to the doorpost or doorframe of the Jewish family's home as a declaration and reminder of their faith, as commanded in the Torah (Deut. 6.9).

destruction by the owners, the Muslims decided to help the Jews in this work, considering the Jews' surprising behavior a victory from Allah—that Allah was using the hands of the Jews to destroy their own houses. Some Muslim commentators confirm this interpretation:[27]

> [This verse Q 59.2-4] refers to the Banū al-Naḍīr, whom the prophet fought and made a treaty of peace and evacuated them to the Levant [Syria]. Abandoning their homes, they started ruining their houses and they even ripped the doors and the wood from the houses. They took whatever they liked and could take. They destroyed their own houses with their own hands and with the hands of the believers.

When I was a little child, my fellow students and I used to repeat these verses (Q 59.2-4) in order to memorize them (but without understanding). The teacher at the mosque (who was my dad) would sometimes explain these verses, telling us how the Prophet expelled the Jews of Banū al-Naḍīr and burned their palm trees, and how his followers helped them ruin their homes. We used to rejoice after the telling of this story, because Allah helped his prophet to triumph over the Jews when Muḥammad expelled them to the Levant (Syria).

I have no doubt that the members of Islamic State who expelled the Christians from Mosul in 2014 were mindful of this earlier event, believing that this expulsion was a victory from Allah against the Christians of Mosul, especially the rich Christians who had beautiful houses. When these Christians refused to convert to Islam, abandoning their homes in less than 48 hours, the Islamic State fighters considered their exodus a divine victory, appropriating the now vacant homes without any work or effort and dividing the properties among themselves. This real estate became the spoils and properties of Islamic State's new Caliphate.

When I saw (and later heard firsthand) what happened to the Christians of Mosul, I was hit by a powerful urge to cry, because I saw how the Christians in Mosul suddenly lost everything. These people had worked all their lives to save their money and build their houses, and then—with little or no warning—they were forced to just leave everything. Compounding this devastating loss was learning that some of their Muslim neighbors had betrayed them to members of Islamic State, who then came and marked the Arabic letter *nūn* (ن) on their

---

[27] See the commentary on Q 59.2-4, *Tafsīr al-Ṭabarī* 28: 30.

houses. (I was told of such an incident during an episode of my television program by one of the displaced Christians who witnessed this evil act.)[28]

Greatly pained by these accounts, I composed a poem concerning this issue and entitled it "*Nūn.*" Shortly after its publication[29] Christian Iraqis circulated it all over the world through various social networking sites; they even shouted it during their demonstrations. On August 30, 2014, Rev. Kamil Ishak, the pastor of St. Jacques Syriac Orthodox Church, read the poem during a huge demonstration in Montreal, Canada, and hundreds of participants chanted its words along with him.

Effect of inflammatory religious texts on Jews and Christians

Hatred towards Christians has been impressed onto my mind and heart since childhood, and the use of the word *Naṣārā* to insult Christians was common in my village. Whenever we wanted to describe a ruthless person, we would say that he was a Christian. In my mind, a Christian was the ruthless infidel who does not believe in Allah. As I grew older, my early assessment was reinforced by the Islamic texts I carefully read. What I learned as I studied these texts is that my community's attitude, beliefs, and behavior deeply echoed these old Islamic teachings. After centuries of generations passing down these teachings, these teachings now run in our blood. We no longer need to rely on schools to learn them, because they have become the stories that grandmothers tell their young grandchildren, an embedded part of the mainstream culture, like inherited cultural genes.

One example of this religious crossover into an established cultural norm is reflected in this *ḥadīth*: "Do not greet the Jews and the Christians before they greet you and when you meet any one of them on the roads force him to go to the narrowest part of it."[30]

So, according to this *ḥadīth*, Muslims are commanded not to greet first a Jew or a Christian that they meet on the road, and they should even push the Jew or Christian to the narrowest part of the road in order to make it difficult for him to pass by.

[28] "Christian Persecution in Iraq" (Episode 386). Narr. Brother Rachid. *Daring Question.* Al Hayat TV. 27 Nov. 2014. Television. (To view YouTube video, see URL: https://www.youtube.com/watch?v=raS7o0zWVjc; alternate source: https://preview.tinyurl.com/y737j829)

[29] Brother Rachid. "*Nūn.*" 24 July 2014. Poem. (To read Arabic poem transcript and hear YouTube audio clip, see URL: https://www.youtube.com/watch?v=G1v-5TgIr50)

[30] *Sahih Muslim,* Book of Salutations and Greetings: Prohibition of saying first al-Salam-u-ʿAlaikum to the people of the book, and how their salutations should be responded (p. 1339); *Ṣaḥīḥ Muslim*, Kītāb al-Salām 2: 1036.

Naturally, Muslims will not be able to exercise this *ḥadīth* in societies where Islamic law does not prevail. But imagine if the Christians had remained in Mosul under the rule of Islamic law. In this scenario, Muslims would have treated these Christians according to this text, and the Christians would have no right to object to this practice because it is considered part of the law of Allah and his Messenger. Even the sheikhs of Saudi Arabia, its universities, and Al Azhar would not be able to deny this text, although they will officially state, "The circumstance is not appropriate for its application." Of course, Islamic State considers that the circumstance is appropriate, and why not? When Islamic State controls large regions, it can apply Islamic law as stated in the religious texts.

The interpretation of this *ḥadīth* has led to disastrous consequences, encouraging extreme discrimination and intolerance. Influential Syrian Sunni jurist and *ḥadīth* scholar al-Nawawī (AD 1233-1277) makes this comment:[31]

> The scholars agree that the greeting of the People of the Book should be returned, if they greet us with *salām*, but we should not say to them, "*Wa 'alaykum al-salām* ("and upon you be peace")." We should say only "'*alaykum* ("upon you")" or "*wa 'alaykum* ("and upon you")"... and [regarding the part of the *ḥadīth*] "if you meet one of them on the road, push him to the narrowest part of it"...[other opinions state that] the *dhimmi* is not left to walk in the middle of the pathway, and he should be forced to walk on its sides if the Muslims are walking through. If the pathway is not crowded then it is acceptable [for the *dhimmi* to walk in the middle of the pathway], and forcing him to the sides should not be done so as to let him fall into a hole or hit by a wall, or something similar, and Allah knows best.

Forcing Christians and Jews to walk on the narrowest edges of the roadway to allow greater passage for Muslims or marking Christian houses with a *nūn* (ن) for later confiscation of the property and expulsion of the inhabitants are blatant examples of overt intolerance and discrimination. This abusive, unjust treatment is based solely on the identity of these groups and not wrongful behavior. (This type of discriminatory treatment is reminiscent of Nazi Germany and its treatment of "inferior" minorities. For example, it required Jews to wear a yellow Star of David to identify and separate them from the "superior" Germans. Later, Jews and other

---

[31] al-Nawawī, *Sharḥ* 14: 121, 123.

minority groups, i.e., gypsies, blacks, homosexuals, Slavic populations, etc., were stripped of their livelihoods, possessions, and homes, and many lost their lives in concentration camps.)

The whole world must fight any ideology that espouses and promotes this kind of intolerance and racism. In the case of Islam, the opposition must begin with its religious texts, because these texts inevitably lead to Muslims fighting and killing others. Any religion that allows this kind of ideology does not merit respect. To defeat Islamic State and other like-minded groups, we must defeat first this intolerant, hate-filled ideology of Islam. Any other course is useless.

How would Muslims react if sacred Christian or Jewish texts, read and taught in churches and synagogues, religiously affiliated universities, and repeated by religious leaders, religious institutions and their satellite channels, commanded this practice: "Do not greet the Muslims before they greet you, and when you meet any one of them on the roads force him or her to go to the narrowest part of it"? Unfortunately, the Arabic Islamic religious texts with these racist teachings are translated into foreign languages to even invade the minds of the Muslim youth born in environments that respect human rights and do not discriminate people on the basis of religion, race, or gender.

The expulsion of the Christians would not have taken place if not for these Islamic religious texts. The "extremists" use these texts as their guide and standard for their declarations and their works. If these texts did not exist, then these extremists would be embarrassed and castigated in front of their followers, for these groups have legitimate Islamic jurists and judges and a *shura* (consultative council) who search the Qur'ān and other religious texts before making these kinds of major decisions.

For example, the Hadith literature justifies the expulsion of Christians, because Muḥammad himself, as well as his Companions after him, forcibly removed Christians and Jews from the vicinity. In one *ḥadīth*, Muḥammad vows to his Companions, "I will expel the Jews and Christians from the Arabian Peninsula and will not leave any but Muslim."[32] 'Umar Ibn al-Khaṭṭāb, who narrated this *ḥadīth* himself, implemented this commandment when he became the second caliph

[32] *Sahih Muslim,* Book of Jihad and Expedition: Evacuation of the Jews from the Hijaz (p. 1091); *Ṣaḥīḥ Muslim,* Kītāb al-Jihād wa al-Sīyar 2: 846.

after Muḥammad's death. He ordered the expulsion of Christian and Jewish communities living in the Arabian Peninsula to Syria and Iraq.

So, the presence of Jews and Christians who would not convert to Islam was not tolerated by Prophet Muḥammad, his Companions, and his successors. Therefore, it should not be surprising that Abū Bakr al-Baghdādī, the self-proclaimed caliph of Islamic State—and supposedly a descendant of the Prophet's family—hates Christians and cannot tolerate their presence in Muslim-held land. His ultimatum to expel them is based on the Hadith literature and replicates the policies of the Prophet and the caliphs toward these two groups of non-Muslims.

Religious fatāwa dependent on religious texts

Even today, fatāwa (Islamic legal rulings) are posted on Saudi Web sites prohibiting the existence of Christians and Jews and all polytheists in the Arabian Peninsula. So what is the difference between Islamic State and Saudi Arabia, which allows religious authorities to post their rulings on these state-sanctioned Web sites without global condemnation? For an example, read the discussion and fatwa given by Ibn Bāz, former Grand Mufti of Saudi Arabia, in response to the following question posed by a Muslim believer:[33]

> **Question:** The Prophet said, "Two religions shall not co-exist in the land of the Arabs."[34] Yet we find in most of the countries of the Arabian Peninsula an intensive presence of non-Muslim labor, so much to the extent of building places of worship for others, whether for Christians or Hindus or Sikhs. What is the position that the governments of these countries must take towards this painful phenomenon of imminent danger [non-Muslim churches]?"

[33] Ibn Bāz, 'Abd al-Aziz. "The Obligation of Expelling the Infidels from the Arabia Peninsula." *Binbaz.org*. Official Web site of al-Imam Abd al-Aziz Ibn Baz. N.d. Web (http://www.binbaz.org.sa/fatawa/1685). See al-Munajjid, "Fatwa no. 104806: Expel the Infidels from the Arabia Peninsula." *IslamQA.info/ar*. Islam Question and Answer, 18 Sept. 2007. Web (https://islamqa.info/ar/104806).

[34] Mālik Ibn Anas, *Muwatta'* 4: 234.

> **Ibn Bāz:** It is true that the Prophet said, "Two religions shall not coexist in the land of the Arabs." And it is true that he commanded the expulsion of the Jews and the Christians from the Peninsula and to keep only Muslims in it. He ordered at his death to remove the infidels from the Peninsula, and this is an approved constant [unchanging] command from the Messenger of Allah. There is no doubt in it, and therefore, the rulers are obliged to implement this commandment just as it was implemented by the Muslim caliph 'Umar [Ibn al-Khaṭṭāb, second caliph] when he expelled and evacuated the Jews from Khaybar [AD 642]. The rulers in Saudi Arabia and in the Gulf and in all the parts of the Arabian Peninsula have to work hard to remove all the Christians, Buddhists, pagans, Hindus and other infidels and to only allow Muslim labor to enter their countries.

These are the words of a high-ranking religious authority in a country that claims today that it is against terrorism and against Islamic State and does not agree with the actions of this organization. Yet simultaneously, it allows the publication of the very same beliefs and views that have produced Islamic State (and precursors, ISIL and ISIS), its doctrines, and its operations.

So, is there a difference between Islamic State and Saudi Arabia? The only apparent difference is that Islamic State implemented these beliefs and commands by using very physical and violent methods in the lands its fighters had overtaken, while Saudi Arabia is content to only publish these same beliefs and apply it in limited, furtive ways, such as forbidding idolaters from entering Mecca.

Muḥammad: model for the treatment of infidels

The hatred against Christians and the persistence in maltreating them is not a new phenomenon but is rooted in Islam. Stories about the prophet Muḥammad and the way he dealt with Christians shape the subconscious of every Muslim who loves the prophet and considers him holy. Muslims continually read about his battles against the polytheists and infidels, conflicts and wars that have been celebrated even up to today. Each year on the seventeenth day of Ramadan, we celebrate the anniversary of the victory of Muḥammad over the infidels at the Battle of Badr, although this victory was more than fourteen hundred years ago.

The Battle of Badr (AD 624) was fought when Muḥammad and his warriors attempted to raid a Quraysh trade caravan on its way back from the Levant (Syria). After their emigration from Mecca to Medina in AD 622, Muḥammad and his followers turned to raiding when they could not sustain themselves economically in other ways. When Muḥammad and his men learned that a particularly wealthy Meccan caravan was heading their way past Medina, they filled up wells along the caravan route to deny water to the Quraysh tribesmen (who left Mecca to protect the caravan) in preparation for their attack. The two forces—Muḥammad and his army of 300 followers and the Meccan contingent with 1000 warriors—met at Badr (near Medina).[35] After a short battle of a few hours, the Muslims claimed victory, taking prisoners and booty.

The Battle of Badr is one of the few battles specifically mentioned in the Qur'ān. This passage (Q 8.12-13; Palmer trans.) casts the Muslims' victory as Allah's retribution to the nonbelievers:

> *When your Lord inspired the angels—'Verily, I am with you; make ye firm then those who believe; I will cast dread into the hearts of those who misbelieve,—strike off their necks then, and strike off from them every fingertip.' That is, because they went into opposition against God and His Apostle; for he who goes into opposition against God and His Apostle—verily, God is keen to punish.*

The beheading of the misbelievers as mentioned in Q 8.12 confirms that this method of killing infidels is not an invention of Islamic State and its precursors, ISIL and ISIS. The Qur'ān and Hadith literature not only report and celebrate the strategy and outcome of this battle, they also claim it was inspired by Allah and supported by angels. From AD 624 until today, Muslims celebrate this victory of the early Muslims, who tried to rob this Quraysh caravan of its goods but ended up battling and beheading the tribesmen who left Mecca to protect the caravan from the Muslims' attack. In truth, this "battle" was just Quraysh tribesmen trying to defend their convoy from Muḥammad and his followers' piratical attack.

While it is true that the Old Testament contains similar stories of violence, pastors and Christian clergy today do not use these stories as model examples for living life today. These stories may provide helpful lessons for guiding a person's spiritual life, but the literal application of historical events involving violence for a specific time, place, and situation is not appropriate, useful, or ethical. Therefore, Christian leaders of all the major denominations would never appear on television, urging

[35] Bunting, Tony. "Battle of Badr." *Brittanica.com*. Encyclopædia Brittanica, Inc., 22 Mar. 2017. Web (https://www.britannica.com/event/Battle-of-Badr).

Christians to encircle and destroy selected cities and nations, emulating Joshua's circumambulatory march and destruction of Jericho (see Bible, Josh. 6) or Saul's slaughter of the hostile Ammonites (1 Sam. 11). Christian theology views these historical events as just that—conflicts and participants of the past—with no divine expectation or command to repeat these actions now in the same places or with the same peoples (or their proxies).

But Muslims still believe that Muḥammad is the supreme role model who must be followed today as in his time as the ideal example in everything: the way he ate, slept, used the toilet, conducted sexual intercourse, and, of course, the way he treated Jews, Christians, pagans, and idolaters. All his behaviors and actions prescribe the precise rules that Muslims follow as the righteous "code of conduct" that should be applied literally today, and Islamic State, Saudi Arabia and Al Azhar agree on this disastrous principle. The difference is that Islamic State has come in order to apply these rules now while the others say that the conditions are not favorable yet.

The Qur'ān itself exalts Muḥammad: *"Ye had in the Apostle of God a good example..."* (Q 33.21; Palmer trans.). He is presented as the perfect example in all aspects, and his teachings are considered the most important even in insignificant or inconsequential matters. Muḥammad is so highly esteemed that Muslims must reject any teachings from others that disagree with his teachings.

The famous Muslim scholar and commentator al-Qurtubī offers this comment about an excellent role model: "The good example is the role model.... He is the person who is looked to by others as an example in everything he does to be imitated...."[36]

Muḥammad's teachings and actions affect and control every facet, no matter how small, in the daily life of a Muslim, as described in this *ḥadīth*:[37]

[36] See the commentary on Q 33.21, *Tafsīr al-Qurtubī* 14: 156.

[37] *Sahih Muslim*, Book of Purification: How to cleanse oneself after relieving oneself (p. 198); *Ṣaḥīḥ Muslim*, Kitāb al-Ṭahāra 1: 135.

> Salman [the Persian, a follower of Muḥammad] said that (one among) the polytheists remarked: "I see that your friend [Muḥammad] even teaches you about the excrement." He replied: "Yes, he has forbidden us that anyone amongst us should cleanse himself with his right hand, or face the Qibla [direction for praying to Mecca]. He has forbidden the use of dung or bone for it, and he has also instructed us not to use less than three pebbles (for this purpose)."

Therefore, any attempt to separate the actions of the Islamic groups from the Islamic religion is doomed to failure; it's an unworkable approach, because they are the groups that are the most attached to the religious texts and the most committed to strictly apply the text declarations and decrees. In fact, the Muslim youth, who read and know that these groups are basing their actions—even their violence—on the religious texts, will dismiss Muslim critics who condemn the violent application. They think that if Muslims are to follow Muḥammad in the little things, why not the bigger things—even if that means fighting, war, and bloodshed.

The solution is not to distort the relationship between Islam and Islamic groups by ascribing "peace" to Islam and "terrorism" to these jihadist Islamic groups. Anyone who reads these texts will find that the Islamic groups are more faithful to the spirit and the letter of the religious texts than those who seek only to beautify the image of Islam.

Dealings with Christians by Muḥammad and his Companions

How did the early Muslims deal with Christian communities? One Arab Christian community (a contemporary of Muḥammad's tribe, the Quraysh) lived in the city of Najrān, an important and thriving trade center (located in the southwestern corner of the Arabian Peninsula) for two major caravan routes. In AD 631 a delegation of Christian scholars from Najrān traveled to Medina to discuss theological matters with Muḥammad after the Christian bishop of Najrān, Abū Harīth Ibn 'Alqamā, received this invitation from Muḥammad:[38]

> In the name of the Lord of Ibrāhīm, Isḥāq and Ya'qūb.
>
> This is a letter from Muḥammad, the Prophet and Messenger of Allah, to the Bishop of Najrān and the people of Najrān:

[38] Ibn Kathīr, *Al-Bidāya* 7: 263. See the commentary on Q 3.59, *Tafsīr Ibn Kathīr* 3: 78.

> If you submit and become Muslims, I praise and glorify the Lord of Ibrāhīm, Isḥāq and Ya'qūb. Now I invite you all to worship Allah instead of worshipping His creatures, so that you may come out of the guardianship of the creatures of Allah and take place under the guardianship of Allah Himself. And in case you do not accept my invitation you must pay *jizya* (tribute), failing which you are hereby warned of war. Peace be with you.

According to the Islamic sources, the Christian delegation of over sixty members spent three days in Medina with Muḥammad for theological discussion and debate, and the two religious groups discovered that they could not agree on a key doctrine concerning the nature of Christ. At this point, Muḥammad received a revelation, which resolved this question for him regarding Christ's divinity.[39] He shared this revelation (Q 3.59-60; Arberry trans.) with the Christian delegation:

> *Truly, the likeness of Jesus, in God's sight, is as Adam's likeness; He created him of dust, then said he unto him, 'Be,' and he was. / The truth is of God; be not of the doubters.*

Unconvinced, the Najrān Christians maintained that Christ is divine and the Son of God. Muḥammad rebuked their position with Q 3.61 (Arberry trans.):

> *And whoso disputes with thee concerning him, after the knowledge that has come to thee, say: "Come now, let us call our sons and your sons, our wives and your wives, our selves and your selves, then let us humbly pray and so lay God's curse upon the ones who lie."*

Muḥammad then requested that the Najrān Christian delegation participate in a ceremony, al-Mubāhala, to challenge their belief by mutually and formally calling on Allah's curse on whichever group—Muslims or Christians—was speaking untruthfully. However, the implementation of the curse may be through the opponent (rather than directly from Allah) and is considered a kind of divine response for the occurrence of the curse.

Given the threat in Muḥammad's letter ("...I invite you all to worship Allah.... And in case you do not accept my invitation...[and do not]

[39] "Chapter 57: Representatives of Najran in Madina." *Al-Islam.org*. Ahlul Bayt Digital Islamic Library Project, 1995-2017. Web (https://www.al-islam.org/the-message-ayatullah-jafar-subhani/chapter-57-representatives-najran-madina). See "Hadith about Najran Christians Praying in the Masjid." *Askaquestionto.us*. N.p., 2009-2017. Web (https://askaquestionto.us/question-answer/miscellaneous/hadith-about-najran-christians-praying-in-the-masjid).

pay *jizya*…you are hereby warned of war") and their predicament in Medina surrounded by Muḥammad's army, it is not surprising that the delegation decided ultimately to withdraw from al-Mubāhala. The Christians concluded that they would be killed following the ceremony—not because Allah would suddenly respond from heaven to Muḥammad and his family's supplications and curse the Christians—but because they knew that Muḥammad could and might eventually implement Allah's "response" with the swords of Muḥammad's army.

Some might argue that the Najrān Christians' withdrawal from al-Mubāhala indicated their fear of Allah's curse and that Islam, and not Christianity, is the true religion. If this analysis was true, why then would Muḥammad pursue a "peace treaty" and the extortion of the tribute instead of claiming a religious victory when the Christians backed down? Shouldn't the retreat mean no tribute? It seems clear that Muḥammad's original "invitation" was really an announcement of war. As the Najrān Christians had only a few options, they chose to pay the tribute to save their lives and the lives of their children.

Thus, the Christian people of Najrān became the first group of people to pay the *jizya*, or tribute, to Muḥammad. They signed a bitter treaty of peace with him, with the particular conditions recorded by Muslim commentators:[40]

> The Messenger of Allah made a treaty with the people of Najrān on the basis that they would give to the Muslims two thousand *hullahs*, [expensive outfits], half in Safar [second month] and half in Rajab [seventh month]. And that they would lend the Muslims thirty coats of mail, thirty horses, thirty camels, and thirty of every type of weapon, for use in their campaigns, for which, the Muslims will stand surety [guarantee the loaned items] until they returned it to them, lest there be any plot or treachery [against Muslims] in Yemen [location of Najrān]. In return for that, no [Christian] church of theirs would be destroyed, and no priest would be expelled, and they would be left to practice their religion, provided they did not do something wrong or consume *ribā* [usury].

Unfortunately for the Najrān Christians, this peace treaty with its promise to allow the presence and tolerance of Christianity in their city was overturned with the ascension of 'Umar Ibn al-Khaṭṭāb, the second Muslim caliph, who expelled them from the Arabian Peninsula only a

---

[40] *Sunan Abū Dawūd*, Book of Kharāj, Fai' and Imārah (Leadership) 3: 521-522.

few years after Muḥammad's death in AD 632. His action highlights the constant problem facing Christians or Jews living under an Islamic state: Their circumstances can radically change with the change of their ruler, especially if the original law dictating their treatment is unjust, inadequate, or open to many different interpretations.

In the case of the Najrān Christians, the Muslim tolerance for their religion would be allowed, according to the peace treaty, unless the Christians "bring something new or take usury." The phrase "bring something new" is an extremely vague condition, because the word *new* is not clearly attached to a particular action. This lack of specificity was exploited when 'Umar Ibn al-Khaṭṭāb exiled the Najrān Christians to Kūfa because their number had greatly increased, and he became afraid that they would revolt against the Muslims.[41]

The expulsion of Christians and Jews did not end at the death of Muḥammad and the demise of the caliphs. The history of the Middle East and North Africa bears strong witness that Islam has persisted since its appearance in the seventh century AD until today to erase the Christian presence from these regions.[42] At the beginning of the seventh century AD, Christianity had spread to most of the Mediterranean world, including North Africa, Egypt, and parts of the Middle East. However, by the AD 630s Muḥammad had united the entire Arabian Peninsula under Islam. After his death, Muslim armies under the successive caliphs helped further Islam's spread into the surrounding lands, eventually controlling territory that stretched from Spain to India.

Christian and Jewish populations that fell under this Muslim control were forced to emigrate, convert, or accept the lesser status and conditions of *dhimmi*, which included paying the *jizya*. Many thousands of others were persecuted and killed. In all these ways, the Muslim empire was able to overwhelm the once dominant Christian populations in the areas it controlled.

By the ninth century AD, Syria, one of the earliest centers of Christianity, then had and now still has a Muslim majority. (Today only

---

[41] Ibn Abū Shayba, *Al-Musannaf* 8: 565. Excerpt: "The people of Najrān had reached forty thousand people...and 'Umar was afraid that they would become stronger than the Muslims and conflict with one another...they [Christians] came to 'Umar, saying: We are in conflict with each other, so evacuate us.... The Messenger of Allah had written a book for them that they shall not be evacuated...[but] 'Umar took advantage on it and he evacuated them...."

[42] Christie, Grazie Pozo. "The List of Victims Is Long Enough." *USNews.com*. US News and World Report, 7 Oct. 2016. Web (http://www.usnews.com/opinion/articles/2016-10-07/stop-the-islamic-states-genocide-of-christians-in-the-middle-east).

10% of its population is Christian.) Egypt, home of one of the oldest Christian churches in existence—the Coptic Church—became a Muslim nation by the end of the twelfth century AD. (Today approximately 11%-15% of Egypt's population is Christian.) Lebanon, the nation with the highest percentage of Christians (approximately 40%) in the Middle East, has had a Muslim majority since the middle of the twentieth century AD. According to the Pew Research Center, "about a fifth of the world's Muslims live in the Middle East and North Africa, but it is the only region where a majority of the population is Muslim."[43] As of 2010, this Muslim population was 93% of the total population and will increase to 94% by 2050.[44] Christianity was once the dominant religion in the Middle East, but now Christians are minority populations in the lands once considered Christianity's "birthplace."

As these Christian populations dwindle—and even disappear—in these regions, their history, contributions, and achievements receive little if any attention or acknowledgment by the Muslim-dominated governments in North Africa and the Middle East. Given this silence, one might think that Christianity never existed in North Africa if it weren't for historical records and the archaeological remains in Algeria and Tunisia and in the Amazigh heritage with its use of the cross in home furnishings and jewelry. Once North Africa was proud of the Church of Carthage before the domination of Islam, but today its remains are in ruins.

Today's North African Muslim nations also give scant acknowledgment to the great philosopher and Christian theologian, Saint Augustine (AD 354-430), whose teachings and writings influenced the development of Western Christianity and Western philosophy. He was born in Thagaste, Numidia (present-day Souk Ahras, Algeria) and was the bishop of Hippo Regius (within present-day Annaba, Algeria) from AD 396 until his death. He is considered one of the most important church fathers in Western Christianity.

The city of ancient Carthage (located in present-day Tunisia) is the birthplace and home of another early church father, the Christian apologist and author Tertullian (c. AD 150-225). He is famous for his use of the

[43] "The Future of World Religions: Population Growth Projects, 2010-2050" (Middle East-North Africa). *PewForum.org*. Pew Research Center, 2 Apr. 2015. Web (http://www.pewforum.org/2015/04/02/middle-east-north-africa/).

[44] Ibid.

term *trinity* to describe Christianity's Holy Trinity of the Father, Son, and Holy Spirit. Supposedly, his conversion to Christianity was influenced by the courageous martyrdom of Christians brutalized and tortured to death in Carthage's amphitheater. His most famous work, *Apologeticus*, a defense of Christians, includes one of his most quoted statements: "the blood of martyrs are the seeds of the church." (See Chapter 50.)

One of the greatest biblical scholars of the early Christian church was Origen (c. AD 184-254), whose most important work and career was spent in Alexandria (Egypt). An extremely prolific writer (perhaps more than 6000 rolls or chapters), he excelled in textual criticism, biblical exegesis, hermeneutics, philosophical theology, and preaching. Unfortunately, few of his writings are extant, though large portions of three commentaries on the Book of John (New Testament) have survived over the centuries.

Saint Mark (d. AD 68), considered by most scholars as the author of the Book of Mark (New Testament), was an important evangelist of the early Christian church. Though not one of Jesus's twelve disciples, he was a devout follower of Jesus and a close friend to the disciples, especially Peter. Mark witnessed the preaching and passion of Jesus Christ and continued Christ's ministry in Egypt. There he founded the Church of Alexandria, the forerunner of both the Coptic Orthodox Church and the Greek Orthodox Church of Alexandria. Mark is credited with the establishment of the Catechetical School of Alexandria, which is the oldest catechetical school in the world, and was one of two major centers for biblical study during early Christian history. According to Coptic tradition, Mark was born in Cyrene (in present-day Libya) and he is honored as the founder of Christianity in Africa.

Another notable Libyan in early Christian history was Simon of Cyrene, who was ordered by Roman soldiers to carry the cross of Jesus Christ as Jesus was taken to his crucifixion. (See Bible: Matt. 27.32, Mark 15.21, Luke 23.26.) Cyrene had a sizable Jewish population during this time, descendants of the Jewish diaspora conducted under Ptolemy I (320 BC). Many of these Jews later converted to Christianity and these converts strongly contributed to the first Gentile (non-Jew) Christian church at Antioch, another important early Christian center.

All this rich Christian history and heritage that have shaped and contributed to the wonderfully vibrant past of North Africa have seemingly evaporated, as we no longer read anything apart from Islamic history in our history books. In Morocco, for example, the study of history begins in elementary school, with just one lesson about the Amazigh (Berbers), the indigenous Moroccans. The rest of the lessons are only about Islamic history and mention very little information about the Christian and pagan history of the region. This paucity implies that this history is unworthy, shameful, or embarrassing to include. Most North Africans have no knowledge of early Christian history, let alone Saint Augustine, Tertullian, or Origen. Muslims do not know that the Christian Church created there was one of the most influential Christian communities that existed at that time, and it used to fight injustice and oppression. This omission in our education is combined with our dedicated attention to create, name, and maintain streets, parks, monuments, cultural sites, cities, etc. of Morocco, Tunisia, and Algeria that primarily highlight our pride in Arab and Muslim leaders and conquerors and their historical significance.

Islam's selective distortion and suppression of North African history

History books in these North African countries mention little about history before Islam. Few monuments, scattered here and there, remain from cultures and communities different from and before Islam. Only researchers seem aware of their significance. This lack of attention and care to these pre-Islam artifacts, monuments, and history is a deliberate suppression of all that is non-Islamic.

Although the Amazigh (Berbers), the indigenous people of North Africa, resisted the multiple invasions of Arab Muslims, they are described in Islam as eager receivers of the new religion. Their Muslim conquerors are depicted as saviors to these regions of "ignorance and darkness." In truth, the Amazigh of North Africa rejected and resisted these invaders and conversion to Islam.

According to Ibn Khaldūn (AD 1332-1406), the famous and extremely influential Arab historiographer, the Amazigh "in Africa and Morocco before Islam were under the rule of the Crusaders and they were all Christians," and they rebelled against the Muslims and their Islam religion twelve times.[45]

Until the eighth century AD, the Amazigh in both Tunisia and Libya continuously rebelled against the Arab Muslim invaders because

[45] Ibn Khaldūn, *Tārīkh Ibn Khaldūn* 6: 121.

of the rampant killing and looting undertaken by these would-be conquerors, particularly when Muslim military commander 'Amr Ibn al-'Āṣ (c. AD 585-664) ruled Egypt under the caliphate rule of 'Umar Ibn al-Khaṭṭāb. Not only did he demand tribute from the residents of Cyrenaica (present-day Libya) in order to leave them alone (let them live), but he required them if necessary to sell their children to pay the tribute to avoid default. Eminent Persian historian al-Balādhurī (d. AD 892) notes this condition in his work, *Kitāb Futūḥ al-Buldān*, stating that 'Amr Ibn al-'Āṣ specified in his decree to the Amazigh of the Luwata (Berber tribal confederation) in Cyrenaica, "You have to sell your children and your women in order to pay the tribute."[46]

Ibn Khaldūn also paints 'Amr Ibn al-'Āṣ unfavorably in his dealings with the Amazigh peoples:[47]

> ['Amr Ibn al-'Āṣ] used the sword with the people of the country because they used to become Muslims only when the Muslim soldiers came, and they apostatized when they [Muslims] left...and he used to invade and send brigades for raiding and looting to make most Berbers [Amazigh] enter Islam.

Ibn Khaldūn also reports elsewhere in his history the Arab Muslims' brutal treatment of the Amazigh if they refused to convert to Islam:[48]

> The Arabs attacked them [Amazigh/Berbers] until there was blood everywhere, and they chased them in the villages, mountains, and deserts until they converted—either freely or unwillingly—to the religion of Islam, and they were led to the state of Egypt.

Ibn Khaldūn's very clear statement documents the horrible suffering of the Amazigh under Muslim rule and its policy of obligatory conversion to Islam.

The Amazigh endured some of the worst treatment under Muslim warlord Mūsā Ibn Nuṣayr (AD 640-716), who led the Arab Muslim armies of the Umayyad caliphate. He was appointed a ruler of Africa by al-Walīd Ibn 'Abd al-Malik (AD 668-715), who was the sixth Umayyad caliph. During this time the Arab Muslim empire reached its zenith, stretching eastward from the Arabian Peninsula into Central Asia and

---

[46] al-Balādhurī, *Kitāb Futūḥ al-Buldān* 1: 265.
[47] Ibn Khaldūn, *Tārīkh Ibn Khaldūn* 3: 12.
[48] Ibid. 7: 9.

India and westward into North Africa and the Iberian Peninsula (present-day Spain and Portugal).

As the ruling governor of Ifriqiya (North Africa), Mūsā Ibn Nuṣayr was most responsible for the horrific killing of the Amazigh, and he is credited for completely exterminating Christianity in North Africa. Kurdish Muslim historian and scholar Ibn Khalkān (AD 1211-1282) writes in his renowned biographical dictionary that "Mūsā...went out as an invader, chasing after the Berbers, and he slaughtered many civilians and enslaved many captives."[49]

According to Islamic sources, the number of captives Mūsā Ibn Nuṣayr enslaved has no parallel in the history of Islam. Ibn Kathīr reports that "there was never heard in Islam of anything similar to the [numbers of] captives of Mūsā Ibn Nuṣayr, the Prince of Al Maghrib."[50] Mūsā Ibn Nuṣayr conquered and occupied a Berber region then-called Saqouma, close to the present-day famous Moroccan city of Fez, enslaving much of the population. Ibn Khaldūn reports this account of the conquest:[51]

> ...when Mūsā Ibn Nuṣayr conquered Saqouma, he wrote to [Caliph] al-Walīd Ibn Abd al-Malik, telling him, "You now have hundred thousand heads [slaves] from Saqouma," and al-Walīd Ibn Abd al-Malik wrote back to him, [replying], "Woe to you! I think this is just one of your lies, but if you are telling the truth, then this is the Judgment Day of the nation."

Mūsā Ibn Nuṣayr's extreme exploitation of the people he conquered, seizing their wealth, land, and resources, was not an isolated action limited to him and perhaps a few other Muslim warlords. Instead, his action reflects a similar pattern of behavior by other Muslim warlords and rulers in other conquered territories, such as Iraq, Syria, and Egypt.[52] The only difference is that the remaining Christians in Egypt and the other countries were able to maintain their resistance. However, with every successive Muslim campaign, the number of remaining Christians in these countries declined, either through the forced compulsion to

[49] Ibn Khalkān, *Wafiyāt al-A'yān* 3: 160.

[50] Ibn Kathīr, *Al-Bidāya* 12: 629.

[51] Ibn Khaldūn, *Tārīkh Ibn Khaldūn* 6: 125; compare with *Ibn Kathīr, Al-Bidāya* 12: 629.

[52] al-Maqrīzī, *Al-Mawā'iẓ* 3: 252. When a famine occurred in Medina, the caliph 'Umar Ibn al-Khaṭṭāb sent a letter to his ruler 'Amr Ibn al-'Āṣ at the time and asked him to send supplies. 'Amr wrote back to him: "From the servant of the King [Allah], 'Amr Ibn al-'Āṣ, to the Commander of the Faithful: I am at your service! I have sent to you camels where the first one is already at your end and the last one is at my end. Peace, and Allah's mercy and blessings be upon you." And so he sent him many camels, where the first one was at Medina and the last one in Egypt, in a line, following one another.

convert to Islam, persecution, death, or the social pressures to conform with the ruling Muslim majority in order to enjoy more political rights and better economic opportunities.

"Oppositional" religious texts

Our conflict with non-Muslims is not contained inside the pages of historical texts but is rooted in our daily lives. Even if this hostility does not appear on the surface (except for a few big events, e.g., church or foreign embassy burnings, mass protest demonstrations, etc.), we live it in the less noticeable details in our daily behavior. In Morocco we call every foreigner a *gawri*. Until recently, I didn't know the meaning of this word. During a phone call with someone from Turkey, he told me that Turks used to call Armenians the same term, *kawri*, which is equivalent to the Arabic word *kāfir* (infidel). So, by calling every foreigner an infidel (*gawri*), we Moroccans have essentially categorized all foreigners as less than Muslims.

My father used to rebuke me if I said "Good morning!" when I woke up early in the morning. He would lecture me, saying that our greeting is "*Al-salāmu 'alaykum!*" (Peace be upon you) while the greeting "Good morning!" is only used by Christians. I also remember similar phone call exchanges with my relatives (e.g., my cousin, whom I consider as a sister and one of my aunt's daughters) and my friends. I would say "Hello," and they would answer "*Al-salām 'alaykum.*" When I asked them, "Why don't you just say 'Hello' like the rest of the people all over the world," they replied, "The greeting of Islam is '*Al-salām 'alaykum,*' but 'Hello' is from the Christians and the infidel West."

We apply similar irrational reasoning to justify our desire for and use of technology from the infidel West. We "Islamize" the West's technology by buying from Western companies the latest smartphones but putting on them Islamic ringtones that might play the call to worship (*adhān*) or "*Allahu Akbar*" or a verse from the Qur'ān—as if to convince ourselves that we are outwitting and defeating these infidels. This need to Islamize things or actions that did not originate from Islam is another religiously inherited psychological "complex" inside of us.

When Abū Bakr al-Baghdādī delivered his first sermon on July 4, 2014, a few days after Islamic State was declared a caliphate and he declared himself Caliph Ibrahim, the news media noticed that he wore his watch on his right wrist. They tried to guess its brand and kind, but very few seemed interested to know why he was wearing it on his right wrist. In fact, why do all Islamic jihadists, including Bin Lāden, al-Ẓawāhirī, and many *mujāhidīn*, wear their watch on their right wrist? Is there some kind of secret message behind it?

The "secret" is that Muslims are commanded to do the opposite of what the polytheists do, especially Jews and Christians. Regarding personal appearance, for example, Muḥammad advises his men in this *ḥadīth* to "[d]o the opposite of what the pagans do. Keep the beards and cut the moustaches short."[53] In another *ḥadīth*, Muḥammad declares, "The Jews and Christians do not dye their hair, so you should do the opposite of what they do."[54] (Because Muḥammad thought that Jews did not dye their hair and commanded his Companions to dye their hair, Osama Bin Lāden observed this *ḥadīth* and used to dye his hair.) When Muḥammad spotted one Companion, 'Abd Allah Ibn 'Amr Ibn al-'Āṣ, wearing two garments "dyed in saffron," Muḥammad told him, "These are the clothes (usually worn by) the nonbelievers, so do not wear them."[55]

The common rule in Islam is "whoever imitates a people becomes one of them."[56] Therefore, a Muslim must not imitate Christians and Jews but do the opposite to what they do in everything, even in speech and appearance.

Researchers wonder at the failure of many young Muslims to fully integrate into Western societies. It is very likely that one reason for this lack of assimilation concerns the demands and expectations of their religion conflicting with the demands and expectations of Western societies. Islam and the Hadith literature demand that Muslims be different from non-Muslims in everything, including speech mannerisms and appearance. How can these Muslims resolve this dilemma, living in the West but told not to follow Western living? The destructive consequence is that the young Muslims who commit themselves to these Islamic rules for living only live physically (marginally) in the West but live mentally in

[53] *Sahih Bukhari*, Book of Dress (p. 1314); *Ṣaḥīḥ al-Bukhārī*, Kītāb al-Libās 5: 2209.

[54] *Sahih Bukhari*, Book of Dress (p. 1315); *Ṣaḥīḥ al-Bukhārī*, Kītāb al-Libās 5: 2210. See *Musnad Aḥmad* 2: 513.

[55] *Sahih Muslim*, Book Pertaining to Clothes and Decoration: It is not permissible for a man to wear clothes of yellow colour (p. 1292); *Ṣaḥīḥ Muslim*, Kītāb al-Libās wa al-Zīna 2: 1000. **Note:** Islamic commentators define the color "saffron" as (solid) red, though English translators define it as the color yellow. (See URL: https://islamqa.info/ar/72878)

[56] *Sunan Abū Dawūd*, Book of Clothing 4: 387. This *ḥadīth* states that whoever "wears a garment of fame and vanity, on the Day of Resurrection Allah will clothe him in a similar garment…. Then He will set it ablaze."

the East—and not in our current time but seventh century AD in the Arabian Peninsula, re-living the problems and enmities of Muḥammad and his Companions and re-forming them for application in the twenty-first century AD.

Beheading of Coptic Christians

On February 15, 2015, Islamic State publicized from their Libyan branch a brutal video depicting the beheading of twenty-one kidnapped Coptic Christians from Egypt. A rolling caption in this video states that these captive Christians are "People of the cross, followers of the hostile Egyptian Church."[57] In the seventh issue of Islamic State's magazine *Dabiq*, the article "Revenge for the Muslimāt Persecuted" declares that the execution of the twenty-one Coptic "crusaders" was to avenge "Kamilia Shehata, Wafa' Constantine, and other sisters who were tortured and murdered by the Coptic Church of Egypt."[58] Islamic and Salafist groups allege that two women, Wafa' Constantine (age 48) and Kamilia Shehata Zakher (age 24) and both married to Coptic priests, had converted to Islam.[59] During their disappearances from their families (Wafa' in December 2004 and Kamilia in July 2010), Coptic Christians and Muslim groups clashed, each claiming that the other was holding the women captive and mistreating them.[60]

In the same article, *Dabiq* mentions the massacre at a Syrian Catholic church, Sayīdat al-Najāt (Our Lady of Salvation) in Baghdad, Iraq, which occurred on October 31, 2010. Nearly sixty people were killed and about eighty more were wounded or maimed. The magazine rebukes condemnation of this massacre by other Islamic groups and leaders by citing this Qur'ānic verse (Q 48.29): *"Muhammed is the Messenger*

---

[57] Islamic State. *A Message Signed with BLOOD to the Nation of the Cross*. Al-Hayat Media Center. 15 Feb. 2015. Web. **Note:** To read the video transcript, see URL: https://myislam.dk/articles/en/durie%20a-message-signed-with-blood-to-the-nation-of-the-cross.php. To view graphic video, see URL: http://schnellmann.org/message-signed-with-blood.html. See "ISIL Video Shows Christian Egyptians Beheaded in Libya." *Aljazeera.com*. Al Jazeera Media Network, 15 Feb. 2015. Web (http://preview.tinyurl.com/pldfxpj).

[58] "Revenge for the Muslimāt Persecuted by the Coptic Crusaders of Egypt." *Dabiq*. Issue 7 (Jan.-Feb. 2015): 30-32. Web (https://clarionproject.org/docs/islamic-state-dabiq-magazine-issue-7-from-hypocrisy-to-apostasy.pdf).

[59] Goodenough, Patrick. "Mass Beheading Video Appeared after ISIS Called on Muslims to Kill 'Crusaders' Everywhere." *CNSNews.com*. Conservative News Service, 15 Feb. 2015. Web (http://www.cnsnews.com/news/article/patrick-goodenough/mass-beheading-video-appeared-after-isis-called-muslims-kill).

[60] "Egyptian Coptic Protesters Freed." *BBC.co.uk*. British Broadcasting Corporation, 22 Dec. 2004. Web (http://news.bbc.co.uk/2/hi/middle_east/4117831.stm); Abdelmassih, Mary. "Muslims in Egypt Demand Release of Alleged Convert to Islam." *AINA.org*. Assyrian International News Agency. 30 Mar. 2011. Web (http://www.aina.org/news/20110329221230.htm).

of Allah; and those with him are harsh against the disbelievers, merciful among themselves...." In other words, Muslims should be violent against misbelievers but merciful among themselves (among true Muslims). The article concludes with this statement: "Finally, it is important for Muslims everywhere to know that there is no doubt in the great reward to be found on Judgment Day for those who spill the blood of these Coptic crusaders wherever they may be found."[61]

On April 15, 2015, Islamic State broadcasted a 39-minute video showing the slaughter of thirty Ethiopian Christians.[62] One group of fifteen was beheaded along a Mediterranean beach; the other group of fifteen was shot in the back of the head in a desert landscape. The video is titled *Until There Came to Them Clear Evidence*, which is a phrase taken from Q 98.1: "*The unbelievers of the People of the Book* [Jews and Christians] *and the idolaters would never leave off; till the Clear Sign came to them*" (Arberry trans.). In the same video, Islamic State also broadcasts pictures of the destruction of churches, Christian tombs, and statues of religious symbols and crosses in areas located in the Iraqi province of Mosul. This destruction by Islamic State was their response to the Christian residents' refusal to pay the tribute or convert to Islam. In the video, one Islamic State member says, "On the land of the caliphate in Libya, we invite Christians to enter Islam now," commenting that these scenes are of African Christians in Libya converting to Islam. But the man himself warns that "those who refuse to convert to Islam will have to face death by the sword."[63] The video describes the Ethiopian Church as a hostile church, because it belongs to a country that fights Islamic groups in Somalia.

Islamic State's killing of Coptic Christians and Ethiopian Christians is a kind of re-enactment of ancient Islamic history. The new "Caliphate" under Islamic State is trying to evoke the glories of Islam's past and its conquests of the Christian countries and territories during the Middle

---

[61] "Revenge for the Muslimāt Persecuted by the Coptic Crusaders of Egypt." *Dabiq*. Issue 7 (Jan.-Feb. 2015): 30-32. Web (https://clarionproject.org/docs/islamic-state-dabiq-magazine-issue-7-from-hypocrisy-to-apostasy.pdf).

[62] McLaughlin, Eliot C. "ISIS Executes More Christians in Libya, Video Shows." *CNN.com*. Cable News Network, 20 Apr. 2015. Web (http://www.cnn.com/2015/04/19/africa/libya-isis-executions-ethiopian-christians/); Shaheen, Kareen. "ISIS Video Purports to Show Massacre of Two Groups of Ethiopian Christians." *TheGuardian.com*. The Guardian, 19 Apr. 2015. Web (https://www.theguardian.com/world/2015/apr/19/isis-video-purports-to-show-massacre-of-two-groups-of-ethiopian-christians).

[63] "Video: Daesh [ISIS] Executed 28 Christian Ethiopians in Libya." *Alarabiya.net*. Al Arabiya Network, 19 Apr. 2015. Web (http://preview.tinyurl.com/zjmk6ek).

Ages by the early Muslim warlords, e.g., 'Amr Ibn al-'Āṣ and Mūsā Ibn Nuṣayr, who forced people to choose Islam, the tribute, or death.

Those who ignore the role of religious texts on the typical Muslim mind-set do not realize the impact of this Muslim conviction that Islam lived its most glorious era during the times of its invasions, conquests, and empire-building, when decisions were routinely made by the sword and the Islamic state was strong. This conviction stokes Islam's religious influence and elevates the self-pride of Arabs in the hearts and emotions of young Muslims. These young people then feel empowered as they read and follow the actions of Islamic State, which make them feel that this new Caliphate is returning Islam to its lost glory and strength using its religious authority, ability, and brutality—by the power of the sword—to subject Jews and Christians to Islam's control.

The painful irony is that the Ethiopian Church was the first Christian community to host the oppressed Qurayshi Muslims in their first migration from Mecca (c. AD 615), when the early Muslims numbered in the dozens. They sought refuge in Abyssinia (present-day Ethiopia) under the protection of the Christian ruler, or Negus. Of him and Abyssinia, Muḥammad said, "[T]he king will not tolerate injustice and it is a friendly country."[64] This Negus supported these early Muslims even though they followed a religion that does not align with Christianity and even refutes core Christian beliefs, e.g., divinity and crucifixion of Jesus Christ. However, when Muḥammad became stronger and his followers now numbered in the thousands, they "forgot" the kindness and hospitality of these Abyssinian Christians. In fact, Muḥammad eventually called for the expulsion of all Christians from the Arabian Peninsula,[65] a command that was fulfilled by his successors.

Now the members of these Islamic groups, the descendants of these early Muslim emigrants, are beheading the descendants of the early Ethiopian (Abyssinian) king who protected their Muslim ancestors. If that Abyssinian Christian Negus hadn't taken in those first Muslim emigrants, perhaps Islam would have died in the seventh century AD.

[64] Ibn Hishām (Ibn Isḥāq), *The Life of Muhammad* 146; Ibn Hishām (Ibn Isḥāq) *Al-Sīra al-Nabawīya* 2: 90. First migration to Abyssinia is mentioned.

[65] *Sahih Muslim,* Book of Jihad and Expedition: Evacuation of the Jews from the Hijaz (p. 1091); *Ṣaḥīḥ Muslim*, Kītāb al-Jihād wa al-Sīyar 2: 846. In this *ḥadīth*, narrated by 'Umar Ibn al-Khaṭṭab, Muḥammad said, "I will expel the Jews and Christians from the Arabian Peninsula and will not leave any but Muslim."

Kamilia Shehata Zakher and Wafa' Constantine

Islamic State mentions the names of two Coptic Christian women, Kamilia Shehata Zakher and Wafa' Constantine, as part of its justification for beheading the twenty-one Egyptian Coptic Christians.

Kamilia Shehata Zakher Mus'ad (full name) was born in Egypt in 1985. She became a junior high school teacher and the wife of Coptic priest. In July 2010, after some heated marital disagreements, she departed from the family home but left no messages or clues about her destination.

Worried that she, as the wife of a Coptic priest, might have been targeted by Muslims, her husband filed a complaint with the local police, stating that she had been kidnapped by hard-line Muslims in Minya. He was guessing that she might have been forced to convert to Islam or that someone had persuaded her to become a Muslim to get out of her marriage. (In the Coptic Christian Orthodox Church, divorce is only permitted in cases of adultery. Islam forbids a Muslim woman to be married to a non-Muslim man. So, if Kamilia became a Muslim, then she could divorce her Christian husband—against the will of the Coptic Church—because he is a non-Muslim.)

When the husband mobilized a demonstration with dozens of Christians, demanding police intervention to help find his wife, the ensuing publicity alerted Kamilia, and she came out of hiding. However, the publicity also aroused local Muslims, who charged (incorrectly) that Kamilia had converted to Islam and had run away from her Christian husband, because she, as a Muslim, could not remain married to him (according to Islamic law).

So Muslims, led by Salafists, held a series of demonstrations, holding up a picture of Kamilia and banners that demanded the return of their "sister" Kamilia or the liberation of their Muslim sisters who (they claimed) were prisoners in the Coptic Church. A "Photoshopped" (digitally edited) picture presenting Kamilia wearing the Islamic *hijāb* was circulated to "prove" that she had converted to Islam, but by then

Kamilia had returned to her husband and all the family was transferred to another place to ensure their safety.[66]

Yet the demonstrations continued, even with the departure of Kamilia and her family from Egypt—even after the fall of President Hosni Mubarak's regime during the January 25 Revolution in 2011. The demonstrations were led by Salafists in front of mosques and pressure was exerted on the church.[67]

Wafa' Constantine, like Kamilia, is also a wife of an Egyptian Coptic Christian priest, though she (born in 1956) is much older than Kamilia and worked as an agricultural engineer. She too was experiencing marital problems. When she separated from her husband in 2004, Salafists circulated propaganda that she had converted to Islam. The Coptic Church staged demonstrations claiming she had been kidnapped and forced to convert to Islam.[68] As the situation fomented increasingly more violent civil unrest and hostile confrontations between Copts and Muslims, the government brought the woman to a Copt Christian cathedral in Cairo. Since then, rumors and various news media offer conflicting reports about Wafa' Constantine and her whereabouts. Depending on the source, she eventually returned to her family, resides in a Copt monastery, or was tortured and killed at a Copt monastery.[69]

To this day, Islamic groups use the cases of Wafa' Constantine and Kamilia Shehata to justify their attacks on Christians in the Middle East—whether or not these Christian targets are Copts. These two women are considered great propaganda value because they are both wives of priests and as such their (alleged) conversion to Islam is more sensational. A story of a priest's wife converting to Islam carries a special

---

[66] "Big Surprise: Appearance of Sister Kamilia Shehata Only on *Daring Question*" (Episode 214). Narr. Brother Rachid. *Daring Question.* Al Hayat TV. 7 May 2011. Television. (To view video, see URL: http://preview.tinyurl.com/gqaf4d3). During my television interview with Kamilia, she told me she and her family had to leave Egypt because she believed the Salafists would kill her once they realized she did not convert and never would leave Christianity. She also felt that her continued presence in Egypt would only extend the crisis and generate more blame toward or persecution of the Coptic Church. Today, she and her family live in a Western country.

[67] **Note:** After my televised interview with Kamilia, hundreds of Salafists the same day attacked the Coptic Orthodox Church of St. Mina in Giza, killing ten and wounding over two hundred parishioners, and burned down the building.

[68] "30 Hurt in Egypt Religious Conversion Dispute." *NBCNews.com.* National Broadcasting Corporation, 8 Dec. 2004. Web (http://www.nbcnews.com/id/6682743/ns/world_news/t/hurt-egypt-religious-conversion-dispute/#.Wm5ePzeIaUl).

[69] Ibid.; Mustafa, Muhammad. "Renewed Controversy over the Disappearance of a Coptic Woman Converted to Islam Four Years Ago." *Aawsat.com.* Middle East, 28 Aug. 2008. Web (http://archive.aawsat.com/details.asp?section=4&article=484599&issueno=10866).

flavor of victory over the Christian church. Likewise, the kidnapping of Christian daughters and marrying them to Muslims also brings euphoria, another instance of Muslim victory over Christianity.

This deep obsession to convert Christian women into Muslims is a complex Muslims have had since the time of Muḥammad up to the present. Even today Coptic female minors get kidnapped and married off to Muslims, while Egyptian security forces as well as Al Azhar collude with Islamic parties to quickly facilitate all the paperwork to recognize these forced marriages to Muslim men and the young wives' "conversion" to Islam. Conversely, if any Muslim girl converts to Christianity, it is impossible to change her religion and her identification documents. She also would run the risk of getting sentenced to prison where she would be tortured by the security forces.

When Al Qaeda in Iraq (AQI) attacked the Syriac Catholic Church of Sayīdat al-Najāt (Our Lady of Salvation Church) in Baghdad on October 31, 2010, the attackers demanded during their assault that the Egyptian Coptic church must release their "sisters" Wafa' Constantine and Kamilia Shehata, the two Coptic women who allegedly converted to Islam and were held by the church against their will.

In October 2014, I personally questioned the "mother of John"[70] and her daughter Joanne after they received political asylum in Australia. Um John (the mother of John) lost four members of her family in this monstrous attack: her husband, Yūnān Kūrkīs al-Sāʿūr; her son John and his wife, Rita Matta; and their four-month-old infant Sandro, who was the youngest martyr in this massacre, where more than fifty people were killed and nearly seventy people wounded.[71] The terrorists were shouting "*Allahu Akbar*" as they were killing the Christians and yelling that it was *ḥalāl* (lawful) to kill the Christians. Witnesses also heard the attackers scream, "We will go to paradise if we kill you and you are going to hell!" They told the Christians inside the church that "all of you are infidels" and then said, "We are here to avenge the burning of the Qur'āns and the jailing of Muslim women in Egypt!" After the massacre, one female

[70] She preferred that I call her "mother of John" in order to keep alive the memory of her son, who was killed in the bloody attack.

[71] "Baghdad Church Siege Survivors Speak of Taunts, Killings, and Explosions." *TheGuardian.com*. The Guardian, 1 Nov. 2010. Web (https://www.theguardian.com/world/2010/nov/01/baghdad-church-siege-survivors-speak). See "The Massacre of Assyrians at Our Lady of Deliverance Church in Baghdad." *AINA.org*. Assyrian International News Agency, 3 Dec. 2010 (Appendix). Web (http://www.aina.org/releases/20101203154244.htm). **Note**: Second source (AINA) includes a listing of related articles connected to this attack and a video recorded interview of one of the survivors.

surviving witness commented, "They hated us and said we were all going to die."[72]

AQI publicly claimed credit for the attack and massacre. It released a statement on the Internet suggesting that it had planned to hold the Christians hostage in the church for at least two days until the two Egyptian women supposedly being held against their will in Coptic churches were released.[73] AQI also threatened to carry future attacks against Christian churches all over the world:[74]

> ...various attacks will be launched against them inside and outside this country, in which their lands will be destroyed, their strength will be undermined, and they will be afflicted by the humiliation that God ordained for them....

In 2015, Islamic State carried out this threat in Libya when its members slaughtered the twenty-one Coptic Christians "to avenge" Wafa' Constantine and Kamilia Shehata. Its act of revenge is but one of a continuing series of such acts, with or without a pretext. Even if there was no Wafa' or Kamilia Shehata, these terrorist groups will fabricate a thousand pretexts.

Zaghlūl El-Naggār, the sheikh who concocted the lie that Wafa' Constantine had been killed by the church, was never put on trial for this deliberate falsehood, although he was sued by a Coptic lawyer for inciting Muslims against the church for spreading these lies. However, it is well known that the Egyptian judicial system will not sympathize with a Christian lawyer against a Muslim sheikh and will never submit him to a trial.[75] Therefore, any sheikh can accuse the Christian church of anything, including murder, witchcraft and sorcery. These manufactured charges will then create a pretext for angry Muslims to attack the church.

---

[72] "Baghdad Church Siege Survivors Speak of Taunts, Killings, and Explosions." *TheGuardian.com*. The Guardian, 1 Nov. 2010. Web (https://www.theguardian.com/world/2010/nov/01/baghdad-church-siege-survivors-speak). See "The Massacre of Assyrians at Our Lady of Deliverance Church in Baghdad." *AINA.org*. Assyrian International News Agency, 3 Dec. 2010 (Appendix). Web (http://www.aina.org/releases/20101203154244.htm).

[73] Roggio, Bill. "Al Qaeda in Iraq Claims Massacre at Christian Church in Baghdad." *LongWarJournal.org*. Foundation for Defense of Democracies (FDD's Long War Journal). 1 Nov. 2010. Web (http://www.longwarjournal.org/archives/2010/11/al_qaeda_in_iraq_cla.php).

[74] Ibid.

[75] "Renewed Controversy over the Disappearance of a Coptic Woman Converted to Islam Four Years Ago." *Aawsat.com*. Middle East, 28 Aug. 2008. Web (http://archive.aawsat.com/details.asp?section=4&article=484599&issueno=10866).

Christians cannot object or prosecute the instigators of these rumors in court.

For example, a senior Islamic scholar in Egypt, Muḥammad Salīm al-'Awā, asserted on Al Jazeera television program *Without Limits*, hosted by journalist Ahmed Mansour, the following comment: "The weapons that Copts bring and store in a church have no other purpose other than to be used in the future against the Muslims."[76] This supposedly moderate Islamic thinker further accuses the Egyptian Coptic Church of planning war against Egyptian Muslims—with no evidence—except to state in the interview that "many people say that the monasteries are full of weapons" and that this effort is "continuous, organized, and systematic."[77] Though his statements are denounced by the Coptic Church, his irresponsible and unsubstantiated comments have not been formally challenged in a court of law.

In another example, Sheikh Muḥammad Ḥassān accused the Atfih Church in Hilwan, south of Cairo, of practicing witchcraft on Muslims in order to justify a Muslim attack on the church, setting it on fire on March 5, 2011. This destruction was followed by Copts demonstrating in front of the Maspero Building, the headquarters of Egyptian television. Sheikh Muḥammad Ḥassān maintains that he tried to intervene between the two groups to reduce the tension, but he still claimed that the Muslims' attack on the church was precipitated by books on witchcraft and the names of Muslim individuals written on paper as targets found in the church.[78] In reality, the incident was caused by a love affair between a young Christian man and a Muslim girl, a relationship considered an insult to the Muslim family because Muslim females are forbidden to marry infidels.[79]

---

[76] "Muhammad Salim Al-Awa, Secretary-General of the International Union of Muslim Scholars: Copts Amass Weapons in Egyptian Churches and are 'Preparing for War against the Muslims.'" *MEMRI.org/tv*. Middle East Media Research Institute TV Monitor Project, 15 Sept. 2010. Television. (See MEMRI Clip #2624: https://www.memri.org/tv/muhammad-salim-al-awa-secretary-general-international-union-muslim-scholars-copts-amass-weapons)

[77] Ibid.

[78] Abdo, Mary. "The Witchcraft of the Atfih Church." *Copts-United.com*. Copts United, 12 Mar. 2011. Web (http://www.copts-united.com/Article.php?I=2819&A=32612).

[79] Ibid. See Nūrī, Sājid. "After the Expulsion of Copts in Beni Suef Crisis: 12 Most Famous Sectarian Conflicts in Egypt." *Elwatannews.com*. El Watan News, 3 June 2015. Web (http://www.elwatannews.com/news/details/742791). **Note:** The Atfih Church attack is #9 in this listing.

Religious texts blameworthy

The justification for the killing of Christians in Iraq and the killing of Egyptian Christians in Libya can be directly traced to the Islamic texts, which feed generation after generation this hatred towards Christians.

Even the details of Islamic State's operation of kidnapping the Egyptians in Libya and slaughtering them show the fruits of this hostility instilled by the religious texts. The twenty-one Coptic Christians who were beheaded on February 15, 2015, were two groups kidnapped separately. The first group, a total of seven men, was kidnapped by a Muslim driver who drove them himself to the terrorist organization. When he returned home, he claimed that they were kidnapped from him. The second kidnapping of fourteen men occurred "at twelve midnight" according to a witness who escaped capture:[80]

> A large number of the organization's terrorists were involved, and the operation was carried out with high accuracy, as they entered only rooms where Copts lived despite the fact that the house was full of Muslim and Christian Egyptians. This shows that whoever broke into the house had prior knowledge of who was in it and which ones were specifically the rooms of the Copts. He stressed the fact that there were Egyptians who took part in informing on their [Christian] colleagues.

What motivates Muslim Egyptians, sharing the same house and food with fellow Christian Egyptian citizens, to betray their Christian roommates to terrorist groups? If religion played no role, what then made these people behave so despicably against their fellow citizens, knowing that they were going to hand them over to such a merciless group? It is definitely the religious texts that taught and brought up generations on a culture of hatred towards Christians.

Muslims are brought up to call Christians "worshippers of the cross" in order to humiliate and denounce them. Books published in Muslim countries and Web sites in the Muslim world condemn Christians as "worshippers of the cross."[81] This hatred of Christianity's sacred symbol, the cross, is rooted in the mentality of Muslims, to the extent that when I was a Muslim I used to feel disgusted whenever I saw a Christian cross.

---

[80] Abū Ḍayf, Muḥammad. "The Mystery of Kidnapping the Victims: Egyptians Took Part in Informing on Them and Driver Handed Them over to Daesh [ISIS]." *Elwatannews.com*. El Watan News, 17 Feb. 2015. Web (http://www.elwatannews.com/news/details/664707).

[81] "A Warning to the Monotheists [Muslims] from the Holidays of the Worshipers of the Cross." *Islamway.net*. Islam Way, 30 Dec. 2014. Web (http://preview.tinyurl.com/hv5fxlu).

For some Muslims, the reason rests in the following famous *ḥadīth*: "Allah's Apostle [Muḥammad] said, 'The Hour will not be established until the son of Mary (i.e., Jesus) descends amongst you as a just ruler, he will break the cross, kill the pigs, and abolish the Jizya tax...."[82] The phrases "break the cross" and "kill the pigs" means that when Jesus returns, he will destroy Christianity by rejecting its central doctrine—his death and resurrection, which Muslims deny—and destroy those Christian practices that do not follow Islamic law. The phrase "abolish the Jizya tax" means that at the Final Hour, Christians can no longer pay a tax to avoid conversion to Islam or death: they must choose one or the other.

Christians, as "worshippers of the cross," appear idolatrous to Muslims; thus, in hating idolatry, they then hate Christians and their sacrilegious practices, e.g., eating of pork. With this Islamic belief, it should not be surprising to see photographs of the *mujāhidīn* in Syria and Iraq breaking the crosses and smashing the icons while attacking Christian churches dating back to the beginning of Christianity.[83] It is their belief that Jesus himself will come back one day to destroy the idols of the Christians and their holy places, and he will literally break them before their eyes.

This *ḥadīth* about the return of Jesus to "break the cross" is the same *ḥadīth* that is cited in the video showing the slaughter of the Coptic Christians, who cry out, "Lord Jesus," as the knives fall.[84] In fact, the title of this video refers to this *ḥadīth*: *A Message Signed with BLOOD to the Nation of the Cross*. This Islamic theology of hatred for all that is Christian is the reason and motivation for these vicious attacks. As more and more Muslims around the world have access to these religious texts and apply to them the most literal conservative interpretation, we shall see more and more Islamic extremism, because these extremist Islamic groups cling to this strict language in the texts.

The Christian cross is the symbol of enmity in the Muslim mind because it is the symbol of the religion in most competition with Islam.

---

[82] *Sahih Bukhari*, Book of Oppressions (p. 564; see pp. 499, 803); *Ṣaḥīḥ al-Bukhārī*, Kītāb al-Maẓālim 2: 876.

[83] Bahā', Jafrā. "Daesh [ISIS] Breaks the Crosses on al-Raqqa Churches and Burns Their Contents." *Alarabiya.net*. Al Arabiya Network, 26 Sept. 2013. Web (http://preview.tinyurl.com/j5oncfl).

[84] Islamic State. *A Message Signed with BLOOD to the Nation of the Cross*. Al-Hayat Media Center. 15 Feb. 2015. Web. (To read the video transcript, see URL: https://myislam.dk/articles/en/durie%20a-message-signed-with-blood-to-the-nation-of-the-cross.php; to view graphic video, see URL: http://schnellmann.org/message-signed-with-blood.html). See Smith II, Michael S. "IS in Libya Threatens Rome." *InsidetheJihad.com*. Downrange, 15 Feb. 2015. Web (https://insidethejihad.com/2015/02/is-in-libya-threatens-rome/).

Therefore, Islam must overcome the cross and "break" it. One way Muslims feel they can "break the cross" is to buy churches in the East and the West and convert them into mosques because this physical conversion of a Christian holy site gives them a sense of victory, of overcoming the cross. For others, greater ecstasy of victory occurs when they physically break the crosses on churches and raise up the flag of Islam.

The beliefs and doctrines of Islam's religious texts, rooted in the hearts of Muslims for generations, have spawned these terrorist groups—Al Qaeda, Boko Haram, and Islamic State—and will continue to spawn others yet to appear on the global radar. It is not possible to eliminate the symptoms without knowing the roots of the disease. The roots are the religious texts that are cited and implemented by Islamic State and Al Qaeda. Yet these texts are also cited in the public domain and government-sponsored media and mosques of Muslim countries, like Qatar and Saudi Arabia, and by the sheikhs all over the Muslim world who cite them in their speeches and videos. But they are too cowardly to actually implement them; they issue fatāwa but expect others to read and implement them. Islamic State implements.

SIX

Declaring a person an infidel (kāfir) is an Islamic disease

One of the most dangerous terms in the Islamic dictionary is *kāfir* (infidel). This term is proclaimed by Muslims against anyone who does not believe in Islam or the Messenger of Islam and anyone who is found guilty of leaving Islam (apostasy). Denial of any essential element of Islam is considered a deeply serious matter.[1] If any Muslim is accused of being a *kāfir*, this means that it becomes lawful to spill his or her blood; it is only enough to label the person as a *kāfir* without explicitly uttering the word "kill." After this point of utterance, his or her life will be under the threat of imminent death. However, even with this understanding, sometimes the word is paired with the command of killing the *kāfir*.

[1] See Fatwa no. 78151: "Emphatically or Unequivocally Known to be Part of the Religion." *Islamweb.net*. Ministry of Endowments and Islamic Affairs of Qatar, 18 Oct. 2006. Web (http://fatwa.islamweb.net/fatwa/index.php?page=showfatwa&Option=FatwaId&Id=78151). Excerpt: An essential part of Islam, "something emphatically and unequivocally known to be part of the religion," means that it is "what is known by all Muslims about the religion...without consideration nor contemplation, whether it is an obligation or a prohibition."

Many Islamic apologists state that the word *kāfir* is just a simple word: It only means that "you are a disbeliever of my beliefs, which makes you a *kāfir* to me, and I'm a *kāfir* to you because I am a disbeliever of your beliefs." Similar prevarication was expressed by the Sheikh of Al Azhar, Ahmed al-Tayeb, during a televised interview on Egypt's Channel One. Excerpts of his comments have been posted in the following online news article:[2]

> The term *kāfir* is an additional term that means to deny something, and Christians deny the message of Muḥammad and we consider them infidels as Muslims. I do not believe in the Trinity and I do not believe in Christianity as it is now, I am considered an infidel according to them. [Then he quotes Q 2.256 "*...whoso disbelieves in Tâghût and believes in God....*"; Palmer trans.] So the believer in God disbelieves in Taghut [idols] and saying that someone is an infidel is not an insult.... Muslims are considered infidels in the sight of Western religious organizations. [He concludes by saying] I advise people from both sides not to play with the word infidel and speaking about beliefs is not a right thing.

In contrast, Egypt's Grand Mufti, Sheikh 'Alī Gom'a, who is a graduate and professor of Al Azhar—and second in authority to Sheikh Ahmed al-Tayeb—categorized Christians as *kuffār* (plural form of *kāfir*) in a video and quoted Q 5.17 ("*They are infidels, who say, verily God is Christ the son of Mary...*"; Sale trans.). He explains that anyone who "thinks the Christ is God, or the Son of God, not symbolically—for we are all sons of God—but attributively, has rejected the faith which God requires for salvation," and is thereby an infidel.[3] He bluntly identifies Christians as infidels based on Qur'ānic text, unlike the Sheikh of Al Azhar who suggests the term is relative and can be used reciprocally.

What then is the danger behind the word *kāfir*? And what does it mean? Does it have a linguistic meaning that only indicates a person to be a "nonbeliever"? Or is it more serious than that?

[2] "Sheikh of Al Azhar on Egyptian Television Says Current Christianity Is Corrupted and I Am Considered an Infidel by Christians." *CoptsToday.com*. Copts Today, n.d. Web (https://www.coptstoday.com/Archive/Detail.php?Id=11780).

[3] Ibrahim, Raymond. "Top Muslim Declares All Christians 'Infidels.'" *MEForum.org*. Middle East Forum, 28 Oct. 2011. Web (http://www.meforum.org/3085/muslim-declares-christians-infidels).

Characteristics of disbelievers in the Qur'ān

The Qur'ān declares in many verses that Christians are infidels. In Q 5.17 (*"They* ***misbelieve***[4] *who say, 'Verily, God is the Messiah the son of Mary'...* "; Palmer trans. with emphasis added), the Christians are "misbelievers" or *kuffār* (infidels) because of their belief in Christ as the Son of God. Another verse, Q 5.73 (*"They misbelieve who say, 'Verily, God is the third of three;' for there is no God but one...* "; Palmer trans.), again means that the Qur'ān considers Christian "misbelievers" or *kuffār* because of their belief in the Trinity, which Muslims incorrectly assert is polytheism—that God, Jesus, and Holy Spirit are three separate gods and not one God that is Father, Son, and Holy Spirit.

In yet another verse (Q 9.30; Palmer trans.), the Qur'ān declares that both Jews and Christians are misbelievers. Christians are misbelievers because of their "incorrect" faith in Christ, and Jews are misbelievers because of their faith in a person called Ezra: *"The Jews say Ezra is the son of God; and the Christians say that the Messiah is the son of God; that is what they say with their mouths, imitating the sayings of those who misbelieved before.—God fight them! How they lie!"*

Less clear-cut is a verse (Q 98.1; Palmer trans.) where the Qur'ān labels the People of the Book (Jews and Christians) as misbelievers but implies an object ("the manifest sign") of the misbelief: *"Those of the people of the Book and the idolaters who misbelieve did not fall off until there came to them the manifest sign."* Does the Qur'ān mean their incorrect Christian or Jewish beliefs or does this text mean a far more serious misbelief—disbelief in Muḥammad, the Qur'ān, Islam? The other verses that describe infidels connect the word "disbelievers" or "misbelievers" with the article *the* (as in "**the** disbelievers"), which is not used to label Muslims but is used to describe non-Muslims, or Muslims who disbelieve in some parts of Islam or some of the Pillars of Islam. This kind of disbelief would make that Muslim an infidel apostate.

The Qur'ān (Q 8.55; Palmer trans.) describes misbelievers as the *"worst of beasts"* and thus removes their humanity: *"Verily,* ***the worst of beasts*** *in God's eyes are those who misbelieve and will not believe"* (emphasis added). Their beastliness is the result of their lack of belief in Muḥammad and his religion. A similar description is found in another verse (Q 98.6;

[4] The English word *misbelieve* in this verse is translated from the Arabic verb *kafara*, which means "to reject belief."

Palmer trans.), where the Qur'ān considers them as the worst of created beings: *"Verily, those who disbelieve amongst the people of the Book and the idolaters shall be in the fire of hell, to dwell therein for aye;* ***they are wretched creatures!****"* (emphasis added). Given these insulting and dehumanizing descriptions, can one still say that the Christian is a *kāfir* in the eyes of the Muslim and the Muslim is an *kāfir* in the eyes of the Christian, relatively speaking? Would a Muslim then accept being described as "the worst of beasts" and "wretched creatures"? Obviously, the word *kāfir* carries significantly more negative connotations in Islam.

No verse in the Qur'ān describes a Muslim or Muslims using the word *kāfir* (infidel) or *kuffār* (infidels). However, one verse (Q 2.256; Palmer trans.) uses the term in question as an action (a verb): *"...and whoso* ***disbelieves***[5] *in Tâghût* [Palmer's note: "idols and demons of the ancient Arabs"] *and believes in God, he has got hold of the firm handle in which is no breaking off; but God both hears and knows"* (emphasis added).

Therefore, the primarily descriptive terms used in the Qur'ān for "misbelievers" resolves the issue, with the intended characterization a critical, prejudiced, and derogatory slur towards those who do not believe in Islam. It is not merely an alternative expression for the term "nonbeliever." The Qur'ān (Q 47.12; Palmer trans.) states that those who disbelieve are just animals that eat: *"...those who misbelieve enjoy themselves and eat as the cattle eat; but the fire* [hellfire] *is the resort for them!"* The Qur'ān (Q 8.65; Palmer trans.) even describes misbelievers as people with no intelligence: *"...If there be of you twenty patient men, they shall conquer two hundred; if there be of you a hundred, they shall conquer a thousand of those who misbelieve, because they are a people who did not discern."* The Qur'ān repeatedly curses misbelievers.

If the term is relative, as the Sheikh of Al Azhar contends, then the cursing of Muslims should also be permissible because they are considered infidels to Christians. So, would the Sheikh of Al Azhar find it acceptable if God curses him or if Christians curse him? When the Qur'ān states, *"...God's curse be on the misbelievers"* (Q 2.89; Palmer trans.), the word "misbelievers" is preceded with the article *the*, i.e., "**the** misbelievers," which means all misbelievers, wherever and whoever they are.

[5] The English word *disbelieve* in this verse is translated from the Arabic verb *yakfur*, which means "to reject belief."

Allah's cursing of the misbelievers is described even more harshly in another verse (Q 33.64; Palmer trans.): *"Verily, God has cursed the misbelievers and has prepared for them a blaze!"* In Q 3.32, Muslims are told that Allah even hates the misbelievers (*"... God loves not misbelievers"*; Palmer trans.) and in Q 2.98 he considers them as his enemies (*"... God is an enemy to the unbelievers"*; Palmer trans.). According to Islamic commentators, this last verse, Q 2.98, concerns the Jews, in the sense that Allah is a personal enemy of the Jews. The respected Muslim commentator al-Ṭabarī states that "this [text] indicates that Allah revealed this verse to rebuke the Jews about their disbelief in Muḥammad, and informing them [Jews] that whoever is an enemy of Muḥammad means that Allah is his enemy."[6]

The Qur'ān also considers misbelievers as criminals who deserve punishment for their disbelief: *"But as for those who disbelieved (it will be said to them): 'Were not Our Verses recited to you? But you were proud, and you were a people who were Mujrimun (polytheists, disbelievers, sinners, criminals)'"* (Q 45.31; Hilâlî-Khân trans.).[7] But Muslims are not categorized as criminals if the term *misbeliever* means only "nonbeliever," because the Qur'ān rejects the pairing of "Muslim" with a sinful, criminal "misbeliever": *"Shall we then make the Muslims like the sinners? / What ails you? How ye judge!"* (Q 68.35-36; Palmer trans.). This massive collection of verses shows that the Qur'ān dedicates a lot of text to describe infidels with contempt and humiliation, placing them in the lowest rankings as notorious sinners and criminals who deserve punishment in the world and in the hereafter.

Muḥammad says in a *ḥadīth*, "If a man says to his brother, 'O Kafir (disbeliever)!' Then surely one of them is such (i.e., a kāfir)."[8] If the term *kāfir* is relative, why then would only one of them become a disbeliever? Wouldn't both be misbelievers in the eyes of each other?

The use of the term *kāfir* in this *ḥadīth* indicates that it is a dangerous term because it means that the accusation alone is enough to criminalize someone; an accused person is no longer protected by secular laws and no longer a citizen. Such an accused Muslim must face this charge under

---

[6] See the commentary on Q 2.98, *Tafsīr al-Ṭabarī* 1: 349.

[7] **Note:** In Arabic, the word *Mujrimun* means "criminals."

[8] *Sahih Bukhari*, Book of Good Manners and Form (p. 1358); *Ṣaḥīḥ al-Bukhārī*, Kītāb al-Adab 5: 2264. See *Sahih Muslim*, Book of Faith: The condition of the faith of one who calls his brother Muslim an unbeliever (p. 91); *Ṣaḥīḥ Muslim*, Kītāb al-Imān 1: 47.

Islamic-based texts instead of the secular laws, which means the term *kāfir* is a discriminatory term. It is a term that ranks such people as second to and thus lower than Muslims. In practice, this ranking means in a community of both Muslims and non-Muslims, the Muslims are considered the first or top class and enjoy more privileges just because they're Muslims, while the non-Muslims, or "infidels," are second-class citizens—and that designation only if they are "peaceful infidels." (See Chapter 7, page 163.) These "peaceful infidels" are those meek, good and humble nonbelievers who accept the rulings of Islam, pay the tribute, but not protest their economic or social conditions, accepting that their status and treatment is at the mercy of Muslims. These infidels are considered less in status than Muslims in everything. Therefore, infidels in general, and Christians in particular, live in daily misery in the Muslim world, whether in Egypt, Iraq, Iran, Pakistan, Syria and the rest of the countries of the Muslim world. Even in Jordan, one of the safest and most hospitable of the Muslim countries, excludes non-Muslims from some jobs (e.g., secret security police) and political positions (e.g., prime minister) that are open to their fellow Muslim citizens.

Value of infidels, enemies of Muslims

Infidels are the enemies of Muslims in every way, according to the Qur'ān: *"...verily, the misbelievers are your obvious foes"* (Q 4.101; Palmer trans.) and *"Let not the believers take the unbelievers for friends, rather than the believers—for whoso does that belongs not to God in anything..."* (Q 3.28; Arberry trans.). This second verse even commands Muslims to shun friendship with people who are non-Muslims, because the infidels are enemies of Allah. Therefore, infidels are the enemies of Muslims, because Allah wants Muslims to take his own enemies as their enemies.

The Qur'ān even tells Muslims to pray for help against infidels: *"...and pardon us, and have mercy on us. Thou art our Sovereign, then help us against the people who do not believe!"* (Q 2.286; Palmer trans.). This supplication is one of the most famous prayers recited by Muslims during their Friday prayers, group prayers, and other occasions. The purpose of this prayer is to ask Allah for help against misbelievers, all misbelievers, whoever and wherever they are, even if they coexist with the believers in the same country...even if they are the neighbors.

The Qur'ān makes it clear that believers should not have nonbelievers as friends. But what happens if a Muslim kills an infidel? In this situation, the Muslim will not receive capital punishment, according to the law or principle of retaliation, "life for a life."[9] Because the Muslim's blood (life) is more precious than the blood of an infidel, the life of the infidel does not have the same value in Allah's sight. Thus, a Muslim is not to be killed for killing an infidel. This exception is a known Islamic ruling based on this *ḥadīth* attributed to Muḥammad: "…no Muslim should be killed for killing an infidel."[10] This same statement is repeated in many Islamic sources, including the *Musnad Ahmad*: The prophet Muḥammad has judged that "a Muslim is not to be killed for [killing] a *kāfir*."[11]

One of the famous commentators of Hadith literature in the Islamic world, Ibn Ḥajar al-'Asqalānī (AD 1372-1449), reports that "not killing a Muslim for killing a *kāfir* is the opinion of the majority."[12] His statement means that Muslim scholars have agreed to apply this ruling, taken from the Hadith literature: No Muslim should be killed in retaliation for killing a *kāfir*. Given these repercussions, does the term *kāfir* now still seem equivalent to "nonbeliever"?

The Sheikh of Al Azhar obviously understands the complexities of the term *kāfir* and its religious ruling, but he simplifies the term in public to "normalize" it and make it acceptable for Christians to hear it without protest. The entire international community, however, should strongly condemn this term, because Arab Christians do not use it at all in their dealings with non-Christians. It is only used by Muslims as an abusive insult. By delineating people into two unequal groups—believers and misbelievers—it reduces the human value of the lesser group. It is even a discriminatory term because it establishes that the life of the Muslim is more precious than the life of a non-Muslim.

The existence of Islamic State today encourages the full understanding and application of this term. For example, if a Christian person living among Muslims accepts to pay the tribute (*jizya*) and all the other arbitrary conditions (which are imposed on him with contempt) to avoid expulsion but still ends up being killed by a Muslim, his Muslim murderer will not receive capital punishment. The Muslim murderer

---

[9] Though the term *infidel* is not specifically mentioned, the law of retaliation is clearly outlined in this verse, Q 2.178 (Palmer trans.): *"O ye who believe! Retaliation is prescribed for you for the slain: the free for the free, the slave for the slave, the female for the female…."*

[10] *Sahih Bukhari*, Book of Fighting for the Cause of Allah (Jihad)(p. 701); *Ṣaḥīḥ al-Bukhārī*, Kītāb al-Jihād wa al-Sīyar 3: 1110.

[11] *Musnad Aḥmad* 2: 372.

[12] al-'Asqalānī, *Fatḥ al-Bārī* 14: 259.

will only pay some kind of indemnity to the family and relatives of his Christian victim, even if he had a prior social or political agreement or contract (treaty) with Muslims.

A similar incident happened in the days of Muḥammad when a Muslim, Hilāl Ibn Umayyah, killed an infidel who had a treaty with the early Muslims. During a sermon to his followers, Muḥammad said, "Have you not seen what your companion Hilāl Ibn Umayyah has done? If I could kill a believer for killing a *kāfir*, I would kill him [Muslim murderer] for it. So pay for his blood [of the infidel]."[13] Muḥammad was confirming and legitimizing in this public sermon this rule against executing a Muslim for killing an infidel. In lieu of his life, the Muslim killer need only pay the *dīya*, or "blood money."[14]

What then is the punishment for a Muslim who deliberately murders an infidel, even someone who is of the People of the Book and has a treaty with Muslims? There will be no worldly punishment for him, but he will receive some punishment in the hereafter. He will be deprived of paradise for a few years, but he will end up eventually in paradise after spending a short period of time in hell—somewhat like Purgatory in Catholic theology. This *ḥadīth* (attributed to Muḥammad) discusses this temporary delay into paradise (Janna): "Whoever killed a person having a treaty with the Muslims, shall not smell the smell of Paradise though its smell is perceived from a distance of forty years."[15] Al-'Asqalānī offers this comment on this *ḥadīth*:[16]

> ...and the meaning of this denial [shall not smell], although it is [stated] generally, is about a certain time from the available logical and transmitted evidence [from the religious texts], that he who dies as a Muslim, even if he [commits]...major sins, is judged as a Muslim, and will not be doomed eternally to hell but will eventually reach Janna [Paradise], even if he is tortured before that.

This earthly pardon and modest spiritual punishment is exactly what encourages Muslims to kill Christian and Jewish infidels. In Egypt, a Muslim has never been executed for killing a Christian, nor will it ever happen under any government that adopts Islamic law, because

[13] al-Bayhaqī, *Al-Sunan al-Kubra* 12: 39.

[14] al-'Asqalānī, *Fatḥ al-Bārī* 14: 258.

[15] *Sahih Bukhari*, Book of Fighting for the Cause of Allah (Jihad)(p. 734); *Ṣaḥīḥ al-Bukhārī*, Kītāb al-Jizya wa al-Mawāda'a 3: 1155.

[16] al-'Asqalānī, *Fatḥ al-Bārī* 14: 257.

the execution of a Muslim for the killing of an infidel contradicts the provisions of Islam based on the Hadith literature.

Even in involuntary manslaughter, when the killing is unintentional (resulting from recklessness or criminal negligence), believers and infidels are judged differently. In these cases, the guilty party must give the family of the victim financial compensation, or "blood money" (*dīya*). If a Muslim unintentionally killed a Christian or a Jew, he or she must give the family half the amount of "blood money" that would be required in the unintended killing of a Muslim. This proportional difference in the blood money is based on a *ḥadīth* attributed to Muḥammad, where he states that the blood money for *dhimmis*, which are non-Muslim citizens of an Islamic state, is half the amount for Muslims.[17] The same proportion is corroborated in another *ḥadīth*: "The apostle of Allah spoke to people on the day of Fatḥ saying, 'O people! ...[A] believer is not to be killed for killing a *kāfir*, and the *kāfir's dīya* is half the *dīya* of the believer....'"[18]

Based on the Hadith literature, the "blood money" (*dīya*) to compensate the family for the unintentional killing of a *kāfir* by a Muslim is half the *dīya* for the unintentional killing of a Muslim. Isn't this difference unjust and discriminatory? Would a Muslim accept living in a country where the blood money required for the unintentional death of a Christian is double the amount that is required for a Muslim? Would he accept living in a country where a Christian is not executed for killing a Muslim, even if deliberately?

With this incontrovertible double standard, how can some Muslims continue to present the term *kāfir* as just a linguistic alternative for the word *nonbeliever*?

Kāfir: term of severe discrimination

The term *kāfir* connotes many discriminatory meanings. In practice, this discrimination is in clear opposition to international conventions on human rights—the civil, social, economic, and political rights of all people.

For example, in Islam it is not permissible to accept the testimony of a *kāfir*, according to the Qur'ān (Q 65.2; Palmer trans.): "*...and bring as witnesses men of equity from among you....*" This verse requires two

[17] al-Nisā'ī, *Sunan al-Nisā'ī al-Sughra* 8: 414.
[18] al-Bayhaqī, *Al-Sunan al-Kubra* 12: 39.

conditions of witnesses regarding the admissibility of their testimony: (1) witnesses must be men "of equity," which means just men of honorable integrity, and (2) witnesses must be "from...you," which means Muslim believers. By omission here, the *kāfir* is then deemed unjust and his or her testimony unacceptable. This unjust behavior of infidels is emphasized in Q 3.151 (Palmer trans.): *"We will throw dread into the hearts of* ***those who misbelieve****, for that they associate that with God which He has sent down no power for; but their resort is fire, and* ***evil is the resort of the unjust****"* (emphasis added).

Muslim scholars uphold the view that the testimony of the infidel is impermissible: The practices of Muḥammad "decided that the testimony of the infidel is not permissible to be taken...but to be taken [only] from Muslims."[19] Noted Muslim exegete Ibn Qudāma (c. AD 1146-1223) states that "the testimony of the infidel against the Muslim is not acceptable at all."[20]

Another example of unequal treatment under the law concerns inheritance. If, upon the death of a Muslim man his son is determined an infidel, this son cannot receive any inheritance from his Muslim father. His siblings can exclude him if they can prove that he is a misbeliever, which aligns with this *ḥadīth* attributed to Muḥammad: "A Muslim cannot be the heir of a disbeliever, nor can a disbeliever be the heir of a Muslim."[21]

All these examples, with their corresponding religious texts and scholarly explanations, show that the term *kāfir* is not just a linguistic alternative for nonbeliever. In fact, it denotes a particular social, civil, and political station that considers all non-Muslims unequal to and as less entitled than Muslims, when it comes to their testimony, their money, and their lives.

The consequences of this discriminatory social status even affect marital relationships. Though a Muslim man can marry an "infidel" (Christian or Jewish) woman, the "infidel" (Christian or Jewish) man cannot marry a Muslim woman, based on the Qur'ān (Q 2.221; Palmer trans.): *"...And wed not to idolatrous men until they believe, for surely a believing slave is better than an idolater, even though he please you...."* According to this verse, Muslim commentators state that Allah has forbidden marriage

[19] See the commentary on Q 5.106, *Tafsīr al-Ṭabarī* 7: 73.

[20] Ibn Qudāma, *Al-Sharḥ al-Kabīr* 4: 172.

[21] *Sahih Bukhari*, Book on Laws of Inheritance (p. 1512); *Ṣaḥīḥ al-Bukhārī*, Kītāb al-Farā'iḍ 6: 2484.

between a Muslim woman (believer) and an "idolatrous" (meaning infidel) man, no matter his "idolatrous" religion: "So do not wed, O believers, any idolater because this is unlawful for you."[22]

Imagine if there were laws in a European country, America, or Canada forbidding Muslim men from marrying Christian women but allowing Christian men the right to marry Muslim women? Wouldn't this law be discriminatory, maybe even racist? Yet the term *kāfir* with its full meaning and application is no less discriminatory when it prohibits marital unions on the basis of religion. In any country when Islamic law (*sharīʿa*) is administered, it becomes impossible for non-Muslim men to marry Muslim women.

For example, if a French man wishes to marry a Moroccan woman, he is asked by the court if he is Muslim, born into a Muslim family. If he was not born a Muslim, he would have to prove with proper documentation that he had converted to Islam. Some couples are forced to marry abroad because of this religious but legal obstacle. Unfortunately, the couple's marriage contract, if drawn up and signed outside the country, will never be officially recognized in Morocco. Similarly, some Moroccan women who wish to marry Christian Arabs, e.g., in Jordan, Egypt, Lebanon or Iraq, feel forced to escape to a European country to solemnize their marriage. Others may obtain and use forged documents or a counterfeit marital contract to circumvent these rulings.

It is indeed an especially tragic situation for Muslim women because they are the most affected by these discriminatory teachings. In spite of the irrational, discriminatory foundation for these teachings, there are still Muslims who want to defend these teachings and apply them in Europe and America under the pretext that they are the best laws for all peoples.

One of the principles of social justice in developed countries is that citizens are given equal access to public jobs. However, Islamic law is not concerned about equal access for all citizens—only for Muslims. Muslims are always given preference because they are considered better than infidels. The life of a Muslim is more important and his testimony more trustworthy than that of the infidel. Therefore, some jobs should be exclusive to Muslims. For instance, the infidel is denied access to any ministerial position in the executive branch of government and any

[22] See the commentary on Q 2.221, *Tafsīr al-Ṭabarī* 2: 224.

judicial position in the judiciary. Both types of positions require the administration of justice, a condition beyond the scope of the "unjust" infidel. Furthermore, any judge must rule according to Islamic law. Since the infidel is a disbeliever of these laws, it would not be appropriate and thus not permissible for him to be a judge. Finally, infidels cannot assume the office of a president or vice president, because these executive positions would make the infidel a guardian over Muslims, a responsibility and hierarchy that is not permissible according to Islamic law.

Sheikh 'Abd al-Ḥayy Yūsuf, a professor in the Department of Islamic Studies at the University of Khartoum, was asked this question: "What is the [Islamic] ruling of a non-Muslim taking the post of a president or vice-president or minister or judge and similar positions?" He provided the following response:[23]

> The scholars unanimously agree that the presidency is not to be given to an infidel. In case the governor becomes a disbeliever, then he must be removed in accordance to the verse "...for God will not give the misbelievers a way against believers" [Q 4.141; Palmer trans.], because the imāma (Islamic political leadership) is a religious position that is intended to protect religion and supervise domestic policy, which is a matter that is not expected to be done by an infidel. Regarding ministries, scholars have distinguished between the ministry of policy development and the ministry for policy implementation, ...[and] have allowed a non-Muslim to handle policy implementation, which is not concerned with policy development and has no impact on decisions, while the ministry of policy development is not handled by a non-Muslim. The judiciary position is like the position of the imāma. It is not permissible for a non-Muslim to handle it, and, likewise, the leadership of the zakāt (Islamic monies) and military command. These four posts (the great imāma, judiciary, zakat and military command) are only handled by trusted Muslims, because they are by their nature religious jobs, and Allah Almighty knows best.

This fatwa is issued by a person highly knowledgeable about Islamic law, a lecturer at an Islamic university. His statement is not an exception in Sudan but a well-known judgment in Islam, confirmed by Islamic scholars, both present and past. Moroccan imam and high judge Abū al-Faḍl 'Ayyāḍ (d. c. AD 1149) states that "scholars have unanimously agreed that the imāma is not given to an infidel, and that if he becomes

[23] Yūsuf, 'Abd al-Hayy. "Eligibility of a Non-Muslim As a President or Vice President." *Meshkat.net*. Islamic Meshkat Net, n.d. 1 June 2017 (last visited). Web (http://meshkat.net/old/node/16444).

an infidel, he must be removed." He added that the same applies if he stopped organizing the prayers and stopped inviting others to pray.[24] Ibn al-Mundhir al-Nisāburī (AD 855-930) reports that the "majority of scholars are of the opinion that the infidel shall have no leadership over a Muslim in any case."[25]

Additional confirmation regarding the prohibition of government positions and other public offices for infidels can be easily found on the Internet. Fatāwa listed and discussed on Web sites in Egypt and Saudi Arabia, for example, show that Christians and Jews cannot obtain sovereign positions because of the religious texts. Christian Egyptians in Egypt cannot hold certain jobs in the intelligence agencies or the presidency. None of these kinds of jobs are open to infidels because Islamic law is the source of Egypt's laws, even though Islamic law does not uniformly take precedence over Egyptian law in all cases.

Rulings on "apostate infidels" and "warrior infidels"

It has been well established in the previous sections that the term *kāfir* is not a simple synonym for "infidel" and carries significant negative and discriminatory repercussions. And this meaning is for the "normal" or "good" infidel.

There are other types of infidels, considered worse than the "good" infidel, that Islam treats with a different logic, such as the apostate infidel.

The apostate infidel is a person who was born a Muslim but then renounced his or her religion or chose to follow Islam but then changed his or her mind and left. This kind of infidel, the apostate infidel, has no rights at all and must be killed. Execution for this kind of apostasy is the consensus of the four Islamic schools of jurisprudence. The only difference among the opinions of these schools is the amount of time given to the apostate to withdraw his or her decision to leave Islam.

This death sentence for apostasy is supported in the Hadith literature, where Muḥammad states, "Whoever changed his Islamic religion, then kill him."[26] In another *ḥadīth*, Muḥammad states, "It is not permissible to take the life of a Muslim who bears testimony (to the fact that there is no god but Allah, and I am the Messenger of Allah), but in one of the three

[24] al-Nawawī, *Sharḥ* 12: 180.
[25] Ibn Qayyīm al-Jawzīya, *Aḥkām Ahl* 2: 787.
[26] *Sahih Bukhari*, Book of Dealing with Apostates (p. 1539); *Ṣaḥīḥ al-Bukhārī*, Kītāb Istitābat al-Murtaīn wa al-Muʿānidīn 6: 2537.

cases: the married adulterer, a life for life, and the deserter of his Din (Islam), abandoning the community."[27]

These pronouncements mean that I, as a former Muslim, fall into this category of "apostate infidel." I was born into a Muslim family, was Muslim at birth ("Muslim from the factory"), but when I grew older and decided to leave Islam, I became an infidel—an "apostate infidel" who, according to Islam, has no right to live. Whoever is placed into this category and his or her words or actions are ruled as apostasy (renunciation of Islam), he or she will be sentenced to death.

The other main type of "bad" infidel is the "warrior infidel." The warrior infidel resists Islam, whether by actions or words. He or she has never accepted or practiced Islam. This kind of infidel has no rights, not even small ones, and must be deprived of everything: money, property, children, spouse, etc.

Ibn Qayyīm al-Jawzīya (AD 1292-1350), an important Muslim jurisconsult, exegete and scholar, states that the *dhimmi* is considered a warrior if he does one or more of these actions:[28]

> If a *dhimmi* refuses to pay the tribute and doesn't let our rules be administered upon them [sic], by this he is breaching the treaty [of peace]...and if he encourages a Muslim to leave Islam...and if he finds fault in or undermines Islam, and they are four things: (1) mentioning Allah, (2) his book, (3) his religion, and (4) his Messenger in a way that he shouldn't.

The Qur'ān (Q 9.12; Palmer trans.) confirms that any infidel who speaks ill of Islam becomes a warrior infidel who must be fought and killed: *"But if they break faith with you after their treaty,* ***and taunt your religion****, then fight the leaders of misbelief; verily, they have no faith, haply they may desist"* (emphasis added).

Often called "Sheikh al-Islam," Abū 'Abd Allāh Muḥammad Ibn Idrīs al-Shāfi'ī (AD 767-820), a Muslim jurist considered one of the four great imams, writes the following comment in his authoritative book of Islamic law, *Kītāb al-Umm*:[29]

---

[27] *Sahih Muslim*, Book Pertaining to the Oath, for Establishing the Responsibility of Murders, Fighting, Requital and Blood-Wit: When it is permissible to take the life of a Muslim (p. 1028); *Ṣaḥīḥ Muslim*, Kītāb al-Qasāma wa al-Muḥāribīn 2: 798.

[28] Ibn Qayyīm al-Jawzīya, *Aḥkām Ahl* 3: 1370.

[29] al-Shāfi'ī, *Kītāb al-Umm* 4: 280.

> If anyone of you mentions Muḥammad, or Allah Almighty's book, or his religion in a way that he should not, in this case, protection of Allah will abandon him, then the protection of the Commander of the Believers, and of all Muslims. What was given to him of security shall be removed, and the Commander of the Believers can lawfully take away his money and life, just like it is lawful to take away the money and lives of the people of war.

Like the apostate infidel who renounces Islam, the warrior infidel—the non-Muslim who resists and fights Islam—will be sentenced to death for any words or actions critical of Islam.

The "good" infidel Christians or Jews may escape execution, but only if they live out life humiliated, disgraced, and despised and do not raise their voices to object to or criticize the Islamic religion. Still, in the best cases, they would be second-class citizens with some measure of protection. But in all cases they would be at the mercy of Muslims, knowing that if they speak or act against the Islamic religion, the Islamic state can legally kill them.

So when some Muslims tell me that they have lived side by side with Christians in Egypt or Iraq or Jordan, I always tell them: You did live side by side with Christians but at their expense, and they have paid the price for that "peace." Over time, many of them have converted to Islam to escape their living situations, which are affected by the limited and limiting financial opportunities and social pressures, and the constant state of religious oppression. Some continue to live as Christians but feel humiliated and frustrated because if they open their mouths to complain, they may be taken to court and tried and even executed for their criticism or opposition. Some just give up and emigrate from their homeland to a non-Muslim country.

The population of Christians has continuously decreased since the seventh century AD in all the Middle East. They have been essentially eliminated in North Africa. Peaceful coexistence of Christians and Muslims living in an Islamic country is a myth. It is a coexistence that leaves a bitter taste in the mouths of Christians, who must silently swallow their pain as they witness their population decrease to the point of extinction, which has already happened in North Africa (Algeria, Morocco, and Tunisia).

Recent application of excommunication (*takfir*) texts

Islamic State applies the Islamic texts of excommunication (*takfir*) and uses them to classify people as infidels or believers. The true Muslim, in the eyes of Islamic State, is the one who follows the Islamic texts and totally abides by their rulings as confirmed by Muslim scholars.

The infidel is defined as one who disbelieves in Islam either partially or totally, by word or action. This definition is the reason Islamic State (and precursors, ISIL and ISIS) has killed many people whom others may consider as Muslims but are certainly infidels in accordance to the rulings set by Muslim scholars. Once Islamic State determines that a person is an infidel, they believe that the life of that person can be lawfully taken. They consider the infidel's disbelief as justification for killing him (or her) in cold blood. This justification explains (though it doesn't excuse) Islamic State's killing of Shiites (whom it considers infidels or apostate infidels) and collaborators with the Syrian or Iraqi governments, and collaborators with the anti-Islamic State coalition countries. All these types of people are accused of apostasy and are marked for execution based on the Hadith literature.

However, Islamic State does not kill Muslims who are under its Islamic laws and do not object to its authority or rule. This policy resembles the administration of Muḥammad in similar circumstances. He did not kill anyone who surrendered to him and lived under his mercy—whether or not that person was a believer in him and his Islam religion or a hypocrite who expressed belief but hid disbelief. All these conquered peoples lived under the shadow of this first Islamic state without too many problems (except for the requisite humiliation and subservience, of course). Still, Muḥammad would not tolerate criticism directed at him, and he would send Companions to get rid of those who would insult him, as he did with the Jewish leader, Ka'b Ibn al-Ashraf, who mocked the prophet through poetry.[30]

---

[30] *Sahih Bukhari*, Book of Fighting for the Cause of Allah (Jihad)(p. 697); *Ṣaḥīḥ al-Bukhārī*, Kītāb al-Jihād wa al-Sīyar 3: 1103. The *ḥadīth* states that the "Prophet said, 'Who is ready to kill Ka'b bin Al-Ashraf who has really hurt Allah and His Apostle?' Muḥammad bin Maslama said, 'O Allah's Apostle! Do you like me to kill him?' He replied in the affirmative. So, Muḥammad bin Maslama went to him (i.e., Ka'b) and said, 'This person (i.e., the Prophet) has put us to task and asked us for charity.' Ka'b replied, 'By Allah, you will get tired of him.' Muḥammad said to him, 'We have followed him, so we dislike to leave him till we see the end of his affair.' Muḥammad bin Maslama went on talking to him in this way till he got the chance to kill him."

Like Muḥammad, Islamic State also kills those who cause trouble or cooperate with its enemies. But it would be incorrect to declare that most of the victims of Islamic State are Muslims, because they are not Muslims in its eyes. The term *Muslim* is a relative term: A Shiite Muslim is a Muslim only in his own view, but in the eyes of the Sunni Muslim he is an infidel; the Sunni Muslim is not a Muslim but an infidel in the Shiite view. And any Muslim who says that he is a Muslim but cooperates with infidels or the West is considered an apostate—which means, it is then permissible to kill him, seize his money, his properties, and his children. This judgment is *sharīʿa* that shows no mercy towards anyone. (For more details, see Chapter 7, page 163.)

Terror begins first with classifying the person as a *kāfir* and then ends with killing the person. Even though classification precedes the killing, it is an extremely dangerous classification. When people are classified as believers and infidels, this distinction means that the ones who are classified as believers are Muslims who must be protected from being killed, while the others, the infidels, are targeted for killing because their blood is of no value in the sight of Allah. The treatment of these two groups by Allah's followers is clear in the Qur'ān (Q 48.29; Arberry trans.): *"Muḥammad is the Messenger of God, and those who are with him are hard against the unbelievers, merciful one to another...."* Muḥammad's followers are to deal harshly with infidels but extend mercy to fellow Muslims. Like Muḥammad's followers, Islamic State expresses vehement opposition against the misbelievers: It kills them without mercy and only shows compassion toward its own members.

Before Islamic State kills a person, it classifies him or her as an infidel in order to make it more acceptable to its followers to kill that person. It looks for legitimate rulings to justify the killing. Islamic history is full of examples of Muslim governments and institutions that have declared, like Islamic State, certain people or people groups as infidels in preparation to "legally" kill them. In fact, the first *takfīr jamāʿī* (mass declaration of people as infidels) began immediately after Muḥammad's death, when several subject people groups, such as the Arab tribes Kināna, ʿAbs, and Dhubyān, stopped sending obligatory monies to Muḥammad's successor, Abū Bakr, the second caliph.[31]

[31] Ibn Kathīr, *Al-Bidāya* 9: 440-444.

Origin of this classification and declaration of people as infidels

Muḥammad imposed an annual obligatory payment, or *zakāt*,[32] on the tribes who converted to Islam, using his authority as the leader of the Islamic nation. This collected money was used to benefit the Muslim community, defray the costs of his military campaigns, recompense the *mujāhidīn* who fought with him, and assist the poor and others.

After Abū Bakr became Muḥammad's successor, problems arose when the Arab tribes who had been subject to Muḥammad assumed that they were finally free from paying this heavy religious tax. Abū Bakr, the first caliph (and a father-in-law to Muḥammad), discussed this matter in a conversation with 'Umar Ibn al-Khattab (another father-in-law of Muḥammad who would become the second caliph), according to this *ḥadīth*:[33]

> ...when the Messenger of Allah...breathed his last and Abu Bakr was appointed as his successor (Caliph), those amongst the Arabs who wanted to become apostates became apostates. 'Umar Ibn al-Khattab said to Abu Bakr: "Why would you fight against the people, when the Messenger of Allah declared, 'I have been directed to fight against people so long as they do not say: There is no god but Allah, and he who professed it was granted full protection of his property and life on my behalf except for a right? His (other) affairs rest with Allah.'" Upon this Abu Bakr said: "By Allah, I would definitely fight against him who severed prayer from Zakat, for it is the obligation upon the rich. By Allah, I would fight against them even to secure the cord (used for hobbling the feet of a camel) which they used to give to the Messenger of Allah (as zakat) but now they have withheld it." Umar Ibn Khattab remarked: "By Allah, I found nothing but the fact that Allah had opened the heart of Abu Bakr for (perceiving the justification of) fighting (against those who refused to pay Zakat) and I fully recognized that the (stand of Abu Bakr) was right."

This *ḥadīth* is referring to Arab tribes that Caliph Abū Bakr considered infidels because they decided not to pay him the *zakāt*. To Abū Bakr, this noncompliance in paying the *zakāt*, which he said was one of the Pillars of Islam, demonstrated their infidelity. As infidels, he could now lawfully take their money and lives, and so he declared war against them. Their

---

[32] *Zakāt* is the third Pillar of Islam. It is a religious obligation to give a "fourth of the tenth," meaning 2.5% of one's wealth to specified recipients. (See Q 9.60.)

[33] *Sahih Muslim*, Book of Faith: Command for fighting against the people so long as they do not profess that [there] is no god but Allah and Muḥammad is his messenger (p. 70); *Ṣaḥīḥ Muslim*, Kītāb al-Imān 1: 131.

refusal to pay the *zakāt* was enough to label them as infidels and not Muslims in his eyes—even if these tribes continued to say the Shahāda (bear witness that there's no god other than Allah and that Muḥammad is the messenger of Allah), prayed, fasted, and pilgrimaged. But 'Umar protested, saying that Muḥammad declared that whoever becomes a Muslim will save his property and his life. Abū Bakr explained to him that whoever refrains from paying *zakāt* is just like the person who refrains from the prayer rituals, one of the cornerstones of the Islam religion. Such behavior means that the person is an infidel and killing him with the sword is permissible.

Islamic State applies the same principle today against Shiite and other Muslim collaborators with the Iraqi or Syrian regimes, or other regimes that are against the Islamic organization. Islamic State considers these Muslims as infidels and therefore it is permissible to deal with them the same way Abū Bakr dealt with the Arab tribes who stopped paying the *zakāt* as soon as Muḥammad died. The rationale is that a person's or a people's abstention from one of the Pillars of Islam is considered an act of apostasy, which requires fighting; hence, the wars of Abū Bakr were based on the process of *takfīr*—classifying and declaring people as infidels—followed by fighting and killing.

For Islamic State and other like-minded groups, it is enough today to classify a group of people as infidels and apostates and "prove" that they have violated one of the Pillars of Islam or one of its fundamental religious elements in order to recruit young enthusiastic Muslims to fight them, seize their money, and take their lives. Therefore, *takfīr* is preparation for killing.

Al-takfīr al-jamā'ī (collective declaration of people as infidels) did not stop with the wars of apostasy conducted by Abū Bakr, the first caliph of Muḥammad. But the phenomenon of *takfīr*, instituted both individually and collectively, has overshadowed all Islamic history since the days of Muḥammad. Many lives have been taken throughout Islamic history because of the policy of *takfīr*.

If *takfīr*—punishment for religious infidelity—is indeed a fundamental tenet in Islam, as confirmed by Muslim scholars, on whom should it be rightfully applied? Given the profound consequences, what are the parameters of *takfīr*?

Excommunication (*takfir*) of Islamic sects

The main difference among Muslims throughout history is not about the application of *takfir* (considering others as infidels), but how and where to draw the distinction between disbelief and faith. How and when is a certain person or a group of people declared infidels? Muḥammad established the initial structure of *takfir*, when he himself declared that the majority of Muslims are infidels and will end up in hell. He stated that his nation will be divided into seventy-three sects. All these sects—except one—will end up in hell:[34]

> The Messenger of Allah stood up among us and said: "Those who came before you of the people of the Book split into seventy-two sects, and this *Ummah* will split into seventy-three sects, seventy-two of which will be in the Fire, and one in Paradise. That is the *Jamā'ah* (main group of Muslims)."

This famous *ḥadīth* is repeated by Muslims and sheikhs, read aloud in Friday sermons, and published in books and religious references. According to this *ḥadīth*, the seventy-two sects that will go to hell are really not Islamic sects. Even though they are named and called "sects," the members of these sects are not true Muslims. And only one sect out of seventy-three will be saved, which is a very small percentage (~1.4%).

Islamic State obviously believes that it is part of this very select group of true Muslims and shows no hesitation in killing members of sects considered Muslim by Western world leaders, Western media, and even the majority of Muslims. Its viewpoint is that the members of these sects are apostates, or agents and infidels who dress like Muslims but do not believe or think like true Muslims. This thinking aligns with the same kind of thinking proclaimed by Muḥammad and his Companions and expressed in the aforementioned *ḥadīth*.

In another *ḥadīth*, Muḥammad describes some people who will act ostensibly as Muslims but inwardly disbelieve and commands his followers to kill them:[35]

---

[34] *Sunan Abū Dawūd*, Book of the Sunnah 5: 154-155.

[35] *Sahih Muslim*, Book of Zakat: Exhortation to kill the Khwarij (p. 590); *Ṣaḥīḥ Muslim*, Kītāb al-Zakāt 1: 474. See *Sahih Bukhari*, Book of Virtues and Merits of the Prophet and his Companions (p. 841).

> There would arise at the end of the age a people who would be young in age and immature in thought, but they would talk (in such a manner) as if their words are the best among the creatures. They would recite the Qur'an, but it would not go beyond their throats, and they would pass through the religion as an arrow goes through the prey. So when you meet them, kill them, for in their killing you would get a reward with Allah on the Day of Judgment.

In yet another *ḥadīth*, Muḥammad provides even more details for identifying these hypocritical believers:[36]

> There will appear some people among you whose prayer will make you look down upon yours, and whose fasting will make you look down upon yours, but they will recite the Qur'an which will not exceed their throats (they will not act on it) and they will go out of Islam as an arrow goes out through the game....

Muḥammad thus ordered his Companions to fight the "fake" Muslims, the ones who disobey the imāms, even though their Islamic prayers may be the best prayers and their fasting may be the best fasting, and they read the Qur'ān and apply the rituals of Islam. They are not authentic Muslims because they do not actually believe wholeheartedly in the Qur'ān or in Islam, and they do not apply it as they should. Muḥammad's subjective declaration here makes speculation about a person's infidelity a matter too dependent upon personal evaluation, which means that anyone in Islam can classify another person as a false or "fake" Muslim.

Some Muslim scholars today consider Islamic State as *khawārij* (false Muslims), including the current Mufti of Saudi Arabia, Sheikh 'Abdul-'Azīz Ibn 'Abdullah al-Sheikh, who used this *ḥadīth* to justify killing them.[37] Islamic State (according to this same *ḥadīth*) considers those who fight against it as the *khawārij*. Each separate group wants to use the *ḥadīth* in its favor and manipulate it to match its opponent, so each side accuses its opponent as the *khawārij*.

The Khawārij (also Khārijites) is an Islamic sect (and classification) produced because of the doctrine of *takfīr*. An early Islamic sect, its application of *takfīr* was considered so extreme by Muslim scholars that they declared it a heretical group and permitted the killing of Khawārij

---

[36] *Sahih Bukhari*, Book of Virtues of the Qur'ān (pp. 1129-1130); *Ṣaḥīḥ al-Bukhārī*, Kitāb Faḍā'il al-Qur'ān 4: 1928.

[37] "Mufti of Saudi Arabia: Daesh [ISIS] and al-Qaeda Are Khawārij." *Arabic.CNN.com*. Cable News Network (Arabic), 19 Aug. 2014. Web (http://arabic.cnn.com/middleeast/2014/08/19/saudi-mufti-isis). Excerpt: "It is lawful to kill them [Daesh/ISIS, Al Qaeda], and we do not count them as Muslims."

using their same doctrine. In other words, Muslim scholars considered the Khawārij as infidels because the Khawārij considered those who are not Khawārij as infidels—creating a neverending cycle of *takfīr* by both groups against each other.

Most historical sources trace the origin of the earliest Khawārij during the fourth caliphate (AD 651-661) when ʿAlī Ibn Abī Ṭālib (Muḥammad's cousin and son-in-law) succeeded the assassinated third caliph, ʿUthmān Ibn ʿAffān. ʿAlī's right to the caliphate was challenged by rival Muʿāwiya Ibn Abū Sufyān. After these two men and their supporters confronted each other at the Battle of Siffīn (AD 657), ʿAlī agreed to arbitration regarding his right to rule. A group of Muslims, eventually known as the Khawārij, opposed the use of arbitration to select caliphs. They believed this judgment belongs to Allah and his Qur'ān and that any Muslim—even if not from Muḥammad's tribe (the Quraysh) or an Arab—could be the leader if he was morally irreproachable. Though the Khawārij considered Muʿāwiya an infidel, they also rejected ʿAlī as a suitable successor because he had agreed to arbitration—and with infidels. (A Khārij later assassinated ʿAlī with a poison-coated sword.)

The Khawārij received this name from their enemies, because they left ʿAlī's army, or side. (The name derives from an Arabic root word that means "to leave," "to exit," or "to get out.") They called themselves al-Shurāt (the Exchangers), because they had traded their earthly, mortal life for the afterlife with Allah. They considered themselves "the community of believers" and others as infidels (misbelievers). This group has also been called al-Muḥakkima (the Ruling Choosers), because they proclaimed that it is only Allah who rules, which means that all rulings should emanate from the Qur'ān and the Hadith literature—not from humans. (Islamic State, Al Qaeda, and other Islamic jihadist organizations make the same proclamations today.)

The Khawārij were memorizers of the Qur'ān, and they set up their own commander of the faithful. They were known for declaring that anyone who committed major sins, such as murder or adultery, is an infidel.

After trying unsuccessfully to diplomatically resolve this religio-political controversy, ʿAlī then declared war against the Khawārij, which means that (in his view) they were no longer Muslims but infidels (i.e., Muslims must not fight Muslims). At the Battle of Nahrawan, his army nearly killed them all (about 4,000 people).[38] (Ironically, this battle took place in present-day Iraq, about twelve miles from Baghdad. The group Al Qaeda in Iraq, or AQI, one of Islamic State's predecessors, began its terrorism in this same area.)

This battle happened only twenty-seven years after the death of Islam's prophet and founder Muḥammad, and during the caliphate of a very important early leader of Islam: 'Alī (Muhummad's cousin and son-in-law and one of his closest Companions), who instigated this bloodshed.

Given this famous early example of *takfir* put into motion by a major Muslim leader, how can people blame Islamic State for similar applications of *takfir* but exonerate Islam? Aren't the mass murders perpetrated by Islamic State (and precursors, ISIL and ISIS) similar to 'Alī's massacre of the Khawārij?

When comparing these actions of 'Alī and Islamic State, the only differences are the dates and the targeted peoples. Fourteen centuries separate the two events. 'Alī attacked the Khawārij while Islamic State targeted a more diverse set of "infidel" groups (Yazidis, Alawites, Shiites, Christians, etc.) However, the place—Iraq—is the same. The religious texts to justify these actions are the same texts. The reason—*takfir* (declaring people infidels)—is the same. And both sets of victims number in the thousands.

Contemporary examples of excommunication (*takfir*)

Takfir is used by sheikhs and Muslim rulers, Islamic groups and institutions. Islamic history is strewn with many known incidents of persons considered infidels and then killed based on this judgment. Religious leaders need only declare a person an infidel to set into motion the final deadly consequences. In these situations, these religious authorities have essentially loaded a revolver when they make these declarations; all they need is a willing follower to take that revolver and use it to eliminate the infidel.

One of the most famous contemporary examples concerns Farag Fouda, a "Muslim" in his own view, but an "infidel" in the eyes of religious leaders—sheikhs, scholars, and leaders of Islamic religious movements—in his country, Egypt. Farag Fouda advocated for human rights, argued for the necessity of adopting a secular government in

[38] 'Imāra, *Izālat al-Shubuhāt* 402.

Egypt, and attacked projects promoting the creation of an Islamic state "utopia" ruled by *sharī'a* in the Middle East. He wrote articles and books critical of Islamic fundamentalism, e.g., *The Absent Truth*, and debated proponents of this idealized Islamic state, such as Muḥammad 'Imāra, Al Azhar Sheikh Muḥammad al-Ghazālī, and Chancellor Ma'mūn al-Huḍaybī, an extremely important figure in the Muslim Brotherhood.

Even though he is a self-proclaimed Muslim, Farag Fouda was declared an infidel after these debates because of his opposition to the belief that Islam should be both a religious and a political state. His opposition precipitated his classification as an infidel in the eyes of his opponents who hold the majority opinion. A symposium of Al Azhar scholars issued a fatwa to declare him an infidel and that he should be killed.[39] Within a week of this fatwa, Farag Fouda was shot by two members of a militant Islamic group, Al-Jamā'a al-Islāmīya ("The Islamic Group") on June 8, 1992. Bystanders and others with Fouda were also injured in the attack, including his son. Fouda did not survive his injuries and died later at the hospital.

When one of the arrested suspects was asked in court about his reason for murdering Farag Fouda, he responded that Fouda was an apostate and any apostate must be killed according to the fatwa of Sheikh 'Umar 'Abdel-Raḥmān, the mufti, or spiritual leader, of Al-Jamā'a al-Islāmīya.[40] However, when he was pressed to submit evidence for this statement, the defendant admitted that he had not read (he was illiterate) any books written by Fouda; he simply heard about Fouda being an infidel from the sheikhs.

Al Azhar scholar and former Muslim Brother Muḥammad al-Ghazālī, who had debated Farag Fouda, volunteered to testify in favor of the suspect during the trial. He also demanded the suspect's acquittal because Farag Fouda was an apostate infidel and had to be killed. So, according to this defense, the suspect was not guilty of murder (because the victim was an apostate infidel), but he had usurped the authority of the state in carrying out the execution himself. But since this action is a minor

---

[39] "The Secrets of the Assassination of Farag Fouda: Terrorists Based It on a Fatwa from Al-Azhar in Killing of Academic." *Elwatannews.com*. El Watan News, 6 June 2015. Web (http://www.elwatannews.com/news/details/744847).

[40] Traboulsi, Karim. "Farag Fouda's Murder: A Sign of Things to Come." *Alaraby.co.uk*. Al-Araby Al-Jadeed (The New Arab), 10 June 2015. Web (https://www.alaraby.co.uk/english/comment/2015/6/10/farag-foudas-murder-a-sign-of-things-to-come).

crime with no punishment under Islamic law, al-Ghazālī argued that the suspect should be freed.

Maḥmūd Mazrū'a, who was then the head of the Department of Faith and Religions at Al Azhar University, also testified, stating that "a man like him [Farag Fouda] was considered an apostate according to the consensus of the Muslims. And the matter did not require a jury to judge him of being an apostate."[41]

Many other sheikhs justified the killing of Farag Fouda and even rejoiced about it. Chancellor Ma'mūn al-Huḍaybī, another adversary in the debate with Fouda, received the news with happiness and justified the act on the radio station Voice of Kuwait.[42] Sheikh 'Abdul Ghaffār 'Azīz authored the book about this assassination, *Who Killed Farag Fouda?,* and concludes that Farag Fouda himself is responsible for his own death because of his blasphemous words and actions.[43]

Many people participated in the plot to murder Farag Fouda, including Muḥammad Abū El'Ela 'Abdrabu, who had provided the weapon. He was released in 2012 by then Egyptian president Mohamed Morsi (who was the Muslim Brotherhood candidate). Upon leaving prison, 'Abdrabu publicly defended the murderers of Farag Fouda and expressed pride in his participation and no regrets because for him Farag Fouda was an infidel.[44]

The court convicted and sentenced all the direct participants, e.g., the shooter, the transportation provider, with terms ranging from imprisonment to executions. However, the indirect participants—those who classified Farag Fouda as an infidel or issued the fatwa of death—were never charged and remain free.

Unfortunately, declaring people infidels is a familiar and disturbing issue in the Muslim world, and there is no law yet in the Muslim world that makes it unlawful for someone to declare another person an infidel

---

[41] Khalil, Magdy. "The Hellish Network That Killed Farag Fouda." *Middle-eastonline.com.* Middle East Online, 22 Feb. 2014. Web (http://middle-east-online.com/?id=171640).

[42] Salem, Hamdi al-Saeed. "Terrorist Mohammed al-Ghazali and His Role in the Assassination of Dr. Faraj Foda." *ArabTimes.com.* Arab Times, 11 June 2014. Web (http://www.arabtimes.com/portal/article_display.cfm?Action=&Preview=No&ArticleID=35595).

[43] Traboulsi, Karim. "Farag Fouda's Murder: A Sign of Things to Come." *Alaraby.co.uk.* Al-Araby Al-Jadeed (The New Arab), 10 June 2015. Web (https://www.alaraby.co.uk/english/comment/2015/6/10/farag-foudas-murder-a-sign-of-things-to-come).

[44] Soage, Ana B. "Faraj Fawda, or the Cost of Freedom of Expression." *MERIA* (Middle East Review of International Affairs) 11.2 (June 2007): n. pag. Web (http://www.rubincenter.org/2007/06/soage-2007-06-03/).

and support the killing of such a person. Classifying and killing people viewed as infidels is still considered the purview of the Islamic clergy.

Farag Fouda was one of 202 people killed by Islamic militants in Egypt in politically motivated assaults between March 1992 and the end of September 1993.[45] And this number accounts for just the killings in one Muslim country over a period of only eighteen months. Sadly, these killings are part of a continuing pattern of killing over accusations of infidelity in other Middle Eastern countries.

Islamic State and its application of *takfir* cannot be considered an exception; the difference rests in the scope of the application of declaring people as infidels or the extent it can be applied. Islamic State leaders are not concerned about Western countries or organizations that would oppose them and advocate for human rights in international forums. While Muslim countries are subject to global pressure and compromises to maintain positive international relationships, Islamic State unapologetically executes individuals it considers as infidels and even boastfully publicizes videos and photographs of the executions on the Internet. Islamic State uses this public forum to deliver and highlight its message to the Muslim world to show that it is not cowardly like the other Muslim regimes. Islamic State is different from those Muslim countries that know the right thing to do but only partially apply it.

Islamic State paints itself as the image of the Islamic state as it was known to Muslims during the time of Prophet Muḥammad and as it is written in the authoritative Islamic literature—the kind of Islamic state that does not fear anyone except Allah and applies his laws no matter the personal cost. Islamic State wants to convince Muslims that it is the desired Islamic state (the resurrection of the old "ideal" Caliphate), which strictly applies the text and the rulings of Allah regarding the apostate infidels. Islamic State claims that the people it kills are not Muslims, despite claims to the contrary, but infidels according to its standard of faith and infidelity. Islamic State insists that it is not carrying out new applications of new beliefs or interpretations of Islam; it is strictly following and applying *takfir*, whose long history began with the very beginnings of Islam.

One Muslim country has forbidden the application of *takfir* (declaring people as infidels). Tunisia formed a new government following the

---

[45] Miller 26.

Tunisian Revolution in 2010. In establishing a new constitution in 2014, the new government criminalized *takfīr* after a conflict with the Renaissance Party (Tunisian branch of Muslim Brotherhood). Chapter 6 of Volume 1 (General Principles) in the Tunisian constitution makes this statement:[46]

> ...The State is committed to spread the values of moderation and tolerance and to protect holy places, and to prevent anyone from undermining them, and is also committed to ban calls for *takfīr* and the incitement of hatred and violence and to fight it.

The direct catalyst for this criminalization of *takfīr* in the Tunisian constitution was the assassination of two Tunisian politicians, Chokri Belaid (February 6, 2013) and Mohamed Brahmi (July 25, 2013). The Tunisian government blames these assassinations on an Islamic extremist cell linked to Al Qaeda.[47] Both politicians were killed with the same weapon, and the alleged gunman, French-born Boubakr al-Hakim, is a Salafist and a weapons smuggler.[48] Because both politicians were members of a left-wing coalition, some attribute their targeted assassinations to political reasons. However, Belaid's widow claims *takfīr* is the reason for her husband's murder.[49]

Whatever the true reason for these assassinations, the subsequent move to include Chapter 6, or the criminalization of *takfīr*, in the country's new proposed constitution met heavy resistance. The Tunisian Islamic Renaissance Party objected to its inclusion,[50] and some deputies resigned after the Tunisian parliament approved this chapter. One of the parliamentarians who resigned, Ahmed al-Smīʿī, stated that Chapter 6 "is contrary to the teachings of the Islamic religion and it legalizes the spread of misbelief, atheism and idolatry and it forbids *takfīr*, which exists in the law of Allah."[51] Another parliamentarian who resigned from

---

[46] *The Constitution of the Republic of Tunisia*. 2014: vol. 1, ch. 6, p. 4. Print and Web. (To download document PDF, see URL: https://www.constituteproject.org/constitution/Tunisia_2014.pdf?lang=ar)

[47] Gall, Carlotta. "Tunisia Says Assassination Has Links to Al Qaeda." *NYTimes.com*. New York Times, 26 July 2013. Web (http://www.nytimes.com/2013/07/27/world/middleeast/tunisia-assassination.html).

[48] Ibid.

[49] al-Khalafāwī, Basma. Interview. Nass Nasma News. 22 Jan. 2014. Television. (To view YouTube video, see URL: https://www.youtube.com/watch?v=yec1RX8mmqw). The wife of Chokri Belaid claims that *takfīr* is the reason for her husband's assassination.

[50] "Tunisia: 'Criminalization of Takfir' Hinder the Adoption of the New Constitution." *Alhurra.com*. Al Hurrah TV, 23 Jan. 2014. Television. (See URL: http://www.alhurra.com/a/Tunisia-assembly-controversial-/242137.html)

[51] Bin Burayk, Khamis. "Tunisian Constitution and the Crisis of Chapter 6." *Aljazeera.net*. Al Jazeera Media Network, 24 Jan. 2014. Web (http://tinyurl.com/jhwtvpu).

the Renaissance Party, 'Azzūz al-Shawwālī (a lecturer at Zaytūna Mosque, who holds a doctorate in Islamic law) commented that "the adoption of Chapter 6 with its general terms is contrary to the teachings of the Islamic religion and conflicts with the legal rulings in the Book of Allah."[52]

Despite the adoption of this constitution (January 26, 2014), thirty-three scholars and Muslim sheikhs have signed a fatwa against this Constitution, which states "what came in the sixth chapter prejudices the greatest and mandatory five pillars of Islam and opens the door wide to atheism and it is contrary to the Islamic faith."[53] Many Islamic groups also disapprove of this Chapter 6 text.

This level of resistance and objection to Chapter 6 indicates that even with this Tunisian prohibition of killing based on *takfir*, many Muslim scholars and leaders consider this exception contrary to Islamic doctrine. Undoubtedly, these Muslim scholars and sheikhs will look for opportunities to remove this text from the Tunisian constitution in future legislation.

[52] Bin Burayk, Khamis. "Tunisian Constitution and the Crisis of Chapter 6." *Aljazeera.net*. Al Jazeera Media Network, 24 Jan. 2014. Web (http://tinyurl.com/jhwtvpu).

[53] Bin Ragab, Muḥammad. "Protesting Tunisian Imams and Sheikhs Reject New Constitution." *Elaph.com*. Elaph Publishing, 26 Jan. 2014. Web (http://elaph.com/Web/news/2014/1/870892.html).

SEVEN

"Nullifiers of Islam" can transform a Muslim into an infidel

If *takfir* is a calamity, then the process for dividing people and classifying them as infidels is a greater calamity. Most Muslims do not know that there are ten nullifiers of Islam, which means ten actions or behaviors a Muslim must avoid; committing one or more of these acts will change a Muslim into an infidel, lowering his or her station to that of Christians and Jews and the rest of the infidels. It is considered a greater sin for a person born a Muslim to disbelieve than for a person born a non-Muslim.

Islamic State has published and posted on social media and its online forums many photographs and articles regarding the lawful use of executions according to the Qur'ān and Hadith literature. Many of the beheadings carried out by its members occur after a fatwa has been issued by a *sharī'a* judge, a person who is knowledgeable about religious rulings and decisions of the main schools of Islamic jurisprudence concerning those who commit religious "violations." Killing apostates is one of the frequently applied punishments. The term *apostate* is a general name that includes anyone who is classified as an infidel or anyone who commits one of the nullifiers of Islam by words or deeds, or both.

Any discussion about the nullifiers of Islam necessitates the inclusion of Arab religious reformer Muḥammad Ibn ʻAbd al-Wahhāb (AD 1703-1792), who founded Wahhabism, a religious movement that dominates the religious and political life in Saudi Arabia even today. Ibn ʻAbd al-Wahhāb allied himself with Muḥammad Ibn Saʻūd (AD 1710-1765), the founder of the first Saudi state and Saud dynasty in AD 1744. Muḥammad Ibn ʻAbd al-Wahhāb was among the first to collect, detail, and explain the nullifiers of Islam. His summarizations of these nullifiers are circulated among Muslim people. His work is still available today as tracts and books on the Internet.

The Web site of Sheikh ʻAbd al-ʻAzīz Ibn Bāz (former Mufti of Saudi Arabia who died in 1999) also explains these nullifiers in detailed posts for those who want to read them.[1] However, the official government Web site, *Dār al-Iftāʼ of Saudi Arabia,* states that there are more than ten nullifiers of Islam. The ten nullifiers are the famous ones but there could be ten other nullifiers.[2]

The online forum of Sheikh Abū Muḥammad al-Maqdisī, the spiritual father of Abū Muṣʻab al-Zarqāwī (key leader of Al Qaeda in Iraq, or AQI, from 2004 until his death in 2006), lists and explains ten nullifiers of Islam with supporting quotations from Muḥammad Ibn ʻAbd al-Wahhāb.[3]

Nullifier #1: Associating partners (*shirk*) in the worship of Allah

Anyone who associates partners (other gods) in his or her worship of Allah is considered a polytheist or an infidel in the sight of Islam: *"Verily, God pardons not associating aught with Him, but He pardons anything short of that to whomsoever He pleases..."* (Q 4.48; Palmer trans.) Polytheism is the greatest sin that one can commit in Islam. Allah can forgive murder and adultery, and one can commit other major sins and remain a Muslim. However, the Muslim who commits the act of polytheism

---

[1] Ibn Baz, Abd al-Aziz. "Nawāqiḍ al-Islām [Nullifiers of Islam]." *Binbaz.org*. Official Web site of al-Imam Abd al-Aziz Ibn Baz, n.d. Web (https://www.binbaz.org.sa/article/575).

[2] See Fatwa no. 221461: "Nullifiers of Islam." *Alifta.net*. General Presidency for Scientific Research and Iftāʼ (Saudi Arabia), 25 Sept. 2013. Web (http://fatwa.islamweb.net/fatwa/index.php?page=showfatwa&Option=FatwaId&Id=221461).

[3] "Al-Iʻlām bi-Tawḍīḥ Nawāqiḍ al-Islām [Awareness of the Nullifiers of Islam]." *Ilmway.com*. N.p., n.d. Web (http://www.ilmway.com/site/maqdis/MS_22706.html).

cannot remain a Muslim, as evidenced in the Hadith literature. When one of the Companions asked Muḥammad, "What is the greatest sin in the Sight of Allah?" Muḥammad replied, "That you set up a rival unto Allah though He Alone created you."[4] Polytheism is an unforgivable sin. Islam renounces any Muslim who commits polytheism—that person becomes a non-Muslim, an infidel.

Muslims generally consider Christians polytheists as well as infidels because they have "associated" Jesus Christ (who is only a human being according to Islam) with Allah in their worship in addition to their disbelief in Islam and Muḥammad's prophethood. (Of course, this Islamic view is not the Christian theological view, which considers Christ as the Word of God manifested in the flesh and not a separate person from God.)

Even Jews are considered polytheists by Muslims, because they worship Ezra, according to the Qur'ān (Q 9.30; Palmer trans.): *"The Jews say Ezra is the son of God; and the Christians say that the Messiah is the son of God; that is what they say... imitating the sayings of those who misbelieved before.—God fight them! how they lie!"* This accusation is untrue—Jews do not worship Ezra, who was a Jewish scribe and priest—but this falsehood does not concern Muslims who uncritically grant it veracity, because the Qur'ān says so.

Being a former Muslim, I know that Muslims ignore what people say concerning Islam, because to Muslims the Qur'ān always states The Truth; anyone who disagrees with its text is a liar, even if he is telling the truth. The only thing that matters to Muslims is the Qur'ān, and if the Qur'ān declares that Jews are polytheists, then that judgment is final.

Concerning this nullifier of Islam, prominent Saudi Sheikh 'Abd al-Azīz Ibn Marzouk al-Tarīfī, concurring with Muḥammad Ibn 'Abd al-Wahhāb's views, makes these comments:[5]

> The blood and money of the polytheist are violable (except those who have a dhimmi pact or a pact): *"...kill the idolaters wherever ye may find them; and take them, and besiege them, and lie in wait for them in every place of observation..."* [Q 9.5; Palmer trans.].

[4] *Sahih Bukhari*, Book of Prophetic Commentary on the Qur'an (Tafsir of the Prophet)(p. 970); *Ṣaḥīḥ al-Bukhārī*, Kītāb al-Tafsīr 4: 1626. See Q 2.22 (Palmer trans.): *"...so make no peers for God, the while ye know!"*

[5] al-Ṭarīfī, *Al-I'lām* 12.

And when the polytheist is killed, his death does not atone for him and he will enter hell and dwell therein forever. The Qur'ān (Q 5.72; Palmer trans.) states, "*...verily, he who associates aught with God, God hath forbidden him Paradise, and his resort is the Fire, and the unjust shall have none to help them.*"

This verse (Q 5.72) also includes this text: "*...but the Messiah said, 'O children of Israel! Worship God, my Lord and your Lord....'*" Islamic scholars interpret this part of the verse to mean that Christians should be prohibited from worshipping Christ. So, if Christians, who are considered "People of the Book," must be pressured to abandon the worship of Christ, then it should follow that the pressure for non-Christians or infidels to abandon their faith must be even greater.

Islamic State has used this reasoning to kill Yazidis, whom it considers infidels, and does not give them any options, because Islamic history does not document the giving of any options to infidels. Muḥammad gave options other than death to Christians (even though Islam considers them polytheists), because they are People of the Book and believe some of the (Islamic) truth. The case is different for the Yazidis, because Muḥammad did not give the Quraysh any options other than Islam or death. In AD 630 Muḥammad entered Mecca with an army of ten thousand fighters. All the Meccan Quraysh who accepted Islam at that time were "converted" by the persuasive power of the sword. According to the Hadith literature, the Muslim fighters killed any Quraysh who they intercepted on their way to Mecca.[6] Correlatively, "infidel" Yazidis face only two choices: conversion to Islam or death. But their conversion to Islam must occur before the sword is on their necks or before Islamic State reaches them. This policy is essentially "repentance before occupation or capture." However, if Islamic State gets hold of them first, it will kill them because no repentance or conversion is accepted after this point.

On August 20, 2014, Islamic State released a video of hundreds of Yazidis who had "converted" to Islam after it had already executed hundreds more who had been caught and did not repent before its

[6] *Sahih Muslim*, Book of Jihad and Expedition: The conquest of Mecca (p. 1102); *Ṣaḥīḥ Muslim*, Kītāb al-Jihād wa al-Sīyar 2: 857. Excerpt: [As narrated by Abū Hurayra] "The Messenger of Allah...said: 'You see the ruffians and the (lowly) followers of the Quraish [Quraysh].' And he indicated by (striking) one of his hands over the other that they should be killed and said: 'Meet me at as-Safa.' Then we went on (and) any one of us wanted that a certain person should be killed, he was killed, and none could offer resistance...."

offensive into the area.[7] This video confirmed the savage August 3 onslaught, when Islamic State attacked the northern Iraqi city of Sinjar and other neighboring cities. Resisters were executed, and residents were told to convert to Islam or die. Almost 200,000 Yazidis fled their homes. About a quarter of them (50,000) took refuge in the Sinjar Mountains but became trapped there without food, water, or medical care.[8] Hundreds remained trapped there, under siege, for about four months (August to December of 2014).

Their dire predicament quickly rallied the international community to intervene: to repel Islamic State and rescue the civilian populations under siege.[9] If not for the international military and humanitarian intervention that finally released the besieged Yazidis, the world would have witnessed one of the largest human massacres in the twenty-first century and probably the largest compulsory conversion to Islam.

Still, hundreds of Yazidis were slaughtered before the international intervention, and thousands of Yazidi women were raped and enslaved, given to the jihadist fighters as "wives" or sold in the slave market,[10] reminiscent of similar practices carried out by the early Muslims after they invaded and occupied new territory during their military campaigns. Writer and politician Adnan Buzān, Secretary-General of the Kurdish Democratic Party-Syria, made these comments during an interview with *Al-Quds* newspaper:[11]

---

[7] Zain al-'Ābidīn, Nadā. "Islamic State Compels Hundreds of Yazidis to Convert to Islam." *Elwatannews.com*. El Watan News, 21 Aug. 2014. Web (http://www.elwatannews.com/news/details/543462). **Note:** The link to the Islamic State video is no longer available on this newspaper Web site.

[8] Salih, Mohammad, and Wladimir van Wilgenburg. "Iraqi Yazidis: 'If We Move They Will Kill Us.'" *Aljazeera.com*. Al Jazeera Media Network, 5 Aug. 2014. Web (http://www.aljazeera.com/news/middleeast/2014/08/iraqi-yazidis-if-move-they-will-kill-us-20148513656188206.html); Smith-Spark, Laura. "Iraqi Yazidi Lawmaker: 'Hundreds of My People Are Being Slaughtered.'" *CNN.com*. Cable News Network, 6 Aug. 2014. Web (http://edition.cnn.com/2014/08/06/world/meast/iraq-crisis-minority-persecution/index.html).

[9] "UN Security Council Condemns Attacks by Iraqi Jihadists." *BBC.com*. British Broadcasting Corporation, 7 Aug. 2014. Web (https://web.archive.org/web/20140808001143/http://www.bbc.com/news/world-middle-east-28699832).

[10] Barnett, David. "Women Who Are Captured by ISIS and Kept as Slaves Endure More Than Just Sexual Violence." *Independent.co.uk*. The Independent, 29 Nov. 2016. Web (http://www.independent.co.uk/news/world/middle-east/isis-sex-slaves-lamiya-aji-bashar-nadia-murad-sinjar-yazidi-genocide-sexual-violence-rape-sakharov-a7445151.html)

[11] Shri, Rima. "Famine, Mass Displacement, and Genocide of Yazidis Fleeing the Sword of Daesh [ISIS] to Hell of Mount Sinjar." *Alquds.co.uk*. Al-Quds al-Arabi, 16 Aug. 2014. Web (http://www.alquds.co.uk/?p=207707).

> ...such crimes are not the first of their kind to be committed against the Yazidi sect. In the era of the Islamic invasions and conquests, such acts were repeated. Today we see the same scenario being repeated with this community again under the banner of Islam, but in fact the goal of ISIS' regulation is devastation and destruction, and the displacement of people from their places...: What law and what religion accept the slaughter of men and the abduction of women?

The United Nations confirmed through the reports it received that the Islamic State fighters made Yazidis choose between conversion to Islam and death, unlike Christians who were given a third option, the tribute (*jizya*). Christof Heyns, UN Special Rapporteur on summary, arbitrary and extrajudicial executions, received reports that "Islamic State fighters are chasing members of minority groups and ordering them to convert to Islam or [expect] death."[12]

The Yazidis are followers of one of the oldest religions in Iraq. This religion is a mixture of beliefs and doctrines taken from Zoroastrianism, Islam, Christianity, and Judaism. They believe in one God, who created the world and placed it under the care of seven angels. The chief angel is Melek Taus, the Peacock Angel. Muslims consider the Yazidis devil worshippers because the story of the Yazidi peacock angel resembles the Islamic story of Iblīs (Satan). To Muslims, the Yazidi belief in the peacock angel makes them not only devil worshippers but polytheists too, a category requiring execution unless they convert to Islam. (One of Islam's primary goals is to erase polytheism from the earth to ensure the oneness of Allah and the world's subjection to him alone, without a partner.)[13]

Most Yazidis are Kurds, and their population today is around one million. Most of them live in Iraq. What has happened to the Yazidis in recent years is a tragedy by all measures, but in the eyes of Islamic State, their destruction is the only and correct action to take concerning them. Muḥammad himself did not spare his own tribe and family, subjecting them to the same two choices—conversion to Islam or the sword—and certainly the Yazidis are not better than the tribe of Muḥammad or his

[12] Shri, Rima. "Famine, Mass Displacement, and Genocide of Yazidis Fleeing the Sword of Daesh [ISIS] to Hell of Mount Sinjar." *Alquds.co.uk*. Al-Quds al-Arabi, 16 Aug. 2014. Web (http://www.alquds.co.uk/?p=207707).

[13] See Q 51.56 (Palmer trans.): *"And I* [Allah] *have not created the ginn and mankind save that they may worship me."* See also Q 8.39 (Palmer trans.): *"Fight them then that there should be no sedition, and that the religion may be wholly God's...."*

clan. To Islamic State, the application of Islamic law is more important than feelings of pity or compassion.

Nullifier #2: Placing intermediaries between Allah and humans

Muḥammad Ibn 'Abd al-Wahhāb states that the second nullifier of Islam is anyone who calls upon others, such as religious leaders, "and asks intercession [to Allah] from them, and seeks reliance in them, has committed disbelief according to the unanimous agreement" of Muslim scholars.[14]

In many Muslim countries, there exists a kind of popular Islam that does not adhere to many strict beliefs contained in the religious books but follows instead cultural or social customs, such as the practice of visiting the tombs of religious leaders and consecrating them.

Sufism, a religious philosophy of Islam, or its inner, mystical, or purely spiritual dimension, encourages Muslims to seek a personal, intimate closeness with Allah. The veneration of Muḥammad is central in Sufism because it holds up Muḥammad as the supreme human role model for emulation and that Islam is the best religion because of Muḥammad. As perfect prophet his saintly power continues through his successors to help guide later Muslims on their spiritual journey to Allah.[15] Therefore, these Sufi beliefs support the erection, use, and protection of shrines.[16]

On the other hand, Islamic and jihadist groups that are trying to apply the *sharī'a* of early Islam oppose these practices and consider them polytheistic. Therefore, Muslims who follow these "polytheistic" practices must be expelled from Islam. For example, most Muslims in Morocco do not view visiting shrines and getting blessings from them a sinful act. But to Islamic State, these Muslims are polytheists and infidels, because they are committing a major sin when they visit and honor religious shrines—a sin so great that they are even committing one of the nullifiers of Islam.

Muḥammad Ibn 'Abd al-Wahhāb fought the sanctification of shrines and worked to demolish them as well as the tombs of Muḥammad and

[14] Ibn Baz, *Subbul al-Salām* 68.

[15] Yachnes, Paul. "Sufism: Name and Origin." *Islam.uga.edu*. Islam and Islamic Studies Resources, 9 Dec. 2000. Web (http://islam.uga.edu/sufismdef.html); "Prophet Muḥammad (S) Was the Original Sufi!" *MuslimObserver.com*. The Muslim Observer (TMO), 3 May 2012. Web (http://muslimobserver.com/prophet-muhammad-s-was-the-original-sufi/).

[16] See al-Alawi, Irfan. "Egyptian Extremism See Salafis Attacking Sufi Mosques." *TheGuardian.com*. The Guardian, 11 Apr. 2011. Web (https://www.theguardian.com/commentisfree/belief/2011/apr/11/salafis-attack-sufi-mosques).

other early Muslim caliphs. In Saudi Arabia there are no religious shrines per se (though the government protects the tombs of Muḥammad and his Companions and allows visitation but no touching). However, some Muslim leaders have demanded the removal of the tomb of the prophet Muḥammad because they believe its presence is forbidden according to the religious texts.[17]

In fact, the graves of all the prophet's family members were destroyed after removing the names of them in 1924, so that people and pilgrims wouldn't know the locations and seek blessings from them. The orders for this destruction were based on many religious texts, including the Qur'ān, which states that the battle against the Quraysh was not because they were misbelievers but because they took patrons, or intercessors, beside him: *"Aye! God's is the sincere religion: and those who take beside Him patrons—'We do not serve them save that they may bring us near to God—' Verily, God...guides not him who is a misbelieving liar"* (Q 39.3; Palmer trans.).

According to this *ḥadīth*, Abū al-Hayyāj al-Asadī reports that 'Alī Ibn Abū Ṭālib (fourth caliph after Muḥammad's death) told him, "Should I not send you on the same mission as Allah's Messenger [Muḥammad]... sent me? Do not leave an image [statue] without obliterating it, or a high grave without levelling it...."[18]

Given these prohibitions against the enshrinement and veneration of grave sites in the religious texts, the demolition of the shrine of Prophet Yūnus (Jonah) by Islamic State should not have been unexpected.[19] To seek blessings from or revere entombed dead people is one of the greatest sins in Islam (a form of idolatry). By bombing this site, Islamic State removed this temptation and avenue toward sin for Muslims.

Islamic State planted and detonated explosive devices in the shrine, which was located east of Mosul, in July 2014 after they captured the city the previous month. A video of this destruction was publicized by the

---

[17] Spillett, Richard. "Will Saudi Arabia MOVE the Remains of Prophet Muḥammad? Controversial Plan for 'Anonymous' Burial to Prevent the Site Itself Being Worshipped." *Dailymail.co.uk*. Telegraph Media Group, 1 Sept. 2014. Web (http://www.dailymail.co.uk/news/article-2740307/Controversial-plan-calls-Saudis-tomb-Prophet-Muḥammad-Fears-idea-stoke-religious-divisions.html).

[18] *Sahih Muslim*, Book of Prayers: Commandment in regard to the levelling of the grave (p. 534); *Ṣaḥīḥ Muslim*, Kītāb al-Janā'iz 1: 429.

[19] Ford, Dana, and Mohammed Tawfeeq. "Extremists Destroy Jonah's Tomb, Officials Say." *CNN.com*. Cable News Network, 25 July 2014. Web (http://www.cnn.com/2014/07/24/world/iraq-violence); "Daesh [ISIS] Blows Up the Shrine of Nabi Yunis [Prophet Jonah] in Iraq." *Alarabiya.net*. Al Arabiya Network, 24 July 2014. Web (http://preview.tinyurl.com/z3q7knm). **Note:** Link to the video footage of the destruction available in these articles.

organization to underscore its adherence to the prohibitions of shrines, a ban not followed by most Muslim countries. On August 23, 2015, Islamic State in Syria destroyed the Roman Temple of Baalshamin, which dates to the first century AD.[20]

Both sites are ancient places constructed many centuries before the rise of both Christianity and Islam. The history of Nebi Yūnus (shrine of Prophet Jonah) predates the king of Assyria, Sennacherib (reign 705-681 BC), who enhanced the area, according to historical records, by enlarging his palace there.[21] The earliest construction of the Temple of Baalshamin dates to the late second century BC and is a United Nations Educational, Scientific, and Cultural Organization (UNESCO) World Heritage site.

However, Islamic State and similar groups do not care about the preservation of ancient places, buildings, and artifacts or World Heritage sites. They only care about Islam and the implementation of its rulings. For these groups, all manifestations of polytheism and idolatry should be destroyed. The caption on Islamic State's published pictures showing the booby-trapping of the temple and its subsequent destruction emphasizes this goal: "The complete destruction of the pagan Baalshamin temple."[22]

In February 2015, Islamic State published a video explaining why it destroyed the archaeological statues in the Mosul Museum, including a human-headed, winged Assyrian bull that dates to the seventh or eighth century BC.[23] The video is titled *Those Who Enjoin What Is Right and Forbid What Is Wrong*. This text is a reference to the Qur'ān (where it also states that Muslims are the best nation produced for mankind): *"Ye were the best of nations brought forth unto man. Ye bid what is reasonable,*

---

[20] Stack, Liam. "ISIS Blows Up Ancient Temple at Syria's Palmyra Ruins." *NYTimes.com*. New York Times, 23 Aug. 2015. Web (https://www.nytimes.com/2015/08/24/world/middleeast/islamic-state-blows-up-ancient-temple-at-syrias-palmyra-ruins.html?_r=2).

[21] See Ensor, Josie. "Previously Untouched 600 BC Palace Discovered under Shrine Demolished by ISIL in Mosul." *Telegraph.co.uk*. Telegraph Media Group, 28 Feb. 2017. Web (http://www.telegraph.co.uk/news/2017/02/27/previously-untouched-600bc-palace-discovered-shrine-demolished); see also Jones, Christopher. "What is the Tomb of the Prophet Jonah?" *GatesofNineveh*. Wordpress, 11 July 2014. Web (https://gatesofnineveh.wordpress.com/2014/07/11/what-is-the-tomb-of-the-prophet-jonah/). **Note:** This article was written before the destruction. The author discusses the destruction in a later article. (See "And Now It's Gone: Shrine of Jonah Destroyed by ISIS," 24 July 2014. Web: https://gatesofnineveh.wordpress.com/2014/07/24/and-now-its-gone-shrine-of-jonah-destroyed-by-isis).

[22] "Islamic State Photos 'Show Palmyra Temple Destruction.'" *BBC.com*. British Broadcasting Corporation, 25 Aug. 2015. Web (http://www.bbc.com/news/world-middle-east-34051870).

[23] Shaheen, Kareen. "ISIS Fighters Destroy Ancient Artefacts at Mosul Museum." *TheGuardian.com*. The Guardian, 26 Feb. 2015. Web (https://www.theguardian.com/world/2015/feb/26/isis-fighters-destroy-ancient-artefacts-mosul-museum-iraq); "ISIS Destroys Mosul Museum Artifacts." *NYTimes.com*. New York Times, 26 Feb. 2015. Web. (To view YouTube video clip, see URL: https://www.nytimes.com/video/world/middleeast/100000003537753/isis-destroys-mosul-museum-artifacts.html)

and forbid what is wrong, believing in God..." (Q 3.110; Palmer trans.). By destroying these statues and artifacts, Islamic State believes it is removing idolatry. During the short video (about five minutes), the narrator presents the reasons for destroying the statues, and then Islamic State fighters are shown destroying them.[24]

In 2001, Afghanistan's Taliban used dynamite to blow up the world's two largest standing Buddhas, situated at the foot of the Hindu Kush mountains. A special edict issued by a Taliban leader ordering the destruction of all non-Islamic statues triggered an international outcry. Despite mediation efforts to stop the destruction of these ancient, 1700-year-old statues, the Taliban were resolved in implementing this edict, and eventually they succeeded with dynamite, after anti-aircraft and tank fire failed to wreck the two statues.[25] Wakīl Aḥmad Mutawakkil, the Taliban's Foreign Minister, explained the rationale for this destruction: "Our decree for destroying these idols is based on the teachings of Islam, and we will not exclude statues from the pre-Islamic era or after Islam."[26]

It is worth noting here that Japan (where Buddhism is one of the major religions) as well as Western nations appealed to Muslim countries, asking them to intervene to stop this barbaric act. Unfortunately, their pleas for preservation of these priceless cultural treasures seemed to fall on deaf ears. For example, on the official Web site of Qatar's Ministry of Endowments and Islamic Affairs, a reader's question regarding the religious legitimacy of the Taliban's destruction received this response:[27]

> **Question:** "What is the Islamic ruling on what the Taliban government is doing regarding the destruction of idols and statues there [Afghanistan]? Is there a legitimate justification for the calls that are raised by some to slander the Taliban?"
>
> **Answer:** "Islamic evidence indicates that it is obligatory to destroy idols and statues, whenever it is accessible for Muslims to do it and whether or not people worship them."

---

[24] "ISIS Destroys Mosul Museum Artifacts." *NYTimes.com*. New York Times, 26 Feb. 2015. Web. (To view YouTube video clip, see URL: https://www.nytimes.com/video/world/middleeast/100000003537753/isis-destroys-mosul-museum-artifacts.html)

[25] Rashid, Ahmed. "After 1700 Years, Buddhas Fall to Taliban Dynamite." *Telegraph.co.uk*. Telegraph Media Group, 12 Mar. 2001. Web (http://www.telegraph.co.uk/news/worldnews/asia/afghanistan/1326063/After-1700-years-Buddhas-fall-to-Taliban-dynamite.html).

[26] Mimut, Mark. "Taliban Insists on the Destruction of the Buddha Statues, Despite International Mediation Efforts and Fears of Reprisals Kills Islamic Architectural Heritage." *Aawsat.com*. Middle East, 9 Mar. 2001. Web (http://preview.tinyurl.com/zsfq3vu).

[27] See Fatwa no. 7458: "Must Remove the Idols." *Islamweb.net*. Ministry of Endowments and Islamic Affairs of Qatar, 19 Mar. 2001. Web (https://preview.tinyurl.com/y84wjlob).

Along with this fatwa, the site quotes from a *ḥadīth* attributed to Muḥammad, where he explains that Allah sent him "to join ties of relationship (with kindness and affection), to break the Idols, and to proclaim the oneness of Allah (in a manner that) nothing is to be associated with Him."[28]

In another *ḥadīth*, 'Alī Ibn Abū Ṭālib states that at a funeral he attended with Muḥammad, the Messenger of Allah said, "If anyone comes to Medina, he must not leave a grave without levelling it or an image without destroying it or an idol without breaking it."[29] After his command was implemented, Muḥammad then said, "Whoever builds up something similar to those [grave sites, images, idols] has disbelieved in what Allah has revealed to Muḥammad."[30]

There are other examples in the Qur'ān that encourage the destruction of idols, including this dialogue between Abraham and his father (Q 21.52-58; Palmer trans.):

> *When he* [Abraham] *said to his father and to his people, 'What are these images to which ye pay devotion?' / Said they, 'We found our fathers serving them.' / Said he, 'Both you and your fathers have been in obvious error.' / They said, 'Dost thou come to us with the truth, or art thou but of those who play?' / He said, 'Nay, but your Lord is Lord of the heavens and the earth, which He originated; and I am of those who testify to this; / and, by God! I will plot against your idols after ye have turned and shown me your backs!' / So he brake them all in pieces, except a large one they had; that haply they might refer it to that.*

Interestingly, these verses were recited by Islamic State in the background of the aforementioned video while its members were toppling and breaking the statues. Yet the whole world condemned the event without fully understanding its precedent and exhortation in the religious texts.

Muḥammad himself had commanded the destruction of statues:[31]

---

[28] *Sahih Muslim*, Book of Prayers: How 'Amr b. 'Abasa embraced Islam (p. 467); *Ṣaḥīḥ Muslim*, Kitāb al-Salāt 1: 371.

[29] *Musnad Ahmad* 1: 140.

[30] Ibid. 1: 223.

[31] *Sahih Muslim*, Book of Jihad and Expedition: Removal of the idols from the vicinity of the Ka'ba (p. 1104); *Ṣaḥīḥ Muslim*, Kītāb al-Jihād wa al-Sīyar 2: 857.

> The Holy Prophet...entered Mecca. There were three hundred and sixty idols around the Ka'ba. He began to thrust them with the stick that was in his hand saying: *"Truth has come and falsehood has vanished. Lo! falsehood was destined to vanish"* [Q 17.81]. Truth has arrived, and falsehood can neither create anything from the beginning nor can It restore to life.

Recently, the following fatwa was posted on an official Saudi Web site forbidding the erection of statues for any reason. This fatwa was given in response to this question: "What is the Islamic attitude towards erecting statues for various purposes?" The fatwa relies on the Hadith literature for the following answer:[32]

> Erecting statues for any purpose is prohibited, whether they were built as a memorial to kings, commanders of armies, prominent figures and reformers, or as a symbol of wisdom and courage, like the statue of the Sphinx, or for any other purpose, and that is done according to the general meaning of the *ṣaḥīḥ* [authentic] *ḥādīths* which forbid that, because it is a pretext that leads to polytheism.

Young Muslims face a major dilemma on this issue. On one hand, they read religious texts that prohibit the erection of statues and command their destruction, while on the other hand, they live in societies that not only consecrate graves and tombs but even build museums for sculptures.

This dilemma—the religious texts and reality—is but one of many. But any and all can create a psychological crisis for and encourage the radicalization of young Muslims. For them the texts are sacred and must be applied on society and not the reverse; society must be subject to the authority of the religious texts. Muslim governments compound this hypocrisy between text and reality by establishing and supporting an educational curriculum that teaches these religious texts to the young and posting the same texts and positions on government-sponsored Web sites, but, in their diplomatic relationships with the West, they denounce the actions of Islamic State and similar groups—even though their own fatāwa agree one hundred percent with the agenda and actions of these militant jihadist organizations.

My father never bought dolls for my sister, because it is *ḥarām* (religiously unlawful), but my mother would go behind his back and buy

32 "What Is Islam's Position Regarding Erection of Statues for Any Purpose?" *Alifta.net.* General Presidency for Scientific Research and Iftā' (Saudi Arabia), n.d. Web (http://preview.tinyurl.com/z52xl27).

the dolls secretly and give them to my sister. She would also warn my sister to hide them lest my father discover them when he got home. She would warn me in particular not to inform on her or my sister.

One time I asked my father the reason for his objection towards dolls, and he responded with a story about Muḥammad, when his wife 'Ā'isha had bought for Muḥammad a reclining cushion with pictures on it:[33]

> ...I ['Ā'isha] bought a cushion with pictures on it. When Allah's Apostle saw it, he kept standing at the door and did not enter the house. I noticed the sign of disgust on his face, so I said, "O Allah's Apostle! I repent to Allah and His Apostle. (Please let me know) what sin I have done." Allah's Apostle said, "What about this cushion?" I replied, "I bought it for you to sit and recline on." Allah's Apostle said, "The painters (i.e., owners) of these pictures will be punished on the Day of Resurrection. It will be said to them, 'Put life in what you have created (i.e., painted).'" The Prophet added, "The angels do not enter a house where there are pictures."

My father did not want the angels to refrain from entering into our house because of my sister's dolls; he did not want to be held accountable on the Day of Resurrection for allowing an image into the house. He believed that the makers of pictures will be punished on the Day of Judgment for attempting to create something similar to what Allah creates, and that Allah will ask them to make these pictures alive. But since they will never be able to bring their creations alive like Allah, they will remain in the torment of hellfire forever. Also, anyone who buys their artistic creations will be contributing to the artists' misbelief and will also be punished along with them.[34]

According to Muḥammad, picture makers, i.e., artists, photographers, etc., will be the most grievously tormented people on the Day of Resurrection.[35] In other words, it is religiously unlawful for anyone to make pictures of any living being, whether human or animal. So according to this Islamic ruling, Walt Disney, who touched and regaled the whole world with his illustrations, Oscar-winning animated films, and revolutionary amusement theme parks, will certainly be grilled in

---

[33] *Sahih Bukhari*, Book of Sales and Trade (p. 477; for similar *ḥadīths*, see pp. 1158, 1325, and 750); *Ṣaḥīḥ al-Bukhārī*, Kītāb al-Bīū' 2: 742.

[34] *Sahih Bukhari*, Book of Sales and Trade (p. 477; for similar *ḥadīths*, see pp. 1158, 1325, and 750); *Ṣaḥīḥ al-Bukhārī*, Kītāb al-Bīū' 2: 742.

[35] *Sahih Bukhari*, Book of Dress (p. 1324); *Ṣaḥīḥ al-Bukhārī*, Kītāb al-Libās 5: 2220. In this *ḥadīth*, Muḥammad tears a curtain with pictures on it that is hanging from 'Ā'isha's chamber and states, "The people who will receive the severest punishment from Allah will be the picture makers."

the fire of hell, because of his artistic creations, such as the beloved, world-recognized fictional character, Mickey Mouse. Allah will ask Walt Disney to give life to Mickey Mouse, Donald Duck and Pluto. But since he won't be able to breathe real life into his creations, Walt Disney will grill in the fire of hell forever.

For these reasons, the art of sculpture does not exist in conservative Muslim countries, such as Saudi Arabia. Conservative Muslims do not hang on the walls of their homes any pictures representing living beings, such as animals and people. Instead, they might hang Qur'ānic verses or natural landscapes. As a consequence, no other types of artistic expression have excelled in the Muslim world except architecture and the art of handwriting, because they do not include images.

If dolls and certain kinds of pictures are prohibited according to the religious texts, how much more severe would it be with shrines and statues? Islamic groups judge ordinary Muslims who do not pay attention to these texts that prohibit against artistic images as Muslims who have gone astray. If these Muslims insist on keeping these bad habits after being warned, then these groups will consider them polytheists who must be punished.

Nullifier #3: Refusing to apply excommunication (*takfir*) to the infidel

According to Muḥammad Ibn 'Abd al-Wahhāb, the third nullifier is anyone who does not hold polytheists to be infidels or has doubts about their disbelief or considers their ways and beliefs to be correct has committed disbelief.[36] For example, when the Qur'ān states that Christians are infidels but a nice Muslim opposes this classification, asserting that Christians are believers and not infidels, such a Muslim is then considered an infidel. To generalize from this example, it means that when Islamic State and similar groups declare a group of people as infidels and kill them, it is not permissible to object. If a group member or any other Muslim objects to this declaration of infidelity and the issuance of punishment (execution), then this Muslim objector will certainly be condemned and eventually share the same fate as that infidel—unless, of course, the objector repents. Then he or she would be spared execution and restored to Islam.

[36] Ibn Baz, *Subbul al-Salām* 98.

Also counted as infidels by Islamic, fundamentalist, and often mainstream groups are all those Muslims who interpret Islam along more contemporary, liberal lines with more tolerance for non-Muslims, befriending others who follow a different religion, or resist the idea of considering others as infidels, because these more temperate Muslims are then defending polytheists and are called infidels in the Qur'ān.

This third nullifier is justified in this verse based on the Qur'ānic story (Q 60.4; Palmer trans.) of Abraham:

> *Ye had a good example in Abraham and those with him, when they said to their people, 'Verily, we are clear of you and of what ye serve beside God. We disbelieve in you: and between us and you is enmity and hatred begun for ever, until ye believe in God alone!'....*

According to this verse, Abraham considered his own people as infidels, and he cuts every relationship with them. He even establishes enmity and hatred between himself and them, which cannot be removed unless they believe in Allah alone without intermediaries or idols.

Thus, the committed Muslim must call those whom the Qur'ān considers polytheists as infidels. He or she must sever any relationship with these infidels and cannot view them as "non-infidels" or even help them in their disbelief in any way.

Imagine the complete isolation of Muslims from the rest of the people of the world who are classified as infidels because of these inhuman, ruthless rulings.

Nullifier #4: Accepting the supremacy of secular over Islamic laws

The fourth nullifier, according to Muḥammad Ibn 'Abd al-Wahhāb, is anyone who believes that the rulings and judgments of others are more complete or surpass the Prophet's guidance (which means he or she then prefers the judgment of false gods, or *ṭaghūt,* over Muḥammad) are infidels.[37] This nullifier makes it obligatory for the Muslim to believe in the supremacy of Islamic law over all other laws in human history because it is divine law and above all human-made laws. No Muslim country should let any human-made laws overrule divine law, because the Qur'ān states that the "*...judgment is only Allah's...* " (Q 6.57; Shakir trans.) and "*...And whoso will not judge by what God hath sent down*[—]*such are the*

[37] Ibn Baz, *Subbul al-Salām* 108.

Infidels" (Q 5.44; Rodwell trans.). This belief—that only Allah has the right to judge—applies to all judges who adjudicate according to human-made rather than Islamic laws or makes rulings according to some Islamic laws but applies human-made laws for other judgments.

Therefore, it is not surprising that Islamic and jihadist organizations consider Muslim countries, such as Iraq, Morocco and Egypt, as infidel countries, because these countries apply Islamic laws on only some issues (estate and family law, e.g., marriage, divorce). However, for punishments for convictions concerning theft or marital infidelity, the laws of these countries do not include the amputation of hands for thieves or the stoning or lashing of adulterers, for example. In this way, these countries demonstrate preference to human-made laws over Islamic (divine) laws.

For this judicial preference, these Islamic organizations have declared jihad against these countries. They seek the destruction of these countries, because they want all judgments to come from Allah; there is no place for human-made rulings. Indeed, Islamic State boasts about not giving any consideration towards human-made laws. Islamic State resolutely defends and administers such Islamic legal punishments as lashing, stoning, and hand amputation despite international condemnation. Allah's law is of more importance to Islamic State and all the other Islamic jihadist groups than any denunciation of these laws (*sharī'a*) by infidel countries.

Foundational to this belief in the supremacy of Allah's judgment is the principle *tawḥīd al-hakimiyya* (the oneness of Allah's sovereignty and law, or the linking of Allah with governance on earth), which some Islamic scholars interpret as forms of authority that translate into legislative, executive, and judicial functions.[38] Ultimate authority, though, resides within the divine alone—or, on this earth, human representatives (*sharī'a*) of the divine will.[39] This view means that "all legitimate worldly powers must necessarily submit to God."[40] This principle conflicts with explicitly secular political systems, where religion and government ("church and state") are separate. However, all Islamic jihadist organizations accept this principle—that Allah must rule alone: *"...nor does He let any one share in His judgment"* (Q 18.26; Palmer trans.).

[38] Mandaville 312.

[39] Ibid.

[40] Eddebo, Johan. "*Tawḥīd al 'uluhiyya*, Secularism, and Political Islam." *Journal of Religion and Society* 16 (2014): 2. Print and Web (http://moses.creighton.edu/jrs/2014/2014-4.pdf).

This principle, which is widely embraced by more traditional, orthodox Muslims, is not understood by Western media when they analyze published statements from Islamic State that refer to this concept. The West fails to see or ignores the strong connection between the posted Islamic State rationale and this religious principle and supporting religious texts.

Many sheikhs of Saudi Arabia bless these strict, orthodox Islamic laws and their often brutal applications. They even witness the lashing and the beheadings in public squares; they do not care what the West says. From their perspective, their Islamic laws are better than all Western laws collectively. To them, no matter how better crafted these human-made laws may seem outwardly, they are still bad inwardly.

I wish to share a story related to this point. I had the honor of interviewing the wife and children of Rā'if Badawī, a Saudi writer, dissident, and activist, who founded and once blogged on the Web site, *Free Saudi Liberals*. I had tears in my eyes when his little daughter, aged 10, told me at the time of the interview that she wished to play with her father and to fall asleep in his arms.[41] But Rā'if Badawī is still languishing in a Saudi Arabian jail even as this book went to press because of his blog writings, where he advocated for the discussion and consideration of liberal ideas and criticized the Islamic religion and the Saudi Arabia regime. He even criticized the Committee for the Promotion of Virtue and the Prevention of Vice, the "religious police" of Saudi Arabia.[42] (His Web site was ordered closed by the court following his arrest in 2012.)[43]

Rā'if Badawī was arrested in 2012, charged with apostasy and other accusations because of his online blog writings, and has been imprisoned ever since. In July 2013 he was convicted and sentenced to seven years in prison and 600 lashes for creating and posting articles on an Internet forum that "violates Islamic values and propagates liberal thought."[44]

---

[41] Badawī, Najwa. Interview by Brother Rachid. *YouTube.com*. YouTube, 19 Nov. 2014. Web (https://www.youtube.com/watch?v=kPpCm_HGFtU).

[42] An agency of the Saudi Arabian government informally known as the Hai'a, these "religious police" patrol the streets to enforce *sharī'a* and are authorized to monitor such matters as dress code, gender separation, and participation in and respect for the daily prayer times. However, in recent years its autonomy and authority have been curtailed. In 2016, its police powers were removed, and its presence is less visible now. Debate over its total abolishment has started but its total removal seems unlikely in the near future.

[43] Black, Ian. "A Look at the Writings of Saudi Blogger Raif Badawi—Sentenced to 1000 Lashes." *TheGuardian.com*. The Guardian, 14 Jan. 2015. Web (https://www.theguardian.com/world/2015/jan/14/-sp-saudi-blogger-extracts-raif-badawi).

[44] "Saudi Arabian Social Website Editor Sentenced to Seven Years Behind Bars and 600 Lashes." *NYDailyNews.com*. Daily News, 30 July 2013. Web (http://www.nydailynews.com/news/world/saudi-arabian-social-website-editor-sentenced-years-behind-bars-600-lashes-article-1.1412811).

The court, in its decision to find Rā'if Badawī guilty as charged, offered this reasoning in the court documents:[45]

> His preference to the law of the infidel West over the law of his own country and its Constitution, which is the Qur'ān and Sunna, is likening him to those about whom Allah says: "... *They* [infidels] *believe in Gibt and Tâghût, and they say of those who misbelieve, 'These are better guided in the way than those who believe These are those whom God has cursed, and whom God has cursed no helper shall he find'"* [Q 4.51-52; Palmer trans.].

On May 7, 2014, Badawī's sentence was increased to 1000 lashes and ten years in prison, and his fine raised to the equivalent of US$267,000.[46] (Initially, he was also charged with apostasy, which carries the death penalty if convicted. But Badawī repented and this charge was dismissed. However, he was not acquitted of "violating" Islam through his writings.)[47]

The flogging was to be distributed over twenty weeks. The first flogging of fifty lashes was implemented on January 9, 2015. Badawī was flogged in a Jeddah public square near a mosque before hundreds of spectators who shouted "*Allahu Akbar*," clapped, and whistled.[48] Subsequent floggings have been postponed because of Badawī's poor physical health according to a medical assessment and recommendation by a Saudi panel of doctors. However, international outcry and pressure by many countries and human rights organizations to stop further floggings of Badawī (United Kingdom called it "cruel, inhumane or degrading punishment")[49] suggests that Saudi officials are aware and mindful of global opinion in this case.

Amnesty International has called Badawī's flogging a "vicious act of cruelty" and states that his only "crime" was "to exercise his right to

---

[45] District of Jeddah v. Rā'if Badawī, No. 3418494, Criminal Court of Jeddah. 20 Feb. 2013. Page 42. Print and Web (http://preview.tinyurl.com/z9lzj5t).

[46] "Saudi Blogger Raif Badawi Gets 10 Year Jail Sentence." *BBC.com*. British Broadcasting Corporation, 8 May 2014. Web (http://www.bbc.com/news/world-middle-east-27318400).

[47] District of Jeddah v. Rā'if Badawī, No. 3418494, Criminal Court of Jeddah. 20 Feb. 2013. Pages 37, 44. Print and Web (http://preview.tinyurl.com/z9lzj5t).

[48] "Saudi Blogger Receives First 50 Lashes of Sentence for 'Insulting Islam.'" *TheGuardian.com*. The Guardian, 10 Jan. 2015. Web (https://www.theguardian.com/world/2015/jan/09/saudi-blogger-first-lashes-raif-badawi); Black, Ian. "Planned Flogging of Saudi Blogger Raif Badawi Postponed Again." *TheGuardian.com*. The Guardian, 23 Jan. 2015. Web (https://www.theguardian.com/world/2015/jan/22/flogging-saudi-blogger-raif-badawi-postponed).

[49] Black, Ian. "Planned Flogging of Saudi Blogger Raif Badawi Postponed Again." *TheGuardian.com*. The Guardian, 23 Jan. 2015. Web (https://www.theguardian.com/world/2015/jan/22/flogging-saudi-blogger-raif-badawi-postponed).

freedom of expression by setting up a website for public discussion."[50] The following excerpts are translations of some of Badawī's writings on his (now closed) Web site, *Free Saudi Liberals*:[51]

> As soon as a thinker starts to reveal his ideas, you will find hundreds of fatwas that accuse him of being an infidel just because he had the courage to discuss some sacred topics. I'm really worried that Arab thinkers will migrate in search of fresh air and to escape the sword of the religious authorities. (August 12, 2010)

> For me, liberalism simply means, live and let live. This is a splendid slogan. However, the nature of liberalism—particularly the Saudi version—needs to be clarified. It is even more important to sketch the features and parameters of liberalism, to which the other faction, controlling and claiming exclusive monopoly of the truth, is so hostile that they are driven to discredit it without discussion or fully understanding what the word actually means. They have succeeded in planting hostility to liberalism in the minds of the public and turning people against it, lest the carpet be pulled out from under their feet. But their hold over people's minds and society shall vanish like dust carried off in the wind. (May 2012, shortly before his arrest)

On September 28, 2010, Badawī argued in a blog post that secularism is "the most important refuge for citizens of a country." Badawī maintained that "secularism respects everyone and does not offend anyone.... Secularism...is the practical solution to lift countries (including ours) of the third world and into the first world."

These kinds of opinions led to the Saudi government's charges of apostasy against Badawī, especially his positive views regarding secularism in a country that elevates Islamic religious law over all other kinds of law, considering Islamic religious law divine and thus flawless. So when Badawī supported on his Web site the separation of governmental and religious institutions in the implementation and execution of laws (as is the case in most Western "infidel" countries), his statements suggested to Saudi authorities that Badawī was exalting Western laws above the religious laws of Saudi Arabia. The prosecution bolstered their case against by him by misrepresenting his full arguments with narrow citations of his

[50] "Saudi Blogger Receives First 50 Lashes of Sentence for 'Insulting Islam.'" *TheGuardian.com*. The Guardian, 10 Jan. 2015. Web (https://www.theguardian.com/world/2015/jan/09/saudi-blogger-first-lashes-raif-badawi).

[51] Black, Ian. "A Look at the Writings of Saudi Blogger Raif Badawi—Sentenced to 1000 Lashes." *TheGuardian.com*. The Guardian, 14 Jan. 2015. Web (https://www.theguardian.com/world/2015/jan/14/-sp-saudi-blogger-extracts-raif-badawi).

writings, i.e., "...the law in the West is better even than Saudi Arabia's law...."[52]

Of course, such an opinion (even if manipulated and taken out of context) is unacceptable in a Muslim country. Therefore, Badawī must be an infidel and must be held accountable for it. The law of Allah is the best of all laws even if it stipulates hand amputation for persons convicted of theft, beheading for other capital crimes, and brutal floggings for people convicted, like Badawī, of "insulting Islam." In his case, he was shackled and brutally flogged (fifty lashes) in front of a mosque after Friday prayers with hundreds of people, standing and cheering as if they were watching a sporting event. His sentence mandates nineteen more of these floggings (if he can survive that long).

This Muslim view—that Islamic law (*sharīʿa*) is better than the West's secular laws—is upheld and protected even while young Muslims see their peers in Western countries enjoying the freedom to practice (or not practice) religion, the freedom to express opinions, and the freedom to petition their government without fear of reprisal. Despite these stark comparisons, Muslims will continually maintain that anyone who claims the laws of the infidel West are better than their own country's Islamic laws is a disgrace and is committing a crime. At least, this position is what Muslims say—even if they inwardly believe otherwise. They will exclaim (with hypocrisy and despite *sharīʿa's* deep flaws): "What good and great laws we have, for our laws are from Allah!"

Nullifier #5: Hating Islamic rules, teachings, and punishments

People who dislike any teachings by Muḥammad—even if they outwardly act on it—are considered infidels. They are infidels even if they pray and fast during Ramadan but dislike praying and fasting.[53] They are infidels if they hate the implementation of the Islamic punishments (*ḥudūd*) for adulterers (stoning) or thieves (hand amputation), because they would then hate what Allah has revealed: *"That is because they were averse from what God has revealed; but their works shall be void!"* (Q 47.9; Palmer trans.).

Whenever Islamic State found any person living within its "Caliphate" jurisdiction who had declared or indicated that he or she hated any of

[52] District of Jeddah v. Rāʾif Badawī, No. 3418494, Criminal Court of Jeddah. 20 Feb. 2013. Page 37. Print and Web (http://preview.tinyurl.com/z9lzj5t).

[53] Ibn Baz, *Subbul al-Salām* 136-137.

the Islamic obligatory religious practices (*fara'iḍ*), e.g., prayers, fasting, or *ḥudūd*, such a person would have faced grave punishment unless he or she repented or denied the previously stated negative opinion. Hating Islamic commands and punishments is disbelief that is worthy of death.

Nullifier #6: Mocking Islam

Anyone who mocks or ridicules any part of the Prophet's religion (Islam) or its rewards or punishments has committed the sixth nullifier.[54] This act of disbelief is detailed in the Qur'ān (Q 9.65-66; Palmer trans.):

> *But if thou shouldst ask them, they will say, 'We did but discuss and jest;' say, 'Was it at God and His signs, and His Apostle, that ye mocked?' / Make no excuse! Ye have misbelieved after your faith; if we forgive one sect of you, we will torment another sect, for that they sinned!*

This nullifier is especially dangerous because it is so encompassing and subjective. Numerous photographs of beheadings posted on Islamic forums show the consequences for those who have allegedly mocked Islam, such as executions carried out by ISIL (and then later, Islamic State) when it occupied and controlled large areas in Iraq and Syria. Often the phrase "killing an apostate" is printed on the pictures. Sometimes the Islamic militants would kill someone who supposedly insulted Allah or the Prophet, because mocking anything Islamic includes insulting the Prophet himself. (See Chapter 14, page 440.)

The case of Saudi blogger Rā'if Badawī is one example regarding this particular nullifier. According to court documents, his sentence was amended to 1000 (from 600) lashes for mocking the religion of Allah. As incriminating evidence, the amendment to the original document cites statements where Badawī described Ramadan as a month of hypocrisy and nuisance and that he reluctantly observed it because he had no choice. The amended document also notes that Badawī asserted that the sword and the Qur'ān are more dangerous than the atomic bomb.[55]

The judge condemned Badawī's comments and opinions by stating that they were contemptuous of his religion and his people and incited

---

[54] Ibn Baz, *Subbul al-Salām* 146.

[55] District of Jeddah v. Rā'if Badawī, No. 3418494; amended. Criminal Court of Jeddah. 2013. Page 51. Print and Web (http://preview.tinyurl.com/nytpff3).

others to look down upon the Qur'ān and Sunna.[56] Badawī was initially found guilty of apostasy because he had committed some nullifiers. However, he retracted his statements (of course from fear of execution), which then released him from Allah's ultimate punishment.[57] Yet he was still sentenced to ten years of imprisonment and 1000 lashes and banned from travelling abroad for ten years following his discharge from prison. (The travel ban means that Rā'if Badawī will only leave one prison cell for a bigger prison: Saudi Arabia.)

This judgment in Badawī's case is considered a lenient decision for the punishment of apostasy, which requires killing by the sword.[58] Committing one or more nullifiers of Islam is not an insignificant act to Muslim-governed states, be it Saudi Arabia or Islamic State.

In another case, a Mauritanian judge delivered the first death sentence for apostasy since the country's independence in 1960 to Muslim blogger and freelance journalist, Mohamed Cheikh Ould M'khaitir. He was convicted and sentenced to death on December 24—Christmas Eve in the West—in 2014.[59] The timing could be a coincidence or an intentional message to young Muslims influenced by or infatuated with the West.

M'khaitir's death sentence resulted from an article he wrote in December 2013 entitled "Religion, Religiosity, and Craftsmen," which he published on the news Web site, *Aqlame*. His article discusses the "marginalized status" of his country's craftspeople, criticizing Mauritania's "caste system and those who use religion to marginalize certain groups

---

[56] **Note:** During the early centuries of Islam, a *sunna* was used to describe Muḥammad's sayings, actions, and approvals, and a *ḥadīth* was used to relate his verbal utterances. This book refers to the organized collections of these *sunnas* and *ḥadīths* as the Sunna or Hadith literature, respectively. (See *The Qur'an: An Encyclopedia* 606.)

[57] District of Jeddah v. Rā'if Badawī, No. 3418494; amended. Criminal Court of Jeddah. 2013. Page 44. Print and Web (http://preview.tinyurl.com/nytpff3).

[58] **Note:** In June 2015, Saudi Arabia's Supreme Court upheld the sentence against Rā'if Badawī. Only a pardon from King Salman (newly crowned in January 2015) can release Badawī from his sentence. In the meantime, his lawyer and human rights activist, Walīd Abū al-Khayr (who is also Badawī's brother-in-law), was charged and convicted of such offenses as "inciting public opinion against the government." (See URL: http://preview.tinyurl.com/l7ouxvu). He has been sentenced to fifteen years of prison, followed by a 15-year travel ban and a large fine (~US$53,000). His wife and human rights defender Samar Badawī (Rā'if's sister) was arrested in January 2016 but released the following day. Since 2014 she has been banned from travel outside the country. In February 2017 she was summoned for more questioning. She has endured continual judicial harassment since her husband's conviction and imprisonment. (See URL: http://preview.tinyurl.com/mlue7tk). As of June 2018, Rā'if Badawī has served six years of his prison term but has not received any more lashes since January 2015. He continues to languish in prison despite international appeals for his immediate release. His wife Ensar Haidar and their three children fled to Canada in 2015 after receiving anonymous death threats.

[59] Buchanan, Elsa. "Who Is Mohamed Cheikh Ould M'khaitir, the Mauritanian Blogger on Death Row for 'Apostasy'?" *IBTimes.co.uk*. International Business Times, 1 Feb. 2017. Web (http://www.ibtimes.co.uk/who-mohamed-cheikh-ould-mkhaitir-mauritanian-blogger-death-row-apostasy-1591453).

of society."[60] M'khaitir also likens this marginalization of today's Mauritanian craftspeople to the prophet Muḥammad's discriminatory policy concerning the Jews of Hijaz[61] (whom he killed) and non-Muslim members of his tribe, the Quraysh (whom he pardoned)—even though only the Quraysh intentionally tried to harm Muḥammad.

Though his article was quickly taken down, it sparked a wave of anger in Mauritania. Protesters called for the young man's execution, which led to his arrest on January 2, 2014. When M'khaitir was finally tried and sentenced to death, he fainted because he did not expect this harsh decision.[62] Inside the court the death sentence was greeted with ululations of joy, while outside in the streets car horns honked and motorcycles fired in celebration.[63]

In its sentencing, the court held that M'khaitir's article "evidenced apostasy as it spoke 'lightly [indifferently, carelessly] of the Prophet Mohammed'"[64] and found the defendant guilty of violating Article 306 of the Mauritanian Penal Code:[65]

---

[60] "The Case of…Mohamed Cheikh Ould M'khaitir." *Globalfreedomofexpression.columbia.edu.* Global Freedom of Expression (Columbia University), n.d. Web (https://globalfreedomofexpression.columbia.edu/cases/the-case-of-mauritanian-blogger-mohamed-cheikh-ould-mkhaitir/).

[61] Ibid.

[62] "Sentenced to Death a Young Mauritanian Mohamed Cheikh Ould Mohamed on Charges of Apostasy." *France24.com/ar.* France 24 (Arabic), 25 Dec. 2014 (updated). Web (http://preview.tinyurl.com/zpk5cng).

[63] "Mauritanian Judiciary Sentenced to Death a Young Man Accused of Apostasy." *Alhurra.com.* Alhurra, 25 Dec. 2014. Web (http://www.alhurra.com/a/prosecution-mauritania-execution-religious-conversion/263843.html).

[64] "The Case of…Mohamed Cheikh Ould M'khaitir." *Globalfreedomofexpression.columbia.edu.* Global Freedom of Expression (Columbia University), n.d. Web (https://globalfreedomofexpression.columbia.edu/cases/the-case-of-mauritanian-blogger-mohamed-cheikh-ould-mkhaitir/).

[65] *Criminal Law of Mauritania.* No. 83-162. 9 July 1983. *Justice.gov.mr.* Official Web site of the Ministry of Justice of the Islamic Republic of Mauritania. Pages 55-56. Print and Web (http://preview.tinyurl.com/zcnzud5).

> Any Muslim, male or female guilty of the crime of apostasy, or said or did anything that implies apostasy, or denies anything of the religion, or mocks Allah, His angels, His books or His prophets, is to be given the opportunity to repent within three days. If the accused does not repent within that period, he/she is to be sentenced to death as an infidel, and all of his/her properties shall be confiscated by the government [treasury of the Ministry of Islamic Affairs]. And if a person who has been sentenced to death for apostasy repents before his/her execution, the Mauritanian Supreme Court will then take the case from the public prosecutor and investigate about the sincerity of his repentance, and accordingly decides to drop the decision of the death penalty and restore his properties to him.... Everyone who turns his back to Islam and turns to misbelief is considered a heretic and shall be punished with death whenever he is found before he was asked to repent, and his repentance shall not be accepted unless he declares it before he is announced a heretic.

Even though Mohamed Cheikh Ould M'khaitir denied these charges of intentionally insulting the prophet Muḥammad, he was still sentenced to the death penalty. In April 2016, the Nouadhibou Court of Appeals upheld this sentence despite M'khaitir admitting that he had made a mistake and asking for forgiveness. In November 2017, an appeals court reduced M'khaitir's death sentence to two years' imprisonment. Because he had already served more than four years in prison, he was set free.[66]

I have personally contacted Mohamed Cheikh's sister, Aeicha Cheikh, via e-mail exchanges (September 10, 2015). She told me that this nightmare had enveloped her sister-in-law, Mohamed Cheikh's wife. The government forcibly and secretly annulled his marriage to his wife, a woman he had married just three months before his arrest in January 2014. His "ex"-wife was forcibly married to someone else, because it is forbidden for a Muslim woman to remain married to an infidel man. This divorce was carried out without his knowledge.

Rā'if Badawī and Mohamed Cheikh Ould M'khaitir are just two examples of the tragedy experienced by Muslim youth who dare to critically discuss Islam. I consider myself in the same camp. Had I not escaped from Morocco, I would have been facing the same situation now.

---

[66] "Africa Highlights: Call to Free Nigeria Shia Muslim Leader, Mauritius Defends Offshore Accounts." *BBC.com*. British Broadcasting Corporation, 9 Nov. 2017. Web (http://www.bbc.com/news/live/world-africa-41926318).

Nullifier #7: Practicing witchcraft

Muḥammad Ibn ʿAbd al-Wahhāb states, "Sorcery includes magic spells that cause a person to hate or love someone or something. So whoever performs it or is pleased with it being done has committed disbelief." [67] As support, Wahhāb cites the Qur'ān (Q 2.102; Palmer trans.): "*...yet these* [two angels at Babylon, Hārūt and Mārūt] *taught no one until they said, 'We are but a temptation, so do not misbelieve'....*

The ruling for sorcerers is death in Islam.[68] In Saudi Arabia, many of those who are arrested and tried on charges of sorcery are sentenced to death, such as Muḥammad Ibn Bakr Ibn Ṣāliḥ al-ʿAlāwī, who was executed on August 5, 2014, for practicing witchcraft.[69] On December 30, 2014, a man in Riyadh was arrested for using magic to make couples love each other.[70] During the (still ongoing) Saudi Arabian-led military intervention in Yemen to combat Houthi rebels, a Riyadh newspaper reported the arrest of a Yemeni accused of entering Saudi Arabia to carry out acts of "sorcery."[71]

Saudi Arabia even has a special police unit for witchcraft and sorcery. It specializes in finding and arresting witches—operating similarly to anti-terrorism units in Western countries. In 2009, it apprehended more than 2000 so-called sorcerers. Saudi Arabia is the only country in the world with a security force (under the direction of the Committee for the Promotion of Virtue and the Prevention of Vice) that specializes in fighting witchcraft and sorcery.[72] The Committee recently drafted a set of rules and punishments to help streamline and regulate the prosecution of persons charged and convicted of sorcery. Article IX stipulates the punishment for a person convicted of sorcery:[73]

---

[67] Ibn Baz, *Subbul al-Salām* 159.

[68] "The Rule of Magic and Magician." *Islamweb.net.* Ministry of Endowments and Islamic Affairs of Qatar, 19 Mar. 2006. Web (http://articles.islamweb.net/media/index.php?id=16904&lang=A&page=article).

[69] "Execution of Two Saudis as Punishment: One a Sorcerer and One a Killer of His Son." *Sabq.org.* Sabq Online Newspaper, 5 Aug. 2014. Web (https://sabq.org/IMhgde).

[70] al-Hazzāʿ, Mājid. "Sorcerer Arrested in Riyadh." *Alarabiya.net.* Al Arabiya Network, 30 Dec. 2014. Web (http://preview.tinyurl.com/hqfrv3w).

[71] al-Zaʾirī, ʿĀdil. "Arresting a Yemeni Suspected of Sorcery for Attempting to Cross the Border." *Alriyadh.com.* Al Riyadh Daily, 15 May 2015. Web (http://www.alriyadh.com/1048424).

[72] al-Rakf, Abdullah. "Saudi Arabia: Hai'i Raid Magicians Abusing the Koran to Draw Closer to the Devil." *Alarabiya.net.* Al Arabiya Network, 17 May 2009. Web (https://www.alarabiya.net/articles/2009/05/17/73053.html).

[73] al-Qarīān, Faīsal. "Execution or 15 Years in Prison for Sorcery and Witchcraft Crimes." *Alyaum.com.* Al Yaum, 6 Jan. 2013. Web (http://www.alyaum.com/article/3067501).

> Whoever has been legally proven that he/she has committed the crime of sorcery, shall be punished with death, and if the competent court deemed—for its own reasons—that the person does not deserve death penalty, then he is to be punished by imprisonment for a term not less than fifteen years and a fine of not less than three hundred thousand riyals, and not more than five hundred thousand riyals [~US$80,000-133,300].

Islamic State shares the same attitude as Saudi Arabia towards sorcery, perhaps because both subscribe to an extremely rigid, fundamentalist form of Islam. Wahhabism, the official, state-sponsored form of Sunni Islam in the Kingdom of Saudi Arabia, is influenced by the Hanbali school of Islam (most conservative of the four major Sunni Islamic schools) and Ibn Taymīya, the medieval Muslim theologian and reformer known for his controversial, iconoclastic teachings. Literal interpretation of the Qur'ān and Hadith literature is a major hallmark of these doctrines. Given the large number of Saudi recruits (second only to Tunisia) and Saudi funding (oil money),[74] it is no wonder that Islamic State's policies, actions, rulings, and fatwas reflect these doctrines, which treat magic and sorcery as credible, serious threats. For both "mainstream" Saudi Arabia and jihadist terrorist groups like Islamic State, anyone engaging in witchcraft must be sentenced to death.

On February 6, 2015, the public beheading by Islamic State of a grey-bearded, elderly man convicted of sorcery was carried out in a village outside the city of Raqqa, Syria.[75] Photographs of this execution were released on affiliated media and reported by an anti-Islamic State activist group, Raqqa is Being Slaughtered Silently, which has been documenting the terrorist group's brutality.

---

[74] See The Soufan Group. *Foreign Fighters: An Updated Assessment of the Flow of Foreign Fighters into Syria and Iraq* (Dec. 2015): 5-10. Print and Web (http://soufangroup.com/wp-content/uploads/2015/12/TSG_ForeignFightersUpdate_FINAL3.pdf); Cockburn, Patrick. "We Finally Know What Hillary Clinton Knew All Along—US Allies Saudi Arabia and Qatar Are Funding ISIS." *Independent.co.uk*. The Independent, 14 Oct. 2016. Web (http://www.independent.co.uk/voices/hillary-clinton-wikileaks-email-isis-saudi-arabia-qatar-us-allies-funding-barack-obama-knew-all-a7362071.html); Shane, Scott. "Saudis and Extremism: 'Both the Arsonists and the Firefighters.'" *NYTimes.com*. New York Times, 25 Aug. 2016. Web (https://www.nytimes.com/2016/08/26/world/middleeast/saudi-arabia-islam.html?_r=0); Williams, Jennifer. "The Saudi Arabia Problem: Why a Country at War with Jihadists also Fuels Them." *Vox.com*. Vox Media, 1 Dec. 2015. Web (http://www.vox.com/2015/12/1/9821466/saudi-problem-isis).

[75] Hall, John. "Islamic State Behead Man…for WITCHCRAFT: Barbaric Execution for 'Invoking Magic' Plunges Middle East Further into the Dark Ages." *DailyMail.co.uk*. Telegraph Media Group,, 9 Feb. 2015. Web (http://www.dailymail.co.uk/news/article-2945684/Beheaded-WITCHCRAFT-Latest-ISIS-execution-Syria-echoes-Dark-Ages-man-killed-invoking-magic.html).

The Islamic State release explains that Islam teaches in its holy texts that sorcery greatly impacts the lives of people and might harm them, even if it is performed from afar through talismans, magic spells, incense, and other magical equipment. According to the Qur'ān, sorcery can cause division between a husband and his wife: *"Men learn from them* [two sorcerers or angels Mārūt and Hārūt[76]] *only that by which they may part man and wife; but they can harm no one therewith, unless with the permission of God, and they learn what hurts them and profits them not"* (Q 2.102; Palmer trans.).

Muslims believe that Muḥammad himself was bewitched at the hand of a Jewish man, named Labīd Ibn al-A'ṣam. This Jew took the Prophet's comb, with his hair sticking to it, and threw it into a well.[77] Muslims believe that this act was a magic spell that affected the mental abilities of Muḥammad, as he was imagining that he had slept with his wives (or other women) when he had not.

If the Prophet himself was bewitched by sorcery, then ordinary Muslims have even more to fear from the power of sorcery. Therefore, a Muslim recites Sura Al-Falaq, or "The Dawn," (Q 113.1-5; Palmer trans.) to ward off witchcraft and envy:

> *Say, I seek refuge in the Lord of the daybreak, / from the evil of what He has created; / and from the evil of the night when it cometh on; / and from the evil of the blowers upon knots; / and from the evil of the envious when he envies.*

Muḥammad would recite this sura and suras Al-Ikhlas (Q 112) and An-Nās (Q 114) before rubbing his hands over various parts of his body

[76] See the commentary on Q 2.102, *Tafsīr al-Ṭabarī* 1: 352-371.

[77] *Sahih Bukhari*, Book of Beginning of Creation (p. 759); *Ṣaḥīḥ al-Bukhārī*, Kitāb Bad' al-Khalq 3: 1192-1193. This *ḥadīth* (as narrated by 'Ā'isha) reports that the Prophet became bewitched and began to think he was doing things that he was not actually doing. One day after praying to Allah he dreamed two men were discussing his bewitchment. One man in the dream revealed that 'Lubaīd bin Al-A'ṣam' [Labīd Ibn al-A'sam] had bewitched Muḥammad with "[a] comb, the hair gathered on it, and the outer skin of the pollen of the male date-palm," which was now in the well of Dharwan. Muḥammad went out to the well and then returned, saying that the date-palms near the well looked like the "heads of devils." When 'Ā'isha asked him if he had removed the comb from the well, Muḥammad said he did not but that he was cured. However, worried that this evil will spread, he had the well filled up with earth. See *Sahih Bukhari*, Book of Medicine (p. 1287); *Ṣaḥīḥ al-Bukhārī*, Kitāb al-Tib 5: 2175. This *ḥadīth* (as narrated by 'Ā'isha) reports that "[m]agic was worked on Allah's Apostle so that he used to think that he had sexual relations with his wives [Arabic uses the word *women* instead of "his wives"] while he actually had not…."

to protect himself from sorcery.[78] This sura (and *ḥadīth*) indicates that Muḥammad feared witches (Q 113.4: *"and from the evil of the blowers upon knots"*), so he taught his followers to seek refuge in Allah from envy, from the evil of magic, and from the evil of the night, because supposedly most magic is performed during the night when the devils are more active.

The second caliph, 'Umar Ibn al-Khaṭṭāb (who was one of the most important early leaders of Islam), wrote an order just one year before his death, which included this directive: "Kill every sorcerer and sorceress."[79] As narrated by Aḥmad and Abū Dāwūd, "Then we killed three sorceresses in one day."[80] Several other important Companions, such as "'Uthmān [Ibn 'Affān], Ibn 'Umar [son of second caliph 'Umar Ibn al-Khattab], Abū Mūsa, Qays Ibn Sa'd, and seven other followers, including 'Umar Ibn 'Abd al-'Azīz, also killed people accused of sorcery."[81]

This early Islamic history of killing people accused of sorcery continues today in "mainstream" Muslim countries like Saudi Arabia, with a special police department allocated for hunting down sorcerers, as well as Islamic terrorist groups like Islamic State. The current application of this policy proves that the investigation, prosecution, and punishment of sorcery and witchcraft have been a part of Islam, both then and now, and seems to derive from the core of Islam itself.

Some Muslim countries do not prosecute and punish sorcery, applying secular laws, similar to such laws in Western countries, over Islamic laws in these matters. If these Muslim countries were to apply the real Islam, they would be obligated to kill all sorcerers.

In Morocco, however, the belief in and tolerated practice of sorcery, or black magic, is widespread throughout the country.[82] Morocco is also host to many shrines and grave sites that venerate Muslim saints of historical or religious importance and are popular sites for pilgrimages

---

[78] *Sahih Bukhari*, Book of Virtues of the Qur'ān (p. 1120); *Ṣaḥīḥ al-Bukhārī*, Kitāb Faḍā'il al-Qur'ān 4: 1916. This *ḥadīth* (as narrated by 'Ā'isha) reports that when the Prophet went to bed at night, "he used to cup his hands together and blow over it after reciting Surat Al-Ikhlas, Surat Al-Falaq, and Surat An-Nas, and then rub his hands over whatever parts of his body he was able to rub, starting with his head, face, and front of his body. He used to do that three times."

[79] al-Quranī, *'Ālam al-Siḥr* 59.

[80] Ibid.

[81] Ibid.

[82] El Mouatassim, Houda. "Witchcraft: A Stigma in the Reputation of Morocco." *MoroccoWorldNews.com*. MoroccoWorldNews, 17 Aug. 2012. Web (https://www.moroccoworldnews.com/2012/08/52277/witchcraft-a-stigma-in-the-reputation-of-morocco/).

by followers.[83] Although Morocco follows the Mālikī Islamic school of thought, it does not apply Mālik's rulings, which command the killing of sorcerers.[84] Morocco ignores this ruling, because its current laws are highly influenced by the laws of France, when Morocco was once its colony. Also, many Moroccan Muslims incorporate Sufism as part of their religious beliefs and are influenced by their cultural heritage, which accepts the construction and veneration of shrines and the practice of sorcery (and even encourages them).

The Pew Research Center has collected and published data regarding Muslim belief in supernatural forces, e.g., jinn, witchcraft, and the evil eye, which are all mentioned in the Qur'ān and Hadith literature.[85] Approximately, half or more Muslims in most of the surveyed countries believe that "jinn exist and that the evil eye is real."[86] Though belief in sorcery or witchcraft is less common, "half or more Muslims in nine of the countries included…say they believe in witchcraft."[87]

Muslim countries where belief in the jinn is extremely strong (greater than 70%) include Afghanistan (70%), Lebanon (73%), Malaysia (77%), Pakistan (77%), Tunisia (79%), Tanzania (83%), Bangladesh (84%), and Morocco (86%). Muslim countries where belief in the evil eye is extremely strong (greater than 70%) include Iraq (72%), Morocco (80%), and Tunisia (90%). Belief in sorcery or witchcraft is strongest (greater than 70%) in Morocco (78%), Tunisia (89%), and Tanzania (92%).[88]

Yet even as high percentages of Muslims in all these countries believe in supernatural forces, such as jinn, as well as the evil eye and sorcery, "most Muslims agree that Islam forbids appealing to jinn or using sorcery."[89]

Still these beliefs in the evil eye and sorcery are problematic for Muslims, because these beliefs instill fear and encourage mistrust of others. For instance, some Muslims will believe that their neighbors are the reason for their misery because their neighbors have "bewitched"

[83] Gray, Martin. "Sacred Sites of Morocco." *SacredSites.com*. Martin Gray, 1982-2016. Web (https://sacredsites.com/africa/morocco/sacred_sites_of_morocco.html).

[84] al-Jazīrī, *Kitāb al-Fiqh* 5: 406. The followers of the Mālikī doctrine state that "the sorcerer is an infidel who must be killed as a sorcerer without having him repent; he must be killed as a heretic."

[85] "The World's Muslims: Unity and Diversity," *Pewforum.org*. Pew Research Center, 9 Aug. 2012. Web (http://www.pewforum.org/2012/08/09/the-worlds-muslims-unity-and-diversity-4-other-beliefs-and-practices/). See Chapter 4: Other Practices and Beliefs.

[86] Ibid.

[87] Ibid.

[88] Ibid.

[89] Ibid.

them. Many Muslim girls and women will blame witchcraft to explain their unwanted singlehood or failed romantic relationships or marriages. These beliefs in the evil eye and sorcery remove personal responsibility for poor decisions or control over life outcomes and ignore just plain chance, from typical Muslim believers all the way to Islamic State.

Nullifier #8: Joining with or supporting infidels against Muslims

Taking infidels for friends and giving them support and assistance against Muslims is an act of disbelief,[90] according to the Qur'ān (Q 5.51; Arberry trans.): *"O believers, take not Jews and Christians as friends; they are friends of each other. Whoso of you makes them his friends is one of them. God guides not the people of the evildoers."*

Saudi Sheikh 'Abdul 'Azīz al-Rājḥī, a professor at the Islamic University of Imām Muḥammad Ibn Sa'ūd in Riyadh, explains this nullifier:[91]

> Joining or supporting [polytheists] means loving the polytheists, which is infidelity and apostasy, and assisting the polytheists against the Muslims. Whoever supports polytheists against Muslims is evidence that he is joining the polytheists, and joining them is apostasy....
>
> The root of this support is love from the heart, which leads to helping and assisting, and being a helper for polytheists against Muslims by [use of] money, weapons, or opinion is a proof that he has joined the polytheists and loves them.

Thus, any Muslim who helps infidels against other Muslims is considered an apostate because he or she has committed a nullifier of Islam. Punishment for this nullifier is death.

Current application of this nullifier occurs in such instances where Islamic State or a similar terrorist group catches a Muslim helping its enemies, e.g., anti-terrorism coalition forces—by planting car bombs amidst their fighters or disclosing the group's whereabouts or headquarters. These informers are considered apostates and must be killed according to Islamic law. Similarly, if a Muslim is caught supporting Iraqi, American, Syrian, or other enemy forces with food, supplies, or other assistance, he (or she) too is considered an apostate who deserves to be killed. For these judgments and capital punishments, Islamic State and related groups rely on this nullifier, which was drafted by Muḥammad Ibn 'Abd al-Wahhāb, who himself cites the Qur'ān to solidify his position.

---

[90] Ibn Baz, *Subbul al-Salām* 194.
[91] al-Rājhī, *Tabsīr al-'Anām* 46.

Muslim and non-Muslim countries that support the United States in its war against Islamic State and other jihadist militant organizations are infidel countries, according to the Qur'ān. These allies are considered infidels in the eyes of the militant jihadist groups too. Therefore, these groups allow and assist violent operations to be carried out in these Muslim countries, e.g., suicide bombers, car bombings, shooting massacres, etc., that can harm the citizens and interests of these countries. These deadly attacks are a form of revenge for the countries' intervention against these groups. When Islamic State broadcasts pictures of this carnage, it describes the victims as traitors and enemy helpers based on this nullifier.

On December 15, 2014, a jihadist forum posted pictures of a mass execution of thirteen men dressed in orange jumpsuits, who were shot dead before an assembled crowd, which included children.[92] The executions were carried out by Islamic State fighters on a large roundabout about four miles east of Tikrit, Iraq, in the afternoon. Residents state that the executed men were "members of an anti-ISIS group of Sunni tribal fighters known as the Knights of Al-Alam who were captured by the jihadists...10 days earlier."[93]

On October 29, 2015, Islamic State released a slickly produced video entitled *Harvest of the Spies* that ultimately shows the execution of four men, dressed in the familiar orange jumpsuits, by four disguised, armed Islamic State fighters clothed in black garb.[94] The video incorporates still scenes and video footage as well as black-and-white and color cinematography. Background music (male singers extolling and encouraging the soldiers) is interwoven with the visual components. The video eventually presents the four prisoners individually giving a final statement, an obviously forced "confession" to supplying information about Islamic State locations and members to the local police or Syrian army. (One of the four men, however, gives no statement.) Then they are shown all together outside in a wooded area claimed to be near the Euphrates River in Syria. It is there where they are shot in the head and killed. The final scene shows one of the executioners stepping squarely in the blood of one of the murdered men and stating (translated from

[92] "ISIS in Iraq Release Pictures of Mass Execution." *Alarabiya.net* (English). Al Arabiya News, 16 Dec. 2014. Web (http://english.alarabiya.net/en/News/middle-east/2014/12/16/ISIS-militants-in-Iraq-release-pictures-of-mass-execution-.html).

[93] Ibid.

[94] Islamic State. *Harvest of the Spies #3—Wilāyat al-Furāt. Jihadology.net.* 29 Oct. 2015. Video. (To view video, see URL: https://preview.tinyurl.com/y9e47mjc).

the Arabic), "We send you this message (accompanied) with your spies' blood!"

On December 20, 2016, Islamic State ignited and burned four men to death in Deir ez-Zor, the largest city in eastern Syria. The men had been arrested three months earlier by Islamic State-led police. They were charged with supporting the Kurdish People's Protection Units (YPG) by providing information about Islamic State movements in local areas. (Islamic State considers the Kurdish government an infidel state.) The Sharī'a Court of Deir-ez-Zor determined that this cooperation with the enemy constituted "conscious abandonment of Islam," and so the men were additionally convicted of apostasy as well as treason and deserved "the most brutal punishment." The immolation of the four men was witnessed by hundreds of spectators, including the victims' families who were forced to attend.[95]

These are but three out of hundreds of examples. These examples clearly show that all those who cooperate with "infidels" or other enemies of true Muslims must be punished to death with no mercy; they are not considered Muslims anyway, because supporting the infidel against Muslims is an act of apostasy. Aiding the enemy is one of the greatest nullifiers in Islam. (For more detailed information about Islamic State operations of mass slaughter and burial, see Chapter 10, page 277.)

Nullifier #9: Believing in religious freedom

People who seek or desire a religion other than Islam, forsaking the law of Muḥammad, are infidels.[96] The Qur'ān clearly supports this statement: *"Whosoever craves other than Islam for a religion, it shall surely not be accepted from him, and he shall, in the next world, be of those who lose"* (Q 3.85; Palmer trans.). In other words, any Muslim who believes that a Christian or a Jew (or others) can keep his or her respective religion and still go to heaven is an infidel. Correlatively, any Muslim who thinks that a person can be spared from Allah's torment without converting to Islam is an infidel.

---

[95] Smith, Samuel. "ISIS Burns 4 Men Alive in Front of Their Parents." *ChristianPost.com*. Christian Media Corporation (CMC) Group, 21 Dec. 2016. Web (https://www.christianpost.com/news/isis-burns-4-men-alive-in-front-of-their-parents-172282/).

[96] Ibn Baz, *Subbul al-Salām* 223.

Sheikh 'Abdul 'Azīz al-Rājḥī (refer to page 192) offers the following comment on this nullifier:[97]

> The meaning of this [ninth nullifier] is the view that anyone could leave the religion of Muḥammad and worship Allah in a way different than the one that the Prophet brought, and he can reach for Allah and be in paradise even if he does not work with the religion of Muḥammad. Some philosophers have said that one can worship through philosophy or through the Sabian religion or Sufism, and that he can reach Allah through Muḥammad or anyone else, or say that they are all the same—this person is an infidel because there is no other way that will lead to Allah except through the Prophet. No one has the authority to forsake the religion of the prophet because his law is...the seal of all laws.

Thus, a Muslim must believe that no human being can be "saved" unless that person believes in the Islam brought by Muḥammad. Anyone in the world who does not believe in Muḥammad will inevitably perish. But if a Muslim thinks otherwise, he will be one of the infidels and will join their ranks and his Islam will be annulled.

Nullifier #10: Turning away from Islam

Turning away from the religion of Allah or not following its teachings is an act of disbelief, or apostasy.[98] Often cited Qur'ānic support for this nullifier is Q 32.22 (Palmer trans.): *"Who is more unjust than he who is reminded of the signs* [verses, revelations, etc.] *of his Lord, and then turns away from them? Verily, we will take vengeance on the sinners!"*

This nullifier encompasses all religious practices and teachings of Islam, making it extremely subjective, because there is no scholarly consensus on all its teachings. Islamic State exploits this lack of clarity, even ambivalence, to classify many people as infidels. For example, it will classify any Muslim who has abandoned prayer as an infidel who has forsaken Islam—an infidel, using Muḥammad's own words as its basis: "Between man and polytheism [*shirk*] and unbelief [*kufr*] is the abandonment of prayer."[99]

---

[97] al-Rājhī, 'Abdul Azīz. "Explaining Nullifiers of Islam." *Saaid.net.* Ṣayd al-Fawā'id, n.d. Web (http://www.saaid.net/Minute/m51.htm).

[98] Ibn Baz, *Subbul al-Salām* 228.

[99] *Sahih Muslim*, Book of Faith: Application of the word "*kufr*" [unbelief] to one who neglects prayer (p. 97); *Saḥīḥ Muslim*, Kitāb al-Iman 1: 52.

The Hadith literature also reports that Muḥammad has even said that the covenant between him and the rest of Muslims is prayer.[100] It means that if a Muslim stops praying, he or she has broken the covenant and will no longer be under the protection of Muslims. The three Islamic schools of thought (which subscribe to the doctrines of al-Mālikī, al-Shāfiʿī, and al-Ḥanbalī) have agreed that whoever neglects praying is to be killed, with slight differences among the schools. The schools of al-Mālikī and al-Shāfiʿī state that the one who neglects praying should be granted a chance to repent. However, if that person does not pray, then he or she shall be punished with death. The Ḥanbalī school offers no chance for reconsideration—the person who neglects to pray should be killed because he or she is an apostate.[101]

The school of al-Ḥanafī differs slightly from the other three Islamic schools. It states that the person is to be beaten and imprisoned until he or she repents and restarts praying. However, if this person refuses to repent and pray, then he or she shall remain in prison until death.[102]

The chairman of the International Union of Muslim Scholars, Egyptian Yūsuf al-Qaraḍāwī (who lives in Qatar), comments on this issue:[103]

> It is the duty of all religious people to ostracize anyone who abandons praying, insisting on leaving it even after advisement.... [I]t is not permissible for a father to give his daughter in marriage to someone who abandons praying because such a person is not a true Muslim and is not worthy of her, nor is he trustworthy to be with her or her children.
>
> The owner of a business must not hire someone who abandons praying because he [the owner] would be helping him to disobey Allah with Allah's money.

Sheikh al-Qaraḍāwī also clarifies the ruling of Islam towards those who abandon praying, according to the Ḥanbalī school:[104]

---

[100] *Musnad Aḥmad* 6: 475. The *ḥadīth* reports that Muḥammad said that the "covenant between us and them [Muslims] is praying; whoever neglects it has disbelieved."

[101] See Fatwa no. 1145: "Ruling Details of the One Who Neglects Praying." *Islamweb.net*. Ministry of Endowments and Islamic Affairs of Qatar, 21 Jan. 2001. Web (http://fatwa.islamweb.net/fatwa/index.php?page=showfatwa&Option=FatwaId&Id=1145). See also al-Mubarakfurī, *Tuḥfat al-Aḥwadhī* 2: 387, and Ibn ʿAbd al-Bar, *Al-Istidhkār* 2: 149.

[102] Ibid.

[103] al-Qaraḍāwī, Yūsuf. "The Duty of Muslims toward the One Who Abandons Prayer." *Archive.IslamOnline.net*. Islam Online (Archive), n.d. Web (https://archive.islamonline.net/?p=21008). This excerpt is taken from one of his fatāwa, which are collected and posted on this Web site.

[104] Ibid.

> Imām Aḥmad says—in one of the most famous narrations about him—that the person who abandons praying is an infidel and an apostate and has no punishment other than death. He must be asked to repent to Allah and turn back to Islam by performing prayers. If he does repent, it must be acceptable or he must be beheaded.

If beheading is the ruling for Muslims who abandon prayer, which is a private matter between a person and his or her Creator, then it should be no surprise when Islamic State and similar Islamic groups kill people for many other reasons.

Personally, I remember my father threatening to beat me whenever I skipped prayer because of laziness. I once asked him, "Is it really appropriate to beat a child in order to force him to pray?" My father told me that the Prophet ordered this discipline. He would refer to this *ḥadīth*: "Command **your children** to **pray** when they reach the **age of seven** and **hit them** if they leave it off when they reach the **age of ten**" (emphasis added).[105] And thereby he closed all the doors of objection, because when the Apostle speaks, objection has no place, because that would mean disbelief and apostasy.

Yet many adult Muslims in Muslim countries do not perform all the five prayers, and some of them do not have the enthusiasm to pray except on Fridays. Still others pray only during religious occasions or during the month of Ramadan. According to a survey of the world's Muslims by the Pew Research Center, religious commitment expressed through the daily prayers (one of the five mandatory Pillars of Islam) varies widely.[106] Unlike mosque attendance, annual giving of alms, fasting, or pilgrimage to Mecca, prayer "is...universally accessible" and is a "useful indicator of religious commitment among Muslims."[107] Despite such accessibility, Muslims in various regions of the world vary in their participation in the five daily prayers, with higher attendance in sub-Saharan Africa, Southeast Asia, South Asia, and across the Middle East and North Africa. These regions average 78%, 78%, 60%, and 69%, respectively. However, Southern-Eastern Europe (25%) and Central Asia

---

[105] *Musnad Aḥmad* 2: 387.

[106] "The World's Muslims: Unity and Diversity," *Pewforum.org*. Pew Research Center, 9 Aug. 2012. Web (http://www.pewforum.org/2012/08/09/the-worlds-muslims-unity-and-diversity-2-religious-commitment/). See Chapter 2: Religious Commitment.

[107] Ibid.

(32%) reveal markedly lower participation percentages.[108] (Interestingly, younger Muslims (ages 18-34) generally pray less frequently than older Muslims (ages 35 and older), especially in the Middle East and North Africa. The greatest difference between these two age groups occurs in Lebanon (+28), followed by the Palestinian territories (+23), Tunisia (+19), and Morocco (+18).[109]

These numbers reflect the fact that Muslims do not uniformly practice the mandatory obligation of the five daily prayers and thus do not adhere to Islam as stated in Islamic texts and teachings. However, Muslims who live in a Muslim country that strictly implements Islam may be harassed by "religious police." Until recently, Saudi Arabia's "religious police," the Hai'a (Committee for the Promotion of Virtue and the Prevention of Vice, or CPVPV), had unchallenged authority to compel people to close their shops and go pray, monitor women's attire, and pressure citizen compliance with other religious obligations. Founder and first monarch of the Kingdom of Saudi Arabia, King 'Abdul 'Azīz (AD 1875-1953) but better known in the West as Ibn Saud, who created this agency during his reign, explained its purpose in a speech to Muslim scholars and prominent people of Mecca:[110]

> We have come to a decision where we shall hire committees in all the Islamic countries, to command people to do what's good and forbid what's evil, most importantly, compelling people to keep the five prayers in congregation and to prompt people to learn their religion.

In 2015 this "committee," or the CPVPV, employed 4000 to 6000 personnel to police the religious and moral behavior of Saudis.[111] It enjoyed considerable latitude, authority, and financial resources in patrolling Saudi streets, shopping malls, and other public spaces to ensure that businesses and citizens follow Islamic laws and edicts. Predictably, this power and authority, unchecked by any formal procedural manual (in fact, Saudi Arabia has no written penal code), resulted in numerous

[108] "The World's Muslims: Unity and Diversity," *Pewforum.org*. Pew Research Center, 9 Aug. 2012. Web (http://www.pewforum.org/2012/08/09/the-worlds-muslims-unity-and-diversity-2-religious-commitment/). See Chapter 2: Religious Commitment.

[109] Ibid.

[110] al-Saad, Nora Khaled. "Committee for the Promotion of Virtue and the Prevention of Vice." *Saaid.net*. Ṣayd al-Fawā'id, n.d. Web (http://www.saaid.net/alsafinh/h42.htm).

[111] "Commission for the Promotion of Virtue and the Prevention of Vice." *ADHRB.org*. Americans for Democracy and Human Rights in Bahrain, 31 Mar. 2015. Page 2. Print and Web (http://www.adhrb.org/wp-content/uploads/2015/04/2015.03.31_Ch.-1-CPVPV.pdf).

unnecessary or even excessively violent altercations between the Hai'a and the populace it monitored.[112] Consequently, such abuse of its power instilled fear, derision, and criticism among many Saudis.[113]

Sadly, it took a fire in a girls' public intermediate school in Mecca in March 2002 to galvanize the nation and generate sufficient moral outrage to overcome its fear of the Hai'a. Fourteen students tragically died in the blaze when the members of the local CPVPV (*mutawwaʿin*) "interfered with rescue efforts because the fleeing students were not wearing the obligatory public attire (long black cloaks and head coverings) for Saudi girls and women."[114] Not only did the religious police prevent civil defense personnel, parents, and others trying to assist by blocking entry into the burning building, but it also forced evacuated girls without proper dress back into the building by beating them.[115]

In April 2016, fourteen years after this horrific and preventable tragedy, the Saudi Cabinet passed new regulations banning members of the CPVPV from "questioning, asking for identification, pursuing, arresting, and detaining any person suspected of a crime, with these duties falling to police and anti-narcotics officers."[116] Additionally, the new regulations formally delineate the qualifications and more limited duties of the *mutawwaʿin*. These regulations also establish a clearer hierarchy of administration and create an advisory committee to counsel the Hai'a president, address abuses, and hold violators accountable.[117]

Saudi Arabia's CPVPV is based on the Islamic doctrine *al-ḥisba* ("accountability"), the "divinely-sanctioned duty for Muslims to intervene when another Muslim is violating God's law,"[118] as dictated by the Qur'ān: "*...command right and forbid wrong....*" (For other verse examples, see Q 3.104, Q 3.110, Q 9.71, and Q 9.112.) However,

---

[112] Lief, Louise. "With Youth Pounding at Kingdom's Gates, Saudi Arabia Begins Religious Police Reform." *CSMonitor.com*. Christian Science Monitor, 23 May 2013. Web (http://www.csmonitor.com/World/Middle-East/2013/0523/With-youth-pounding-at-kingdom-s-gates-Saudi-Arabia-begins-religious-police-reform).

[113] Hilleary, Cecily. "Saudi Religious Police Work to Improve Image." *VOANews.com*. Voice of America, 27 Mar. 2013. Web (http://www.voanews.com/a/saudi-religious-police-polishing-their-image/1629922.html).

[114] "Saudi Arabia: Religious Police Role in School Fire Criticized." *HRW.org*. Human Rights Watch, 14 Mar. 2002. Web (https://www.hrw.org/news/2002/03/14/saudi-arabia-religious-police-role-school-fire-criticized).

[115] Ibid.

[116] "Haia Can't Chase, Arrest Suspects." *ArabNews.com*. Arab News, 14 Apr. 2016. Web (http://www.arabnews.com/featured/news/910016).

[117] Ibid.

[118] Vidino, Lorenzo. "Hisba in Europe? Assessing a Murky Phenomenon." *European Foundation for Democracy* (June 2013): 6. Print and Web (http://www.css.ethz.ch/content/dam/ethz/special-interest/gess/cis/center-for-securities-studies/pdfs/Hisba_in_Europe.pdf).

some Islamic jurists contend that only rulers (government) have this right though some Islamic fundamentalist groups insist that the duty of *al-ḥisba* is incumbent on all Muslims.[119]

Islamic State (and precursors, ISIL and ISIS) has had its own committee of "religious police," which it called the Ḥisba, in the areas and cities under its control. The Ḥisba would patrol the streets in cars and visit shops to ensure that every Muslim was dutifully following *sharīʿa* and obligatory Islamic practices. For example, the Ḥisba would force people to close their shops and go to prayers during the five daily prayer times. Anyone who refused to obey would have his or her shop permanently closed and undergo questioning in a court based on Islamic law. The shopkeeper may face additional penalties as well.

The following excerpt details an ISIS directive distributed in Raqqa, Syria, regarding the activities of businesses and pedestrians during prayer times:[120]

> Every store owner must close his shop ten minutes before the call, and likewise, every man walking in the streets must go to the mosque to perform the duty of Allah, and not to delay or sit down to talk in the streets while Muslims are in their mosques.... [W]hoever is found with his shop open during prayer time, or in the streets outside the mosques, his shop will be closed and he will be called in for a legitimate accountability.

The Ḥisba would also accost smokers to confiscate and burn their cigarettes—and sometimes more. The severed head of an Islamic State official was found in January 2015 with a cigarette in its mouth and a note attached to the corpse: "Smoking is not permissible, Sheikh."[121] Smoking is a vice especially repellant to Islamic State, which considers it a "slow suicide."[122]

Another mission of the Hisba is to monitor dress codes, especially women's clothing and the wearing of the full-face veil. As Islamic State

---

[119] Vidino, Lorenzo. "Hisba in Europe? Assessing a Murky Phenomenon." *European Foundation for Democracy* (June 2013): 6. Print and Web (http://www.css.ethz.ch/content/dam/ethz/special-interest/gess/cis/center-for-securities-studies/pdfs/Hisba_in_Europe.pdf).

[120] "Activists: Daesh [ISIS] Imposes the Full Veil and Bans Smoking and Immoral Songs in Raqqa." *Arabic. CNN.com*. Cable News Network (Arabic), 20 Jan. 2014. Web (http://arabic.cnn.com/middleeast/2014/01/20/qaeda-riqa-syria-islamic-rules).

[121] Winsor, Morgan. "ISIS Beheads Cigarette Smokers: Islamic State Deems Smoking 'Slow Suicide' Under Sharia Law." *IBTimes.com*. International Business Times, 12 Feb. 2015. Web (http://www.ibtimes.com/isis-beheads-cigarette-smokers-islamic-state-deems-smoking-slow-suicide-under-sharia-1815192).

[122] Ibid.

tightened its control in Mosul (after its fall to the terrorist organization in June 2014), it increasingly required more coverage of the woman's body, until only her eyes could be seen—behind a film of black cloth. Any violator of this strict dress code must turn over her husband's identification (ID) card. He would have to appear in court. He may then be forced to pay a sizable fine, or he or his wife may be sentenced to a whipping. One woman was whipped 21 lashes with a metal-tipped cable for the offense of lifting up her veil to eat a spoonful of food at a picnic.[123]

The use of "religious police" and the application of a stringent form of *sharī'a* (Islamic law) are all draconian measures to regulate and punish Muslims for perceived immoral behavior, improper attire and grooming, and less-than-observant religious conduct, especially concerning one's attendance and observance of the daily prayers—one of the mandatory five Pillars of Islam.

The extreme efforts by Islamic groups like Islamic State and conservative Muslim countries like Saudi Arabic to control and monitor when and how Muslims pray stems from the actions of Muḥammad himself regarding this matter. He used to get angry when his followers did not join him during prayers. The Hadith literature reports that Muḥammad considered ordering a person to lead the people in prayer and "then burn the houses with their inmates (who have not joined the congregation)."[124]

If the Prophet of Islam views death an appropriate punishment for those who are absent from the congregational prayers, then why would his followers believe otherwise? If Muḥammad wanted to burn his followers simply because they did not come to pray behind him, how much more severe the punishment if they did some other sin—such as apostasy?

Those pundits who argue that Islamic State and similar Islamic groups have nothing to do with Islam, claiming that these jihadist terrorist groups do not know or understand the true doctrine of Islam, are the same people who believe that "Islam" is the religion that is practiced by the ordinary Muslims in Muslim countries. However, the "Islam" practiced by these "ordinary Muslims" is a lenient form of the religion (fortunately for us non-Muslims), as reflected by statistics regarding the

---

[123] Callimachi, Rukmini. "For Women under ISIS, a Tyranny of Dress Code and Punishment." *NYTimes.com.* New York Times, 12 Dec. 2016. Web (https://www.nytimes.com/2016/12/12/world/middleeast/islamic-state-mosul-women-dress-code-morality.html).

[124] *Sahih Muslim*, Book of Prayers: Excellence of prayers in congregation and grim warning for remaining away from it (p. 376); *Ṣaḥīḥ Muslim*, Kītāb al-Masājid wa Mawāḍi' al-Ṣalāt 1: 293.

religious commitment of Muslims in the Muslim countries, such as the varying percentages of Muslims who do not regularly observe the daily prayers.

Yet if "ordinary Muslims" practice Islam just as it is presented in the religious texts and as it was practiced by Prophet Muḥammad, then the world would see an Islamic State in every Muslim country.

EIGHT

Inception and rise of Islamic State mirrors Islam

Examining how Islam was founded will help those who earnestly want to understand how the radical Islamic groups came to be. It is simply because these groups refer to Islam's fundamental teachings as their root and Muḥammad as their inspirer. They look up to Muḥammad's model of war tactics and invasions as their guideline: when he raided and when he fled, when he truced and when he accepted conditions. Everything they do strictly follows the Sunna of Muḥammad to the letter. They know their religious teachings inside out and turn to no other source for reference. The religious texts saturate them with the history of Islam and its conquests, with every action of Muḥammad heavily detailed. They are proud of Muḥammad's victories over neighboring tribes and his unification of the Arabian Peninsula and Islam's later conquests during the seventh and eighth centuries AD of such regions as Mesopotamia, Persia, northern Africa, Iberia (Spain), Gaul (France), central Asia, Sindh (Pakistan), and Caucasus (parts of Russia).

They sincerely believe that if Muḥammad, a lowly Meccan shepherd, could achieve these amazing accomplishments, then they can and should parallel today what he did during his life. Muḥammad's leadership style is the footprint or the "main plan" that should be followed by all Muslim leaders. Muḥammad set a high benchmark as he was not only a prophet but a remarkable military leader as well. For Muslims, he was indeed inspired of Allah to do the best.

Islam is founded by Muḥammad and his teachings based on the revelations he supposedly received from Allah. He subsequently shared these revelations with a few members from his family circle, such as his wife Khadīja, and close friends, such as fellow tribesman Abū Bakr (and later, a father-in-law of Muḥammad) and cousin ʿAlī Ibn Abī Ṭālib. Then the call started to spread only between close friends and relatives.

Similarly, today's Islamic terrorist groups are usually founded by one person. For example, Abū Muṣʿab al-Zarqāwī, an Islamic militant from Jordan, personally formed and led the militant jihadist group 'Jamaʿat al-Tawhid wal-Jihad in the 1990s (until his death in 2006).[1] Prior to America's entrance into the 2003 Iraqi War, he approached selected individuals, people close to him (family and friends), in Kurdistan to organize "sleeper cells" in Baghdad to attack US targets. He mobilized people and weaponry the exact way as Muḥammad in tactics and secrecy.

When Muḥammad began to experience hostility from some of the Meccan tribes, he tried to publicize his call beyond Mecca. After persecution from his own tribe, Muḥammad felt forced to emigrate, and he called those followers who emigrated with him the Muhājirīn (Emigrants), and he called those who welcomed and supported him and his fellow emigrants, the Anṣār (Helpers).

Emigration was imposed by Muḥammad over his followers; it became a duty that every Muslim must do. Anyone who refused to emigrate was considered a rebel, if not an infidel. Ibn Kathīr cites in his respected commentary the opinion of Companion and "Interpreter of the Qur'ān" Ibn Abbas (AD 619-687), who holds that the refusal to emigrate is an act punishable by death, according to Q 4.89 (Arberry trans.):

[1] Weaver, Mary Anne. "The Short, Violent Life of Abu Musab al-Zarqawi." *TheAtlantic.com*. Atlantic Media, July/Aug. 2006. Web (https://www.theatlantic.com/magazine/archive/2006/07/the-short-violent-life-of-abu-musab-al-zarqawi/304983/). **Note:** In 2004, this group changed its name to Tanzim Qaidat al-Jihad fi Bilad al-Rafidayn, or Jihad's Base (Al Qaeda) in Mesopotamia.

"...[The phrase] *'then, if they turn their backs,'* means 'did not emigrate' [and so] then *'take them, and slay them wherever you find them'....*"[2]

Islamic terrorist groups like Islamic State accept this interpretation and incorporate it into their recruiting outreach along with promises of assistance and housing for those who decide to leave their homelands to join these groups. Al Qaeda's Osama Bin Laden established a network of guesthouses (Bayt al-Anṣār, or "House of Comrades") for housing, vetting, and assigning recruits from Arab countries joining his organization.[3] These centers formed the core of Al Qaeda in Pakistan and Afghanistan. Of course, Osama Bin Laden understood and exploited the religious significance to Muslims of the name, Bayt al-Anṣār.

The early Muslim emigrants (Muhājirūn) who arrived in Medina were destitute with little resources, financial or otherwise. Muḥammad asked the Anṣār, the people of the Medinan Aws and Khazraj tribes who supported him, to give aid and shelter to the emigrants. So each Anṣār invited an emigrant (or sometimes an emigrant family) into his house and provided support and shelter. The hospitality of one Anṣār was so generous that he offered to divorce one of his wives and give her to his emigrant house guest in order to take care of his guest's emotional and sexual needs as well as his housing needs. The *ḥadīth* about this incident reports that Muḥammad paired emigrant 'Abdul Raḥmān Ibn Auf with host Sa'd Ibn al-Rabī', an Anṣār eager to share his wealth and possessions with his guest:[4]

> I'm the richest among the Anṣār, so I will give you half of my wealth and you may look at my two wives and whichever of the two you may choose I will divorce her, and when she has completed the prescribed period (before marriage) you may marry her.

Like the welcoming homes of the Anṣār that were used to assist and shelter the early Muslim emigrants, the network of guest houses, or Bayt al-Anṣār, in Pakistan and Afghanistan provided a haven for the foreign Al Qaeda recruits, where they received care, assistance, and training before being sent off later to the battlefronts. ISIS (and its successor, Islamic State) sweetened this support by offering recruits Muslim wives

---

[2] See the commentary on Q 4.89, *Tafsīr al-Ṭabarī* 4: 189.

[3] World Heritage Encyclopedia. "Al Anṣār Guesthouse." *Ebooklibrary.org*. World eBook Library, n.d. Web (http://www.ebooklibrary.org/articles/Al_Anṣār_guest_house).

[4] *Sahih Bukhari,* Book of Sales and Trade (p. 465); *Ṣaḥīḥ al-Bukhārī,* Kītāb al-Biyū' 2: 722. See Ibn Kathīr, *Al-Bidāya* 4: 563-564.

and sex slaves, which is a very attractive proposition to Arab Muslim men who generally marry in their thirties because of the limited access to women and the high cost of marriage in their homelands.[5]

Islamic State (and precursors, ISIL and ISIS) uses the term Muhājirīn (Emigrants) to refer to foreigners who join its ranks from European countries, Australia, North America, or even from Arab countries. Today's Anṣār (or Helpers), have been the Sunni Syrians and Iraqis, native-born citizens of the regions once controlled by ISIS (and later, Islamic State), who admire and support this Islamic group, while the foreign fighters resemble the early emigrant guests who took shelter in the houses of the Medinan Anṣār.

The Qur'ān clearly describes the Muhājirīn and the Anṣār, as exemplified in Q 8.72 (Khalifa trans.):

> *Surely, those who believed, and emigrated, and strove with their money and their lives in the cause of GOD, as well as those who hosted them and gave them refuge, and supported them, they are allies of one another....*

Given the pivotal ramifications of the Anṣār help to the early floundering Muslims, it should be no surprise that ISIS promised housing and monthly stipends to help pay for living expenses and other necessities to motivate people to join and solidify their allegiance to this organization. Besides, Muḥammad used a similar strategy after he arrived in Medina. He brought together the Muhājirīn with the Anṣār into a brotherly union and asked the Anṣār to provide the necessities for the Muhājirīn:[6]

> [As narrated by Abū Hurayra] [t]he Anṣār said (to the Prophet), "Please divide the date-palm trees between us and them (i.e., emigrants)." The Prophet said, "No." The Anṣār said, "Let them (i.e., the emigrants) do the labor for using the gardens and share the date-fruits with us." The emigrants said, "We accepted this."

In this way, Muḥammad initiated a mutually beneficial relationship between the Anṣār and the Muhājirīn, where the Muhājirīn offered their labor in exchange for half of the date-fruit harvest. By developing strong relationships between the Muhājirīn and the Anṣār, where they shared

[5] Bloom, Mia. "How ISIS Is Using Marriage as a Trap." *HuffingtonPost.com.* The Huffington Post, 2 Mar. 2015. Web (http://www.huffingtonpost.com/mia-bloom/isis-marriage-trap_b_6773576.html).

[6] *Sahih Bukhari*, Book of Merits of the Helpers in Madinah (Ansaar)(p. 885); *Ṣaḥīḥ al-Bukhārī*, Kitāb Fada'il al-Sahaba 3: 1378.

everything and encouraged intermarriage, Muḥammad was later able to easily assemble and mold them into a loyal, unified fighting force.

Similarly, Islamic jihadist groups have adopted many of the same methods used by Muḥammad to strengthen ties among their followers to secure full allegiance in times of battle and military combats, maintain morale, and reduce the likelihood of desertion or treason. The Qur'ān (Q 8.74; Palmer trans.) also uplifts and rewards this relationship between emigrants and helpers who work together for the cause of Allah: *"Those who believe and have fled and fought strenuously in God's cause, and those who have given a refuge and a help, those it is who believe; to them is forgiveness and generous provision due."*

ISIS attraction to young Muslims

Why did young Muslims emigrate from Europe, America, and other countries to join ISIS? An invitation alone might have worked with some prospective recruits, but it would be impossible to persuade thousands of young French, American, Australian, and Belgium Muslims simply by telling them that they would be better off with ISIS than by remaining in their stable, wealthy homelands. They might have been receptive if they had failed to achieve a steady rewarding career or a satisfying emotional relationship, and consequently felt resentment toward or blamed their own community or society for their woes. Perhaps they committed some sins for which they wished to seek forgiveness.

All of these reasons, whether individually or jointly, could have heightened the attraction of the land of "rebellion," making it too irresistible for some young Muslims who eagerly wanted to exchange a life of unfulfilling social duties or professional and personal failures for the promise of a house, a salary, a wife (or more), and even Yazidi girls purchased as sex slaves.

But these remain ancillary reasons. There must have been more conclusive reasons that would motivate young Muslims to engage in such a dangerous enterprise, when the risk for losing one's own life is extremely high.

A common thread in Islam is the use of invitation but with intimidation—similar to the "carrot and the stick" idiom. A Muslim does nothing without being invited or intimidated, as expressed in the Qur'ān: *"Work not confusion in the earth after the fair ordering (thereof). And call on Him in fear and hope. Lo! the mercy of Allah is nigh unto the good"* (Q 7.56; Pickthall trans.). The word "fear" in this verse refers to the torment of Allah, while "hope" refers to his paradise and bliss. Thus, when Muslims appeal to Allah, they desire to be with him in heaven but know they will enter the fires of hell if they commit evil on earth; goodness is encouraged through the eternal threat of punishment.

Fear is an essential aspect in the Islamic faith, and young Muslims are subject to its influence. They absorb, through reading and listening to the Islamic texts over the years, that if an Islamic caliphate is established that applies the law of Allah, then emigration to this Islamic state is obligatory for every Muslim. At that point, it would simply not be permissible to abide in the land of disbelief *(dār al-kufr)* when a true Islamic state, the one everyone has been expecting and waiting for, has finally materialized.

This doctrine is promoted heavily in most Islamic mosques, because it is a principle that is expressed in both the Qur'ān and the Sunna. For example, in one *ḥadīth*, Muḥammad states, "I am not responsible for any Muslim who stays among polytheists.... Their fires should not be visible to one another."[7] By this text, Muḥammad absolves himself of any responsibility for the welfare of any Muslim who would reside among or near polytheists and suggests that Muslims should not live near infidels but should migrate toward and reside among other Muslims—in this case, Muḥammad's Islamic state in Medina. The Qur'ān specifically states the duty of Muslims to emigrate to and with other believers: "*...As for those who believe, but do not emigrate with you* [Muḥammad], *you do not owe them any support, until they do emigrate...* " (Q 8.72; Khalifa trans.).

In this manner, Muḥammad, along with corroborating Qur'ānic text, intimidated his followers by urging the early emigrants to sever their relationship with those followers who did not flee with them—essentially treating them as if they were not Muslims. Other Qur'ānic verses (e.g., Q 4.97; Hilâlî-Khân trans.) even warn of eternal damnation for those believers who do not emigrate if they have the opportunity:

> *Verily! As for those whom the angels take (in death) while they are wronging themselves (as they stayed among the disbelievers even though emigration was obligatory for them), they (angels) say (to them): "In what (condition) were you?" They reply: "We were weak and oppressed on earth." They (angels) say: "Was not the earth of Allah spacious enough for you to emigrate therein?" Such men will find their abode in Hell—What an evil destination!*

---

[7] *Sunan al-Tirmidhī* 2: 387.

Therefore, emigration is considered obligatory and living among the polytheists a fearsome—and only a temporary—predicament. Thus, many young people who did decide to emigrate to Islamic State's caliphate believed that living in Western countries is dangerous—it may even be one of the greatest sins a Muslim can commit. Muḥammad himself stated, "Anyone who associates with a polytheist and lives with him, then he is like him."[8]

To better understand this dilemma facing Muslims living in non-Muslim countries, one only needs to visit Muslim Web sites that counsel Muslims on religious matters. On one such Web site, *IslamQA* (founded by Saudi sheikh Muḥammad Sālih al-Munajjid who provides information according to the Salafi school of thought), an American Arab now residing in a Muslim country sought advice about returning to America:[9]

> I have been advised by several Muslims who are knowledgeable in Islam against living in a *kāfir* [infidel] country (America). I am an American/Arab who has lived in America all my life but for a few months now I have been living in an Arabic country. However, things are getting hard for me to continue living here (lack of income, housing, etc.), and I am considering going back to America. Also another strong reason is that the health care system is better and free [in America] for my wife who is ill. Please give me as much a detailed answer from the *ḥadīth* and Qur'ān as you can as I don't know for sure if I should strive to continue living here or go back to America regarding Islam.

This reader would not have asked this question if place of residence for Muslims was an issue that did not involve sanctions. In all likelihood, he must have harbored doubts or encountered criticism, which prompted him to seek advice from a Muslim cleric to solve this problem for him from an Islamic point of view. Sheikh Muḥammad Sālih al-Munajjid gave this response:[10]

---

[8] *Sunan Abū Dawūd*, Book of *Jihād* 3: 372.

[9] al-Munajjid, Muḥammad Sālih. "Fatwa no. 27211: Should He Go Back and Live in a *Kāfir* [Infidel] Country?" *IslamQA.info/en*. Islam Question and Answer, 14 Apr. 2003. Web (https://islamqa.info/en/27211).

[10] Ibid. **Note:** Al-Munajjid cites Sheikh al-'Uthaymīn regarding legitimate reasons for staying in an infidel country: (1) The Muslim must be secure in his or her faith and maintain enmity and hatred toward all non-Muslims—no befriending, and (2) the Muslim should be able to practice his faith openly and without restriction. Business and medical treatment are permissible, but the Muslim should consider these reasons as temporary conditions and should return to the land of Islam once these conditions are resolved.

> ...The basic principle is that it is *harām* [prohibited] to settle among the *mushrikīn* [polytheists] and in their land. If Allah makes it easy for a person to move from such a country to a Muslim country, then he should not prefer that which is inferior [i.e., living in a non-Muslim country] to that which is better [living in a Muslim country] **unless he has an excuse which permits him to go back.** [Emphasis added to text not included in Arabic version of this answer.]
>
> We advise you, as others have, not to go and live in a *kāfir* country, **unless you are forced to go there temporarily, such as seeking medical treatment that is not readily available in a Muslim country.** [Emphasis added to text not included in Arabic version of this answer.]
>
> Note that whoever gives up a thing for the sake of Allah, Allah will compensate him with something better. And that with hardship comes ease, and that whosoever fears Allah and keeps his duty to Him, He will make a way for him to get out (from every difficulty), and He will provide him from (sources) he never could imagine. You should also note that preserving one's capital is better than taking a risk in the hope of making a profit; the Muslim's capital is his religion, and he should not risk it for the sake of some transient worldly gain.

The publication of this fatwa is not simply to answer this particular question but is considered a reference of high importance for all Muslims who are having the same issues about residency. This fatwa maintains that it is unlawful for Muslims to live in "lands of disbelief" unless obligated. It is also unlawful to remain in infidel countries when there are Muslim countries that apply the law of Allah.

This ruling regarding residency is part of the religious doctrine of Islam, just as in the days of Muḥammad, when the early Muslims were not allowed to remain in the same place with the polytheists if the Muslims were able to emigrate and join the state of Allah's apostle. This newly established Islamic state needed them in the army and in all sorts of trades and crafts.

The questions and answers presented on this Web site highlight the importance and supreme authority of Islam in the daily lives and decisions of devout Muslims. Unfortunately, Western political analysts and leaders, who search for local causes to explain this exodus of young people to join Islamic State and similar groups, fail to include religious reasons in their investigations. They do not acknowledge or understand the mind-set of devout Muslims, who want to abide by their religion and will feel guilty and disgraced if they do not. Instead, these Western "experts" and leaders unreasonably condemn these people, who desire to follow the tenets of their religion, deeply believing it is right, by expecting—even demanding—that these young people act contrary to their conscience.

To exclude the psychological state of Muslims and their intense desire to be committed to their religion from the equation is a grave mistake made by Westerners regarding the phenomenon of Islamic State and similar Islamic groups. They greatly underestimate these groups and continually denounce them as unfaithful to their religion and its doctrine. But the majority of these groups vehemently believe that they are following Allah's way, the absolute truth, and that death for the sake of the absolute truth should be the wish of every human who is right with himself (or herself) and with Allah.

Obligatory emigration from "infidel" countries to the land of Islam

In early 2015, Islamic State published a pamphlet addressed to its followers and other Muslims entitled, *Allegiance Must Be to Islam, Not to Homelands.*[11] The clear purpose of this pamphlet is to encourage Muslims to give their loyalty to Islam and not to their homelands, because the emigration from the "lands of disbelief" to the land of Islam is a key point emphasized by Islamic State in recruiting young people to join it. The pamphlet refers to Muḥammad, "the greatest of mankind," and his Companions who obeyed Allah's command to leave their homes, properties, and relatives to emigrate to a foreign (to them) land—Medina—because it was "the land of Islam and an Islamic state." Islamic State claims in the pamphlet that its caliphate in Iraq and Syria is also an Islamic state and as such, has become today's "land of emigration" and "an Islamic state" for Muslims. The pamphlet cites Q 4.97 (refer to page 208) to reinforce this obligation for emigration.[12]

The pamphlet also warns Muslims who would prefer to remain in their homelands and thus dishonor their obligation to emigrate to an Islamic state and those Muslims who flee "the regions of the Islamic state" to seek refuge in non-Muslim countries: "What then will Allah Almighty say on the Day of Resurrection about those who are so-called Muslims…?"[13]

Interestingly, this pamphlet is printed only in Arabic, which signifies that Islamic State considers even Arab Muslim countries as "lands of

[11] Islamic State. *Allegiance Must Be to Islam, Not to Homelands.* Al-Himma Library, Feb. 2015. Print and Web (http://preview.tinyurl.com/jhwyzlb).
[12] Ibid.
[13] Ibid.

disbelief," which Muslims must leave to join Islamic State (or regions under its control). If Islamic State considers even Arab Muslim countries as infidel countries, then their condemnation of Western countries would be even stronger and the need for Muslims to emigrate from them even more urgent.

Secondly, the pamphlet seeks to evoke an emotional response, appealing to the Muslim readers' religious sensibilities and devotion, by suggesting that the emigration of Muḥammad and his Companions is no different than the emigration of today's young Muslims to territories under Islamic State control. These words re-stimulate the euphoria and pride Muslims feel about Islam's wars, victories, and conquests—a history passionately instilled in and eulogized by Muslim children throughout their childhood. The text commemorates as it sentimentally recalls the glorious days of the early steadfast Muslims who were eager to emigrate with the Prophet and his Companions, escaping to save their religion and preparing for the major confrontation with the polytheists and infidels.

These powerful feelings of religious pride undoubtedly are present in the minds of many of those who decide to join Islamic State. It would be difficult for any Muslim, convinced of Islam's authenticity and the sincerity of the Islamic State cause, to resist these feelings and not join the *mujāhidīn*. The high risk for death does not frighten or deter them because Muḥammad and his Companions were unafraid. Possible imprisonment does not faze them because they believe in Allah's protection. They will recount events from Islamic history where they believe divine intervention spared the Prophet from harm.

One such story concerns Muḥammad's miraculous escape with his Companion Abū Bakr from the hands of their Quraysh pursuers when the two men secretly left Mecca for Medina at midnight. The night he planned to flee Mecca, Muḥammad asked his cousin 'Alī Ibn Abī Ṭālib to act as a decoy by wrapping himself in Muḥammad's green mantle and sleeping in Muḥammad's bed. Muḥammad managed to slip past the Quraysh would-be assassins lurking about his home by reciting some verses from the Qur'ān to them while Allah blinded them.[14] The following morning, when the Quraysh discovered the deceit, the tribal leaders organized a hunt for the two Muslims, but they failed to find

[14] See Ibn Hisham (Ibn Isḥāq), *The Life of Muḥammad* 222-224; Ibn Hishām (Ibn Isḥāq), *Al-Sīra al-Nabawīya* 2: 309. See the commentary on Q 8.30, *Tafsīr al-Qurtubī* 7: 397.

them hiding in a cave because Allah sent a spider to spin a web over the cave entrance.[15] In some accounts, Allah also commanded two doves to make a nest and lay eggs at the cave entrance.[16] The Quraysh concluded from the unbroken web (or the nesting doves) that no one was inside and did not search the cave.

This story cannily resembles an earlier legend ascribed to Saint Felix of Nola (d. c. AD 250), a Christian priest who was persecuted for his faith by the Roman emperor Decius. Saint Felix helped his bishop hide from soldiers in a vacant building, aided by a spider that spun a web over the door to make the site seem abandoned.[17]

These kinds of stories have become a fundamental part of the Muslim heritage and affect the Muslim listeners' emotions, often eliciting tears when heard during Friday mosque services and repeated by the Muslim teachers at school. I am confident that the young Muslims who have emigrated to join Islamic State or a similar jihadist group were inspired and guided by these stories as a basis for their decisions. Like Muḥammad and his ruses to help him slip out of Mecca undetected by the Quraysh, these young Muslims may lie to their families and airport authorities to conceal their identity and camouflage their journey to these groups in order to escape from their homelands without detection or apprehension. They may even recite the same verses Muḥammad recited during the night of his Hijra from Mecca, such as Q 36.9 (Palmer trans.): *"and we will place before them a barrier, and behind them a barrier; and we will cover them and they shall not see."* According to the Muslim view, Allah may deceive the enemy to rescue the believers, even if cheating, lies, and other deceptive means are used in the process. Allah's willingness to engage in craftiness and scheming to safeguard Muḥammad on the night of his escape is recorded in Q 8.30 (Palmer trans.): *"And when those* [Quraysh] *who misbelieve were crafty with thee to detain thee a prisoner, or kill thee, or drive thee forth* [from Mecca]*; they were crafty, but God was crafty too, for God is best of crafty ones!"*

Given the Qur'ān's approval and Muḥammad's own life examples, why should people wonder that Muslim British twin sisters of Somali

[15] See the commentary on Q 8.30, *Tafsīr al-Qurtubī* 8: 144. See also *Tafsīr Ibn Kathīr* 7: 61-63 and Ibn Kathīr, *Al Bidāya* 4: 451.

[16] See the commentary on Q 9.40, *Tafsīr al-Qurtubī* 8: 145. See also Ibn Kathīr, *Al Bidāya* 4: 452-453.

[17] Butler, Alban. "January 14: St. Felix of Nola, Priest and Confessor." *The Lives of the Saints*. Vol. 1 (Jan. 1866). Print and Web (http://www.bartleby.com/210/1/142.html).

origin copied Muḥammad's use of deception during his Hijra when they pretended to be sleeping in their beds but had really fled their home and travelled first by plane to Istanbul and then by bus to Raqqa, Syria, to join ISIS.[18] What makes these smart sixteen-year-olds leave the modern British city of Manchester to join ISIS in war-torn Raqqa? What convinced them to make such a decision that would end their relationship with their parents forever and the chances of getting back to Britain without dire consequences? What made them willing to risk their lives?

Western analysts may answer these questions by blaming the girls' actions on brainwashing. But can brainwashing happen so suddenly and to the two sisters, who were both planning to study medicine, at the same time? The only rational way to comprehend their willingness to accept (or disregard) these risks is to examine their Muslim religious belief system and its powerful drive to support and encourage such behavior. To the Western world, it seems incomprehensible for anyone to give up everything—family, home, livelihood, security—for nothing in return. But to these Muslim girls and others who believe as they do, they are leaving "the world" behind for the religious promises of Islam.

The Qur'ān clearly promises eternal religious rewards to any Muslim who emigrates and leaves everything behind for the cause of Allah, as exemplified in Q 9.20-21 (Arberry trans.):

> *Those who believe, and have emigrated, and have struggled in the way of God with their possessions and their selves are mightier in rank with God; and those—they are the triumphant; / their Lord gives them good tidings of mercy from Him and good pleasure; for them await gardens wherein is lasting bliss.*

These Qur'ānic promises to believing migrants of Allah's blessings, both now and in paradise, are the greatest incentives for today's young Muslim migration, from Arab and Western countries alike, to join jihadists—particularly Islamic State. These young Muslim recruits also find Qur'ānic permission to deceive and leave their families in service to Allah, if their families are unbelievers:

[18] Robinson, Martin. "'I Love the Name Terror Twin...I Sound Scary': What Schoolgirl Who Fled to Syria and Married an ISIS Fighter Said after Hearing Her Nickname." *Daily Mail.co.uk*. Telegraph Media Group, 8 Aug. 2014. Web (http://www.dailymail.co.uk/news/article-2718746/I-love-Terror-Twin-I-sound-scary-What-schoolgirl-fled-Syria-married-Isis-fighter-said-hearing-nickname.html).

> *O believers, take not your fathers and brothers to be your friends, if they prefer unbelief to belief; whosoever of you takes them for friends, those—they are the evildoers. / Say: 'If your fathers, your sons, your brothers, your wives, your clan, your possessions that you have gained, commerce you fear may slacken, dwellings you love—if these are dearer to you than God and His Messenger, and to struggle in His way, then wait till God brings His command; God guides not the people of the ungodly.'* (Q 9.23-24; Arberry trans.)

The great Muslim exegete al-Ṭabarī makes this statement regarding this passage: "Do not take your fathers and brothers as allies and friends...and prefer staying where they live over emigration to the land of Islam."[19] These verses clearly urge Muslims to emigrate from their "infidel" countries, leaving behind their parents, friends, and relatives, to the lands of Islam, whether it was the Islamic state under Muḥammad in seventh century AD or today's "caliphate" under Islamic State in twenty-first century AD. This Islamic command to emigrate from non-Muslim lands has been in effect continuously since Muḥammad's time. Muḥammad reaffirmed this directive in a *ḥadīth*, stating, "Emigration will not cease as long as disbelievers exist."[20]

This emigration requirement is valid today because the battle with disbelievers still exists. Islamic State recognizes and upholds this requirement in honoring Muḥammad's commands. In its magazine *Dabiq*, which targets foreigners, the topic of emigration based on Qur'ānic and Hadith literature is discussed in one edition with the front cover headline, "Call to Hijrah [Emigration]." On page 26, Muslim professionals are admonished for postponing their jihad to complete their graduate studies; their number one priority should be "to repent and answer the call to hijrah, especially after the establishment of the Khilāfah [Caliphate]."[21] (ISIS formally declared a new Islamic caliphate on June 29, 2014, after it took control of territory in Syria and Iraq and changed its name to Islamic State.)[22] Muslim professionals are urged to share their expertise to build the needed infrastructure for the new caliphate and tend to their fellow Muslims. Otherwise, their lack of

[19] See the commentary on Q 9.23, *Tafsīr al-Tabarī* 10: 69 and *Tafsīr Ibn Kathīr* 7: 164.

[20] Ibn Ḥabbān, *Ṣaḥīḥ Ibn Ḥabbān* 5: 131.

[21] "Introduction: Hijrah from Hypocrisy to Sincerity." *Dabiq*. Issue 3 (Aug. 2014): 25-26. Print and Web (http://www.ieproject.org/projects/dabiq3.pdf).

[22] Bradley, Matt. "ISIS Declares New Islamist Caliphate." *WSJ.com*. Wall Street Journal, 29 June 2014. Web (http://www.wsj.com/articles/isis-declares-new-islamist-caliphate-1404065263).

obedience will become evidence used against them on Judgment Day. The article stresses that this call is particularly obligatory for students who have prioritized their studies over jihad. Their emigration from the land of disbelief (*dār al-kufr*) to the land of Islam (*dār al-Islam*) and jihad is "more obligatory and urgent" than studying for years exposed "to doubts and desires that will destroy their religion and thus end...any possible future of jihād."[23] If religious appeals are not persuasive enough, Islamic State adds in a later section that "money and accommodations for yourself and your family" will be provided to those who take up the call and emigrate.[24]

In the eighth issue of *Dabiq*, Umm Sumayyah al-Muhājirah (Umm Sumayyah "the Emigrant"), the female author of a six-page article entitled "The Twin Halves of the Muhājirīn [Emigrants]" appeals to female readers to leave their families and homelands and emigrate to the lands of the Islamic State. Besides citing verses from the Qur'ān (e.g., Q 9.100, Q 4.97, Q 60.10) to support the obligatory ruling regarding *hijra* for women as well as men, she attempts to inspire readers with stories of resolute, honorable female emigrants and the hardships and sacrifices they endured to reach Islamic State.[25]

As an emigrant herself, she explains the advantages of being shielded against the influence of drifting from the right path of Islam and joining other Muslims in their jihad and strengthening them. She says that emigration means exiting from disbelief and entering in belief.[26]

She also refers to Ibn Kathīr's interpretation of Q 4.97 and quotes from his commentary: "'The āyah [verse] indicates the general obligation of hijrah. So everyone who lives amongst the mushrikīn [polytheists] while being able to perform hijrah and not being able to establish his religion, then he is wronging himself and committing sin....'"[27]

On page 28 of the same edition is a photo of a young man, pulling a suitcase toward a departure gate at an airport, with the caption, "Abandon the Lands of Shirk [Disbelief]." Page 29 displays another man, carrying a backpack, with the Islamic State flag in the background. The caption

[23] "Introduction: Hijrah from Hypocrisy to Sincerity." *Dabiq*. Issue 3 (Aug. 2014): 26. Web (http://www.ieproject.org/projects/dabiq3.pdf).
[24] Ibid. 33.
[25] Sumayyah, Umm. "The Twin Halves of the Muhājirīn." *Dabiq*. Issue 8 (Mar.-Apr. 2015): 32-37. Web (https://azelin.files.wordpress.com/2015/03/the-islamic-state-e2809cdc481biq-magazine-8e280b3.pdf).
[26] Ibid. 32.
[27] See the commentary on Q 4.97, *Tafsīr Ibn Kathīr* 4: 228. Umm Sumayyah quotes his commentary in her article (p. 33).

below reads, "And Come to the Land of Islam." Both pages include *ḥadīths* that discourage residency in the land of disbelief.[28]

Emigrants' significance in Islamic jihadist organizations

The title *al-Muhājirah* (the Emigrant) used by author Umm Sumayyah is not a frivolous addition and is frequently used by many Islamic State fighters who come from homelands other than Iraq and Syria. This designation is a source of pride for many Muslim males and females, because the early followers who migrated with Muḥammad were honored by him with this title.

The Hijra, or emigration of Muḥammad from Mecca to Medina, is considered the ground zero of Islam. Even Islam's calendar begins with this event. Those Muslims who emigrated with Muḥammad, establishing the first Muslim community in Medina, became the first Islamic state and nucleus of his eventual military force. During Muḥammad's first battle, the Battle of Badr, against his Quraysh tribesmen, about a quarter of his fighters were Emigrants—out of 314 fighters, 83 were Emigrants.[29]

Foreign fighters have formed the bulk of Islamic State's military force. Iraqi Prime Minister Ḥaydar al-'Abādī estimated that the number of foreign fighters within the organization was about sixty percent of the total number (60,000) in 2015, though other estimations conflict with these figures.[30]

According to a report from the United Nations' Security Council, the number of foreign fighters joining jihadist groups in 2015 reached 25,000 and perhaps as many as 30,000.[31] These figures mean that the number of emigrants who fled to join Islamic State had been equal to or surpassed the number of local supporters. Nearly a fifth were "residents or nationals of Western European countries."[32]

---

[28] *Dabiq*. Issue 8 (Mar.-Apr. 2015): 28-29. Web (https://azelin.files.wordpress.com/2015/03/the-islamic-state-e2809cdc481biq-magazine-8e280b3.pdf).

[29] Ibn Hishām (Ibn Isḥāq), *The Life of Muḥammad* 330, 336; Ibn Hishām (Ibn Isḥāq) *Al-Sīra al-Nabawīya* 3: 164.

[30] Shri, Rima. "Between London [January 2015] and Paris Conferences [June 2015]: 'Islamic State' Records a Rise in the Number of Fighters." *Alquds.co.uk*. Al-Quds al-Arabi, 6 June 2015. Web (http://www.alquds.co.uk/?p=352996).

[31] Ibid.

[32] Neumann, Peter R. "Foreign Fighter Total in Syria/Iraq Now Exceeds 20,000; Surpasses Afghanistan Conflict in the 1980s." *ICSR.info*. International Centre for the Study of Radicalisation and Political Violence, 26 Jan. 2015. Web (http://icsr.info/2015/01/foreign-fighter-total-syriairaq-now-exceeds-20000-surpasses-afghanistan-conflict-1980s/).

It is unremarkable that many of them originated from France, Germany, United Kingdom, Belgium, and the Netherlands because these countries are home to many Muslim communities, especially Muslims from North Africa (Morocco and Algeria, in particular).[33] The Arab world also contributed to these foreign fighter totals (September-October 2015): Tunisia (6000); Saudi Arabia (2500); Jordan (2000+) and Morocco (1200), my country of origin.[34] These numbers signify the importance of emigration in the hearts of these foreign fighters, who have committed themselves to the same religious directive—to physically defend fellow Muslims in areas of conflict around the world—that has inspired jihad amongst Muslims in other earlier political conflicts and warfare.

With the loss of Raqqa, the administrative capital of Islamic State, in October 2017 as well as tighter borders and heavier fighting, the emigration of foreign fighters dramatically slowed to a standstill. At one time 2000 foreign recruits a month were crossing the Turkey-Syria border to join Islamic State, but now many of these foreign fighters are leaving the battlefield. Collected data indicates that about "30% of the approximately 5000 residents of the European Union" from the Syrian and Iraqi battlefronts "had returned home."[35] Some, however, have chosen not to return to their European homelands but to countries in South East Asia, "whether or not advised to do so by IS leaders."[36]

But celebration over this heartening news should be tempered with the worry that this decline "may be the beginning of a new stage, one in which would-be fighters choose to carry out attacks at home rather than travel abroad, and battle-hardened veterans seek out new land for conflict."[37] According to a Soufan Center report, a realization of this threat will depend heavily on the "attitude and ability of the surviving

---

[33] Hackett, Conrad. "5 Facts about the Muslim Population in Europe." *PewResearch.org*. Pew Research Center, 19 July 2016. Web (http://www.pewresearch.org/fact-tank/2016/07/19/5-facts-about-the-muslim-population-in-europe/).

[34] The Soufan Group. *Foreign Fighters: An Updated Assessment of the Flow of Foreign Fighters into Syria and Iraq* (Dec. 2015): 7-10. Print and Web (http://soufangroup.com/wp-content/uploads/2015/12/TSG_ForeignFightersUpdate_FINAL3.pdf).

[35] The Soufan Center. *Beyond the Caliphate: Foreign Fighters and the Threat of Returnees.* (Oct. 2017): 10. Print and Web (http://thesoufancenter.org/wp-content/uploads/2017/10/Beyond-the-Caliphate-Foreign-Fighters-and-the-Threat-of-Returnees-TSC-Report-October-2017.pdf).

[36] Ibid.

[37] Witte, Griff, Sudarsan Raghavan, and James McAuley. "Flow of Foreign Fighters Plummets As Islamic State Loses Its Edge." *WashingtonPost.com*. The Washington Post, 9 Sept. 2016. Web (https://www.washingtonpost.com/world/europe/flow-of-foreign-fighters-plummets-as-isis-loses-its-edge/2016/09/09/ed3e0dda-751b-11e6-9781-49e591781754_story.html?utm_term=.4d3ccfbbfd03).

members...of over 40,000 foreigners who flocked to join IS...before and after the declaration of the caliphate in June 2014.... [I]t is inevitable that some will remain committed to...violent jihad...."[38]

The active, foreign Muslim response and application of these religious teachings regarding the obligatory emigration to pursue jihad gathered momentum during the (and still ongoing) Israeli-Palestinian hostilities (beginning full-scale with the 1947-1948 civil war), the Soviet-Afghan War (1978-1989), the intervention of American forces in Iraq (Persian Gulf War, 1990-1991; Iraq War 2003-2011), the Bosnian War (1992-1995) and the First and Second Chechen Wars (1994-1996; 1999-2000).

With all these successive conflicts, many Muslims, who were raised with and believed in the obligatory duty to emigrate to these troubled areas to help their Muslim brethren, heeded this call. During the Soviet-Afghan War, it is estimated that over 20,000 foreigners came to join Afghanistan's *mujāhidīn*.[39] (Osama Bin Laden, a wealthy Saudi, helped funnel money, arms, and fighters to the *mujāhidīn*. He founded Al Qaeda in 1988.) The continuous religious appeal for foreign Muslim jihadists over the past forty years, along with increasingly deeper funding (through oil money), greater and easier travel access, and faster and far-reaching communication ultimately created the critical mass necessary to eventually produce Islamic State and enable it to grow quickly.

During 1992 to 1993 when I was studying at the University of Hassan II at Casablanca, students who supported the Moroccan Islamic association, Al-'Adl wal Ihsan (Justice and Charity),[40] used to organize rallies and weeks of awareness to motivate fellow students to unite with Muslims around the world. They would demonstrate holding pictures of murdered Palestinian children, bloody body parts of killed Bosnian Muslims, and Israeli or Serbian soldiers attacking Muslims. I used to see many angry young Muslims shouting slogans and denouncing the

---

[38] The Soufan Center. *Beyond the Caliphate: Foreign Fighters and the Threat of Returnees.* (Oct. 2017): 7. Print and Web (http://thesoufancenter.org/wp-content/uploads/2017/10/Beyond-the-Caliphate-Foreign-Fighters-and-the-Threat-of-Returnees-TSC-Report-October-2017.pdf).

[39] Neumann, Peter R. "Foreign Fighter Total in Syria/Iraq Now Exceeds 20,000; Surpasses Afghanistan Conflict in the 1980s." *ICSR.info*. International Centre for the Study of Radicalisation and Political Violence, 26 Jan. 2015. Web (http://icsr.info/2015/01/foreign-fighter-total-syriairaq-now-exceeds-20000-surpasses-afghanistan-conflict-1980s/).

[40] This Moroccan Islamic group was founded by an extremely charismatic leader, Sheikh Abdesslam Yassine (d. AD 2012), who called for regime change in Morocco, advocating for the transformation of Morocco into an Islamic state based on and ruled by *sharī'a*. Though the Moroccan government has never permitted the group to become a political party, its followers are still vocal and influential. Today, Mohammad Abbadi is secretary-general of this group, and Yassine's daughter, Nadia, is leader of the feminist branch.

silence of Arab governments concerning these atrocities and appealing to fellow Muslims to unite in jihad against their enemies. These protesters would use the Islamic Arabic term *nafīr*, which is a public call to action requiring any member of a jihadi group to travel to a country selected for a holy war in the name of Allah.[41]

They particularly highlighted jihad as their prime goal and would remind Muslims of Muḥammad's victorious battles and conquests, chanting jihadi Qur'ānic verses that promise victory and empowerment, as well as jihadist songs—the same songs that I have heard on videos produced by Al Qaeda and Islamic State. All these activities and events were seen and heard by the university administration and security forces. The authorities' lack of response suggests agreement or acquiescence with the activities of this officially illegal Muslim group.

I wonder how many other universities were overrun by such speech in Morocco back in the 1990s when Al-'Adl wal Iḥsān was the dominating student group? How many mosques and universities in the Arab Muslim world were and still are allowing such speeches and activities with this viewpoint?

Behold, the time has come for the Islamic world to reap what it has been planting in the hearts of its students. For yesterday's students are today's fighters. Those fiery speeches and politically charged activities have not gone unheeded; they have produced a generation that has only one concern and that is fighting and going to war—jihad—on behalf of all Muslims. There is no need to wonder why there are thousands of fighters from Tunisia, Morocco, and Saudi Arabia ready to emigrate to groups like Islamic State. Anyone who attended these kinds of Muslim universities and heard these students' speeches and Friday sermons would never wonder. Only extreme security measures by the governments of Tunisia, Morocco, Saudi Arabia, and others have limited undoubtedly countless numbers of these fighters willing to emigrate and become jihadists. A poll undertaken in 2015 by Al Jazeera supports this claim. To the question, "Do you consider the advancement of the Islamic State

[41] Kochavi, Adi, and Rachael Levy. "Jihadis Are Seething at Russia Over Crimea—Will It Boil Over?" *CounterJihadReport.com*. Counter Jihad Report, 20 Mar. 2014. Web (https://counterjihadreport.com/tag/nafir/). **Note:** *Nafīr* "was declared in the early stages of the conflicts in Syria and Egypt, and it helped spark jihadi migrations into these nations."

in Iraq and Syria a benefit to the region?" over 81 percent of the 56,000 respondents said, "Yes."[42]

If the minds of these young Muslims had not already been readied for this militant jihadist mind-set, the propaganda of Islamic State would not have encountered such alarming susceptibility in young people. Young Muslims in Europe would not have so quickly and easily joined Islamic State and similar groups if they had not heard repeatedly the incitant religious speeches convincing them that the Islamic nation confronts an infidel world continually conspiring to destroy it. Emigration to an Islamic state, wherever jihad is necessary, is the first step toward restoring Islam's past glories.

Today France, Germany, Great Britain, and Belgium are inundated with mosques that openly broadcast hate speech about infidels or non-Muslims without fear of punishment. These Muslim speakers and leaders exploit the democratic principle and Western laws upholding freedom of religion to shield their inflammatory and subversive rhetoric from legal challenges and charges. Hypocritically, these Muslims believe in freedom of religion when they can benefit by it, but they will deny that same freedom for religions other than Islam in Muslim countries.

But should this freedom of religion allow the freedom of speech that denigrates and advocates violence toward those of different religious beliefs?

Effect of emigrant leadership on ISIS escalation

Many of the founders of the Islamic groups that arose during the last fifty years were emigrants. Abū Muṣ'ab al-Zarqāwī, founder of Jamā'at al-Tawḥīd wal-Jihād (Organization of Monotheism and Jihad), was a Jordanian who emigrated to Iraq, where he pledged an oath of allegiance to Osama Bin Laden and renamed his group Qā'idat al-Jihād fī Bilād al-Rāfidayn (Jihad's Base in Mesopotamia). At this point, his group was a branch of Al Qaeda, but over time it eventually evolved through subsequent mergers and changes into Islamic State. (See page 204.) Bin Laden, a founder of Al Qaeda, was himself an emigrant from Saudi Arabia, and his successor, Ayman al-Ẓawāhirī (b. AD 1951), another emigrant, was born and raised in Egypt.

---

[42] "Poll: Do You Consider the Advancement of the Organization of Islamic State in Iraq and Syria a Benefit to the Region?" *Aljazeera.net*. Al Jazeera Media Network, 22-28 May 2015. Web (http://www.aljazeera.net/votes/pages?voteid=5270).

Another founder of Al Qaeda and a mentor to Osama Bin Laden was 'Abd Allāh 'Azzām (AD 1941-1989), also known as the "Father of the Afghani Jihad." He too was an emigrant. A Palestinian Sunni scholar and theologian, he left his homeland to help the Afghan *mujāhidīn* against the Soviet army. He was instrumental in organizing guest houses in Pakistan and military training camps in Afghanistan for foreign fighters. In one of his books, *Join the Caravan*, Azzam urges Muslims everywhere to come to the defense of Muslim victims of aggression, wrest Muslim lands from foreign domination, and protect and defend the Islam religion.[43] He also preached that jihad was the fighting and killing of all occupiers of Muslim lands and that jihad was a **global obligation**, an unprecedented expansion of a Muslim's duty to fight against enemies of Islam[44] (emphasis added).

Emigrants can also be found among the roster of Islamic State leaders. One of the most important field commanders in the organization (before his death in 2016 as a result of an American airstrike) was Abū 'Umar al-Shīshānī, or Abū Omar the Chechen.[45] Born Tarkhan Batirashvili, this Georgian Chechen veteran of the 2008 Russo-Georgian War became a jihadist after his discharge. Before joining Islamic State, he fought with a variety of Islamic military groups in Syria's civil war and was the leader of the rebel group Katībat al-Muhājirīn (Emigrants Brigade) and its successor, Jaysh al-Muhājirīn wal-Anṣār (Army of Emigrants and Supporters). These groups consisted of foreign fighters, including those with Chechen origins.[46]

In 2014, Abū 'Umar al-Shīshānī appeared with ISIL spokesman Abū Muḥammad al-'Adnānī in an Arabic-language ISIL video entitled, *Breaking of the Borders.*[47] During the short video, ISIL fighters perform a

---

[43] Azzam, Abdullah. *Join the Caravan*, 1987, 1991 (2nd English ed.). *English.Religion.info*. Religiscope, 1 Feb. 2002. Web (http://english.religion.info/2002/02/01/document-join-the-caravan/).

[44] Azzam, Abdullah. *Defence of the Muslim Lands: The First Obligation after Iman*, 1979, 2002 (2nd English ed.). Trans. Brothers in Ribatt. *English.Religion.info*. Religiscope, 1 Feb. 2002. Web (http://english.religion.info/2002/02/01/document-defence-of-the-muslim-lands/).

[45] "Islamic State Confirms Key Commander Omar Shishani Dead." *BBC.com*. British Broadcasting Corporation, 13 July 2016. Web (http://www.bbc.com/news/world-middle-east-36789635).

[46] al-Shishani, Murad Batal. "Syria Crisis: Omar Shishani, Chechen Jihadist Leader." *BBC.com*. British Broadcasting Corporation, 3 Dec. 2013. Web (http://www.bbc.com/news/world-middle-east-25151104).

[47] Strickland, Adam. "Iraq: ISIL Leaders al-Adnani and al-Shishani Celebrate 'Dissolution of Sykes-Picot Borders.'" *Fundforfallenallies.org*. Fund for Fallen Allies, 1 July 2014. Web (http://fundforfallenallies.org/news/2014/07/01/iraq-isil-leaders-al-adnani-and-al-shishani-celebrate-dissolution-sykes-picot). **Note:** Article includes a transcript summary and English translation of ISIL video *Breaking of the Borders*. See Islamic State of Iraq and al-Sham (ISIS). *Breaking of the Borders. Jihadology.net*. Al-I'tisām Media. 29 June 2014. Video. (To view video, see URL: http://preview.tinyurl.com/yd8yhfaf)

symbolic demolition of the border between Syria and Iraq by dismantling a boundary berm. Al-ʿAdnānī repudiates the borders set into place by the West (Sykes-Picot Agreement)[48] in Islamic lands, claiming these divisions were intended to prevent Muslims from moving to their lands and thus weaken the Islamic nation. (His claim evokes the conspiracy theory, the Islamic belief that the infidel world is constantly trying to convert or destroy the Islamic world. See Chapter 1, page 20.) He praises the *mujāhidīn* for confronting and battling the infidels and working to restore the Caliphate, so that Allah's law will at last prevail in one Muslim Caliphate.

One of the most prominent emigrants within the jihadist Islamic organization was "Jihadi John," who appeared in several ISIL videos. Though dubbed "Jihadi John" by the media—in part because of his British accent—his real name was Muḥammad Jassim Emwazi. He was born in 1988 in Kuwait but moved with his parents to live in London when he was six years old. He studied at Westminster University, where he earned a degree in information systems and business management.[49]

His radicalization appears to have started during his teen years. He and his friends and associates were impressed and influenced by Muslim scholar and sheikh, Hānī al-Sibāʿī.[50] Emwazi first joined jihadist militant groups in Syria in 2012 or 2013 and then later joined the ranks of ISIL.[51]

His public persona as propagandist and representative began in August 2014, when he appeared in a shocking and grisly video. Masked and dressed in black, he blames the American government for its "aggression toward the Islamic State" and threatens US President Barack Obama with "bloodshed of your people" if he denies "the Muslims their rights

---

[48] "Sykes-Picot Agreement." *Brittanica.com*. Encyclopædia Brittanica, Inc., 2017. Web (https://www.britannica.com/event/Sykes-Picot-Agreement).

[49] Topping, Alexandra, Josh Halliday, and Nishaat Ismail. "Who is Mohammed Emwazi? From Shy, Football-Loving Boy to ISIS Killer." *TheGuardian.com*. The Guardian, 13 Nov. 2015. Web (https://www.theguardian.com/uk-news/2015/mar/02/who-is-mohammed-emwazi-from-lovely-boy-to-islamic-state-executioner).

[50] Ibid. **Note:** Hānī al-Sibāʿī is an Egyptian Muslim scholar who was a member of Egyptian Islamic Jihad. He lives now in London as a political refugee and supports Al Qaeda, which refers to his teachings. Efforts to deport him have been unsuccessful. Current Al Qaeda leader Ayman al-Ẓawāhirī considers him one of four scholars that Muslims should follow.

[51] Ibid.; Mekhennet, Souad, and Adam Goldman. "'Jihadi John': Islamic State Killer Is Identified as Londoner Mohammed Emwazi." *WashingtonPost.com*. The Washington Post, 26. Feb. 2015. Web (http://preview.tinyurl.com/mhv58k8).

of living in safety under the Islamic Caliphate."[52] After uttering these statements, the black-cladded terrorist beheads American journalist James Foley and threatens to kill another hostage, Steven Sotloff, an American-Israeli journalist.[53]

In September 2014, Steven Sotloff was beheaded by "Jihadi John" (Emwazi) as a "second message to America" to stop air strikes in Iraq. The execution was again posted online in a video and followed the same scenario: Emwazi, masked and dressed in black, brandishing a knife, with Sotloff dressed in an orange jumpsuit kneeling before him. Sotloff reads a message, obviously scripted by his captors, before Emwazi concludes with more threats to the United States (and to yet another captive) and then kills Sotloff.[54] (See Chapter 9, page 252).

Before his own targeted death in November 2015 by a US drone strike,[55] Emwazi had purportedly beheaded or participated in the killings, with each instance then posted online, of these abducted men: David Haines, British aid worker (September 2014); Alan Henning, British aid worker (October 2014); Peter Kassig, American Army veteran and aid worker, along with nearly two dozen Syrian soldiers (November 2014); Haruna Yukawa and Kenji Goto, Japanese nationals (January 2015).[56]

"Jihadi John" is one of the emigrants who was masterfully exploited by Islamic State as an extremely effective and compelling propaganda tool because he could deliver the organization's messages to the West in English and he himself emigrated from a Western country. Islamic State also capitalized on his riveting presence on camera and his steeliness in carrying out these atrocities, quickly realizing his words and actions would command immediate attention and devastate the victims' families, demoralize its enemies, and thrill its supporters. The identification of

---

[52] "IS Beheads Captured American James Wright Foley, Threatens to Execute Steven Joel Sotloff." *News.SITEintelgroup.com*. SITE Intelligence Group, 19 Aug. 2014. Web (http://preview.tinyurl.com/mg23aga).

[53] Ibid.

[54] Carter, Chelsea J., and Ashley Fantz. "ISIS Video Shows Beheading of American Journalist Steven Sotloff." *CNN.com*. Cable News Network, 9 Sept. 2014. Web (http://www.cnn.com/2014/09/02/world/meast/isis-american-journalist-sotloff/).

[55] Osborne, Samuel, and Henry Austin. "ISIS Confirms 'Jihadi John' Was Killed in Drone Strike." *Independent.co.uk*. The Independent, 19 Jan. 2016. Web (http://www.independent.co.uk/news/world/middle-east/isis-confirms-jihadi-john-is-dead-a6822016.html).

[56] Khomami, Nadia. "Mohammed Emwazi: Who Were His Victims?" *TheGuardian.com*. The Guardian, 13 Nov. 2015. Web (http://preview.tinyurl.com/n6t9yfs); Hall, John. "ISIS Mass Beheading Video Took Up to Six HOURS to Film and Cost $200,000: Forensic Analysis of Syrian Soldier Murders Reveals Clues That Could Help Nail Jihadi John." *DailyMail.co.uk*. Telegraph Media Group, 8 Dec. 2014. Web (http://preview.tinyurl.com/odwrbnn).

"Jihadi John" and his capture or elimination became a top priority for Western forces. Though the Western allies were reasonably certain he had been killed by an air strike in November 2015, his death was not confirmed by Islamic State until January 2016. His death carried great symbolic significance for the United States and its allies, because, up to that time, they had been largely ineffective in crippling Islamic State or removing it from the territory it had overtaken and controlled in Syria and Iraq.[57]

As an emigrant, Emwazi's role as "executioner-in-chief" and leading propagandist rather than a military field position was unique. Half or more of the striking forces of Islamic State are emigrants.[58] Hundreds of foreign fighters from Chechnya,[59] with battle-hardened experience from their war against the Russians, have been extremely useful to Islamic State for their firsthand knowledge and application of military tactics and their training and familiarity with different types of weapons. Islamic State has used these jihadist Chechen fighters to provide logistical and military support and training for the various battalions and the newly recruited fighters.

Besides this exploitation of and reliance on experienced emigrant fighters, Islamic State depends on emigrants for its suicide attacks. They have been the spearhead for opening difficult and well-fortified military targets. For example, before each mounted attack by a military force, a series of suicide attacks is carried out to disable or help destroy targeted forts.

Islamic State finds the use of emigrants in suicide attacks an advantageous strategy. For these acts of "martyrdom," Islamic State tends to select young emigrants, who are separated from their families, their homeland social ties and familiar social surroundings, rather than local supporters who often have families and many social relations and responsibilities—connections that complicate making the decision to kill one's self and others. Also, these foreign jihadists are generally enthusiastic

---

[57] Osborne, Samuel, and Henry Austin. "ISIS Confirms 'Jihadi John' Was Killed in Drone Strike." *Independent.co.uk*. The Independent, 19 Jan. 2016. Web (http://www.independent.co.uk/news/world/middle-east/isis-confirms-jihadi-john-is-dead-a6822016.html).

[58] Thorp, Gene, and Swati Sharma. "Foreign Fighters Flow to Syria." *WashingtonPost.com*. The Washington Post, 27 Jan. 2015. Web (https://www.washingtonpost.com/world/foreign-fighters-flow-to-syria/2015/01/27/7fa56b70-a631-11e4-a7c2-03d37af98440_graphic.html?utm_term=.63198ff05c56).

[59] The Soufan Group. *Foreign Fighters: An Updated Assessment of the Flow of Foreign Fighters into Syria and Iraq*. (Dec. 2015): 14. Print and Web (http://soufangroup.com/wp-content/uploads/2015/12/TSG_ForeignFightersUpdate_FINAL3.pdf).

recruits (they sacrificed and traveled great distances to join) who have already been immersed in and are committed to the martyrdom ideology before they even left their homelands.[60]

Islamic State, in fact, has a special battalion called Katībat al-Istishhādīyin, or "Martyrs Battalion." Most of its members are foreign fighters. British newspaper *Daily Mail* states that Islamic State focuses on foreigners for the suicide operations because most of them have no experience in fighting, and thus they have no military value in the confrontations—unless they are used in suicide attacks.[61] According to the newspaper article, Islamic State experienced a shortage of suicide bombers in early 2015 after dozens of would-be suicide bombers either deserted the "Martyrs Battalion," defected to rival militias, or fled the battlefield without carrying out their suicide mission. Islamic State set up roadblocks, intensified security checks, and threatened summary execution for any deserter or defector in an effect to halt the rebellion.[62]

Several reasons for these defections include (1) Islamic State defeat in the critical battle for the northern Syrian town of Kobane, despite the efforts of many suicide bombers (suggesting wasteful use of lives); (2) fear of dying at the hands of Kurdish fighters; (3) loss of several high-ranking Islamic State commanders to sustained airstrikes from Western and Arab warplanes (which would reduce morale); (4) realization that training camps for new recruits separates the foreigners with little military experience from the others and prepares them for suicide operations.[63]

One British security source mentioned that some of the young Muslims who travel to Syria, "thinking they will be treated like equal brothers by IS find out very quickly that they are being told to strap on suicide vests and prepare for Jannah [heaven].... [I]t's hardly surprising that they [would] have cold feet about these missions."[64]

Muḥammad also relied on his Emigrants in his combat operations. Although the Emigrants formed about a quarter of his army in the Battle

---

[60] al-Manūrī, Hanān. "The Secret behind Daesh [ISIS] Preference for Foreign Fighters." *Alarabiya.net*. Al Arabiya Network, 11 Dec. 2014. Web (http://preview.tinyurl.com/zqznb6h).

[61] Verkaik, Robert, and John Hall. "Is ISIS Running Out of Suicide Bombers? Terror Group Suffers Shortage of Martyrs after Dozens of Fighters Desert or Defect to Rival Militias." *DailyMail.co.uk*. Telegraph Media Group, 9 Feb. 2015. Web (http://preview.tinyurl.com/ndtxl8o).

[62] Ibid.

[63] Verkaik, Robert, and John Hall. "Is ISIS Running Out of Suicide Bombers? Terror Group Suffers Shortage of Martyrs after Dozens of Fighters Desert or Defect to Rival Militias." *DailyMail.co.uk*. Telegraph Media Group, 9 Feb. 2015. Web (http://preview.tinyurl.com/ndtxl8o).

[64] Ibid.

of Badr, for example, according to Islamic historical records almost half of those who died were emigrants: six out of every fourteen people.[65]

As of early 2017, the percentage of foreign fighters used in Islamic State's suicide bombing missions actually declined even though the number of such missions escalated, "rising from 61 bombings in December 2015 to a record-breaking 132 in November 2016."[66] Only 20 percent of these bombers were foreign fighters, while the rest were Iraqi or Syrian (local fighters).[67] Unlike the earlier bombings by primarily foreign fighters against civilian targets, more recent suicide bombings carried out by local fighters are chiefly against military targets, its use increasingly a strategic military tactic.[68]

Local supporters' role within Islamic jihadist groups

What is the duty and place of the local supporters of Islamic groups like Islamic State? Some Islamic leaders consider them the incubator, the future, of the establishment of a pure Islamic state. Medina was Muḥammad's incubator, while the Sunni areas of Iraq and Syria are the "Medina" for today's Islamic State. Just as people in Medina welcomed Muḥammad and formed an alliance with him against the Meccan Quraysh, the predominantly Sunni regions in Iraq and Syria welcomed ISIL (precursor to Islamic State) and formed an alliance with it against the Syrian Alawites (Syrian President Bashar al-Assad is himself an Alawite) and the Iraqi Shiites.

Islamic State and similar groups seek to follow Muḥammad's plan and applications for establishing an Islamic state. They study Muḥammad's biography and the Hadith literature to guide them in the formulation of their military tactics and war plans. They note, for example, that once Muḥammad consolidated his control over the communities in and around Medina, creating a safe haven for himself and his followers, he used Medina as his base for launching raids and battles and exterminating or expelling enemy tribes. His effort—to destabilize surrounding regions by fomenting conflict among the various tribes and undertaking a

---

[65] Ibn Qayyīm al-Jawzīya, *Zādu al-Ma'ād* 3: 169; see chapter "The Battle of Badr."

[66] Grierson, Jamie. "ISIS Has Industrialized Martyrdom, Says Report into Suicide Attacks." *TheGuardian.com*. The Guardian, 28 Feb. 2017. Web (https://www.theguardian.com/world/2017/feb/28/isis-has-industrialised-martyrdom-says-report-suicide-attacks).

[67] Ibid.

[68] Winter, Charlie. "War by Suicide: A Statistical Analysis of the Islamic State's Martyrdom Industry." *The International Centre for Counter-Terrorism – The Hague* 8.3 (2017). Print and Web (https://icct.nl/publication/war-by-suicide-a-statistical-analysis-of-the-islamic-states-martyrdom-industry/).

campaign of violence to expose the weakness of rival leaders and attract followers—has been described by a modern-day jihadist strategist, Abū Bakr Nājī, as Muḥammad's plan to create a spreading network of "regions of savagery."[69] From these "regions of savagery," Muḥammad then "managed" these "regions of savagery," areas that had succumbed to social and political chaos and barbarism, by instituting measures to restore order and establishing an Islamic state.[70]

Abū Bakr Nājī's book, *Idārat al-Tawaḥḥush: Akhtar Marhala sa-Tamurru biha al-'Umma* (*The Management of Savagery: The Most Critical State Through Which the Umma Will Pass*) was posted online in 2004 (and translated into English in 2006). Called the "*Mein Kampf* of jihad" by *The Washington Post* newspaper, its manifesto has become a key blueprint for Islamic State's goals, policies, and justification. (The author's name, Abū Bakr Nājī, is believed to be a pseudonym for an unidentified strategist or strategists of Al Qaeda's politico-military doctrine.)[71]

Early in his book, Nājī discusses the use of the "administration of savagery" in Islamic history:[72]

> The administration of savagery has been established in our Islamic history various times. The first example of it was the beginning of the Islamic state in Medina.... Of course, Medina was not suffering from savagery before the hijra of the Prophet...but it was previously administered by tribes like the Aws and the Khazraj with an order that resembled the order of the administration of savagery. When Muḥammad...emigrated to Medina and its leadership elements gave allegiance to him, Medina in that first period was administered by the Muslims with a similar order (to that of the Aws and Khazraj); however, it was an ideal order for the administration of savagery....

As a *mujāhīd* and a leader in Al Qaeda, Nājī states that "...even if we generally follow in the footsteps of the Prophet...and his Companions..., we only accept that our policies in any jihadi action are Sharia policies...."[73]

The "footsteps of the Prophet," which Nājī boldly outlines in his book as stages necessary for the establishment of an Islamic state, have become the instructions set for Islamic State and similar groups. This

---

[69] Nājī, *Idārat al-Tawaḥḥush* 12, 16-17.
[70] Ibid. 17-18.
[71] Polk, William R. "Sayyid Qutub's Fundamentalism and Abu Bakr Naji's Jihadism." *MEPC.org*. Middle East Policy Council, 1 Dec. 2013. Web (http://www.mepc.org/commentary/sayyid-qutubs-fundamentalism-and-abu-bakr-najis-jihadism).
[72] Nājī, *Idārat al-Tawaḥḥush* 12.
[73] Ibid.

strategy is basically a three-stage process: Stage 1, "the power of vexation and exhaustion," Stage 2, "administration [management] of savagery," and Stage 3, "power of establishment—establishing the state."[74] In Stage 1, Nājī recommends that jihadists instigate a civil war within Islam by undertaking "a merciless campaign of violence in Muslim lands to polarize the population, expose the inability of the state to maintain control, attract followers, and create a spreading network of 'regions of savagery.'"[75]

Nājī provides a list of factors to consider when selecting which regions or zones would be most susceptible for waging Stage 1. He also counsels that jihadists start small and select two or three remote regions or states with weak ruling regimes, poor border control, and peoples who support Islamic jihadism. By maintaining constant warfare and violence from various fronts within these selected regions, as well as attracting new young recruits with attention-getting operations and well-crafted propaganda, jihadists can exhaust and eventually dislodge these regimes—thus creating chaos and savagery in these regions or states and win over more supporters.[76]

Once Stage 1 is completed, then jihadists can begin Stage 2 (administration or management of these "regions of savagery"), taking control of the chaos and filling the political vacuum by "establishing internal security, providing food and medical treatment, securing the borders against the invasion of enemies, establishing Sharia law, [and] establishing a fighting society at all levels and among all individuals."[77]

America unwittingly assisted Islamic State, emboldening it to launch Stage 1 in Syria (2013), Iraq (2014), and Libya (2014). When the US withdrew its troops from Iraq (completed in 2011) and heavily limited its involvement in abating the growing political unrest in Libya (after the overthrow of Muammar el-Qaddafi) and the Syrian Civil War, ISIS and its allied groups seized the moment to attack and terrorize vulnerable regions within these three countries, successfully creating several zones

---

[74] Nājī, *Idārat al-Tawaḥḥush* 15.

[75] Tapson, Mark. "The Management of Savagery." *Frontpage,* 26 Oct. 2014. Web blog post. *CounterJihadReport.com.* Counter Jihad Report, 13 Nov. 2015. Web (https://counterjihadreport.com/2015/11/13/the-management-of-savagery).

[76] Nājī, *Idārat al-Tawaḥḥush* 16-17.

[77] Tapson, Mark. "The Management of Savagery." *Frontpage,* 26 Oct. 2014. Web blog post. *CounterJihadReport.com.* Counter Jihad Report, 13 Nov. 2015. Web (https://counterjihadreport.com/2015/11/13/the-management-of-savagery/). See Nājī, *Idārat al-Tawaḥḥush* 17-18.

of savagery.[78] In time, Islamic State asserted its control over these chaotic regions and established Raqqa as its capital with secondary capitals in the Sunni areas of Iraq, i.e., Mosul and other cities.

The Management of Savagery was not inspired by the author's imagination; he based his book on the Prophet's biography, especially the military and political actions that Muḥammad undertook when he created "regions of savagery" after his emigration to Medina. For example, Muḥammad's alliance with the Aws and Khazraj, the two main Arab tribes of Medina, was a strategic compact to advance mutual interests and cement blood kinship. (As Muḥammad's maternal family was from Medina,[79] it seems in this situation that he was seeking refuge and closer kinship with his maternal uncles in opposition to the Meccan Quraysh, the tribe of his paternal uncles.) These early alliances helped Muḥammad when he turned to raiding and warfare (i.e., Nājī's Stage 1) after his emigration to Medina.

Prior to his emigration to Medina, Muḥammad made two pledges, each one made secretly at al-'Aqaba, between himself and the Anṣār, or Helpers, from Medina who were recent converts to Islam. At the first pledging (AD 621), twelve Anṣār from the Medinan tribes of Aws and Khazraj gave Muḥammad their allegiance "after the manner of women," i.e., an allegiance not based on fighting. The following year, seventy-three Anṣār from the same tribes, Aws and Khazraj, met Muḥammad and pledged allegiance to and protection of Muḥammad and his Emigrants.[80] This second pledge included a guaranteed response to a call to arms:[81]

> The apostle [Muḥammad] smiled and said: "Nay, blood is blood and blood not to be paid is blood not to be paid for [meaning, he would treat blood revenge and its obligation as common to both parties]. I am of you and you are of me. I will war against them that war against you and be at peace with those at peace with you."

[78] See Ignatius, David. "How ISIS Spread in the Middle East—And How to Stop It." *TheAtlantic.com*. Atlantic Media, 29 Oct. 2015. Web (https://www.theatlantic.com/international/archive/2015/10/how-isis-started-syria-iraq/412042/).

[79] Ibn Hishām (Ibn Isḥāq), *The Life of Muḥammad* 228; Ibn Hishām (Ibn Isḥāq), *Al-Sīra al-Nabawīya* 2: 353. When Companion and Ansār Abū Umāmā died, his tribe, the Banū al-Najjar came to Muḥammad, asking him to appoint a replacement. Muḥammad responded, "You are my maternal uncles, and we belong together so I will be your leader." See al-Halabī, *Al-Sīra al-Ḥalabiya* 2: 245. See also *Ṣaḥīḥ Bukhari*, Book of Belief (p. 20); *Sahih al-Bukhari*, Kītāb al-'Īmān 1: 23: "When the Prophet came to Medina, he stayed first with his grandfathers or maternal uncles from Anṣār…."

[80] Ibn Hishām (Ibn Isḥāq), *The Life of Muḥammad* 201-204; Ibn Hishām (Ibn Isḥāq), *Al-Sīra al-Nabawīya* 2: 268.

[81] Ibn Hishām (Ibn Isḥāq), *The Life of Muḥammad* 203-204; Ibn Hishām (Ibn Isḥāq), *Al-Sīra al-Nabawīya* 2: 268.

Islamic State exploits this same strategy, "rooted in tribal traditions," by encouraging its fighters to marry women from the local communities under its control to solidify ties between the jihadis and the local communities.[82] These relationships thus foster kinship and friendship and increase loyalty and commitment among all parties. Consequently, Islamic State has enjoyed protection and support among many Sunni tribes in Syria and Iraq, because many of its members are related by kinship or marriage or both.

Under its current leader Abū Bakr al-Baghdādī, Islamic State has capitalized on and advertized the allegiances it has made with various local Sunni tribes. It has posted and published pictures of tribal elders pledging allegiance to Islamic State during meetings with its members. In June 2015, Fallujah clan elders (Sunni Iraqis) pledged their allegiance to al-Baghdādī and their "support and solidarity" with Islamic State.[83] Earlier, in late March 2015, Islamic State published a video showing tribal leaders representing thirty Sunni Iraqi clans of Nineveh pledging allegiance to al-Baghdādī in a huge celebration in a luxurious Mosul hall.[84]

All these videos have served as propaganda to ostentatiously herald and magnify the "achievements" of the Caliphate in order to uplift the morale of followers and dishearten and dismay the enemy. At the same time they also show how Islamic State seeks political and religious "kinship" with local tribes for its benefit in trying to further its own gains on the ground.

If it were not for the Medinan Anṣār, Islam would never have survived. Muḥammad understood very well the value of the Anṣār who sheltered, provisioned, and protected Muḥammad and his fellow Emigrants. To express his appreciation of their loyalty and love, Muḥammad stated in one *ḥadīth*, "Love for the Anṣār is a sign of faith and hatred for the Anṣār is a sign of hypocrisy."[85] Without that early pledged contingent of Aws and Khazraj tribesmen, Muḥammad would not have been able to fight or conquer an ant. Similarly, Islamic State would never have been able

[82] Hafez, Mohammed M. "The Ties That Bind: How Terrorists Exploit Family Bonds." *CTC Sentinel* 9.2 (Feb. 2016): 15-17. *Combating Terrorism Center at West Point*. Print and Web (https://ctc.usma.edu/posts/the-ties-that-bind-how-terrorists-exploit-family-bonds). Excerpt: A New America study (Nov. 2015) of 474 foreign fighters from 25 Western countries discovered that one-third had "a familial connection to jihad… through relatives currently fighting…marriage…or some other link to jihadis from prior conflicts…."

[83] "The Elders of the Fallujah Clans Pledges Allegiance to al-Baghdadi and Attacks on the Government." *Aljazeera.net*. Al Jazeera Media Network, n.d. Web (http://preview.tinyurl.com/jx882b7).

[84] "Video: Iraqi Tribal Leaders Publicly Pledge Allegiance to al-Baghdadi." *Vetogate.com*. Vetogate, 1 Apr. 2015. Web (http://www.vetogate.com/1561193).

[85] *Sahih Bukhari*, Book of Belief (p. 14); *Ṣaḥīḥ al-Bukhārī*, Kītāb al-'Īmān 1: 14-15.

to continue and survive in Iraq and Syria without the help of the local tribes.

When Muḥammad made his first pledge of allegiance with the twelve Medinan Anṣār at al-'Aqaba, he was anxious to find a new location for himself and his small band of followers. His hometown of Mecca had become increasingly hostile to him and his message; he knew that he and his followers could no longer remain there and be safe. No doubt he was greatly heartened when seventy-three Anṣār agreed to a second pledge of allegiance promising even more support and a new home for his followers the following year.

After the second pledge at al-'Aqaba, Muḥammad's paternal uncle, al-'Abbas Ibn 'Abd al-Muttalib (who was very protective of his nephew though he was only three years older), pressed the Khazraj and Aws tribesmen to confirm the authenticity and commitment of their allegiance to Muḥammad:[86]

> O people of al-Khazraj (the Arabs used the term to cover both Khazraj and Aus). You know what position Muḥammad holds among us. We have protected him from our own people who think as we do about him. He lives in honour and safety among his people, but he will turn to you and join you. If you think that you can be faithful to what you have promised him and protect him from his opponents, then assume the burden you have undertaken. But if you think that you will betray and abandon him after he has gone out with you, then leave him now. For he is safe where he is.

Obviously, the uncle (on Muḥammad's behalf) wanted reassurance from these two tribes that his nephew was not going to leave Mecca (which was increasingly hostile to Muḥammad and his followers) for an uncertain and possibly equally volatile environment in Medina without any support or protection.

In turn, the Aws and Khazraj needed a leader or mediator who would treat each tribe fairly and help reduce conflict between them. Additionally, a man who was blessed by Allah, a prophet, symbolized divinely appointed authority and could act as a powerful talisman for his people and his allies. With perhaps these thoughts in mind, they pledged their allegiance to Muḥammad and agreed to defend him and fight with him in his wars: "By Him [Allah] Who sent you with the truth

[86] Ibn Hishām (Ibn Isḥāq), *The Life of Muḥammad* 203; Ibn Hishām (Ibn Isḥāq), *Al-Sīra al-Nabawīya* 2: 266.

we will protect you as we protect our women. We give our allegiance and we are men of war possessing arms...."[87] Convinced that Muḥammad was inspired by Allah, they wanted to benefit from Muḥammad's special power, moral authority, and likely (in their minds) ability to reward them with Allah's favor.

Yet at the same time the two tribes wanted Muḥammad's promise that he would not desert them if they helped him and fought with and for him—particularly if their support of him may mean breaking their pledged alliances with other tribes:[88]

> Oh apostle, we have ties with other men (he meant the Jews) and if we sever them perhaps when we have done that and God will have given you victory, you will return to your people and leave us?

As was mentioned earlier, it was at this point during the second meeting at al-ʿAqaba that Muḥammad expressed his unity with them and pledged his alliance to these two tribes: "I am of you and you are of me. I will war against them that war against you and be at peace with those at peace with you."[89] The interests of these two parties—the Anṣār and the Meccan Muslims—were mutual as both wanted to work together for the promotion of Islam and the protection of its followers. These mutual interests are the same interests that exist between Sunni tribes and Islamic State.

In the early history of Islam, the pursuit of alliances with local tribes had been a political and military strategy for Muḥammad, which has been since replicated in modern times by Islamic State. However, this same strategy was also employed in 2006 by thirty local Sunni tribal groups in Iraq who sought the help of and worked together with US forces to rid their province, Al-Anbar, of Al Qaeda in Iraq (AQI) and its foreign fighters, who were subjecting the region to horrific violence. Called the Anbar Awakening, this alliance of local Sunni tribes, in partnership with US forces, managed to clear AQI insurgents from the city of Ramadi and

---

[87] Ibn Hishām (Ibn Isḥāq), *The Life of Muḥammad* 203; Ibn Hishām (Ibn Isḥāq), *Al-Sīra al-Nabawīya* 2: 267.

[88] Ibn Hishām (Ibn Isḥāq), *The Life of Muḥammad* 203; Ibn Hishām (Ibn Isḥāq), *Al-Sīra al-Nabawīya* 2: 267.

[89] Ibn Hishām (Ibn Isḥāq), *The Life of Muḥammad* 204; Ibn Hishām (Ibn Isḥāq), *Al-Sīra al-Nabawīya* 2: 267-268.

much of the Euphrates River Valley, denying AQI access to one of its most critical bases in Iraq.[90]

Because this model in combating jihadists in central Iraq's Al-Anbar province—once Iraq's most violent—was so successful, it was adopted in other regions tormented by AQI and helped neutralize its strength and support.[91]

Unfortunately, the success of the Anbar Awakening was short-lived. Though it was a speedy and effective way to curtail the violence and spread of AQI, it failed in the end because of the withdrawal of US forces, the less-than-uniform nature of the Awakening organization itself, "composed of numerous local elements roused to action by a wide array of cultural, political, and economic considerations,"[92] and an Iraqi government dominated by Shiite leaders who demonstrated sectarian preferences in policy decisions by prioritizing Shia over Sunni areas and showing "little interest in making concessions" to Sunnis.[93]

As the incompetence and corruption increased under the leadership of Iraqi Prime Minister Nouri al-Maliki (a Shiite), AQI-affiliated fighters remobilized and rebranded themselves as ISIS.[94] Civil war erupted in 2014, with Iraqi insurgents and ISIS fighting the central government of Iraq. Sunni tribes in the Anbar province who once banded together to oust AQI were now divided. Many Sunni tribes threw their support to ISIS because they distrusted and feared the Shiite-dominated government of al-Maliki.

And in this way, these Sunni tribes in northern and western Iraq who supported the foreign fighters of ISIS and other jihadists became the incubator of Abū Bakr al-Baghdadī's caliphate on June 29, 2014–just

---

[90] Kagan, Kimberly. "The Anbar Awakening: Displacing Al Qaeda from Its Stronghold in Western Iraq." *UnderstandingWar.org*. Institute for the Study of War and *Weekly Standard.com*, 21 Aug. 2006-30 Mar. 2007. Web (http://www.understandingwar.org/report/anbar-awakening-displacing-al-qaeda-its-stronghold-western-iraq). See Klein, Joe. "Is al-Qaeda on the Run in Iraq?" *Time.com*. Time Inc., 23 May 2007. Print and Web (https://preview.tinyurl.com/y6vgj96w). **Note:** Though an alliance with the tribes "was proposed by U.S. Army intelligence officers as early as October 2003, this proposal was rejected by L. Paul Bremer's Coalition Provisional Authority on the grounds that 'tribes are part of the past. They have no place in the new democratic Iraq.'"

[91] McCormack, David. "Understanding the Anbar Awakening." *WeeklyStandard.com*. Clarity Media Group, 22 Dec. 2010. Web (http://www.weeklystandard.com/understanding-anbar-awakening/article/524770).

[92] Ibid.

[93] Klein, Joe. "Is al-Qaeda on the Run in Iraq?" *Time.com*. Time Inc., 23 May 2007. Print and Web (https://preview.tinyurl.com/y6vgj96w).

[94] al-Ali, Zaid. "How Maliki Ruined Iraq." *ForeignPolicy.com*. Foreign Policy, 19 June 2014. Web (http://foreignpolicy.com/2014/06/19/how-maliki-ruined-iraq/).

as the Aws and Khazraj tribes of Medina were the incubator in seventh century AD of the Islamic state of Prophet Muḥammad Ibn 'Abd Allāh.

NINE

Raiders and criminal gangs are a past and present part of Islam

At the beginning of Islam, Muḥammad needed men and money to be able to live and support the Emigrants (Muhajirīn) who moved with him to live in Medina. The brotherly hospitality that was established between the Emigrants (Muhajirīn) and the Helpers (Anṣār) was just a temporary arrangement for Muḥammad and his Emigrants, because the Anṣār would not be able to financially support the families of the Emigrants for a lengthy time. Therefore, Muḥammad had to find alternative ways to generate revenue other than his group's reliance on charity in order to extend his control and influence and prompt fighters to join his forces. Only then could he hope to begin his plan to establish Islam over the entire region.

Muḥammad also wanted to take revenge on his own tribe, the Quraysh, and take it over by force. His revenge was two-fold: (1) retaliation for the Meccan tribe's rejection of him and his call and subsequent persecution of him and his followers and (2) economic support of his followers.

But to properly execute this plan, Muḥammad needed to raise money, mobilize more men, and provide a convincing reason for them to invade the targets that had been already set.

At that time, some Arab tribes made their livelihood by raiding and looting passing caravans and enemy tribes. One year after settling in Medina, Muḥammad decided to pursue a similar course and set out to find vulnerable targets, particularly Meccan Quraysh caravans.[1] Muḥammad concluded that his tribe, the Quraysh, would be easy pickings from a well-planned attack. Muḥammad had lived nearly his entire life among his Quraysh tribesmen and had worked during his early adult years as a camel driver and caravan manager. He knew well the members of this tribe and the terrain of the region surrounding Mecca. He knew the Meccan caravans would pass within eighty miles of Medina, with Mecca a distance twice as far, on their trade route. (This disadvantageous position meant the Muslims would only need to deal with the caravan escorts during any raid.)[2] Additionally, his continuing tribal relationships with some of the Quraysh tribesmen allowed him to keep abreast of their news and travels.

Given their still small numbers, Muḥammad and the Emigrants went out in raiding parties searching first for Quraysh caravans, because they carried valuable trade goods but generally posted few guard escorts. Muḥammad could not yet invade the Quraysh in its own backyard of Mecca because of the huge imbalance of Quraysh fighters compared to the much smaller number of Muslims.

The Muslims' early raids were unsuccessful in directly harming the Quraysh. In one early raid, Muḥammad and his men tried to intercept a Quraysh caravan at Waddān (al-'Abwā') but found instead a caravan of the Banū Ḍamra, a neighboring tribe to the Quraysh. After some negotiation, the two groups signed a treaty of nonaggression. The Banū Ḍamra also agreed not to side with the Quraysh against the Muslims. Muḥammad and his men returned to Medina without starting war. This

[1] Ibn Hishām (Ibn Isḥāq), *The Life of Muḥammad* 281; Ibn Hishām (Ibn Isḥāq), *Al-Sīra al-Nabawīya* 3: 29. Muḥammad "went forth raiding in Safar [second month of Islamic calendar] at the beginning of the twelfth month from his coming to Medina."

[2] Watt, *Muḥammad at Medina* 2.

raid, or "expedition" (a term Muslims use to characterize these sorties) was later called the Expedition (Raid) of al-'Abwā'.[3]

Muḥammad selected his uncle Ḥamza to lead Emigrants to the seashore, near Al-Īs, for another of the earliest expeditions (March AD 623).[4] This group encountered three hundred seasoned Meccan fighters led by Amr Ibn Hishām, or Abū al-Ḥakam (which means "Father of Wisdom" but he was derisively called Abū Jahl, or "Father of Ignorance," by the early Muslims), an arch enemy of Muḥammad. A Quraysh tribesman intervened, and the two groups separated without fighting, the Emigrants returning to Medina with (again) no booty. This incident has been called the Expedition of Ḥamza Ibn 'Abd al-Muttalib, or the Saif al-Baḥr after the location.[5]

The Anṣār were not keen to participate in Muḥammad's raids because only Muḥammad and the Emigrants needed the money. Consequently, Muḥammad sent out raiding parties comprised of only Emigrants (Muhajirīn).[6] On one such raid or "expedition," a Muslim group of "sixty or eighty riders" led by Companion 'Ubayda Ibn al-Ḥārith tried to intercept (again) a Quraysh caravan but refrained from attacking when the Muslims saw that the caravan was heavily protected with two hundred armed Quraysh riders. Thus no fighting took place, and the Muslims returned back to Medina empty-handed. But one Muslim, Sa'd Ibn Abū Waqqāṣ, did shoot an arrow, "the first arrow to be shot in Islam."[7] This incident (April AD 623)[8] has since been chronicled in Islamic history as the Expedition of 'Ubaydah Ibn al-Ḥārith.[9]

Muḥammad himself led a group of Muslims for one of the expeditions, the second raid under his personal leadership. (During his absences from Medina, Muḥammad would assign a surrogate to be in charge of the city, an appointment that indicates that Muḥammad was now ruler of

---

[3] *History of al-Ṭabarī* 7: 12. See Ibn Hishām (Ibn Isḥāq), *The Life of Muḥammad* 281; Ibn Hishām (Ibn Isḥāq), *Al-Sīra al-Nabawīya* 3: 30. Muḥammad "reached Waddān [his first raid], which is the raid of al-'Abwā'.... The B. [Banu] Damra there made peace with him.... Then he returned to Medina without meeting war...."

[4] Watt, *Muḥammad at Medina* 339. See *History of al-Ṭabarī* 7: 10.

[5] Ibn Hishām (Ibn Isḥāq), *The Life of Muḥammad* 283; Ibn Hishām (Ibn Isḥāq), *Al-Sīra al-Nabawīya* 3: 35.

[6] Ibn Hishām (Ibn Isḥāq), *The Life of Muḥammad* 281; Ibn Hishām (Ibn Isḥāq), *Al-Sīra al-Nabawīya* 3: 31. Once Muḥammad returned to Medina after the incident at Waddan, he "sent Ubaydah b. al-Ḥārith b. al-Muṭṭalib with sixty or eighty riders from the emigrants, there not being a single one of the Anṣār among them [on the next raid]."

[7] Ibn Hishām (Ibn Isḥāq), *The Life of Muḥammad* 281; Ibn Hishām (Ibn Isḥāq), *Al-Sīra al-Nabawīya* 3: 31.

[8] Watt, *Muḥammad at Medina* 340.

[9] Ibn Hishām (Ibn Isḥāq), *The Life of Muḥammad* 281; Ibn Hishām (Ibn Isḥāq), *Al-Sīra al-Nabawīya* 3: 31.

Medina.) He went as far as Buwāt along the caravan route. He failed to find any Quraysh, and so he too returned to Medina with nothing to show for his effort, a mission sometimes called the Raid of Buwāṭ (September AD 623).[10]

A few months later (December AD 623),[11] Muḥammad set off with his cousin and Companion Alī Ibn Abū Ṭālib on another, and ultimately, unsuccessful raid later called the Raid of al-'Ushayra. Interestingly, the boredom in looking and waiting for Quraysh caravans to attack and plunder apparently prompted 'Alī and another Companion, 'Ammār Ibn Yāsir, to watch some men of another tribe "working at a well and on the date palms" until sleep overcame them.[12] Though these Emigrants were not experienced farmers or artisans, one wonders what would have happened to the history of Islam—indeed the world—if these early Muslims had tried harder to learn these legitimate forms of employment rather than focusing all their energy into becoming successful raiders.

Killing and looting finally occurred during an incident Islamic sources call the Expedition of 'Abd Allah Ibn Jahsh, or the Raid of Nakhla (January AD 624).[13] For this mission, Muḥammad directed this Companion (and eventual brother-in-law) to lead eight Emigrants and spy on the Quraysh. Once they had some worthy news to share, they were to return to Muḥammad.[14]

During this mission, a small Quraysh caravan, led by 'Amr Ibn al-Ḥaḍramī, passed by the Emigrants. The men of the caravan became nervous when they saw the group of Emigrants encamped near them but then concluded that the Emigrants were on a pilgrimage because it was a sacred month.

Now Arabs at that time considered four months of the year as holy or sacred,[15] and fighting and war were prohibited during this period. All

[10] Ibn Hishām (Ibn Isḥāq), *The Life of Muḥammad* 285; Ibn Hishām (Ibn Isḥāq), *Al-Sīra al-Nabawīya* 3: 38. See Watt, *Muḥammad at Medina* 340, and *History of al-Ṭabarī* 7: 13.

[11] Watt, *Muḥammad at Medina* 340.

[12] Ibn Hishām (Ibn Isḥāq), *The Life of Muḥammad* 285-286; Ibn Hishām (Ibn Isḥāq), *Al-Sīra al-Nabawīya* 3: 40.

[13] Watt, *Muḥammad at Medina* 340.

[14] Ibn Hishām (Ibn Isḥāq), *The Life of Muḥammad* 286-287; Ibn Hishām (Ibn Isḥāq), *Al-Sīra al-Nabawīya* 3: 42-43. Muḥammad gave 'Abd Allah Ibn Jahsh a letter and "ordered him not to look at it until he had journeyed for two days, and to do what he was ordered to do." After two days, Ibn Jahsh read the letter's contents, which gave him instructions for travel and the command to spy on the Quraysh: "...find out for us what they are doing."

[15] Four months—Rajab, Dhū-l-Qi'da, Dhū-l-Hijja, and Muharram—were once considered sacred by medieval Arab tribes. During these months, Arabs had to cease from any fighting and allow trade caravans to travel freely without fear of attack.

the Arab tribes honored these months and regarded fighting at any time during this sacred time a grave crime, an indefensible breach of customs and traditions.

However, the Emigrants, looking at the little-protected Quraysh caravan with its trade goods of dry raisins, leather, and other merchandise and no doubt feeling angry and revengeful over their past persecution by the Quraysh, debated the merits of attacking the caravan. In the end, these Companions of Muḥammad decided to attack the peaceful caravan, killing everyone they could and taking all the property, even though it was the last day of Rajab (a sacred month).[16]

One of the Emigrants shot an arrow at ʿAmr Ibn al-Ḥaḍramī, the leader of the caravan, and killed him. Of the remaining three Quraysh men, two surrendered and one escaped. The Emigrants then seized the camels and all the trade goods packed upon them, plus the two captives, and headed back to Medina. Before they reached Muḥammad, they divided the spoils among themselves and allocated one-fifth of the plunder for their prophet.[17]

Muḥammad's initial reaction upon their return was harsh condemnation. He was shocked that a simple exploratory mission resulted in a profound breach in well-known and obligatory tribal customs. Even so, he did not denounce the attack itself (with its bloodshed and stealing) but its launch during a sacred month.[18] The raiders were also reproached by the rest of their fellow Muslims for their action, and the Jews "turned this raid into an omen against the apostle."[19] The Quraysh in Mecca said that "Muḥammad and his companions have violated the sacred month, shed blood therein, taken booty, and captured men."[20]

With all the bad press by followers, friends and foes, Muḥammad quickly realized that he was losing control of the situation and needed to find a solution that would quell the uproar and restore his reputation. Fortuitously, Muḥammad received a revelation, Q 2.217 (Palmer trans.), that bailed him out of his predicament:

---

[16] Ibn Hishām (Ibn Isḥāq), *The Life of Muḥammad* 287; Ibn Hishām (Ibn Isḥāq), *Al-Sīra al-Nabawīya* 3: 44-45.

[17] Ibn Hishām (Ibn Isḥāq), *The Life of Muḥammad* 287; Ibn Hishām (Ibn Isḥāq), *Al-Sīra al-Nabawīya* 3: 44-45.

[18] Ibn Hishām (Ibn Isḥāq), *The Life of Muḥammad* 287-288; Ibn Hishām (Ibn Isḥāq), *Al-Sīra al-Nabawīya* 3: 45.

[19] Ibn Hishām (Ibn Isḥāq), *The Life of Muḥammad* 288; Ibn Hishām (Ibn Isḥāq), *Al-Sīra al-Nabawīya* 3: 45.

[20] Ibn Hishām (Ibn Isḥāq), *The Life of Muḥammad* 288; Ibn Hishām (Ibn Isḥāq), *Al-Sīra al-Nabawīya* 3: 45.

> *They will ask thee of the sacred month,—of fighting therein. Say, 'Fighting therein is a great sin; but turning folks off God's way, and misbelief in Him and in the Sacred Mosque, and turning His people out therefrom, is a greater* [sin] *in God's sight; and sedition is a greater sin than slaughter.' They will not cease from fighting you until they turn you from your religion if they can; but whosoever of you is turned from his religion and dies while still a misbeliever; these are those whose works are vain in this world and the next; they are the fellows of the Fire, and they shall dwell therein for aye.*

According to this verse, Allah himself approves of the killing of the caravan's leader, taking the two men as captives, and looting the caravan, even if these heinous actions occurred during a sacred month. Such otherwise unforgivable acts are absolved or vindicated because of the Quraysh's disbelief in Allah, especially since they had prevented Muslims from practising their faith and expelled them from the Sacred Mosque (namely, the Ka'ba and its surroundings). Disbelief in Allah by non-Muslims and efforts to dissuade Muslims from their religion or obstruct their religious practices are judged in Allah's eyes as greater religious offenses than killings of disbelievers by Muslims during the sacred months.

After the revelation of this verse (Q 2.217) and its apparent justification of the actions committed by 'Abd Allah Ibn Jahsh and his men, Muḥammad took possession of the two captives and the share of the booty that his men had set aside for him. His men had divided the spoils before returning to Medina, allocating one-fifth for Muḥammad, a division commonly practiced by Arab bandits where one-fifth is distributed to the leader and the rest of the bandits divide the remaining four-fifths among themselves. After this incident, Muḥammad received the revelation of Q 8.41 (Palmer trans.), that divinely codified this same division of spoils, an Islamic rule still considered valid among Mujāhidīn to this day:

> *and know that whenever ye seize anything as a spoil, to God belongs a fifth thereof, and to His Apostle, and to kindred and orphans, and the poor and the wayfarer; if ye believe in God and what we have revealed unto our servants on the day of the discrimination,—the day when the two parties met; and God is mighty over all.*

Then Muḥammad demanded a swap with the Quraysh: his two caravan captives for two Muslims held captive in Mecca. However, he stipulated that he would not set the two Quraysh men free until his two Companions were released and had arrived safely to Medina, stating, "If you kill them, we will kill your two friends."[21]

However, Muḥammad did not fully comply with his promise. According to Islamic sources, one of the two captives became a Muslim and stayed with Muḥammad, while the other one returned to his people.[22]

Battle of Badr

Less than two months after the expedition of 'Abd Allah Ibn Jahsh and his eight fellow Emigrants, the Muslims heard about a huge Quraysh merchant caravan, loaded with Quraysh money and merchandise, that would be traveling close to Medina on its way back from Syria. Abū Sufyān (also known as Sakhr Ibn Harb), a powerful Quraysh tribal leader, and thirty to forty Quraysh tribesmen were escorting this caravan.[23]

What a great opportunity for achieving some economic stability for Muḥammad and his Companions, if they could get their hands on this Quraysh treasure; they would no longer have to rely so heavily on the hospitality of the Anṣār. And overpowering this convoy would satisfy political and emotional needs as well. Attacking the caravan, absconding with its goods and money, and perhaps killing some of the Quraysh escorts would cause the Quraysh severe trade losses, weaken their strength, and help avenge for the persecution the Muslims endured in Mecca.

The moment Muḥammad heard the news about the approaching convoy, he said, "This is the Quraysh caravan containing their property. Go out to attack it, perhaps Allah will give it as a prey."[24] Though some of Muḥammad's followers eagerly supported his summons, others were not very enthusiastic about the prospect of fighting, "because they had not thought that the apostle would go to war."[25] These feelings of apprehension and resistance to Muḥammad's new, aggressive direction

---

[21] Ibn Hishām (Ibn Isḥāq), *The Life of Muḥammad* 288; Ibn Hishām (Ibn Isḥāq), *Al-Sīra al-Nabawīya* 3: 46.

[22] Ibn Hishām (Ibn Isḥāq), *The Life of Muḥammad* 288; Ibn Hishām (Ibn Isḥāq), *Al-Sīra al-Nabawīya* 3: 46.

[23] Ibn Hishām (Ibn Isḥāq), *The Life of Muḥammad* 289; Ibn Hishām (Ibn Isḥāq), *Al-Sīra al-Nabawīya* 3: 48.

[24] Ibn Hishām (Ibn Isḥāq), *The Life of Muḥammad* 289; Ibn Hishām (Ibn Isḥāq), *Al-Sīra al-Nabawīya* 3: 48.

[25] Ibn Hishām (Ibn Isḥāq), *The Life of Muḥammad* 289; Ibn Hishām (Ibn Isḥāq), *Al-Sīra al-Nabawīya* 3: 48.

have been captured and expressed in this Qur'ānic verse (Q 8.5-7; Hilâlî-Khân trans.):[26]

> *As your Lord caused you (O Muḥammad SAW) to go out from your home with the truth, and verily, a party among the believers disliked it; / Disputing with you concerning the truth after it was made manifest, as if they were being driven to death, while they were looking (at it). / And (remember) when Allah promised you (Muslims) one of the two parties (of the enemy i.e. either the army or the caravan) that it should be yours, you wished that the one not armed (the caravan) should be yours, but Allah willed to justify the truth by His Words and to cut off the roots of the disbelievers (i.e. in the battle of Badr).*

Abū Sufyān, the leader of the Quraysh caravan, heard that Muḥammad and his Companions were plotting to attack the convoy. He sent a messenger to Mecca, urging his fellow tribesmen to come out and defend their property and men from Muḥammad and his followers.[27] Not surprisingly, Abū Sufyān later changed the customary return route of the caravan and headed toward Yanbu, located along the coastline of the Red Sea when he suspected the Muslims were nearby.[28] The Meccan response to this appeal was immediate. Nearly every man and all but one tribal leader "prepared quickly" to come to the aid of the caravan.[29]

When Muḥammad learned that the Meccan Quraysh were setting out to protect the caravan, he assembled a council with both his Muhajirīn (Emigrants) and the Ansār (Helpers), to discuss the situation and how to proceed. The Muhajirīn were steadfast and vowed to "fight resolutely" with Muḥammad. However, Muḥammad needed the support of the Ansār, because they "formed the majority" and had only pledged their protection and only within their territory. He "was afraid that the Ansār would not feel obliged to help him unless he was attacked by an enemy."[30] To his relief, the Ansār also staunchly declared their support and obedience and agreed to help Muḥammad fight the Quraysh.[31]

---

[26] See the commentary on Q 8.7, *Tafsīr al-Ṭabarī* 9: 126.

[27] Ibn Hishām (Ibn Isḥāq), *The Life of Muḥammad* 289; Ibn Hishām (Ibn Isḥāq), *Al-Sīra al-Nabawīya* 3: 48.

[28] Ibn Hishām (Ibn Isḥāq), *The Life of Muḥammad* 295; Ibn Hishām (Ibn Isḥāq), *Al-Sīra al-Nabawīya* 3: 60.

[29] Ibn Hishām (Ibn Isḥāq), *The Life of Muḥammad* 291; Ibn Hishām (Ibn Isḥāq), *Al-Sīra al-Nabawīya* 3: 51.

[30] Ibn Hishām (Ibn Isḥāq), *The Life of Muḥammad* 294; Ibn Hishām (Ibn Isḥāq), *Al-Sīra al-Nabawīya* 3: 58.

[31] See the commentary on Q 8.7, *Tafsīr al-Ṭabarī* 9: 126. See also Ibn Hishām (Ibn Isḥāq), *The Life of Muḥammad* 294; Ibn Hishām (Ibn Isḥāq), *Al-Sīra al-Nabawīya* 3: 58.

In the meantime, Abū Sufyān had shepherded the caravan safely out of range and from the danger of attack by the Muslims. He sent word to the Quraysh, thanking them for rushing to his aid and inviting them to turn back to Mecca. A few Meccan tribes accepted this proposal and returned home, not wishing to initiate a war and risk lives when the reason for their military assembly—protecting the caravan and its escort—no longer existed. However, most of the Quraysh, perhaps to avenge the killing of 'Amr Ibn al-Ḥaḍramī or destroy the Muslims and stop their raiding, decided to challenge Muḥammad and his army.[32]

The inevitable showdown between the Muslims and the Quraysh army occurred on March 15, AD 624, at Badr (more correctly, Badr Hunayn), a small market centre located at the junction of a caravan route and situated in a plain surrounded by steep hills and sand dunes.[33] Muḥammad and his three hundred followers, both Muhajirīn (Emigrants) and Anṣār (Helpers), were facing an army of one thousand Quraysh tribesmen—Muḥammad's own people.[34] This confrontation was decidedly personal for these combatants: fathers would be fighting sons and brothers would be fighting brothers; in short, many of the Muslims, especially the Emigrants, would be fighting (and killing) their relatives.

Several Qur'ānic verses revealed after this battle support and vindicate those Muslims who fight for Allah, even elevating fighting above praying and almsgiving (see Q 4.77) and promising certain admittance into paradise through martyrdom (see Q 3.195):

> *Such believers as sit at home—unless they have an injury—are not the equals of those who struggle in the path of God with their possessions and their selves. God has preferred in rank those who struggle with their possessions and their selves over the ones who sit at home; yet to each God has promised the reward most fair; and God has preferred those who struggle over the ones who sit at home for the bounty of a mighty wage.* (Q 4.95; Arberry trans.)

[32] Ibn Hishām (Ibn Isḥāq), *The Life of Muḥammad* 296; Ibn Hishām (Ibn Isḥāq), *Al-Sīra al-Nabawīya* 3: 61.

[33] *The Qur'an: An Encyclopedia* 108, 421.

[34] Bunting, Tony. "Battle of Badr." *Brittanica.com*. Encyclopaedia Brittanica, Inc., 22 Mar. 2017. Web (https://www.britannica.com/event/Battle-of-Badr).

> *Hast thou not regarded those to whom it was said, 'Restrain your hands, and perform the prayer, and pay the alms'? Then, as soon as fighting is prescribed for them, there is a party of them fearing the people as they would fear God, or with a greater fear, and they say, 'Our Lord, why hast thou prescribed fighting for us? Why not defer us to a near term?' Say: 'The enjoyment of this world is little; the world to come is better for him who fears God; you shall not be wronged a single date-thread.'* (Q 4.77; Arberry trans.)

> .... *And those who emigrated, and were expelled from their habitations, those who suffered hurt in My way, and fought, and were slain—them I shall surely acquit of their evil deeds, and I shall admit them to gardens underneath which rivers flow.' A reward from God! And God with Him is the fairest reward.* (Q 3.195; Arberry trans.)

Muḥammad's army held up two black flags as it advanced to meet the Quraysh army. One of the banners was called *Rāyat al-ʿUqāb* (Banner of the Eagle).[35] Hadith literature describes the flags as square in shape with white writing on a black background.[36] (Islamic or jihadist organizations, such as Islamic State, Al Qaeda, and Boko Haram, use a similar black flag. White writing at the top of the banner reads, "There is no god but Allah. Muḥammad is the messenger of Allah," the Islamic declaration of faith known as the Shahada. Underneath is a solid white circle with black writing that reads, from bottom to top the following phrases: "Muḥammad | the messenger of | Allah."[37] The circle symbolizes the Prophet's seal and matches the inscription engraved on Muḥammad's personal ring.) [38]

Muḥammad and his forces reached the battle site first. As part of his battle strategy, Muḥammad had his men stop up all the nearby wells, so the enemy would not have any water to drink, but constructed for themselves a cistern so that they would have plenty of water during the

[35] Ibn Hishām (Ibn Isḥāq), *The Life of Muḥammad* 292; Ibn Hishām (Ibn Isḥāq), *Al-Sīra al-Nabawīya* 3: 45.

[36] *Sunan al-Tirmidhī* 5: 266. The flag was just a piece of cloth, "black with white writing in a square shape."

[37] Gander, Kashmira. "ISIS Flag: What Do the Words Mean and What Are Its Origins." *Independent.co.uk*. The Independent, 6 July 2015. Web (http://www.independent.co.uk/news/world/middle-east/isis-flag-what-do-the-words-mean-and-what-are-its-origins-10369601.html).

[38] *Sahih Bukhari*, Book of Dress (pp. 1311, 1312); *Ṣaḥīḥ al-Bukhārī*, Kītāb al-Libās 5: 2205 and Kītāb al-Khumus 3: 1131. Muḥammad wore a silver ring he had made for himself and was later worn by the next three caliphs: Abū Bakr, 'Umar, and 'Uthman, who lost it when it fell into a well. The "engraving of the ring was in three lines: [The word] 'Muḥammad' was one line, 'Apostle' in another line,' and 'Allah' in a third line...."

upcoming battle.[39] Temperatures at that time of year (March) would have been hot, ranging from 85 to 95 degrees Fahrenheit.[40] Obviously, such a plan would be effective in weakening the enemy. But was it ethical? Water was held sacred by these Arabs; therefore, it probably did not cross the minds of the Quraysh that the Muslims would deny them water before attacking them with swords. Even in armed conflicts, there were "rules" traditionally upheld by warring Arab parties. But as earlier reported, Muḥammad had already breached one of these covenants honored by all the Arab tribes when he absolved Companion 'Abd Allah Ibn Jahsh for killing 'Amr Ibn al-Ḥaḍramī, the Quraysh caravan leader, during a sacred month and keeping the spoils of the raid. Muḥammad's action—to prevent enemy access to water in preparation for the battle—exhibits not only Machiavellianism over morality but also a startling ruthlessness in pressing for this attack to slaughter his own tribesmen by thirst and the sword.

In contrast, 'Utba Ibn Rabī'a, one of the Quraysh leaders, even on the eve of battle, counselled retreat so that no one would end up guilty of killing a blood relative:[41]

> "O people of Quraysh! By God, you will gain naught by giving battle to Muḥammad and his companions. If you fall upon him, each one of you will always be looking with loathing on the face of another who has slain the son of his paternal or maternal uncle or some man of his kin. Therefore turn back and leave Muḥammad to the rest of the Arabs. If they kill him, that is what you want; and if it be otherwise, he will find that you have not tried to do to him what you (in fact) would have liked to do."

Unlike Muḥammad, 'Utba put this upcoming battle in human terms and understood the ramifications of killing others, especially people related to them by blood ties, over nebulous causes.

Islamic accounts report that seventy Quraysh were killed and seventy were captured during the Battle of Badr.[42] Only fourteen of Muḥammad's

---

[39] Ibn Hishām (Ibn Isḥāq), *The Life of Muḥammad* 296-297; Ibn Hishām (Ibn Isḥāq), *Al-Sīra al-Nabawīya* 3: 63.

[40] Weather Spark. "Average Weather in Medina (Saudi Arabia)." *Weatherspark.com.* Cedar Lake Ventures, Inc. Web (https://weatherspark.com/y/101175/Average-Weather-in-Medina-Saudi-Arabia).

[41] Ibn Hishām (Ibn Isḥāq), *The Life of Muḥammad* 298; Ibn Hishām (Ibn Isḥāq), *Al-Sīra al-Nabawīya* 3: 65.

[42] Ibn Hishām (Ibn Isḥāq), *The Life of Muḥammad* 337-339; Ibn Hishām (Ibn Isḥāq), *Al-Sīra al-Nabawīya* 3: 174. **Note:** The English translation of this source states that 50 Quraysh were killed and 43 taken captive (pages 338 and 339, respectively). The original Arabic source reports 70 killed and 70 taken captive.

Companions were killed: six Muhajirīn and eight Anṣār.[43] Muḥammad demanded a ransom of four hundred to four thousand dirhams in exchange for each captive he had.[44]

A ransom of four hundred to four thousand dirhams was a considerable amount during this time period, when fifty dirhams a year was considered by Muḥammad a yearly income sufficient to maintain a comfortable living standard.[45] Even if the lower figure of four hundred dirhams is accurate, that means Muḥammad managed to get in exchange for each captive an amount that would comfortably support eight people for an entire year. With possibly seventy captives, the total ransom collected would be able to support nearly six hundred (or more exactly 560) people for a year. (If one thousand dirhams, with four thousand dirhams requested only for the most important captives, was the more typical ransom, then the total collection would have been 70,000 dirhams, enough to support 1400 people for a year.)

The Muslim victory at Badr was a game changer for the fledgling (and even floundering) movement. It elevated the status of Muḥammad and his religion while it destroyed the leadership and prestige of the Meccan Quraysh, a dominant, wealthy tribe in the region. The tremendous emotional impact of this military success, given the considerable odds, is reflected even in the Qur'ān, in which much of Q 8 describes and extolls this event.

Besides the Qur'ān, the glorification of this battle and its Muslim combatants has been perpetuated in the Hadith literature. The Islamic biography of Muḥammad provides a detailed list of the battle participants, including classifications of "Those Who Died as Martyrs," "Polytheists Who Were Slain, and "Polytheists Who Were Taken Prisoner." Those Muslims who survived the battle were given a portion of the booty and later rewarded with a yearly stipend of "five thousand (Dirhams) each.... 'Umar [second caliph] said, 'I will surely give them more than what I

---

[43] Ibn Hishām (Ibn Isḥāq), *The Life of Muḥammad* 336-337; Ibn Hishām (Ibn Isḥāq), *Al-Sīra al-Nabawīya* 3: 166.

[44] Islamic sources report different amounts for the ransoming of the Battle of Badr captives: Al-Ṭabarī, *Tafsīr al-Ṭabarī* 10: 30. (Commentary on Q 8.67 reports each ransom = 4000 dirhams); Ibn Kathīr, *Al-Bidayah* 5: 168 (Each ransom = 400 to 4000 dirhams); *Sunan Abū Dawūd*, Book of *Jihād* 3: 310 (Ransoms "fixed...at 400"). See Ibn Hishām (Ibn Isḥāq), *The Life of Muḥammad* 311; Ibn Hishām (Ibn Isḥāq), *Al-Sīra al-Nabawīya* 3: 100. This source reports that one prisoner, Abū Waḍḍā' Ibn Ḍubayra al-Sahmī, was released when his wealthy son paid "4000 dirhams."

[45] *Sunan Abū Dawūd*, Book of Zakāt 2: 282. When asked what amount of wealth is sufficient for independent living, Muḥammad replied, "Fifty *Dirham*, or its equivalent in gold."

will give to others.'"[46] The martyrs of this battle were promised the most superior of heavenly paradises.[47]

Pragmatically speaking, the victory at the Battle of Badr provided an incredible financial windfall for the economically struggling Muslims. The Emigrants no longer had to depend on or require the generous hospitality of the Anṣār. Now the Muslims had funding to expand and provision a large army and go from raiding to conquest. The title of Q 8 seems to express this financial and military optimism: Al Anfāl, or "The Spoils of War."

Battle of Badr captives

Muḥammad did not demand ransom for all the captives. In fact, he had several Quraysh captives killed as his army returned to Medina. He ordered his cousin 'Alī to behead al-Naḍr Ibn al-Ḥārith, a well-traveled Arab doctor.[48] Islamic sources imply this execution was done to remove a vocal critic of Muḥammad's prophethood.[49] According to Muslim commentators, a few Qur'ānic verses allude to al-Naḍr Ibn al-Ḥārith's mockery of Muḥammad, such as accusing the Prophet of plagiarism:

> *But when our verses were rehearsed to them they said, 'We have already heard.—If we pleased we could speak like this; verily, this is nothing but tales of those of yore.'* (Q 8.31; Palmer trans.)[50]

---

[46] *Sahih Bukhari*, Book of Military Expeditions Led by the Prophet (p. 949); *Ṣaḥīḥ al-Bukhārī*, Kītāb al-Maghāzī 4: 1475.

[47] *Sahih Bukhari*, Book of Military Expeditions Led by the Prophet (p. 939); *Ṣaḥīḥ al-Bukhārī*, Kītāb al-Maghāzī 4: 1462-1463. A woman whose son was killed during the Battle of Badr asked Muḥammad if her son was now in Paradise. He replied, "May Allah be merciful to you! Have you lost your senses? Do you think there is only one Paradise? There are many Paradises and your son is in the (most superior) Paradise of Al-Firdaus."

[48] Shahîd vol. 2, pt. 2, p. 179.

[49] See the commentary on Q 8.31, *Tafsīr Ibn Kathīr* 7: 63-64. For the English source, see *Tafsīr Ibn Kathīr* (p. 1962). Al-Nadr "visited Persia and learned stories of some Persian kings, such as Rustum and Isphandiyar.... Whenever the Prophet would leave an audience in which Al-Nadr was sitting, Al-Nadr began narrating to them the stories that he learned in Persia, proclaiming afterwards, 'Who, by Allah, has better tales to narrate, I or Muḥammad?' When Allah allowed the Muslims to capture Al-Nadr in Badr, the Messenger of Allah commanded that his head be cut off before him, and that was done, all thanks are due to Allah." See also Ibn Hishām (Ibn Isḥāq), *The Life of Muḥammad* 308; Ibn Hishām (Ibn Isḥāq), *Al-Sīra al-Nabawīya* 3: 93.

[50] See the commentary on Q 8.31, *Tafsīr Ibn Kathīr* 7: 63-64. For the English source, see *Tafsīr Ibn Kathīr* (pp. 1961-1962). According to this commentator, al-Nadr would narrate Persian stories after Muḥammad left his audience and remark, "Who, by Allah, has better stories to narrate, I or Muḥammad?"

> *And amongst men is one who buys sportive legends, to lead astray from God's path, without knowledge, and to make a jest of it; these, for them is shameful woe!* (Q 31.6; Palmer trans.)[51]
>
> *They will ask thee of the spirit. Say, 'The spirit comes at the bidding of my Lord, and ye are given but a little knowledge thereof.'* (Q 17.85; Palmer trans.)[52]

Muḥammad (about whom Q 21.107 states, *"We have only sent thee as a mercy to the worlds"*; Palmer trans.) also commanded the execution of another captive, 'Uqba Ibn Abū Mu'ayṭ, who begged him to spare his life, asking "Who will look after my children, O Muḥammad?" To this appeal, Muḥammad reportedly said, "Hell" and had 'Uqba beheaded.[53] (Like al-Naḍr, 'Uqba had been a critic of Muḥammad when the prophet began his call in Mecca. 'Uqba ridiculed Muḥammad both verbally and physically, claiming he was a false prophet and even spitting on him.[54] One time, he made a public butt of Muḥammad, when he placed the entrails or fetus of a slaughtered camel on Muḥammad's back while he was prostrated in prayer. Muḥammad had to remain in that position until the heavy waste was removed by his daughter while the Quraysh leaders laughed so hard they fell over themselves.[55])

Muḥammad's lack of mercy toward these two captives appears to be a human act of revenge for the mockery and bullying Muḥammad endured during his early call in Mecca rather than divine punishment for their lack of belief in Islam. Men of their stature would have commanded a high ransom. The difference in their treatment—quick execution—suggests a personal reason.

According to Muslim commentator al-Ṭabarī, Muḥammad consulted his Companions before deciding the fate of the rest of the captives:[56]

---

[51] al-Suyutī, *Asbāb al-Nuzūl al-Qur'ān* 202; al-Waḥidī, *Asbāb Nuzūl* 356. According to these sources, al-Nadr tempted people with food, drink, and entertainment to persuade them to abandon Islam.

[52] al-Suyutī, *Asbāb al-Nuzūl* 168. According to this source, al-Nadr and 'Uqba Ibn Abū Mu'ayṭ posed three theological questions (including this one about the spirit), supplied to them by Medinan Jewish elders, to Muḥammad to test his authenticity and legitimacy as a prophet.

[53] *Sunan Abū Dawūd*, Book of *Jihād* 3: 307-308. See Ibn Hishām (Ibn Isḥāq), *The Life of Muḥammad* 308; Ibn Hishām (Ibn Isḥāq), *Al-Sīra al-Nabawīya* 3: 93.

[54] Ibn Hishām (Ibn Isḥāq), *The Life of Muḥammad* 164; Ibn Hishām (Ibn Isḥāq), *Al-Sīra al-Nabawīya* 2: 147.

[55] *Sahih Muslim*, Book of Jihad and Expedition: The persecution of the holy prophet...at the hands of infidels and hypocrites (pp. 1111-1112); *Ṣaḥīḥ Muslim*, Kitāb al-Jihād wa al-Sīyar 2: 863. See *Sahih Bukhari*, Book of Virtues of the Prayer Hall (p. 129); *Ṣaḥīḥ al-Bukhārī*, Abūāb Sutrat al-Musallī 1: 194.

[56] See the commentary on Q 8.67, *Tafsīr al-Ṭabarī* 10: 32. See also *Sahih Muslim*, Book of Jihad and Expedition: The help with angels in Badr and the permissibility of the spoils of war (pp. 1088-1089); *Ṣaḥīḥ Muslim*, Kītāb al-Jihād wa al-Sīyar 2: 843-844.

> The Messenger of God...said: "What do you say about those captives?" Abū Bakr said: "O Messenger of God, they are your people and kindred. So keep them alive and ask them to turn to God in repentance so that God may accept their repentance." And 'Umar said: "O Messenger of God, they disbelieved you and drove you out. So bring them forward and behead them!" 'Abd Allah Ibn Rawāḥa said: "O Messenger of God, you are in a valley which abounds in firewood. So throw them into it and set it on fire."

The Companions' answers presented different degrees of harshness regarding the treatment of the Quraysh captives. Muḥammad responded to their advice with silence, took the opinion of Abū Bakr, and demanded ransom from the Quraysh in exchange for the lives of their tribesmen, now held captive by the Muslims.

However, after collecting the ransom money, Muḥammad claimed that Allah sent down upon him Q 8.67. Its directive aligns with 'Umar's suggestion: *"It has not been for any prophet to take captives until he hath slaughtered in the land! Ye wish to have the goods of this world, but God wishes for the next, for God is mighty, wise!"* (Palmer trans.). After the revelation of this verse, Muḥammad and Abū Bakr cried, reproaching themselves for not slaughtering all the captives.[57] According to Muslim commentator Ibn Kathīr, this verse means that it is "not (fitting) for the Prophet that he should have prisoners of war until he has fought (his enemies thoroughly) in the land." Men desire "the goods of this world, but Allah desires...the Hereafter...."[58]

Muḥammad faced a dilemma in how to handle the Badr captives. If he ransomed them, he could generate much needed funding, but if he killed them, he could satisfy his revenge. His eventual resolution is interesting in several ways. Why, for instance, does Muḥammad ask his Companions first (instead of Allah) for advice concerning the fate of the captives? Why does Muḥammad follow Abū Bakr's advice and ransoms the captives instead of killing them? Why does the revelation of Q 8.67 come to Muḥammad after the captives are ransomed? What would have happened to Muḥammad and his army if he had followed 'Umar's advice and had not ransomed the captives but beheaded them all?

---

[57] See the commentary on Q 8.67, *Tafsīr al-Ṭabarī* 10: 32. See also *Sahih Muslim*, Book of Jihad and Expedition: The help with angels in Badr and the permissibility of the spoils of war (pp. 1088-1089); *Ṣaḥīḥ Muslim*, Kītāb al-Jihād wa al-Sīyar 2: 843-844.

[58] See the commentary on Q 8.67, *Tafsīr Ibn Kathīr* 7: 119-120. For the English translation, see *Tafsir Ibn Kathir* (p. 2013). See also the commentary on Q 8.67, *Tafsīr al-Ṭabarī* 10: 32.

Captives of jihadists and the choices of execution and ransom

Today's Islamic jihadist groups generally favor killing rather than ransoming their captives. To them, the choice of ransom is only acceptable in exceptional cases, such as when there is an urgent need for money or a particularly important interest. One such exceptional case was when Islamic State released forty-nine people (forty-six Turkish citizens, three Iraqi consulate employees) who were taken hostage when ISIS invaded Mosul, Iraq, in June 2014, and held them captive for three months. Initially, the government of Turkey "insisted that no military actions had been taken and that no ransoms were paid" to obtain the release of these hostages.[59] However, the Turkish government would not explain "why or how the captives were transported from Mosul in Iraq to Raqqa in Syria" before their return to Turkey.[60] During the time Islamic State held the captives, Turkey did not join the Western coalition in its military campaign against the terrorist group. In its negotiations to release the hostages, Turkey undoubtedly wanted to avoid any belligerent action that might jeopardize the treatment and return of the hostages.[61] In turn, Islamic State may have wanted neighboring Turkey's abstention from the Western coalition, given its location (reduce another hostile front) and its porous border, which had provided Islamic State with a pathway for its foreign fighters and access to oil and other necessities it needed to solidify and expand its control in Iraq. (In October 2014, less than one month after the release of the hostages, Turkey finally joined the Western coalition to fight Islamic State in Iraq and Syria.)[62]

For most captives, especially Americans, ISIS (and later, Islamic State) has abused them and exploited their captivity and eventual public execution for propaganda purposes. The majority of these captives have been decapitated—a practice often used by Muḥammad and his followers when dispatching their captives. All Islamic terrorist groups, including ISIS, count the United States as their worst enemy. They celebrate these beheadings, publicizing the brutally graphic executions worldwide for all

---

[59] Hubbard, Ben, Sebnem Arsu, and Ceylan Yeginsu. "Turkey Obtains Release of Hostages Held in Iraq." *NYTimes.com*. New York Times, 20 Sept. 2014. Web (https://www.nytimes.com/2014/09/21/world/middleeast/dozens-of-turkish-hostages-held-by-islamic-state-are-freed.html).

[60] Ibid.

[61] Lowen, Mark. "Turkish Hostages Held by IS in Iraq Released." *BBC.com*. British Broadcasting Corporation, 20 Sept. 2014. Web (http://www.bbc.com/news/world-europe-29291946).

[62] Hunter, Isabel. "War against ISIS: Turkey Joins Western Coalition in Fight to Stop Militants." *Independent.co.uk*. The Independent, 2 Oct. 2014. Web (http://www.independent.co.uk/news/world/middle-east/war-against-isis-turkey-joins-western-coalition-in-fight-to-stop-militants-9771253.html).

to witness, as a way to deeply wound, demoralize, and humiliate their arch enemy.

Like millions of people, I followed the heart-rending news story of freelance journalist, Steven Sotloff, who was abducted in 2013 by ISIS. After the ISIS beheading of James Foley, also a freelance journalist, Steven's mother Shirley Sotloff broke her family's self-imposed silence and pleaded with ISIS leader Abū Bakr al-Baghdādī to spare her son's life: "I ask you to use your authority to spare his life and to follow the example set by the Prophet Muḥammad, who protected People of the Book [Christians and Jews]."[63] I deeply sympathized with this desperate mother who was compelled by her love and grave concern to make this public appeal. Unfortunately, this poor mother, like most Westerners, does not realize is that if al-Baghdādī were to truly follow Muḥammad's example, he would not feel any compunction in killing her son in cold blood and telling her that the fire of hell will eternally burn her son. Muḥammad did no less in the way he treated his captives al-Naḍr and 'Uqba after the Battle of Badr victory.

The West is uninformed and naïve to think that Islamic State (and its precursors, ISIL and ISIS) does not follow Muḥammad whenever it shows no mercy on those whom it considers infidels. In reality, Islamic State **is** following the example of Muḥammad because its purpose and policies are dictated and guided by the Qur'ān, the Hadith literature, Sunna, and Muḥammad's biography, all of which detail the Prophet's words, deeds, and commands. For Islamic State and similar groups, the rulings and commands in Islam's holy books take precedence over the internationally ratified laws of the Geneva Conventions regarding the humane treatment of prisoners of war and civilians during military conflicts—let alone some insignificant mother's plea.

Muḥammad showed no compassion to the families of the men who fought during the Battle of Badr—on either side. Even before the event, he knew in particular that his Emigrants would be fighting against their close relatives, the Quraysh. One of his followers, Abū Ḥudhayfa, would be fighting against his brother Walīd Ibn 'Utba, his uncle Shayba Ibn Rabī'a, and his father 'Utba Ibn Rabī'a, a high-ranking Quraysh tribal leader. When Abū Ḥudhayfa and the other Muslims were told by Muḥammad

---

[63] Callimachi, Rukmini. "U.S. Captive's Mother Issues Plea to ISIS." *NYTimes.com*. New York Times, 27 Aug. 2014. Web (https://www.nytimes.com/2014/08/28/world/middleeast/steven-sotloff-isis-hostage.html).

before the battle's commencement to spare a few Quraysh—including Muḥammad's own paternal uncle al-'Abbās Ibn 'Abd al-Muṭṭalib (refer to Chapter 8, page 232)—claiming they had been "forced to come out against their will and have no desire to fight us," Abū Ḥudhayfa asked incredulously, "Are we to kill our fathers and our sons and our brothers and our families and leave al-'Abbās?"[64] (Apparently, Muḥammad had compassion for his own family, even if they were infidels.)

Soon after this outburst, Abū Ḥudhayfa witnessed the deaths of his brother, uncle, and father in a traditional champion combat duel at the hands (swords) of three peers among the Emigrant Muslims before the actual battle began.[65]

After the Muslims had won the battle, Muḥammad ordered his men to throw the dead Quraysh into a pit. As the corpse of 'Utba was dragged over to the pit's edge, Muḥammad noticed that Abū Ḥudhayfa was sad, his face drained of color. The Prophet asked him if Abū felt "deeply the fate" of his father and received this chilling response:[66]

> "No…I have no misgivings about my father and his death, but I used to know my father as a wise, cultured, and virtuous man and so I hoped that he would be guided to Islam. When I saw what had befallen him and that he had died in unbelief after my hopes for him it saddened me."

If Muḥammad's own followers believed that their prophet had the authority to lead them into battle against their own family members, forsaking all human relationships for the cause of Islam, what chance does an infidel American mother have to dissuade Abū Bakr al-Baghdadī, who proclaimed himself caliph of Islamic State in 2014, to release her son? Muḥammad is his supreme role model and he considers himself Muḥammad's modern-day standard-bearer.

The early Muslims' angst-filled dilemma of fighting and killing one's own relatives undoubtedly colored their morale and jubilation in the

---

[64] Ibn Hishām (Ibn Isḥāq), *The Life of Muḥammad* 301; Ibn Hishām (Ibn Isḥāq), *Al-Sīra al-Nabawīya* 3: 73.

[65] Ibn Hishām (Ibn Isḥāq), *The Life of Muḥammad* 298-299; Ibn Hishām (Ibn Isḥāq), *Al-Sīra al-Nabawīya* 3: 66. Prior to the three-champion duel, 'Utba Ibn Rabī'a had tried to persuade the Quraysh not to battle the Muslims, return to Mecca, and "leave Muḥammad to the rest of the Arabs." He did feel an obligation to avenge the death of their tribesman 'Amr Ibn al-Ḥaḍramī (the slain caravan leader) but not a bloodwit against all the Muslims. In the three-champion combat, he (and his brother and son) also refused to duel with any Anṣār, saying, "We have nothing to do with you." The three were killed by Hamza, 'Alī, and Ubayba.

[66] Ibn Hishām (Ibn Isḥāq), *The Life of Muḥammad* 307; Ibn Hishām (Ibn Isḥāq), *Al-Sīra al-Nabawīya* 3: 86.

Battle of Badr and subsequent battles. In time, the Qur'ān itself (Q 58.22; Palmer trans.) weighs in to settle this matter:

> *Thou shalt not find a people who believe in God and the last day loving him who opposes God and His Apostle, even though it be their fathers, or their sons, or their brethren, or their clansmen. He has written faith in their hearts, and He aids them with a spirit from Him; and will make them enter into gardens beneath which rivers flow, to dwell therein for aye! God is well pleased with them, and they well pleased with Him: they are God's crew; ay, God's crew, they shall prosper!*

According to Muslim commentator Ibn Kathīr, this verse refers to the Battle of Badr and several of Muḥammad's closest Companions who killed infidel relatives during the onslaught: Abū 'Ubayda Ibn al-Jarrāḥ (who killed his infidel father); Muṣ'ab Ibn 'Umayr (who killed his infidel brother); 'Umar Ibn al-Khaṭṭāb (who killed his infidel uncle); Abū Bakr (who intended to kill his infidel son); and Ḥamza and 'Alī, Muḥammad's paternal uncle and cousin, respectively, who killed several of their relatives.[67] In other words, this verse affirms that only those who oppose infidels—even their own relatives—in the cause of Allah, will enter paradise and receive Allah's blessings.

Ibn Kathīr further explains that Allah views these actions—killing infidel relatives—as a testament to the high religious character of these Muslim fighters, and Allah will compensate and reward them for these killings:[68]

> When the believers became enraged against their relatives and kindred in Allah's cause, He [Allah] compensated them by being pleased with them and making them pleased with Him from what He has granted of eternal delight, ultimate victory and encompassing favor.

So, in the end, Shirley Sotloff's plea to save her son was not ignored by a singular particularly sadistic or amoral man; it was ignored by the teachings and actions of Muḥammad and Islamic texts that encourage and glorify the killing of *"those who disbelieve."*

---

[67] See the commentary on Q 58.20-22, *Tafsīr Ibn Kathīr* 8: 86. For the English translation, see *Tafsīr Ibn Kathīr* (pp. 5088-5089).

[68] See the commentary on Q 58.20-22, *Tafsīr Ibn Kathīr* 8: 86. For the English translation, see *Tafsīr Ibn Kathīr* (p. 5090).

After the video of the beheading of Steven Sotloff was posted online September 2, 2014, a spokesman for the Sotloff family, Barak Barfi, gave a public statement on behalf of the family to the press.[69] He also gave a statement in Arabic, challenging the leader of ISIS to a debate regarding whether or not the Qur'ān encourages violence. In his remarks directed toward Abū Bakr al-Baghdādī, he posed this question: "You said Ramadan is a month of mercy but where is your mercy?"[70]

Barak Barfi's question to al-Baghdādī is puzzling. Doesn't Barfi know that the Battle of Badr occurred during the month of mercy and forgiveness—Ramadan—a battle where the early Muslims killed their own relatives? Even though the Battle of Badr was the outcome of a Muslim plan to attack and plunder a commercial caravan, it has been celebrated ever since as a divinely blessed victory on the seventeenth day of Ramadan every year. In fact, many Qur'ānic verses that discuss the use of violence against nonbelievers "came" to Muḥammad after this first large-scale engagement between the Muslims and their enemies, including Q 8.12 (Palmer trans.):

> *When your Lord inspired the angels—'Verily, I am with you; make ye firm then those who believe; I will cast dread into the hearts of those who misbelieve,—strike off their necks then, and strike off from them every finger tip.'*

In this verse, Allah affirms his unwavering support of Muḥammad and his followers through his angels as he clearly urges beheading and fingertip amputation of *"those who misbelieve."* There is no mention of mercy because of Ramadan.

During his media presentation, Barak Barfi also cites a Qur'ānic verse (Q 2.190) rebuking al-Baghdādī by stating that the Qur'ān is a book of peace. Though he recites the verse in Arabic he does not seem to fully appreciate the occasion and circumstances surrounding the revelation of this verse: *"Fight in God's way with those who fight with you, but transgress not; verily, God loves not those who do transgress"* (Palmer trans.). Barfi does not seem to know (or will not acknowledge) that conditions specified

---

[69] Carter, Chelsea J., and Faith Karimi. "Slain Journalist's Family Accuses ISIS Leader of Violating Islam with Execution." *CNN.com*. Cable News Network, 4 Sept. 2014. Web (http://www.cnn.com/2014/09/03/world/meast/isis-beheading-videos/).

[70] "A Spokesman for the Sotloff Family Challenges Baghdadi in Arabic: '*Waylaka*' [Doom to You]...Ready to Debate You by Qur'ān...Where Is Your Mercy?'" *Arabic.CNN.com*. Cable News Network (Arabic), 4 Sept. 2014. Web (http://arabic.cnn.com/middleeast/2014/09/04/isis-beheading-videos).

in a Qur'ānic verse can be supplanted by different—even opposing—conditions presented in verses revealed later.

According to highly respected Orientalist Nöldeke, this second sura (Sura al-Baqara) is the "earliest of the Medinan suras."[71] Islamic scholars point out that two of the conditions in Q 2.190 (*"Fight in God's way with those who fight with you"* and *"transgress not"*) have both been abrogated, or nullified, by verses revealed later. In this case, the first condition (*"Fight in God's way with those who fight with you"*) has been abrogated by Q 9.36 (*"...but fight the idolaters, one and all, as they fight you one and all"*), Q 2.191 and Q 4.91 (*"...kill them wherever/wheresoever ye find them..."*), Q 9.29 (*"Fight those who believe not in God and in the last day..."*), and the Sword verse, Q 9.5 (*"...kill the idolaters wherever ye may find them..."*).[72] The second condition (*"transgress not"*) has been abrogated by Q 9.36 and Q 9.5. These abrogations mean that Muslims are no longer restricted from initiating fighting in the cause of Allah (jihad).

Additionally, Muslim commentator Ibn Kathīr explains that the second condition (*"transgress not"*) means that Muslims are prohibited from "killing women, children, and old people who do not participate in warfare, killing priests and residents of houses of worship, burning down trees and killing animals without real benefit."[73] Yet, with the abrogation of the first condition, Muslims can still initiate the fighting. Some Islamic scholars would even argue that the abrogation of the second condition by Sword verse Q 9.5 means that Muslims, in the cause of jihad, are not prevented from killing women, children, and the elderly.[74] (See Chapter 16, page 496.)

Thus, selecting and quoting a Qur'ānic verse out of context with little understanding or attention to its history and sequence is unwise, and in Barak Barfi's situation, undermines his argument. Instead of rigorously

---

[71] Noldeke, et al. *History of the Qur'ān* 141.

[72] Ibn al-Jawzī, *Nawāsikh* 179. **Note:** Most Islamic accounts maintain that the ninth chapter, Sura al-Tawba, was the last sura given by Muḥammad, and the majority of Islamic scholars agree that this sura was revealed all at once. (See Ibn 'Āshūr, *Tafsīr* 10: 86.)

[73] See the commentary on Q 2.190, *Tafsīr al-Ṭabarī* 2: 111. See also the commentary on Q 2.190, *Tafsīr Ibn Kathīr* 473. For the Arabic source, see *Tafsīr Ibn Kathīr* 2: 214.

[74] *Sahih Bukhari*, Book of Fighting for the Cause of Allah (Jihad)(pp. 693-694); *Ṣaḥīḥ al-Bukhārī*, Kītāb al-Jihād wa al-Sīyar 3: 1097. See *Ṣaḥih Muslim*, Book of Jihad and Expedition: Permissibility of killing women and children in the night raids, provided it is not deliberate (p. 1076); *Ṣaḥīḥ Muslim*, Kītāb al-Jihād wa al-Sīyar 2: 832-833. The *ḥadīth* in *Sahih Bukhari* states that Muḥammad "was asked whether it was permissible to attack the pagan warrior at night with the probability of exposing their women and children to danger. The Prophet replied, 'They (i.e., women and children) are from them (i.e., pagans)'...."

challenging Abū Bakr al-Baghdādī with a Qur'ānic verse that would truly question or invalidate the ideology and policies of Islamic State, Barfi inadvertently defended Islam and thus dishonored his friend, Steven Sotloff. Barfi's ill-advised Qur'ānic examples only underscored the close alignment and compatibility of Islamic State with Islamic doctrine.

Abū Bakr al-Baghdādī can easily find verses, including Q 2.190, to justify and support Islamic State's abduction, imprisonment, and finally, execution by decapitation of Steven Sotloff. As an American Israeli, Sotloff is by default an enemy of Islam because America and Israel are fighting Muslims (*"Fight in God's way with those who fight with you..."*). Possible prohibitions against the killing of captives (*"transgress not"*) are reserved for only women, children, and the elderly.[75] Unfortunately for Steven Sotloff, he was not from one of these protected groups.

Regrettably, many people think and act like Barfi concerning Islamic groups. Although they witness the atrocities of Islamic State and similar groups and rightfully condemn them, they do not understand the truth: Not only is there a strong correlation between these ugly deeds and Islam, these actions of al-Baghdadi are completely compatible with the deeds of Muḥammad.

Barak Barfi is foolish and naïve to challenge Abū Bakr al-Baghdadī to a debate about the Qur'ān, especially when he has already selected such flawed verses to present his opening argument. Al-Baghdadī is not an illiterate, mentally unstable person whose agenda and actions are based on personal whims. He has been a professor and educator and is a recognized preacher. He is a "graduate of the Islamic University in Baghdad, where he finished his academic studies (BA, MA and PhD)" and possesses a comprehensive knowledge in Islamic culture, history, Hadith literature, Sunna, and jurisprudence (*sharī'a*).[76] As the leader and self-proclaimed "Caliph" of Islamic State, he has surrounded himself with advisors and clergy with similarly deep knowledge of the Qur'ān and Hadith literature, who would not hesitate to inform al-Baghdadī if any of his goals and policies breached Islamic law, Hadith literature

[75] See the commentary on Q 2.190, *Tafsīr al-Ṭabarī* 2: 111. See also the commentary on Q 2.190, *Tafsīr Ibn Kathīr* 473. For the Arabic source, see *Tafsīr Ibn Kathīr* 2: 214.

[76] Insite Blog on Terrorism and Extremism. "A Biography of Abu Bakr al-Baghdadi." *SITEintelgroup.com*. SITE Intelligence Group, 12 Aug. 2014. Web (http://news.siteintelgroup.com/blog/index.php/entry/226-the-story-behind-abu-bakr-al-baghdadi).

(Muḥammad's practices), or the Qur'ān. His methodology is supported by Islamic doctrine.

For this reason, many terrorist operations take place during the month of Ramadan as jihad in the cause of Allah. For example, the attack by Islamic State on two beachside hotels in Sousse, Tunisia, on June 26, 2015, killing at least thirty-nine tourists, occurred during Ramadan.[77] An Islamic State suicide bomber not only struck the Al-Imām al-Ṣādiq Shiite Mosque in Kuwait City (capital and largest city of Kuwait) during Ramadan, but he also carried out his plan as the packed worshippers were observing this holy month during Friday prayers. The explosion killed at least twenty-seven and injured 227 worshippers.[78] The expulsion of thousands of Assyrian Christians from Mosul, Iraq, in July 2014, after Islamic State took control of the city, also occurred during the holy month of Ramadan.[79]

The list goes on and on. Ramadan is actually the month of Islamic jihad—not a month of mercy, as Mr. Barfi thinks.

The ISIS videos of executions where captives are shown being beheaded are extremely disturbing, regardless of the race or religion of these people. These graphic and unapologetic scenes of brutality are traumatizing viewers, the final visuals taking only a minute but haunting them for days, weeks, or longer afterward. However, in the Muslim world, Muslims are repeatedly taught (just as I once was taught as a former Muslim) to celebrate and glorify these kinds of killings as noble acts of bravery. Our preachers cry "*Allahu Akbar*" while they teach us that the slaughtering and beheading of non-Muslims are all part of Muḥammad's Hadith literature and Sunna, the collective works that detail his words and deeds.

---

[77] Mosendz, Polly. "Report: ISIS Claims Responsibility for Tunisia Hotel Attack." *Newsweek.com*. Newsweek, 26 June 2015. Web (http://www.newsweek.com/least-19-dead-terrorist-attack-tunisian-resort-hotel-347193); "Tunisia Attack on Sousse Beach 'Kills 39.'" *BBC.com*. British Broadcasting Corporation, 27 June 2015. Web (http://www.bbc.com/news/world-africa-33287978). **Note:** The month of Ramadan in 2015 was June 18 to July 17.

[78] Robinson, Martin, and Tom Wyke. "Suicide Bomb Rips through Kuwaiti Mosque after Friday Prayers Killing at Least 27 Worshippers as ISIS Claims Responsibility." *DailyMail.co.uk*. Telegraph Media Group, 26 June 2015. Web (http://www.dailymail.co.uk/news/article-3140525/Suicide-bomb-rips-Kuwaiti-mosque-Friday-prayers-killing-13-worshippers-ISIS-claims-responsibility.html). **Note:** Islamic State considers Shiite Muslims as polytheists and heretics and not true Muslims.

[79] "Iraqi Christians Flee after ISIS Issue Mosul Ultimatum." *BBC.com*. British Broadcasting Corporation, 18 July 2014. Web (http://www.bbc.com/news/world-middle-east-28381455). **Note:** The month of Ramadan in 2014 was June 28 to July 27.

For instance, these Islamic narrations report that at the time of the Battle of Badr, Muḥammad considered the Quraysh leader Amr Ibn Hishām, or Abū al-Ḥakam ("Father of Wisdom), a hateful enemy and called him instead Abū Jahl ("Father of Ignorance"). When Abū al-Ḥakam fell to the ground, his foot severed during the combat, he was approached by 'Abd Allāh Ibn Mas'ūd, one of Muḥammad's closest Companions. (Muḥammad had ordered a search for Abū al-Ḥakam's body.) Finding Abū al-Ḥakam still alive, Ibn Mas'ūd placed his foot upon the mortally wounded man's neck. (Undoubtedly, Ibn Mas'ūd revelled in this reverse of circumstances. During his Meccan childhood, Ibn Mas'ūd had been a lowly shepherd while Abū al-Ḥakam was one of the prominent figures in his tribe.) As Abū al-Ḥakam was taking his final breaths, he allegedly said to Ibn Mas'ūd, "You have climbed high, you little shepherd!"[80] At this point, Ibn Mas'ūd then pulled out his sword and beheaded him. He triumphantly threw the head before Muḥammad, saying, "This is the head of the enemy of God, Abū Jahl."[81] Muḥammad responded by thanking Allah.[82]

The practice of beheading is a *sunna*, a teaching or deed, of Muḥammad and endorsed in the Qur'ān. Its application was honored by his closest Companions, such as 'Abd Allāh Ibn Mas'ūd. The members of Islamic organizations know this fact very well. The Islamic Jordanian-Palestinian writer, Abū Muḥammad al-Maqdisī, one of the most prominent theorists of jihad organizations in the world, defended the execution method of decapitation when al-Zarqāwī (initial leader of Al Qaeda in Iraq, or AQI) beheaded some American hostages, especially Nicholas Berg, an American freelance radio-tower repairman. In one of his sermons, al-Maqdisī made this comment:[83]

> Cutting off heads is a part of this religion. Indeed, slaughtering Allah's enemies is part of this religion, as it is written in the biography of the leader of the Mujahidin [Muḥammad] in accordance with his jihad and the call of the Prophet to his people.

[80] Ibn Hishām (Ibn Isḥāq), *The Life of Muḥammad* 304; Ibn Hishām (Ibn Isḥāq), *Al-Sīra al-Nabawīya* 3: 80. See Ibn Kathīr, *Al-Bidaya* 5: 135-137.

[81] Ibn Hishām (Ibn Isḥāq), *The Life of Muḥammad* 304; Ibn Hishām (Ibn Isḥāq), *Al-Sīra al-Nabawīya* 3: 80.

[82] Ibn Hishām (Ibn Isḥāq), *The Life of Muḥammad* 304; Ibn Hishām (Ibn Isḥāq), *Al-Sīra al-Nabawīya* 3: 80.

[83] "Daesh [ISIS] Debaters Respond to al-Maqdīsī: 'You Have Already Defended Zarqawi's Cutting Heads and Necks.'" *Arabic.CNN.com.* Cable Network News (Arabic), 18 Aug. 2014. Web (https://arabic.cnn.com/middleeast/2014/08/18/maqdessi-isis-zarqawi).

Al-Maqdisī is correct in stating that the bloody killing of enemies is a part of Islam. Early in his call, Muḥammad himself threatened his own tribesmen, the Quraysh, with violence when he was still living among them: "Will you listen to me, O Quraysh? By him who holds my life in His hand I bring you slaughter."[84]

Muḥammad made this pronouncement before he migrated to Medina (AD 622) and before he formed his army, which means that he waited for several years for the opportunity to carry out his threat. But Islamic sources show that he later established the permission and use of slaughtering. His statements and later behavior disprove all claims made by people who state that Islam's early wars were only defensive. Muḥammad's threats of slaughtering his foes before the first Islamic battles have been documented in the Islamic sources.

These threats to slaughter infidels are also found in Islam's holiest book:

> *And when ye meet those who misbelieve—then striking off heads until ye have massacred them, and bind fast the bonds!...*" (Q 47.4; Palmer trans.)
>
> *When your Lord inspired the angels—'Verily, I am with you; make ye firm then those who believe; I will cast dread into the hearts of those who misbelieve,—strike off their necks then, and strike off from them every finger tip.'* (Q 8.12; Palmer trans.)

Therefore, the slaughtering—and, in particular, the beheading of infidels—is advocated not only in the Hadith literature and the biography of Muḥammad but also in the Qur'ān.

Muḥammad's words, deeds, and teachings have constructed the foundation for the goals and policies of Islamic State, which is a continuation of these seventh century AD acts. If people today feel horrified because of these barbaric acts committed by ISIS (Islamic State) and similar groups, then they should research the origin or inspiration behind today's ruthless and bloodthirsty acts and the acts of Muḥammad and his Mujāhidīn. If Muḥammad, Islam's Prophet and supreme role model, had not slaughtered people, then Islamic groups would not have been able to justify their acts or easily find Islamic texts that report and celebrate this kind of behavior.

---

[84] Ibn Hishām (Ibn Isḥāq), *The Life of Muḥammad* 131; Ibn Hishām (Ibn Isḥāq), *Al-Sīra al-Nabawīya* 2: 41. See *History of al-Ṭabarī* 6: 102.

The famous exegete Abū 'Abd Allah al-Qurṭubī (AD 1214-1273) presents the following comment regarding Q 47.4:[85]

> It has been said that the meaning [of this phrase *"then striking off heads"*] is: intentionally strike heads. He [Allah] said: *"striking off heads"* instead of "kill them," because this expression contains a harshness and emphasis that are not found in the word *kill.* It describes killing in its ugliest manner, i.e., cutting the neck and making the organ, which is the head of the body, to fly off [the body].

So, according to this highly regarded Muslim commentator, the Qur'ān's terminology here regarding this particular method of killing is deliberate, presumably to heighten the enemies' shock and terror at the prospect of such brutal and bloody killing.

Islamic State totally understands the emotional power of using decapitation—with even just one captive. The main purpose of these publicly shared videos of these executions, where the helpless captive is shown kneeling and then beheaded by his jihadist executioner, is to both terrorize people as well as create a commanding, invincible image of the jihadists in order to demoralize and frighten their enemies before the next confrontation. To make more fearsome the method of killing over the fear of death itself has proven to be an extremely effective military strategy for ISIS and later, Islamic State. The slaughtering and take-no-prisoners approach by these fighters as they began seizing territory, taking control of cities in the Anbar province in northern Iraq, apparently unnerved the much larger Iraqi army, which fled in panic when ISIS turned its sights on Mosul, Iraq's second largest city, in early June 2014. (Later analysis also suggests poor discipline, missing leadership, and disorganization among the Iraqi forces.) The tens of thousands of Iraqi army soldiers and federal police chose to drop their weapons (some even discarded their uniforms) and other military equipment, munitions, and vehicles rather than face and fight the much smaller terrorist group (which numbered about 1500).[86] The swiftness of the city's fall by the greatly outnumbered jihadist terrorist group, compounded by the anemic Iraqi defense,

---

[85] See the commentary on Q 47.4, *Tafsīr al-Qurṭubī* 16: 230.

[86] Carter, Chelsea J., Salma Abdelaziz and Mohammed Rawfeeq. "Iraqi Soldiers, Police Drop Weapons, Flee Posts in Portions of Mosul." *CNN.com.* Cable Network News, 13 June 2014. Web (http://www.cnn.com/2014/06/10/world/meast/iraq-violence/); Sly, Liz, and Ahmed Ramadan. "Insurgents Seize Iraqi City of Mosul as Security Forces Flee." *WashingtonPost.com.* The Washington Post, 10 June 2014. Web (https://www.washingtonpost.com/world/insurgents-seize-iraqi-city-of-mosul-as-troops-flee/2014/06/10/21061e87-8fcd-4ed3-bc94-0e309af0a674_story.html?utm_term=.92b2c1e5d126).

widespread desertion, and piles of discarded uniforms and military matériel, stunned the whole world.

When the ISIS forces infiltrated Mosul, they made examples of Iraqi soldiers that they captured. They "hanged…soldiers and lit them ablaze, crucified them, and torched them on the hoods of Humvees."[87] The use of terrorism, which is embraced and routinely implemented by Islamic State and similar groups, is a Qur'ānic method for religious warfare par excellence:

> *Prepare ye against them what force and companies of horse ye can, to make the enemies of God, and your enemies, and others beside them, in dread thereof. Ye do not know them, but God knows them! and whatever ye expend in God's way He will repay you; and ye shall not be wronged.* (Q 8.60; Palmer trans.)

In this verse, the Qur'ān commands Muslims to be prepared against the enemy and to display their power in order to terrorize the enemy. Surely, today's execution videos of beheadings by Islamic groups certainly serve this purpose. Muḥammad himself was famous for commanding his followers to *"strike off* [the] *necks"* of infidels, i.e., "I was sent to strike the necks and bind fast the bonds."[88] It seems as though the use of decapitation became so customary that Muḥammad's followers would ask the Prophet, "Shall we strike his neck O Messenger of Allah?" when determining a sentence for a person they felt deserving of death.[89]

Slaughtering and beheading have always been a part of Islamic history and have become part of our Islamic culture. We Muslims have been taught that it is a normal practice that should be carried out on infidels as they are the enemies of Allah. Because Muḥammad and his Companions applied it against infidels and their enemies, then it is not wrong for today's Muslims or Islamic groups to apply it against their infidel enemies; these acts have a strong foundational base in Islamic doctrine, literature, and tradition.

---

[87] Parker, Ned, Isabel Coles, and Raheem Salman. "Special Report: How Mosul Fell—An Iraqi General Disputes Baghdad's Story." *Reuters.com*. Reuters, 14 Oct. 2014. Web (http://www.reuters.com/article/us-mideast-crisis-gharawi-special-report-idUSKCN0I30Z820141014).

[88] See the commentary on Q 8.12, *Tafsīr al-Ṭabarī* 9: 133.

[89] al-Mubarakfurī, *Tuḥfat al-Aḥwadhī*, Kitāb al-Dīyāt (Book of Blood Money) 4: 546. According to this source, Muḥammad commanded beheading whenever he wanted to kill anyone until it became common place among his Companions. So whenever they saw a man whom they thought deserved killing, one of them would say: "Messenger of Allah, let me behead him."

Therefore, if we want to confront Islamic and similar Islamic jihadist groups over these barbaric acts of terrorism, then we have to confront the Islamic sources.

Muḥammad and the nomadic bandits (*al-sa'ālīk*)

Muḥammad also formed alliances with nomadic groups of bandits called *al-sa'ālīk*. These criminals became marauding vagabonds after they were disowned by their tribes for their crimes and created their own roving communities. The banishment by a tribe of its lawless members was the tribe's way to dodge responsibility and compensation for any criminal behavior these wayward members might commit upon other tribes. In this way, if any of these banished members raided, kidnapped, or killed people of a different tribe, the native tribe would not have to pay compensation or blood money to or face war with the injured tribe.

Iraqi historian Jawād 'Alī (AD 1907-1987) who wrote *Al-Mufaṣṣal fi Tārīkh al-'Arab Qabla al-Islām*, one of the largest and most well-known encyclopaedias about the history of pre-Islamic Arabs, offers this description:[90]

> *Al-sa'ālīk* are a people who have rebelled against their families, clans and tribes for many reasons...and they rely on themselves to protect their lives and on their strength to provide for their own needs by raiding [along] roads and attacking scattered Arab neighborhoods, both individuals or communities.... That is why they would sometimes gather together to form groups united by a single purpose.

Muḥammad attracted these nomadic criminal bandits. When they witnessed how his call challenged the status quo, causing extreme turmoil and controversy among his Quraysh tribesmen (and, later, other nearby tribes), perhaps they saw in him a kindred spirit, a kind of a rebel against his tribe and its customs. No doubt his eventual migration to Medina to escape the growing hostility of the Quraysh leadership to his call and his small band of followers resonated with these banished vagabond raiders.

Abū Dharr al-Ghifārī was one of the first of these nomadic bandits to join the call of Muḥammad. The highly respected Muslim scholar and historian al-Dhahabī (AD 1274-1348) provides these details about this particular bandit:[91]

---

[90] 'Alī, *Al-Mufaṣṣal* 10: 128.
[91] al-Dhahabī, *Sīyar* 3: 383-384.

> Abū Dharr was a man who knew how to target [roads and attack travellers]. He was brave, attacking roads by himself and victimizing isolated groups in the darkness before dawn on horseback or on foot as if he was a lion. He came to a district to take whatever he could, but then Allah cast Islam in his heart.

Abū Dharr al-Ghifārī was born to the Ghifār clan, a branch of the Banū Kināna tribe.[92] The Ghifār clan was known at that time for raiding pilgrims and caravans.[93] He was the fourth or fifth person who believed in Muḥammad and became a Muslim.[94] After converting to Islam, he returned to his tribe at Muḥammad's request to convince them to become Muslims. Muḥammad also told Abū Dharr to rejoin him once he heard the news that the Muslims have achieved victory.[95] His brother, mother and half of his tribe embraced Islam. The other half embraced Islam after Muḥammad migrated to Medina.[96] Muḥammad loved the Ghifārī because they were strong fighters who were skillful at raiding and looting. Muḥammad set aside a special prayer for the tribe: "...and may Allah forgive Ghifār!"[97] Muḥammad also compared the Ghifār more favorably to other groups:[98]

> Al-Aqra' bin Habis said to the Prophet, "Nobody gave you the pledge of allegiance but the robbers of the pilgrims (i.e., those who used to rob the pilgrims) from the tribes of Aslam, Ghifar, Muzaina."... The Prophet said, "Don't you think that the tribes of Aslam, Ghifar, Muzaina...are better than the tribes of Banū Tamim, Banū Amir, Asad, and Ghatafān?" Somebody said, "They were unsuccessful and losers!" The Prophet said, "Yes, by Him in Whose Hands my life is, they (i.e., the former) are better than they (i.e., the latter)." Abu Huraira said, "(The Prophet said), '(The people of) Banū Aslam, Ghifar and some people of Muzaina (or some people of Juhaina or Muzaina) are better in Allah's Sight (or on the Day of Resurrection) than the tribes of Asad, Tamim, Hawazin and Ghatafān.'"

---

[92] Watt, *Muḥammad at Medina* 81.

[93] al-Dhahabī, *Sīyar* 3: 384. Abū Dharr said about his tribe that "there were people who would loot the pilgrims."

[94] *History of al-Ṭabarī* 6: 87; see al-Dhahabī, *Sīyar* 3: 383-384.

[95] *Ṣaḥīḥ al-Bukhārī*, Kītāb al-Manāqib 3: 1294-1295; *Sahih Bukhari*, Book of Virtues and Merits of the Prophet and his Companions (pp. 820-821). **Note:** The English translation differs from the Arabic original source, which also mentions parenthetically that Muḥammad asked Abū Dharr to hide his conversion from the Quraysh until he learned of the Muslims' victory.

[96] al-Dhahabī, *Sīyar* 3: 382.

[97] *Sahih Bukhari*, Book of Virtues and Merits of the Prophet and his Companions (pp. 818); *Ṣaḥīḥ al-Bukhārī*, Kītāb al-Manāqib 3: 1293.

[98] *Sahih Bukhari*, Book of Virtues and Merits of the Prophet and his Companions (pp. 819); *Ṣaḥīḥ al-Bukhārī*, Kītāb al-Manāqib 3: 1294.

The reaction of the Quraysh when they learned that these nomadic bandit groups, like the Ghifār, were converting to Islam is allegedly recorded in a Qur'ānic verse (Q 46.11; Palmer trans.):

> *And those who misbelieve say of those who believe, 'If it had been good, they would not have been beforehand with us therein;' and when they are not guided thereby, then will they say, 'This is an old-fashioned lie.'*

Some Muslim commentators explain that the verse is about the pagan Quraysh who dismissed the conversion of the ill-regarded lawless bandit clans like the Ghifār by saying if Islam was authentic and good, then (good) Quraysh would have accepted and converted first—not the wicked low-status nomadic bandit clans.[99] The Quraysh knew these groups very well and considered them their inferiors, merely roving bands of thieves and robbers. The Quraysh could not imagine such unprincipled, disreputable people embracing anything that was decent, good, and pure. Yet these were the kinds of people who sought out Muḥammad at the beginning of his call and accepted him and his new religion in Mecca, with more joining after he moved to Medina.

Abū Baṣīr is another bandit who embraced Islam. He created a diplomatic controversy when he escaped imprisonment in Mecca to join Muḥammad at Medina.

In AD 628, Muḥammad and a few thousand followers left Medina to embark on a pilgrimage to Mecca. The Quraysh prevented their entry into the city despite Muḥammad's assurances that the pilgrims were peaceful and only wanted to venerate the Ka'ba and perform the *umra* (another type of pilgrimage). After a tense standoff, the two sides negotiated a ten-year armistice, the Treaty of Ḥudaybīya. One clause in the document stipulates that citizens from Mecca entering Medina would be permitted to return to Mecca (if they so wanted); however, Muslims from Medina who entered Mecca would not be permitted to return to the Muslims, even if Muḥammad himself requested the transfer. This clause angered many Muslims.[100]

When Abū Baṣīr reached Muḥammad in Medina, the terms of the treaty were in effect, and Muḥammad felt politically obligated to return Abū Baṣīr to the Quraysh in Mecca. Abū Baṣīr protested, saying, "Would you return me to the polytheists who will seduce me from my religion?"

---

[99] See the commentary on Q 46.11, *Tafsīr al-Qurṭubī* 16: 190.

[100] Ibn Hishām (Ibn Isḥāq), *The Life of Muḥammad* 504; Ibn Hishām (Ibn Isḥāq) *Al-Sīra al-Nabawīya* 4: 50.

But Muḥammad did not relent: "Go, for God will bring relief and a way of escape for you and the helpless ones with you."[101]

During the forced return trip, Abū Baṣīr managed to elude his two guard escorts after killing one of them. Once more, he made his way back to Muḥammad. This time he told Muḥammad that the Prophet's obligation to hand him over (again) was now over; he, Abū Baṣīr, would now protect himself in his religion. He then relocated to the region of Dhū'l Marwa by the seashore," where he led other Meccans who had converted to Islam in killing and raiding:[102]

> About seventy men attached themselves to him, and they so harried Quraysh, killing everyone they could get hold of and cutting to pieces every caravan that passed them, that Quraysh wrote to the apostle begging him by the ties of kinship to take these men in, for they had no use for them; so the apostle took them in and they came to him in Medina.

According to Islamic sources, as many as seventy Quraysh Muslims were able to escape Mecca and become renegades with apparently no condemnation by Muḥammad for breaking the Treaty of Hudaybīya or for choosing this violent livelihood. He apparently made no effort to force their return to Mecca or to stop their criminal activities. Was his silence on their killing and raiding his tacit approval or willing acceptance of their banditry because they were not attacking Muslims? And when the Quraysh begged him to take them in (despite the terms of the treaty, which indicates their desperation), Muḥammad welcomed them when they came to him in Medina and received them as champions.

Islamic State and bandits

A similar situation exists in the world today. Islamic State accepts—even recruits—those Muslims who reject their own societies and governments and wish to show their deep discontent through violence, especially Muslims who harbor hatred toward the West, i.e., European nations and the United States. These disgruntled and disillusioned Muslims find shelter in Islam to carry out their revengeful activities without guilt, because, according to Islam, their violence toward "the infidels" will be counted as heroic and glorious acts, not unlike the celebrated acts

---

[101] Ibn Hishām (Ibn Isḥāq), *The Life of Muḥammad* 507; Ibn Hishām (Ibn Isḥāq) *Al-Sīra al-Nabawīya* 4: 57.

[102] Ibn Hishām (Ibn Isḥāq), *The Life of Muḥammad* 508; Ibn Hishām (Ibn Isḥāq) *Al-Sīra al-Nabawīya*. 4: 58. See *Sahih Bukhari*, Book of Conditions (pp. 629-630); *Ṣaḥīḥ al-Bukhārī*, Kītāb al-Shirūt 2: 974.

of the bandit gangs during the early history of Islam. For in the eyes of Muḥammad, Abū Baṣīr (and the seventy men with him) was not a murderer but a righteous Muslim just doing his duty and striving for the victory of his fellow Muslims.

Like Muḥammad, Islamic State eagerly accepted and absorbed many fighters who split from Al-Nusrah Front, which is affiliated with Al Qaeda, and other Islamic groups inside Syria. Even if these fighters had committed crimes while members of their former group, they were not held accountable for their previous crimes when they joined Islamic State—precisely the same reaction by Muḥammad when the bandit gangs joined him in Medina. Muḥammad disregarded the criminal activities committed by these bandits before they accepted Islam, because "Islam annuls anything that was before it."[103]

Tunisian Aḥmad al-Ruwaysī (also known as Abū Zakaryā al-Tūnisī) represents one of the best contemporary examples regarding this Islamic doctrine of annulling past crimes. He was convicted of criminal and drug-related issues and sentenced to fourteen years' imprisonment in 2006. However, in 2011 when he escaped with thousands of prisoners during the Tunisian revolution, al-Ruwaysī became a leader of Anṣār al-Sharī'a Tunisia, an Islamic terrorist group. He soon fled to Libya, "where he helped run a training camp and smuggled arms back into Tunisia."[104] He was also believed to be the mastermind of several attacks in Tunisia.[105] He became wanted by the Tunisian Ministry of the Interior for assassinating Tunisian political leaders, Chokri Belaid and Mohamed Brahmi, in 2013.[106] He later pledged allegiance to Islamic State, joining its forces in the Libyan city of Sirte. He became one of its most active and dangerous members until he was killed by a Libyan militia group in March 2015.[107]

---

[103] *Musnad Aḥmad* 5: 231. This commentator states, "Islam annuls what was before it [crimes] and the emigration annuls what [crimes] was before it."

[104] Joscelyn, Thomas. "US Confirms Death of High-Profile Tunisian Islamic State Assassin." *LongWarJournal.org*. Foundation for Defense of Democracies (FDD's Long War Journal), 12 Dec. 2016. Web (http://www.longwarjournal.org/archives/2016/12/us-confirms-death-of-tunisian-islamic-state-leader-involved-in-high-profile-assassinations.php).

[105] "IS Commander 'Killed in Libya.'" *TimesofMalta.com*. Allied Newspapers Ltd., 18 Mar. 2015. Web (http://www.timesofmalta.com/articles/view/20150318/world/IS-commander-killed-in-Libya-.560416).

[106] Masi, Alessandria. "Tunisian ISIS Leader Abu Zakariya al-Tunisi Reportedly Killed in Libya Fighting Near Sirte." *IBTimes.com*. International Business Times, 17 Mar. 2015. Web (http://www.ibtimes.com/tunisian-isis-leader-abu-zakariya-al-tunisi-reportedly-killed-libya-fighting-near-1849704).

[107] al-Qizani, Mufida, and Minia al-'Arafawi. "From Elios the Fortuneteller to Abu Zakariya [al-Tunisi] the Terrorist." *Assabah.com.tn*. As Sabah, 17 Mar. 2015. Web (http://preview.tinyurl.com/jyh9jca).

Another prominent example is the self-proclaimed "Caliph" of Islamic State himself: Abū Bakr al-Baghdādī. In 2003, after the American invasion in Iraq, al-Baghdadi helped found a "Sunni militia violently opposed to the United States and its allies," the Army of the People of the Sunna and Communal Solidarity.[108] He was arrested in Fallujah in 2004 but was classified as a "civilian detainee," which means the arresting authorities were unaware of his jihadist activities.[109] During his detention, al-Baghdādī "hid his militancy and devoted himself to religious instruction."[110] He provided religious leadership by leading prayers, preaching Friday sermons, and teaching religious classes to prisoners. He also inserted himself into the camp's politics by acting as a negotiator and mediator between rival prisoner groups. Above all, he courted Sunni Arabs "who had served in Saddam's military and intelligence services."[111] Their purge from power after Saddam Hussein's regime was overthrown left them disenfranchised, angry, and resentful. Al-Baghdādī exploited their disaffection in order to win their allegiance and their valuable military expertise. By the time Abū Bakr al-Baghdādī was released from Camp Bucca, he had "a virtual Rolodex for reconnecting with his co-conspirators and protégés: They had written one another's phone numbers in the elastic of their underwear."[112]

In 2002, the administration of US President George W. Bush established a military prison at Guantanamo Bay, Cuba, to hold, interrogate, and prosecute detainees for war crimes as part of its "War on Terror." Since its opening, more than 700 detainees have been housed there. (As of January 2017, the detention camp now holds 41 detainees.)[113] In 2014 US media reported that of the 620 detainees released from the camp, "180 have returned or are suspected to have returned to the battlefield." Some of the sources state that of the 180 recidivists, about twenty to thirty (with most

---

[108] Kort, Alicia. "How ISIS Leader Abu Bakr al-Baghdadi Came to Be." *Newsweek.com*. Newsweek, 24 Sept. 2016. Web (http://www.newsweek.com/abu-bar-al-baghdadi-isis-499594).

[109] Ibid.

[110] McCants, William. "Who Exactly Is Abu Bakr al-Baghdadi, the Leader of ISIS?" *Newsweek.com*. Newsweek, 6 Sept. 2015. Web (http://www.newsweek.com/who-exactly-abu-bakr-al-baghdadi-leader-isis-368907).

[111] Ibid.

[112] Ibid.

[113] "Guantanamo Bay Naval Station Fast Facts." *CNN.com*. Cable Network News, 7 Mar. 2017. Web (http://www.cnn.com/2013/09/09/world/guantanamo-bay-naval-station-fast-facts/).

operating inside Syria) have "either joined ISIS or other militant groups in Syria, or are participating with these groups from outside countries."[114]

A more startling example is US citizen Douglas McAuthur McCain, who became the first American foreign fighter to die fighting for Islamic State in late August 2014. Prior to his involvement with jihadist terrorism, he too had been convicted of various minor crimes: disorderly conduct (2000); misdemeanor theft (2001); and marijuana possession (2003). McCain also continued to drive despite a suspended driver's license—and got caught for that offense too.[115] Though he didn't become a convert until his twenties (he was raised in a Christian family), his life of frequent moves and petty crime, lacking ambition and close community ties, strongly resembles the lives of the early "bandit gangs" who eventually joined Muḥammad. According to expert Richard Barrett of The Soufan Group, McCain's path to ISIS is similar to other foreign fighters who joined ISIS. They "often operate somewhere on the fringes of society" and are "disaffected, aimless, and lacking a sense of identity or belonging."[116]

One disturbing trend with today's foreign ISIS fighters who converted to Islam after convictions for minor crimes is the impetus for the conversion: imprisonment. Chief Inspector Dame Anne Owers of Great Britain reports that nearly a third of the prisoners in British prisons adopted Islam while serving their sentence.[117] Some prison inmates stated that their reasons for converting to Islam included "protection of belonging to a gang and perceived material perks offered to Muslims," which often included more time outside of their cells, better food, and exclusion from work and education on Fridays to permit attendance for prayers.[118] Unfortunately, these "convenience Muslims" put themselves at risk of being recruited and indoctrinated by more extremist Muslims within the prison system. In time, the bonds of fellowship and protection strengthen between the new converts and their Muslim mentors, and the

---

[114] "Sources: Former Guantanamo Detainees Suspected of Joining ISIS, Other Groups in Syria." *FoxNews.com*. Fox Entertainment Group, 30 Oct. 2014. Web (http://www.foxnews.com/politics/2014/10/30/sources-former-guantanamo-detainees-suspected-joining-isis-other-groups-in.html).

[115] McCoy, Terrence. "How Douglas McAuthur McCain Became the First American to Die Fighting for the Islamic State." *WashingtonPost.com*. The Washington Post, 27 Aug. 2014. Web (https://www.washingtonpost.com/news/morning-mix/wp/2014/08/27/how-douglas-mcarthur-mccain-became-the-first-american-to-die-fighting-for-the-islamic-state/?utm_term=.12c70180f466).

[116] Ibid.

[117] "Prisoners Convert to Islam to Win Perks and Get Protection from Powerful Muslim Gangs." *DailyMail.co.uk*. Telegraph Media Group,, 8 June 2010. Web (http://www.dailymail.co.uk/news/article-1284846/Prisoners-converting-Islam-protection-powerful-gangs.html).

[118] Ibid.

new converts feel empowered knowing that their past "sins" or criminal offenses are annulled in the eyes of Islam. By the time they leave prison, they are well on their way to becoming jihadists and perhaps as new recruits for ISIS (and later, Islamic State).

Former inmates of Camp Bucca, Iraq, where Islamic State's Abū Bakr al-Baghdādī was once detained, echo these prophetic sentiments. One inmate stated to a reporter that when a new prisoner came in, his peers would "teach him, indoctrinate him, and give him direction so he leaves [as] a burning flame."[119] The goal was to prepare these new recruits so thoroughly that when they were finally released, they were "ticking time bombs."[120] Another inmate stated that "If there was no American prison in Iraq, there would be no [ISIS] now.... Bucca was a factory. It made us all. It built our ideology."[121] The camp was nicknamed "The Academy," and al-Baghdādī was considered one of the faculty members during his brief internment.[122] A PBS Frontline documentary, *The Secret History of ISIS*, televised on May 17, 2016, reports that the US prisons that detained Iraqis "swept up by US forces during the early days of the invasion" eventually became "jihadi universities."[123] Imprisoned jihadists took advantage of this confinement with thousands of other Iraqi inmates "to network with other jihadists, capable jihadists" as well as recruit and train new jihadists.[124]

Horrific terrorist attacks in France in recent years have shown that Islamic radicalization in prisons can produce "homegrown" attacks—terrorist acts perpetrated by French citizens who became Muslims or radicalized Muslims while in French prisons (e.g., *Charlie Hebdo* terrorist attack, January 2015). Increasingly, Muslims "constitute a disproportionate majority of the French penal population—an estimated 60%, as opposed to 8% in society at large—and the proportion of Islamic radicals among the country's 68,000 prisoners is growing."[125]

---

[119] McCants, William. "Who Exactly Is Abu Bakr al-Baghdadi, the Leader of ?" *Newsweek.com*. Newsweek, 6 Sept. 2015. Web (http://www.newsweek.com/who-exactly-abu-bakr-al-baghdadi-leader-isis-368907).

[120] Ibid.

[121] Ibid.

[122] Ibid.

[123] Taddonio, Patrice. "How US Prisons in Iraq Became 'Jihadi Universities' for ISIS." *PBS.org*. Frontline (WGBH Educational Foundation), 17 May 2016. Web (http://www.pbs.org/wgbh/frontline/article/how-u-s-prisons-in-iraq-became-jihadi-universities-for-isis/).

[124] Ibid.

[125] de Bellaigue, Christopher. "Are French Prisons 'Finishing Schools' for Terrorism?" *TheGuardian.com*. The Guardian, 17 Mar. 2016. Web (https://www.theguardian.com/world/2016/mar/17/are-french-prisons-finishing-schools-for-terrorism).

American prisons are not immune to this phenomenon and have also become targets for radicalization by militant Wahhabi and Salafist Muslim groups. Even as far back as 2006, law enforcement, including then FBI Director Robert Mueller, warned that prisons were "fertile ground" for militant Islamic extremists.[126] A 2010 law enforcement bulletin from the FBI titled "Prisoner Radicalization" states that prisons "literally provide a captive audience of disaffected young men easily influenced by charismatic extremist leaders."[127] Unlike Camp Bucca, the American detention center in Iraq where released and radicalized detainees headed out to join ISIS, the newly converted but violence-prone Muslim ex-convicts released from US prisons are more likely to commit terrorist acts in their American homeland. According to Patrick Dunleavy, former deputy inspector general of the New York State Police Criminal Intelligence Unit and author of the 2011 book, *The Fertile Soil of Jihad: Terrorism's Prison Connection*, Islamic terrorist groups "no longer need handlers in direct contact to bring the crazy guy along and convince him to do their will. They can do it online and unilaterally."[128]

On September 25, 2014, ex-convict Alton Nolen, "a Muslim convert with a lengthy rap sheet," entered Vaughan Foods, a food processing plant based in Moore, Oklahoma, with a large knife and beheaded Colleen Hufford and then stabbed Traci Johnson, two female employees. Nolen had been suspended from the company after a complaint filed by Johnson earlier in the day. Though Nolen had grown up in a non-denominational Christian church, he is believed to have converted to Islam while in prison serving time on various convictions, including drug charges, assaulting a police office, and escaping detention.[129] Controversy surrounds the characterization of the attack, with law officials and media describing it as an incident of workplace violence, but others, including then Texas Governor Rick Perry, labelled the attack as a terrorist act

[126] "Oklahoma Beheading Suspect Likely Radicalized behind Bars, Say Experts." *FoxNews.com*. Fox Entertainment Group, 30 Sept. 2014. Web (http://www.foxnews.com/us/2014/09/30/oklahoma-beheading-suspect-likely-radicalized-behind-bars-say-experts.html).

[127] Ibid.

[128] Ibid.

[129] Ohlheiser, Abby. "What We Know about Alton Nolen, Who Has Been Charged with Murder in the Oklahoma Beheading Case." *WashingtonPost.com*. The Washington Post, 30 Sept. 2014. Web (https://www.washingtonpost.com/news/post-nation/wp/2014/09/30/what-we-know-about-alton-nolen-who-has-been-charged-with-murder-in-the-oklahoma-beheading-case/?utm_term=.116ba7666cd2); "Oklahoma Beheading Suspect Likely Radicalized behind Bars, Say Experts." *FoxNews.com*. Fox Entertainment Group, 30 Sept. 2014. Web (http://www.foxnews.com/us/2014/09/30/oklahoma-beheading-suspect-likely-radicalized-behind-bars-say-experts.html).

because of Nolen's belief in a conservative form of Islam, his shouting of Qur'ānic verses during the attack, and the method of the killing (beheading). Was his attack based on revenge or religion? Ryan Mauro, a national security analyst and adjunct professor of Homeland Security (research institute Clarion Project), believes it could be both: "There is a false debate about whether this was an act of murder by someone who happened to have radical Islamic beliefs, or whether this was a radical Islamic terrorist attack," Mauro said. "It can be both. He [Nolen] believed that such violence qualifies as a jihad and chose a target, his former place of employment, that he wanted revenge upon."[130]

These examples are representative of many imprisoned Muslims (some converting to Islam while in prison) who find purpose, meaning, and a welcoming refuge in Islam—not for personal reformation and future responsible citizenship but for the application and justification for more crimes and violence. Only now, this violence is characterized as sacred, a holy jihad for the cause of Allah—exactly the reasons Muḥammad proclaimed when he turned the criminal violence of the roving bandits into holy jihad with him. He took advantage of their destructive energy to serve his cause: the spread of Islam.

The majority of the elite leaders in Islamic State are Iraqis, just like "Caliph" Abū Bakr al-Baghdādī.[131] Muḥammad's closest confidants were likewise his fellow Quraysh tribesmen; Muḥammad's successors were also from his Quraysh tribe. Placing the highest trust in and sharing the most important intelligence with subordinates who are closest to the leader in terms of familial or ethnic relationships or nationality is not unusual. However, al-Baghdādī has selected and assigned to high leadership positions in his jihadist terrorist organization many men who once had a key military role in the army of former Iraqi dictator, Saddam Hussein. These men acted like criminal gangsters on behalf of Saddam, but they have now declared their repentance and redirected their service from the Arab Socialist Baa'th Party to ISIL/Islamic State—for the cause of Allah.

130 "Oklahoma Beheading Suspect Likely Radicalized behind Bars, Say Experts." *FoxNews.com*. Fox Entertainment Group, 30 Sept. 2014. Web (http://www.foxnews.com/us/2014/09/30/oklahoma-beheading-suspect-likely-radicalized-behind-bars-say-experts.html); Ohlheiser, Abby. "What We Know about Alton Nolen, Who Has Been Charged with Murder in the Oklahoma Beheading Case." *WashingtonPost.com*. The Washington Post, 30 Sept. 2014. Web (https://www.washingtonpost.com/news/post-nation/wp/2014/09/30/what-we-know-about-alton-nolen-who-has-been-charged-with-murder-in-the-oklahoma-beheading-case/?utm_term=.116ba7666cd2).

131 "Top 20 ISIS Leaders Are Iraqis except One Syrian." *Alarabiya.net*. Al Arabiya Network, 18 Sept. 2014. Web (http://preview.tinyurl.com/jzuvqyq).

Among these leaders were Abū Muslim al-Turkmānī, Deputy Leader of ISIL (before his death in August 2015), and Abū 'Abdul-Raḥmān al-Bilāwī, ISIL Military Chief (before his death in June 2014).[132]

The medieval Arab nomadic bandits justified their actions, claiming their raiding and looting was a message from Allah; the money and property that they stole was only their livelihood, which was sent to them from Allah for them to punish the wealthy. In other words, they were tools used to fulfill divine will. Jawād 'Alī makes this observation:[133]

> Therefore, Arab *sa'ālīk*, thieves, and bandits used to consider the spoils, which they would get through looting and extortion of the sword, as blessings, because the money is not lawful when held with stinginess and ingratitude. So Allah has sent them [*sa'ālīk*] to it [the money/spoils] and made it their livelihood.

Muḥammad's acceptance and application of this *sa'ālīk* mind-set is addressed in Islamic commentaries in Q 2.104 (*"O believers, do not say, 'Observe us,' but say, 'Regard us'; and give ear; for unbelievers awaits a painful chastisement"*; Arberry trans.). Muslim commentator Ibn Kathīr explains that the verse is Muḥammad declaring that his livelihood (as given and blessed by Allah) is predicated on the threat (and use) of force:[134]

> I [Muḥammad] was sent with the sword just before the Last Hour, so that Allah is worshipped alone without partners. My sustenance was provided for me from under the shadow of my spear. Those who oppose my command were humiliated and made inferior, and whoever imitates [by statements, deeds, clothes, feasts, acts of worship, etc.] a [disbelieving] people, he is one of them.

Thus, Muḥammad and Islam came from the same *sa'ālīk* environment. He turned its customs, tribal rules, booty practices, and raiding culture into a holy religion, for which we are still paying the price.

Islamic State accentuated these religiously sanctioned *sa'ālīk* practices and customs in its military and political policies. Like the nomadic Arab bandits of Muḥammad's day who raided and looted the neighboring tribes, Islamic State invaded cities and then expelled the citizens, especially Christians, from their homes, forcing them to leave behind

---

[132] "Top 20 ISIS Leaders Are Iraqis except One Syrian." *Alarabiya.net*. Al Arabiya Network, 18 Sept. 2014. Web (http://preview.tinyurl.com/jzuvqyq).

[133] 'Alī, *Al-Mufaṣṣal* 10: 129.

[134] See the commentary on Q 2.104, *Tafsīr Ibn Kathīr* (p. 280). For the Arabic source, see *Tafsīr Ibn Kathīr* 2: 5-6. See also *Ṣaḥīḥ al-Bukhārī* 3: 1067.

nearly all of their belongings. It then took possession of the abandoned property and possessions, which were then considered as booty and a blessing from Allah.

When ISIS captured the city of Mosul in June 2014, the defeated Iraqi army hastily withdrew from the city, leaving behind vehicles, weapons, and other matériel. To ISIS, this discarded military equipment was war booty, treasure that Allah had snatched from the Iraqi army and given to ISIS. ISIS had also captured oil refineries in both Iraq and Syria. The revenue that ISIS, and then later Islamic State, received from the oil it smuggled to other countries provided critical financial resources for its "livelihood." (Of course, the captured oil refineries are a blessing from Allah.) The priceless artwork, antiquities, and artifacts that ISIS/Islamic State took from museums and archaeological or historical sites and sold on the black market were also considered booty taken—with Allah's blessing—from their enemies. It and other Islamic jihadist groups have also raised money by abducting and then ransoming selected captives.

Islamic State had an unprecedented profitable year in 2014. A conservative estimate of its cash and revenues was US$1.5 billion.[135] According to the US Treasury, RAND Corporation, and other sources, its financial assets came in part from seized bank assets (US$500 million to $1 billion), oil (US$480 million), antiquities (US$100 million), taxes (US$48 million/month), and ransom payments (US$20 million).[136] The livelihood of Islamic State was indeed under the shadow of its spear.[137]

The modus operandi of Islamic State is indeed contemporary *sa'laka* (raiding) par excellence, with no regard to boundaries or countries—just like Muḥammad who chose not to respect or tolerate the customs, traditions, religious beliefs and practices of the neighboring "infidel" tribes, because, for him, these people must either submit to him or become legitimate targets to dominate or destroy.

---

[135] Lister, Tim. "Is ISIS Going Broke?" *CNN.com*. Cable News Network, 29 June 2016. Web (http://www.cnn.com/2016/03/04/middleeast/isis-finance-broke-lister/).

[136] Ibid.

[137] **Note:** Though Islamic State is probably still the richest terrorist organization in the world, its fortunes have declined since 2014. One study reports that Islamic State's annual revenue now in 2017 is less than half its 2014 annual revenue. Research findings suggest the decrease in revenue results from loss of territory. Islamic State has been forced to relinquish approximately 62 per cent of its mid-2014 "peak" territory it controlled in Iraq, and 30 per cent in Syria. This loss of territory means fewer people and businesses to tax and less control of natural resources, e.g., oil. (Source: International Centre for the Study of Radicalisation and Political Violence (ICSR). "Caliphate in Decline: An Estimate of Islamic State's Financial Fortunes." 2017. Page 3. Print. (See URL: http://icsr.info/wp-content/uploads/2017/02/ICSR-Report-Caliphate-in-Decline-An-Estimate-of-Islamic-States-Financial-Fortunes.pdf)

Islamic State followed this same plan of conquer and conquest, which is based on the Qur'ān, Hadith literature, Sunna, and the Prophet's biography. For Islamic State there were only two choices: submit to it and its conditions or await its heinous assault and the raiding and killing by its own *sa'ālīk*.

TEN

The Islamic legacy of captivity, murder, expulsion, and destruction is revived

June 12, 2014, marks the date of one of the most horrific massacres in recent Iraqi history. Though ISIL (also known as ISIS and later, Islamic State) claimed responsibility for this operation and publicized it through two released videos, accusations of a conspiracy between Sunni Iraqi tribesmen and ISIL further deepened the anger and grief over this tragedy.

ISIL and Camp Speicher massacre

After the fall of Mosul by June 10, ISIL fighters quickly headed the next day toward Tikrit. Meanwhile, thousands of young Iraqi Air Force cadets stationed at Camp Speicher, which is based outside Tikrit, were apparently given a fifteen-day leave. Assured by their commanding officers they would have safe passage to Samarra, hundreds left the base on foot, unarmed and dressed in civilian clothes. As the cadets walked down the main highway, some of them, escorted by local tribesmen, eventually entered Tikrit, where the tribesmen handcuffed them and then handed them over to ISIL fighters. The ISIL fighters separated the Shia cadets from the others and marched them to the old palace grounds of Saddam Hussein and executed them. Other cadets were captured by ISIL fighters along the highway. These men were transported in vehicles or marched into the desert or to the Tigris River. There, hundreds of these (mostly Shia) cadets were lined up, hands tied behind their back, and shot in shallow trenches by masked ISIL soldiers.[1] The violent, cold-blooded nature and organization of these mass killings stunned and horrified the world.

Families of the murdered cadets and the few survivors who managed to escape accused the government and local Sunni people of betraying the cadets to ISIL. During an Iraqi parliament session in September 2014, the victims' families charged government authorities of "selling our sons" to ISIL and demanded an accounting of the dead and missing cadets.[2]

ISIL (ISIS) boasted on its Twitter accounts and other social media platforms that its fighters executed 1700 cadets. Satellite imagery and photographs have confirmed some of these staged killings.[3] At least two mass graves found near Tikrit contained many of the murdered cadets, most of whom were Shiites.[4] (Though the estimated total death toll is frequently mentioned as 1700, some sources suggest the exact number

[1] "Daesh, Saddam's Henchmen, Third Party: Who Was Behind the Killing of 1700 Troops in the Speicher Massacre in Iraq?" *Arabic.CNN.com.* Cable News Network (Arabic), 10 Sept. 2014. Web (http://arabic.cnn.com/middleeast/2014/09/10/iraq-speicher-massacre); Salman, Raheem. "Survivors Demand Justice after Iraq Massacre." *Reuters.com.* Reuters, 5 Sept. 2014. Web (http://www.reuters.com/article/us-iraq-crisis-massacre-idUSKBN0H021L20140905); Loveluck, Louisa. "ISIL Releases New Video of 2014 Speicher Massacre of Shia Army Recruits." *Telegraph.co.uk.* Telegraph Media Group, 12 July 2015. Web (http://www.telegraph.co.uk/news/worldnews/islamic-state/11734606/Isil-releases-new-video-of-2014-Speicher-massacre-of-Shia-army-recruits.html); Shum, Mike, Greg Campbell, Adam B. Ellick, and Mona El-Naggar. "Surviving an ISIS Massacre." *NYTimes.com.* New York Times, 3 Sept. 2014. Web (https://www.nytimes.com/2014/09/04/world/middleeast/surviving-isis-massacre-iraq-video.html?mcubz=1&_r=0); Michael, Tom. "Taste of Their Own Vile Medicine: ISIS Jihadis Involved in Notorious Camp Speicher Massacre Pictured in Orange Jumpsuits Moments before Being Hanged in Front of Victims' Families." *TheSun.co.uk.* The Sun, 23 Aug. 2016. Web (https://www.thesun.co.uk/news/1655654/isis-jihadis-involved-in-notorious-camp-speicher-massacre-pictured-in-orange-jumpsuits-moments-before-being-hanged-in-front-of-victims-families).

[2] Fayyad, Mu'd. "Speicher Massacre: Government Tried to Hide Its Details, Victims' Families Make It Public Case." *Aawsat.com.* Middle East, 13 Nov. 2014; edited 6 Sept. 2014. Web (http://aawsat.com/home/article/176296); "Daesh/Saddam's Henchmen, Third Party: Who Was Behind the Killing of 1700 Troops in the Speicher Massacre in Iraq?" *Arabic.CNN.com.* Cable News Network (Arabic), 10 Sept. 2014. Web (http://arabic.cnn.com/middleeast/2014/09/10/iraq-speicher-massacre); Heine, Debra. "What Happened at the Speicher Massacre in Iraq?" *Breitbart.com.* Breitbart News Network, 4 Sept. 2014. Web (http://www.breitbart.com/blog/2014/09/04/what-happened-at-the-camp-speicher-massacre-in-iraq).

[3] "ISIS Commits Mass Murder, Advertises It: Iraq Executions Detailed." *RT.com.* RT (formerly *Russia Today*), 27 June 2014; edited 17 Sept. 2014. Web (https://www.rt.com/news/168916-isis-iraq-war-crimes).

[4] Ibid.

may be more or less this amount. According to the Ministry of Human Rights in November 2014, the total number of missing persons and murdered victims is 1997 but indicated that the investigation was still ongoing.)[5] ISIL claimed exclusive responsibility for these mass killings, but survivor eyewitness accounts and other evidence implicate others, such as former members of the Arab Socialist Baʿath Party (Iraq Region), in helping and assisting ISIL in the organization and implementation of this atrocity.[6]

This massacre is one of the most horrific mass executions in the modern history of Iraq, a monstrous war crime by all standards. But did ISIL dream up this murderous undertaking from its own imagination? Or, is there a parallel to this atrocity in the Islamic heritage? Can ISIL "justify" it from Islamic religious texts and the biography of Muḥammad?

The moment I saw the disturbing, gruesome photographs of the executed cadets, I immediately retrieved without any effort similar images in my mind, when I, as a young man, read the biography of the Prophet in my father's library for the first time. My mental pictures were of the seventh-century AD Jews of Banū Qurayẓa, a Jewish tribe that dwelled near Medina, the city that took in Muḥammad and his followers when they emigrated from Mecca. (Eventually, Medina became the headquarters of Muḥammad's supreme commandership and the springboard for his conquests into the surrounding areas, similar to the function of the city of Raqqa in Syria for Islamic State, 2014-2017.)

The story of the Banū Qurayẓa requires contemplation and discussion because it is emblematic of the profound changes in the focus and tone of Muḥammad's mission after the Muslim victory at the Battle of Badr. Unfortunately, the story of the Banū Qurayẓa, as orchestrated by Muḥammad and his Muslim army, ends with their extermination. With its demise, Muḥammad (and, later, his successors) began a methodical process of expelling other non-Muslim tribes living in the Arabian Peninsula.

---

[5] Human Rights: "The Total Number of Speicher Missing Persons and Massacres Reach 1997." *AlSumeria.tv.* Al Sumaria News, Nov. 2014. Web (http://preview.tinyurl.com/jmjm4yw).

[6] Fayyad, Muʿd. "Speicher Massacre: Government Tried to Hide Its Details, Victims' Families Make It Public Case." *Aawsat.com.* Middle East, 13 Nov. 2014; edited 6 Sept. 2014. Web (http://aawsat.com/home/article/176296); "Daesh, Saddam's Henchmen, Third Party: Who Was Behind the Killing of 1700 Troops in the Speicher Massacre in Iraq?" *Arabic.CNN.com.* Cable News Network (Arabic), 10 Sept. 2014. Web (http://arabic.cnn.com/middleeast/2014/09/10/iraq-speicher-massacre).

Muḥammad and the Jewish tribes

Even before Muḥammad migrated to Medina from Mecca (Hijra, June AD 622), the three major Jewish tribes of Medina had made it plain that they considered him an imposter. Undoubtedly, their rejection of his claim of prophethood—particularly when he presented himself as the last of a long line of prophets beginning with Adam and including Abraham, Moses, and Jesus—greatly interfered with his efforts to convince others that he was Allah's messenger and Islam was the true message. Obviously, for Muḥammad to succeed, it was critically important for him to either win their acceptance and support or find a way to diminish or remove their influence.

A few months before the Hijra, at the second pledge of al-'Aqaba, which was a secret meeting between Muḥammad and Muslim converts from Medina, he asked them (members of the Khazraj and Aws, Arab tribes) for their loyalty and protection. (For more information about the first and second pledges of al-'Aqaba, see Chapter 8, page 227.) Before they gave him their full consent, one man informed Muḥammad that they already had ties with the Jews; pledging allegiance to Muḥammad would sever those ties, and he was concerned about the consequences of breaking this prior pact. Muḥammad persuasively promised that their blood was his blood: "I am of you and you are of me. I will war against them that war against you and be at peace with those at peace with you."[7] This covenant with the Arab Khazraj and Aws tribesmen thus ominously signaled Muḥammad's future hostile intentions toward the Jews.

Shortly after Muḥammad emigrated to Medina, he drafted a constitution or charter establishing an amicable alliance among the major Medinan tribes, both Arab and Jewish, and the Muslim Emigrants from Mecca. This alliance delineated the rights, duties, and relationships of all the parties.[8] It also maintained that "the Jews have their religion and the Muslims have theirs."[9] But Muḥammad's seeming tolerance for religions other than Islam would soon fade.

Muḥammad's tolerant attitude toward the Jews started to change less than two years after his arrival to Medina and after he and his followers

---

[7] Ibn Hishām (Ibn Isḥāq), *The Life of Muḥammad* 203-204; Ibn Hishām (Ibn Isḥāq), *Al-Sīra al-Nabawīya* 2: 266.

[8] Ibn Hishām (Ibn Isḥāq), *The Life of Muḥammad* 231-233; Ibn Hishām (Ibn Isḥāq), *Al-Sīra al-Nabawīya* 2: 346-350.

[9] Ibn Hishām (Ibn Isḥāq), *The Life of Muḥammad* 233; Ibn Hishām (Ibn Isḥāq), *Al-Sīra al-Nabawīya* 2: 349.

(and later his ally, the Anṣār) began their raids. Emboldened by their spectacular victory in the Battle of Badr (March AD 624), Muḥammad and his followers resumed their military "expeditions," but the outcomes of the next several raids and skirmishes were unsatisfactory, producing little to no booty, captives, or enemy casualties.[10]

Muḥammad then began to threaten neighboring tribes of Medina. He approached the Banū Qaynuqā', a wealthy Jewish tribe of artisans and traders, with this warning: "O Jews, beware lest God bring upon you the vengeance that He brought upon Quraysh and become Muslims. You know that I am a prophet who has been sent—you will find that in your scriptures and God's covenant with you."[11] The Banū Qaynuqā' retorted, "O Muḥammad, you seem to think that we are your people. Do not deceive yourself because you encountered a people with no knowledge of war and got the better of them; for by God if we fight you, you will find that we are real men!"[12]

According to several Islamic sources, the following incident became the catalyst for the physical attack on and dispelling of the Banu Qaynuqa'.[13] Some Jews decided to play a trick on an Arab woman, who was doing business in the Qaynuqā' marketplace. One of them attached part of her skirt to the ground where she was seated in such a way that she became partially uncovered when she stood up. A Muslim who witnessed this trick was angered and insulted by this act and the ensuing laughter. He killed the Jewish prankster and was in turn killed by the other Jews present at the scene.

When Muḥammad heard about the incident and the killings, he declared war against the Banū Qaynuqā' and besieged them until they surrendered unconditionally.[14] Some sources report that 'Abd Allah Ubayy Ibn Salūl,[15] a prominent leader from the Arab Khazraj tribe, appealed to Muhamman to spare the Banū Qaynuqā'.[16] In the end, the Banū Qaynuqā' people were given three days to leave Medina. They had

---

[10] Watt, *Muḥammad at Medina* 340.

[11] Ibn Hishām (Ibn Isḥāq), *The Life of Muḥammad* 363; Ibn Hishām (Ibn Isḥāq), *Al-Sīra al-Nabawīya* 3: 224.

[12] Ibn Hishām (Ibn Isḥāq), *The Life of Muḥammad* 363; Ibn Hishām (Ibn Isḥāq), *Al-Sīra al-Nabawīya* 3: 224.

[13] Watt, *Muḥammad at Medina* 209; Ibn Hishām (Ibn Isḥāq), *Al-Sīra al-Nabawīya* 3: 225.

[14] Ibn Hishām (Ibn Isḥāq), *The Life of Muḥammad* 363; Ibn Hishām (Ibn Isḥāq), *Al-Sīra al-Nabawīya* 3: 226. See Watt, *Muḥammad at Medina* 209.

[15] **Note:** 'Abd Allah Ubayy Ibn Salūl was later labeled the leader of "the Hypocrites" (al-Munāfiqūn), the "fake" Muslims in Medina who outwardly practiced Islam but internally disbelieved and were enemies of Muḥammad.

[16] Ibn Hishām (Ibn Isḥāq), *The Life of Muḥammad* 363; Ibn Hishām (Ibn Isḥāq), *Al-Sīra al-Nabawīya* 3: 226.

to leave behind all arms, their property, and most of their possessions.[17] This ultimatum seems particularly harsh—to punish an entire tribe by expelling them from the region—for the actions of a few people.

During the year following the Muslim victory at the Battle of Badr and Muḥammad's expulsion of the Banū Qaynuqā' from Medina, the Quraysh leaders of Mecca prepared to avenge their losses. On March 23, AD 625, the Meccans engaged the Muslims in a second military encounter, the Battle of Uḥud, in a valley located below Mount Uḥud, which is north of Medina.[18] This time, the Quraysh got the upper hand—with the help of Muḥammad's archers. Muḥammad had commanded a contingent of arches to stay in position and protect the Muslims' flank. However, they left their post, yelling "Booty, booty!" and chasing Meccan women who were fleeing the battle.[19] The Muslim pursuers were attacked by the Meccan cavalry and many were killed. In the chaos, the Muslims were routed and suffered more casualties.

Despite heavy protection from his followers, even Muḥammad was wounded, suffering facial cuts and a broken tooth.[20] His uncle Ḥamza was killed and his body was mutilated.[21] The Meccans eventually withdrew from the battle site and returned to Mecca, leaving the Muslims to bury their dead, instead of pressing their advantage. As for Muḥammad and his followers, their severe defeat after the Battle of Uḥud was a sobering and humiliating aftermath after their jubilant euphoria following their victory at the Battle of Badr.

Muslim morale was low after this defeat; sixty-five names (Emigrants and Anṣār) are listed as martyrs in Islamic sources.[22] In their minds, the surviving Muslim fighters believed that they could not lose if Allah was on their side. Soon after the Battle of Uḥud, Muḥammad responded with Q 3.152[23] (Hilâli-Khân trans.), which places blame for the defeat on the Muslim fighters who disobeyed Muḥammad's orders and elected to loot rather than protect their fellow fighters during the battle:

---

[17] Ibn Hishām (Ibn Isḥāq), *The Life of Muḥammad* 363-364; Ibn Hishām (Ibn Isḥāq), *Al-Sīra al-Nabawīya* 3: 226. See Watt, *Muḥammad at Medina* 209-210.

[18] Watt, *Muḥammad at Medina* 340.

[19] *History of al-Ṭabarī* 7: 113; Ibn Hishām (Ibn Isḥāq), *The Life of Muḥammad* 379; Ibn Hishām (Ibn Isḥāq), *Al-Sīra al-Nabawīya* 3: 262.

[20] Ibn Hishām (Ibn Isḥāq), *The Life of Muḥammad* 379; Ibn Hishām (Ibn Isḥāq), *Al-Sīra al-Nabawīya* 3: 264.

[21] Ibn Hishām (Ibn Isḥāq), *The Life of Muḥammad* 376, 387; Ibn Hishām (Ibn Isḥāq), *Al-Sīra al-Nabawīya* 3: 253, 277.

[22] Ibn Hishām (Ibn Isḥāq), *The Life of Muḥammad* 401-403; Ibn Hishām (Ibn Isḥāq), *Al-Sīra al-Nabawīya* 3: 317.

[23] Watt, *Muḥammad at Medina* 23.

And Allah did indeed fulfil His Promise to you when you were killing them (your enemy) with His Permission; until (the moment) you lost your courage and fell to disputing about the order, and disobeyed after He showed you (of the booty) which you love. Among you are some that desire this world and some that desire the Hereafter. Then He made you flee from them (your enemy), that He might test you. But surely, He forgave you, and Allah is Most Gracious to the believers.

So, according to this verse, Allah punished the Muslims with defeat because of their disobedience and greed but also expresses his forgiveness and promise for future grace. In other words, this defeat at the Battle of 'Uḥud was just a test and not a final divine judgment.

Yet Muḥammad's next major military engagement is not again with the Quraysh of Mecca but with the Banū al-Naḍīr, a Jewish tribe that lived near Medina.[24] (Perhaps their closer proximity and lesser strength made this tribe a more attractive target—and thus a better chance for a victory to elevate the morale of his fighters.)

A few months after the Battle of Uḥud, Muḥammad, along with some of his Companions, set out to see the tribal leaders of the Banū al-Naḍīr. He wanted their help in raising the blood money he was obligated to pay for two men who were killed by one of his followers. (Notice that this request for financial help was made less than two years after the very profitable Battle of Badr, an outcome that challenges Muḥammad's need for additional funds.) The leaders of the Banū al-Naḍīr agreed to contribute to this blood money. "Yes, Abū al-Qāsim [another name for Muḥammad], we will help you on what you desire, from what you have asked from us."[25]

As the tribesmen consulted among themselves, Muḥammad sat outside by the wall of one of the village houses. Then, abruptly, he got up and left the village, returning to Medina without telling his Companions Abū Bakr, 'Umar, 'Alī, and a few others who had all accompanied him on this mission. Eventually the Companions rejoined Muḥammad in Medina. He explained to them that a divine warning informed him that the Jews were plotting to drop a large stone on him from above the wall

[24] Ibn Hishām (Ibn Isḥāq), *The Life of Muḥammad* 437-438; Ibn Hishām (Ibn Isḥāq), *Al-Sīra al-Nabawīya* 3: 388. See *History of al-Tabarī* 7: 158-159. See also Watt, *Muḥammad at Medina* 211.

[25] Ibn Hishām (Ibn Isḥāq), *The Life of Muḥammad* 437; Ibn Hishām (Ibn Isḥāq), *Al-Sīra al-Nabawīya* 3: 387. See the commentary on Q 59.2, *Tafsīr Ibn Kathīr* 13: 474. See also *History of al-Tabarī* 7: 157-158.

where he had been sitting and thus kill him. Then Muḥammad ordered his Companions "to prepare for war and to march against them."[26]

The Banū al-Naḍīr had taken refuge inside their forts when Muḥammad and his men came upon them. The Muslims besieged the Banū al-Naḍīr for six or fifteen days, depending on the source.[27] At that point, Muḥammad ordered that the palm-trees be cut down and burned.[28] The Banū al-Naḍīr called out to Muḥammad, "Muḥammad, you have prohibited wanton destruction and blamed those guilty of it. Why then are you cutting down and burning our palm-trees?"[29] (Muḥammad would later justify his destruction of the palm-trees as divine permission with Q 59.5 (Palmer trans.): *"What palm trees ye did cut down or what ye left standing upon their roots was by God's permission, and to disgrace the workers of abomination."*) With much of their main livelihood—indeed future in Medina—now in ashes, the frightened Jews surrendered to the Muslims, asking for deportation (instead of execution) in exchange for their property (except for what they could carry on camels) and their armaments. Muḥammad agreed to these terms.

Muḥammad and his men then expropriated all the lands, houses, discarded possessions, and remaining palm-trees and divided the spoils among the Emigrants (with a few exceptions).[30] Muḥammad asserted that the deportation of the Banū al-Naḍīr was Allah's plan and punishment for the Jewish tribe's opposition to Allah and Muḥammad, Allah's representative. Muḥammad presented Q 59.1-4 (Palmer trans.) to support his claim:

---

[26] Ibn Hishām (Ibn Isḥāq), *The Life of Muḥammad* 437; Ibn Hishām (Ibn Isḥāq), *Al-Sīra al-Nabawīya* 3: 388. See *History of al-Ṭabarī* 7: 157-158.

[27] Ibn Kathīr, *Al-Bidāya* 5: 535.

[28] Ibn Hishām (Ibn Isḥāq), *The Life of Muḥammad* 437; Ibn Hishām (Ibn Isḥāq), *Al-Sīra al-Nabawīya* 3: 388.

[29] Ibn Hishām (Ibn Isḥāq), *The Life of Muḥammad* 437; Ibn Hishām (Ibn Isḥāq), *Al-Sīra al-Nabawīya* 3: 388.

[30] Ibn Hishām (Ibn Isḥāq), *The Life of Muḥammad* 437-438; Ibn Hishām (Ibn Isḥāq), *Al-Sīra al-Nabawīya* 3: 389. See *History of al-Ṭabarī* 7: 160.

What is in the heavens and in the earth celebrates God's praises; He is the mighty, the wise! / He [Allah] *it was who drove those of the people of the Book who misbelieved forth from their houses, at the first emigration;*[31] *ye did not think that they would go forth, and they thought that their fortresses would defend them against God; but God came upon them from whence they did not reckon, and cast dread into their hearts! They ruined their houses with their own hands and the hands of the believers; wherefore take example, O ye who are endowed with sight! / Had it not been that God had prescribed for them banishment, He would have tormented them in this world; but for them in the next shall be the torment of the Fire! / that is because they opposed God and His Apostle: and whoso opposes God, verily, God is keen to punish!*

Isn't Muḥammad's policy and treatment of the Banū al-Nadir similar to Islamic State's policy and treatment of the Mosul Christians who were forced to leave behind their houses and possessions and walk away from the city on foot? (See Chapter 5, page 103.)

Muḥammad expelled the Jews of Banū al-Naḍīr, evacuating them from their village with the understanding that their banishment would be permanent. Muḥammad claimed that this banishment was divinely ordered. Not only was this removal divinely ordered, it was predestined and the Banū al-Naḍīr should be thankful that Allah had decided not to torment or kill them at the hands of his prophet, Muḥammad. Their eternal torment will happen upon death, according to Q 59.3 (cited above).

I have encountered this Muslim mind-set of the "mercifulness" of expelling non-Muslims during an episode on my TV program *Daring Question* from a Muslim caller living in Sweden. He was a supporter of ISIS but apparently was unafraid to announce his full name on my live show. "Was Muḥammad a Mercy for the Worlds?" was my subject for this episode. I asked this caller, "So what ISIS is doing to Christians in Mosul considered merciful?" He responded, "Yes, isn't it merciful to only expel rather than kill them?"[32] As a former Muslim, I understand this kind of thinking, because it is based on Qur'ānic doctrine. As already exemplified in Q 59.3, Allah and Muḥammad are presented as merciful because they

---

[31] **Note:** This phrase *"at the first emigration"* refers to this forced expulsion of the Banū al-Naḍīr to Khaybar, where many of them settled after leaving Medina. Those Jews who settled in Khaybar were later expelled from there during the reign of 'Umar, the second caliph. (See Wherry 4: 129; footnote 2.)

[32] "Was Muḥammad a Mercy for the Worlds?" (Episode 370). Narr. Brother Rachid. *Daring Question.* Al Hayat TV. 7 Aug 2014. Television. (To view YouTube video, see URL: https://www.youtube.com/watch?v=kh8ie-gg68o)

did not participate in the killing of the Jews of Banū al-Naḍīr but only in their swift and permanent evacuation from their houses. What a mercy!

Muḥammad continued his military "expeditions," i.e., attacks. (The Arabic word is *al-ghazū*, which means "going out to seek and plunder an enemy").[33] This term *al-ghazū* refutes those who claim that Muḥammad's raids and battles were only defensive actions. In fact, most of his battles were offensive engagements, and, in several instances, Muḥammad would try to surprise his enemies to maximize and maintain an early advantage. In the military expedition of Dhāt al-Riqā', Muḥammad and his followers selected the Banū Tha'laba and Banū Muḥārib of Ghatafān[34] (some tribes living east of Medina) for attack in order to isolate the Quraysh. However, when the two opposing armies approached each other, "no fighting took place, because they feared one another."[35] (This military expedition was merely little more than one month after the siege and surrender of the Banū al-Naḍīr.) During this encounter, Muḥammad led his followers in a new kind of prayer, now commonly called the Fear Prayer.[36]

Within a couple of months after this military draw, Muḥammad and his army set out to Badr and waited there about a week for Quraysh leader Abū Sufyān, who was leading an army out from Mecca. (This military expedition has been called various names: Expedition of al-Sawīq, Badr al-Maw'id, the last or other expedition of Badr.)[37] During this military expedition no fighting took place because Abū Sufyān turned back before reaching Badr because drought affected available forage for the caravan animals.[38]

A six-month cessation of military action followed this "nonevent" with the Quraysh. In late summer of AD 626, Muḥammad set out on

[33] Ibn Manẓūr, *Lisān al-'Arab* 3253.

[34] Ibn Hishām (Ibn Isḥāq), *The Life of Muḥammad* 445; Ibn Hishām (Ibn Isḥāq), *Al-Sīra al-Nabawīya* 3: 401. *History of al-Tabari* 7: 161.

[35] Ibn Hishām (Ibn Isḥāq), *The Life of Muḥammad* 445; Ibn Hishām (Ibn Isḥāq), *Al-Sīra al-Nabawīya* 3: 401. See also *History of al-Tabari* 7: 161.

[36] *Sunnah.com*: *Ṣaḥiḥ Bukhari*, Book of Military Expeditions led by the Prophet. Web (https://sunnah.com/bukhari/64/171). This *ḥadīth* reports that Muḥammad "set out for the battle of Dhat-ur-Riqa' at a place called Nakhl and he met a group of people from Ghaṭafān, but there was no clash (between them); the people were afraid of each other" and so Muḥammad "offered the two raka'āt [bows] of the Fear prayer." For more details about this type of prayer, see *Sahih Bukhari*, Book of Fear Prayer (p. 219); *Ṣaḥīḥ al-Bukhārī*, Abwab Salāt al-Khawf 1: 319. See also Q 4.102.

[37] Ibn Hishām (Ibn Isḥāq), *The Life of Muḥammad* 447-448; Ibn Hishām (Ibn Isḥāq), *Al-Sīra al-Nabawīya* 3: 410-411.

[38] *History of al-Tabari* 7: 165. See Ibn Hishām (Ibn Isḥāq), *The Life of Muḥammad* 449; Ibn Hishām (Ibn Isḥāq), *Al-Sīra al-Nabawīya* 3: 411.

the military expedition of Dūmat al-Jandal, an oasis in northern Arabia.[39] According to some Islamic sources, Muḥammad had heard that some tribes in that area were raiding, plundering, and heading toward Medina.[40] To take the enemy tribes by surprise, Muḥammad and his men marched by night and hid by day. Even so, they failed to find these marauding tribes. However, Muḥammad's forces did capture the raiders' livestock, and the Muslim presence compelled the inhabitants in that area to flee. On the return to Medina, Muḥammad made a truce with 'Uyaynah Ibn Ḥisn (leader of one of the Ghatafān tribes), concerning pasturelands for his tribe's herds because of the drought.[41]

As Muḥammad's military expeditions and raids increased against the Jewish tribes and other neighboring tribes, the expelled Jews of Banū al-Naḍīr (many of whom had migrated to Khaybar, located north of Medina) encouraged the Arab tribes to fight Muḥammad and his followers. Though the Banū al-Naḍīr were obviously driven by personal reasons—their desire to avenge their subjugation, dispossession, and banishment by Muḥammad—Muḥammad and his Muslims had become a mounting threat to all their non-Muslim neighbors, Jewish and Arab alike, with the growing frequency and belligerence of the Muslims' threats, military expeditions, raids, enslavement, expulsions, torture, and assassinations. As a result, Jewish and Arab tribes, including the Quraysh of Mecca, formed a military confederacy to confront Muḥammad and his Muslims at Medina with the goal of removing them once and for all from the region.[42] This Meccan confederacy combined three (or two) armies for a total of 10,000 men and included 600 or more horsemen. The Quraysh, led by Abū Sufyān, and its closest allies constituted one of the armies with 4000 men. Muḥammad had only 3000 men to oppose this huge force.[43]

The strategy of the confederacy was to besiege the Muslims at Medina and force them to surrender. From Muḥammad's perspective, this upcoming battle was a defensive war for the Medinans, though the Meccan coalition most likely considered it a (defensive) retaliation for

---

[39] *History of al-Tabari* 8: 4; footnote 16.

[40] al-Mubarakpuri, *Sealed Nectar*, 193. See *History of al-Tabari* 8: 4-5.

[41] al-Mubarakpuri, *Sealed Nectar*, 193; *History of al-Tabari* 8: 5. See Ibn Hishām (Ibn Isḥāq), *The Life of Muḥammad* 449; Ibn Hishām (Ibn Isḥāq), *Al-Sīra al-Nabawīya* 3: 410.

[42] Ibn Hishām (Ibn Isḥāq), *The Life of Muḥammad* 450; Ibn Hishām (Ibn Isḥāq), *Al-Sīra al-Nabawīya* 3: 416-417. See *History of al-Tabari* 8: 6-7.

[43] Watt, *Muḥammad at Medina* 36.

the raids and military expeditions undertaken by Muḥammad against them. This perception—that these battles and military expeditions were defensive actions by the Muslims and offensive actions by his enemies—is a common theme in the Islamic sources. (ISIS, and later Islamic State, used the same declarations when it attacked targets in Syria and in Iraq and in Turkey.)

When Muḥammad learned about the Meccan confederacy and its plan to attack Medina, he prepared for this assault by having his followers dig a trench around the northern parts of the city open to cavalry attack. Muḥammad was informed of this new tactic (previously unknown in Arabia) through Salmān the Persian, who advised its construction.[44] Tools to dig this large ditch were borrowed from the Banū Qurayẓa,[45] a Jewish tribe that lived at the oasis of Medina.

Reading different narrations, it seems that the Jewish tribes never signed any formal agreement with Muḥammad to help him in his war preparations; the Medina covenant was signed between the Emigrants (Muhajirīn) and Helpers (Anṣār) on the behalf of the Jews as their allies (though no Jewish tribal leader representatives were present). The Banū Qurayẓa stayed neutral in this war, but still Islamic sources try to justify the war against them.

According to Islamic sources, the Meccan confederacy arrived into the area as the Muslims completed their trench. Ḥuyyay Ibn Akhṭab, leader of the Jewish Banū al-Naḍīr, approached Ka'b Ibn Asad al-Quraẓī, leader of the Banū Qurayẓa, to support the Meccan confederacy. Ka'b vehemently refused but "Ḥuyyay kept on wheedling" him until Ka'b finally agreed when Ḥuyyay promised to enter Ka'b's fort and "await his fate" should the Meccan army fail to kill Muḥammad.[46]

Hearing rumors of this transaction, Muḥammad sent the Arab leaders of the Aws and Khazraj tribes, Sa'd Ibn Mu'ādh and Sa'd Ibn 'Ubāda, respectively, to meet with Ka'b to confirm this report. The Banū Qurayẓa denied having a treaty with Muḥammad, and the two Sa'ds and the tribe "reviled" each other.[47] Sa'd Ibn Mu'ādh, "a man of hasty temper," and his partner returned to Muḥammad with the discouraging news.[48]

---

[44] Watt, *Muḥammad at Medina* 37.

[45] al-Ḥalabī, *Al-Sīra al-Ḥalabīya* 2: 404.

[46] Ibn Hishām (Ibn Isḥāq), *The Life of Muḥammad* 453; Ibn Hishām (Ibn Isḥāq), *Al-Sīra al-Nabawīya* 3: 423.

[47] Ibn Hishām (Ibn Isḥāq), *The Life of Muḥammad* 453; Ibn Hishām (Ibn Isḥāq), *Al-Sīra al-Nabawīya* 3: 424.

[48] Ibn Hishām (Ibn Isḥāq), *The Life of Muḥammad* 453; Ibn Hishām (Ibn Isḥāq), *Al-Sīra al-Nabawīya* 3: 424.

In January AD 627, the Battle of the Trench (also called the Battle of the Confederates) between the Meccan confederacy and the Medinan Muslims commenced.[49] Sura al-Aḥzāb (Q 33), or "The Confederates," mentions this battle in several passages. For the first twenty days, the Meccan confederation maintained a siege around the Muslims without fighting "except for some shooting with arrows."[50]

During this siege, some Quraysh on horseback tried to breach the trench, but they were repelled when several of their leaders were killed in single combat. Some Muslims were injured as well during this battle. Sa'd Ibn Mu'ādh himself was wounded, the vein in his arm severed by an arrow.[51] As the siege wore on, Muḥammad and his Muslims "remained in fear and difficulty."[52]

At this point, Nu'aym Ibn Mas'ūd (of the Arab Ghatafān tribe), who had secretly converted to Islam, approached Muḥammad and offered his services. Muḥammad sent him to "awake distrust" and foment division among the Arab and Jewish tribes of the Meccan confederacy. Muḥammad justified this duplicity by saying that "war is deceit."[53] So Nu'aym met with the Banū Qurayẓa, the Quraysh, and the Ghatafān, telling each tribe in turn of planned betrayal by the others.[54]

Nu'aym's clandestine mission was aided by the advent of inclement weather, and the Meccan confederacy soon broke apart with the different tribes leaving the monthlong siege of Medina to return home to their own region—except for the Banū Qurayẓa people because Medina was their home.[55]

Slaughter of the Banū Qurayẓa

The following morning after the siege ended, all the Muslims put down their weapons, no doubt feeling that a heavy burden on them had been

---

[49] Ibn Hishām (Ibn Isḥāq), *The Life of Muḥammad* 450-453; Ibn Hishām (Ibn Isḥāq), *Al-Sīra al-Nabawīya* 3: 416-417.

[50] Ibn Hishām (Ibn Isḥāq), *The Life of Muḥammad* 450-454; Ibn Hishām (Ibn Isḥāq), *Al-Sīra al-Nabawīya* 3: 435-436.

[51] Ibn Hishām (Ibn Isḥāq), *The Life of Muḥammad* 454-458; Ibn Hishām (Ibn Isḥāq), *Al-Sīra al-Nabawīya* 3: 430-431.

[52] Ibn Hishām (Ibn Isḥāq), *The Life of Muḥammad* 454-458; Ibn Hishām (Ibn Isḥāq), *Al-Sīra al-Nabawīya* 3: 425.

[53] Ibn Hishām (Ibn Isḥāq), *The Life of Muḥammad* 458; Ibn Hishām (Ibn Isḥāq), *Al-Sīra al-Nabawīya* 3: 433-434. See *Sunan Abū Dawūd*, Book of Jihad 3: 275.

[54] Ibn Hishām (Ibn Isḥāq), *The Life of Muḥammad* 458-460; Ibn Hishām (Ibn Isḥāq), *Al-Sīra al-Nabawīya* 3: 433-434.

[55] Ibn Hishām (Ibn Isḥāq), *The Life of Muḥammad* 459-460; Ibn Hishām (Ibn Isḥāq), *Al-Sīra al-Nabawīya* 3: 434-435.

removed. But within hours, Muḥammad declared war on the Banū Qurayẓa, claiming that the angel Gabriel appeared to him and gave him a command from heaven: "God commands you, Muḥammad, to go to Banū Qurayẓa. I am about to go to them to shake their stronghold."[56] Despite the Jewish tribe's earlier assistance by providing the Muslims tools to dig their defensive trenches and remaining neutral during the siege (their agreement with Ḥuyyay Ibn Akhṭab notwithstanding), Muḥammad moved to punish them. (Apparently, his maxim, "war is deceit," only applies to Muslims; perceived enemies are held to a higher standard.)

Muḥammad sent 'Alī forward with an army to the forts of the Banū Qurayẓa. When Muḥammad caught up with his men at the forts, he called out to the Banū Qurayẓa: "You brothers of monkeys, has God disgraced you and brought His vengeance upon you?"[57]

After twenty-five days of the Muslims' siege, the Jews grew desperate, exhausted and terrified. (As promised, Ḥuyyay Ibn Akhṭab, leader of the Banū al-Naḍīr, was with them and did not leave with the rest of the Meccan confederacy.) Ka'b Ibn Asad, leader of the Banū Qurayẓa, told his tribe they had three alternatives: convert to Islam, kill their families (so they wouldn't be enslaved) and fight, or fight on their Sabbath and take Muḥammad by surprise. The tribe would not accept any of these options and asked Muḥammad to send them Abū Labāba, a leader of the Arab Aws tribe, an ally of the Banū Qurayẓa, for counsel. He told them to accept Muḥammad's judgment but then tacitly indicated they would be slaughtered by the Muslims.[58]

The Banū Qurayẓa finally submitted to Muḥammad, perhaps hoping their judgment would be expulsion, as was done with the Banū Qaynuqā'. The Khazraj, Arab ally of the Banū Qaynuqā', was involved in that judgment and swayed Muḥammad to be merciful. Likewise, the Arab ally of the Banū Qurayẓa, the Aws, wanted to pronounce judgment over the Banū Qurayẓa. But this time, Muḥammad—and not the tribe—selected the judge: Sa'd Ibn Mu'ādh, Muḥammad's emissary to the Banū Qurayẓa,

---

[56] Ibn Hishām (Ibn Isḥāq), *The Life of Muḥammad* 461; Ibn Hishām (Ibn Isḥāq), *Al-Sīra al-Nabawīya* 3: 436.

[57] Ibn Hishām (Ibn Isḥāq), *The Life of Muḥammad* 461; Ibn Hishām (Ibn Isḥāq), *Al-Sīra al-Nabawīya* 3: 436-437.

[58] Ibn Hishām (Ibn Isḥāq), *The Life of Muḥammad* 461-462; Ibn Hishām (Ibn Isḥāq), *Al-Sīra al-Nabawīya* 3: 439-440. **Note:** Abū Labāba immediately repented for warning the Jews and bound himself to one of the pillars in the mosque until he was forgiven by Allah for his betrayal of Muḥammad. Muḥammad later released him.

who had been rebuffed and reviled by the tribe and now lay dying from a mortal wound to his arm.[59] When he became fatally wounded, Sa'd Ibn Mu'ādh had implored Allah to grant him martyrdom but not let him die "until I have seen my desire [revenge] upon the Banū Qurayẓa."[60] So, not surprisingly, in his appointed role as judge, he pronounced that the Banū Qurayẓa "men should be killed, the property divided, and the women and children taken as captives."[61]

Was Muḥammad pleased with this judgment? Yes. Not only was he pleased, but he stated so to Sa'd Ibn Mu'ādh: "You have given the judgment of Allah above the seven heavens."[62] The judgment was quickly carried out, perhaps the next day:[63]

> Then they [Banū Qurayẓa] surrendered, and the apostle confined them in Medina.... Then the apostle went out to the market of Medina... and dug trenches in it. Then he sent for them [adult men] and struck off their heads in those trenches as they were brought out to him in batches. Among them was the enemy of Allah Ḥuyyay Ibn Akhṭab [leader of the Banū al-Naḍīr] and Ka'b Ibn Asad their chief. There were 600 or 700 in all, though some put the figure as high as 800 or 900. As they were being taken out in batches to the apostle they asked Ka'b what he thought would be done with them. He replied, "Will you never understand? Don't you see that the summoner never stops and those who are taken away do not return? By Allah it is death!" This went on until the apostle made an end of them.

In just one day and in the presence of Muḥammad, some 600 to 900 Jewish men were dragged out into Medina's public marketplace to be beheaded, their headless corpses thrown into the freshly dug trenches. They received no sympathy or mercy, because of their refusal to support Muḥammad or believe in his prophethood and their willingness to

---

59 Ibn Hishām (Ibn Isḥāq), *The Life of Muḥammad* 463-464; Ibn Hishām (Ibn Isḥāq), *Al-Sīra al-Nabawīya* 3: 443.

60 Ibn Hishām (Ibn Isḥāq), *The Life of Muḥammad* 457; Ibn Hishām (Ibn Isḥāq), *Al-Sīra al-Nabawīya* 3: 431. See Ibn Kathīr, *Al-Bidāya* 6: 87-88.

61 Ibn Hishām (Ibn Isḥāq), *The Life of Muḥammad* 464; Ibn Hishām (Ibn Isḥāq), *Al-Sīra al-Nabawīya* 3: 443. See *History of al-Tabari* 8: 27-41, and Watt, *Muḥammad at Medina* 214.

62 Ibn Hishām (Ibn Isḥāq), *The Life of Muḥammad* 464; Ibn Hishām (Ibn Isḥāq), *Al-Sīra al-Nabawīya* 3: 443. See *Ṣaḥiḥ Muslim*, Book of Jihad and Expedition: Justification for killing those guilty of breach of trust and making the people of the fort surrender on the arbitration of a just person (pp. 1091-1092); *Ṣaḥīḥ Muslim*, Kītāb al-Jihād wa al-Sīyar 2: 846-847. Several *ḥadīths* on this judgment state that Muḥammad told Sa'd Ibn Mu'ādh, "You have adjudged by the decision of The King [Allah]." See also Ibn Kathīr, *Al-Bidāya* 6: 90: "The Messenger of Allah…said, "You have judged them with the judgment of Allah and the judgment of His Messenger."

63 Ibn Hishām (Ibn Isḥāq), *The Life of Muḥammad* 464; Ibn Hishām (Ibn Isḥāq), *Al-Sīra al-Nabawīya* 3: 444-445.

accept the judgment on their unconditional surrender from a mortally wounded former ally (now a Muslim convert), a man of hasty temper,[64] who had previously suffered ridicule from their leaders.

ISIL imitation of Banū Qurayẓa slaughter

How is this slaughter of the Banū Qurayẓa in seventh-century AD not the exact type of atrocity committed by today's ISIL fighters when they dug trenches and killed hundreds of young Iraqi cadets from Camp Speicher? Was their inspiration this account taken from the biographical annals of the prophet Muḥammad?

When I saw the pictures and read the news about the Camp Speicher massacre and reflected on its similarities to the beheading of the Jews of the Banū Qurayẓa in Muḥammad's biography, I imagined the young men crying out as they slowly walked to their death, their hands tied, as Muḥammad sat and watched his Companions cutting off the heads, one head after another, from morning to evening—a long day of killing that exhausted the executioners. Even for the members of the Banū Qurayẓa who were not beheaded that day—the young children and women—the day was still full of fear and anguish. I remember reading that the face, armpits, and genitals of the young boys were examined for any traces of beard or pubic hair to separate them from the adult men. Those boys with no such signs of physical maturity were spared—but taken as slaves. One of the child survivors gave this account: "We were presented to the Messenger of Allah on the Day of Qurayẓa. Those whose pubic hair had grown were killed, and those whose pubic hair had not yet grown were let go. I was one of those whose pubic hair had not yet grown, so I was let go."[65] In another narration, the survivor states, "I was the first to be judged by Sa'd. They brought me to him, and I was thinking that he would kill me, but they uncovered my genitals and saw that I had not yet grown any pubic hair, so they took me as captive."[66]

Muḥammad himself supervised the process of separating the boys from the adult men and the subsequent killing. He also supervised the division of the spoils and the division of the women and children. He

[64] Ibn Hishām (Ibn Isḥāq), *The Life of Muḥammad* 453; Ibn Hishām (Ibn Isḥāq), *Al-Sīra al-Nabawīya* 3: 424.

[65] *Sunan al-Tirmidhī* 5: 195. See Ibn Hishām (Ibn Isḥāq), *The Life of Muḥammad* 466; Ibn Hishām (Ibn Isḥāq), *Al-Sīra al-Nabawīya* 3: 448.

[66] Ibn Ḥabbān, *Ṣaḥīḥ Ibn Ḥabbān* 5: 100.

even sold some female captives to buy horses and weapons to restock his war chest for future military expeditions.[67] However, Muḥammad took for himself a beautiful woman, Rayḥāna, of the tribe.[68] She remained in his possession as his concubine (because she wanted to remain a Jew) the rest of her life.[69]

Division of female captives among Muḥammad and his followers

Other Jewish tribes feared becoming the next target for a Muslim attack. So they began to fortify themselves, equipping themselves to withstand any sudden attack, because Muḥammad attacked the Jews of Banū Qurayẓa, Banū al-Naḍīr and Banū Qaynuqāʿ even though these tribes did not initiate any military aggression against the Muslims.

However, from Muḥammad's perspective, any non-Muslim tribe making defensive preparations is committing a crime that justifies an attack. He applied this kind of thinking within a year after the Muslim attack on the Banū Qurayẓa (January AD 627).[70] When he heard that the Arab tribe Banū al-Muṣṭaliq was preparing for war, Muḥammad and his followers (both Emigrants and Helpers) set out with a large force to surprise the Banū al-Muṣṭaliq with a pre-emptive assault.[71] Muḥammad's men surprised the Banū al-Muṣṭaliq while the tribesmen were watering their cattle at a watering hole. The Muslims "killed those who fought and imprisoned others."[72] With this rout, the Muslims were able to claim complete victory and carried out the now familiar pattern of killing the captured men, enslaving the women and children, and appropriating and dividing the spoils.[73]

Once again, Muḥammad, as commander of the victorious Muslims, exercised his "right" to select the most valuable female captive, the beautiful Jūwayriyya Bint al-Ḥārith, daughter of the Banū al-Muṣṭaliq chief. She agreed to marry Muḥammad to escape enslavement under

---

[67] Ibn Hishām (Ibn Isḥāq), *The Life of Muḥammad* 466; Ibn Hishām (Ibn Isḥāq), *Al-Sīra al-Nabawīya* 3: 450.

[68] Ibn Kathīr, *Al-Bidāya* 8: 233.

[69] Ibn Hishām (Ibn Isḥāq), *The Life of Muḥammad* 466; Ibn Hishām (Ibn Isḥāq), *Al-Sīra al-Nabawīya* 3: 450.

[70] Watt, *Muḥammad at Medina* 341.

[71] Ibn Hishām (Ibn Isḥāq), *The Life of Muḥammad* 490; Ibn Hishām (Ibn Isḥāq), *Al-Sīra al-Nabawīya* 4: 13-14.

[72] *Sunnah.com*: *Sahih Muslim*, Book of Jihad and Expeditions. Web (https://sunnah.com/muslim/32/1); *Ṣaḥīḥ Muslim*, Kītāb al-Jihād wa al-Sīyar 2: 828.

[73] Ibn Hishām (Ibn Isḥāq), *The Life of Muḥammad* 490-493; Ibn Hishām (Ibn Isḥāq), *Al-Sīra al-Nabawīya* 4: 13-14. See *History of al-Tabarī* 8: 51-56.

another Muslim. When Muḥammad married her, her family became his in-laws. So Muḥammad set them free (about a hundred families), but the rest of the captives were divided among his followers.[74]

After their successful raid on the Banū al-Muṣṭaliq,[75] the Muslim fighters faced a dilemma regarding their female captives. They knew if they satisfied their sexual lust with any of their female slaves and pregnancy occurred, the market value of that pregnant female slave would drop. So the men asked Muḥammad if they had the right to practice *'azl* (coitus interruptus) during sexual intercourse with a female captive to prevent impregnation and thus retain her market value. (A captive woman without a child was considered more valuable than one with a child.) According to this *ḥadīth*, Muḥammad gave this response:[76]

> [As narrated by Abu Said Al-Khudri]...during the battle with Banū al-Muṣṭaliq they (Muslims) captured some females and intended to have sexual relations with them without impregnating them. So they asked the Prophet about coitus interruptus. The Prophet said, "It is better that you should not do it, for Allah has written whom He is going to create till the Day of Resurrection."

The men's concern centered not on the morality or religious "legality" of sexual intercourse (rape) of a (most likely unwilling) female captive but the morality or religious "legality" of practicing some type of natural contraception during the sexual act. Muḥammad advised them not to practice coitus interruptus, giving the reasoning that the creation of a soul is up to Allah; sexual intercourse with or without the ejaculation of semen will not change the destiny of Allah. Therefore, according to Muḥammad's response, it is not forbidden to practice incomplete intercourse, but Allah will enable conception if he chooses no matter what they do.

The next major military expedition against a Jewish tribe, the Khaybar, occurred in May AD 628.[77] Just two months before this attack, Muḥammad had signed a ten-year armistice in March with the Meccan Quraysh (commonly called the Treaty of Hudaybīya). With the signing

---

[74] Ibn Hishām (Ibn Isḥāq), *The Life of Muḥammad* 493; Ibn Hishām (Ibn Isḥāq), *Al-Sīra al-Nabawīya* 4: 19. See *History of al-Tabarī* 8: 56-57.

[75] Ibn Kathīr, *Al-Bidāya* 6: 181. The date of this raid differs depending on the source: AH 4 (Mūsa Ibn 'Uqba), AH 5 ('Urūa, al-Waqidi), or AH 6 (Ibn Isḥāq).

[76] *Sahih Bukhari*, Book of Oneness, Uniqueness of Allah (pp. 1656-1657) and Book of Wedlock, Marriage (p. 1167); *Ṣaḥīḥ al-Bukhārī*, Kītāb al-Maghāzī 4: 1516, and Kītāb al-Nikāh 5: 1998.

[77] Watt, *Muḥammad at Medina* 341.

of this compact, Muḥammad received written assurance that his strongest enemy would not be seeking or engaging in hostilities against him and the Medinan Muslims for an extensive period.[78] Was the timing of this agreement and his sudden attack on the Khaybar so soon afterward just a coincidence or a deliberate move emboldened by the Meccans' pragmatic pacifism (to avoid a costly war) toward the Muslims?

Muḥammad and his army marched quickly and secretly toward Khaybar. Their early morning first attack caught the Jews of Khaybar off guard:[79]

> We [Muslim army] met the workers of Khaybar coming out in the morning with their spades and baskets. When they saw the apostle and the army they cried, "Muḥammad with his force," and turned tail and fled. The apostle said, "*Allahu Akbar!* Khaybar is destroyed. When we arrive in a people's square it is a bad morning for those who have been warned."

Notice the documentation in the Islamic sources regarding Muḥammad's use of the phrase "*Allahu Akbar*" as a battle cry when attacking and killing infidels.

Khaybar was a collection of several groups of strongholds, many of which were built on hilltops for protection. Muḥammad and his army began to attack each group in turn. During this progressive siege, the Muslims killed many of the Jewish fighters and captured their women and children. After they had conquered and taken possession of two forts, the rest offered little resistance, and terms of surrender were drawn up.[80] Muḥammad spared the lives of most of the Khaybar Jews, though many were expelled and had to leave their wealth to the Muslims. Others negotiated to stay so they could continue to farm their orchards. They offered to give half the harvest each season to the Muslims. Muḥammad agreed to these conditions but with the caveat that "if we wish to expel you we will expel you."[81]

Of the Jewish women captured during this siege and battle of Khaybar, Muḥammad selected for himself (yet again) a beautiful female

[78] Watt, *Muḥammad at Medina* 47-48.

[79] Ibn Hishām (Ibn Isḥāq), *The Life of Muḥammad* 511; Ibn Hishām (Ibn Isḥāq), *Al-Sīra al-Nabawīya* 4: 69. This account also found in the Ḥadīth literature. For an example, see *Sahih Bukhari*, Book of Call to Prayers (p. 149); *Ṣaḥīḥ al-Bukhārī*, Kitāb al-Adhān1: 221.

[80] Watt, *Muḥammad at Medina* 218. See Ibn Hishām (Ibn Isḥāq), *The Life of Muḥammad* 511, 515; Ibn Hishām (Ibn Isḥāq), *Al-Sīra al-Nabawīya* 4: 79-80.

[81] Ibn Hishām (Ibn Isḥāq), *The Life of Muḥammad* 515; Ibn Hishām (Ibn Isḥāq), *Al-Sīra al-Nabawīya* 4: 82.

captive of high status: Ṣafīya Bint Ḥuyyay Ibn al-Akhṭab.[82] She was the daughter of Banū al-Naḍīr chief Ḥuyyay Ibn Akhṭab (beheaded earlier by Muḥammad after the military expedition to the Qurayẓa)[83] and now a widow of Kināna Ibn al-Rabī' (tortured and beheaded on Muḥammad's orders), the treasurer of the Banū al-Naḍīr.[84]

Despite this horrific personal loss in her life—the direct result of Muḥammad's actions—Muḥammad moved quickly to "free" her so he could "marry" her and thus fulfill his sexual desire for her. Incredibly, he seemed to show no qualms in consummating his marriage with a young woman whose father and husband he had brutally executed. Apparently, his followers had misgivings because one of them posted himself, armed with his sword, outside Muḥammad's tent during the "wedding" night. When Muḥammad saw this guard the following morning, the guard said, "I was afraid for you with this woman for you have killed her father, her husband, and her people…so I was afraid for you on her account."[85]

The Hadīth literature reports that Ṣafīya once said, "There was none more hateful to me than Allah's Messenger as he killed my father and husband."[86] This *ḥadith* also states that Muḥammad kept apologizing to her regarding this matter until that "feeling of hatred vanished" from her.[87]

But did her feelings of grief (and perhaps rage) over the execution of her father and husband ever vanish, especially as the murderer was the same person who then sexually violated her? How would any woman feel towards someone who killed her dearest people and then pressured her into sexual intercourse? When ISIS leaders sexually abused female captives, the media unreservedly labelled it "rape."[88] How are these actions any different than the immoral actions of Muḥammad with his female captives as reported in his biography and Hadith literature? These

[82] *Sahih Bukhari*, Book of Sales and Trade (p. 501); *Ṣaḥīḥ al-Bukhārī*, Kītāb al-Biyū' 2: 778. According to this *ḥadīth*, "the beauty of Safiya…was mentioned to him [Muḥammad] and her husband had been killed while she was a bride. Allah's Apostle selected her for himself…."

[83] Ibn Hishām (Ibn Isḥāq), *The Life of Muḥammad* 464; Ibn Hishām (Ibn Isḥāq), *Al-Sīra al-Nabawīya* 3: 445, 4: 70.

[84] Ibn Hishām (Ibn Isḥāq), *The Life of Muḥammad* 514-515; Ibn Hishām (Ibn Isḥāq), *Al-Sīra al-Nabawīya* 4: 70.

[85] Ibn Hishām (Ibn Isḥāq), *The Life of Muḥammad* 517; Ibn Hishām (Ibn Isḥāq), *Al-Sīra al-Nabawīya* 4: 85.

[86] Ibn Ḥabbān, *Ṣaḥīḥ Ibn Ḥabbān* 5: 233.

[87] Ibid.

[88] Goldman, Adam, and Greg Miller. "Leader of Islamic State Used American Hostage as Sexual Slave." *WashingtonPost.com*. The Washington Post, 15 Aug. 2015. Web (https://www.washingtonpost.com/world/national-security/leader-of-islamic-state-raped-american-hostage/2015/08/14/266b6bf4-42c1-11e5-846d-02792f854297_story.html?utm_term=.e01a38a3df8b).

texts are an integral part of an Islam-based curriculum, which Muslims must consider as exemplary behavior to emulate, because Muḥammad is the Messenger of Allah and a teacher for all humankind.

ISIS and Muḥammad's treatment of female captives

I was not surprised when I heard that ISIS fighters were publicly trafficking captured Yazidi women, because I know that Muḥammad and his Companions considered this economic activity as a law coming from Allah. Indeed, the Qur'ān makes it lawful and establishes rules for its correct application: "*...then marry*[89] *what seems good to you of women, by twos, or threes, or fours; and if ye fear that ye cannot be equitable, then only one, or what your right hands possess...*" (Q 4.3; Palmer trans.). Thus, in Islam a man is limited to four wives. However, there is no limit for "what his right hand possesses," i.e., female slaves. In practice, Muḥammad and his Companions used to take as many women as they wanted during their military campaigns but divided the captured women equitably among themselves, so each Companion received his appropriate share of female captives. The Muslim fighter was also allowed to sell, buy, or exchange the captives in any manner that he wished.

Muḥammad's acquirement of a Jewish captive after the Battle of Khaybar exemplifies the early Muslims' system of human trafficking. Though she was initially given away to a Companion by Muḥammad, sight unseen, he changed his mind when he realized her status and value. He then offered that Companion another female captive in exchange for Safiya:[90]

> We conquered Khaybar, took the captives, and the booty was collected. Diḥya came and said, "O Allah's Prophet! Give me a slave girl from the captives." The Prophet said, "Go and take any slave girl." He [Dihya] took Ṣafiya Bint Ḥuyyay. But then a man came to the Prophet and said, "O Allah's Apostle! You gave Ṣafiya Bint Ḥuyyay to Diḥya and she is the chief mistress of the tribes of Qurayẓa and Naḍīr and she befits none but you." So the Prophet said, "Bring him along with her." So Diḥya came with her and when the Prophet saw her, he said to Diḥya, "Take any slave girl other than her from the captives."

---

[89] **Note:** The Arabic word is *inkaḥū*, a graphic term that refers to a person's availability (not necessarily voluntary consent) to engage in sexual intercourse. English translators have substituted this Arabic word with the subtler, less provocative word *marry*.

[90] *Sahih Bukhari*, Book of Prayer (pp. 99-100); *Ṣaḥīḥ al-Bukhārī*, Kītāb al-Salāt fī al-Thiyāb 1: 145-146.

The distribution and bartering of female captives after the early Muslims' military expeditions, battles, and campaigns were routine proceedings for the Prophet and his followers. Consequently, human trafficking was a normal and routine occurrence for ISIS when it attacked and subdued a population within a targeted territory. By engaging in this activity, ISIS members believed they were honoring Muḥammad's way of life and restoring the glories of their Muslim ancestors.

Muḥammad and his followers commonly used their female infidel captives for sexual purposes. Similarly, ISIS fighters felt entitled to use their Yazidi female captives for sexual purposes as well, relying on the Qur'ān and Hadith literature for guidance. A description of this treatment has been publicized on the American radio station Sawa, which broadcasted an eyewitness account of a Yazidi survivor concerning the treatment of girls and women after capture by ISIS fighters:[91]

> After taking our group to Sinjar, they [ISIS fighters] gathered us in a big hall that contained sixty girls, women, and young men. But then they separated the young men from the group and moved the women and children to Mosul, while the girls were forced to stay with the ISIS members, who severely tortured any girl who refused to obey their orders.

Doesn't this treatment compare with the actions of Muḥammad and his men when they raided and battled with non-Muslim tribes? Didn't they separate young men from girls and children? Didn't they kill the young men but kept the girls, distributing them among themselves? In the Sawa radio broadcast, the young female Yazidi survivor confirmed that ISIS captured "about three thousand women, girls, and children."[92]

Amnesty International, a nongovernmental organization focused on human rights, published a document in 2014 summarizing the experiences and treatment of hundreds, possibly thousands, of Yazidi men, women, and children abducted and held captive by ISIS. Young women, including little girls as young as 12, "were separated from their parents and older relatives and sold, given as gifts or forced to marry IS fighters and their supporters. Many [had] been subjected to torture and ill-treatment, including rape and other forms of sexual violence,

[91] Ali Mendi, Samira. "Yazidi Maria Tells Her Story: What Daesh [ISIS] Did to Us." *Radiosawa.com*. Radio Sawa, 12 Mar. 2015. Web (https://www.radiosawa.com/a/isis-iraq-yazidi-women-sex-slaves/267701.html).

[92] Ibid.

and have likewise been pressured into converting to Islam."[93] Amnesty International notes that the violations and abuses documented in this report constitute as "war crimes" and "crimes against humanity" according to international humanitarian law (IHL, the laws of war) and Resolution 1820 (2008) of the United Nations Security Council. Not only are all these acts prohibited, but the perpetrators (civilian or military individuals or groups) will be held criminally responsible for "assisting in, facilitating, aiding or abetting the commission of a war crime."[94]

If the torture, rape, executions, enslavement, imprisonment, family separation, and other forms of violence against the abducted Yazidi people by ISIS (and later, Islamic State) are classified as "war crimes" and "crimes against humanity," how does a person classify the actions of Muḥammad and his men concerning their captives? Didn't Muḥammad separate Ṣafīya Bint Ḥuyyay from her family—in fact, he permanently isolated her by executing her father and husband—and then forced sexual intercourse upon her? Didn't his followers separate hundreds of young girls from their parents by abducting them and holding them captive for use as sex slaves or trade (or both)? Didn't Muḥammad accept a slave girl, Maria al-Qibṭiya (Mary the Copt), as a gift from the Muqauqis Christian ruler of Alexandria (Egypt)? Though she was never officially his wife, she bore him a son, Ibrāhīm.[95]

If Muḥammad is the supreme role model of Islam, whose every action must be respected and imitated, then Muslims face a major problem. How can Muslims criticize the actions of conservative believers who try to live their lives according to Muḥammad's example without criticizing the Prophet himself? If Muḥammad was just a role model for a designated historical time period, then there would not be a problem. However, in Islamic sources, Muḥammad is a role model who is not limited to time and place; he remains the perfect role model even in the twenty-first century. Though his actions are arguably war crimes and crimes against humanity according to today's world view, they are considered in the eyes of his most ardent followers and ISIS (and later, Islamic State) as just

[93] Amnesty International. *Escape from Hell: Torture and Sexual Slavery in Islamic State Captivity in Iraq*. London: Amnesty International, 2014. See page 4. Print and Web (https://www.amnesty.org/en/documents/mde14/021/2014/en/).

[94] Ibid. See page 15.

[95] Ibn Hishām (Ibn Isḥāq), *The Life of Muḥammad* 653; Ibn Hishām (Ibn Isḥāq), *Al-Sīra al-Nabawīya* 1: 328.

religious rituals and worship of Allah, which they must fight to uphold for religious devotion and glorification.

Muḥammad would also employ the tempting promise of female captives to increase his fighters' motivation and gain their support for his proposed expeditions and raids. He might mention an alluring characteristic as enticement: "Fight and you will have the spoils of the daughters of yellow [blonde-haired people]," a reference to Byzantine women.[96]

As a matter of fact, Islam decrees that Muslim men will have women in the earthly world and in the hereafter. For instance, he is permitted to take women as captives of war. If a Muslim man dies as a martyr, there will be many women waiting for him in paradise: "[H]e is married to seventy-two wives from the wide-eyed virgins."[97]

Some Islamic sources report that some of Muḥammad's Companions were reluctant to have sexual intercourse with female captives because the women were already married.[98] But Muḥammad gave the men permission with Q 4.24 (Palmer trans.): *"...and married women, save such as your right hands possess...."* A married woman becomes lawful for sexual intercourse once she completes her menses. Her captivity annuls her marriage to her (polytheistic) husband.[99] By reciting this and other verses from the Qur'ān, Muḥammad removed their reservations concerning the religious lawfulness of sexual intercourse with married female captives. No matter how immoral or shameful this behavior might seem initially to these followers, what good Muslim would argue with the Book of Allah?

---

[96] See the commentary on Q 9.49, *Tafsīr al-Ṭabarī* 10: 105.

[97] *Sunan al-Tirmidhī* 5: 246. The *ḥadīth*, repeated in many narrations, reports that the "martyr has six privileges with God: his sins are pardoned when the first drop of blood falls; he is shown his seat in paradise; he is safe from the punishment of the grave and secure from the great terror (i.e. hell); a crown of dignity is placed on his head one jewel of which is worth more than the world and all that is therein; and he is married to seventy two dark-eyed virgins; and he makes successful intercession for seventy of his relatives." (See Kītāb Faḍā'il al-Jihād, ch. "Fī Thawāb al-Shahīd.")

[98] See *Sahih Muslim,* Book of Marriage: It is permissible to have sexual intercourse with a captive woman after she is purified (of menses or delivery) in case she has a husband, her marriage is abrogated after she becomes captive (pp. 847-848); *Sunnah.com*: *Ṣaḥīḥ Muslim*, Book of Suckling. Web (https://sunnah.com/muslim/17/43); *Ṣaḥīḥ Muslim*, Kītāb al-Riḍā' 1: 666. Excerpt: The Muslim fighters "took captives (women) on the day of Autas who had their husbands. They were afraid (to have sexual intercourse with them) [until] this verse [Q 4.24] was revealed: *'and women already married, except those whom your right hands possess.'"* In other words, the women become religiously lawful for sexual intercourse with their Muslim captors after their menses had ended. Variations of this *ḥadīth* can be found in the Hadith literature.

[99] See *Sahih Muslim,* Book of Marriage: It is permissible to have sexual intercourse with a captive woman after she is purified (of menses or delivery) in case she has a husband, her marriage is abrogated after she becomes captive (pp. 847-848); *Sunnah.com*: *Sahih Muslim*, Book of Suckling. Web (https://sunnah.com/muslim/17/43); *Ṣaḥīḥ Muslim*, Kītāb al-Riḍā' 1: 666.

And if the Qur'ān—considered Allah's book for all times and all places—permits sexual intercourse with (rape of) married female captives, then acceptance of this primitive, barbaric policy by some of today's Muslims should come as no surprise.

In fact, ISIS (Islamic State) not only accepted this policy—it encouraged and applied it in areas under its control and derided Muslim groups and governments that would dare criticize them for implementing these practices. It openly and boastfully published stories about the people it had taken captive, justifying this enslavement with verses and passages from the Qur'ān, Hadīth literature, and the biography of Muḥammad. Islamic State even accused the Muslim world of dishonoring and disgracing Islam for its abandonment of this "custom." It maintained that it follows a more authentic Islam by reviving this abandoned *sunna*—holding Yazidi women, for example, in captivity and selling them in the slave markets.

A 2014 article in the magazine *Dabiq*, which is published by Islamic State, addresses the use of slavery in modern times.[100] The article contends that experts in Islamic jurisprudence and Islamic law (*fuqahā'*) have classified the Yazidis as a *mushrik* (polytheistic) group and therefore do not deserve the same treatment as other non-Muslim but monotheistic groups, such as Jews and Christians, who have not been enslaved but given the option to pay the *jizya*:[101]

> [Therefore, after conquering the Sinjar region] the Yazidi women and children were then divided according to the Sharī'ah amongst the fighters of the Islamic State who participated in the Sinjar operations, after one fifth of the slaves were transferred to the Islamic State's authority to be divided as khums [one fifth].

The article compares the selling of the enslaved Yazidi families by Islamic State fighters to the *mushrikīn* (polytheists) who were sold by Muḥammad and his Companions.[102] The article further justifies this policy concerning the enslaved Yazidi population with this comment:[103]

---

[100] "The Revival of Slavery before the Hour." *Dabiq*. Issue 4 (Aug.-Sept. 2014): 14-17. Web (http://www.ieproject.org/projects/dabiq4.pdf).
[101] Ibid. 15.
[102] Ibid.
[103] Ibid. 17.

> ...one should remember that enslaving the families of the kuffār and taking their women as concubines is a firmly established aspect of the Sharī'ah that if one were to deny or mock, he would be denying or mocking the verses of the Qur'ān and the narrations of the Prophet..., and thereby apostatizing from Islam.

The article also points out that "slavery has been mentioned [in Hadith literature] as one of the signs of the Hour as well as one of the causes behind al-Malhamah al-Kubrā [Final Battle and End Times]."[104]

If Islamic State holds up the Qur'ān, *sharī'a*, and Muḥammad's actions to legitimize and justify its use of slavery, how can critics then claim that it does not represent Islam in any way? What Muslim groups or sects do represent true Islam? Wouldn't it be those groups that institute or revive the Sunna of the Messenger of Islam and follow it?

In the last century, Muslim countries have officially abolished slavery—not because they are convinced that it is a crime but from international pressure. Slavery is a part of Islamic law, and therefore Muslim countries have been among the last countries in the world to abolish slavery, e.g., Qatar (1952),[105] Yemen[106] and Saudi Arabia (1962).[107] Still, Qatar, Yemen, Saudi Arabia, and other Muslim countries have waited even longer to ratify the1926 Slavery Convention,[108] an international treaty prohibiting slavery and human trafficking.[109]

The Islamic Republic of Mauritania in North Africa has tried three times to abolish slavery within its borders. Even though the country "officially" ratified the 1926 Slavery Convention in 1986 and established stronger penalties in 2007, "the practice remains pervasive, with an estimated half million Mauritanians enslaved, about 20 percent of the

[104] "The Revival of Slavery before the Hour." *Dabiq*. Issue 4 (Aug.-Sept. 2014): 15. Web (http://www.ieproject.org/projects/dabiq4.pdf).

[105] Finn, Tom. "Qatar Slavery Museum Aims to Address Modern Exploitation." *Reuters.com*. Reuters, 18 Nov. 2015. Web (http://www.reuters.com/article/us-qatar-slaverymuseum-doha-idUSKCN0T71XH20151118).

[106] "Slaves in Impoverished Yemen Dream of Freedom." *Alarabiya.net*. Al Arabiya Network, 21 July 2017. Web (http://www.alarabiya.net/articles/2010/07/21/114451.html).

[107] Halabi, Romina. "Contract Enslavement of Female Migrant Domestic Workers in Saudi Arabia and the United Arab Emirates." *Human Rights and Contemporary Slavery* (2008): 43. *Human Rights and Human Welfare*. Web (http://www.du.edu/korbel/hrhw/researchdigest/slavery/index.html).

[108] United Nations. "Slavery Convention." *United Nations Treaty Collection*. 212:1, 2861 (1955) Geneva: League of Nations, 1926; New York: United Nations (amended by the Protocol), 1953. 17-25. Web (https://treaties.un.org/doc/Publication/UNTS/Volume%20212/v212.pdf).

[109] United Nations. "Penal Matters." *Status of Treaties*. 14 July 2017. Ch. XVIII, No. 2: Slavery Convention, signed at Geneva on 25 September 1926 and amended by the Protocol. Web (https://treaties.un.org/Pages/ViewDetails.aspx?src=TREATY&mtdsg_no=XVIII-2&chapter=18&lang=en). Document lists participants (countries) and respective dates of participation, signature, and ratification.

population."[110] These Mauritanian slaves are forbidden to own property, have a last name, or even have legal custody of their own children.[111]

And at the time of this book's publication, no legal fatwa has been issued by Muslim religious institutions to legally prohibit slavery—because it is impossible! Islamic law not only permits but legalizes slavery. Islam's Prophet Muḥammad himself considered that any slave who escaped from his master became an infidel, which means he is thus deserving of death.[112] Even if the slave managed to escape capture or death, Allah would never accept his prayers.[113] In other words, the escaped slave would face eternal damnation.

Saudi sheikh Ṣāliḥ al-Fūzān, who is a member of the General Presidency of Scholarly Research and Iftā' in Saudi Arabia, presents this position, regarding the legality of slavery and the Qur'ān:[114]

> This ruling [slavery] is related to the Qur'ān and it cannot be abolished as long as there is *"jihād in the way of Allah"* [see Q 2.218] because slavery is a part of it [jihad]...that is the ruling of Allah, with no favoritism or courtesy to anyone. If slavery was wrong, Islam would have announced it, as it did regarding usury and adultery. Islam is brave and does not please people.

Muḥammad and his followers possessed slaves.[115] Muḥammad even established rules regarding the selling and buying of slaves,[116] and especially the sexual use of female slaves.[117] Therefore, if Islamic State is following the rules established by Muḥammad concerning slavery, then

[110] Fisher, Max. "The Country Where Slavery Is Still Normal." *TheAtlantic.com*. Atlantic Media, 28 June 2011. Web (https://www.theatlantic.com/international/archive/2011/06/the-country-where-slavery-is-still-normal/241148).

[111] Ibid.

[112] *Sahih Muslim*, Book of Faith: Calling the fugitive slave as infidel (p. 94); *Ṣaḥīḥ Muslim*, Kitāb al-Imān 1: 49. According to several *ḥadīths*, Muḥammad stated that any slave who "fled from his master committed an act of infidelity as long as he would not return to him," and in such cases, the master's "responsibility with regard to him [the slave] was absolved," and the slave's prayers to Allah would "not [be] accepted."

[113] *Sahih Muslim*, Book of Faith: Calling the fugitive slave as infidel (p. 94); *Ṣaḥīḥ Muslim*, Kitāb al-Imān 1: 49.

[114] "News of ISIS Enslavement of Yazidi Women Angers Member of Saudi Shura [Council]: Activists Reply with [Contradicting] Video of al-Fuzan. *Arabic.CNN.com*. Cable News Network (Arabic), 12 Aug. 2014. Web (https://arabic.cnn.com/middleeast/2014/08/11/fawzan-issa-iraq-twitter).

[115] Ibn Qayyīm al-Jawzīya, *Zādu al-Ma'ād* 1: 111. This source reports that Muḥammad owned many male slaves and listed at least twenty-eight names. Concerning women slaves, the source lists nine names but does not give the entire total. Muḥammad eventually did set free some of the men.

[116] al-Bayhaqī, *Al-Sunan al-Kubra* 13: 458. Examples of these rules include "no separation between a mother and her son" and "no separation between siblings."

[117] For examples, see *Sahih Muslim*, Book of Marriage: It is forbidden to have intercourse with a pregnant slave-woman (p. 838). See also *Sunnah.com*: *Muwatta Malik*, Book of Marriage. Web (https://sunnah.com/urn/511270); *Ṣaḥīḥ Muslim*, Kitāb al-Nikāḥ 1: 657.

no one can accuse it of not applying Islam in this matter. Those Muslim countries that do not apply Islamic law regarding slavery are only bowing to international pressure, because they cannot state publicly that "right-hand possession" (slavery) is unlawful according to Islamic law.

Islamic State has never desired or sought this kind of acquiescence. For this Islamic jihadist group, obedience is to Allah: "There is no obedience to the creation [created beings, i.e., humans] in disobedience to the Creator."[118] In other words, anyone in authority is not to be obeyed, if he does not rule according to Allah's laws. Therefore, applying the laws of Allah concerning slavery, including the selling and gifting of captive "polytheistic" women, is proper and religiously lawful. This view about slavery is the real Islam, as Muslims read about it from the early books, the Qur'ān and its commentaries, the Hadith literature, and the biography of Muḥammad.

Jābir Ibn 'Abd Allah, one of Muḥammad's Companions, relates in a *ḥadith* that the buying and selling of women were common, normal transactions in the eyes of Muḥammad; he never prohibited Muslims from engaging in human trafficking: "We would sell our concubines, the mothers of our own children, and the prophet among us, and considered nothing wrong with that."[119] Imam al-Shāfi'ī or "Sheikh al-Islam," one of the four great imams and founder of the Islamic al-Shāfi'ī school (*fiqh*), documents the Muslims' sale of captured Jewish women and children. He also mentions Muḥammad's own slave sale and his leadership in dividing all the remaining captives:[120]

> The Apostle of Allah took captive women and their children from Banū Qurayẓa, and he sold them from the polytheists. Then a Jewish merchant, namely Abū al-Shaḥim, purchased a woman and her sons from the prophet. And the Apostle of Allah divided all the remaining captives into three groups. He then sent the first group to Tihama and the second to Najd and the third to the Levant, and there they were all sold in exchange for horses, weapons, camels and money.

As documented in all the Islamic sources (Qur'ān, Hadith literature, biography, etc.), Muḥammad enslaved female captives. He divided them among his followers, who undoubtedly enjoyed receiving this human

---

[118] *Musnad Ahmad* 2: 376. According to a *ḥadīth*, "There is no obedience to a creation in disobedience to Allah almighty."

[119] Ibid. 4: 266.

[120] al-Shāfi'ī, *Kitāb al-'Umm* 7: 599.

"booty," for personal possession or sale. Muḥammad himself also kept or sold his female captives, and generally selected female captives of high status and beauty.

ISIS, and later Islamic State, followed the same pattern today in the way it treated the populations it captured. And young Muslims, wanting to be like their Prophet Muḥammad, are electrified by the successful military exploits of ISIS (Islamic State)—the invasions, the beheadings, the enslavement or expulsion of entire city populations. These actions remind them of Muḥammad and his campaigns and convince them that ISIS (Islamic State) is honoring Islam and Muḥammad by killing "infidel" men and humiliating their families (women and children).

In November 2014 Islamic State created a brochure, which it published on the Internet and distributed copies to its followers, entitled *Questions and Answers on Taking Captives and Slaves*. It contains more than two dozen questions[121] about the treatment of captives and slaves, where Islamic State answers the questions in accordance to Islamic law. The following four sets of questions and answers is an excerpt from this brochure:[122]

> **Q1. What is al-Sabi?**
> Al-Sabi is a woman from among Ahl al-Harb [the people of war] who has been captured by Muslims.
>
> **Q2. What makes al-Sabi permissible?**
> What makes al-Sabi permissible (i.e., what makes it permissible to take such a woman captive) is her unbelief. Unbelieving women who were captured and brought into the abode of Islam are permissible to us, after the imam distributes them among us.
>
> **Q3. Can all unbelieving women be taken captive?**
> There is no dispute among the Ulama [Islamic scholars] that it is permissible to capture unbelieving women who are characterized by Kufr Asil [original unbelief], such as the al-Kitābīyat (women from among the People of the Book, i.e., Jews and Christians) and polytheists....

---

[121] **Note:** Several editions of this pamphlet, particularly in Arabic, present thirty to thirty-two sets of questions and answers. This English edition lists twenty-seven sets but set number 23 is missing or the listing has been incorrectly numbered.

[122] Diwan al-Buhouth Wal-Iftaa (Departments of Scholarly Research and Verdicts in the Islamic State). *Questions and Answers on Taking Captives and Slaves*. Al-Himma Library, Nov. 2014. Print and Web. (For the English translation, see URL: http://preview.tinyurl.com/yap4jngu). See Smith, Amelia. "ISIS Publish Pamphlet on How to Treat Female Slaves." *Newsweek.com*. Newsweek, 9 Dec. 2014. Web (http://www.newsweek.com/isis-release-questions-and-answers-pamphlet-how-treat-female-slaves-290511).

Q4. Is it permissible to have [sexual] intercourse with a female captive?
It is permissible to have sexual intercourse with the female captive. Allah the almighty said: *"Who (the believers) guard their chastity (5) Except from their wives or the captives and slaves that their right hands possess, for then they are free from blame (6)" (Surat al-Mu'minoun)* [Q 23.5-6.].

All these questions and answers are based on the Islamic religion and on the comments and statements of significant Muslim scholars about Islamic history. Those who would dismiss these views concerning the treatment of captives and slaves must read the Islamic texts before insisting that Islamic State does not represent the real Islam. For Islamic State is genuinely following the religion and the life of Muḥammad and his Companions.

I ask those who try to separate Islamic State from Islam in order to exonerate the Islamic religion: Where has Islamic State gone astray? Has it committed any act that contradicts Islam or is contrary to the actions of Islam's prophet Muḥammad?

Muḥammad: perennial aggressor until death

Muḥammad continued his military expeditions until his death in AD 632. For the most part, Muḥammad and his army were successful in the later military campaigns after the Muslims' triumphant battle against the Jews of Khaybar. During the Battle of Khaybar, he besieged two forts of Khaybar until the people inside surrendered and asked him to spare their lives. Muḥammad agreed but took possession of all their property. In the end, the people of Khaybar asked Muḥammad to employ them on their now confiscated lands and share equally in the harvest. Muḥammad agreed—but with the condition that the Jews could be expelled at any time.[123]

No doubt, the relatively easy subjugation of the Khaybar by the Muslims frightened the nearby smaller Jewish tribes, like the people of Fadak, who soon asked Muḥammad "to let them go and spare their lives and they would leave him their property, and he did so."[124] The lands of the Fadak became the personal property of Muḥammad

[123] Ibn Hishām (Ibn Isḥāq), *The Life of Muḥammad* 515; Ibn Hishām (Ibn Isḥāq), *Al-Sīra al-Nabawīya* 4: 79-82.

[124] Ibn Hishām (Ibn Isḥāq), *The Life of Muḥammad* 515; Ibn Hishām (Ibn Isḥāq), *Al-Sīra al-Nabawīya* 4: 81.

because the Muslims "had not driven horses or camels against it," i.e., received the lands without battle.[125]

Notice that any property that was given up without a fight became the personal property of Muḥammad. Notice also the euphemistic term "peace treaty" used by Muslims to describe the surrender arrangements of the Khaybar: the Jews' offer to farm their own seized lands and give half the harvest to their conquerors so they would not be further attacked or expelled from the region. A "peace" treaty with such an unbalanced, unjust set of conditions seems more like a forced payoff by the Jews for self-preservation. Haven't ISIS (Islamic State) fighters employed the same policy—accept money payments, i.e., girls, bribes or forced payoffs, in exchange for neutrality or exemption from attack?[126]

The following year (September AD 629), Muḥammad sent out an army of three thousand fighters to make war with the Byzantines, but his army returned home to Medina, routed and defeated. Early Islamic accounts characterize this Battle of Mu'ta as a humiliating loss.[127] Undaunted, Muḥammad himself led a huge army of ten thousand warriors a few months later (January AD 630) to conquer Mecca, the city of his own native tribesmen, the Quraysh.[128] According to the Hadith literature, Muḥammad ordered his followers to kill all Quraysh tribesmen who might stand in their way in their conquest of Mecca:[129]

> [Companion Abū Hurayra narrates that Muḥammad said the following text to the Anṣār.] O ye Assembly of the Ansar, do you see the ruffians of the Quraysh? They said: Yes. He said: See, when you meet them tomorrow, wipe them out. He hinted at this with his hand, placing his right hand on his left and said: You will meet us at al-Safa'. (Abū Hurayra continued): Whoever [Quraysh] was seen by them [Anṣār] that day was put to death.

[125] Ibn Hishām (Ibn Isḥāq), *The Life of Muḥammad* 515-516, 523; Ibn Hishām (Ibn Isḥāq), *Al-Sīra al-Nabawīya* 4: 82, 99.

[126] Swanson, Ana. "How the Islamic State Makes Its Money." *WashingtonPost.com*. The Washington Post, 18 Nov. 2015. Web (https://www.washingtonpost.com/news/wonk/wp/2015/11/18/how-isis-makes-its-money/?utm_term=.94d4d523ac09). See Saul, Heather. "ISIS in Libya: Families Forced to Marry Girls as Young as 12 to Fighters for Protection as Clinics See Growing Number of Miscarriages and STDs." *Independent.co.uk*. The Independent, 12 May 2015. Web (http://www.independent.co.uk/news/world/europe/isis-in-libya-families-forced-to-marry-girls-as-young-as-12-to-fighters-for-protection-as-clinics-10244257.html).

[127] Ibn Hishām (Ibn Isḥāq), *The Life of Muḥammad* 531-536; Ibn Hishām (Ibn Isḥāq), *Al-Sīra al-Nabawīya* 4: 131-132. One excerpt states that the men "began to throw dirt at the [returning] army" when it approached Medina and yelled, "You runaways, you fled in the way of God!"

[128] Ibn Hishām (Ibn Isḥāq), *The Life of Muḥammad* 544-545; Ibn Hishām (Ibn Isḥāq), *Al-Sīra al-Nabawīya* 4: 150, 184. See Watt, *Muhammad at Medina* 66.

[129] *Sahih Muslim*, Book of Jihad and Expedition: The conquest of Mecca (p. 1102); *Ṣaḥīḥ Muslim*, Kītāb al-Jihād wa al-Sīyar 2: 856-857.

According to Islamic sources, including the Hadith literature, this dire plight was averted for most of the Meccans because of Quraysh leader, Abū Sufyān, who interceded for his tribe.[130] Muḥammad declared that any Quraysh who entered "the house of Abū Sufyān" would "be safe."[131] With this offer of general amnesty, most of the Meccans then went inside their houses, and Muḥammad and his men entered and took control of Mecca with little resistance, executing "whoever was seen by them that day" as well as a handful of specifically named people.[132] (Most of these executed persons were critics of Muḥammad or had committed some specific misdeed.)[133]

However, this general amnesty did not include religious acceptance or tolerance of the Meccans' paganism. Muḥammad telegraphed his deeper intention when he ordered the collection, breaking, and burning of all the idols surrounding the Ka'ba.[134] Afterward, the Meccans who had surrendered were gathered together "to do homage" to Muḥammad. With his Companion 'Umar below him, "imposing conditions" that they promised to obey Allah and his prophet, Muḥammad received and dealt with the men and then the women. In this manner, most of Mecca "converted" when they formally submitted to Muḥammad and their lives were spared.[135]

Thus Muḥammad's policy with polytheists was plain: fight and kill them or force them to convert. On his deathbed, he added another

---

[130] *Sahih Muslim,* Book of Jihad and Expedition: The conquest of Mecca (pp. 1102-1104); *Ṣaḥīḥ Muslim,* Kītāb al-Jihād wa al-Sīyar 2: 856-857. See Ibn Hishām (Ibn Isḥāq), *The Life of Muḥammad* 547-548; Ibn Hishām (Ibn Isḥāq), *Al-Sīra al-Nabawīya* 4: 155-157. See also *History of al-Ṭabarī* 8: 171-173, and Watt, *Muḥammad at Medina* 66.

[131] *Sahih Muslim,* Book of Jihad and Expedition: The conquest of Mecca (p. 1102); *Ṣaḥīḥ Muslim,* Kītāb al-Jihād wa al-Sīyar 2: 856-857. See Ibn Hishām (Ibn Isḥāq), *The Life of Muḥammad* 547-548; Ibn Hishām (Ibn Isḥāq), *Al-Sīra al-Nabawīya* 4: 157.

[132] Ibn Hishām (Ibn Isḥāq), *The Life of Muḥammad* 550; Ibn Hishām (Ibn Isḥāq), *Al-Sīra al-Nabawīya* 4: 167-169. See Watt, *Muḥammad at Medina* 67-68. See also *Sunnah.com*: *Ṣaḥīḥ Muslim,* Book of Jihad and Expeditions. Web (https://sunnah.com/muslim/32/106); *Ṣaḥīḥ Muslim,* Kītāb al-Jihād wa al-Sīyar 2: 857.

[133] Watt, *Muḥammad at Medina* 68.

[134] *Sahih Muslim,* Book of Jihad and Expedition: Removal of the idols from the vicinity of the Ka'ba (p. 1104); *Ṣaḥīḥ Muslim,* Kītāb al-Jihād wa al-Sīyar 2: 857. According to several *ḥadīths* and other Islamic sources, Muḥammad "entered Mecca [where there] were three hundred and sixty idols around the Ka'ba. He began to thrust them with the stick that was in his hand, saying, 'Truth has come and falsehood has vanished. Lo! Falsehood was destined to vanish....'" See *Sahih Bukhari,* Book of Oppressions and Book of Prophetic Commentary on the Qur'an (pp. 564, 1035, respectively). See also Ibn Hishām (Ibn Isḥāq), *The Life of Muḥammad* 552; Ibn Hishām (Ibn Isḥāq), *Al-Sīra al-Nabawīya* 4: 176.

[135] Ibn Hishām (Ibn Isḥāq), *The Life of Muḥammad* 553-554.

component to this plan: expulsion of polytheists "from the territory of Arabia...."[136]

With the conquest of Mecca, Muḥammad quickly turned his sights toward subduing Arab tribes in the surrounding region that were rivals and long-standing enemies of the Quraysh, particularly the Hawāzin and Thaqīf. Fortified with about two thousand Quraysh troops, Muḥammad and his army of 12,000 set out northward to battle the much larger Arab confederation, which Islamic sources claim numbered 20,000 warriors.[137] At this Battle of Ḥunayn, only four weeks after his conquest of Mecca, Muḥammad and his followers achieved another important military and political victory.[138]

During the Battle of Ḥunayn, the Thaqīf abandoned the battlefield to seek safety inside their own fortress walls at al-Ṭā'if. Eventually, the Muslims overcame the remaining and disorganized Arab tribes. Some of the defeated fighting men managed to escape but over six thousand men were taken prisoner or killed. Their women, children, animals, and goods (all of which accompanied the men during this campaign) "fell into the hands of the Muslims."[139]

Immediately after this spoils-rich victory, Muḥammad and his army marched directly to al-Ṭā'if to attack the Thaqīf and any other members of the Arab confederacy taking refuge there. The Muslims besieged the fortress for a couple of weeks (even using catapult-type machines according to some Islamic sources) but were unable to breach the walls and gain access.[140] Stalemated, Muḥammad ended the siege, divided the extensive booty among his followers, and returned to Medina in late spring to prepare for the next military campaign.[141]

Over the next several months, Muḥammad mobilized men and resources for an ambitious raid in late fall of AD 630. His target was the Byzantine army. Many of Muḥammad's followers were less than enthused in confronting the Byzantine army, a formidable opponent respected for its fighting ability, and with the timing of the raid, as the Muslims

---

[136] *Sahih Muslim,* Book of Bequests: He who has not anything with him to will away should not do it (p. 994); *Ṣaḥīḥ Muslim*, Kītāb al-Waṣīya 2: 771.

[137] Watt, *Muḥammad at Medina* 72.

[138] Ibid. 70-72. See Ibn Hishām (Ibn Isḥāq), *The Life of Muḥammad* 566-576; Ibn Hishām (Ibn Isḥāq), *Al-Sīra al-Nabawīya* 4: 229.

[139] Watt, *Muḥammad at Medina* 72.

[140] *History of al-Tabarī* 9: 22-25.

[141] Watt, *Muḥammad at Medina* 73-75; Ibn Hishām (Ibn Isḥāq), *The Life of Muḥammad* 587-597; Ibn Hishām (Ibn Isḥāq), *Al-Sīra al-Nabawīya* 4: 257-258.

were suffering from a drought and high temperatures.[142] Despite these challenges, Muḥammad eventually raised an army of 30,000 warriors and set off to wage war with the Byzantines at Tabūk.[143] Muḥammad and his men did not encounter any Byzantine army there but, according to Islamic sources, made "peace" treaties with various tribes; the people agreed to pay a head tax and the Muslims spared their lives.[144]

Even when Muḥammad was extremely ill and near death, he ordered his people to go on a military expedition to Syria (to wage war with the Byzantines) and selected his freed slave Usāma Ibn Zayd Ibn Ḥāritha[145] to command the army and "lead the cavalry into the territory of al-Balqā' and al-Dārūm in the land of Palestine."[146] When some of the people were "tardy in joining the expedition" and "criticized the leadership" of Usāma, Muḥammad sternly chided his followers and reiterated his support of Usāma as military commander.[147]

According to Islamic sources, Muḥammad continually organized raids and military expeditions after his first raid, when he and his followers were settled in Medina after the Hijra (AD 622), until his death (AD 632). He never sought regional peace, and the Qur'ān does not call for peace, except in the case of Muslim defeat: *"Then faint not, nor cry for peace while ye have the upper hand; for God is with you and will not cheat you of your works!"* (Q 47.35; Palmer trans.). This verse treats peace as a military tactic, a temporary cessation of hostilities, and not as the final goal.

In his ten years of active military planning and supervision, Muḥammad "took part personally in twenty-seven raids," which included fighting "in nine engagements [battles]: Badr; Uḥud; al-Khandaq, Qurayẓa; al-Muṣṭaliq; Khaybar; the occupation; Ḥunayn; and al-Tā'if."[148] He sent

---

[142] *History of al-Tabari* 9: 47-48; Ibn Hishām (Ibn Isḥāq), *The Life of Muḥammad* 602; Ibn Hishām (Ibn Isḥāq), *Al-Sīra al-Nabawīya* 4: 291-292.

[143] Watt, *Muḥammad at Medina* 343.

[144] Ibn Hishām (Ibn Isḥāq), *The Life of Muḥammad* 607-608; Ibn Hishām (Ibn Isḥāq), *Al-Sīra al-Nabawīya* 4: 335-336.

[145] Usāma Ibn Zayd Ibn Ḥāritha was the son of Muḥammad's freed slave Zayd Ibn Ḥāritha, whom he adopted as a son. During his childhood, Usāma was treated like a grandson by Muḥammad. Usāma's first military encounter as a Muslim fighter was the Battle of the Trench.

[146] Ibn Hishām (Ibn Isḥāq), *The Life of Muḥammad* 652, 678; Ibn Hishām (Ibn Isḥāq), *Al-Sīra al-Nabawīya* 4: 385, 386, 423.

[147] Ibn Hishām (Ibn Isḥāq), *The Life of Muḥammad* 679; *Sunnah.com: Sahih Bukhari,* Book on the Companions of the Prophet. Web (https://sunnah.com/bukhari/62/78).

[148] Ibn Hishām (Ibn Isḥāq), *The Life of Muḥammad* 659-660; Ibn Hishām (Ibn Isḥāq), *Al-Sīra al-Nabawīya* 4: 394.

out thirty-eight military missions and raiding parties.[149] However, some Muslim scholars state that the total is fifty-six brigades.[150] Given this possible range of eighty-three (27+56) to sixty-five (27+38) military operations over ten years, Muḥammad and his army conducted, on average, one military operation every forty-four to fifty-six days.

Can any person, who plots and launches a battle or raid on average every forty-plus days, be considered an emissary of peace deserving of the Nobel Peace Prize?

Muḥammad was a man of war par excellence. He easily found reasons to initiate wars and expended great effort to marshal sufficient money, supplies, equipment, animals, and troops to carry out his campaigns. Sometimes he would employ diplomacy before embarking on a military campaign, but these written communications to neighboring rulers were nothing more than "invitations" to embrace Islam (i.e., surrender to Muḥammad) coupled with the threat of warfare if the invitations were not accepted.[151] These letters only offered two options: (1) submit to Muḥammad and his new religion or (2) risk war with the Muslims and possibly suffer trade interruptions, raiding, and looting at best or lose their property, possessions, wives, and children, and their lives at worst.

Included in the content of these letters (as narrated in the Hadith literature) is the phrase "*aslim taslam*" ("accept Islam and you will be saved").[152] This phrase only promises a conditional peace; it grants peace in return for accepting Islam—or else there will be war.

Isn't this phrase part of the same "diplomacy" practiced by Islamic terrorist groups today? Didn't Al Qaeda threaten the West many times to meet its demands, or else it must face war? Islamic State has followed the same course. After it established its presence and control in an area,

---

[149] Ibn Hishām (Ibn Isḥāq), *The Life of Muḥammad* 660; Ibn Hishām (Ibn Isḥāq), *Al-Sīra al-Nabawīya* 4: 394.

[150] al-Nawawī, *Sharḥ* 12: 153. This source reports that several *ḥadīths* in *Sahih Muslim* differ in the total number of military expeditions led by Muḥammad and brigades led by others. Ibn Sa'd and others mention twenty-seven military expeditions and fifty-six brigades. See *Sahih Muslim*, Book of Jihad and Expedition: The number of wars waged by the holy prophet (pp. 1129-1131); *Ṣaḥīḥ Muslim*, Kītāb al-Jihād wa al-Sīyar 2: 880-881.

[151] Ibn Hishām (Ibn Isḥāq), *The Life of Muḥammad* 652-653; Ibn Hishām (Ibn Isḥāq), *Al-Sīra al-Nabawīya* 4: 386. Muḥammad "sent out some of his companions in different directions to the kings of the Arabs and the non-Arabs inviting them to Islam in the period between al-Hudaybiya [treaty] and his death."

[152] See *Sahih Bukhari*, Book of Revelation (p. 11); *Ṣaḥīḥ al-Bukhārī*, Kītāb Bad' al-Waḥī 1: 8-9. This *ḥadīth* is an account of a meeting between Abū Sufyān, a leader of the infidel Quraysh, and Heraclius, at a time when the Quraysh had a truce with the Muslims. Heraclius asked Abū Sufyān questions about Muḥammad and to translate a letter from the prophet. The first part of the letter includes this text: "Furthermore I invite you to Islam, and if you become a Muslim you will be safe.... "

it sent letters to the neighboring regions or countries, "inviting" them to embrace Islam. If they refused, Islamic State then declared war against them and their interests wherever they are.

Isn't this policy following in the footsteps of Muḥammad, the Prophet of Islam?

ELEVEN

For Islamic terrorists, jihad is an Islamic decree

At the time of Muḥammad's death, his army, now led by Usāma Ibn Zayd Ibn Ḥāritha, was preparing to invade the Roman Byzantine Empire in Syria. Muḥammad died before achieving this vision of conquering an entire non-Muslim empire and making it a part of an Islamic state. However, his Companions accomplished this mission after his death even as he could not during his lifetime. In fact, the early Islamic state became a great empire by AD 750, its borders stretching from China to France and encompassing the entire Arabian Peninsula, Egypt and Nubia (Sudan), North Africa, Iberia (Spain), Armenia, and Persia (Iran and Afghanistan). Did this expansion occur because of the conquered peoples' love for Islam—or the swords of the Muslims?

Who instructed and incited the Muslims to invade? Wasn't the instigator their own supreme role model, Muḥammad? And why did his Companions launch other wars and invasions after his death? The truth of the matter is that the early Islamic state continued to expand, thanks to its military forces and not to religious persuasion or philosophical debate. The much touted "Golden Age of Islam" (AD 750-1258) during the 'Abbāsid caliphate, when the Muslim world became the intellectual center for science, philosophy, medicine, and education and the remarkable Bayt al-Hikma ("House of Wisdom") in Baghdad promoted scholarly research and preserved and translated ancient classical writings, the Muslim empire was already widespread. Therefore, one cannot say that the persuasive power of the Qur'ān and Hadith literature was the primary tool for the relatively sudden and extensive "conversion" to Islam by the peoples conquered by the early Muslims. In fact, the Qur'ān and related writings were not available to the general public. Muḥammad himself had no compiled, written Qur'ān in his possession.[1] In reality, the main means of persuasion was the sword and the rule of *aslim taslam* ("accept Islam and you will be saved"). Peoples who did not accept Islam were not saved from the sword of the Islamic state.

How can entire nations be persuaded to embrace one religion, where the total populace suddenly chooses the same religion? Islamic books boast of the Muslim conquests of Egypt, Morocco and Andalusia (southern Spain), using the Arabic term *fath*,[2] which means "opening," a "clearing up of a doubtful situation," a "judgment," and "victory."[3] The use of this Arabic term in reference to these Muslim conquests "is derived from this conception of the conquest of Mecca as a judgement or clearing-up" between Muḥammad and his followers and the pagans.[4] The year in which Muḥammad and his troops conquered Mecca is called *'Ām al-Fatḥ* ("The Year of Conquest"): Allah opened the way for Muḥammad to conquer Mecca after it was shut in the face of Islam. As with the conquest of Mecca, the conquests of Egypt, Morocco, and Andalusia demonstrate to Muslims that these countries were closed in the face of Islam, but Allah granted the Muslims victory in "opening" them up to Islam through conquest and subjugation.

---

[1] **Note:** Today there are two separate versions of the Qur'ān, based on the Reading of Hafs and the Reading of Warsh. The 'Uthmānic codex (AD 650), the first major compilation of a written Qur'ān, lacked textual standardization, which generated multiple readings and interpretations and thus inconsistencies and ambiguity. The introduction of dotting and diacritical markings to the Arabic language, which help to clarify spellings, grammar, and other linguistic issues, was not applied to the Qur'ān until the tenth century AD.

[2] See Ibn Manẓūr, *Lisān al-'Arab* 3338. This highly respected, comprehensive dictionary defines *fatḥ* (singular) and *futūḥāt* (plural) as "to conquer."

[3] Watt, *Muhammad at Medina* 66.

[4] Ibid. 66-67.

The Qur'ān itself discusses conquest. One entire chapter (Q 48) is named Sura al-Fatḥ ("The Conquest") and includes the submission of the Jews of Khaybar and the conquest of Mecca.[5] Another chapter (Q 110), Sura al-Naṣr ("The Victory"), succinctly describes conquest in its three verses: *"When there comes God's help and victory, / And thou shalt see men enter into God's religion by troops, / Then celebrate the praises of thy Lord, and ask forgiveness of Him, verily He is relentant!"* (Palmer trans.). This Qur'ānic text associates the conquest of Islam first with military victory before the entrance into Islam by the conquered multitudes.

Forcibly subjecting people to accept Islam is clearly sanctioned according to the biography of Muḥammad, the Hadith literature, and the Qur'ān. One Qur'ānic verse (Q 3.110; Palmer trans.) declares that the early Muslim followers of Muḥammad *"were the best of nations brought forth unto man. Ye bid what is reasonable, and forbid what is wrong, believing in God. Had the people of the Book believed, it would have been better for them...."* A Companion of Muḥammad, Abū Hurayra (one of the most identified narrators of the *ḥadīths*), explains that this verse means that true Muslims "are the best of peoples ever raised up for mankind" and as the best of peoples they "bring them [non-Muslim war captives] with chains on their necks till they embrace Islam."[6]

Islamic State and its precursors, ISIL and ISIS, have applied similar principles. Though Islamic State presented three options in July 2014 to the Mosul Christians of Iraq—Islam, *jizya*,[7] or expulsion—its leadership only presented two options the following month to the Yazidis (considered idolaters by Islamic State): conversion to Islam or death.[8] Hundreds of Yazidis, victims and eyewitnesses of Islamic State brutality, spoke of executions of husbands and fathers, forced "marriages" of young women to its fighters, forced group conversions to Islam, enslavement of

---

[5] See Wherry, *Comprehensive Commentary of the Qur'an* 4: 58, and Nöldeke et al., *History of the Qur'ān* 174-175.

[6] *Sahih Bukhari*, Book of Prophetic Commentary on the Qur'an (p. 992); *Ṣaḥīḥ al-Bukhārī*, Kītāb al-Tafsīr 4: 1660.

[7] **Note:** The *jizya*, or head tax, is a Qur'ānic law according to Q 9.29 (Palmer trans.): *"Fight those who believe not in God and in the last day, and who forbid not what God and His Apostle have forbidden, and who do not practice the religion of truth from amongst those to whom the Book has been brought,* ***until they pay the tribute by their hands and be as little ones***" (emphasis added).

[8] **Note:** The two options presented to the Yazidis are based on the Sword verse, or Q 9.5 (Palmer trans.): *"But when the sacred months are passed away, kill the idolaters wherever ye may find them; and take them, and besiege them, and lie in wait for them in every place of observation; but if they repent, and are steadfast in prayer, and give alms, then let them go their way...."*

young girls, and sequestration of young boys for jihadist training.[9] In a video recorded interview, one witness relates how Islamic State fighters surrounded the house and then separated the Yazidi inhabitants. The Yazidi men were ordered to convert to Islam but they refused. The girls were ferried away in three cars. When the remaining women and children were allowed to leave, they saw that all the men had been killed.[10] In other reports, Yazidis who converted to Islam did so under compulsion.[11] This tactic, using the threat of death to force conversion to Islam, was the same tactic used centuries before by Muḥammad and his followers.

It is worth mentioning that many Yazidi girls and women, who endured multiple rapes and sometimes torture during their sexual enslavement by Islamic State fighters before their escape or liberation, then suffered community ostracism for their "defilement." They pleaded with their religious leaders to overturn Yazidi religious tradition and allow them to return to their faith, an action that emphasizes their intense desire to be a Yazidi and not a Muslim "convert." (Yazidi supreme spiritual leader, Khurto Hajji Ismail, agreed and welcomed them back. A new ceremonial ritual, similar to a baptism, to accept and heal these survivors has been created and instituted.)[12]

Ibn Taymīya, the controversial medieval Sunni Muslim theologian, scholar, and jurisconsult whose views and interpretations have greatly influenced contemporary Wahhabism, Salafism, and jihadism, makes this comment about the imposition of Islam: "The structure of the religion [Islam] is in the guiding Book [Qur'ān] and the conquering sword [jihad]."[13]

It was the sword and not the Qur'ān of Muḥammad that induced the Arab tribes and then their neighbors to "accept" Islam until the Muslims had established at last an empire. This empire formation happened rapidly. During Muḥammad's Meccan period, which lasted thirteen years, his followers numbered in the dozens. During the later Medinan

---

[9] "Iraq: Forced Marriage, Conversion for Yezidis." *HRW.org*. Human Rights Watch, 11 Oct. 2014. Web (https://www.hrw.org/news/2014/10/11/iraq-forced-marriage-conversion-yezidis).

[10] Ibid. **Note:** Eyewitness account occurs 0:00-0:22 minutes in the article's video.

[11] Ibid. **Note:** Eyewitness account and ISIS documentation occur approximately 2:00-2:45 minutes in the article's video.

[12] Graham-Harrison, Emma. "'I Was Sold Seven Times': The Yazidi Women Welcomed Back into the Faith." *TheGuardian.com*. The Guardian, 1 July 2017. Web (https://www.theguardian.com/global-development/2017/jul/01/i-was-sold-seven-times-yazidi-women-welcomed-back-into-the-faith). **Note:** Many of the captured and enslaved Yazidi girls and women chose suicide to escape rather than accept their plight. (See URL: http://www.cnn.com/2015/10/05/middleeast/yazidi-women-suicide-in-isis-captivity/index.html)

[13] Ibn Taymīya, *Majmū' Fatāwā* 10: 13.

period, when Muḥammad and his followers had emigrated to Medina from Mecca, he had accumulated more than 10,000 followers in ten years.[14]

Why wasn't Muḥammad able to persuade his fellow Quraysh tribesmen to embrace Islam during the first thirteen years of his call in Mecca, when he was reciting the Qur'ān to them? The Qur'ān reports that the Quraysh mocked Muḥammad at that time when he hadn't yet assembled an army: *"And when they saw thee they only took thee for a jest, 'Is this he whom God has sent as an apostle?'"* (Q 25.41; Palmer trans.). The Quraysh even mocked the Qur'ān itself, ridiculing Muḥammad for ordering his followers not to sit with the nonbelieving Quraysh when the Qur'ān was the subject of conversation: *"He hath revealed this to you in the Book, that when ye hear the signs of God disbelieved in and mocked at, then sit ye not down with them until they plunge into another discourse..."* (Q 4.140; Palmer trans.).

So what happened to change the Quraysh from mockers to believers of Islam? Was it a coincidence that they were suddenly persuaded in Muḥammad's final years, when his army contained thousands of warriors? One answer is given by Syrian poet, Abū Tammām (c. AD 804-845): "The sword is more sincere than books; / on its edge is the boundary between seriousness and frivolity."[15]

The sword of Muḥammad was eloquently more honest than his Qur'ān; with his sword, he won his fights.

Jihad a source of livelihood

Muḥammad never hid the fact that warfare nurtured his call. He even boasted of the spoils collected from his raids and battles. He once baldly stated, "My sustenance was provided for me from under the shadow of my spear. Those who oppose my command were humiliated and made inferior...."[16] In other words, the sword does not just bring people to Islam; it also provides a livelihood for any Islamic state and their princes.

[14] Ibn Hishām (Ibn Isḥāq), *The Life of Muḥammad* 545; Ibn Hishām (Ibn Isḥāq), *Al-Sīra al-Nabawīya* 4: 153. According to this source, Muḥammad went to Mecca with an army of "10,000 Muslims."

[15] *Sharḥ Diwan Abū Tammām* 1: 32.

[16] See the commentary on Q 2.104, *Tafsīr Ibn Kathīr* (p. 280). For the Arabic source, see *Tafsīr Ibn Kathīr* 2: 5-6. See also *Ṣaḥīḥ al-Bukhārī* 3: 1067.

This exact policy has been adopted by today's Islamic State. Warfare is not only a vehicle for defeating and subjugating the enemy, it is also a source of livelihood.

An article in the fourth issue of Islamic State's magazine *Dabiq* refers to the aforementioned *ḥadīth* with this comment:[17]

> This hadīth indicates that Allah did not send His messenger to endeavor to seek the dunyā [world], nor to gather the dunyā and its treasures, nor to strive to seek its causes, rather He sent him as a caller to His tawhīd [monotheism] with the sword.

In summary, Allah did not send Muḥammad to peacefully earn his livelihood through hard work but to fight and convert infidels with his sword.

Muḥammad began his prophethood at the age of forty. Prior to his call, Muḥammad was a caravan agent and then a trader after his marriage to his first wife Khadīja, a widow of means. Once he began to preach and share his revelations to others, he no longer engaged in trading enterprises. When he and his small band of followers fled from Mecca to Medina during the Hijra (AD 622), they had to rely on the charity of the Medinan Anṣār, or Helpers, who took in the Muslim emigrants and eventually converted to Islam. Within a year, Muḥammad and his band of followers were raiding passing caravans to support themselves and their families, a "career path" that led to larger-scale military expeditions and battles and a nearly continuous cycle of warfare for the remainder of his life.[18]

Muḥammad's Companions similarly became lifelong soldiers after embracing Islam and giving up the pursuit of more peaceable occupations, such as herding, farming, trading, and the like. For example, Abū Bakr, Muḥammad's best friend and father of his wife 'Ā'isha, gave

---

[17] al-Hanbalī, Ibn Rajab. "My Provision Was Placed for Me in the Shade of My Spear." *Dabiq*. Issue 4 (Sept.-Oct. 2014): 10. Web (http://www.ieproject.org/projects/dabiq4.pdf).

[18] See *Sahih Muslim*, Book of Jihad and Expedition: Fai' (property taken from the enemy without a formal war)(p. 1083); *Ṣaḥīḥ Muslim*, Kītāb al-Jihād wa al-Sīyar 2: 839. See *Ṣaḥīḥ al-Bukhārī*, Kītāb al-Jihād wa al-Sīyar 3: 1064. These *ḥadīths* report that when Muḥammad expelled the Banū al-Naḍīr, "the properties abandoned by Banū al-Naḍīr were the ones which Allah bestowed upon His Apostle for which no expedition was undertaken either with horses or camels. These properties were particularly meant for the Holy Prophet.... He would meet the annual expenditure of his family from the income thereof, and would spend what remained for purchasing horses and weapons as preparation for Jihad." See also Q 59.6 (Palmer trans.), which also addresses the awarding of spoils from expelled peoples to supplement Muḥammad's income: *"and as for the spoils that God gave to His Apostle from these (people) ye did not press forward after them with horse or riding camel; but God gives His Apostle authority over whom He pleases, for God is mighty over all!"*

up his business enterprises to be Muḥammad's advisor and an active participant in treaties and military campaigns for the rest of his life as a Muslim. Chosen by prominent Companions to be the successor, or first caliph, after Muḥammad's death in AD 632, Abū Bakr unified Arabia through a series of military campaigns during his brief two-year reign by successfully forcing apostate and other rebellious tribes to re-embrace or adopt Islam.[19]

Close Companion (and another father-in-law) of Muḥammad, 'Umar Ibn al-Khaṭṭāb, who is considered one of the early stalwarts of Islam, also had no profession after embracing Islam other than being a Muslim warrior and military strategist. Not only did he participate in all the major Muslim battles, sieges, and other military campaigns, he greatly accelerated the political and religious reach of the early Islamic empire through vigorous military campaigns and conquests as the second caliph. (Abū Bakr, on his death bed, appointed 'Umar in his final will and testament.) At 'Umar's death (AD 644), the Islamic empire included "conquered territories across Syria, Palestine, Mesopotamia and Persia" as well as parts of Egypt and North Africa.[20]

These two men represent most of the other Companions and followers of Muḥammad who all subsisted from the spoils they amassed from the raids, military expeditions, battles, and expulsions, and the institution of the *jizya* (head tax) they imposed on subject non-Muslim peoples. These early Muslims primarily derived their income from the taking, trading, or selling of the defeated enemy's possessions, property, and animals. Captives were sold or kept for free labor and other services. Thus, the early Muslims' financial means did not come from the sweat of their brow from daily labor on the farm or in the marketplace but from overcoming other peoples and seizing the fruits of their hard work—and using Allah and his religion to justify the appropriation.

Why then should people be surprised today when Islamic State has made its living in similar fashion: confiscating the money, possessions, and property from the citizens of every city or region under its control? As Muslims, we learn from an early age that Muḥammad is the supreme model, who was divinely presented to mankind, and his prophethood

[19] Crawford 89-90. See *Sunnah.com*: *Sahih Muslim*, Book of Faith. Web (https://sunnah.com/muslim/1/32); *Ṣaḥīḥ Muslim*, Kitāb al-Imān 2: 857.

[20] Crawford 202, 208.

was the best era for the Islamic nation. His actions set the standard, a guideline for the Islamic nation to follow upon his death.

Muḥammad's conduct in the cause of Allah—jihad—became the aspirational model for subsequent generations of dutiful Muslims. It proved to be the most effective way to spread Islam and extend its control over the world; indeed, it became the fastest way to get money and women. If jihad had not been so successful, Muḥammad would not have imposed it on his followers, even though he knew how much they hated it. In response to their qualms and distaste over the escalating bloodshed, he recited Q 2.216 (Hilâlî-Khân trans.): *"Jihad (holy fighting in Allah's Cause) is ordained for you (Muslims) though you dislike it, and it may be that you dislike a thing which is good for you and that you like a thing which is bad for you. Allah knows but you do not know."*

Besides reciting verses from the Qur'ān, Muḥammad used other means to persuade his followers to love the idea of jihad. He told them that martyrdom during fighting demonstrated the highest degree of faith and promised that martyrs would receive many more rewards in paradise. He himself repeatedly declared in front of them that he would love to die in a battle and then become resurrected in order to die again as a martyr:[21]

> [According to a narration of Abū Hurayra, the] Prophet said, "By Him in Whose Hands my life is! Were it not for some men amongst the believers who dislike to be left behind me and whom I cannot provide with means of conveyance, I would certainly never remain behind any *sariya*ʿ (army unit) setting out in Allah's Cause. By Him in Whose Hands my life is! I would love to be martyred in Allah's Cause and then get resurrected and then get martyred, and then get resurrected again and then get martyred and then get resurrected again and then get martyred."

If Muḥammad himself professed his eager willingness to die carrying a sword while fighting for the sake of spreading Islam, how then could his followers, who believed him to be Allah's chosen and blessed messenger, aspire to do less? When devout Muslims read these texts, they feel commanded to strongly love and follow their prophet, their perfect role model, in all his steps—especially if they really want to be true Muslims who apply the Sunna of the Prophet.

[21] *Sahih Bukhari,* Book of Fighting for the Cause of Allah (p. 646); *Ṣaḥīḥ al-Bukhārī,* Kītāb al-Jizya wa al-Muwādaʿa 3: 1030. Similar versions of this *ḥadīth* are found in several narrations of Abū Hurayra. See *Sahih Bukhari,* Book of Belief (p. 19); *Ṣaḥīḥ al-Bukhārī,* Kitāb al-Imān 1: 22.

Osama Bin Laden, the founder of Al Qaeda in the late 1980s who was killed by a US Navy Seals operation in May 2011, commented publicly on jihad, referring to this *ḥadīth*, in a 40-minute video intercepted and translated in 2007 before its publication on several Islamic Web sites:[22]

> So be alert, be wise and think. What is this status that the best of mankind wished for himself? He [Muḥammad] wished to be a martyr. He himself said, "By him in whose hands my life is! I would love to attack [raid] and be martyred, then attack [raid] again and be martyred, then attack [raid] again and be martyred...."
>
> So this whole broad life is summarized by him [Muḥammad] who was inspired by God, the Lord of the heavens and earth, praised and exalted is he. This glorious prophet who was inspired by God summarized this entire life by these words. He wished upon himself this status. Happy is the one who was chosen by God as a martyr.

The words of Muḥammad powerfully affect the mind of the Muslim person. The more his words and sayings are reverently repeated, the more likely the predisposed Muslim listener will surrender to them. Jihadists quote Muḥammad's words and sayings to remind and focus Muslims.[23]

However, the foundation of these words and beliefs has already been placed into our minds by the religious education we received and then reinforced during the successive stages of our lives—that is to say, the Islamic principle that one is to love and seek death and hate life.

Islam and the culture of death

Muḥammad guaranteed paradise for those who fought for the cause of Allah, for the sake of Islam. He urged his followers to take up jihad:[24]

> Allah has undertaken to look after the affairs of one who goes out to fight in His way believing in Him and affirming the truth of His Apostles. He is committed to his care that He will either admit him to Paradise or bring him back to his home from where he set out with a reward or (his share of) booty....

[22] "'New' Al-Qaeda Tape May Contain Old Clip of Bin Laden." *CNN.com*. Cable News Network, 15 July 2007. Web (http://www.cnn.com/2007/WORLD/meast/07/14/bin.laden.video). This video, produced by Al-Sahab Media, is available on jihadist Web sites and YouTube. Many of the commenters on these YouTube videos wish Paradise for Osama Bin Laden, considering him a hero who stood up to America. Some of the replies label him, "The Lion of Islam." (See URLs: http://www.jpost.com/Middle-East/Online-jihadis-eulogize-lion-of-Islam-bin-Laden; https://in.reuters.com/article/idINIndia-56832820110506)

[23] See Q 51.55 (Palmer trans.): "*And remind; for, verily, the reminder shall profit the believers.*"

[24] *Sahih Muslim*, Book on Government: The merit of Jihad and campaigning in the way of Allah (p. 1169); *Ṣaḥīḥ Muslim*, Kītāb al-Imāra 2: 907-908.

Muḥammad guaranteed his Muslim fighters that they would either enter paradise (if they were killed) or receive a portion of the spoils, e.g., money, female captives, etc. (if they survived the battle). No matter the "destination" (eternal or earthly home) after the battle, Muḥammad promised his Muslim fighters that their material, physical, and sexual needs would be fulfilled. He even described paradise with images that would greatly appeal to the imaginations of Arabs who lived in and traveled through arid deserts, where the intense heat can kill:

> [The inhabitants] *"will see there neither excessive heat of the sun, nor the excessive bitter cold, (as Paradise there is no sun and no moon)."*
> (Q 76.13; Hilâlî-Khân trans.)

> [Paradise has] *"gardens beneath which rivers flow...."*
> (See Q 2.25, Q 3.15, and Q 4.13; Palmer trans.)

> [Paradise has] *"thornless lote trees...tall trees with piles of fruit...outspread shade...."*
> (Q 56.28-30; Palmer trans.)

Anyone living in the Arabian Peninsula, which suffers greatly from the cruelties of nature, would very much like all these things—especially for the ordinary believer. However, the Muslim martyr will receive and enjoy much more in paradise than an idyllic setting and freedom from thirst and hunger, for he will encounter "things which have not been seen by an eye, or heard by an ear, or imagined by a human being."[25]

Muḥammad told his followers that paradise is under the shadows of the swords of the *mujāhidīn*, as they will find their swords [paradise] the moment they fall dead during the fight: "...the gates of Paradise are under the shadows of the swords."[26] A Muslim martyr is also forgiven all his sins except his debts.[27]

---

[25] **Note:** *Sahih Bukhari* includes *ḥadīths* where Muḥammad declares that Allah has prepared for his pious worshippers "such things as no eye has ever seen, no ear has ever heard of, and nobody has ever thought of." (See *Sahih Bukhari*, Book of the Beginning of Creation, p. 754, and Book of Prophetic Commentary on the Qur'an, p. 1059; *Ṣaḥīḥ al-Bukhārī*, Kītāb Bad' al-Khalq 3: 1185.) An earlier version of this statement can be found in the Bible: "However, as it is written: 'What no eye has seen, what no ear has heard, and what no human mind has conceived'—the things God has prepared for those who love him—" (*NIV*, 1 Cor. 2.9; see Isa. 64.4. The Jewish prophet Isaiah began his ministry in 740 BC, which means his writings predate *Sahih Bukhari* sixteen centuries or even more.)

[26] *Sahih Muslim*, Book on Government: In proof of the martyr's attaining paradise (p. 1182); *Ṣaḥīḥ Muslim*, Kītāb al-Imāra 2: 918.

[27] *Sahih Muslim*, Book on Government: One who is killed in the way of Allah will have all his sins blotted out except debt (p. 1174); *Ṣaḥīḥ Muslim,* Kītāb al-Imāra 2: 911.

Muḥammad even promised the Muslim martyr who dies in the cause of Allah special privileges:[28]

> The martyr has six privileges with God: his sins are pardoned when the first drop of blood falls; he is shown his seat in paradise; he is safe from the punishment of the grave and secure from the great terror (i.e. hell); a crown of dignity is placed on his head one jewel of which is worth more than the world and all that is therein; and he is married to seventy-two dark-eyed virgins; and he makes successful intercession for seventy of his relatives.

I repeatedly heard these *ḥadīths* in sermons, informal conversations, and during religious occasions. They were discussed among my father and his friends who are religion specialists. These are *ḥadīths* commonly known by many ordinary Muslims, and specialists know them by heart.

If these *ḥadīths* were planted in our minds since our childhood, and we believe that they are the divine truth about the path to paradise for Muslims, then is it any wonder that many young Muslims who wish to take their religion seriously end up joining jihadist groups? In the view of these earnest young men, these groups are the only groups able to provide the legitimate environment for jihad according to all the Islamic religious texts. The promises given in these religious texts are the essential incentives for the religious person who believes that there is a hereafter life (the manifestation of these promises) and will give up everything—family, livelihood, and even his or her life—in order to be worthy of its attainment.

We Muslims learn from Islam to love and prefer death over life. Muḥammad taught us how to die—but never how to live—for Allah's sake. Thus, we frequently hear a phrase included by leaders of jihadist groups in their statements: "We are a people who desire death as ardently as you desire life." This phrase summarizes the tragedy that we live every day in our Islamic world: We glorify death over everything and consider dying a heroic act. In contrast, we despise life and all its comforts and advantages. Hence, our youth never learn how to love or how to love life itself; they only learn that real life begins after death, while the earthly life before death is trivial and holds little value.

This Islamic view about death and life was established and reinforced during the early history of Islam. The statement, "We are a people who

[28] *Musnad Aḥmad* 5: 117; *Sunan al-Tirmidhī* 5: 246. (See Kītāb Faḍā'il al-Jihād, ch. "Fī Thawāb al-Shahīd.")

desire death as ardently as you desire life," was spoken by one of the greatest military leaders of early Islam, Khālid Ibn al-Walīd (AD 585-642). A Quraysh clansman who initially opposed Muḥammad, he eventually converted to Islam and participated in Muḥammad's later raids and battles. He earned the nickname "Sayf Allāh" and "Sayf Allāh al-Maslūl," or "The Drawn Sword of Allah," after his valiant exploits during the Battle of Mu'ta against the Roman Byzantine Empire (AD 629). As military commander after Muḥammad's death, he was instrumental in consolidating the entire Arabian Peninsula under one caliphate. Abū Bakr, the first caliph, sent Khālid with a large Muslim army to the Persian Empire to conquer its richest province (modern day Iraq). Khālid wrote and sent the following letter to the enemy leaders before he prepared for battle:[29]

> ...*Aslim Taslam* [Accept Islam and you will be safe] or agree that you and your people will be under our protection as *dhimmis* [Christians and Jews allowed to practice their religion but under unjust and humiliating conditions] and agree to pay the [yearly] *jizya* [tribute]. Otherwise, you will have only yourself to blame for the consequences, for I bring to you men who desire death as ardently as you desire life.

Khālid and his Muslim forces quickly won several consecutive victories and ultimately gained control of the lower Mesopotamia region. Under his military leadership, he would eventually expand the Islamic caliphate to include the conquest of the Sassanid-Persian and Roman Syrian empires as well as subdue rebel Arab tribes challenging the caliphate.

In 2014, a member of Islamic State quoted from Khālid's menacing letter (from over fourteen centuries ago) in a video, which was posted online: "...I swear we are a people who love death for the sake of God just as you love to live. I swear we are a people who love drinking blood. We came to slaughter you.... We love dying for God as much as you love life."[30] The 26-year-old speaker, an Arab-Israeli man named Rabīʿ Shiḥāda (also known as "the Palestinian slayer") was threatening to slaughter the

---

[29] Ibn Kathīr, *Al-Bidāya* 9: 513. See *History of al-Ṭabarī* 11: 7.

[30] "'We Love Drinking Blood,' Says ISIS 'Vampire.'" *Alarabiya.net.* Al Arabiya Network (English) 17 Sept. 2014. Web (https://english.alarabiya.net/en/News/middle-east/2014/09/17/-We-love-drinking-blood-says-ISIS-vampire-.html); Moore, Jack. "ISIS: Arab-Israeli 'Vampire' Says Terror Group 'Loves Drinking Blood.'" *IBTimes.co.uk.* International Business Times, 17 Sept. 2014. Web (http://www.ibtimes.co.uk/isis-arab-israeli-vampire-says-terror-group-loves-drinking-blood-1465936). **Note:** The original video footage on YouTube has been posted and removed many times. (See first speaker on YouTube video: https://www.youtube.com/watch?v=0dQkvps2Kzk). Readers can also visit the Web site of newspaper *Al-Yawm al-Sābiʿ* and search for video footage titled "Video: Member of ISIS Confesses "We Are a People Who Love to Drink Blood."

Muslim Alawite sect in Syria.[31] Before joining ISIS, he was a husband and father studying mechanical engineering.[32] According to the newspaper *Al-Yawm al-Sābi*, he was not regarded as an extremist among those close to him back in his Arab hometown of Sepphoris near Nazareth.[33]

This "Palestinian slayer" is not the only one who has announced that he belongs to a people, "the nation of Islam," that loves death as much as its enemies love life. Ismail Haniya,[34] senior official and recently elected political bureau chief of Ḥamās,[35] declared in one of his speeches, "We are a people who love death as our enemies love life."[36]

The official Web site of the Ministry of Endowments and Islamic Affairs in Qatar posted the following question by a reader: "Who said 'I brought you a people who love death as you love life'?" The fatwa answers that Khālid Ibn al-Walīd made this statement and includes the historical context when he issued these words. The fatwa concludes with this comment: "May Allah be pleased with Khālid, and may Allah grant the *umma* [Islamic nation] more people like him in a time where this *umma* has been humiliated."[37]

If this statement had not been spoken by one of Islam's renowned early Muslims and a Companion of Muḥammad, Khālid Ibn al-Walīd,

---

[31] "'We Love Drinking Blood,' Says ISIS 'Vampire.'" *Alarabiya.net.* Al Arabiya Network (English) 17 Sept. 2014. Web (https://english.alarabiya.net/en/News/middle-east/2014/09/17/-We-love-drinking-blood-says-ISIS-vampire-.html); Moore, Jack. "ISIS: Arab-Israeli 'Vampire' Says Terror Group 'Loves Drinking Blood.'" *IBTimes.co.uk.* International Business Times, 17 Sept. 2014. Web (http://www.ibtimes.co.uk/isis-arab-israeli-vampire-says-terror-group-loves-drinking-blood-1465936). **Note:** The original video footage on YouTube has been posted and removed many times. (See first speaker on YouTube video: https://www.youtube.com/watch?v=0dQkvps2Kzk). Readers can also visit the Web site of newspaper *Al-Yawm al-Sābi'* and search for video footage titled "Video: Member of ISIS Confesses "We Are a People Who Love to Drink Blood."

[32] Ibid.

[33] Ibid.

[34] **Note:** Ismail Haniya is a senior political leader and formerly the prime minister of the Palestinian National Authority. Though he was dismissed from this office by President Mahmood Abbas in June 2007, Haniya continued to exercise his authority. He was elected Hamās political chief in May 2017 and is predicted to become head leader of Hamās in the near future. On January 31, 2018, the US designated him as a "global terrorist."

[35] **Note:** Hamās is a Palestinian Sunni Islamic fundamentalist organization and has acted as the de facto government authority of the Gaza Strip after it took over this region in 2007. Hamās is considered a terrorist organization by the US, Israel, the European Union, and other countries and international organizations. However, most Muslim countries consider Hamās a legitimate jihadist Islamic organization.

[36] "The Positions and Statements of Hamas's New Political Bureau Head Isma'il Haniya: 'We Are Truly a People Who Love Death as much as Our Enemies Love Life.'; Bin Laden Was a 'Muslim Mujahid... May Allah Cover Him with His Mercy, next to the Prophets, the Righteous, and the Martyrs.'" *MEMRI.org.* Middle East Media Research Institute (MEMRI), 9 May 2017. Special Dispatch No. 6914. Web (https://www.memri.org/reports/compilation-of-isma'il-haniya-statements).

[37] See Fatwa no. 97623: "Say: I Brought You People Who Love Death as You Love Life." *Islamweb.net.* Ministry of Endowments and Islamic Affairs of Qatar. 10 July 2007. Web (http://preview.tinyurl.com/yc9nwg5e).

and recorded in the early Islamic historical sources, then it wouldn't be so frequently repeated by many Muslims. Islamic fighters in Iraq and Syria today cite the words of Khālid Ibn al-Walīd, because in their view he is the Muslim example to emulate in their fight against infidels and their battles against the enemies of Islam. (The tomb of Khālid Ibn al-Walīd still exists today in a mosque bearing his name in the heavily shelled ruins of Homs, once an important industrial center in Syria before the war.)

Islamic State fighters are not the only jihadists who have adopted this policy of preferring and seeking death over life. All Islamic organizations have adopted this approach, including the Muslim Brotherhood, which is considered by the West as less radical when compared to Islamic State. But is it? The flag of the Muslim Brotherhood displays **two** crossed swords beneath the Qur'ān on a green field. Between the hilts of the two swords are the words "And prepare," which is a phrase taken from Q 8.60 (Rodwell trans.): *"Make ready...*[prepare] *against them what force ye can, and strong squadrons whereby ye may strike terror into the enemy of God and your enemy, and into others...whom ye know not, but...God knoweth...."* According to Ibn Kathīr's commentary, this part of the verse means that "Allah commands Muslims to prepare for war against disbelievers, as much as possible, according to affordability and availability."[38]

If the phrase "And prepare" and its reference to Q 8.60 are not sufficiently obvious, the motto of the Muslim Brotherhood succinctly declares its specific purpose and goal: "Allah is our objective. The Prophet is our leader. The Qur'ān is our law. Jihad is our way. Dying in the way of Allah is our highest hope."[39] Could there be any clearer statements to illustrate the relationship between Islam and the culture of death?

The West and the culture of life

In the summer of 2014, I visited New York City with my small family. We decided to visit the National September 11 Memorial and Museum, the place where the twin towers of the World Trade Center were destroyed on September 11, 2001. Although this horrific event happened about thirteen years earlier, the memory of it has never left my mind. I remembered how I followed the news from Morocco with my American friend when I was at his home. (See Chapter 1, page 32.) And now, here

[38] See the commentary on Q 8.60, *Tafsīr Ibn Kathīr* 7: 109.

[39] Vidino, Lorenzo. "The Muslim Brotherhood's Conquest of Europe," *Middle East Quarterly* 12.1 (2005): 25. Print and Web (http://www.meforum.org/687/the-muslim-brotherhoods-conquest-of-europe).

I was, standing in the same place that I saw being destroyed that long ago fall day. The televised scenes were terrible, and the photographs in the newspapers and on the Internet sites were heartrending images of blood, rubble, and signs of death everywhere. I could not imagine then that America would ever be able to rise from such a devastating strike. It was very tough emotionally on the American people, let alone their economy and important symbols of their progress and civilization.

I observed how the two enormous, recessed reflecting pools, each fringed on all four straight sides with continuously flowing waterfalls, were built within the footprints of the North and South Towers. The thunderous sound of the falling water absorbs the noises of the city. From the surrounding plaza, visitors get a panoramic view of the two pools and waterfalls, which offer a serene vision of hope and reflection on the continuation of life.

This Memorial Plaza includes an eight-acre park with nearly 400 white oak trees, a beautiful garden where people may eat, sit, or stroll. Within this grove is a Callery pear tree, now known as "The Survivor Tree." It was discovered three weeks after the attack at Ground Zero, severely damaged and burned. The tree was rescued, rehabilitated and replanted at the memorial in 2010, displaying new smooth branches protruding from its gnarled stumps. Protected now by only a simple fence, it stands "as a living reminder of resilience, survival, and rebirth."[40] Its story is a symbol of life overcoming death.

The names of 2983 victims—2977 killed in the September 11 attacks and six killed in the 1993 World Trade Center bombing—are inscribed on seventy-six bronze plates affixed to the wall parapets surrounding the pools and their waterfalls. An algorithm was used to arrange the victims' names on the plaques according to their relationships ("meaningful adjacencies") to one another, i.e., proximity at the time of the attacks, company or organization affiliations, etc. According to Edith Lutnick, executive director of the Cantor Fitzgerald Relief Fund, the victims' names "are surrounded by the names of those they sat with, those they worked with, those they lived with and, very possibly, those they died

[40] "The Survivor Tree." *911memorial.org*. National September 11 Memorial and Museum, 2017. Web (https://www.911memorial.org/survivor-tree).

with."[41] This arrangement honors individual as well as collective loss for the surviving families and the nation.

As I stood there at this memorial with my wife and children and gazed upon the pools, the waterfalls, the plaques, and the plaza park grounds, I contemplated the message that this memorial design is delivering to the entire world. While it acknowledges the tremendous grief and loss caused by these attacks and commemorates the lives of those who perished, this memorial unmistakably is life-affirming. From the cascading waterfalls of life-giving water to the graceful grove of deciduous trees that undergo nature's cycle of rebirth every year (not to mention the Survivor Tree), this memorial design proclaims the clear message that America and its people wish to bring life out of death.

This memorial is no humiliating graveyard but a place of beauty and renewal, the victims' names immortalized for all time. Its design is a great uplifting message about life and hope after so many innocent deaths. It rebukes the negative message of Khālid Ibn al-Walīd and instead proclaims to terrorists, "We are a people who desire life more than you desire death!"

Islam's denigration of the worldly life

Why does the West love life, while our Muslim fathers and our religion teach us to love death? Why do they teach us to despise life and to glorify death? My own father always reminded us children of death and the insignificance of the worldly life, often in connection with this *ḥadīth*: "If the world to Allah was equal to a mosquito's wing, then He would not allow the disbeliever to have a sip of water from it."[42] This *ḥadīth* means that the world in Allah's sight is contemptible; for this reason, Allah lets infidels enjoy the good things of the world, because if the world was valuable he would have prevented infidels from enjoying it. By extension, the fact that infidels do enjoy the world is the greatest evidence for the insignificance of the world in Allah's sight.

---

[41] Dunlap, David. "Constructing a Story, with 2982 Names." *NYTimes.com*. New York Times, 4 May 2011. Web (http://www.nytimes.com/2011/05/05/nyregion/on-911-memorial-constructing-a-story-name-by-name.html).

[42] *Sunnah.com*: *Jami' at-Tirmidhī*, Chapters on Zuhd. Web (https://sunnah.com/tirmidhi/36/17).

The Qur'ān confirms this view in Q 9.55 (Palmer trans.): *"Let not their wealth please you nor their children, God only wishes to torment them therewith in the life of this world, and that their souls may pass away while still they misbelieve."* (Compare with Q 3.178 and Q 2.212.) No doubt, Muḥammad's earliest followers, who were mostly poor and low in status (in fact, some were slaves), were comforted by the Qur'ān's condemnation of the infidels' worldly goods, asserting that Allah will torment the affluent infidels for the accumulation of their earthly treasures and deny their souls at death. In this particular verse, the Qur'ān warns believers not to admire the riches and families of the affluent infidels. Instead they should feel reassured and even vindicated, knowing that Allah allows the disbelievers to attain such wealth so that they may experience hardship in getting their wealth and suffer the consequences for having it; they will be punished both in this world and the hereafter for their disbelief.

I remember how we used to see many foreign tourists in the markets of our town, taking pictures and riding on luxurious buses, wearing beautifully elegant clothes and carrying impressive cameras. I particularly remember asking my father about the French tourists: Why did Allah give the infidels so many good things, much more than us Muslims? Why doesn't Allah give us similar things as we are better than they are? My father would simply answer that it is because Allah has given them the world—here—in order to torment them—there—in the hereafter. We Muslims are promised the hereafter, and for this reason we are deprived of the world's offerings.

This thinking is based on certain verses in the Qur'ān and the Hadith literature. These religious texts promise eternal life in the hereafter, while they castigate people who focus on their earthly life, trying to improve it so that they can live the longest life possible with the least amount of pain. To refute this worldly but meaningful and purpose-driven living, we Muslims are compelled to seek arguments to justify our backwardness and our regression behind the rest of the developed world. Religion, of course, is the best apologetic defense.

Many *ḥadīths* within this context forbid Muslims from being distracted by the life of the world, urging them instead to engage in jihad, as Muḥammad told his followers: "When you enter into *'Ēnah* transactions,[43] take hold of the tails of cattle, and are content with farming, and you forsake *Jihād*, Allah will cause humiliation to prevail over you and will not withdraw it until you return to your religion."[44] This *ḥadīth* means Muslims who work as traders, businessmen, ranchers, or farmers will suffer humiliation throughout their lives, a humiliation that will never be lifted until they return to their religion. In this case, returning to religion means embracing jihad.

This *ḥadīth* has been cited in Islamic State's magazine *Dabiq* to incite its Muslim readers to jihad. After citing and discussing this *ḥadīth*, the writer concludes his article with this comment: "So the best condition for the believer is that his time is spent in obedience of Allah, jihād fī sabī-lillāh [jihad in the cause of Allah], and da'wah [the call] for His obedience."[45]

This religious priority of jihad over more domestic forms of employment has affected the behavior of many young Muslim men living in Western countries who subscribe to this view. They spend their lives dependent on their hosting Western countries, collecting social benefits, while working to spread the call of Islam. They consider the money of the West lawful for them to take, because Westerners are infidels. Their unemployment, supported by state aid, enables them to be like the Messenger of Allah—unencumbered and fully free for preaching and jihad.

A representative example is Riḍā Ṣiyām, a man of Egyptian origin and German nationality, who joined Islamic State and became an administrator in its Office of Education in Mosul, when it was under ISIS control, until his death in 2014. (He was killed during a military attack.) Previously, he had lived in Germany for more than fifteen years. During all that time, he received about three thousand euros a month from government benefits while spending his time promoting Islam and the call to carry the banner of jihad against infidel countries, like Germany.[46] Are not his actions the highest level of exploitation? But where has it come from and what is the reason for it? Doesn't religious thought play a role?

---

[43] **Note:** An *'ēnah* transaction "means to sell something for a price to be paid at a later date, then to buy it back for a lower price (to be paid immediately); this is a trick used to circumvent the prohibition on lending with interest." See *Sunan Abū Dawūd*, Book of *al-Ijārah* (The Book of Employment) 4: 123.

[44] *Sunan Abū Dawūd*, Book of *al-Ijārah* (The Book of Employment) 4: 123.

[45] al-Hanbalī, Ibn Rajab. "My Provision Was Placed for Me in the Shade of My Spear." *Dabiq*. Issue 4 (Sept.-Oct. 2014): 12. Web (http://www.ieproject.org/projects/dabiq4.pdf).

[46] "The Truth about the Egyptian Dhul-Qarnayn, the Second Man in ISIS." *Albawabhnews.com*. Al-Bawabh News, 14 Dec. 2014. Web (http://www.albawabhnews.com/965885).

Jihad and fighting in the cause of Allah is mentioned in the Qur'ān more than thirty times. One representative example is Q 3.157 (Arberry trans.): *"If you are slain or die in God's way, forgiveness and mercy from God are a better thing than that you amass* [in wealth]*."* The Qur'ān has never urged believers to live for the cause of Allah—not in a single verse! Instead it consistently and scornfully characterizes the worldly life as despised and inconsequential, as exemplified in Q 29.64 (Palmer trans.): *"This life of the world is nothing but a sport and a play; but, verily, the abode of the next world, that is life,—if they did but know!"* Another verse (Q 6.32; Palmer trans.) reinforces this view that the earthly life is but a momentary amusement; the real meaning to life is through death: *"The life of this world is nothing but a game and a sport, and surely the next abode were better for those who fear. What! do they not understand?"*

Another Qur'ānic verse (Q 57.20; Palmer trans.) likens the affluent life of this world to vegetation that springs up after rain showers and delights the vain and boastful disbelievers. But this vegetation, like the riches of the earth, will wither and turn yellow, becoming useless and of no value:

> *Know that the life of this world is but a sport, and a play, and an adornment, and something to boast of amongst yourselves; and the multiplying of children is like a rain-growth, its vegetation pleases the misbelievers; then they wither away, and thou mayest see them become yellow; then they become but grit. But in the hereafter is a severe woe, and forgiveness from God and His goodwill; but the life of this world is but a chattel of guile.*

The verse concludes that the life of this world is nothing more than the deceitfulness of material things.

Still more verses condemn the contemptibility and arrogance of the present world, maintaining Allah has control over everything. (See Q 10.24 and Q 18.45.)

This Islamic view contends that death and the hereafter are not only superior but are to be desired to life in the present world. This view is a kind of trade, or swap, or a deal. A person sells his worldly life for a price and sacrifices his worldly life in exchange for his "life," i.e., death in the hereafter. Of course, according to the Qur'ān, this "deal" is profitable, because the worldly life is of trivial worth compared to death in hereafter, or the Second Life.

One of the clearest Qur'ānic verses that encourages this kind of life trade or swap is Q 9.111 (Sher 'Alī trans.):

> *Surely, Allāh has purchased of the believers their persons and their property in return for the Garden they shall have; they fight in the cause of Allāh, and they slay and are slain—a promise that He has made incumbent on Himself in the Torah, and the Gospel, and the Qur'ān. And who is more faithful to his promise than Allāh? Rejoice, then, in your bargain which you have made with Him; and that it is which is the supreme triumph.*

This verse maintains that Allah has bought the believers from themselves, but they must sacrifice themselves for his sake. In return, he has promised three times (or in three places, i.e., through the Jewish Torah, the Christian New Testament and the Muslim Qur'ān) to give them paradise. Therefore, they must be overjoyed because they are the ones who will benefit from this deal.

If Allah gave his believers their lives, why is he then asking them to kill themselves for him?

Other verses in the Qur'ān similarly extol the virtue of trading the worldly life for death and "life" in the hereafter through jihad, such as Q 4.74 (Hilâlî-Khân trans.): *"Let those (believers) who sell the life of this world for the Hereafter fight in the Cause of Allah, and whoso fights in the Cause of Allah, and is killed or gets victory, We shall bestow on him a great reward."*

Some of the early Muslims found the "invitation" of jihad oppressive and resisted it because they preferred their worldly life over promises with no tangible evidence of a bountiful, lavish life in the hereafter. The Qur'ān (Q 9.38; Palmer trans.) reproaches this reluctance: *"O ye who believe! what ailed you when ye were told to march forth in God's way, that ye sank down heavily upon the earth? were ye content with the life of this world instead of the next? but the provision of this world's life is but a little to the next."* This verse challenges the fainthearted not to succumb to the temptations of the worldly life, reminding them of its little pleasures compared to the greater and permanent pleasures in the afterlife.

These types of verses are essential in understanding the mentality of the *mujāhidīn*, because religion is the foundation in the mind-set of believers who are involved in jihad operations.

To most Westerners, it seems illogical for a Muslim Australian doctor like Tareq Kamleh[47] to sacrifice his career, family, and life in a Western developed country and choose to travel to Syria for a harsh life fighting in league with ISIS—exchanging a peaceful, stable, and productive life for an uncertain, violent, and likely deadly one with the jihadists. However, according to the Qur'ān, his decision is not only logical but also profitable, given the lavish rewards he will receive in paradise for his martyrdom.

Since leaving Australia and posting propaganda videos for ISIS, Kamleh is now wanted by Australian authorities on several issues and a warrant for his immediate arrest (should he return) has been issued.[48] Undeterred, Kamleh declared in an open letter to the Australian Health Practitioner Regulation Agency (AHPRA) posted on his Facebook page that he had "no concern" if his medical registration or citizenship is revoked.[49] Two years later, he posted a video addressed to US President Donald Trump, stating that Islamic State is "eagerly awaiting" US troops and their ultimately futile attempt to destroy Islamic State. In his remarks to the US President, Tareq asserts, "We love death more than you love life," and adds, "Is it that you love this life more than you love the life after? But the enjoyment of this life is only but little."[50]

This logic may never be understood by Westerners, but it is rational logic for those who were raised in Muslim families and influenced by the teachings of Islam, especially its doctrine about exchanging the worldly life with the life after death. According to Islam, the personal decision to seek death and places of war for the sake of Allah is one of the best choices of life. Muḥammad esteemed the jihadist in this *ḥadīth*:[51]

---

[47] Mills, Tammy, Patrick Hatch, and Rachel Olding. "Australian Islamic Doctor Tareq Kamleh's Sudden Change after Mystery Trip in 2013." *SMH.com*. Sydney Morning Herald, 28 Apr. 2015. Web (http://www.smh.com.au/national/australian-islamic-state-doctor-tareq-kamlehs-sudden-change-after-mystery-trip-in-2013-20150427-1mui3m.html). **Note:** Tareq Kamleh was born to a Palestinian Muslim father (who had immigrated to Australia) and a German Catholic mother who converted to Islam after marriage. His father lived a "largely secular life after moving to Australia," while his mother's "strict religious views influenced the rest of the family."

[48] Davidson, Helen. "ISIS Doctor Tareq Kamleh: 'I Don't Care about Losing Australian Citizenship." *TheGuardian.com*. The Guardian, 21 June 2015. Web (https://www.theguardian.com/australia-news/2015/jun/21/isis-doctor-tareq-kamleh-i-dont-care-about-losing-australian-citizenship#img-1).

[49] Ibid.

[50] Roy, Ananya. "Who Is Australia's Dr. Jihad? Tareq Kamleh Calls for More Attacks on the West in New ISIS Video." *IBTimes.co.uk*. International Business News, 4 July 2017. Web (http://www.ibtimes.co.uk/who-australias-dr-jihad-tareq-kamleh-calls-more-attacks-west-new-isis-video-1628809).

[51] *Sahih Muslim*, Book of Government: Merit of Jihad and of keeping vigilance (over the enemy)(p. 1176); *Ṣaḥīḥ Muslim*, Kītāb al-Imāra 2: 913.

> Of the men he lives the best life who holds the reins of his horse (ever ready to march) in the way of Allah, flies on its back whenever he hears a fearful shriek, or a call for help [the sound of war], flies to it seeking death at places where it can be expected....

Thus, those Muslims who seek to fight for the cause of Allah in places of death—like the *mujāhidīn* from all parts of the world who have joined Islamic State to fight in Iraq, Syria, and other places of destruction and death in the Middle East—have made the best decision in their earthly life.

Imagine yourself as a committed, devout Muslim who believes Muḥammad spoke these words. What then are your options? You would either obey and remain a devout Muslim or ignore these words and become a disobedient Muslim—and perhaps subject to accusations of apostasy.

Hereafter temptations as jihad bait

We Muslims are brought up in Islam by the idiomatic carrot and stick, or, according to Islamic jurists, the policy of "enticement and intimidation." In Islam, the promise of paradisiacal pleasure and enjoyment is the "enticement" while the threat of hellfire torment is the "intimidation."

This policy has the same logic as Muḥammad's rationale for jihad. To "entice" people to desire death by fighting for the sake of Allah, Muḥammad made death seem less terrifying—perhaps, even exciting—when coupled with such sensual pleasures in paradise for the Muslim martyr. At the same time, Muḥammad intimidated his followers by warning them not to delay their response to the call of jihad, because passivism would mean disobedience and eventually incur the wrath and punishment of Allah. The following Qur'ānic verse (Q 48.16; Palmer trans.) clearly addresses those believers who delay their jihad:

> *Say* [O Muḥammad] *to those desert Arabs who were left behind, 'Ye shall be called out against a people endowed with vehement valour, and shall fight them or they shall become Muslims. And if ye obey, God will give you a good hire; but if ye turn your backs, as ye turned your backs before, He will torment you with grievous woe!'*

Further enticements aimed at Muslim men to answer the call of jihad can be found in other verses and the Hadith literature that specifically mention beautiful virgins (houris) awaiting all martyrs. These beautiful women of paradise embody all the physical attributes most desired by Arab men, such as big bright eyes, where the white sclera sharply contrasts with the black iris and pupil (*"And bright and large-eyed maids / like hidden pearls"*), and chastity (*"Bright and large-eyed maids kept in their tents.... Whom no man nor ginn has deflowered before them"*). (See Q 56.22-23 and Q 55.72, 74, respectively; Palmer trans.) Another verse (Q 56.37) describes these heavenly virgins as *"darlings of equal age (with their spouses),"* which means that they are all "very loving to their men, and of the same young age."[52] Muslim commentators state that the description of the heavenly virgins' breasts is another Qur'ānic measurement of beauty: *"Verily, for the pious is a blissful place,—gardens and vineyards, / and girls with swelling breasts of the same age as themselves, / and a brimming cup"* (Q 78.31-34; Palmer trans.).

An important point to remember is that the wide-eyed virgins are the reward for every Muslim man who fears Allah and not just for the Muslim martyr. However, the Allah-fearing "ordinary" Muslim will be awarded only two virgins in paradise: "Everyone of them [Muslim men in paradise] shall have two wives, each of whom will be so beautiful, pure and transparent that the marrow of the bones of their legs will be seen through the flesh."[53] (Notice the detail about the extreme whiteness of these women, whiteness to the point of near transparency, where the marrow beneath their bones and flesh can be seen within their legs!) The jihadist martyr will be awarded many, many more virgins: seventy-two virgins for every martyr.[54] Each one of these virgins is more important and valuable than the world, according to Muḥammad: "And if a houri [paradise virgin] from Paradise appeared to the people of the earth, she would fill the space between Heaven and the Earth with light and pleasant scent and her head cover is better than the world and whatever is in it."[55]

Intellectuals do not think that the concept of heavenly virgins to motivate the *mujāhidīn* is of great importance. Yet if it is of no importance, how do they explain the large number of respected Islamic books that have allocated special chapters to describe those heavenly virgins? For example, *Ṣaḥīḥ al-Bukhārī*, one of the most trusted and respected collections of *ḥadīths*, contains an entire chapter titled "The

---

[52] See the commentary on Q 56.35-37, *Tafsīr al-Ṭabarī* 27: 103.

[53] *Sahih Bukhari*, Book of the Beginning of Creation (p. 755); *Ṣaḥīḥ al-Bukhārī*, Kitāb Bad' al-Khalq 3: 1188.

[54] *Musnad Aḥmad* 5: 117.

[55] *Sahih Bukhari*, Book of Fighting for the Cause of Allah (Jihad) (p. 646); *Ṣaḥīḥ al-Bukhārī*, Kitāb al-Jihād 3: 1029-1030.

Wide-Eyed Virgins and Their Description."[56] Similar chapters can be found in *Sunan al-Tirmidhī* ("Description of the Women of Paradise")[57] and *Musnad al-Dārmī* ("Description of the Houris [Heavenly Virgins]").[58] All these religious books would not have included these special chapters with *ḥadīths* about these virgins of paradise if this subject was not of high importance or interest. These *ḥadīths* help to shape jihadi culture in the Muslim world, and sex is certainly an important factor for jihad.

The Qur'ān mentions in several verses about the neverending pleasures of the afterlife, including the very appealing promise of unlimited sexual gratification: *"Verily, the fellows of Paradise upon that day shall be employed in enjoyment; / they and their wives, in shade upon thrones, reclining"* (Q 36.55-56; Palmer trans.). The respected Muslim commentator al-Ṭabarī explains that the "work they are employed to do is a bliss; they will be deflowering virgins, and playing and enjoying, and keeping busy from what the people of hell are facing."[59] In fact, according to Hadith literature, Allah will give the Muslim man in paradise endurance for nearly continuous sexual intercourse:[60]

> ...the Messenger of Allah said, "In paradise, the believer will be given such and such strength [for sexual intercourse] for women." Anas [a Companion] said, "I asked, 'O Allah's Messenger, will one be able to do that' [and Muḥammad] said, "He will be given the strength of a hundred [men]."

Because of the abundance of this and other pleasures in the hereafter, no one who enters paradise would ever wish to return to this earthly world—except the martyr. He does desire to return to the earthly world—not to live in it—but to be killed again as a martyr in order to have a double taste of hereafter bliss, according to Muḥammad:[61]

---

[56] *Ṣaḥīḥ al-Bukhārī*, Kitāb al-Jihād 3: 1029-1030. **Note:** English version of *Sahih Bukhari* does not include this chapter heading about the heavenly virgins.
[57] *Sunan al-Tirmidhī* 7: 245.
[58] *Musnad al-Dārmī*, Kitāb al-Riqāq 3: 1777; see page 1871.
[59] See the commentary on Q 36.55-56, *Tafsīr al-Ṭabarī* 32:14.
[60] See the commentary on Q 56.35-37, *Tafsir Ibn Kathir*; *Sunan al-Tirmidhī* 7: 249.
[61] *Sahih Bukhari*, Book of Fighting for the Cause of Allah (pp. 645-646); *Ṣaḥīḥ al-Bukhārī*, Kitāb al-Jihād 3: 1029.

> Nobody who dies and finds good from Allah (in the Hereafter) would wish to come back to this world even if he were given the whole world and whatever is in it, except the martyr who, on seeing the superiority of martyrdom, would like to come back to the world and get killed again (in Allah's Cause).

In other words, the pleasures the martyr enjoys in paradise are so incredibly spectacular, he is exuberantly enthusiastic about returning to his earthly life to kill (again) and be killed for the sake of Allah to repeat this entry and immersion in the pleasures of paradise.

The immense amount of literature about jihad that is paired with the sexual pleasures of the hereafter have impacted the conscious and subconscious minds of young Muslims. Discussions about the sexual pleasures of paradise are heard in the mosques and schools and read in the school curriculums and the official Web sites of Muslim Arab governments. Of course, this discussion is highly visible in the published teachings and main literature of jihadist groups.

There is not a single jihadist Web site that does not discuss the physical pleasures that the martyr will enjoy just as soon as he dies. Muḥammad declares that the martyr will not feel extreme pain at the point of death: "What the martyr will feel when being killed is just like what anyone feels after being bitten [by an insect]."[62] The Qur'ān (see Q 47.15; Rodwell trans.) promises that when his life ends, the infinite journey of joys and pleasures in paradise begins, including pleasures forbidden to him (e.g., drinking wine), during his earthly life:

> *A picture of the Paradise which is promised to the God-fearing! Therein are rivers of water, which corrupt not: rivers of milk, whose taste changeth not: and rivers of wine, delicious to those who quaff it; And rivers of honey clarified: and therein are all kinds of fruit for them from their Lord!....*

And don't forget that there will be continuous sex.

The young chaste Muslim, who has never experienced sexual intercourse, finds himself in a sexual delirium when he hears the imam in his mosque describing the wide-eyed, voluptuous virgins of paradise. His body begins to shake and his imagination runs wild, conjuring images of the virgins who are waiting for him. He imagines himself deflowering their virginity, one after the other, in neverending pleasure, while, in reality, he is single and unmarried because of tremendous social,

[62] *Musnad Aḥmad* 2: 575.

economic, and even religious restrictions. Everything he desires may be inaccessible or unavailable to him because of these pressures. Even if he is fortunate enough to experience such worldly or sensual pleasures, he will always feel guilt and remorse, because he knows that he is violating the teachings of his religion and will end up in hell if he continues to enjoy them. In the end, he is left with just one choice: martyrdom. And jihad is the perfect way to achieve religious salvation and reward himself with all these sexual pleasures without any fears or pressures—only the blessings of Allah.

The promise of these sexual pleasures in the hereafter are considered a highly important motivation in any comprehensive jihadist research study, for sexual pleasure was and still is a real existing motivation for jihad.

Jihad and sex in the world and the hereafter

Muḥammad used the enticement of sexual pleasure and gratification in the world and in the hereafter to motivate Muslims to fight for the cause of Allah. For the jihadists still living in the world, Muḥammad exploited the use of the "temporary" marriage (which was later termed *al-mut'a*) for sexual "enjoyment."[63] For martyred jihadists, he promised the tantalizing prospect of permanent marriages with wide-eyed virgins in the hereafter, ready and willing to engage in fulfilling and neverending sexual pleasure.

During the military expeditions of early Islam, Muḥammad permitted his followers to "enjoy" women for short periods of time by paying these women money or goods in return for sexual favors—not unlike the kinds of legalized sexual transactions in some of today's European countries, where prostitution is lawful and regulated. During the conquest of Mecca, Muḥammad permitted this recourse to his men to help relieve their sexual needs:[64]

[63] **Note:** These *mut'a* marriages are still contracted today, especially in Shiite Islam. In Iran, for example, sexual relations outside of marriage is a punishable crime, and convicted adulterers are stoned to death. However, a man and a woman may contract a *mut'a* for a specific time period (minutes to more than 99 years) and a specific amount of remuneration, payable to the woman. (See URLs: http://www.motherjones.com/politics/2010/03/temporary-marriage-iran-islam/; http://www.thedailybeast.com/islams-sex-licenses)

[64] *Sahih Muslim*, Book of Marriage: Temporary marriage and its prohibition for all times to come (p. 808); *Ṣaḥīḥ Muslim*, Kitāb al-Nikah 1: 633.

> Rabi' Ibn Sabra reported that his father went on an expedition with Allah's Messenger...during the Victory of Mecca, and we stayed there for fifteen days (i.e., for thirteen full days and a day and a night), and Allah's Messenger...permitted us to contract temporary marriage with women.

Some *ḥadīths* state that this type of "temporary" marriage continued until the caliphate of 'Umar Ibn al-Khaṭṭāb, according to one of Muḥammad's Companions, Jabīr Ibn 'Abd Allah: "We contracted temporary marriage by giving a handful of the dates or flour as a dower during the lifetime of Allah's Messenger...and during the time of Abū Bakr until 'Umar forbade it...."[65]

Permitting the use of the "temporary marriage" was Muḥammad's strategy to maintain high morale among his fighters. It is generally recognized that soldiers engaged in war need some kind of sexual relief, and Muḥammad's men were no different and complained about the lack of sexual relations when they were gone for extended periods of time from their wives:[66]

> ...We were on an expedition with Allah's Messenger...and we had no women with us. We said: Should we not have ourselves castrated? He (the Holy Prophet) forbade us to do so. He then granted us permission that we should contract temporary marriage for a stipulated period giving her a garment....

It is a common practice for today's jihadists to set up hastily arranged marriages, particularly when they know they will soon be facing hard or dangerous fighting. Widows of martyrs are encouraged to quickly remarry another jihadist (given the shortage of women). In regions of heavy fighting, these "serial" marriages become more frequent, with a widow moving from one martyr to the next like a bag of goods.[67]

Islamic State has exploited the "marriage crisis" for many men in Arab countries who remain unmarried because of its high cost. (More than fifty percent of these Arab men aged 25-29 are single.) By promising potential unmarried recruits a wife (and even more than one), Islamic

---

[65] *Sahih Muslim*, Book of Marriage: Temporary marriage and its prohibition for all times to come (p. 807); *Ṣaḥīḥ Muslim*, Kitāb al-Nikah 1: 632.

[66] *Sahih Muslim*, Book of Marriage: Temporary marriage and its prohibition for all times to come (p. 806); *Ṣaḥīḥ Muslim*, Kitāb al-Nikah 1: 632.

[67] Walsh, Nick, Salma Abdelaziz, Mark Phillips, and Mehamed Hasan. "ISIS Brides Flee Caliphate as Noose Tightens on Terror Group." *CNN.com*. Cable News Network, 17 July 2017. Web (http://www.cnn.com/2017/07/17/middleeast/raqqa-isis-brides/index.html).

State appealed to the sexual desires of its young fighters while ensuring the recruits stay and not defect because of the added responsibilities and constraints of caring for a wife (or more), a house, and, later, children. To prospective brides, it promised a "wonderful husband and a free house with top-of-the-line appliances" and higher religious status should their husband become a martyr.[68]

Islamic State also "instituted a payment system" where married couples were "paid a stipend for every child" they had.[69] This policy was intended to grow Islamic State as it lost its martyred fighters in the cause of Allah, because the children of these couples would "ensure the longevity of the group: they are the "new generation ready to be trained [and] brainwashed…."[70]

According to Islamic State, all these types of marriages are considered religiously legal based on the prophet's biography, the Hadith literature and related Qur'ānic verses and their interpretations. Islamic State has a religion committee that decides the lawfulness of speech and behavior and determines the punishment for those individuals who commit an unlawful act. The rulings of this committee are based on Islam's religious texts, Muḥammad's words, behavior and teachings, and the application of these teachings by the subsequent caliphs. Therefore, Islamic State would not have supported the use of sexual enticements, such as the promise of brides and sex slaves, to encourage fighter recruitment or morale if it did not find such evidence for this policy in the Islamic sources. Most Sunni Muslims hold that Muḥammad "permanently forbade *mut'a* before his death. [However,] Shi'i Muslims…continue to regard it as legal."[71] Despite this difference, the promise of sexual enticements on earth or in the hereafter to manipulate Muslims still exists, no matter the religious euphemism or purpose. Word choice may vary, but the means are the same.

The international news and television network France 24 revealed samples of Twitter text of Islamic State members who presented descriptions about sex in the hereafter to entice potential recruits. One jihadist encouraged his friends to volunteer for a suicidal operation with

---

[68] Bloom, Mia. "How ISIS Is Using Marriage as a Trap." *HuffingtonPost.com*. The Huffington Post, 2 Mar. 2015. Web (http://www.huffingtonpost.com/mia-bloom/isis-marriage-trap_b_6773576.html).
[69] Ibid.
[70] Ibid.
[71] *The Qur'an: An Encyclopedia* 391.

these three tweets: (1) "Allow me to quickly invade your minds with some of their beautiful descriptions [referring to the wide-eyed virgins]...and that is in order for you to look away from the beauty of the world, and to keep your eyes focused upward where the beautiful virgins are...." (2) "Perhaps I might be a reason for one of you to be involved in one of the works [meaning, a suicidal operation]...." (3) "Just imagine, my beloved brother...when a man encounters his virgin in paradise, she makes him sit on her lap and have him drink honey from a silver cup. Then she wipes his mouth with her mouth...."[72] (Jihadist groups have even stooped to posting photographs of their dead fighters on social media platforms to celebrate their martyrdom, exclaiming that the smiles on the corpses indicate that they were now with the heavenly virgins in paradisial bliss.)[73]

This fantasy of a paradise full of beautiful virgins has inspired a plethora of poems and spoken songs, which are often chanted by jihadists, such as the ISIS fighters in preparation for their suicide missions and terrorist attacks. One of these poem songs is *Nashīd Yā Khāṭib al-Ḥūr*, a famous jihadist song known by heart by every dedicated *mujāhid*:[74]

> O you who would propose to the beautiful virgins,
> seeking love communion with them in the paradise of the living....
> Hasten then, for your journey is just an hour of time,
> It is a beautiful paradise with a beautiful bliss....
> its bliss is everlasting, not an ending bliss.

This poem is but one example of many other spoken songs easily found on the Internet, where *mujāhidīn* sing about their longing for the virgins of paradise. They will confess that they are running out of patience because of their keen desire to meet their maidens.

Hundreds of videos of sheikhs describing these virginal maidens of paradise as well as hundreds more of fatāwa discussing them are posted

---

[72] "The 'Sexual' Temptation to Encourage Jihadists to Carry Out Suicide Bombings." *France24.com*. France 24, 22 Apr. 2015. Web (http://preview.tinyurl.com/hqrknoe).

[73] Warrick, Joby. "Islamist Rebels in Syria Use Faces of the Dead to Lure the Living." *WashingtonPost.com*. The Washington Post, 4 Nov. 2013. Web (https://www.washingtonpost.com/world/national-security/islamist-rebels-in-syria-use-faces-of-the-dead-to-lure-the-living/2013/11/04/10d03480-433d-11e3-8b74-d89d714ca4dd_story.html?utm_term=.e91183613096); "MEMRI, Cyber, and Jihad Lab." *MEMRI.org*. Middle East Media Research Institute (MEMRI), 4 Nov. 2016. Web (http://cjlab.memri.org/lab-projects/tracking-jihadi-terrorist-use-of-social-media/warning-graphic-on-telegram-jihadis-disseminate-death-photos-of-martyrs-noting-their-beatific-smiles-scent-of-musk-emanating-from-their-bodies-and-the-virgins-awaiting-them-in/).

[74] Ibn Qayyīm al-Jawzīya, *Al-Qaṣida al-Nūniya* 217, 218. **Note:** The origin of this poem song can be traced to the writings of Ibn Qayyīm al-Jawzīya, an important Muslim scholar, theologian, and spiritual writer from Damascus.

on the Internet. Despite this deluge of detailed comment and discussion about these "wide-eyed virgins" in the Islamic religious sources and online, Muslim countries continue to express surprise when their youth leave to join the *mujāhidīn*, recruited in part by these enticements of neverending sexual pleasure in the hereafter. These young men have heard and dreamed about this vision of paradise as a sexual playground since their childhood. How then can these Muslim countries criticize these young men for leaving to fight in the cause of Allah when they have been taught from birth to believe in and sanctify a paradise overflowing with sensual pleasures and death over life?

It is not possible to eliminate this terrorist ideology until these Muslim governments, imams, and scholars are pressured to invalidate and then expunge these teachings. Terrorism is born and sustained with every incitement to die for the sake of Allah to ensure eternal bliss. It is born and sustained with every incitement to exchange the worldly life for holy sex and the hereafter bliss that is sponsored by Allah himself in the Gardens that exist in the imagination of Arabs.

TWELVE

The Islamic caliphate dream has become a nightmare

The glory of the Islamic nation lies in its past. The past has been so ingrained in us that we Muslims are not inspired to live for the future. I grew up admiring the bravery of Muḥammad and his Companions, proudly recalling the glories of the Islamic empire and such leaders as the Berber Muslim commander Tāriq Ibn Ziyād,[1] who allegedly gave the following motivational speech to his army before his bloody but decisive victory at the Battle of Guadalete in AD 711, which led to the successful Muslim invasion and conquest of Hispania:[2]

---

[1] **Note:** Different Islamic sources report that Tāriq Ibn Ziyād gave his speech on a mountaintop that was later named after him (Jabal al-Tariq, or "Tariq's Mountain"). This site is better known today as the Rock of Gibraltar.

[2] al-Maqqari 241-242; Ibn Khalkān, *Wafiyāt al-A'yān* 3: 161.

> Oh my warriors, whither would you flee? Behind you is the sea, before you, the enemy. You have left now only the hope of your courage and your constancy. Remember that in this country you are more unfortunate than the orphan seated at the table of the avaricious master. Your enemy is before you, protected by an innumerable army; he has men in abundance, but you, as your only aid, have your own swords, and, as your only chance for life, such chance as you can snatch from the hands of your enemy....
>
> Remember that if you suffer a few moments in patience, you will afterward enjoy supreme delight. Do not imagine that your fate can be separated from mine, and rest assured that if you fall, I shall perish with you, or avenge you....

The purpose of Tāriq Ibn Ziyād's assault was to exalt and promote the religion of Islam and to conquer Andalusia (southern Spain) for the Muslims. In his famous speech, Tāriq tells his troops that Caliph al-Walīd Ibn 'Abd al-Malik[3] (AD 668-715) had chosen them for this holy mission from among all his Arab warriors, asserting that this decision proved the caliph's "confidence in your intrepidity. The one fruit which he desires to obtain from your bravery is that the word of God shall be exalted in this country, and that the true religion shall be established here. The spoils will belong to yourselves."[4]

This speech was one of the history lessons we learned in elementary school. I had to memorize it by heart, and I still remember it as though I had just learned it yesterday.

And I still remember the words of the Arab Muslim general, 'Uqba Ibn Nāfi' (AD 622-683), who led the Muslim expansion into Maghreb (North Africa), including present-day Algeria, Tunisia, Libya, and Morocco. Upon reaching the Atlantic coast, he allegedly rode his horse into the sea and exclaimed, "O Allah, I have reached my target, and if the sea had not prevented me, I would have galloped on forever, upholding your faith and fighting the unbeliever, until everyone believes in you."[5]

Muslims have reigned over one of the greatest empires of the world. Books, movies, and television programs as well as mosque sermons and school curriculums generously cover these achievements of the Muslim Empire, and pride in these accomplishments form our character and

[3] **Note:** Also known as Al-Walid I, this Muslim caliph undertook and oversaw the greatest expansion of the Islamic caliphate during his reign, which at one point stretched from Spain to India.

[4] al-Maqqari 241-242; Ibn Khalkān, *Wafiyāt al-A'yān* 3: 161.

[5] al-Mālikī, *Kitāb Riyāḍ al-Nufūs* 1: 39.

intensify our nostalgia for our past. With such a celebrated history, we Muslims today wonder, "Why do Muslims live today so miserably on so many levels? Why are our countries divided and antagonistic toward each other?" The answer we always hear from our religious leaders is that we need to return to Islam in order to reclaim our past glories.

Returning to Islam means to reinstate an Islamic caliphate. All major Islamic groups call for the return of an Islamic caliphate: Al Qaeda, Ḥamās, Boko Haram, Al Shabaab, and Islamic State. Even the Muslim Brotherhood calls for the return of an Islamic caliphate.[6] Even Muslim countries headed by kings or presidents spread this teaching of an Islamic caliphate through the state curriculum and Web sites and through religious scholars—that the institution of a caliphate is a lawful matter and that it will return one day. An Islamic caliphate is the dream desired of all Muslims all over the world.

How can these heads of state believe in an Islamic caliphate yet remain in power? Why don't they just waive their own authority and dedicate themselves to teaching their countrymen that caliphate rule is the true and legitimate rule set by the caliphs since the first Islamic state?

Sheikh Yūsuf al-Qaraḍāwī, an intellectual leader of the Egyptian Muslim Brotherhood who currently lives in Qatar, does not deny the idea of the Islamic State caliphate; he only denies the legitimacy of Abū Bakr al-Baghdādī as leader because he lacks the qualifications of a caliph.[7] In other words, if another organization, such as the Muslim Brotherhood, had taken the initiative and announced an Islamic caliphate, Sheikh Yūsuf al-Qaraḍāwī would have backed it.

The Web site of the Ministry of Social Affairs in Qatar states in a published legitimate fatwa that the "re-establishment of the caliphate is the legitimate duty of all Muslims."[8] The fatwa even asserts that an Islamic caliphate should be the top priority for Muslims to institute "material and moral" order, providing the world with "the living example

[6] **Note:** The Muslim Brotherhood was established in 1928, or four years after the caliphate was abolished in a resolution by the Turkish National Assembly on March 3, 1924.

[7] "Al-Qaraḍāwī: 'Khadafah [ISIS Caliphate]' Does Not Meet the Required Conditions." *DW.com/ar*. Deutsche Welle (Arabic), 26 July 2014. Web (http://preview.tinyurl.com/zc8qf44).

[8] See Fatwa no. 1411: "Re-Establishing the Caliphate Is a Legitimate Duty for Muslims." *Islamweb.net*. Ministry of Endowments and Islamic Affairs of Qatar, 27 July 1999. Web (http://fatwa.islamweb.net/fatwa/index.php?page=showfatwa&Option=FatwaId&Id=1411).

of combining the religious and the secular" in contrast to those (Western) countries that are "hostile to Islam" and work to silence it:[9]

> The first thing that the Islamic call needs in this era is to establish the House of Islam, or the State of Islam, which adopts the message of Islam as a doctrine, a system, and a civilization. And to assess its entire life, material and moral, on the basis of this comprehensive message. And to open its door to every believer who wants to emigrate from the land of infidelity, injustice and innovation....

And as soon as ISIS announced its caliphate and its new name, Islamic State, the International Union of Muslim Scholars (IUMS), based in Qatar and led by Sheikh Yūsuf al-Qaraḍāwī, issued a statement explaining its position on this caliphate: "We all dream of the Islamic caliphate following the path of prophecy or prophethood, and we wish from the bottom of our hearts that it takes place today before tomorrow...."[10] The entire statement also includes this comment:[11]

> The Islamic caliphate and its return once again is a matter of longing, which all of us yearn for. All our minds think about it and all our hearts desire it, but it has its legitimate rules and requires great and deep preparations at all levels....

The difference between IUMS and Islamic State lies only in the formalities but not the essence of this matter. Neither disputes the need and desire to restore the Islamic caliphate. In general, both agree that the restoration of the Islamic caliphate is essential to combat disbelief, but IUMS questions whether Islamic State satisfies the required conditions decreed by the religious texts.

These religious texts are filled with pronouncements that the Islamic caliphate will only be restored following the "way of prophethood," which means that the correct and successful means for establishing the ideal Islamic state must follow the methodology of Prophet Muḥammad. Muslims cannot deny this fact, or else they would be at odds with the heavy legacy of these explicit texts, which go back from the beginning of Islam to this date. These religious texts all underline the need to

---

[9] See Fatwa no. 1411: "Re-Establishing the Caliphate Is a Legitimate Duty for Muslims." *Islamweb.net*. Ministry of Endowments and Islamic Affairs of Qatar, 27 July 1999. Web (http://fatwa.islamweb.net/fatwa/index.php?page=showfatwa&Option=FatwaId&Id=1411).

[10] "Statement by the World Federation of Muslim Scholars Regarding a Declaration Urging the Islamic Caliphate." *Manaratweb.com*. Manarat Web, 6 July 2014. Web (http://preview.tinyurl.com/ycrdsl73).

[11] Ibid.

properly install an authentic Islamic state—under one banner—in order to victoriously confront and defeat infidelity, which, in the eyes of Islam, is one religion.[12]

Roots of caliphal succession conflict

When Muḥammad died, he did not leave a will. If he had done so, he could have designated his successor or provided rules regarding the methodology for the successive transfer of power over the caliphate. The Qur'ān also does not provide any verse to specifically help guide changes in leadership. So his Companions gathered together in a meeting to appoint a successor to Muḥammad—to be "the Caliph." This famous meeting in the Islamic sources has been called the Saqīfa. Named after the house where this crucial meeting took place, this event, attended by Muḥammad's close Companions, determined Muḥammad's successor.

During this meeting, a dispute regarding the caliphal succession arose between the Anṣār, or Helpers (the Medinans who supported Muḥammad when he and his small band of followers emigrated to Medina during the Hijra in AD 622), and the Muhājirīn (Emigrants). Several suggestions were presented, including a dual form of leadership, where an emir from the Anṣār and another emir from the Muhājirīn would share the rule and administration of the caliphate.

However, this proposal was not accepted by some of the Companions, especially 'Umar Ibn al-Khaṭṭāb, one of the most important people who arranged this assembly. He suggested that Abū Bakr, a father-in-law of Muḥammad and one of his earliest followers, become the caliph. After some heated debate Abū Bakr was eventually accepted as the next caliph, and the meeting participants pledged their allegiance to him.[13]

The discussion regarding the successor to Muḥammad and the eventual selection of Abū Bakr occurred as 'Alī Ibn Abū Ṭālib (Muḥammad's cousin and most prominent son-in-law) and the rest of Muḥammad's family were preoccupied with the funeral arrangements and burial of Muḥammad. By arranging the succession meeting during this time, the participants were able to minimize consideration of close Companion and family relative 'Alī, a powerful contender because of his important blood and marital ties to Muḥammad. Once the meeting participants

[12] This phrase, "infidelity is one religion," is often repeated by Muslim scholars. For an example, see the commentary on Q 109.6, *Tafsīr Ibn Kathīr* 14: 487.

[13] Ibn Kathīr, *Al-Bidāya* 8: 84-86.

selected Abū Bakr and pledged their allegiance to him, the Islamic caliphate—now under a new leader—became fait accompli.

This event—the transfer of leadership from Muḥammad to Abū Bakr by circumventing ʿAlī—is generally considered the spark that ignited the eventual dogmatic schism between two groups of early Muslims: ʿAlī and Muḥammad's family (Āhl al-Bayt) and Muḥammad's other Companions (many from the Quraysh tribe). This hostile division became known as Islam's Shiite-Sunni conflict, and it continues to this day. The causes of wars between Shiite Iran and the Sunni Saudi Arabia or any other proxy war that represents their interests in the region can be traced, as a rule, to this event. Isn't it both strange and sad to see the Muslim world today still bitterly split and influenced by this 1400-year-old conflict?

After Muḥammad's death and the installation of Abū Bakr as the next Muslim leader, some Arab tribes that had been forced to convert to Islam (i.e., under the sword) had stopped paying the *zakāt*, believing that this obligatory religious tax burden was cancelled upon the death of the person (Muḥammad) who had established it. However, Abū Bakr and the other Companions considered this refusal an act of apostasy:[14]

> ...when the Messenger of Allah...breathed his last and Abu Bakr was appointed as his successor (Caliph), those amongst the Arabs who wanted to become apostates became apostates. 'Umar b. Khattab said to Abu Bakr: Why would you fight against the people, when the Messenger of Allah declared: I have been directed to fight against people so long as they do not say: There is no god but Allah, and he who professed it was granted full protection of his property and life on my behalf except for a right? His (other) affairs rest with Allah. Upon this Abu Bakr said: By Allah, I would definitely fight against him who severed prayer from Zakat, for it is the obligation upon the rich. By Allah, I would fight against them even to secure the cord (used for hobbling the feet of a camel) which they used to give to the Messenger of Allah (as zakat) but now they have withheld it. 'Umar b. Khattab remarked: By Allah, I found nothing but the fact that Allah had opened the heart of Abu Bakr for (perceiving the justification of) fighting (against those who refused to pay Zakat) and I fully recognized that the (stand of Abu Bakr) was right.

Abū Bakr and his generals embarked on several military campaigns to force these errant Arab tribes to re-embrace Islam and resume the *zakāt*

[14] *Sahih Muslim*, Book of Faith: Command for fighting against the people so long as they do not profess that there is no god but Allah and Muḥammad is his messenger (p. 70); *Ṣaḥīḥ Muslim*, Kitāb al-Imān 1: 31.

payments. These campaigns became known as the Ridda Wars or Wars of Apostasy. Some of these Arab tribes still considered themselves Muslims because they continued to perform the prayers and follow Muḥammad's teachings; they just chose not to pay the *zakāt* after Muḥammad died, because Muḥammad had established the *zakāt* with them. But Abū Bakr equated the paying of the *zakāt* with the daily praying and declared that these tribes were not acting like Muslims to withhold the *zakāt*. One of the Arabs, Mālik Ibn Nuwayrah, protested to Khālid Ibn al-Walīd (one of Abū Bakr's generals; see Chapter 11, page 321) just before his death about this judgment:[15]

> Are you going to kill me when I am a Muslim who prays facing the qiblah? Khālid said to him: If you were a Muslim you would not have withheld the zakat and you would not have told your people to withhold it. By Allah you will not sleep until I kill you.

These Wars of Apostasy (Ridda Wars) reveal the willingness of the early caliphate to confront and even militarily attack peoples who claimed to be practicing Muslims if they did not follow a particular ruling. This policy is no different than today's Islamic terrorist groups that attack and kill Muslims who do not support their interpretation and application of the Qur'ān. For those who say that Islamic State and similar groups are not representative of Islam because most of their victims are Muslims, then know that most of the victims of Caliph Abū Bakr's military campaigns were Muslims too.

After the death of Abū Bakr (AD 634), 'Umar Ibn al-Khaṭṭāb became the caliph, his succession the result of Abū Bakr's personal nomination in his last will and testament and not by a vote.[16] 'Umar Ibn al-Khaṭṭāb was a fellow Quraysh Emigrant and one of Muḥammad's closest Companions and a son-in-law. His caliphate lasted until his assassination in AD 644. He lingered several days after reportedly being stabbed by a Persian slave. On his deathbed, he too wanted to influence the selection of his successor and appointed a handpicked committee of six close Companions of the Prophet to elect a successor from among themselves.[17]

A few days after 'Umar's death, 'Uthmān Ibn 'Affān, another of Muḥammad's close Companions and a son-in-law, became the next

---

[15] al-Wāqidī, *Kitāb al-Ridda* 107.

[16] Ibn Kathīr, *Al-Bidāya* 9: 574.

[17] *History of al-Ṭabarī* 14: 91-92. This committee included 'Abd al-Raḥmān Ibn 'Awf, Sa'd Ibn Abī Waqqāṣ, Talha Ibn 'Ubayd Allah, 'Uthmān Ibn 'Affān, 'Alī Ibn Abī Ṭālib, and Zubayr Ibn al-'Awam.

caliph. Like Abū Bakr and 'Umar, 'Uthman was also a Quraysh Emigrant. Up to this point, no caliph after the death of Muḥammad was from the family house of Muḥammad or the Anṣār (Helpers).

'Uthmān[18] was assassinated in AD 656 by Muslim rebels who objected to his policies and perceived nepotism. The following day, 'Alī Ibn Abū Ṭālib was declared the caliph after a meeting held in the Al-Masjid al-Nabawi Mosque. An extremely close confidant of the Prophet, 'Alī was Muḥammad's paternal first cousin and a son-in-law. He accepted Islam as a child when he lived in Muḥammad's household as a foster son and later married Muḥammad's favorite daughter Fatima. He led and fought valiantly in major battles under Muḥammad's leadership during the early military campaigns. With his installation as the fourth caliph, the caliphate was finally given to a man from the Banū Hashīm—the family house of Muḥammad.

Many Muslims then and now believe Muḥammad intended 'Alī to be his successor. 'Alī Ibn Abū Ṭālib himself believed that the family house of Muḥammad, the Banū Hashīm, was the more legitimate line of succession. However, he accepted and supported the installation and caliphates of Abū Bakr, 'Umar, and 'Uthmān, even when his allegiance was sometimes sought after the decision of successor had already been made by others.

Unfortunately for 'Alī, his short-lived caliphate of five years was heavily marked throughout by controversy and conflict among the Muslim communities. (This period of time has been called the First Fitna, or First Islamic Civil War.) One of 'Uthmān's appointees (and relatives), Mu'āwiya, who at that time was the governor of Syria, refused to acknowledge 'Alī as the new caliph. Mu'āwiya faulted 'Alī for not quickly finding and punishing 'Uthmān's assassins and vowed revenge. One Muslim group supportive of 'Alī turned against him when he was forced to agree to arbitration regarding caliphal succession after an indecisive battle (Battle of Siffīn, AD 657) against Mu'āwiya's forces. This group, later known as the Kharijites,[19] protested that Allah alone decides

[18] **Note:** According to Islamic sources, 'Uthmān's corpse was left unburied for three days. When his family received permission to move the body to a grave, "people lay in wait…by the road, armed with stones." Only five people attended his funeral. (See *History of al-Tabari* 15: 246-250; see also Ibn Kathīr, *Al-Bidaya* 10: 325-326.)

[19] "Khārijite." *Britannica.com.* Encyclopædia Brittanica, Inc., 2017. Web (https://www.britannica.com/topic/Kharijite).

(see Q 6.57) and that the Qur'ān commands Muslims to fight those groups that rebel (see Q 49.9).

Even Muḥammad's widow, 'Ā'isha, got swept up in these conflicts. She criticized 'Alī, demanding that he find and punish 'Uthmān's murderers before involving himself with other caliphate matters. She then enlisted the support of two other Companions (who were also her brothers-in-law), Talha Ibn 'Ubayd Allah and Zubayr Ibn al-'Awam, and 'Uthmān's powerful clan, the Banū Ummaya. Together this rebel army marched out from Mecca. It entered and conquered Basra, and then quickly imprisoned and executed seventy of the Basran governor's officers. This action was followed by the execution of 400 more men charged in the fatal attack on 'Uthmān.

Meanwhile, 'Alī attempted to increase his support so that he could successfully confront this insurgent army. Reinforced with Arab tribesmen from Kūfa, he and his army marched to Basra. When his army reached the city outskirts, 'Alī attempted to avert battle by negotiating a peaceful resolution with the rebel leaders. Both sides seemed genuinely anxious to avoid bloodshed between the two rival Muslim armies.

However, some of 'Alī's supporters had been involved in the attack on 'Uthmān and feared a peaceful compromise would eventually lead to their execution. So they and other rebel tribes launched a night attack to create confusion between 'Alī's forces and some Basran tribes. The chaos soon enveloped both sets of armies, each believing the other had instigated the treachery. At the end of this disorganized battle, tens of thousands lay dead or wounded. Talha, disabled by an arrow wound, died later in Basra. 'Ā'isha, seated in her litter atop her camel, was eventually captured unharmed, after seventy warriors protecting her were killed and her camel was hamstrung. (Zubayr was murdered as he was performing his prayers after he left the battlefield.)

This horrific onslaught, the first between two Muslim armies, became known as the Battle of the Camel (AD 655).[20] Its unbelievable carnage (10,000 dead) seemed to have little effect in removing growing misunderstandings among the various tribes within the Muslim community or solidifying 'Alī's position and power.

[20] "Battle of the Camel." *NewWorldEncyclopedia.org*. New World Encyclopedia, 20 May 2016 (last mod.). Web (http://www.newworldencyclopedia.org/entry/Battle_of_the_Camel). See Ibn Kathīr, *Al-Bidāya* 10: 431-469.

In AD 661, 'Alī Ibn Abū Ṭālib was assassinated by 'Abd al-Raḥmān Ibn Maljam, a Khārijite, who struck 'Alī with a poisoned sword while he was praying in the Kūfa mosque.[21] (The Khārijites also tried to assassinate Mu'āwiya and 'Amr Ibn al-'As but failed.) Like 'Uthmān Ibn 'Affān, 'Alī was also killed by Muslims.[22]

After the death of 'Alī, his eldest son Ḥasan became caliph but abdicated six or seven months later to Mu'āwiya, who then became the next caliph and the second Umayyad caliph after 'Uthmān. Since Mu'āwiya controlled Egypt and Syria and commanded the largest force in the Muslim empire, Ḥasan obviously saw the wisdom in removing himself from public life.[23]

These conflicts over caliphal rule and succession were triggered by fanatical tribalism. When Umayyad caliph Mu'āwiya was succeeded by his son, Yazīd, the caliphal succession became Umayyad, or belonging to the Banū Umayya, and not to the Banū Hāshim, the tribe of Muḥammad. This line of succession continued for about the next ninety years, when the most extensive expansion of the Islamic empire took place and included the invasions and the conquest of North Africa and Andalusia (southern Spain).

In AD 750 the Umayyad caliphate was overthrown by descendants of Muḥammad's youngest uncle, 'Abbās Ibn 'Abd al-Muttalib, and their supporters. During the previous thirty years, members of this family plotted to regain control of the Muslim caliphate, believing that the Umayyads had illegitimate claims to the caliphate and convincing other discontented Muslim tribes through skillful propaganda that the family house of the Prophet was the only legitimate line of succession. After the successful revolt against and ouster of Marwan II (who then became the last Umayyad caliph), the first 'Abbāsid caliph, Abū al-'Abbās, was installed. The resulting 'Abbāsid caliphate reigned until AD 1258, when the Mongols invaded the empire and destroyed and sacked its capital, Baghdad.

During its five centuries of power, the 'Abbāsid caliphate built a new city, Baghdad, to be the empire's capital. It emphasized "membership in the community of believers rather than Arab nationality" and maintained

[21] Ibn Kathīr, *Al-Bidāya* 11: 12-15, 17-18.

[22] Ibid. 10: 306-309.

[23] Ibid. 11: 131-133. See Little, Donald P. "Mu'āwiya I." *Brittanica.com*. Encyclopædia Brittanica, Inc., 7 Sept. 2017. Web (https://www.britannica.com/biography/Muawiyah-I).

that laws must be based on the religion of Islam (the beginnings of *sharīʿa*).[24] Its first century was notable for its promotion of business, trade, industry, arts, and science and the introduction of Islam's "Golden Age." (See Chapter 11, page 313.)

The first ʿAbbāsid caliph Abū al-ʿAbbās (c. AD 721-754) earned the caliphal title "The Blood-Shedder" (Al-Saffāh) for brutally and quickly dispatching his Umayyad rivals. One story recounts that he invited all remaining Umayyad male family members to a dinner party where they were all murdered before the first course was served.[25] He also had some of this family's graves in Damascus dug up and looted, and the bodies mutilated.[26] "The Blood-Shedder" died from smallpox in AD 754, only four years into his reign.

Another colorful ʿAbbāsid caliph, Hārūn al-Rashīd (c. AD 766-809), ruled for about ten years during the zenith of the Muslim empire. His extremely wealthy family and court were famous for their conspicuous consumption. Though he was a lover, connoisseur, and patron of the arts, he would summarily imprison or execute people, including a close friend.[27]

Other caliphates followed the ʿAbbāsid caliphate after its fall in the thirteenth century, but these were not as consequential as the Ottoman Empire (c. AD 1300-1923), which "grew to be one of the most powerful states in the world" during the fifteenth and sixteenth centuries and lasted about six centuries. Ever since its fall and partitioning into separate nations and the official abolition of the caliphate after World War I, the Muslim world has been trying to put it back together.

This admittedly thumbnail sketch summarizing the Islamic caliphates since Muḥammad paints a caliphate legacy filled with assassinations, vengeful bloodletting, court extravagances, and sometimes hedonistic, unsavory, or vicious behavior by caliphs who should be the supreme religious leaders.

Yet the Muslim world dreams and prepares for the restoration of such a caliphate.

---

[24] "ʿAbbāsid Dynasty." *Brittanica.com*. Encyclopædia Brittanica, Inc., 8 Sept. 2017. Web (https://www.britannica.com/topic/Abbasid-dynasty).

[25] Roberts, *History of the World* 347-348.

[26] Ibn Kathīr, *Al-Bidāya* 13: 258-259.

[27] Watt, William Montgomery. "Hārūn al-Rashīd." *Brittanica.com*. Encyclopædia Brittanica, Inc., 9 Sept. 2017. Web (https://www.britannica.com/biography/Harun-al-Rashid).

Textual support of caliphate

The Islamic texts present the blueprint for the establishment of a Muslim caliphate and exalts the first century of Islam as the ideal standard. Despite all the conflicts, wars, and shed blood, Muslims consider it the best century because Muḥammad declared it so in the Hadith literature: "The best people are those living in my generation, and then those who will follow them, and then those who will follow the latter...."[28] His assessment is considered true, despite the heavy loss of life from the battles against non-Muslims during Muḥammad's life and from the bloody conflicts between rival Muslim factions following his death. For example, during just one of these Muslim clashes, the Battle of the Camel (when supporters of 'Alī and 'Ā'isha were fighting each other), Islamic sources report that thousands of fighters died, from "ten thousand killed" and countless wounded,[29] to fifteen thousand men killed, "ten thousand from the people of Basra and five thousand dead from the people of Kūfa."[30]

Sheikhs and imams on pulpits, satellite channels, and Internet Web sites constantly repeat this *ḥadīth* to assert that the Islamic caliphate line of succession and the role of the prophethood path ("prophetic methodology") were foretold by Muḥammad:[31]

> "Prophethood will remain among you for as long as Allaah Wills it to be. Then Allaah Will Raise it when He Wills to Raise it. Then there will be the reign [in Arabic, *caliphate*] that follows the prophetic methodology [Abū Bakr to Hasan]. And it will last for as long as Allaah Wills it to last. Then Allaah Will Raise it when He Wills to Raise it. Then there will be an oppressive reign [according to the 'Abbāsid rulers, this reign refers to the first half of the Umayyad dynasty], and it will remain for as long as Allaah Wills it to Remain. Then Allaah Will Raise it when He Wills to Raise it. Then there will be tyrannical reign [according to the 'Abbāsid rulers, this reign refers to the second half of the Umayyad dynasty] and it will remain for as long as Allaah Wills it to Remain. Then He Will Raise it when He Wills to Raise it. Then there will be a reign that follows the prophetic methodology ['Abbāsid dynasty]."

[28] *Sahih Bukhari*, Book of Companions of the Prophet (p. 852); *Ṣaḥīḥ al-Bukhārī*, Kītāb Fadā'il Ashāb al-Nabī 3: 1335.

[29] Ibn Kathīr, *Al-Bidaya* 19: 473-474.

[30] *History of al-Tabari* 16: 164.

[31] See Fatwa no. 36833: "Then There Will Be a Rule Following the Prophetic Methodology." *Islamweb.net*. Ministry of Endowments and Islamic Affairs of Qatar, 2 Apr. 2013. Web (http://www.islamweb.net/emainpage/index.php?page=showfatwa&Option=FatwaId&Id=36833); *Musnad Aḥmād* 5: 342.

Muslims today interpret this prophetic methodology differently. Many believe that Muslims are still living in the oppressive-tyrannical times and that these negative times included the ʿAbbāsids. Though there is little agreement as to the beginning and end times of the oppressive and tyrannical reigns, greater agreement revolves over the opinion that the foretold caliphate is yet to come.

As this *ḥadīth* was written down and published during the ʿAbbāsid caliphate, it should not be surprising that its text seems to present the ʿAbbāsid caliphate as "a reign that follows prophetic methodology." One wonders when the political bias occurred during its transference from oral to written form over the course of two centuries. Obviously, someone during this process wanted the ʿAbbāsid caliphate to look like a legitimate rule that corresponds with the sayings of the Prophet. In fact, much of the writing and scholarship (which flourished during the ʿAbbāsid reign), such as the biography of Muḥammad by Ibn Isḥaq as well as some Hadith literature and books of *fiqh* (Islamic religious laws and rulings), were commissioned or at least influenced by ʿAbbāsid rulers.[32] Consequently, many statements attributed to Muḥammad in these writings and literature, especially those in praise of the ʿAbbāsid reign or its rulers, should be viewed with circumspection if not some skepticism.[33]

For Sunni Muslims, however, the aforementioned *ḥadīth* has been adopted as established belief, and no argument will persuade them that it is not authentic despite content with clear political connotations. The Qur'ān itself testifies that Muḥammad cannot predict the future or know the unseen: *"Say, 'I do not say to you that I possess the treasures of GOD. Nor do I know the future.... I simply follow what is revealed to me...'"* (Q 6.50; Khalifa trans.).

Even so, this *ḥadīth* has become the justification for those who call for a succession based on the prophethood path, because supporters of this

---

[32] Goldziher, *Muslim Studies* 2: 54. **Note:** Goldziher, one of the founders of modern Islamic studies in Europe, states that there was "official pressure" by ʿAbbāsid rulers "to eradicate" *ḥadīths* favorable to the Ummayad dynasty: "For example, al-Bukhārī can no longer give any *manāqib* of Muʿāwiya [Ummayad ruler] as sound *ḥadīths*.... [T]hese as well as anything friendly to the Umayyads were officially suppressed and destroyed. In contrast, a large number of *ḥadīths* were circulated, which were intended to show the people the unworthiness of that [Umayyad] dynasty."

[33] Ibid. 2: 44. **Note:** Goldziher suggests that the fabrication of and interpolation of *ḥadīths* began very early for political and other reasons; in other words, this process was not restricted to one particular Islamic caliphate or dynasty: "...it is not surprising that, among the hotly debated controversial issues of Islam, whether political or doctrinal, there is none in which the champions of the various views are unable to cite a number of traditions, all equipped with imposing *isnāds* [chain of Muslim authorities attesting to the historical authenticity of a particular *ḥadīth*, e.g., a Companion.]."

position believe that today's era is an "oppressive reign," with rulers who are forcibly imposed upon the Muslim people; these rulers should be removed and replaced with a caliph (*khilafah*) based on the prophethood path.

Famous Saudi sheikh Muḥammad al-'Arifī explained this *ḥadīth* in a passionate speech on January 11, 2013, in Cairo's Amr Ibn al-'As mosque (when the Muslim Brotherhood held political power in Egypt), calling on Muslims for solidarity and for jihad against Syria's President Bashar al-Assad. After reading out loud the *ḥadīth*, al-'Arifī made this comment:[34]

> We are waiting for the Islamic Caliphate. I swear to God that the Islamic caliphate is coming as if I am looking at it with my eyes now. What is happening today in the Islamic countries is now a union of the nation's scholars and events.... [This speech predates the announcement of the Islamic State (caliphate) by ISIS on June 29, 2014.]

Sheikh al-'Arifī was thrilled when the Muslim Brotherhood assumed power in Egypt soon after the overthrow of President Hosni Mubarak during the Egyptian Revolution in 2011. Sheikh al-'Arifī anticipated the inevitable rise of an Islamic caliphate in all the neighboring Muslim countries and predicted the collapse of Syria and the expansion and control of the Muslim Brotherhood or Islamic groups over it. (In his Cairo speech, the sheikh predicted the near future establishment of an Islamic caliphate and suggests that the current stage is the era of the "oppressive reign," which means a king or political leader who is forcibly imposed on people, including the monarchy of Saudi Arabia. In other words, all these kings and presidents of Muslim countries are not legitimate and will be removed as soon as the caliphate is established.)

Muslims believe that when the Islamic caliphate is re-established, there must be just one successor, and all those who are fighting to take power from him are to be killed. In one *ḥadīth* Muḥammad states, "When oath of allegiance has been taken for two caliphs, kill the one for whom the

[34] "'Arifī Invites Egyptians to Support Syria: Caliphate Is Coming, I Can See It with My Own Eyes." *Archive.Arabic.CNN.com*. Cable News Network (Arabic), 14 June 2013. Web (http://archive.arabic.cnn.com/2013/middle_east/6/14/egypt.syria). (To view his hour-long speech, see YouTube video: https://www.youtube.com/watch?v=yCh2pNanjO4). (To view excerpts of the Cairo speech with English subtitles, see YouTube video: https://www.youtube.com/watch?v=D1JJoVmiluM; the excerpt occurs approximately 2:10 minutes.) See Fick, Maggie. "Egypt Brotherhood Backs Syria Jihad, Denounces Shi'ites." *Reuters.com*. Reuters, 14 June 2013. Web (http://www.reuters.com/article/us-syria-crisis-sunnis-brotherhood/egypt-brotherhood-backs-syria-jihad-denounces-shiites-idUSBRE95D0NL20130614).

oath was taken later."[35] As an example, when 'Alī declared himself the caliph after 'Uthmān's death and Mu'āwiya contested his caliphate, 'Alī should have killed and not negotiated with Mu'āwiya.

ISIS caliphate announcement

ISIS formally announced on June 29, 2014, via an MP3 audio file entitled *This is the Promise of Allah*, the establishment of an Islamic caliphate and declared "Abū Bakr al-Baghdādī" as the name of the new caliph.[36] (Abū Bakr al-Baghdādī's birth name is Ibrāhīm 'Awwād Ibrāhīm.) Official ISIS spokesman Abū Muḥammad al-'Adnānī recorded the message and includes the demand that all Muslims "pledge allegiance" to the new caliph.

The title of the audio file states that this new caliphate is a promise from Allah. Experts on Islamic groups contend that this title is a reference to Q 24.55 (Arberry trans.):

> *God has promised those of you who believe and do righteous deeds that He will surely make you successors in the land, even as He made those who were before them successors, and that He will surely establish their religion for them that He has approved for them, and will give them in exchange, after their fear, security: 'They shall serve Me, not associating with Me anything.' Whoso disbelieves after that, those—they are the ungodly.*

On the audio file, al-'Adnānī actually begins his statement by first reciting this verse in order to remind Muslims that an Islamic caliphate is a promise from Allah to Muslims, and that Allah will grant them the succession of the entire earth because they are more worthy of it than infidel regimes; Muslims are to spread the religion of Allah and bring all nations under true submission and worship of him. But this promise about succession is not just about taking power, according to al-'Adnānī:[37]

---

[35] *Sahih Muslim*, Book on Government: When the oath of allegiance has been obtained for two caliphs (p. 1158); *Ṣaḥīḥ Muslim*, Kītāb al-Imāra 2: 899.

[36] "Da'ash [ISIS] 'Declares Islamic State' Caliphate and Allegiance to al-Baghdadi." *Alarabiya.net.* Al Arabiya Network, 29 June 2014. Web (http://preview.tinyurl.com/hdeyq2e). See Bradley, Matt. "ISIS Declares New Islamist Caliphate." *WSJ.com.* Wall Street Journal, 29 June 2014. Web (https://www.wsj.com/articles/isis-declares-new-islamist-caliphate-1404065263); "ISIS Rebels Declare 'Islamic State' in Iraq and Syria." *BBC.com.* British Broadcasting Company, 30 June 2014. Web (http://www.bbc.com/news/world-middle-east-28082962).

[37] al-'Adnānī, *This is the Promise of Allah* [English transcript] 1; audio file: http://www.dailymotion.com/video/x3u3iol.

> ...That is the reality of succession, which Allah created us for. It is not simply kingship, subjugation, dominance, and rule. Rather, succession is to utilize all that for the purpose of compelling the people to do what the Sharīʿa (Allah's law) requires of them concerning their interests in the hereafter and worldly life, which can only be achieved by carrying out the command of Allah, establishing His religion, and referring to His law for judgment....

Al-ʿAdnānī includes in his message a comparison concerning the status—past and present—of the Islamic *umma* (nation or community). The harsh contrast between yesterday's glories and today's disappointments rests heavily on the conscience of every young Muslim. Most Muslims believe that detachment from religion is the reason—not poor education, mismanagement, or dictatorship—for the backwardness and degeneration of Muslim countries. Al-ʿAdnānī seems to agree, as he states that Allah's promise of an Islamic caliphate will only be fulfilled when Muslims have faith in Allah and submit to him in everything with a "level of obedience that makes your lusts, inclinations, and desires to be in compliance with what the Prophet came with...."[38]

After comparing the past and present status of the *umma*, al-ʿAdnānī rallies his listeners:[39]

> ...O umma of Muḥammad (peace be upon him), you continue to be the best umma and continue to have honor. Leadership will return to you. The God of this umma yesterday is the same God of the umma today, and the One who gave it victory yesterday is the One who will give it victory today.
>
> The time has come for those generations that were drowning in oceans of disgrace, being nursed on the milk of humiliation, and being ruled by the vilest of all people, after their long slumber in the darkness of neglect—the time has come for them to rise. The time has come for the umma of Muḥammad (peace be upon him) to wake up from its sleep, remove the garments of dishonor, and shake off the dust of humiliation and disgrace for the era of lamenting and moaning has gone, and the dawn of honor has emerged anew. The sun of jihad has risen. The glad tidings of good are shining. Triumph looms on the horizon. The signs of victory have appeared.
>
> Here the flag of the Islamic State, the flag of tawḥīd (monotheism), rises and flutters. Its shade covers land from Aleppo to Diyala....

---

[38] al-ʿAdnānī, *This is the Promise of Allah* [English transcript] 1; audio file: http://www.dailymotion.com/video/x3u3iol.

[39] Ibid. 4.

These words clearly reveal that the crisis of Muslim youth is a crisis created by religion, created by adhering to the religious past and not apologizing for any of it. For Muslim youth consider early Islam's invasions as victories and occupying and ruling other countries as successes. These victories and successes are venerated because they culminated (in their minds) into the best form of rule on earth—even though this early Islamic caliphate was built on the bloody skulls of people, the ravaging of women, and the enslavement of children. This nostalgia for Islam's past and the desire to restore it throbs in the heart of every young devout Muslim.

Through his tone and text, al-'Adnānī appeals to these typical young Muslim men who have been filled with the teachings of Islam, addressing them using certain terminology to stir up these yearnings while subduing potential opposition with carefully selected Qur'ānic verses. His intent is to evoke the long-awaited dream of an Islamic caliphate in his listeners and encourage its realization:[40]

> ...The umma has not tasted honor since it lost it. It is a dream that lives in the depths of every Muslim believer. It is a hope that flutters in the heart of every mujāhid muwahhid (monotheist). It is the khilāfah (caliphate). It is the khilāfah—the abandoned obligation of the era....

Besides the ploy of emotional appeal, al-'Adnānī enlists the use of authoritative religious texts to buttress his remarks. In the 34-minute audio file, he cites twenty-five Qur'ānic verses and four *ḥadīths*, plus the noteworthy Islamic interpretations.[41] The huge repertoire of religious texts and Islamic jurisprudence indicates that his statements have been skillfully drafted and refined with a skill that only highly knowledgeable and experienced jurists and imams in the Muslim world can match.

Among the texts used by al-'Adnānī in his message is Q 2.30: *"And when your Lord said to the angels, I am going to place in the earth a khalif..."* (Shakir trans.). In his explanation of this verse, al-'Adnānī cites highly respected Muslim exegete al-Qurṭubī (AD 1214-1273):[42]

---

[40] al-'Adnānī, *This is the Promise of Allah* [English transcript] 4; audio file: http://www.dailymotion.com/video/x3u3iol.

[41] Ibid. 1-11.

[42] Ibid. See the commentary on Q 2.30, *Tafsīr al-Qurtubī* 1: 279. **Note:** Another English translation of al-Qurtubī's commentary of this passage by Aisha Bewley (203) reads, "This āyat is sound evidence for having a leader and a khalif who is obeyed so that he will be a focus for the cohesion of society, and the rulings of the khalifate will [be] carried out. None of the Imams of the Community disagree about the obligatory nature of having such a leader...."

> ...This verse is a fundamental basis for the appointment of a leader and khalīfah (caliph) who is listened to and obeyed so that the umma is united by him and his orders are carried out. There is no dispute over this matter between the umma nor between the scholars....

According to al-Qurtubī, Muslim scholars unanimously agree on the mandatory nature of the caliphate. Thus, the audacity of ISIS to declare itself the Islamic caliphate was an embarrassment for today's religious scholars who have been advocating for one throughout these many years but have been unable to implement it. With the ISIS declaration on June 29, 2014 as Islamic State, the long-awaited vision of an Islamic caliphate materialized into a reality that could not be ignored.

Moreover, al-'Adnānī admonishes Muslims, reminding them that failure to declare a legitimate caliphal succession is a punishable sin:[43]

> ...Therefore, the shūrā (consultation) council of the Islamic State studied this matter after the Islamic State—by Allah's grace—gained the essentials necessary for khilāfah, which Muslims are sinful for if they do not try to establish. In light of the fact that the Islamic State has no shar'ī (legal) constraint or excuse that can justify delaying or neglecting the establishment of the khilāfah such that it would not be sinful, the Islamic State—represented by ahlul-halli-wal'aqd (its people of authority), consisting of its senior figures, leaders, and the shūrā council—resolved to announce the establishment of the Islamic khilāfah, the appointment of a khalīfah for the Muslims, and the pledge of allegiance to the shaykh (sheikh)....

The ISIS declaration brought into existence an Islamic caliphate—Islamic State—headed by one caliph—Abū Bakr al-Baghdadī. If the required conditions of the one caliphate and one caliph are met, then the rest of the Islamic states and kingdoms must be abolished. Otherwise, they become by default illegitimate opponents of a legitimate succession, and they must be fought and overcome.

Islamic State followed the precedent set by the early Companions. Its shūrā council of the *mujāhidīn* gathered in a meeting, just like Muḥammad's Companions at the Saqīfa meeting shortly after the Prophet's death, to choose and pledge allegiance to a caliph.

---

[43] al-'Adnānī, *This is the Promise of Allah* [English transcript] 5; audio file: http://www.dailymotion.com/video/x3u3iol.

Obviously mindful of this first caliphal pledge of allegiance, al-ʿAdnānī urges all Muslims to support Abū Bakr al-Baghdadī:[44]

> ...We clarify to the Muslims that with this declaration of khilāfah, it is incumbent upon all Muslims to pledge allegiance to the khalīfah Ibrāhīm [Abū Bakr al-Baghdadī] and support him (may Allah preserve him). The legality of all emirates, groups, states, and organizations, becomes null by the expansion of the khilāfah's authority and arrival of its troops to their areas....

A legitimate declaration of an Islamic caliphate is supported by the teachings of Muslim scholars and clerics. Many of today's imams state that they dream of an Islamic caliphate and envision its possibility in the near future. Young people, groomed by their religious teachers and imams since childhood to yearn for and work toward one Islamic caliphate, are especially susceptible to sophisticated propaganda wrapped in Qur'ānic verses and these Islamic teachings by Islamic organizations.

The fruition of this indoctrination among Muslim youth means that when ISIS made its proclamation of an Islamic caliphate, this long-held dream of a unified Islamic state became a nightmare for those Muslim countries that have allowed—even encouraged—these teachings of an inevitable Islamic caliphate and legitimate caliphal succession on their national Web sites and curriculum yet at the same time disregarded them in public policy. When young Muslims began leaving their countries to join Islamic State's caliphate, these countries could not credibly refute the establishment of an Islamic caliphate because they had supported and promoted this doctrine. Their only recourse has been to question the legitimacy of Islamic State's caliphate and its appointed caliph.

It is not a coincidence that the leader of Islamic State chose to rename himself after the first Muslim caliph after Muḥammad's death: Abū Bakr. (Recall that the birthname of Abū Bakr al-Baghdādī is Ibrāhīm ʿAwwād Ibrāhīm.) Abū Bakr al-Baghdādī's obvious intention is to portray Islamic State as the restoration of the first caliphate at the time of Abū Bakr. Like Abū Bakr who fought against apostate tribes (the Ridda Wars) when he became the caliph, Abū Bakr al-Baghdādī has declared war on those Muslim countries that Islamic State considers in a state of apostasy and are not living the true Islam.

---

[44] al-ʿAdnānī, *This is the Promise of Allah* [English transcript] 5; audio file: http://www.dailymotion.com/video/x3u3iol.

Part of Islamic State's belligerence and condemnation toward most of the Muslim world stems from the dismemberment of the Ottoman Empire and the abolition of the caliphate following the end of World War I. During the Great War, several of the Allied Powers—Great Britain, France, imperial Russia (and later Italy)—secretly agreed to divide up the Ottoman Empire (after its predicted fall) among the interested parties. The final arrangement, the Sykes–Picot Agreement (named after the two main negotiators), was completed in 1916.[45] In partitioning and redrawing the borders of this immense region, the dissemblers arbitrarily cut through ethnic, linguistic, and religious lines, ignorant or uncaring of the impact on these affected communities. Today's current boundaries of Iraq, Syria, Lebanon, and Jordan still reflect the decisions of this agreement.[46]

This partitioning of the Middle East is considered sacrilegious and against Islamic doctrines in the eyes of Islamic State. It blames the affected Muslim countries for their defeatist submission to the Western infidels, who divided up the Ottoman Empire according to Westerners' instructions and self-interests. Islamic State believes the time has come for one state to restore the Islamic caliphate, a caliphate that will liberate the Muslim world from the infidel Western idols of secularism, democracy and all foreign values, as stated in its declaration:[47]

> ...By Allah, if you disbelieve in democracy, secularism, and nationalism, as well as all the other garbage and ideas from the west, and rush to your religion and creed, then by Allah, you will own the earth, and the east and west will submit to you. This is the promise of Allah to you. This is the promise of Allah to you....

Shortly before the declaration of the caliphate, ISIS published a propaganda video entitled *Breaking of the Borders* (i.e., borders between

---

[45] "A Century On: Why Arabs Resent Sykes-Picot." *Interactive.Aljazeera.com*. Al Jazeera Media Network/ Al Jazeera Centre for Studies, 18 Sept. 2017. Web (https://interactive.aljazeera.com/aje/2016/sykes-picot-100-years-middle-east-map/).

[46] **Note:** After World War I, the Sykes-Picot Agreement was replaced by the 1920 San Remo Resolution. The four main countries represented at this conference—Great Britain, France, Japan, and Italy—agreed to provisionally recognize Syria and Mesopotamia but not Palestine. Mandates over several of the territories carved out of the prior Ottoman Empire were claimed by Great Britain (Palestine, Iraq) and France (Syria, Lebanon), and a peace treaty agreement with Turkey was drafted. Great Britain and France also signed an agreement to share Iraqi oil, including its production and delivery to Mediterranean ports.

[47] al-'Adnānī, *This is the Promise of Allah* [English transcript] 6; audio file: http://www.dailymotion.com/ video/x3u3iol.

Syria and Iraq).[48] (See Chapter 8, page 221.) Through symbolic imagery, Qur'ānic and *ḥadīth* references, and poetry, this twelve-minute video evokes the desire of a unified Islamic nation and the removal of Western-established borders between Muslim countries. The opening scene shows a breached earthen wall with ISIS vehicles lumbering through the now opened border. The video's voice-over chanting begins with a verse from a poem:[49] "Receive the glad tidings, O my nation / For we have crossed the borders / Of the grandchildren of the apes / They are no longer on our lands."

Soon Abū 'Umar al-Shīshānī and Abū Muḥammad al-'Adnānī are shown, prostrating in thankful prayer (Sajdat al-Shukr) and leading the rest of the fighters. The clear message from this scene is that the destruction of this earthen border wall between two Muslim countries is a victory from Allah and a reminder of a *sunna* Muslims learned from Muḥammad: "...when the Prophet heard any news that made him glad, he would fall down prostrating to Allah, may He be exalted."[50]

During this video, ISIS members speak, one at a time. When it is al-'Adnānī's turn to speak, he begins with a clear reference to Muḥammad ("...and may peace and blessings be upon he who was sent with sword in hand as a mercy to all Creation") and then continues with the following statements:[51]

> The promise of Allah (may He be exalted and glorified) included the words of His Prophet, the truthful and trustworthy: "Then shall the Caliphate arise upon the path of the prophethood." What then, after the dissolution of these borders? The borders of humiliation! And after the smashing of this idol? The idol of patriotism! What could come next other than the establishment of the Caliphate upon the path of the prophethood? Should God, may He be blessed and exalted, permit it? It shall be achieved, not merely hoped for...the borders will be erased from the map and removed from the hearts.

'Adnānī is claiming that the purpose of the Caliphate is the unification of the Islamic nation under one banner and the declaration of jihad to

---

[48] Islamic State of Iraq and al-Sham (ISIS). *Breaking of the Borders. Jihadology.net.* Al-I'tisām Media, 29 June 2014. Video. (To view video, see URL: http://preview.tinyurl.com/yd8yhfaf)

[49] Ibid.

[50] al-Bayhaqī, *Al-Sunan al-Kubra* 3: 334; see Chapter "Prostration of Thankfulness."

[51] Islamic State of Iraq and al-Sham (ISIS). *Breaking of the Borders. Jihadology.net.* Al-I'tisām Media, 29 June 2014. Video. (To view video, see URL: http://preview.tinyurl.com/yd8yhfaf) **Note:** Al-'Adnānī's statement occurs approximately 3:40 to 4:50 minutes in the video.

subjugate the whole world, just as Muḥammad did and his Companions after him. The first Companion to carry on Muḥammad's work was his successor Abū Bakr.

And now with Islamic State's Abū Bakr al-Baghdadī, Muslims have their second Abū Bakr to restore the glories lost by the *umma*. To ISIS and its supporters, this Abū Bakr will revive the caliphate through Islamic State.

Prescribed conditions of the caliph

Does this new caliph, Abū Bakr al-Baghdadī, fulfill all the required conditions? One condition stipulates that the caliph must be Qurayshi in order for Muslims to accept his leadership. For this reason, al-'Adnānī clarifies in the ISIS declaration of the Islamic caliphate that the "khalīfah Ibrāhīm [Abū Bakr al-Baghdadī], may Allah preserve him, has fulfilled all the conditions for khilāfah mentioned by the scholars" and the "people of authority in the Islamic State" in Iraq have pledged allegiance to him as the rightful "imam and khalīfah for the Muslims everywhere."[52] Al-'Adnānī and the religious authoritative leaders of Islamic State know very well the Islamic legitimate conditions of a successor, so they did not just arbitrarily choose Ibrāhīm 'Awwād Ibrāhīm.

The most important consideration is confirmation that Abū Bakr al-Baghdādī is a descendant of the Prophet. Having this lineage would prove he is Qurayshi; only a Qurayshi is deserving of the caliphate, according to the words of Muḥammad: "the Caliphate is in Quraysh"[53] and the "Caliphate will remain among the Quraysh even if only two persons are left (on the earth),"[54] and "[a]uthority of ruling will remain with Quraish, and whoever bears hostility to them, Allah will destroy him as long as they [Quraysh] abide by the laws of the religion [Islam]."[55] Al-'Adnānī documents al-Baghdādī's lineage and upbringing and alludes to these *ḥadīths* in his statement.

The other condition is that allegiance must be pledged to the new caliph. This pledge of allegiance is not required of the general Muslim

[52] al-'Adnānī. *This is the Promise of Allah* [English transcript] 5; audio file: http://www.dailymotion.com/video/x3u3iol.

[53] *Musnad Aḥmād* 5: 202.

[54] *Sahih Muslim*, Book on Government: The people are subservient to the Quraish and the caliphate is the right of the Quraish (pp. 1137-1138); *Ṣaḥīḥ Muslim*, Kītāb al-Imāra 2: 882; See *Sahih Bukhari*, Book on Virtues and Merits of the Prophet and His Companions (p. 816).

[55] *Sahih Bukhari*, Book on Virtues and Merits of the Prophet and His Companions (pp. 815-816); *Ṣaḥīḥ al-Bukhārī*, Kītāb al-Manāqib 3: 1289.

population; in actuality, religious authoritative leaders pledge their allegiance to the new caliph. For instance, during the pledge of allegiance to the first appointed caliph, Abū Bakr ("Caliph of Muslims"), not all the early Muslims were present at that installation meeting. Only a small group of people, representing just a small category of Muslims (Emigrants and Helpers) participated in that first caliphal pledge. When 'Uthmān Ibn 'Affān was appointed the third caliph, only six people participated in this decision.[56] Therefore, based on these historical examples and the Hadith literature, it would be difficult for any Muslim jurist or scholar to challenge this succession as invalid on the pretext that it does not meet the required conditions, because these conditions have been shown to be very flexible in the past. Essentially, the Islamic religious sources support any caliphal succession as long as the new caliph is from the Quraysh and is chosen by a group of Muslims.

However, when ISIS declared Islamic State as the new caliphate and Abū Bakr al-Baghdādī the new caliph, Sheikh Yūsuf al-Qaraḍāwī, chairman of the IUMS, objected, proclaiming the declaration as a "falsehood."[57] IUMS issued a formal denouncement, stating that the ISIS declaration "does not meet several legitimate conditions," particularly the principle that the caliph must be a representative from the entire Muslim nation and not a certain Muslim organization.[58] These objections seem strange because none of the caliphs of earlier Islamic states ever met this condition. In fact, when has the entire Muslim nation agreed on and pledged allegiance to one successor in all of Islam's history? Hasn't the historical pattern been a small group of people making this caliphal decision for the rest of the Muslim nation? Have the Shiites and Sunnis ever agreed on one successor? Did 'Alī willingly yield the first caliphate to Abū Bakr or did Abū Bakr deviously take it? Did all Muslims agree to choose 'Umar as the second caliph and 'Uthmān as the third caliph?

Furthermore, Abū Bakr al-Baghdādī is a religious scholar and holds a doctorate in Islamic law;[59] he once even worked as an imam of a

---

[56] *History of al-Tabari* 14: 91-92.

[57] "Al-Qaradawi Considers the Declaration of Caliphate in Iraq Legally Invalid." *Alquds.co.uk*. Al-Quds al-Arabi, 5 July 2014. Web (http://www.alquds.co.uk/?p=189112).

[58] Ibid.

[59] Insite Blog on Terrorism and Extremism. "A Biography of Abu Bakr al-Baghdadi." *SITEintelgroup.com*. SITE Intelligence Group, 12 Aug. 2014. Web (http://news.siteintelgroup.com/blog/index.php/entry/226-the-story-behind-abu-bakr-al-baghdadi).

mosque in Samarra, a city north of Baghdad, Iraq.[60] So, in addition to his reported lineage as a descendant of the Quraysh tribe, Abū Bakr al-Baghdādī possesses sufficient religious authority through his extensive religious education and upbringing: He has fulfilled all the necessary required conditions. Even if he has forcefully instituted his authority, some Muslim scholars claim that this imposition does not disqualify his caliphal succession and thus it should not be contested.

Al-'Adnānī underscores the legitimacy of the ISIS declaration by quoting highly venerated and influential Arab Muslim jurist and theologian Ahmad Ibn Hanbal, or "Imām Aḥmad" (AD 780-855; founder of the Ḥanbalī doctrine), to clarify the Islamic ruling, especially for those committed Muslims who seek to know the opinion of the Islamic law regarding this caliphate: "Imam Ahmad (may Allah have mercy upon him) said…'It is not permissible for anyone who believes in Allah to sleep without considering as his leader whoever conquers them by the sword until he becomes caliph and is called Amīrul Mu'minīn (the leader of the believers), whether this leader is righteous or sinful.'"[61]

This situation of a forced caliphal succession has precedence in Islamic history. When 'Abd al-Malik Ibn Marwān (AD 646-705) became the fifth Umayyad caliph in AD 685 after the death of his father Marwan I, he faced opposition from several Muslim factions, particularly 'Abd Allah Ibn al-Zubayr,[62] who had been named caliph in Mecca. ('Abd al-Malik resided in Damascus.) 'Abd al-Malik Ibn Marwān appointed al-Ḥajjāj Ibn Yūsuf as his general and ordered him to deal with all the rebel groups. After subduing the smaller factions, al-Ḥajjāj focused his attention on Ibn al-Zubayr, who was entrenched in Mecca. Al-Ḥajjāj and his Syrian troops besieged Mecca, using trebuchets and other means, for over six months.[63] Al-Ḥajjāj finally achieved a brutal victory when the outnumbered Meccans gave up the way stations, and Ibn Zubayr was killed in the ensuing fighting.[64] (His decapitated body was crucified

---

[60] "Profile: Abu Bakr al-Baghdadi." *BBC.com.* British Broadcasting Corporation, 15 May 2015. Web (http://www.bbc.com/news/world-middle-east-27801676).

[61] al-'Adnānī. *This is the Promise of Allah* [English transcript] 5; audio file: http://www.dailymotion.com/video/x3u3iol. See Ibn Duwaiyan, *Manār al-Sabīl* 2: 399.

[62] 'Abd Allah Ibn al-Zubayr (AD 624-692) was an Arab Companion whose maternal grandfather was Abū Bakr, the first caliph. Ibn al-Zubayr refused to pledge his allegiance to Yazid I, who became the second Umayyad caliph in AD 680, and offered his support instead to 'Alī's son, Husayn. When Husayn was assassinated that same year, the Meccan people pledged their allegiance to Ibn al-Zubayr.

[63] *History of al-Ṭabarī* 21: 225; see footnotes 801, 802.

[64] Ibid. 21: 225-232.

and his head delivered to Caliph 'Abd al-Malik.)[65] Al-Ḥajjāj, acting as an extension of 'Abd al-Malik, ruthlessly compelled the defeated Muslim groups to submit to him. And yet 'Abd al-Malik Ibn Marwān was called the "Caliph of the Muslims."[66]

Therefore, it should not be surprising that someone like Abū Bakr al-Baghdādī can be declared the caliph based on the consultation and decision of his exclusive Islamic group, because he knows very well that taking power "by the sword" has historical precedence and is acceptable according to Islamic law.

Caliphates of the past and today

The *mujāhidīn* and members of Islamic groups will take on for themselves alternative names that they know are familiar to and will resonate within the Muslim world. These nicknames will often be the names of early renowned Muslim leaders or early followers heralded for their piety, a special gift, or a courageous act. For example, jihadist Abū Muṣ'ab al-Zarqāwī (see Chapter 8, page 203) chose the name *Muṣ'ab* because it is the name of an early Companion, Muṣ'ab Ibn 'Umayr, who was known as an early ambassador for Islam[67] and died a martyr in the Battle of Uḥud while defending Muḥammad.[68] As already mentioned, Abū Bakr al-Baghdādī chose the name *Abū Bakr*, reviving the name of the first Muslim caliph, which paired powerfully with Muslims with the subsequent ISIS declaration of the new caliphate.[69]

To strengthen the connection between the first Muslim caliph, Abū Bakr, and the ISIS declaration of the new caliphate and its new caliph Abū Bakr al-Baghdādī, al-Baghdādī included text in his inaugural speech as caliph that was nearly a carbon copy of Abū Bakr's first sermon, when he was given the caliphate after the death of Muḥammad, as reported in his biography:[70]

---

[65] *History of al-Ṭabarī* 21: 226; see footnote 807.

[66] Ibn Duwaiyan, *Manār al-Sabīl* 2: 399.

[67] *History of al-Ṭabarī* 6: 127-130.

[68] Ibid. 7: 121; *Tafsīr al-Ṭabarī* 4: 93.

[69] Mosendz, Polly. "How the Head of ISIS Got His Name." *Newsweek.com*. Newsweek, 8 Nov. 2014. Web (http://www.newsweek.com/abu-bakr-al-baghdadi-abu-dua-invisible-sheikh-awwad-ibrahim-ali-al-badri-al-282939).

[70] Ibn Hishām (Ibn Isḥāq), *The Life of Muḥammad* 687; Ibn Hishām (Ibn Isḥāq), *Al-Sīra al-Nabawīya* 4: 450.

> Abū Bakr said after praising God: "I have been given authority over you but I am not the best of you. If I do well, help me, and if I do ill, then put me right.... Obey me as long as I obey God and His Apostle, and if I disobey them you owe me no obedience."

Abū Bakr, the first Muslim caliph, uttered these words after the pledge of allegiance by the Saqīfa meeting participants, followed by the sworn fealty to Abū Bakr by "the people...as a body."[71]

Similarly, Abū Bakr al-Baghdādī repeated much of the same ideas, if not always identical language, in his first Friday sermon, which was broadcasted from the Great Mosque in Mosul on the sixth day of Ramadan. The length of this speech (together with the prayers) was about twenty-one minutes and included the following text:[72]

> ...I am the *wālī* (leader) who presides over you, though I am not the best among you, so if you see that I am right, assist me.... If you see that I am wrong, advise me and put me back on the right track, and obey me as long as I obey God in you....

The first sermons of early Muslim caliph Abū Bakr and Islamic State's caliph Abū Bakr al-Baghdādī are unmistakably parallel. Does this close similarity indicate that Islamic State is trying to imitate if not directly replicate the text stated in the Prophet's biography? The religious leaders of these Islamic military organizations know Islam more than the mainstream (mostly government-appointed) sheikhs. These Islamic organizations don't just read Islamic holy texts to observe it for blessings only—they try to apply it. In contrast, the sheikhs who hold official religious positions of leadership try to please the authorities by beautifying or glossing over the texts of jihad and fighting when reading and explaining them but are silent about their implementation.

---

[71] Ibn Hishām (Ibn Isḥāq), *The Life of Muḥammad* 687; Ibn Hishām (Ibn Isḥāq), *Al-Sīra al-Nabawīya* 4: 450. **Note:** In June 2012, newly elected Egyptian president Mohamed Morsi of the Muslim Brotherhood used similar language in his acceptance speech: "I will be available to you. Help me fulfill my role before God." See Haggag, Mohamed, Hany Osman, and Ismail Refaat. "Video: President Morsi in His First Speech after His Arrival to the Throne: Without the Martyrs' Blood in the Revolution, There Would Be No Freedom...I Will Be Impartial toward Everyone...." *Youm7.com*. Youm 7 [The Seventh Day], 24 June 2012. Web (http://preview.tinyurl.com/zjape9o).

[72] Strange, Hannah. "Islamic State Leader Abu Bakr al-Baghdadi Addresses Muslims in Mosul." *Telegraph.co.uk*. Telegraph Media Group, 5 July 2014. Web (http://www.telegraph.co.uk/news/worldnews/middleeast/iraq/10948480/Islamic-State-leader-Abu-Bakr-al-Baghdadi-addresses-Muslims-in-Mosul.html; to view video of speech, see URL: http://preview.tinyurl.com/jet6v7d).

When my father, an imam, would read, all day and all night, the "fighting" verses,[73] I would always ask him why he was content to read them only—why not implement them? He would answer me by saying that his circumstances did not enable him to implement them. This response means that if he were in better circumstances to put them into action, he would try to do so, and this opinion applies to the other sheikhs.

Those sheikhs whose "circumstances" do not enable or allow them to embark on jihad themselves will instead incite their followers and issue fatāwa explaining the texts. Yet, when a chance for implementation appears, these same sheikhs quietly retreat from their earlier fiery calls for action, leaving the poor enthusiastic youth to stand, abandoned, in front of the cannon. These hypocritical sheikhs are only too willing to motivate the sons of the *umma* to seek martyrdom through jihad—just not their own sons or themselves.

But Islamic State has taken upon itself the responsibility of seriously applying the texts on the ground. And the young enthusiastic Muslims, weary of listening to the impotent reprimands of their country's religious leaders while watching their nation collapsing under political, economic, and social crises, are receptive to the visceral message and action of Islamic State and similar Islamic groups. These Islamic groups welcome these passionate young Muslims, channeling their desire to restore the glories of the past by entreating them to join their jihadi ranks and take up the sword with them.

The goal of Islamic State and similar groups is not new; the dream of an all-encompassing Islamic caliphate has been established and nurtured in these young Muslims, repeatedly reinforced through various educational means and pressed into their consciousness and subconsciousness, so that they are especially prepared to receive, accept, and respond to calls and movements claiming they will restore the glories of this so-called dream caliphate.

Islamic State has massacred many people of the Shiite Muslim sect, slandering them with various ugly names as a way to degrade and deny their Muslim belief. In most videos that show their execution by Islamic

[73] These are Qur'ānic verses, such as the Sword verse (Q 9.5), that direct Muslims to fight non-Muslims until they accept Islam. These verses include (but are not limited to) Q 9.29 (*"Fight those who believe not in God..."*; Palmer trans.) and Q 9.73 (*"O Prophet, struggle with the unbelievers and hypocrites, and be thou harsh with them..."*; Arberry trans.). See Meselmani, *The Sword Verse: Qur'ānic Weapon Against Peace?*

State fighters (and precursors, ISIL and ISIS), the captives are called out as "apostates," "Safavid army,"[74] and "Rawāfiḍ."[75] ISIS fighters called the Shiite Alawites in Syria the "Nuṣayrī-'Alawīs."[76] All these names are derived from old Islamic sects with the purpose of using them to insult these particular religious groups and denounce them as apostates and not true followers of Islam. Why?

This religious name-calling and labeling began during the first civil wars when Caliph Abū Bakr launched military campaigns against Muslims whom he considered apostates because they stopped paying the *zakāt* (religious financial obligation) after Muḥammad died. Therefore, when today's politicians, writers, and journalists state that Islamic State (and precursors, ISIL and ISIS) has killed more Muslims than non-Muslims, as a pretext to show that Islamic State has nothing to do with Islam, they must be either dismissive or ignorant of historical examples, such as the first caliph, Abū Bakr, who also killed more Muslims than non-Muslims. The fourth caliph 'Alī Ibn Abū Ṭālib killed four thousand of his former followers, the Kharijites, during the Battle of Nahrawān (AD 659).[77] During the already mentioned Battle of the Camel, tens of thousands of Muslims died as a result of a political conflict between 'Ā'isha and 'Alī (AD 656).[78] Nearly seventy thousand Muslims were killed in the Battle of Ṣiffīn (AD 657), a military engagement between the forces of the two rival caliphs, 'Alī and Mu'awiyah, battling for dominance.[79] If all these early Muslims were killed during the best era of Islam, why should the killing of Muslims by Islamic groups today be judged "un-Islamic"?

So, given this overwhelming historical precedence, how can people deny that Islamic State is an Islamic entity because it is fighting against other Islamic groups? If this perceived principle—Muslims do not fight against Muslims—is applied to the early Muslim leaders, such as Abū

---

[74] This term *Safavid* refers to the Safavid dynasty in Iran that was fighting against the Ottoman Empire.

[75] This term *Rawāfiḍ*, or Rejecters, refers to Muslim Shiites who reject the caliphal legitimacy of Abū Bakr, 'Umar, and 'Uthmān, accepting only 'Alī and his descendants. Sunni Muslims condemn this rejection as contemptible.

[76] This term *Nuṣayrī* refers to the *Nusayriyyah*, an extreme Shiite sect with a doctrine that is a mixture of Islamic, Gnostic, and Christian beliefs. Sunni Muslims consider Nusayris as heretics for their belief in 'Alī as the incarnation of God, the reincarnation of men, and the rejection of the Qur'ān and praying practices associated with Sunni tradition.

[77] Ibn Kathīr, *Al-Bidāya* 9: 203-204.

[78] Ibid. 10: 469-470.

[79] Ibn Abū Shayba, *Al-Musannaf* 8: 725. Excerpt: The "number of the dead on the day of Ṣiffīn reached seventy thousand, and when they were not able to count them, they put a cane on each body then they counted all the canes."

Bakr, 'Ā'isha, 'Alī, Mu'āwiya, and 'Abd Allah Ibn al-Zubayr, then all of them would be considered non-Muslims. Moreover, the Qur'ān itself does not support this principle of Muslims not fighting other Muslims. It explains that fighting between Muslims is probable; in fact, it is even permissible for Muslims to fight against a certain group of Muslims until they submit to the rule of Allah: *"If two parties of the believers fight, put things right between them; then, if one of them is insolent against the other, fight the insolent one till it reverts to God's commandment. If it reverts, set things right between them equitably, and be just. Surely God loves the just"* (Q 49.9; Arberry trans.).

I have previously explained in earlier sections of this book that Shiites are considered infidels and not Muslims, according to Sunnis. Targeting Shiites is a high priority for Sunni-supported Islamic State, because fighting the close enemy comes before fighting the distant enemy. It prioritizes the killing of the close enemy—infidels and apostates—because in its eyes these two groups are more dangerous than the far enemy. This policy is one of the most important differences between Islamic State and Al Qaeda. (Occasionally, some member or supporter of Islamic State or precursors ISIL and ISIS may have carried out an individual terrorist operation in the West, but this kind of action has not been generally pursued by this organization until it began to lose territory in Syria and Iraq. Its policies and tactics have been changing recently because it has been the facing increasing attacks from multiple fronts.) Foremost for Islamic State has been the cleansing of the land within its Islamic caliphate of all apostate Shiites before recovering the rest of the foreign lands for the caliphate.

Even Islam's great imams and scholars of the past consider the Shiites as infidels. The famous (and controversial) medieval *faqīh* Ibn Taymīya discusses the first instance of Muslim heresy:[80]

> ...the first heresy that occurred in Islam was the heresy of the Kharijites and the Shiites. It occurred during the succession of...'Alī Ibn Abū Ṭālib, and so he punished the two sects. The Kharijites fought him and so he killed them. And as for the Shiites, he burned most of them with fire.

This is the same 'Alī that Shiites revere as the only legitimate caliph among the four caliphs installed during the Rashidun caliphate, the first

[80] Ibn Taymīya, *Majmū' Fatāwā* 3: 279.

caliphate established after Muḥammad's death. Even Sunnis honor him for his critical role as one of Muḥammad's closest Companions and one of his most talented military leaders and fighters as well as 'Alī's personal relationship through blood and marriage to the Prophet. Yet Islamic sources report that this important symbol of Islam, i.e., "Prince of the Believers," burned Muslim Shiites with fire and killed thousands of other Muslims.

Ibn Taymīya is even more negative about Alawite Shiites:[81]

> These people who are called Nuṣayrīyyah (Nusayris) and other varieties of Al-Qarāmiṭa Al-Baṭiniyya are more *kuffār* (infidels) than Jews and Christians, and even more *kuffār* than polytheists. And their damage to the nation of Muḥammad is far greater than the damage of infidel fighters.

So with these historical examples of important Muslim leaders (e.g., 'Alī) and scholars (e.g., Ibn Taymīya) castigating—and even killing—Shiites, should it be surprising to see Islamic State (and precursors) focus its attacks against Shiites wherever its fighters find them? Personally, I wasn't surprised when ISIL brutally treated the captured Camp Speicher cadets by killing hundreds of them and dumping them in mass graves.[82] (Most of the cadets were Shiites.)

Since Muḥammad's death, hostility and bloodshed between two major Muslim sects, Sunni and Shiites, have never ceased because of Muslim leaders and caliphs of one sect targeting the other. Imams and scholars demonizing one sect over another does not adequately honor Allah or practice true Islam. Consequently, this centuries-old religious blood feud influences Sunnis to sympathize and support Islamic State, because they both agree that Shiites are as bad as (or worse than) Jews and Christians. There is no room for coexistence between these two sects as long as the past still manipulates the conscience and emotions of these Muslims.

"Reality" and illusion of a caliphate

Although Muslim countries do not have an official caliphate, they have tried to implement it in such a way to give their citizens the perception

[81] Ibn Taymīya, *Majmū' Fatāwā* 35: 143.

[82] See "ISIS Militants Executed Up to 770 Iraqi Troops in Tikrit—Report." *RT.com*. RT (formerly Russia Today), 4 Sept. 2014. Web (https://www.rt.com/news/184893-isis-mass-execution-iraq/). See also Baker, Aryn. "ISIS Claims Massacre of 1700 Iraqi Soldiers." *Time.com*. Time Inc., 15 June 2014. Web (http://time.com/2878718/isis-claims-massacre-of-1700-iraqis).

that they are close to a caliphate to gain religious legitimacy. For example, when the Alaouite dynasty (the family of the current ruler of Morocco, King Mohammed VI) forcibly took control of the country from the Saadi dynasty in the seventeenth century AD, it claimed descent from the Prophet Muḥammad, through his daughter Fatima and her husband 'Alī. Since then, each king of Morocco is called the "Prince of Believers," a religious title similar to "caliph," which means "successor." (The first Muslim leader to be named "Prince of Believers" was second caliph 'Umar Ibn al-Khaṭṭāb; the first caliph Abū Bakr was called "Caliph of the Muslims." It would have been confusing to call 'Umar "Caliph of the Caliph of the Apostle of Allah," i.e., "Successor of the successor of Muḥammad," and so this new title, "Prince of Believers" was created. 'Umar was the first to be given this title in the history of Islam.)[83]

Today the King of Morocco holds this title, for he is considered a Qurayshi and a descendant of Prophet Muḥammad. With this title, he assumes religious authority as well as political power over his country, and his role and position hints of the possibility of a caliphate under a Qurayshi caliph.

Because religion was used during Islam's history for the assimilation and rule over conquered peoples, many Muslim people today still do not choose their leaders based on their wisdom, credentials, and experience through democratic means. More consideration is given to the relationship of blood pedigree and kinship, and the bloodline of the "king" is considered more honorable than the rest of the bloodlines or races; therefore, he is deemed worthy to judge and rule over those with a less honorable bloodline. This Muslim gravitation to form a state ruled by a "honorable" Qurayshi stems from Islam's teachings about the caliphate, where the Quraysh are exalted, considered the best to rule over all other Muslims. This religious belief is really a form of discrimination or even racism.

A similar ruler succession process occurred with the formation of the Kingdom of Jordan in 1924. Ḥusayn Ibn 'Alī (c. AD 1853-1931), a Hashemite Arab leader, was the Sharif and Emir of Mecca (which indicates he is a descendant of Muḥammad through Fatīma and 'Alī) in 1908, and in 1916 he led the Arab revolt against the Ottoman Empire, proclaiming himself the "King of the Hijaz" (King of the Arab countries)

---

[83] Ibn Sa'd, *Al-Ṭabaqāt al-Kubra* 3: 281.

as well. After the end of World War I and the collapse and partitioning of the Ottoman Caliphate and the abolition of the caliphate, he announced himself "Caliph of all Muslims" in March 1924. However, Ibn Sa'ūd (soon to become the first monarch and founder of today's Saudi Arabia) invaded his kingdom, and Ḥusayn, facing defeat, abdicated in favor of his eldest son 'Alī in October 1924 and then fled to Cyprus. The following year the Saudi forces succeeded in taking over the Hijaz and incorporating it with the rest of Saudi Arabia. 'Alī and his family fled to Iraq.

Ḥusayn's other sons, 'Abdullah and Faisal, were installed with British support as the King of Jordan and King of Iraq, respectively. If not for their genealogy, they would not have been able to be the kings of these two countries.

This Hashemite dynasty continues to rule Jordan (current leader is King Abdullah II), but a bloody military coup in Iraq in 1958 effectively terminated its Hashemite rule and succession. Young King Faisal II, his regent (and relative) 'Abd al-llah, and the prime minister Nuri al-Sa'id were killed, and various military and political leaders of no particular religious heritage have governed Iraq ever since. Some Muslim countries, such as Egypt, are governed through military rule, but all Muslim countries are generally governed through some sort of religious or military rule (or a combination of both types); true representative democracy is a superficiality.

Saudi Arabia's government presents the example of a marriage between kingship and religion. In eighteenth-century AD, the Arab religious leader and theologian, Muḥammad Ibn 'Abd al-Wahhab, preached an austere form of Islam, advocating that Muslims follow and practice the basic tenets of their religion, or "pure" Islam. (See Chapter 7, page 164.) His teachings and actions produced considerable controversy, and he faced possible assassination or exile. At this point, he was introduced to a powerful Arab emir, Muḥammad Ibn Sa'ūd (d. AD 1765). In AD 1744, the two men forged an alliance of mutual noninterference: Ibn 'Abd al-Wahhab agreed not to block Ibn Sa'ūd's plans to conquer the entire Arabian Peninsula, and, in return, Ibn Sa'ūd agreed to support Ibn 'Abd al-Wahhab's strict interpretation of Islam.[84] Marriage between

[84] "A Chronology: The House of Saud." *PBS.org.* Frontline (WGBH Educational Foundation), 1 Aug. 2005. Web (http://www.pbs.org/wgbh/pages/frontline/shows/saud/cron/); Ibn Ghalib, Hisham. "Salafi Saudi Arabia in the Field of Power." *Studies.Aljazeera.net.* Al Jazeera Media Network, 11 Apr. 2013. Web (http://studies.aljazeera.net/ar/reports/2013/04/20134794152127903.html).

emir Muḥammad Ibn Sa'ūd's son, 'Abd al-'Azīz, and sheikh Ibn 'Abd al-Wahhāb's daughter, "sealed the deal," and the First Saudi state (Emirate of Diriyah) was created.

The basic structure of this religious-political agreement between the Sa'ūd family and Wahhabis continued from that time up to (and beyond) the official establishment of the Kingdom of Saudi Arabia in 1932, when Ibn Sa'ūd (full name: 'Abd al-Aziz Ibn 'Abd al-Rahman Ibn Faisal Ibn Turki Ibn 'Abd Allah Ibn Muḥammad Ibn Sa'ūd), a direct descendent of Muḥammad Ibn Sa'ūd, founded it and reigned as its first monarch. As the first king of Saudi Arabia, Ibn Sa'ūd promoted and enforced a religious and political system based on Wahhabism. He also married daughters from all the important tribal clans and influential clerical families to solidify political and religious relationships.[85] Thus, he perpetuated the Sa'ūd family policy of mixing politics and religion to achieve and maintain religious authority and legitimacy regarding its monarchy. In 1986, King Fahd (AD 1921-2005), the fifth monarch of the Al Saud family to rule the Kingdom of Saudi Arabia, changed his title "His Majesty" to *Khādim al-Ḥaramayn al-Sharīfayn* ("The Custodian of the Two Holy Mosques"),[86] to signify and reinforce his religious authority.

Muslim countries will not be liberated nor enjoy a democratic atmosphere until they are liberated from these beliefs that dictate that a certain person is more honorable than others and is entitled to rule over others (which is far from democracy), and that the ruler who has the appropriate religious qualifications is more eligible to hold power and kingship than others. Those who believe in such ideas are still living in the Middle Ages. Muslim youth must be freed from these constraints of the past, the past that has kept them bound for fourteen centuries, so that they can catch up with today's modern civilization.

Yet Islamic State and similar Islamic groups continually emphasize and elevate Islam's past to whip up desire and dedication to this dream of a caliphate. The Islamic State slogan "Remain and Expand" is to remind itself and the world that the state of its caliphate has not ended and that it seeks to expand, like the early caliphates, in order to fulfill all its rightful

---

[85] "A Chronology: The House of Saud." *PBS.org*. Frontline (WGBH Educational Foundation), 1 Aug. 2005. Web (http://www.pbs.org/wgbh/pages/frontline/shows/saud/cron/).

[86] "King Fahd Ibn 'Abd al-Aziz al-Sa'ud." *MOFA.gov.sa*. Kingdom of Saudi Arabia Ministry of Foreign Affairs, 25 July 2014. Web (http://www.mofa.gov.sa/EServ/VisitingSaudiArabia/aboutKingDom/SaudiArabiaKings/Pages/KingFahadAbulAziz.aspx).

religious attributes. This slogan is a kind of psychological reassurance that is published by Islamic State and practiced by its members. Its fighters have even forced captives to recite it.[87]

The dream of the return of the caliphate has become an obsession for the majority of young Muslims, including Islamic State. This dream has exhausted the strength, creativity, and energy of young Muslims who try to find a reason to struggle for its sake and a formula for establishing it. For example, young members of the Muslim Brotherhood are struggling for the return of the Islamic caliphate based on the prophethood path, just like the young members of Al-'Adl wal Iḥsān (Justice and Charity) in Morocco and other similar Islamic groups. Eventually, they will all lose their youth for this illusion. For the dream of the return of the caliphate will not be fulfilled for many reasons, the most important being that it is just an illusion. And illusion is different from reality. And this illusion remains an illusion even if it possesses all of our being.

Reclaiming the Islamic caliphate has become a religious obsession among young Muslims. But because of these Islamic military organizations and terrorist groups, it has turned into a nightmare, a nightmare that kills innocents and fights for an imaginary empire that exists only in the minds of its believers. It is a delusional dream because reality in today's modern world imposes new relationships between and among countries, with different kinds of objectives and alliances. Is it even reasonable that all these Muslim countries can be ruled by one man under one entity?

In recent history, the Arab world has already witnessed unsuccessful efforts to establish alliances among themselves. In 1958, then Egyptian President Gamal Abdul Nasir wanted to unify the Arab world and started by forming a political union (United Arab Republic) with Syria, but this alliance lasted only three years (1958-1961). Iraq and Jordan, both initially instituted with Hashemite monarchies, have enjoyed deep ties since their establishment after World War II, especially during the 1970s through the 1990s, but the current crisis of Islamic State, the Syrian civil war, and Iranian influence in Iraq's politics have created tension between the two countries. There have also been attempts to unite the five countries of the Arab Maghreb (Morocco, Algeria, Tunisia, Libya, Mauritania), but all these attempts ultimately failed. With all these real

---

[87] "Video: When Members of al-Nusra Are in the Grip of ISIS." *Alarabiya.net*. Al Arabiya Network, 9 Dec. 2014. Web (http://preview.tinyurl.com/zu8jc4s). In the video, captured fighters of the Victory Front are forced to slap each other and repeat the Islamic State slogan, "Remain and Expand."

failed attempts at Arab/Muslim unification, what is the likelihood of the caliphate dream, where all Muslims are governed by one caliph? As long as there are divisions among religious doctrines and differences among races, then it is impossible to make this caliphate dream come true.

In spite of this impossibility, Islamic religious institutions urge young people to look to the past and to separate themselves from the future instead of encouraging them to work, to make an effort to integrate into the new world and accept cultural differences. In this way, these religious institutions have contributed in the creation of a dysfunctional generation of young people, a generation whose present is pulled down by the past, a lost generation that cannot ascertain the causes of its backwardness in the world because it believes that being "distant from religion" is the main factor for their own backwardness and the advancement of others. This generation even thinks that the entire world is plotting to separate them from their religion, and, therefore, they should tightly cling to their religion and make it the sole component of their identity, rejecting all other aspects (family, friends, country, etc.). Muslim youth will never advance to the future unless they bury their past, because it continues to impede their progress forward.

THIRTEEN

Decapitating and burning infidels is lawful (*ḥalal*)

Many people say that Islam is a religion of peace; the slaughtering seen on media and publicized by Islamic State (and precursors, ISIL and ISIS) has nothing to do with Islam, because the prophet Muḥammad was *"sent as a mercy to the worlds"* (Q 21.107; Palmer trans.). How then can this kind of slaughter—such as decapitation, burning, and crucifixion—be permissible actions according to Muḥammad's Sunna and commands? Commonly used apologetics to defend Islam insist that Islamic State is but a small Muslim minority that has hijacked the right or true religion followed by most Muslims and severely distorted it. However, anyone who reads Muḥammad's biography and examines the Hadith literature and the Qur'ān will find a great number of verses, texts, and deeds that indicate the sacred endorsement of violence. Devout Muslims believe that these texts are applicable for all time, even in the twenty-first century.

Although some Qur'ānic verses do advocate for peace, many verses authorize and urge violence. It must also be emphasized that the "peace" verses came to Muḥammad at the beginning of his call, when he was weak and had no army. The "violence" verses came during the last ten years of Muḥammad's call, when he had thousands of followers and a strong army. Therefore, those Muslim scholars who believe in the abrogation, or nullification, of verses (an opinion shared by the majority of Muslim scholars and theologians throughout Islam's history) state that the later "jihad" verses have abrogated the earlier "peace" verses.

Yet even if we accept some Muslims' rejection of the doctrine of abrogation (although it is accepted by the majority of Muslim exegetes and scholars), we still face a disturbing dilemma: How do we explain Muḥammad's violence and his killing of others? Was all that violence undertaken in self-defense? Was attacking other tribes just an act of self-defense? Was the attacking—and looting—of convoys more acts of self-defense? Was the violence committed after the death of Muḥammad by his Companions and the subsequent caliphs also acts of self-defense? Were the military campaigns of tens of thousands of Muslim fighters from the Middle East who invaded and conquered Africa before crossing seas to attack Europe actions of self-defense? Common sense does not accept simplistic interpretations that blindly defend its own faith while overlooking facts and difficult questions.

After his migration to Medina (Hijra, AD 622), Muḥammad quickly evolved into a professional fighter, who made his living primarily from his raiding and military campaigns. Killing became a normal, common practice. For example, he possessed nine swords, each with its own name.[1] One of his swords was called *Dhu-l-fiqār* ("The One with Vertebrae" or "The Toothed One"), because it had "teeth" resembling the series of segmented bones along the human backbone. Muḥammad used this weapon for decapitation. Eventually, Muḥammad gave this sword as a gift to his son-in-law (and paternal cousin) 'Alī.

This sword has been mentioned in books and depicted in films. I still remember its appearance in the film *The Message*, an epic historical drama about Muḥammad and the beginnings of Islam (released in Arabic 1976 and in English 1977). In the movie, it was a scissor-like double-bladed sword, like a serpent. During one scene, the sword's bearer, 'Alī, is not

[1] Ibn Qayyīm al-Jawzīya, *Zādu al-Ma'ād* 1: 126.

visible, but his sword is shown cutting the necks of the polytheists, the enemies of Islam.

Muḥammad had another sword named *Al-'Aḍb* ("The Sharp Cutter").[2] He also had a sword that was named *Al-Battār* ("The Amputator"),[3] because it was used to cut up the organs of corpses. Muḥammad also owned seven shields, six bows, and five spears.[4] In short, he developed into a well-equipped, well-experienced soldier of war par excellence.

When Muḥammad lived in Mecca at the beginning of his call (AD 610), during its "peace"-filled stage, he did engage in verbal, if not physical, hostile actions. For instance, Muḥammad threatened those Meccans who resisted his call by mocking his message or ridiculing his religious practices (but did not physically hurt him). Once, he was circumambulating around the Ka'ba and temple, passing by each time a group of Meccans, who were making fun of him. On his third revolution, he stopped and addressed them, saying, "Will you listen to me, O Quraysh? By him who holds my life in His hand I bring you slaughter."[5] (The word *slaughter* in the English translation is *al-dhabh* in the original Arabic, which means "decapitation, or killing by striking the necks.") By these words, Muḥammad warned his Quraysh critics of his intent to kill them—by beheading them—a threat he fulfilled years later when he and his army battled the Quraysh.

The aforementioned *ḥadīth* is cited by many Muslim scholars both in the Muslim world and the West. Egyptian scholar Hānī al-Sibā'ī[6] refers to it when he defends the decapitation of Nicholas Berg (the abducted American freelance radio tower repairman) in 2004 by Al Qaeda *mujāhidīn* in Iraq:[7]

---

[2] Ibn Qayyīm al-Jawzīya, *Zādu al-Ma'ād* 1: 126.

[3] Ibid.

[4] Ibid 2: 41.

[5] Ibn Hishām (Ibn Isḥāq), *The Life of Muhammad* 131; Ibn Hishām (Ibn Ishaq), *Al-Sīra al-Nabawīya* 2: 41.

[6] Hānī al-Sibā'ī was a member of the Egyptian Islamic Jihad and is used as a scholarly reference by Al Qaeda, which he supports. Al Qaeda leader Ayman al-Zawahīrī considers him one of four scholars Muslims everywhere should follow. He currently lives in London as a political refugee despite efforts to deport him for suspected terrorist activities.

[7] "Director of London's Al-Maqreze Centre for Historical Studies Hani Sibai: There Are No 'Civilians' in Islamic Law; The Bombing Is a Great Victory for Al-Qa'ida, Which 'Rubbed the Noses of the World's 8 Most Powerful Countries in the Mud." *Terrorism-info.org.il.* Intelligence and Terrorism Information Center, 12 July 2005. Page 3. Print and Web (http://www.terrorism-info.org.il/Data/pdf/PDF_255%20E_2.pdf). **Note:** This document contains transcript excerpts from television interviews with Hānī al-Sibā'ī (Al Jazeera TV, July 8, 2005) and Lebanese Arab News Broadcast (ANB) TV (February 22, 2005).

> "Do these people [Al Qaeda] base themselves on Islamic law or not? They claim that they do, and to support it, they say that slaughtering appeared in a hadith by the Prophet.... The Prophet told the Quraysh tribe: 'I have brought slaughter upon you,' making this gesture [making the sign of beheading with his hand on his neck]...."

Moroccan Sheikh Muḥammad al-Fizāzī also confirms the authenticity of this *ḥadīth* and cites it to defend the use of decapitation in Islam.[8] Kuwaiti Sheikh Nabīl al-'Awaḍī, in his series on the Prophet's biography, also cites and interprets the same *ḥadīth*, stating that Muḥammad was threatening his Quraysh tribesmen with decapitation in the event of war with them.[9] And a fatwa listed on Qatar's official Web site of the Ministry of Endowments and Islamic Affairs affirms that this *ḥadīth* is authentic and that Muḥammad's threat was directed toward the Quraysh fighters.[10] In summary, this *ḥadīth* regarding Muḥammad's threat of "slaughter," i.e., beheading, is well-known in the Muslim world and is widely cited by Islamic sheikhs and Muslim governments.

In fact, striking necks and inflicting slaughter is mentioned in a Qur'ānic verse before such text was written down in the Hadith literature. Q 47.4 (Palmer trans.) advises Muslims how to kill their enemies when they confront them: *"And when ye meet those who misbelieve—then striking off heads until ye have massacred them, and bind fast the bonds!...."* The highly renowned thirteenth-century Muslim exegete al-Qurṭubī offers this interpretation:[11]

> [The verse] states *"then striking off heads"* [Khalifa trans. *"strike the necks"*] instead of "kill them," because this expression emphasizes a harshness not found in the word *kill*, and it describes killing in its ugliest manner, i.e., cutting off the neck and making the organ, which is the head of the body, to fly off [from the body].

Al-Qurṭubī contends that the Qur'ān intentionally uses the phrase *"striking off heads"* (or *"strike the necks"*) to specify the harshness of the killing.

---

[8] al-Fizāzī, Muḥammad. "This Is Palestine, So What Is the Solution?" Islambi. 16 July 2009. Lecture. (To view YouTube video, see URL https://www.youtube.com/watch?v=aGIi5AkPq_I)

[9] al-'Awaḍī, Nabīl. "Al-Sira al-Nabawiya Series" (Episode 7). Al-Watan (Kuwaiti) TV. 25 July 2011. Television. (To view YouTube video, see URL: https://www.youtube.com/watch?v=NWg2gMfJzxs)

[10] See Fatwa no. 220189: "Authenticity of Hadith: I Have Brought Slaughter to You." *Islamweb.net*. Ministry of Endowments and Islamic Affairs of Qatar, 18 Sept. 2013. Web (http://fatwa.islamweb.net/fatwa/index.php?page=showfatwa&Option=FatwaId&Id=220189).

[11] See the commentary on Q 47.4, *Tafsīr al-Qurṭubī* 16: 230.

Another Qur'ānic verse (Q 8.12; Palmer trans.) uses similar phrasing in the same context of slaughtering enemies. However, in this verse Allah is addressing the angels to help Muslims in their wars against the infidels: *"When your Lord inspired the angels—'Verily, I am with you; make ye firm then those who believe; I will cast dread into the hearts of those who misbelieve,—strike off their necks then, and strike off from them every finger tip.'"* In this verse, the killing emphasizes not only the cutting off the heads but also the fingertips. Another well-regarded Muslim commentator, al-Ṭabarī, confirms (and perhaps expands) this meaning: "Allah has ordered the believers...to kill the infidels by attacking them with the sword.... Allah has commanded Muslims to strike off the heads, necks, hands, and legs of the polytheists."[12] Strangely, some people have argued that the word *sword* is never mentioned in the Qur'ān and its absence proves the Qur'ān is a holy book of peace.[13] Then how does a person strike those necks and cut off those heads—with a fork or a spoon...or with a sword? These "combat" verses explicitly detail the killing process: *"striking off heads"* and *"strike off their necks."* Trying to vindicate the Qur'ān with this argument is like a Mafia leader pleading "not guilty" because he himself did not use the word *gun* that was used to kill his enemy even though he gave the command to kill to one of his subordinates.

Islam and beheadings

An Islamic State member, nicknamed "Abū 'Ā'isha al-Gharīb," wrote an article entitled "The Obvious Response to the Deniers of the Slaughtering of Infidels and Apostates" and disseminated it on the Web site, *JustPaste.it.*[14] He claims Islamic law allows Muslims to slaughter their enemies, the infidels and apostates, and bases his argument on evidence he presents from the Qur'ān, Sunna, Muḥammad's biography, and the later policies of Muḥammad's Companions. He uses these sources to powerfully disprove all the objections that the work of Islamic State has nothing to do with Islam.

---

[12] See the commentary on Q 8.12, *Tafsīr al-Ṭabarī* 9: 132-133.

[13] This pretext is used by apologists of Islam, especially in the West, e.g., Muslim preacher Aḥmad Dīdāt and Yūsuf Estes.

[14] al-Gharīb, Abū 'Ā'isha. "The Obvious Response to the Deniers of the Slaughtering of Infidels and Apostates." *JustPaste.it.* JustPaste.it, 14 Aug. 2014. Web (https://justpaste.it/gmmr).

Among the references that he includes in his treatise are Q 47.4 and Q 8.12, and the *ḥadīth* about Muḥammad's threat to slaughter (behead) the Quraysh. (These Qur'ānic verses and *ḥadīth* have been mentioned earlier in this chapter.) He also discusses Muḥammad's slaughter of the Jewish tribe, the Banū Qurayẓa, and their mass burial in a trench that he had dug for them. Prior to this fate, the Jews consulted one of Muḥammad's Companions, Abū Lubāba, to determine whether they should submit to Muḥammad. When the weeping women and children beseeched him ("Oh Abū Lubāba, do you think that we should submit to Muḥammad's judgment?"), he answered, "Yes," and "pointed with his hand to his throat" to indicate that surrender would mean slaughter.[15]

Abū 'Ā'isha refers to other events in Muḥammad's life, including the instance where Muḥammad sent some of his followers to kill a Jewish leader and poet named Ka'b Ibn al-Ashraf, who was openly critical of Muḥammad. After they killed him (using a deceitful ruse), they returned to Muḥammad and "handed the head" to him, and he "entertained [mindfully held] Allah's praise for their success."[16] Abū 'Ā'isha also mentions the story where 'Abd Allāh Ibn Mas'ūd, a close Companion of Muḥammad, beheaded Quraysh leader Amr Ibn Hishām or Abū al-Ḥakam (derisively called "Abū Jahl," or "Father of Ignorance," by the Muslims), who was mortally wounded during the Battle of Badr. Ibn Mas'ūd's testimony is reported in the Islamic sources: "Then I cut off his head and brought it to the apostle saying, 'This is the head of the enemy of Allah, Abū Jahl'.... [A]nd I threw his head before the apostle and he gave thanks to Allah."[17]

The article's author closes with a story famous in the Muslim world: Khālid Ibn 'Abd Allāh al-Qasrī (d. AD 743). He was an Umayyad leader whose most notable political achievement was his appointment as governor of Mecca and then later Iraq. During his governorship of Iraq, Khālid had a Muslim scholar, al-Ja'd Ibn Dirham, arrested for his heretical teachings. The convicted scholar was then tied to a column of the Wasīt mosque on 'Īd al-Aḍḥa (Feast of the Sacrifice), which is a Muslim religious celebration to commemorate Prophet Abraham's willingness to

[15] al-Gharīb, Abū 'Ā'isha. "The Obvious Response to the Deniers of the Slaughtering of Infidels and Apostates." *JustPaste.it.* JustPaste.it, 14 Aug. 2014. Web (https://justpaste.it/gmmr). See Ibn Hishām (Ibn Isḥāq), *The Life of Muhammad* 462; Ibn Hishām (Ibn Isḥāq), *Al-Sīra al-Nabawīya* 3: 440.

[16] al-Mubarakpuri, *Sealed Nectar* 289. For the Arabic source, see al-Mubarakpuri, *Al-Raḥīq al-Makhtūm* 1: 220.

[17] Ibn Hishām (Ibn Isḥāq), *The Life of Muhammad* 304; Ibn Hishām (Ibn Isḥāq), *Al-Sīra al-Nabawīya* 3: 80.

sacrifice his son[18] to demonstrate his obedience to God. Khalīd addressed the people before he slaughtered this man:[19]

> "Oh People, perform the sacrifice, may Allah accept them from you. I am going to offer al-Ja'd Ibn Dirham in sacrifice, for indeed he claims that Allah did not take Ibrāhīm as His friend nor did He speak to Mūsa [Moses]. Most Perfect is He and exalted is He from what al-Ja'd Ibn Dirham says." He [Khālid] then went down from the pulpit and slaughtered him.

This governor of an early Islamic state, the Umayyad caliphate, actually sacrificed a human being, a Muslim man, on 'Īd al-Aḍḥa by slaughtering him like he was a lamb—livestock—in the presence of imāms, sheikhs and religious scholars, and no one objected. Medieval Muslim theologian Ibn Taymīya comments that "Khālid Ibn 'Abdallāh al-Qasrī killed him [al-Ja'd Ibn Dirham] with the approval of the scholars of Islam."[20]

Before Islamic State gave itself the prerogative to behead and slaughter its hostages in front of cameras, its judicial committee had undoubtedly consulted the Qur'ān, Sunna, and Hadith literature and reviewed the Muslim scholars' and jurists' statements, rulings, and commentary as well as studied the precedents in Islamic history pertaining to the slaughtering of people—certainly, the cases involving the prophet Muḥammad himself and later imitated by his Companions. This survey of all these sources should leave no room for doubt that the use of slaughter was implemented by Muḥammad and was followed by others and blessed by Muslim scholars.

The black-garbed executioner is Islamic State's ugliest symbol. In the its published videos he is shown masked and hooded as he stands by the chained helpless victims, who have no clue when the actual beheading will take place, because of the repeated "rehearsals" during the filming. Eventually, they no longer resist after all the trial runs, so that the actual filmed and broadcasted scene looks as though everyone is just acting. The final scene of the decapitated head, placed on top of the prone body of the victim, repulses any normal viewer, and, at the same time, evokes similar images of Islam's past, written down in its historical records. The

---

[18] **Note:** Christians and Jews believe that Abraham was commanded by God to sacrifice his son Isaac but was prevented from carrying out the act by an angel sent by God (Bible, Gen. 22.1-18). Though most Muslims believe the son who was nearly sacrificed was Ishmael (and not Isaac), Muslim scholars continue to debate the identity of which son was offered in sacrifice.

[19] al-Bayhaqī, *Al-Sunan al-Kubra* 15: 285.

[20] Ibn Taymīya, *Minhāj al-Sunnati* 3: 165.

decapitation of James Foley[21] is no different from the decapitation of Abū al-Ḥakam ("Abū Jahl"), whose head was tossed by his executioner Ibn Mas'ūd before Muḥammad. And the decapitation of Steven Sotloff[22] is no different from the decapitation of Ka'b Ibn al-Ashraf, whose head was handed over to Muḥammad, who then congratulated his followers, saying, "Cheerful faces are yours."[23]

Many more heads were cut off...the head of David Haines,[24] a British aid worker, and his fellow citizen Alan Henning,[25] the head of American Peter Kassig,[26] and the heads of eighteen Syrian soldiers,[27] and many others. All these hostages were decapitated by Islamic State at the hand of Muḥammad Emwazī ("Jihadi John"; see Chapter 8, page 221) and other Islamic State fighters.

This savage method of killing has been legitimized, because it is based on the life and actions of Muḥammad Ibn 'Abd Allāh, the Messenger of Islam, and on his teachings. He gave this brutal practice its power, justification, and legality. If the prophet Muḥammad had not authorized and practiced himself this kind of savage killing, the same method of execution would not be carried out today by Abū Bakr al-Baghdadī and his followers. If Muḥammad, the most holy Muslim, used savagery and beheading in his wars and judgments, how can believing Muslims then criticize these practices? Are Muslims more honorable than their prophet

[21] "Islamic State Beheads American Journalist James Foley." *Leaksource.wordpress.com.* Leak Source, 19 Aug. 2014. Web (https://leaksource.wordpress.com/2014/08/19/graphic-video-islamic-state-beheads-american-journalist-james-foley). **Note:** Islamic State first published this video entitled *A Message to America* on YouTube.

[22] "Islamic State Beheads American Journalist Steven Sotloff." *Leaksource.wordpress.com.* Leak Source, 2 Sept. 2014. Web (https://leaksource.wordpress.com/2014/09/02/graphic-video-islamic-state-beheads-american-journalist-steven-sotloff). **Note:** Islamic State first published this video entitled *A Second Message to America* on YouTube.

[23] Ibn Sa'd, *Al-Ṭabaqāt al-Kubra* 2: 33; al-Mubarakpuri, *Sealed Nectar* 289. For the Arabic source, see al-Mubarakpūrī, *Al-Raḥīq al-Makhtūm* 1: 220.

[24] "Islamic State Beheads British Aid Worker David Haines." *Leaksource.wordpress.com.* Leak Source, 13 Sept. 2014. Web (https://leaksource.wordpress.com/2014/09/13/graphic-video-islamic-state-beheads-british-aid-worker-david-haines). **Note:** Islamic State first published this video entitled *A Message to the Allies of America* on YouTube.

[25] "Islamic State Beheads British Aid Worker Alan Henning." *Leaksource.wordpress.com.* Leak Source, 3 Oct. 2014. Web (https://leaksource.wordpress.com/2014/10/03/graphic-video-islamic-state-beheads-british-aid-worker-alan-henning). **Note:** Islamic State first published this video entitled *Another Message to America and Its Allies* on YouTube.

[26] "Islamic State Claims Beheading of Former US Army Ranger/Aid Worker Peter Kassig." *Leaksource.wordpress.com.* Leak Source, 16 Nov. 2014. Web (https://leaksource.wordpress.com/2014/11/16/graphic-video-islamic-state-claims-beheading-of-former-u-s-army-rangeraid-worker-peter-kassig). **Note:** Islamic State first published this video entitled *Even Though the Infidels Abhor It* [Q 9.32] on YouTube.

[27] Ibid. **Note:** The mass execution of the captive Syrian soldiers and pilots by Islamic State fighters appears in the second video on this Web page.

if they refrain from slaughtering others just because it is a brutal act? Are they more honorable than the Companions and other followers close to Muḥammad if they refuse to cut off heads because they think it is a horrible act?

When Muslims consider the Islamic sources and history and the actions and policies of Muḥammad and the early Companions as sacred texts and behavior that must be protected from all criticism, then the fight against terrorism will continue. We cannot fight terrorism without fighting the ideology behind it, its intellectual roots, especially if these roots are considered sacred and have been engrained in our lives and thinking since childhood because they are an integral and inseparable part of religion.

Islamic State and Islamic legal punishments (*ḥudūd*)

On July 29, 2015, the Syrian Observatory for Human Rights (SOHR) announced that Islamic State had executed more than 3000 people within thirteen months since the declaration of its caliphate.[28] Victims were shot, beheaded, crucified, stoned, thrown off high buildings, and burned alive. Some of the victims had hands or legs amputated or were killed in mass executions. All these actions were carried out and documented in audio recordings and videos by Islamic State.

I feel sick to my stomach when I review these videos, trying to study their relationship with Islamic *sharīʿa*. I try to understand each of these acts from a religious perspective, through my eyes as a former Muslim. So I always ask this question: Does this act have any legal basis in the Qurʾān or in the Sunna, and the rulings of Muslim scholars and sheikhs? In other words, are there precedents for this act recorded in Islamic history and justified by religious texts?

Unfortunately, I find that the rulings made by Islamic State have been applied according to Islamic law. Even before the rulings are implemented, Islamic State representatives often publicly read a statement explaining the charges and its legal ruling. These statements always contain Qurʾānic verses and teachings or sayings made by Prophet Muḥammad to support

---

[28] "170 Children and Women among 3000 Beheaded by ISIS in Last 13 Months." *Syriahr.com*. Syrian Observatory for Human Rights (SOHR), 29 July 2015. Web (http://preview.tinyurl.com/jfqmzns); "Syria: 170 Children and Women Beheaded by ISIS in Last 13 Months, Says SOHR." *IBTimes.co.in*. International Business Times, 29 July 2015. Web (http://www.ibtimes.co.in/syria-170-children-women-beheaded-by-isis-last-13-months-says-sohr-640954).

the ruling. Islamic State does not implement rulings without fortifying itself with religiously lawful evidence to avert criticism by its members and followers; otherwise, they will demand such evidence, and this challenge will create conflicts and divisions. Islamic State is careful to include all supporting religious evidence to ensure that its followers will never turn against it. If its followers ever determine that it is not implementing the true religion of Islam but inventing punishments without relying on the authoritative religious texts, then its illegitimate actions would be equivalent to apostasy.

I have spent long hours viewing a series of videos released by media outlets of Islamic State: *Breaking of the Borders*, *The Clashing of Swords*, *The Flame of War*, *Healing of the Heart*, and *Even Though the Infidels Abhor It.* All these videos include Qur'ānic verses and Islamic songs, with prostrate *mujāhidīn* praying and reading the Qur'ān. The same videos then show them killing people with machine guns in front of the cameras. Are these Islamic State fighters doing all this killing without believing that they are performing a holy religious duty? What makes them think that they will go to paradise, and that by cutting off hands and heads they are pleasing Allah? Their religious conviction is based on the religious texts.

Punishment for thievery (*ḥadd al-sariqa*)

I have seen many Islamic State-publicized pictures and recordings of thieves having their hands amputated and then being treated in a hospital. The Islamic State members who carry out these punishments even explain that the cutting is performed by specialists and not by amateurs. They embrace the now handless person to comfort him because he is a Muslim who was subjected to the rule of Allah.

So, from where did Muslims get this idea for punishment? Of course, the Qur'ān itself is one source of this ruling: *"The man thief and the woman thief, cut off the hands of both as a punishment, for that they have erred;—an example from God, for God is mighty, wise"* (Q 5.38; Palmer trans.). Muḥammad himself carried out this punishment, as reported in a *ḥadīth* narrated by his wife 'Ā'isha.[29] Another *ḥadīth* states that he had

[29] *Ṣaḥiḥ Bukhari*, Book of Limits and Punishments Set by Allah (p. 1519); *Ṣaḥīḥ al-Bukhari*, Kitāb al-Ḥudūd 6: 2493. As narrated by 'Ā'isha, the Prophet "cut off the hand of a lady, and that lady used to come to me, and I used to convey her message to the Prophet and she repented...."

cut the hand of a man from the wrist joint.[30] Muḥammad even hung the amputated hand of a thief around the thief's neck as a warning to others.[31] The early caliphs also punished thieves with hand amputation.[32]

Saudi Arabia continues to implement this punishment in public squares to this day.[33] (Incidentally, Saudi Arabia still beheads criminals, usually convicted drug smugglers, in public squares.)[34] Strangely, while the great Western countries have all condemned Islamic State for its public beheadings, they maintain diplomatic relations with Saudi Arabia with little pressure to force it to stop this barbaric and public form of state punishment as Islamic State. In fact, Saudi Arabic and Islamic State will carry out beheadings for the same convictions, such as apostasy.[35]

Saudi Arabia and Islamic State are not exceptions in this context. Sudanese law, for example, punishes the crime of theft with hand amputation too.[36] The Mauritanian penal code details a progressive form of amputation for repeated thievery, according to Article 351:[37]

---

[30] Ibn Abū Shayba, *Al-Musannaf* 6: 528. In this narration, the "prophet had cut the hand of a man from the wrist joint."

[31] *Sunan Abū Dawūd*, Book of Legal Punishments 5: 49. In this narration, "Fadalah bin 'Ubaid was asked about hanging the thief's hand around his neck—is it Sunnah? He said: 'A thief was brought to the Messenger of Allah...and his hand was cut off, then he ordered that it be hung around his neck.'" **Note:** This *ḥadīth* is reported in several Islamic books, e.g., *Musnad Ahmad, Sunan al-Tirmidhī, Al-Sunan al-Kubra* (al-Bayhaqi).

[32] See the commentary on Q 5.38, *Tafsīr al-Qurṭubī* 6: 175. According to this commentary, "Abū Bakr cut off the hand of a man from Yemen for stealing a necklace, and 'Umar cut off the hand of Ibn Sumra, the brother of 'Abdul Raḥmān Ibn Sumra. There is no dispute about it."

[33] "Saudi Arabia Cuts Off Thief's Hand as Punishment." *Haaretz.com*. Haaretz, 15 Dec. 2014. Web (https://www.haaretz.com/middle-east-news/1.631994); "Execution of the Rule of Robbery by Cutting Off the Hand at the Wrist in the Meccan Area." *Alriyadh.com*. Al Riyadh Daily, 15 Dec. 2014. Web (http://www.alriyadh.com/1003804).

[34] "Saudi Arabia Beheads Syrian Drug Trafficker." *MiddleEastEye.net*. Middle East Eye, 10 Feb. 2015. Web (http://www.middleeasteye.net/news/saudi-arabia-beheads-syrian-drug-trafficker-527769623). See "Execution of a Death Sentence on a Syrian Drug Smuggler in Riyadh." *Sabq.org*. Sabq Online Newspaper, 31 July 2015. Web (https://sabq.org/kcDgde).

[35] Spencer, Richard. "Saudi Arabia Court Gives Death Penalty to Man Who Renounced His Muslim Faith." *Telegraph.co.uk*. Telegraph Media Group, 24 Feb. 2015. Web (http://www.telegraph.co.uk/news/worldnews/middleeast/saudiarabia/11431509/Saudi-Arabia-court-gives-death-penalty-to-man-who-renounced-his-Muslim-faith.html); Hilali, Ahmed. "'Initial Decision' to Implement the Legal Punishment of Apostasy on a Citizen Who Assaulted the Divine." *Alhayat.com*. Al Hayat, 23 Feb. 2015. Web (http://preview.tinyurl.com/hmqtmnc).

[36] See *Sudanese Penal Code*. 1991: ch. 17 (Offences against Property), art. 171. First point (1) reads, "Whoever commits Sariqah Hadiyah [crime of theft] shall be punished with amputation of the right hand from the wrist." European Country of Origin Information Network. Page 44. Print and Web (https://www.ecoi.net/file_upload/1329_1202725629_sb106-sud-criminalact1991.pdf).

[37] *Criminal Law of Mauritania*. No. 83-162. 9 July 1983: art. 351. *Justice.gov.mr*. Official Web site of the Ministry of Justice of the Islamic Republic of Mauritania. Page 67. Print and Web (http://preview.tinyurl.com/zcnzud5).

> The thief is punished by cutting off his right hand from the elbow, and then by cutting off his left leg from the joint. If he steals again, then by cutting off his left hand from the elbow. If he steals a third time, then by cutting off his right leg from the joint. If he steals a fourth time, then by beating him, and imprisoning him if he steals a fifth time.

I am not sure how such an offender could steal for a fifth time with no hands or legs.

The 22-member Arab League (formerly the League of Arab States) has also decided to sanction hand amputation for thievery in a unified penal code agreed upon by the justice ministers in Arab countries.[38] It is important to note that the minimum amount of theft for this permanently disabling punishment has not been universally determined yet in Islam. Some Muslim scholars state any theft equivalent to a quarter of a dinar in gold, as in the time of the Prophet,[39] which is held to mean in today's terms as 1.0625 gram of gold.[40] However, the Hadith literature reports that the theft's value for hand amputation may be as trivial as the cost of an egg or a rope: "The Prophet said, 'Allah curses a man who steals an egg and gets his hand cut off, or steals a rope and gets his hands cut off'…."[41]

Islamic State has not been the first Islamic state to initiate these punishments nor is it the only Muslim country that applies it. As detailed earlier, the origins for this punishment for theft are in the Qur'ān and the Sunna, though its application by Muslim countries may differ. Some Muslim countries have replaced hand amputation with imprisonment for offenders convicted of theft because of international pressure (and not because this change reflects "true" Islam). Other Muslim countries continue to apply parts of foreign (and more humane) laws, like Morocco (once a French protectorate), which still includes some French-influenced laws. However, somewhat isolated Muslim countries, such as Mauritania

---

[38] League of Arab States. *United Arab Penal Code*. 1996: art. 153. *CARJJ.org*. Arab Center for Legal and Judicial Research (sub-organ of the League of Arab States). Page 122. Print and Web (https://carjj.org/sites/default/files/united-arab-criminal-law-part1.pdf).

[39] *Ṣaḥiḥ Muslim*, Book Pertaining to Punishments Prescribed by Islam: Punishment for theft and the minimum limit according to which it is imposed upon an offender (pp. 1036,1037); *Ṣaḥīḥ Muslim*, Kitāb al-Ḥudūd 2: 803-804. As narrated by 'Ā'isha, the prophet said, "The hand of a thief should not be cut off but for the theft of a quarter of a dinar and upwards."

[40] See Fatwa no. 317767: "Minimum Value of Stolen Property that Entails Penalty for Theft." *Islamweb.net*. Ministry of Endowments and Islamic Affairs of Qatar, 28 Feb. 2016. Web (http://www.islamweb.net/emainpage/index.php?page=showfatwa&Option=FatwaId&Id=317767).

[41] *Ṣaḥīḥ Bukhārī*, Book of Limits and Punishments Set by Allah (p. 1516); *Ṣaḥīḥ al-Bukhārī*, Kitāb al-Ḥudūd 6: 2490.

and Sudan, either ignore or attract little international pressure to change these brutally harsh sentences. A large rich country like Saudi Arabia, which also prefers to strictly follow Islamic law, can dismiss international pressure or the voices of human rights organizations because of its influential control over global oil supply and pricing.

Predictably, Muslim critics denounce those Muslim countries that include laws introduced by non-Muslim ("infidel") countries. In their view, such inclusion now categorizes these Muslim countries as "infidel" countries as well, because they are enacting laws from non-Islamic sources rather than divine law: "*...for whoso will not judge by what God has revealed, these be the misbelievers*" (Q 5.44; Palmer trans.).

Even though the barbaric punishment for thievery (hand amputation) was an Arab custom before the emergence of Islam,[42] its continued use—whether by Islamic State or other Muslim countries dominated by Islamic law as a sanctified Islamic ruling—has made it a human disaster.

Punishment for piracy or banditry (*ḥadd al-ḥirāba*)

During the height of its power as a self-proclaimed caliphate, Islamic State published on a weekly basis images of punishments and killings that it had applied on convicted apostates and those who had insulted Islam. It also applied the punishment for piracy or banditry, or *ḥadd al-hirāba*, which is cross-amputation (cutting off the hand and the foot on alternate sides) as well as slaughter (decapitation) and crucifixion—all punishments mentioned in the Qur'ān (Q 5.33; Pickthall trans.):

> *The only reward of those who make war upon Allah and His messenger and strive after corruption in the land will be that they will be killed or crucified, or have their hands and feet on alternate sides cut off, or will be expelled out of the land. Such will be their degradation in the world, and in the Hereafter theirs will be an awful doom.*

Islamic State applied *ḥadd al-hirāba* against those found guilty of the crime of "highway robbery" or "corruption in the land," which can be defined very loosely. Generally, this punishment is related to anyone (with or without weapons) who attacks people on the road.

---

[42] See the commentary of Q 5.38, *Tafsīr al-Qurṭubī* 6: 175. According to this commentary, "the thief's hand was cut off in the *jahiliyah* [pre-Islamic era], and the first man whose hand was cut off in *jahiliyah* was al-Walīd Ibn al-Mughīra. Then Allah ordered that it should be cut in Islam too."

Islamic State is not the only one that has followed this ruling and its punishment. From time to time, Saudi Arabia has followed this ruling, *ḥadd al-ḥirāba*, and carried out its punishment. For example, on March 27, 2013, a Yemeni was executed (beheaded and crucified) for the crime of murder, rape, and road robbery.[43] On August 4, 2009, a gang leader was sentenced to death (decapitation) and then crucified for three days as a punishment for the robbery of gold shops; six gang members were sentenced according to *ḥadd al-hirāba*.[44] On November 20, 2014, two Saudi men were punished with *ḥadd al-hirāba* for raping a girl, robbery, and drug and alcohol intoxication.[45]

Ḥadd al-hirāba (amputation and cross-amputation for robbery/ banditry) is not limited to the criminal codes of Saudi Arabia and Islamic State. Mauritania's penal code specifies that anyone who is found guilty of road robbery is to be punished by either killing, crucifixion, cross-amputation (right hand and left foot), or exile from his country and imprisonment in another town. Any person who helps the perpetrator(s) with information and resources, even if not present during the commission of the crime, will receive the same punishment.[46] Sudan, another Muslim country governed by *sharī'a*, includes similar provisions in its criminal code:[47]

> Whoever commits [the crime of] Ḥaraba shall be punished with: - (a) Execution or execution and thereafter crucifixion if his acts resulted in murder or rape. (b) Amputation of the right hand and left foot if his act resulted in grievous bodily harm or theft of property which amounts to the required minimum (Nisab) for theft punishable with amputation (Sariqah Hadiya)....

---

43 "Saudi Authorities Carry Out Barbarism in Yemen [after] a Pakistani Was Killed after Being Raped." *France24.com/ar.* France 24 (Arabic), 28 Mar. 2013. Web (http://preview.tinyurl.com/jtkdap3). See "Saudi Arabia Executes, Crucifies Yemeni Murderer." *DailyTelegraph.com.au.* Nationwide News, 27 Mar. 2013. Web (http://www.dailytelegraph.com.au/news/world/saudi-executes-crucifies-yemeni-murderer/news-story/f02e573ee79f2a76346a1d2665135f80).

44 "Death and 3 Days' Crucifixion of a Gang Leader for the Robbery of Gold Shops and the 22 Gang Members Sentenced to Ḥirāba and Prison." *Okaz.com.sa.* Okaz, 4 Aug. 2009. Web (http://preview.tinyurl.com/htrcm48).

45 "The Interior Carries Out Ḥadd al-Ḥirāba against Citizens." *Alriyadh.com.* Al Riyadh Daily, 22 Nov. 2014. Web (http://www.alriyadh.com/996474).

46 *Criminal Law of Mauritania.* No. 83-162. 9 July 1983: art. 354. *Justice.gov.mr.* Official Web site of the Ministry of Justice of the Islamic Republic of Mauritania. Page 68. Print and Web (http://preview.tinyurl.com/zcnzud5).

47 *Sudanese Penal Code.* 1991: ch. 17 (Offences against Property), art. 168. European Country of Origin Information Network. Page 43. Print and Web (https://www.ecoi.net/file_upload/1329_1202725629_sb106-sud-criminalact1991.pdf).

Arab Ministers of Justice, in the unified penal law of the Arab League, have adopted *ḥadd al-hirāba* by the cutting off the right hand and the left foot, or cross-amputation.[48]

People today may believe that the use of crucifixion as punishment is a relic of ancient history, when, in fact, it is still a painful reality in the twenty-first century. Incredibly, this barbaric practice exists in the era of the Internet with countries that still crucify convicted citizens. Such a punishment for any crime is heinously inhumane, and the international community must reject it and condemn those who implement it.

Even so, the Qur'ān and Hadith literature support its use and seem to endorse yet another gruesome type of punishment. This punishment was instigated by Muḥammad himself after a group of eight men killed his shepherd and stole his camels. Muḥammad sent some of his followers to pursue and capture these men. When the culprits were presented to him, Muḥammad immediately sentenced them:[49]

> The Prophet ordered…some iron pieces to be made red hot, and their eyes were branded with them and their hands and feet were cut off and were not cauterized. Then they were put at a place called Al-Harra [a rocky land in Medina], and when they asked for water to drink they were not given [any] till they died….

Some Islamic accounts state that when they pleaded for water, Muḥammad refused and responded with "fire," meaning to burn them.[50] Like the punishment of crucifixion with a living victim, this prolonged death sentence—leaving the eight men sightless and exposed to the elements with no food or drink, their amputated limbs untreated, seems excessively cruel and unjust.

I have yet to see any videos or photographs where Islamic State members have heated nails and inserted them into the eyes of their captives, like Muḥammad, but when Islamic State crucifies people, it is only applying Islamic law. Not only was this punishment (and others equally gruesome) carried out or ordered by Muḥammad, verses in the

[48] League of Arab States. *Unified Arab Penal Code*. 1996: art. 157.2. *CARJJ.org*. Arab Center for Legal and Judicial Research (sub-organ of the League of Arab States). Page 126. Print and Web (https://carjj.org/sites/default/files/united-arab-criminal-law-part1.pdf).

[49] *Sahih Bukhari*, Book of Punishment of Disbelievers at War with Allah and His Apostle (p. 1521); *Ṣaḥīḥ al-Bukhārī*, Kitāb al-Muḥāribīn min Ahl al-Kufr wa al-Ridda 6: 2496.

[50] See the commentary on Q 5.33, *Tafsir al-Qurṭubī* 6: 158.

Qur'ān support and promulgate its use, verses in Islam's holiest book, which Muslims believe are valid for all times and places.

Punishment of scourging (*ḥadd al-jald*)

Islamic State imposes the penalty of public scourging or whipping for unlawful sexual relationships and alcohol consumption. The punishment of scourging is presented in the Qur'ān with specific conditions, as in Q 24.2 (Palmer trans.): *"The whore and the whoremonger. Scourge each of them with a hundred stripes, and do not let pity for them take hold of you in God's religion...and let a party of the believers witness their torment."* This verse clearly commands that the scourging take place in a public setting with no show of pity by the administrator or witnesses of the punishment.

The Qur'ān also specifies scourging as punishment for another crime: false accusation against a Muslim woman regarding illicit sexual intercourse. In this case, the accuser becomes a criminal if he or she cannot produce four witnesses to corroborate the charge of unlawful sexual intercourse, as specified in Q 24.4 (Palmer trans.): *"but those who cast (imputations) on chaste women and then do not bring four witnesses, scourge them with eighty stripes, and do not receive any testimony of theirs ever, for these are the workers of abomination."*

Muslim exegetes have long known that these verses (Q 24.2 and Q 24.4) refer to an infamous event (Al-Ifk, or "The Fabricated Incident") involving Muḥammad's favorite wife 'Ā'isha, who was accused of adultery. As narrated by 'Ā'isha "when the apostle of Allah had recited to people the story which was revealed with my innocence, he then ordered the two men and woman who slandered me to be scourged as a punishment."[51] So two men (one of the men was Muḥammad's favorite poet, Ḥassān Ibn Thābit) and a woman were scourged because they accused 'Ā'isha of committing adultery.

Scourging was also used to punish people caught drinking alcoholic beverages during early Islam. The Hadith literature reports that Muḥammad scourged wine drinkers during his rule in Medina, a policy adopted by the caliphs who followed him: "He [Muḥammad] gave him [person who had drunk wine] forty stripes with two lashes. Abū Bakr also did that, but when 'Umar (assumed the responsibilities) of the Caliphate,

[51] al-Bayhaqī, *Al-Sunan al-Kubra* 12: 499; *Sunan Abū Dawūd*, Book of Legal Punishments 5: 85.

he consulted people and...the mildest punishment (for drinking) [was] eighty (stripes)...."[52] (Apparently, 'Umar had to double the punishment in order to eliminate the habit of drinking alcohol.) The Hadith literature not only reports these punishments for alcohol consumption but also describes the tools used to scourge and beat people. In one *ḥadīth*, 'Anas, a servant of Muḥammad, states, "The Prophet beat a drunk with palm-leaf stalks and shoes."[53]

Saudi Arabia's government carries out thousands of lashings every year. A Riyadh newspaper reports that this type of punishment "has reached astronomical numbers."[54] For example, the court sentenced an intoxicated man to 40,000 lashes, divided over many weeks, which means it could take years to complete the punishment.[55]

One scourging judgment by the Saudi Arabian government that has been highlighted around the world concerns blogger Rā'if Badawī, who was sentenced by the court to a thousand lashes, ten years in prison, a large fine (US$267,000), and a ten-year travel ban after his release from prison.[56] Rā'if Badawī's "crime" was his audacity in creating and maintaining an online forum for writers like himself to raise and discuss problematic issues in the country and Islam and defend liberalism. On January 9, 2015, the first fifty lashes were administered as he knelt in front of Al-Jafālī mosque in Jeddah immediately after the Friday prayer.[57] The punishment took place under an increased security presence. Although photography was prohibited, some spectators were still able to photograph the scene of Rā'if Badawī's thin body being scourged with fifty lashes in front of a large crowd by members of the Committee for the Promotion of Virtue and the Prevention of Vice (CPVPV, or

---

[52] *Sahih Muslim*, Book Pertaining to Punishments Prescribed by Islam: Prescribed punishment for (drinking) wine (p. 1048); *Ṣaḥīḥ Muslim*, Kītāb al-Ḥudūd 2: 815.

[53] *Musnad Aḥmād* 3: 955.

[54] al-Miflih, Hayam. "Flogging Punishment Has Reached an Astronomical Number of Lashes." *Alriyadh.com*. Al Riyadh Daily, 5 Apr. 2009. Web (http://www.alriyadh.com/420182).

[55] Ibid.

[56] "Saudi Arabia: Supreme Court Confirms Prison Sentence and Lashes against Blogger Raif Badawi." *France24.com/ar*. France 24 (Arabic), 6 July 2015. Web (http://preview.tinyurl.com/zdc8e7f); "Saudi Supreme Court Upholds Verdict against Blogger Raif Badawi." *TheGuardian.com*. The Guardian, 7 June 2015. Web (https://www.theguardian.com/world/2015/jun/07/saudi-supreme-court-upholds-raif-badawi-blogger-verdict).

[57] Saul, Heather. "Raif Badawi: Saudi Arabia Publicly Flogged Liberal Blogger and Activist Accused of 'Insulting Islam.'" *Independent.co.uk*. The Independent, 9 Jan. 2015. Web (http://www.independent.co.uk/news/world/middle-east/raif-badawi-saudi-arabia-urged-to-halt-flogging-of-liberal-blogger-sentenced-to-1000-lashes-9967008.html).

Saudi religious police). It was a scene that brought to mind some of the draconian practices of the medieval era.

Many countries in the European Union (EU) condemned this punishment. Martin Schulz, then President of the European Parliament (the directly elected parliamentary institution of the EU), demanded that Saudi Arabia stop the "medieval" punishment of scourging entirely and compared it to the kinds of barbaric punishments implemented by ISIS:[58]

> He "cannot see any difference between the operations of beheading that are carried out by members of ISIS before publishing them on social media and the scourging punishment or execution that is imposed by a country like Saudi Arabia in public squares."

British newspaper *The Independent* denounced Saudi Arabia as "another brutal theocracy that tolerates no dissent and has an automatic death sentence for apostasy" and lambasted some British political leaders for their unwillingness to protest—and even accept—these barbaric actions because they "have the support of the vast majority of the Saudi population." The article's news reporter then extrapolated this acquiescent attitude with a possibly similar future relationship with ISIS:[59]

> It would seem grotesque to suggest that Britain might eventually recognize the ISIS caliphate as a state, sell it arms, solicit its investment and then offer only the politest rebuke when innocent heads are sliced off. It is, however, no more grotesque than how we already conduct our official dealings with Saudi Arabia, ...which, like ISIS, is hell-bent on spreading Wahhabi fanaticism far beyond its borders.

Though this punishment is most prevalent in Saudi Arabic, it inevitably is applied in other Muslim countries when political upheaval occurs, as in Libya now, in Afghanistan during the time of the Taliban rule, and in the areas that have been controlled by Islamic State.

Still, the punishment of scourging exists in the laws of other Muslim countries, even if it is not as actively applied as in Saudi Arabia. According to Sudanese criminal law, children may be flogged as a "means of discipline" if the offender is at least ten years old and the flogging

[58] "European Parliament Calls on Saudi Arabia to Abolish Flogging." *DW.com/ar*. Deutsche Welle (Arabic), 23 Jan. 2015. Web (http://preview.tinyurl.com/zfz5k29).

[59] Wheen, Francis. "UK Ministers Have Started to Defend Saudi Arabia's Flogging of Raif Badawi—It's Breathtaking." *Independent.co.uk*. The Independent, 16 June 2015. Web (http://www.independent.co.uk/voices/comment/saudi-arabia-is-teaching-isis-a-lesson-in-cruelty-yet-the-uk-continues-to-defend-them-10324161.html).

does "not exceed twenty lashes."[60] The penalty for drinking, possessing, or manufacturing alcohol is a flogging of "forty lashes if he is a Muslim."[61] Sudan also criminalizes sexual relations between a man and a woman who are not married to each other. If an unmarried man has sexual intercourse with a woman, he must be flogged "a hundred times," and he may also be "banished for one year" in addition to the flogging.[62] Slandering the reputation of chaste women carries another harsh penalty in Sudanese criminal law: "Whoever commits Qadhf [casts a false accusation of sexual immorality] shall be punished with flogging [of] eighty lashes."[63]

Mauritania's criminal code punishes the unmarried adulterer "with one hundred lashes in public, and imprisonment and exile for one year."[64] Mauritanian law also punishes the person found guilty of drinking alcohol with eighty lashes,[65] and eighty lashes also for the person found guilty of slandering Muslim men or women innocent of adultery.[66]

These severe laws in these Muslim countries are not aberrations within the Muslim world. Indeed, the Arab League has adopted a unified penal code that calls for scourging as a punishment for certain cases, e.g., alcohol consumption, slander, fornication.[67] Besides the support for and application of these types of laws and punishments in some Muslim countries and organizations, one must also include the countless fatāwa (rulings) of Muslim scholars and sheikhs, who publicize their opinions

---

[60] *Sudanese Penal Code.* 1991: ch. 4 (Measures of Care and Correction—Reform), art. 47. European Country of Origin Information Network. Page 21. Print and Web (https://www.ecoi.net/file_upload/1329_1202725629_sb106-sud-criminalact1991.pdf).

[61] *Sudanese Penal Code.* 1991: ch. 9 (Offences Affecting Safety and Public Health), art. 78; see (1). European Country of Origin Information Network. Page 27. Print and Web (https://www.ecoi.net/file_upload/1329_1202725629_sb106-sud-criminalact1991.pdf).

[62] *Sudanese Penal Code.* 1991: ch. 15 (Offences against Honour, Reputation, and Public Morals), art. 146; see (1)(b) and (2). European Country of Origin Information Network. Page 39. Print and Web (https://www.ecoi.net/file_upload/1329_1202725629_sb106-sud-criminalact1991.pdf).

[63] *Sudanese Penal Code.* 1991: ch. 15 (Offences against Honour, Reputation, and Public Morals), art. 157; see (3). European Country of Origin Information Network. Page 41. Print and Web (https://www.ecoi.net/file_upload/1329_1202725629_sb106-sud-criminalact1991.pdf).

[64] *Criminal Law of Mauritania.* No. 83-162. 9 July 1983: art. 307. *Justice.gov.mr.* Official Web site of the Ministry of Justice of the Islamic Republic of Mauritania. Page 56. Print and Web (http://preview.tinyurl.com/zcnzud5).

[65] *Criminal Law of Mauritania.* No. 83-162. 9 July 1983: art. 341. *Justice.gov.mr.* Official Web site of the Ministry of Justice of the Islamic Republic of Mauritania. Pages 64-65. Print and Web (http://preview.tinyurl.com/zcnzud5).

[66] *Criminal Law of Mauritania.* No. 83-162. 9 July 1983: art. 341. *Justice.gov.mr.* Official Web site of the Ministry of Justice of the Islamic Republic of Mauritania. Page 65. Print and Web (http://preview.tinyurl.com/zcnzud5).

[67] League of Arab States. *United Arab Penal Code.* 1996: arts. 141, 144, 149. *CARJJ.org.* Arab Center for Legal and Judicial Research (sub-organ of the League of Arab States). Pages 116, 118, 119. Print and Web (https://carjj.org/sites/default/files/united-arab-criminal-law-part1.pdf).

online. A simple click via one's favorite search engine will result in hundreds of Web sites with detailed fatāwa authenticating such laws and punishments based on Islamic law.

Therefore, to say that the acts of Islamic State are crimes not related to Islam is a bogus claim, because all the Muslim countries that apply these inhumane punishments use the same religious texts that Islamic State and similar groups use to guide and justify their barbarism. So, instead of futilely insisting that Islamic State is separate from Islam, we must examine the sources of these punishments and discover why Muslim governments have adopted them—including Islamic State.

Punishment of stoning (*ḥadd al-rajm*)

One of the most abominable punishments revived by Islamic State is death by stoning. In 2014, Islamic State released a chilling video showing a young woman, accused of adultery, standing next to her father (who is surrounded by militants) and asking him for forgiveness. But he refuses to forgive her. Then the militants ask her to repent and ask Allah's forgiveness before she is put to death. Her father then proceeds to tie her up before he leads her to a hole in the ground, where she is then stoned to death by both the militants and her own father.[68]

In early January 2015, Islamic State published pictures of its militants in the province of Nineveh in Iraq, reading a statement near a fully veiled woman, who is lying on the ground, apparently dead after being stoned.[69]

Stoning has also been carried out against women in several cities in Syria, sometimes in the marketplace or bazaar after the night prayer (*ṣalāt al-'ishā'*).[70] Once, a car was filled with stones and driven to the stoning site so that the Islamic State militants could stone the victim more quickly and easily. According to the Syrian Observatory for Human Rights (SOHR),

---

[68] Svirsky, Meira. "Video: Father Helps ISIS Militants Stone Daughter as per Sharia." *ClarionProject.org*. Clarion Project, 21 Oct. 2014. Web (https://clarionproject.org/video-islamic-state-stones-young-woman-accused-adultery-50). **Note:** This publicized case is the first of its kind to happen in the eastern countryside of Hama in Syria.

[69] "The Organization of the Islamic State Continues to Spread Terror on the Internet...and the Western World." *Alquds.co.uk*. Al-Quds al-Arabi, 17 Jan. 2015. Web (http://www.alquds.co.uk/?p=281157); Withnall, Adam. "ISIS Throws 'Gay' Men Off Tower, Stones Woman Accused of Adultery and Crucifies 17 Young Men in 'Retaliatory' Wave of Executions." *Independent.co.uk*. The Independent, 18 Jan. 2015. Web (http://www.independent.co.uk/news/world/middle-east/isis-throws-gay-men-off-tower-stones-woman-accused-of-adultery-and-crucifies-17-young-men-in-9986410.html).

[70] "Organization of the 'Islamic State' Stoning a Woman on Charges of Adultery." *Syriahr.com*. Syrian Observatory for Human Rights (SOHR), 28 July 2015. Web (http://preview.tinyurl.com/hcuz4br). **Note:** English translation of this article is abridged.

the implementation was carried out in the municipal stadium of the city of Raqqa.[71] During the last five months of 2014, SOHR documented twelve cases of death by stoning carried out by Islamic State.[72]

Stoning continues to be practiced in other areas where Islamic militant groups rule or control. On December 14, 2009, Ḥizbul Islam (an Islamic group in Somalia) stoned a man to death for adultery. The Islamic militants buried 48-year-old Muḥammad Abū Bakkār Ibrāhīm in a deep hole up to his neck before pelting him with rocks. They forced the villagers to watch the punishment, which took place twenty miles southwest of the capital city, Mogadishu.[73] In September 2014, Al Shabaab, an Islamic jihadist group based in East Africa with links to Al Qaeda, carried out the same punishment against a Somali woman.[74] The Taliban, another Islamic organization, carried out the stoning of two people in 2010 and filmed the scene in a video that was later circulated on Web sites and newspapers.[75]

Stoning is a known Islamic punishment. While it is true that there is not a specific verse now in the Qur'ān that dictates its use, Muslims believe that such a verse did exist at one time. Many consider its ruling still valid. This view is supported by a *ḥadīth* where 'Umar Ibn al-Khaṭṭāb, the second caliph and a son-in-law of Muḥammad, discussed the punishment of stoning in one of his sermons:[76]

---

[71] Organization of the 'Islamic State' Stoning a Woman on Charges of Adultery." *Syriahr.com*. Syrian Observatory for Human Rights (SOHR), 28 July 2015. Web (http://preview.tinyurl.com/hcuz4br). **Note:** English translation of this article is abridged.

[72] "Observatory: Documentation of 12 'Death by Stoning' Operations on Charges of Adultery within 5 Months." *Arabic.CNN.com*. Cable News Network (Arabic), 23 Dec. 2014. Web (https://arabic.cnn.com/middleeast/2014/12/20/sohrstoning-five-month).

[73] "Pictured: Islamic Militants Stone Man to Death for Adultery in Somalia as Villagers Are Forced to Watch." *DailyMail.co.uk*. Telegraph Media Group, 15 Dec. 2009. Web (http://www.dailymail.co.uk/news/article-1235763/Pictured-Islamic-militants-stone-man-death-adultery-Somalia-villagers-forced-watch.html).

[74] "Somali Woman Stoned to Death for Marrying Four Men Secretly." *Alriyadh.com*. Al Riyadh Daily, 28 Sept. 2014. Web (http://www.alriyadh.com/980187).

[75] "Shocking Footage Emerges of Taliban Stoning Couple to Death." *Telegraph.co.uk*. Telegraph Media Group, 27 Jan. 2011. Web (http://www.telegraph.co.uk/news/worldnews/asia/afghanistan/8287154/Shocking-footage-emerges-of-Taliban-stoning-couple-to-death.html).

[76] *Sahih Bukhari*, Book of Punishment of Disbelievers at War with Allah and His Apostle (p. 1528); *Ṣaḥīḥ al-Bukhārī*, Kītāb al-Muḥāribīn min Ahl al-Kufr wa al-Ridda 6: 2504.

> 'Umar sat on the pulpit...and having glorified and praised Allah, he said, "Now then, I am going to tell you something which (Allah) has written for me to say.... Allah sent Muhammad with the Truth and revealed the Holy Book to him, and among what Allah revealed, was the Verse of the Rajam (the stoning of married person (male and female) who commits illegal sexual intercourse), and we did recite this Verse and understood and memorized it. Allah's Apostle did carry out the punishment of stoning and so did we after him.
>
> I am afraid that after a long time has passed, somebody will say, 'By Allah, we do not find the Verse of the Rajam in Allah's Book,' and thus they will go astray by leaving an obligation which Allah has revealed. And the punishment of the Rajam is to be inflicted to any married person (male and female), who commits illegal sexual intercourse, if the required evidence is available or there is conception or confession...."

In another *ḥadīth*, a man came to Muḥammad and confessed to the Prophet that he had committed illegal sexual intercourse. When Muḥammad asked him, "Are you insane?" He replied, "No." At that point, Muḥammad told his Companions, "Go and stone him to death."[77]

Muḥammad also ordered the stoning of a Jewish couple for adultery, when the Jews brought the two people to him to ask about his judgment regarding adultery.[78] In yet another *ḥadīth*, Muḥammad made this comment after an Aslam tribesman, Mā'iz Ibn Mālik, was stoned after confessing adultery: "Whenever we set forth on an expedition in the cause of Allah, some one of those connected with us shrieked (under the pressure of sexual lust) as [like] the bleating of a male goat. It is essential that if a person having committed such a deed [unlawful sexual relations] is brought to me, I should punish him...."[79]

The following (in)famous *ḥadīth* seems particularly sadistic because the stoning was delayed for many months (perhaps over a year), likely leading the Ghāmidīa woman who confessed her adultery, which

---

[77] *Sahih Bukhari*, Book of Divorce (pp. 1181-1182); *Ṣaḥīḥ al-Bukhārī*, Kītāb al-Talāq 5: 2020.

[78] *Sahih Bukhari*, Book of Punishment of Disbelievers at War with Allah and His Apostle (p. 1525); *Ṣaḥīḥ al-Bukhārī*, Kītāb al-Muḥāribīn min Ahl al-Kufr wa al-Ridda 6: 2499-2500. Ibn 'Umar reported that "Allah's Apostle ordered a Jewish couple to be stoned to death for adultery, and so the Jews brought the couple to him to stone them." See *Sahih Muslim*, Book Pertaining to Punishments Prescribed by Islam: Stoning to death of Jews and other dhimmis in case of adultery (pp. 1045-1046); *Ṣaḥīḥ Muslim*, Kītāb al-Ḥudūd 2: 812.

[79] *Sahih Muslim*, Book Pertaining to Punishments Prescribed by Islam: He who confesses his guilt of adultery (p. 1042); *Ṣaḥīḥ Muslim*, Kītāb al-Ḥudūd 2: 809.

resulted in pregnancy, to hope she would eventually be pardoned and her judgment removed:[80]

> [After refusing her requests to "purify" her, Muḥammad] said: "Well if you insist upon it, then go away until you give birth to (the child). When she was delivered she came with the child (wrapped) in a rag and said: "Here is the child whom I have given birth to." He said: "Go away and suckle him until you wean him." And when she weaned him, she came to him (the Holy Prophet) with the child who was holding a piece of bread in his hand. She said: "Allah's Apostle, here is he as I have weaned him and he eats food." He (the Holy Prophet) entrusted the child to one of the Muslims and then pronounced punishment. And she was put in a ditch up to her chest and he commanded people and they stoned her. Khālid Ibn al-Walīd came forward with a stone which he flung at her head and there spurted blood on the face of Khālid and so he abused her....

But Muḥammad stopped Khālid from cursing her, because he said that she had repented and was cleansed from her sins when she surrendered without resistance to the stoning.

The Hadith literature contains many other examples of Muḥammad ordering his followers to execute the punishment of stoning[81] as well as narrations about his close Companions (and early caliphs), who carried out death-by-stoning sentences because they were following the Prophet's example and Sunna. One *ḥadīth* reports that 'Alī Ibn Abū Ṭālib (Muḥammad's son-in-law and the fourth caliph) had a woman stoned to death on a Friday (Islamic sabbath day) and justified it by stating, "I have stoned her according to the tradition of Allah's Apostle."[82] 'Umar Ibn al-Khaṭṭāb (one of Muḥammad's fathers-in-law and the second caliph) states in another *ḥadīth* that "Allah's Messenger...awarded the punishment of stoning to death (to the married adulterer and adulteress)

---

[80] *Sahih Muslim*, Book Pertaining to Punishments Prescribed by Islam: He who confesses his guilt of adultery (p. 1044); *Ṣaḥīḥ Muslim*, Kītāb al-Ḥudūd 2: 810-811. **Note:** In a different version of this *ḥadīth*, Muḥammad relents and states they should not stone her because there is "none to suckle" the infant. But one of the Anṣār offers to take responsibility for the infant, and the woman "was then stoned to death." (See *Sahih Muslim*, p. 1043.)

[81] *Sahih Bukhari*, Book of Peacemaking (p. 616); *Ṣaḥīḥ al-Bukhārī*, Kītāb al-Ṣulḥ 2: 959. Muḥammad ordered a follower, a man named Unais, to "'go to the [adulterous] wife of this (man) and stone her to death.' So, Unais went and stoned her to death."

[82] *Sahih Bukhari*, Book of Punishment of Disbelievers at War with Allah and His Apostle (p. 1523); *Ṣaḥīḥ al-Bukhārī*, Kītāb al-Muḥāribīn min Ahl al-Kufr wa al-Ridda 6: 2498. See *Sahih Muslim*, Book Pertaining to Punishments Prescribed by Islam: Prescribed punishment for an adulterer and an adulteress (pp. 1039, 1040); *Ṣaḥīḥ Muslim*, Kītāb al-Ḥudūd 2: 806. According to Muḥammad, Allah has ordained that "in case of [a] married male committing adultery with a married female, they shall receive one hundred lashes and be stoned to death."

and, after him, we also awarded the punishment of stoning...."[83] In other words, the use of stoning as a method of execution was formally established from the beginnings of Islam when Prophet Muḥammad ordered its implementation against those men and women who had committed certain sins, e.g., adultery. The early caliphs continued to implement it because they wanted to obey and follow "the Sunna of Muḥammad."

Sunni theologian and ascetic Ibn Qudāma states that "it has been proven that the apostle of Allah had practiced stoning, by his words and his deeds, according to narrations that are similar to *al-ḥadīth al-mutawātir* [which refers to recurrent *ḥadīths* that are ensured by many lines of transmission, according to Muslim scholars]."[84] Ibn Qudāma emphasizes the consensus among Muslim scholars regarding the lawfulness of stoning, and he too believes that the adulterous married man or woman must be stoned to death: "...and this is the opinion of all the scholars of Islam, including the companions and early followers, and after them the scholars of all countries and all eras. There is no one who disagrees except the Kharijites."[85]

The two major sects of Islam, Sunni and Shiite, agree concerning the ruling of stoning. Since 1982, the Iranian Penal Code of the Shiite Islamic Republic of Iran has instituted the punishment of stoning.[86] Published documented reports from Amnesty International and the International Committee Against Execution (ICAE) account for 150 executions by stoning in post-revolutionary Iran during 1980 to 2009.[87] Of this number, forty-four percent were women, a percentage that far exceeds female arrest rates and rates of commission in any other Muslim country.[88]

---

[83] *Sahih Muslim,* Book Pertaining to Punishments Prescribed by Islam: Stoning of a married adulterer (p. 1040); *Ṣaḥīḥ Muslim,* Kitāb al-Ḥudūd 2: 806.

[84] Ibn Qudāma, *Al-Mughnī* 12: 307.

[85] Ibid.

[86] Kusha, Hamid R., and Nawal H. Ammar. "Stoning Women in the Islamic Republic of Iran: Is It Holy Law or Gender Violence?" *Arts and Social Sciences Journal* 5.1 (January 2014): 2. Print and Web (https://www.omicsonline.org/open-access/stoning-women-in-the-islamic-republic-of-iran-is-it-holy-law-or-gender-violence-2151-6200.1000063.pdf). **Note:** The Islamic Republic of Iran was founded in 1979 after the victory of the Iranian Revolution and the overthrow of the Pahlavi dynasty and has been in power ever since.

[87] Ibid.

[88] Ibid. 1.

Sudan, a Sunni Muslim country, specifies in its criminal law execution by stoning for any married man convicted of adultery.[89] Another Sunni Muslim country, Mauritania, has also institutionalized since 1983 execution by stoning in its criminal law code:[90]

> Every person, a male or a female, accused of adultery, and the accusation is confirmed—by four witnesses, or by his/her own confession, or by pregnancy—that he/she committed an act of adultery voluntarily, this person is punishable with one hundred lashes in public, and imprisonment and a one-year exile if unmarried. If he/she was married, the punishment is stoning to death in public. There is no exile for the woman. Punishment with lashes and stoning for a pregnant woman will be postponed until she gives birth. Punishing with lashes will be postponed for a sick person until he/she recovers.

Although (Sunni) Qatar's Ministry of Endowments and Islamic Affairs does not actually apply the punishment of stoning, it affirms its legality, according to a fatwa as recent as December 2004:[91]

> Stoning a married person (adulterer/adulteress) to death is not only permissible in Islam; rather, it is an obligation that is agreed upon in a consensus by all the scholars.... [According to Ibn Qudāma] "the Prophet confirmed the stoning in words and actions (practice).... [and] Allah has revealed (this punishment) in His Book (Quran) but the writing of the verse was abrogated but its ruling is still effective... **and it is a duty to implement it to the Day of Resurrection**. [**Note:** Boldfaced text not shown in English translation.]

If Qatar, like Saudi Arabia, believes that the punishment for married adulterers is stoning, as practiced by Muḥammad and affirmed by his Companions and Muslim scholars, then why hasn't Qatar instituted its use in its criminal law code?

Even Jordan, a Muslim country that has historically enjoyed positive foreign relationships with Western countries, includes on one of its official governmental Web sites, *Dār al-Iftā' of Jordan* (General Iftaa' Department

---

[89] *Sudanese Penal Code.* 1991: ch. 15 (Offences against Honour, Reputation and Public Morals), art. 146 (1)(a). European Country of Origin Information Network. Page 44. Print and Web (https://www.ecoi.net/file_upload/1329_1202725629_sb106-sud-criminalact1991.pdf).

[90] *Criminal Law of Mauritania.* No. 83-162. 9 July 1983: art. 307. *Justice.gov.mr.* Official Web site of the Ministry of Justice of the Islamic Republic of Mauritania. Page 56. Print and Web (http://preview.tinyurl.com/zcnzud5).

[91] See Fatwa no. 86838: "Punishment for Adultery." *Islamweb.net.* Ministry of Endowments and Islamic Affairs of Qatar, 9 Dec. 2004. Web (http://www.islamweb.net/emainpage/index.php?page=showfatwa&Option=FatwaId&Id=86838).

of Jordan), this Fatwa no. 752 (May 24, 2010): "The punishment for the married adulterer is stoning to death and for the unmarried adulterer is flogging."[92]

Similarly, Saudi Arabia's official governmental Web site, *General Presidency for Scientific Research and Iftā'*, has issued this fatwa in response to a question about the validity of stoning in Islam: "Stoning to death, for the act of adultery of married men or women, exists firmly in the texts and deeds of the Islamic law."[93]

More disturbing is the adoption of stoning as execution by the Arab League in its *Unified Arab Criminal Code*. Approved in 1996 by all the ministers of justice of its representative Arab members, Article 141 states that "the punishment of a married man who commits adultery is stoning to death."[94]

These formalized, instituted criminal law codes concerning the issue of stoning can be easily found in individual Muslim countries as well as established Muslim political organizations and indicate that the implementation of stoning is not a punishment unique to Islamic State or is contrary to Islam. In fact, the kinds of punishments that Islamic State has implemented are an integral part of Islam.

There are states that recognize and implement this punishment like Islamic State, and there are those who recognize but do not implement it because the circumstances are not appropriate, like Qatār, Jordan, and the rest of the Arab League states. On the other hand, Islamic State is more consistent by implementing Islamic rulings it claims are authentic. So, it should not be surprising to see young idealistic Muslim people support and then join it, because they judge that their homeland country is acting like a "disbeliever" or a "hypocrite" when the government claims to recognize Islamic law yet does not implement it.

Punishment for homosexual acts

No less horrifying than execution by stoning for adultery are the punishments implemented by Islamic State against accused homosexuals.

[92] See Fatwa no. 752: "Does the Punishment of Stoning the Adulterer Include the Widow and the Divorced?" *Aliftaa.jo*. General Iftaa' Department of Jordan, 24 May 2010. Web (http://www.aliftaa.jo/Question.aspx?QuestionId=752#.WeZChmiPKUl).

[93] See Fatwa no. 1883 (tenth question): "Denial of Stoning." *Alifta.net*. General Presidency for Scientific Research and Iftā' (Saudi Arabia), n.d. Vol. 22, p. 27. Web (http://preview.tinyurl.com/y7p3wkam).

[94] League of Arab States. *United Arab Penal Code*. 1996: art. 141. *CARJJ.org*. Arab Center for Legal and Judicial Research (sub-organ of the League of Arab States). Page 116. Print and Web (https://carjj.org/sites/default/files/united-arab-criminal-law-part1.pdf).

One publicized video and other documentation show Islamic State members hurling a blindfolded gay man, arms tied behind, from a building top in front of a large, jeering crowd.[95]

On August 24, 2015, the United Nations Security Council held an "historic" meeting on the plight of homosexuals in areas controlled by Islamic State to discuss the atrocities committed against homosexuals by Islamic State militants and hear some of the horrific testimonies by victims and witnesses. Jessica Stern, Executive Director of the International Gay and Lesbian Rights Commission, stated that Islamic State has claimed responsibility for and documented the killing of thirty or more people on "charges of doing 'the work of the people of Lot[96]' [reference to homosexual acts]." [97] Subhi Nahas, a gay Syrian refugee, described the escalation since 2011 of attacks by rebel militias, armed groups, and even Syrian government troops on gay people. Another guest speaker, "Adnan," using a pseudonym for protection, spoke by telephone to the Council that he, as a gay Iraqi, "had to leave a society where 'being gay means death.'"[98]

In December 2014, Islamic State sentenced and executed a man convicted of homosexuality ("act of the people of Lot") and then published photographs of the execution, where the young convicted man was thrown to his death from a three-story building, with this announcement: "Like the Muslim Caliph Abū Bakr…the Islamic court in the Euphrates state [Wilayet al-Furāt province] ruled a man who did

---

[95] Hall, John. "Hurled to His Death in Front of a Baying Mob: ISIS Barbarians Throw 'Gay' Man Off Building in Another Sickening Day in Jihadi Capital of Raqqa." *DailyMail.co.uk*. Telegraph Media Group, 4 Mar. 2015. Web (http://www.dailymail.co.uk/news/article-2978890/ISIS-barbarians-throw-gay-man-building-bloodthirsty-crowds-Syria.html).

[96] **Note:** In Islam, Lot was a nephew of Abraham and a prophet sent to give God's message to the sinful people of Sodom and Gomorrah, twin cities known for their extreme sexual misconduct. Lot was later told by two angels to leave the region, and God destroyed both cities for their wickedness. Compare with the earlier Old Testament account in the Bible (Gen. 19.1-16).

[97] "A 'Historic' Session of the Security Council on the Persecution of Homosexuals." *DW.com/ar*. Deutsche Welle (Arabic), 25 Aug. 2015. Web (http://preview.tinyurl.com/j6o32r6); "A 'Historic' Session of the Security Council on the Atrocities of the 'Islamic State' against Homosexuals." *France24.com/ar*. France 24 (Arabic), 25 Aug. 2015. Web (http://preview.tinyurl.com/jbvao4k).

[98] Westcott, Lucy. "Gay Refugees Addresses U.N. Security Council in Historic Meeting on LGBT Rights." *Newsweek.com*. Newsweek, 25 Aug. 2015. Web (http://www.newsweek.com/gay-refugees-addresses-un-security-council-historic-meeting-lgbt-rights-365824).

the act of the people of Lot [practiced sodomy] must be thrown off the highest point in the city and then stoned to death."[99]

In July 2014, the first execution of this kind—sentencing men to death for acts "of the people of Lot" by flinging them off the roof of a tall building—was carried out in the ancient city of Palmyra, when two young men were thrown off a high building for being accused of sodomy.[100] In the following months, more such executions of men accused of homosexuality were carried out. Sometimes, stoning or beheading (or, more mercifully, shooting) was implemented after the victims fell to the ground—even if they did not survive the fall.

From where did Islamic State get these sentences for punishing those who commit "acts of the people of Lot"? Why do these sentences somewhat vary from place to place or from one executioner to another? At first observation, these punishments only appear to be different ways of execution. While the majority of Islamic schools of jurisprudence opine that the killing of homosexuals is an obligatory duty, specific punishment for homosexual activity does not exist in the Qur'ān. The Qur'ān only speaks about Allah's punishment to "the people of Lot" because they have committed the "abominable sin" of homosexual behavior.[101] According to the Qur'ān, Allah punished the people of Sodom and Gomorrah by raining stones down upon them from the sky. This depiction is the apparent inspiration for Muslims' stoning homosexuals or throwing them off a high place or both.

The Hadith literature states, "If you find any persons engaged in homosexuality, kill both the active and the passive partner."[102] This *ḥadīth* is included in Islamic State's written report of the two young men who were sentenced and killed in Palmyra. It is most likely that the two young

---

[99] "Pictures: Da'ash [ISIS] Kills a Man on Charges of Homosexuality through 'Throwing [Him from] High' and 'Stoning.'" *Arabic.CNN.com*. Cable News Network (Arabic), 10 Dec. 2014. Web (https://arabic.cnn.com/middleeast/2014/12/10/isis-new-pics-killing); Adams, Sam. "ISIS Fighters Throw Man Off Roof of Building then STONE Him to Death for Being GAY." *Mirror.co.uk*. Mirror Online, 10 Dec. 2014. Web (http://www.mirror.co.uk/news/world-news/isis-fighters-throw-man-roof-4784798).

[100] "The Organization of the 'Islamic State' Carries Out the First 'Throwing High' Operation in Palmyra." *Syriahr.com*. Syrian Observatory for Human Rights (SOHR), 24 July 2015. Web (http://preview.tinyurl.com/zqgncox).

[101] See Q 27.54-58; Q 7.80-84; Q 26.160-173. In these passages, God punishes Sodom and Gomorrah by raining down on them "a rain," "a rain (of stones)," or a "shower (of brimstone)," depending on the English translation.

[102] *Musnad Aḥmād* 1: 94; *Sunan al-Tirmidhī* 4: 627. See *Sunnah.com*: *Jami' at-Tirmidhi*, Book of Legal Punishments (Al-Hudud). Web (https://sunnah.com/tirmidhi/17/40).

men were together, caught in the sexual act, and so this *ḥadīth* was cited as a basis for implementing the punishment.

The Hadith literature also includes a *ḥadīth* where Muḥammad says, "Stone the upper [person on top of the other] and the lower, stone them both."[103] This *ḥadīth* is considered the basis for those who apply the punishment of only stoning for homosexual acts.

Those Muslims who kill homosexuals by throwing them off the highest point in the city are following instead the opinion of Ibn 'Abbās, a cousin and close Companion of Muḥammad and one of the most important Muslim scholars in the first era of Islam. When he was asked, "What is the punishment for the person who does the acts of the people of Lot?" he answered, "Find the tallest building in the village and throw the homosexual down from its roof with his head down. Then stone him to death."[104]

Medieval Sunni theologian Ibn Taymīya makes this comment concerning the various punishments mentioned in the Hadith literature concerning homosexuals:[105]

> The companions did not dispute concerning the ruling that the homosexual is to be executed, but they differed concerning the method. It was narrated about [first caliph] Abū Bakr that he ordered him [homosexual] to be burned, and from others [companions] that he is to be killed. And it was narrated from some of them [companions] that a wall is to be knocked down on top of him until he dies beneath it. And it is said that both should be detained in the foulest of places until they die. It was narrated from some of them that he should be taken up to the highest place in the village and thrown down from it, and to be followed with stones, as Allah did to the people of Lot.... This was the view of the majority of the *salaf* [considered the pious predecessors: first three generations of Prophet Muhammad, his Companions, their successors and the successors of the successors]. They said: because Allah stoned the people of Lot, and stoning is prescribed for the adulterer [and therefore] by analogy the stoning of the homosexual.

In his comment, Ibn Tamīya confirms that the early Muslims agreed that homosexuals must be killed; they only disagreed upon the method of

---

103 Ibn Māja, *Sunan Ibn Māja* 2: 856; see chapter Kītāb al-Ḥudūd regarding "the one who does the acts of the people of Lot."

104 al-Bayhaqī, *Al-Sunan al-Kubra* 12: 460; see chapter Kītāb al-Ḥudūd, regarding "the punishment of the homosexual."

105 Ibn Taymīya, *Majmū' Fatāwā* 28: 335.

execution. He refers to Ibn 'Abbās (death by throwing off the homosexual from a high place and then stoning him) and 'Abd Allah Ibn al-Zubayr (suffocation from detainment in a malodorous place). Abū Bakr and 'Alī reportedly had homosexuals burned to death.[106]

On the Web site *Islam Question and Answer*, founded by Saudi sheikh Muḥammad Ṣāliḥ al-Munajjid and one of the most popular Salafi Web sites in the Arabic-speaking world, one reader posted this question regarding the punishment for homosexuality: What is the punishment for homosexuality? Is there any differentiation between the one who does it [homosexual act] and the one to whom it is done? To this question, the sheikh gave a detailed (see selected excerpts) response:[107]

> ...Executing the homosexual is obligatory punishment, as the companions of the Messenger of Allah were unanimously agreed, and as is clearly indicated by the Sunnah of the Messenger of Allah, and there is no evidence to the contrary; rather this is what his companions and the Rightly-Guided Caliphs did.... The companions of the Messenger of Allah agreed unanimously that the homosexual is to be executed, and none of them differed concerning that. Rather they differed as to the method of execution....
>
> ...It is stated [in Islamic sources] that Khālid Ibn al-Walīd found a man among one of the Arab tribes with whom men would have intercourse as with a woman. He wrote to [first caliph] Abū Bakr... and so Abū Bakr...consulted the companions. 'Alī Ibn Abū Ṭālib had the strongest opinion of all of them, and he said: "No one did that but one of the nations [i.e., Sodom and Gomorrah], and you know what Allah did to them. I think that he should be burned with fire." So Abū Bakr wrote to Khālid and he had him burned.

Egyptian Muslim scholar and *ḥadīth* master al-Ḥāfiẓ al-Mundhirī states that "Abū Bakr burned the homosexuals, and so did 'Alī, 'Abd Allah Ibn al-Zubayr, and Hishām Ibn 'Abd al-Malik, after killing them with the sword or stoning them."[108]

Only one of the four religious Sunni Islamic schools of jurisprudence (*fiqh*), the Hanafi, does not call for the killing of homosexuals.[109] But this school's doctrine is the exception and not the general rule.

---

[106] al-Jazīrī, *Kitāb al-Fiqh* 5: 127.

[107] al-Munajjid, Muḥammad. "Fatwa no. 38622: Sodomy Punishment." *IslamQA.info/ar.* Islam Question and Answer, 14 Mar. 2006. Web (https://islamqa.info/ar/38622).

[108] al-Jazīrī, *Kitāb al-Fiqh* 5: 127.

[109] See al-Jazīrī, *Kitāb al-Fiqh* 5: 127.

Yet Islamic State is not unique in its insistence to kill people who commit homosexual acts. Several Muslim countries have adopted laws to criminalize and punish homosexuality—with death sentences in some cases. In Mauritania, "Every Muslim accused [of homosexual acts], and the accusation is confirmed by witnesses or by his/her own confession that he/she has committed the crime of sodomy shall be punished by stoning in public."[110] Sudan also criminalizes and harshly punishes homosexual acts:[111]

> Any man who inserts his penis or its equivalent into a woman's or a man's anus or permitted another man to insert his penis or its equivalent in his anus is said to have committed Sodomy. Whoever commits Sodomy shall be punished with flogging [by] one hundred lashes and he shall also be liable to five years' imprisonment. If the offender is convicted for the second time he shall be punished with flogging [by] one hundred lashes and imprisonment for a term which may not exceed five years. If the offender is convicted for the third time he shall be punished with death or life imprisonment.

The death penalty for homosexuality is an Islamic rule. Those Muslim countries that do not apply it do so—not because they believe Islam forbids the killing of homosexuals—but because of international legal, diplomatic, and economic reasons. For example, Morocco sentences convicted homosexuals with imprisonment that varies from six months to three years and fines of 200 to 1000 dirham.[112] Yet acts of homosexuality are treated more harshly than the crime of adultery in Morocco, where the maximum sentence for adultery is only one year.[113] These sentences differ from Islamic rulings because Morocco was once a French protectorate and thus its laws have been influenced by this earlier colonial relationship. Also, Morocco wishes to participate within the international community, which brings with its membership the recognition and protection of human rights.

---

[110] *Criminal Law of Mauritania*. No. 83-162. 9 July 1983: art. 308. *Justice.gov.mr*. Official Web site of the Ministry of Justice of the Islamic Republic of Mauritania. Page 56. Print and Web (http://preview.tinyurl.com/zcnzud5).

[111] *Sudanese Penal Code*. 1991: ch. 15 (Offences against Honour, Reputation, and Public Morals), art. 148; see (1)(2)(a)(b)(c). European Country of Origin Information Network. Page 39. Print and Web (https://www.ecoi.net/file_upload/1329_1202725629_sb106-sud-criminalact1991.pdf).

[112] *Moroccan Penal Code*. 12 Mar. 2018: ch. 8 (Immorality Violations), art. 489. *Justice.gov.ma*. Morocco Ministry of Justice. Page 167. Print and Web (To download document PDF, see URL: https://preview.tinyurl.com/ybbstr2b).

[113] Ibid.

The Muslim countries that adopt criminal codes that are contrary to Islam do not willingly apply these more humane "human-made" sentences but do so under coercion through international pressure and circumstances. If these countries could avoid or ignore these international strictures, they would certainly try to change these sentences and revert their punishments specifically to the era of Muḥammad.

The execution of homosexuals for their sexual behavior by Islamic State is a policy that began since the era of Muḥammad. It continues in some form in other Muslim countries to this day. Islamic State did not originate this policy; it only revived a punishment as it was reported in the Sunna of the Prophet, his successors, his Companions and their followers and confirmed by Muslim scholars during the centuries. Therefore, to condemn Islamic State for these brutal punishments and executions, we must condemn the sources from which it derived these policies.

Punishment of immolation, or burning alive with fire

One of the most gruesome videos in the history of Islamic State shows captive Jordanian pilot Mu'āth al-Kasāsbeh being burned alive. The video was released through one of Islamic State's media outlets (Furqān Foundation for Media Production) and titled *The Healing of Breasts*, a phrase that refers to a Qur'ānic verse (Q 9.14; Palmer trans.): *"kill them! God will torment them by your hands, and disgrace them, and aid you against them, and heal the breasts of a people who believe."* The context clarifies the message intended by Islamic State: Killing and tormenting Islam's enemies shames them as it heals the hearts and minds of the believers and satisfies their need for revenge. Renowned Muslim exegete al-Ṭabarī explains that the pain in the chests of Muslim believers will be relieved and healed by humiliating, defeating, and killing infidels.[114] Clearly, Islamic State, in citing this Qur'ānic reference, wants to intimidate its enemies, acknowledge the hatred and rage its followers feel toward the international coalition strikes, and satiate their desire for revenge. The capture (and torture/killing) of Mu'āth al-Kasāsbeh provided Islamic State with an opportunity to deliver this message.

[114] See the commentary on Q 9.41, *Tafsīr al-Ṭabarī* 10: 64.

On December 24, 2014, the plane of this 26-year-old Jordanian pilot went down in Syria, the first warplane lost since the US-led air strikes began against Islamic State three months earlier.[115]

The pilot ejected from the plane, falling into the Euphrates River, as the plane fell from the sky. His plane either suffered a malfunction or was struck by enemy missile file.[116] Islamic State fighters retrieved the fallen pilot from the river and quickly, jubilantly, proclaimed his capture. Among the photographs Islamic State published on Web sites and supporters' Twitter accounts was a photograph of prostrating militants. The photograph's caption reads: "ISIS militants prostrating in thankfulness to Allah after capturing the apostate Jordanian pilot." One photograph of the captured pilot includes a caption that reads, "The first picture of the Jordanian apostate pilot who was arrested after his plane was shot down." His identification cards were published as well as photographs of the equipment that was found with him. (The word *apostate* here is very important, because it connotes a religious meaning that would become relevant in the choice of punishment used to execute the pilot.)

The video of the pilot's burning was released on February 3, 2015, but some analysts believe that this brutal execution was carried out about a month earlier. The 23-minute video includes an introduction outlining the aggression of the coalition countries against Islamic State, especially Jordan, followed by the confession of the pilot Mu'āth al-Kasāsbeh and details of his mission. He is also forced to reveal the names and workplaces of several of his fellow Royal Jordanian Air Force pilots. Their names and photographs are displayed at the end of the video, with a bounty offer of 100 gold dinars for each Jordanian Air Force pilot killed.

The video is cleverly and skillfully assembled to maximize the Islamic terrorist group's justification in the torturing and burning alive of the pilot with extremely graphic imagery. About midway in the video, scenes of coalition fighter planes blowing up highways and buildings are

---

[115] "ISIS Fighters Capture Jordanian Pilot after Plane Came Down over Syria." *TheGuardian.com*. The Guardian, 24 Dec. 2014. Web (https://www.theguardian.com/world/2014/dec/24/islamic-state-shot-down-coalition-warplane-syria).

[116] Behn, Sharon. "IS Hold Jordanian Pilot; US Denies Claim F-16 Jet Shot Down." *VOANews.com*. Voice of America News, 24 Dec. 2014. Web (https://www.voanews.com/a/activists-islamic-state-fighters-shoot-down-warplane/2571759.html); "ISIS Captures a Jordanian Pilot 'but He Did Not Drop His Plane.'" *DW.com/ar*. Deutsche Welle (Arabic), 24 Dec. 2014. Web (http://preview.tinyurl.com/hfvnreo). The United States and Jordanian officials stated that mechanical problems caused the plane to crash, while Islamic State claimed that its fighters had hit the plane with a heat-seeking missile.

followed by photographs of wounded or dead children—many burnt. The following segment shows Mu'āth dressed in an orange jumpsuit, walking along the bombed ruins of some buildings. Armed Islamic State soldiers, identically clothed and hooded in combat gear, stand in a row near him. As Mu'āth looks out upon the empty ruins, flashback scenes of other destruction and killed civilians interrupt his view, as if to suggest that the coalition (and his role in it) is to blame for all the destruction (and his fate).

Then next major scene shows Mu'āth (head down as if to suggest remorse for his crimes) confined in a large outdoor black steel cage, his orange jumpsuit now wet (with some combustible fluid). A militant ignites a long torch, which he then uses to light a combustible "trail" leading to the cage. In seconds, the area in the cage and Mu'āth are on fire. Vainly, Mu'āth struggles to escape the cage, screaming and hopping in agony. Minutes later his shell of a body collapses backward in the cage and a bulldozer dumps a load of rock over the cage, extinguishing the fire and destroying the cage bars. As the bulldozer backs up, using its bucket to level the area, the camera zooms in on Mu'āth's exposed burnt hand.[117]

Some viewers may wonder why the pilot seems so calm throughout most of the video recording and shows no resistance until it is too late. The careful, artistic nature of the short film, with the computerized special effects and music and its well-organized composition, indicate that many rehearsals and retakes were carried out beforehand. The repeated shoots no doubt lulled Mu'āth into thinking he was only being used as a propaganda tool to facilitate negotiations with Jordan and the international coalition. When Mu'āth realized that the final scene would include his fatal burning, it came as a surprise. Otherwise, he would have expressed resistance by screaming or yelling before the fire reached him inside the cage.

The final minutes of this video contain images no compassionate human can handle seeing without extreme shock and anguish.[118] At the end of Mu'āth's burning, a voice-over quotes Ibn Taymīya:[119]

[117] "WARNING, EXTREMELY GRAPHIC VIDEO: ISIS Burns Hostage Alive." *FoxNews.com*. Fox Entertainment Group, 3 Feb. 2015. Web (http://video.foxnews.com/v/4030583977001/?#sp=show-clips).

[118] Ibid.

[119] Ibn Taymīya, *Majmū' Fatāwā* 28: 314. See Ibn Mufliḥ, *Kītāb al-Furū'* 6: 218.

...[I]f the infidels mutilate the Muslims, then the Muslims have the right to do the same or they have the right to let it go, and patience is better. But they [Muslims] cannot be patient with them [infidels] if mutilation encourages them [infidels] to believe [in Islam] or prevent them from attacking [the Muslims].

Essentially, Ibn Taymīya is stating that the mutilation of bodies is lawful jihad if used to encourage disbelievers to believe in Islam or to deter the disbelievers from engaging in hostilities against believers.

Islamic State issued a statement after the publication of the video clarifying the religiously lawful support for its burning of the Jordanian pilot. The fatwa was prepared before the release of the video, which indicates that the organization was aware that it would face objections, even from its followers. Issued on January 19, 2015, Fatwa no. 60 presents the following text in answer to the expected question ("What is the ruling on burning the *kāfir* [disbeliever] with fire until he dies?"):[120]

[...] The Ḥanafis and Shāfi'īs [two of the four main schools of Sunni jurisprudence, the others being Maliki and Hanbali] have permitted it, considering the saying of the Prophet, "Fire is only to be administered as punishment of God" as an affirmation of humility. Al-Muhallab [early Islamic theologian, d. c. AD 702] said: "This is not an absolute prohibition, but rather on the path of humility."

Al-Hafiz ibn Hajar [Egyptian Islamic theologian, AD 1372-1449] said: "What points to the permissibility of burning is the deeds of the Companions, and the Prophet put out the eyes of the Uraynians with heated iron...while Khalid ibn al-Waleed [Companion of Muḥammad who participated in early Muslim conquests in the Levant] burnt people of those who apostatized."

And some of the Ahl al-'Ilm [Muslim scholars] have been of the opinion that burning with fire was prohibited originally, but then on retaliation it is permitted, just as the Prophet did to the people of Urayna, when he put out the eyes of the Uraynians with fire—in retaliation—as is related in Sahih [reliable] tradition, and this brought forth the words together among the proofs.

By presenting evidence from the Hadith literature, the Sunna of Muḥammad, and commentary by respected Muslim theologians in its Fatwa no. 60, Islamic State anticipated and successfully (in its view) refuted

[120] al-Tamimi, Aymenn Jawad. "Islamic State Justification for Burning Alive the Jordanian Pilot: Translation and Analysis." *Aymennjawad.org*. Aymenn Jawad al-Tamimi's Blog, 4 Feb. 2015. Web (http://www.aymennjawad.org/2015/02/islamic-state-justification-for-burning-alive).

any religious objections to its burning alive of Mu'āth al-Kasāsbeh—thus making its fatwa a valid legitimate religious ruling.

But where did Islamic State derive this ruling of burning a person alive with fire? Does it have precedent in Islamic history? Did Muḥammad or his Companions ever burn alive people? The Qur'ān (Q 16.126; Palmer trans.) states, *"But if ye punish, punish (only) as ye were punished. . . ."* This verse gives Muslims the right to punish others with the same tool(s) that was (were) used to punish them. Islamic State has used this verse to help justify the burning of the Jordanian pilot. To Islamic State, the punishment of immolating the pilot just simulates the burning of homes, buildings, and people from the bombs used to attack Islamic State by the international coalition forces. This type of quid pro quo punishment is part of the argument Islamic State uses to justify its various kinds of barbaric killings. Yet it is a strong religious pretext that sheikhs cannot reject as long as Muslims have the right to punish with the same punishment they have received.

In a similar context, Islamic State strung up four Iraqi Shiite fighters with chains before they burned them alive. The four men were suspended from a children's swing set by chains attached to their hands and feet, just like slaughtered animals trussed for roasting, and then set on fire. The video of this horrific killing was posted online with the title, *But If Ye Punish, Punish (Only) As Ye Were Punished,* which refers to the aforementioned Q 16.126.[121] The burning of the four Iraqi Shiite fighters, which was video recorded and then publicized online, appears to be in response to a video posted online in late August 2015 showing the blackened corpse of an Islamic State fighter suspended face down from an electricity pylon.[122] The short time interval between this burning by an Iraqi militant and the Islamic State burning of the four Iraqi fighters as well as the similar style and method of the burnings indicate an "eye-for-an-eye" relationship.

---

[121] "21+ WARNING: ISIS Burns Four Iraqi Shi'ite Fighters Alive (VERY GRAPHIC)." *TLVFaces.com.* TLV Faces, 31 Aug. 2015. Web (http://www.tlvfaces.com/21-warning-isis-burns-four-iraqi-shiite-fighters-alive-very-graphic); "ISIS 'Roasts' Members from the Popular Mobilization Forces." *Alarabiya.net.* Al Arabiya Network, 31 Aug. 2015. Web (http://preview.tinyurl.com/jfv8azz).

[122] Verkaik, Robert. "'We Will Cut You Like Shawarma': Gruesome Video Shows 'Angel of Death' Iraqi Fighter Carving Flesh Off the Charred Body of an 'ISIS Fighter He Burned to Death.'" *DailyMail.co.uk.* Telegraph Media Group, 28 Aug. 2015. Web (http://www.dailymail.co.uk/news/article-3214167/We-cut-like-shawarma-Gruesome-video-shows-Angel-Death-Iraqi-fighter-carving-flesh-charred-body-ISIS-fighter-burned-death.html). At one point in this video, Iraqi warrior, Ayyub al-Rabaie, known as Abu Azrael ("Angel of Death") faces the camera and says, "ISIS, this will be your fate. We will cut you like *shawarma*" and then carves a chunk of charred flesh from the dead man's leg.

This principle of responding in the same manner to ill will by others is a Qur'ānic principle, as stated in Q 2.194 (Palmer trans.): "...*and whoso transgresses against you, transgress against him like as he transgressed against you....*" The Qur'ān also depicts Allah himself punishing people with fire and delighting in their continual torment. Whenever the skins of the disbelievers are burned, he just replaces them with new skins to be burned: "*Verily, those who disbelieve in our signs, we will broil them with fire; whenever their skins are well done, then we will change them for other skins, that they may taste the torment...*" (Q 4.56; Palmer trans.).

Allah's Messenger, Muḥammad, threatened to burn his Muslim followers who failed to pray in congregation with him:[123]

> Allah's Apostle said, "By Him in Whose Hand my soul is I was about to order for collecting firewood (fuel) and then order Someone to pronounce the Adhan for the prayer and then order someone to lead the prayer then I would go from behind and burn the houses of men who did not present themselves for the (compulsory congregational) prayer...."

If Muḥammad wanted to burn his followers in their homes just because they failed to pray with him in congregation, how much more would he punish enemies who bombed him? I do not think he would have treated them better than his followers. Recall that Muḥammad sent some of his men to pursue eight men from 'Uraina who had stolen his camels and killed his shepherd. Muḥammad commanded to have them killed in a most heinous manner without any trial and before any Qur'ānic verses were revealed: First, their hands and feet were cut off and then nails were heated and inserted in their eyes; they were left to die in the desert without water or other provisions.[124] Some Islamic accounts report that Muḥammad also had them burned.[125] (Since Muḥammad had to use fire to heat the nails, some Muslim scholars have concluded that the use of fire as punishment against enemies is therefore permissible.)

'Alī Ibn Abū Ṭālib was one of Muḥammad's closest Companions, based on his blood and familial relationships with the prophet and longtime association as an early believer of Islam. Some Muslims, then and now (e.g., Shiites) considered and consider him the "heir-apparent"

[123] *Sahih Bukhari*, Book on Call to Prayers (p. 156); *Ṣaḥīḥ al-Bukhārī*, Kitāb al-Adhān 1: 231.

[124] *Sahih Bukhari*, Book of Fighting for the Cause of Allah (pp. 694-695); *Ṣaḥīḥ al-Bukhārī*, Kitāb al-Jihād wa al-Sīyar 3: 1099.

[125] See the commentary on Q 5.33, *Tafsir al-Qurṭubī* 6: 158.

after Muḥammad's death. As the fourth caliph, he was also one of Islam's founders. Therefore, his actions, by all these connections, are considered an extension of Muḥammad's teachings and wishes. According to the Hadith literature, he too burned people, including nonbelievers, apostates, and idolaters.[126]

Islamic State identified Mu'āth al-Kasāsbeh as an apostate in some of its publicized photographs. The Zanādiqa are described in some *ḥadīths* as a people who had left Islam and thus became apostates. Al-Bukhārī places this story in his respected collection of *ḥadīths* in a chapter regarding Islamic rulings of apostates. Close Companion and fourth caliph 'Alī Ibn Abū Ṭālib permitted the burning to death of apostates as well as homosexuals. Would he pardon a person like Mu'āth al-Kasāsbeh, who is considered an apostate fighter by Islamic State?

First caliph Abū Bakr burned a person, commonly known as Al-Fajā'a, because he apostatized and later killed some Muslims:[127]

> ...he [Abū Bakr] deputed a column to get the man back. The column succeeded and he [Al-Fajā'a] was brought to al-Baqī' [cemetery on the southeast side of Medina where many Companions were buried], where his hands were chained to the back of his neck. He was then thrown on top of a fire and was roasted to death while chained.

What Islamic State did to Mu'āth al-Kasāsbeh is similar to what Abū Bakr ordered done to Al-Fajā'a, a Muslim who apostatized and then participated in the killing of Muslims. As far as Islamic State is concerned, Mu'āth al-Kasāsbeh was born a Muslim but then apostatized because he followed the regime of his own country and fought for his country Jordan instead of fighting for the caliph. Not only was Mu'āth an apostate, he was an apostate fighter who fought against and participated in the killing of Muslims who were fighting for Islamic State. So, in the eyes of Islamic State, it had the right to kill him—just as Abū Bakr, the first caliph, when he ordered that Al-Fajā'a be killed. In short, Abū Bakr al-Baghdādī, the caliph of Islamic State, is simply replicating the caliphal

---

[126] *Sahih Bukhari,* Book of Dealing with Apostates (p. 1539); *Ṣaḥīḥ al-Bukhārī,* Kītāb 6: 2537. This *ḥadīth* reports that some "Zanādiqa (atheists) were brought to 'Alī and he burnt them...." **Note:** Variations of this *ḥadīth* describe these people as "atheists," "apostates," or "idolaters," who worshipped idols in secret. See al-'Asqalānī, *Fatḥ al-Bārī* 14: 270. Also, some narrations report that 'Alī killed these people first and then burned their bodies.

[127] Ibn Kathīr, *Al-Bidāya* 6: 319.

actions of Abū Bakr, the first caliph. Furthermore, at least four of the early caliphs also used fire to execute death sentences.

Egyptian Muslim scholar al-Ḥāfiz al-Mundhirī states that "four caliphs have burned homosexuals: Abū Bakr, 'Alī Ibn Abū Ṭālib, 'Abd Allah Ibn al-Zubayr and Hishām Ibn 'Abd al-Malik."[128] Islamic State bases its actions on the abundant evidence it finds in Islamic sources; it knows that its actions are not an exception in the Muslim world. The same actions were practiced by Muḥammad and his Companions and the successors after him. No one can denounce Islamic State without criticizing the Islamic foundations that predicate its policies and actions.

After burning alive the Jordanian pilot and posting the video of it online, a wave of condemnation swept the Arab world. I was following the reactions, especially the reactions of the sheikhs, because I knew that they would try to contain the religious dilemma unleashed by Islamic State by this burning. I surfed online for fatāwa that supports the burning of enemies with fire. In short time, I discovered that the official Web site of Qatar's Ministry of Endowments and Islamic Affairs includes a fatwa that blatantly permits and justifies the killing of people by burning them to death. To the question, "How can we reconcile the Prophet's ban on burning with fire with Abū Bakr's burning of Iyās Ibn 'Abd Yalīl [the person who was known as Al-Fajā'a,] during the Ridda Wars (apostasy wars)," the fatwa, in part, presents this response:[129]

> The Prophet's ban is valid. According to the honorable *ḥadīth,* the Prophet said: "only the God of fire may punish with fire"... [However], religious scholars were divided on whether this ban is absolute, or is only meant to [instill] humility [towards God]. [Shafi'i jurisprudent] Ibn Hajar [Al-'Asqalani] said in his book *Fath Al-Bari*: "This ban is not meant to prohibit [burning], but only to [instill] humility. The actions of the Prophet's Companions indicate that burning is permissible. The Prophet blinded members of the 'Uraina tribe with a hot iron. [Caliph] Abu Bakr punished criminals by burning in the presence of the Prophet's Companions, and [the Prophet's Companion] Khalid Ibn Al-Walid [also] burned people from among the apostates. Most of the scholars of Medina permitted the burning of horses and chariots with the people inside....

---

[128] al-Jazīrī, *Kitāb al-Fiqh* 5: 127.

[129] Fatwa no. 71480: "Abu Bakr Burning Iyas Ibn 'Abd Yalil." *Islamweb.net.* Ministry of Endowments and Islamic Affairs of Qatar, 7 Feb. 2006. Web. **Note:** This fatwa is no longer available on this Web site. (To read complete fatwa now accessible on the MEMRI Web site, see URL: https://www.memri.org/reports/fatwa-qatari-government-website-execution-burning-permitted-under-certain-circumstances)

> ...There is no doubt that Iyās Ibn ʿAbd Yalīl's deed justified his burning. May Allah maximize the reward of the Caliph of the Messenger of Allah for his zeal for Islam.

This fatwa was deleted from the Web site on February 3, 2015 (just hours after the video of the burning was posted), when tweets posted on Twitter pointed to it.[130] Soon afterward, proposals to ban books authored by Ibn Taymīya from entering Jordan were discussed by Jordanian authorities, because Islamic State included quotations from his books at the end of the its video to maintain that the mutilation of dead bodies is permissible according to the religious texts.[131]

It is worth noting that some *ḥadīths* declare that the burning alive of people is forbidden; only Allah can punish with fire.[132] However, many Muslim scholars do not count this punishment ban as lawful. They explain that its cancellation is only a sign of humility from Muḥammad, who banned its use in order to leave that task for Allah alone.[133] (Muslim scholars offer this explanation, even though it really does not reconcile Muḥammad's ban with his own practice of burning people and that of the Companions and early caliphs after Muḥammad's death.)

Islamic State innovation and expansion of Muḥammad's punishments

The videos Islamic State has posted online of its horrific executions are infamous not only for their barbarism but also for their repugnant variety. Of course, these online publications are being used as a sick propaganda tool aimed to intimidate and terrorize, a psychological war to demoralize enemy soldiers and frighten away spies and potential infiltrators.

An example of an Islamic State video particularly directed toward enemy spies is *If You Return, We Will Return*, dated June 23, 2015. Its title refers to Q 17.8 (Palmer trans.): *"... but if ye return we will return, and we have made hell a prison for the misbelievers."* The original context of the

---

[130] Ibrahim, Raymond. "Qatar Published Fatwa in 2006 Permitting Burning People—Removes It after ISIS Burns Pilot." *RaymondIbrahim.com*. Raymond Ibrahim, 7 Feb. 2015. Web (http://raymondibrahim.com/2015/02/07/qatar-published-fatwa-in-2006-permitting-burning-people-removes-it-after-is-burns-pilot).

[131] "Jordan Reserves the Writings of Ibn Tamiya." *Aljazeera.net*, Al Jazeera Media Network, 8 June 2015. Web (http://preview.tinyurl.com/nhr4wg7).

[132] *Sahih Bukhari*, Book of Fighting for the Cause of Allah (p. 694); *Ṣaḥīḥ al-Bukhārī*, Kītāb al-Jihād wa al-Sīyar 3: 1098. In this *ḥadīth*, Muḥammad sent his men on a military mission and said, "If you find so-and-so and so-and-so, burn both of them with fire." But when the men departed, Muḥammad said, "I have ordered you to burn so-and-so and so-and-so, and it is none but Allah Who punishes with fire, so, if you find them, kill them [instead]."

[133] al-ʿAsqalanī, *Fatḥ al-Bārī* 6: 259.

passage (which includes this verse) concerns Allah's threat toward the Jews, where Allah reminds the Jews that he had once *"sent over them servants of ours, endued with violence"* (Q 17.5; Palmer trans.) to punish them for their evilness. In Q 17.8, Allah warns that he will return to punish them again if they renew their evilness. Islamic State has appropriated this verse to warn enemy spies or infiltrators that if they enter the caliphate lands and are caught, they will be severely punished.

In the first segment of this short video, Islamic State fighters load three men clad in the familiar orange prison jumpsuits, their hands bound behind their back, into a waiting car. A masked militant then blows up the car with a rocket-propelled grenade. The men inside the car can be heard screaming as they burn to death. The video then cuts to the second segment. Several masked Islamic State militants load five men into a large cage and then lock its door. The cage is lifted over a deep swimming pool and then slowly lowered into it until the five men inside the cage are completely submerged. An underwater camera shows the men struggling to escape but they ultimately drown. In the third and final segment, seven captives are kneeling, their hands tied behind them. A masked militant ties a long explosive "necklace" consecutively around each man's neck, connecting the entire group. The explosive necklace is detonated, severing their heads.[134] What motivates Islamic State to act with so much cruelty in executing and punishing those whom it describes as spies?

Islam's Allah tells his angels on the Day of Judgment to punish the disbeliever: *"Take him and fetter him, / then in hell broil him! / then into a chain whose length is seventy cubits force him! / verily, he believed not in the mighty God"* (Q 69.30-33; Palmer trans.). This god finds pleasure in tormenting his victims: *"On the day when the torment shall cover them from above them and from beneath their feet, and He* [Allah] *shall say, 'Taste that which ye have done!'"* (Q 29.55; Palmer trans.). This depiction of Allah as a brutally cruel tormentor is not very different from Muḥammad, his prophet, who carried out similarly sadistic tortures, e.g., cutting off the hands and feet of the eight 'Uraina men before piercing their

[134] "Video: 3 Executions in 'New' Methods Carried Out by Daesh [ISIS]." *Alarabiya.net*. Al Arabiya Network, 23 June 2015 (last update). Web (http://preview.tinyurl.com/jdjk3mn). **Note:** The images are so extremely graphic, this news source does not present the entire footage. See Charlton, Corey. "Has ISIS Found a Sadistic New Way to Kill? Ominous Warning of New Video Is Released Featuring Prisoners Surrounded by Islamists on Horseback." *DailyMail.co.uk*. Telegraph Media Group, 26 Aug. 2015 (last update). Web (http://www.dailymail.co.uk/news/article-3210469/ISIS-introducing-new-killing-style-Ominous-warning-terror-group-s-latest-video-depicting-horrific-murder-released-featuring-prisoners-surrounded-Islamists-horseback.html).

eyes with heated nails and leaving them to die in the desert[135] and the torture and beheading of Kināna Ibn al-Rabi'.[136] Though Muḥammad did not have rocket-propelled grenades or explosive dynamite at his disposal, he and Islamic State are absolutely no different from each other in their brutal torture and execution of their enemies—only the tools and methods differ, given the different eras and resources. For instance, Muḥammad's use of catapults, which he launched against the people of al-Ṭā'if,[137] can be compared to Islamic State's use of rocket launchers. On the basis of this incident, some Islamic scholars have concluded that as long as Muḥammad permitted the destruction of the enemies with the catapult, then the use of drowning enemies in water is also permissible: "It was reported by 'Alī Ibn Abī Ṭālib that the Prophet has set up the catapult against the people of aṭ-Ṭā'if, and flooding the enemy with water is similar to that."[138]

Yet the Islamic books and Hadith literature report even worse and more numerous atrocities than those committed by Islamic State and similar Islamic terrorist groups today. One early Muslim leader who comes quickly to mind is the Companion Khālid Ibn al-Walīd, whom Muḥammad nicknamed "Sayf Allāh" ("The Sword of Allah").[139] He was appointed military commander near the end of Muḥammad's life and was instrumental as a ruthless enforcer and empire expander during the caliphate of Abū Bakr. He had Muslim Mālik Ibn Nuwayra, tribal chief of the Banū Yarbu', killed because he refused to pay the *zakāt* (religious obligatory tax) to first caliph Abū Bakr. Not only did he kill Mālik Ibn Nuwayra, but he "took [raped] his wife," who was known for her beauty.[140] Some Muslim historians state that Khālid placed the head of Mālik Ibn

---

[135] *Sahih Bukhari*, Book of Fighting for the Cause of Allah (pp. 694-695); *Ṣaḥīḥ al-Bukhārī*, Kītāb al-Jihād wa al-Sīyar 3: 1099.

[136] Ibn Hishām (Ibn Isḥāq), *The Life of Muhammad* 515; Ibn Hishām (Ibn Isḥāq), *Al-Sīra al-Nabawīya* 4: 79. Muḥammad had Kinana Ibn al-Rabi' ("who had the custody of the treasure of Banū al-Naḍīr") tortured to extract information about the location of the remaining treasure (as some had been found). A fire was kindled "with flint and steel on his chest until he was nearly dead. Then the apostle delivered him [Kināna] to Muḥammad Ibn Maslama and he struck off his head, in revenge for his brother Mahmud."

[137] Ibn Hishām (Ibn Isḥāq), *The Life of Muhammad* 587, 589; Ibn Hishām (Ibn Isḥāq), *Al-Sīra al-Nabawīya* 4: 255. See *Sunan al-Tirmidhī* 8: 38.

[138] Ibn Qudāma, *Al-Kāfi* 4: 268.

[139] *Musnad Aḥmād* 6: 406.

[140] Ibn Kathīr, *Al-Bidāya* 6: 322.

Nuwayra in a pot, cooked it, and ate from it.[141] Many Muslims protested Khālid's actions, primarily because Mālik was a Muslim. (Punishment for murdering a Muslim and fornicating with the murdered man's wife is stoning.) Even 'Umar[142] pressed Abū Bakr to dismiss him, saying, "In this sword there really is forbidden behavior."[143] However, Caliph Abū Bakr did not reject Khālid despite insistent calls for his removal, replying in a now famous statement among Muslims, "I will not sheathe a sword that God has drawn against the unbelievers."[144]

Hints of Khalid's later perverse, sadistic behavior are evident when Muḥammad "sent Khalid forth as a missionary" to "the lower part of the flat country." When the people of that locale, the Banū Jadhima, saw him, they "grasped their weapons," distrustful of this fearsome Muslim military commander. He told them to lay down their arms as "everybody has accepted Islam." Despite their misgivings, the people were persuaded to lay down their arms. At this point, "Khālid ordered their hands to be tied behind their backs and put them to the sword, killing a number of them."[145] When Muḥammad heard this news, he bemoaned the killings—but never disciplined, demoted, or removed Khālid from his position as chief of the army.

Because of his exceptional and successful military leadership (he helped to unite all of Arabia for the first time in history under one unified caliphate), including victory in over a hundred battles, Khālid's shocking excesses were overlooked or excused, e.g., the killing of a defenseless woman "while men gathered around her"[146] and gathering people into a livestock corral and burning them alive.[147]

Even 'Umar, who had protested Khālid's killing of Mālik Ibn Nuwayra and urged first caliph Abu Bakr to punish him, gave this

---

[141] Ibn Kathīr, *Al-Bidāya* 6: 322. According to this source, Khālid Ibn al-Walīd ordered one of his men to strike the neck of Mālik Ibn Nuwayra. Khālid "then ordered his [Mālik's] head and he combined it with two stones and inserted into a cooking pot. And Khalid ate from it that night to terrify the apostate Arab tribes and others. And it was said that Mālik's hair created such a blaze that the meat was so thoroughly cooked."

[142] **Note:** When 'Umar Ibn al-Khattab became the second caliph after Abū Bakr's death, one of his first official acts was to dismiss Khālid Ibn al-Walīd from the army.

[143] *History of al-Ṭabarī* 10: 101-102, 103-104.

[144] Ibn Kathīr, *Al-Bidāya* 6: 322; *History of al-Ṭabarī* 10: 101-102, 103-104.

[145] Ibn Hishām (Ibn Isḥāq), *The Life of Muhammad* 561; Ibn Hishām (Ibn Isḥāq), *Al-Sīra al-Nabawīya* 4: 196-197.

[146] Ibn Hishām (Ibn Isḥāq), *The Life of Muhammad* 576; Ibn Hishām (Ibn Isḥāq), *Al-Sīra al-Nabawīya* 4: 226.

[147] al-Dhahabī, *Siyar* 3: 231.

reason regarding Khālid Ibn al-Walīd's dismissal from the army when 'Umar became the second caliph:[148]

> I have not dismissed Khalid because of my anger or because of any dishonesty on his part, but because people glorified him and were misled. I feared that people would rely on him. I want them to know that it is Allah who gives us victory; and there should be no mischief in the land.

According to this public statement, 'Umar did not dismiss Khālid for his brutality or for killing a Muslim. 'Umar dismissed him because of his *fame*. In other words, his conquests and the subjugation of peoples on behalf of the caliphate—brutality notwithstanding—were lauded and admired among the early Muslims.

Islamic State has not been advocating or following policies that are contrary to the Islamic schools of jurisprudence or contrary to the policies and rulings of the prominent early leaders of Islam. Its doctrine isn't just some new heresy or just an organization falsely claiming to be Muslim. It justifies its actions and policies on the Islamic texts, rulings, and historical precedents and uses them to confront those Muslim sheikhs and other critics who insist that Islamic State's behavior is not representative of Islam. But these sheikhs only condemn Islamic State because they want to exonerate Islam from accusations of terrorism; they avoid any sincere scrutiny of Islamic State and its relationship with Islam.

The bitter truth we all must face is that Islamic State applies Islam strictly and follows in the footsteps of those who brought Islam and spread it in the entire world—in the footsteps of the first Muslim generation, the generation of Muḥammad and his Companions. While it is true that Islamic State does not represent all Muslims in the world, its application of Islam adheres more closely to Islam's teachings, prohibitions, and punishments that are provided in the Qur'ān and Sunna, the sacred Islamic texts of all Muslims.

---

[148] Akram, *Sword of Allah* 488.

FOURTEEN

Je suis Charlie ("I am Charlie") | *Je suis* Muḥammad ("I am Muḥammad")

When I first heard about the attack on the office of the French satirical weekly magazine *Charlie Hebdo*, I tried contacting Zaynab al-Ghazawī, a Moroccan friend who works as a journalist for this very same publication. I was almost certain that if she were there she would have been among the victims, because she is known for her bold views as an atheist and former Muslim. She publicly called upon Moroccans to eat publicly during Ramadan and to protect religious freedom, opinions that caused her problems with the Moroccan authorities even before she joined *Charlie Hebdo*.

Luckily, she was on a holiday in Morocco when the massacre happened. There, she heard the news that her colleagues and some of her close friends were killed by two gunmen. What a shock for any person to find out that his or her coworkers have been brutally murdered only because they used their pen to criticize a certain religion. It is unbelievable that this kind of response to free expression of the press is still happening in the twenty-first century.

Twelve people were killed and eleven wounded in the military-style attack that took place on January 7, 2015.[1] Two French Muslim brothers of Algerian origin, Chérif Kouachi (age 32) and Said Kouachi (age 34), carried out the attack, shouting "*Allahu Akbar*" while shooting the people inside the office and later declaring, "We have avenged the Prophet Muḥammad. We have killed Charlie Hebdo!"[2]

A publicized jihadist "hit list"

Among the targeted victims was the editor of *Charlie Hebdo*, Stéphane Charbonnier, who was known professionally as Charb. Two years earlier, he was one of nearly a dozen people included on an "enemies of Islam" list published in the 2013 spring issue of Al Qaeda's jihadist recruitment magazine *Inspire*.[3] On one page of a two-page spread is a photograph of the American pastor Terry Jones with a superimposed handgun shooting him in the head and the caption: "Yes We Can. A Bullet a Day Keeps the Infidel Away. Defend Prophet Muḥammad Peace Be Upon Him."[4] On the opposite page is the "wanted" list with eleven names (some misspelled), including the name of Stéphane Charbonnier. Some of the names include a "headshot" photograph.[5] Though no explanation is provided with the names to explain their presence on this hit list, most are publicly known for their criticism of Muḥammad or some of Islam's teachings and practices:[6]

---

[1] "Manhunt after Deadly Charlie Hebdo Terrorist Attack." *France24.com/en*. France 24 (English), 7 Jan. 2015; updated 8 Jan. 2015. Web (http://www.france24.com/en/20150107-live-blog-gun-shots-french-paris-charlie-hebdo-satirical-magazine); Henderson, Barney, Andrew Marszal, and David Millward. "Paris Charlie Hebdo Attack: January 7 As It Happened." *Telegraph.co.uk*. Telegraph Media Group, 7 Jan. 2015. Web (http://www.telegraph.co.uk/news/worldnews/europe/france/11332098/Paris-Charlie-Hebdo-attack-January-7-as-it-happened.html).

[2] Vale, Paul. "Paris Gunman Shouts 'We Have Avenged the Prophet Muḥammad' in Newly Released Video Footage." *HuffingtonPost.co.uk*. The Huffington Post, 13 Jan. 2015. Web (http://www.huffingtonpost.co.uk/2015/01/13/paris-killer-shouts-we-have-avenged-the-prophet-mohammed-in-newly-released-video_n_6464448.html). See Bergen, Peter, and Emily Schneider. "How the Kouachi Brothers Turned to Terrorism." *CNN.com*. Cable Network News, 10 Jan. 2015. Web (http://edition.cnn.com/2015/01/09/opinion/bergen-brothers-terrorism/index.html).

[3] Bennett, Dashiell. "Look Who's on Al Qaeda's Most-Wanted List." *TheAtlantic.com*. Atlantic Media, 1 Mar. 2013. Web (https://www.theatlantic.com/international/archive/2013/03/al-qaeda-most-wanted-list/317829).

[4] "Wanted: Dead or Alive for Crimes against Islam." *Inspire*. Issue 10 (Spring 2013): 14-15. Print and Web (https://info.publicintelligence.net/InspireWinter2013.pdf).

[5] Ibid.

[6] See Zavadski, Katie. "These 10 People Were Also Named Al Qaeda's Most Wanted." *NYMag.com*. New York Magazine, 14 Jan. 2015. Web (http://nymag.com/daily/intelligencer/2015/01/who-are-inspires-10-other-most-wanted.html).

Carsten Juste

In September 2005, Danish large-circulation newspaper *Jyllands-Posten*, under then editor-in-chief Carsten Juste, published twelve editorial cartoons, most depicting Prophet Muḥammad, including one where the prophet is wearing a bomb-shaped turban.[7] Publication (and re-publication in 2008) of these cartoons led to protests, a boycott of Danish products, violent demonstrations, rioting, and attacks on Danish and other European embassies in several Muslim countries in 2006 and more violence again in 2008.[8] In 2008, Danish police foiled an assassination plot to kill one of the cartoonists.[9] (See **Kurt Westergaard.**)

Terry Jones

Pastor Terry Jones of Christian Dove World Outreach Center in Florida announced in July 2010 that he planned to burn two hundred Qur'āns on the ninth anniversary of the September 11 terrorist attacks. International outrage from media coverage of this proposed event resulted in violent protests in the Middle East and Asia. He subsequently cancelled this event, only to hold a mock trial of the Qur'ān on March 20, 2011 and burned a Qur'ān in the church sanctuary for its "crimes against humanity." Afghan protesters in the city of Mazar-i-Sharif reacted by attacking the United Nations Assistance Mission, killing more than a dozen people (including two beheadings) and injuring scores more.[10] The pastor received over three hundred death threats after the burning.[11]

---

[7] "Cartoons of Muḥammad." *AINA.org*. AINA Syndicated News and Assyrian International News Agency, 2 Jan. 2006. Web (http://www.aina.org/releases/20060201143237.htm).

[8] Vick, Karl. "Cartoons Spark Burning of Embassies." *WashingtonPost.com*. The Washington Post, 5 Feb. 2006. Web (http://www.washingtonpost.com/wp-dyn/content/article/2006/02/04/AR2006020401208.html); "Muslims Protest Danish Muḥammad Cartoons." *NBCNews.com*. National Broadcasting Corporation, 15 Feb. 2008 (updated). Web (http://www.nbcnews.com/id/23186467/ns/world_news-europe/t/muslims-protest-danish-Muḥammad-cartoons/#.Wfipm7pFyUk).

[9] "Police Foil Plot to Kill Muḥammad Cartoonist." *NBCNews.com*. National Broadcasting Corporation, 2 Dec. 2008. Web (http://www.nbcnews.com/id/23125346/ns/world_news-europe/t/police-foil-plot-kill-Muḥammad-cartoonist#.WfjHFrpFyUk).

[10] Najafizada, Enayat, and Rod Nordland. "Afghans Avenge Florida Koran Burning, Killing 12." *NYTimes.com*. New York Times, 1 Apr. 2011. Web (http://www.nytimes.com/2011/04/02/world/asia/02afghanistan.html?_r=1&hp); "'Hold Islam Accountable': U.S. Pastor Defiant after His Koran-Burning Publicity Stunt Led to Two UN Staff Being Beheaded and Five Others Murdered." *DailyMail.co.uk*. Telegraph Media Group, 2 Apr. 2011 (updated). Web (http://www.dailymail.co.uk/news/article-1372442/Pastor-Terry-Jones-defiant-Koran-burning-led-2-UN-staff-beheaded.html).

[11] Mann, Camille. "Pastor Terry Jones Receiving Death Threats after Quran Burning." *CBSNews.com*. CBS (Columbia Broadcasting System) Corporation, 4 Apr. 2011. Web (https://www.cbsnews.com/news/pastor-terry-jones-receiving-death-threats-after-quran-burning).

Kurt Westergaard

This professional cartoonist contributed the most controversial and famous drawing—Prophet Muḥammad wearing a bomb in his turban—in the highly publicized September 30, 2005, issue of *Jyllands-Posten.* (See **Carsten Juste.**) Though Westergaard has been recognized in much of the West as a "symbol of the freedom of the press and of expression,"[12] he has been the target of many death threats and once barely escaped an ax-wielding Somali Muslim, who broke into his home in 2009.[13]

Geert Wilders

This Dutch politician founded and currently leads the PVV (*Partij voor de Vrijheid*), or Party for Freedom in the Netherlands. However, he is best known for his criticism of Islam and the "Islamisation of the Netherlands," which generates controversy in his homeland and abroad. In 2008, he published online the short film *Fitna,*[14] which uses selected Qur'ānic verses, media clips, and newspaper clippings to argue that Islam encourages terrorism, anti-Semitism, and violence against women, homosexuals, and infidels, and promotes Islamic universalism.[15] In 2012, he wrote the book *Marked for Death: Islam's War against the West and Me*, which chronicles his political journey and his personal ordeal from his open criticism of Islamic ideology.[16] He began receiving death threats in 2003 and, after the assassination of fellow Dutch citizen Theo van Gogh in 2004, Wilders has not lived in his own house but is constantly moved for his protection. A security detail is part of his daily routine.[17]

---

[12] "Merkel Defends Press Freedom, Condemns Koran-Burning." *Spiegel.de.* Der Spiegel, 9 Sept. 2010. Web (http://www.spiegel.de/international/germany/award-for-danish-Muḥammad-cartoonist-merkel-defends-press-freedom-condemns-koran-burning-a-716503.html).

[13] Sjølie, Marie Louise. "The Danish Cartoonist Who Survived an Axe Attack." *TheGuardian.com.* The Guardian, 4 Jan. 2010. Web (https://www.theguardian.com/world/2010/jan/04/danish-cartoonist-axe-attack).

[14] *Fitna.* Script by Geert Wilders and Scarlet Pimpernel. Dir. and prod. Scarlet Pimpernel. LiveLeak, 27 Mar. 2008. Web. (To view film, see URL: https://www.youtube.com/watch?v=2HlptyGvlIY)

[15] "Iran Warns Netherlands Not to Air Controversial 'Anti-Muslim' Film." *FoxNews.com.* Fox Entertainment Group, 21 Jan. 2008. Web (http://www.foxnews.com/story/2008/01/21/iran-warns-netherlands-not-to-air-controversial-anti-muslim-film.html).

[16] Hartwell, Ray. "Book Review: 'Marked for Death.'" *WashingtonTimes.com.* The Washington Times, 13 June 2012. Web (http://www.washingtontimes.com/news/2012/jun/13/how-free-speech-led-to-jihad).

[17] Fjordman. "Geert Wilders: Marked for Death." *FrontPageMag.com.* FrontPage Magazine, 10 May 2012. Web (http://www.frontpagemag.com/fpm/131756/geert-wilders-marked-death-fjordman).

Lars Vilks

This Swedish artist and sculptor unleashed Muslim wrath with a series of drawings caricaturing Prophet Muḥammad as a roundabout dog (Swedish type of street installation). After several art galleries rejected showing his drawings for "security concerns" and fear of violence, a regional Swedish newspaper *Nerikes Allehanda* published one of the drawings in August 2007, as part of an editorial about self-censorship and freedom of expression and religion.[18] Other Swedish newspapers published all the drawings. Among the protests and death threats Vilks received following their publication, Al Qaeda's call for his assassination is particularly odious: a bounty of US$100,000 "for the one who kills this criminal" and US$150,000 if he is "slaughtered [beheaded] like a lamb."[19] Vilks has also been assaulted by Muslim protesters and continues to be a target of assassination attempts. In 2015, he survived an attack by a Muslim gunman, who managed to kill one attendee and wound three police officers at a guarded seminar about free speech.[20] (See Chapter 3, page 67.)

Stéphane Charbonnier

As editorial director of the French satirical magazine *Charlie Hebdo*, Charbonnier was "instrumental in a series of defiant campaigns" promoting free speech on a variety of provocative issues, including Islam and the prophet Muḥammad.[21] The *Charlie Hebdo* offices were firebombed in 2011, just before the magazine published a spoof issue advertised as guest-edited by Prophet Muḥammad. From that time forward, Charbonnier and two coworkers received police protection. Before the *Charlie Hebdo* massacre in 2015, a man was arrested in 2012 for urging on a jihadist Web site the beheading of Charbonnier.[22] Charbonnier is the first person on this Al Qaeda hit list to be assassinated.

---

[18] [English translation] Stroman, Lars. "The Right to Ridicule a Religion." *Nerikes Allehanda*. 30 Aug. 2007 (archived from original, 28 Aug. 2007). Print and Web (https://web.archive.org/web/20070830163657/http://www.na.se/artikel.asp?intId=1209676).

[19] "Al-Qaida Places Bounty on Cartoonist." *JPost.com*. Jerusalem Post, 15 Sept. 2007. Web (http://www.jpost.com/International/Al-Qaida-places-bounty-on-cartoonist).

[20] "Copenhagen Shooting: One Dead in Deadly Seminar Attack." *BBC.com*. British Broadcasting Corporation, 14 Feb. 2015. Web (http://www.bbc.com/news/world-europe-31472423).

[21] Somaiya, Ravi. "Charlie Hebdo Editor Made Provocation His Mission." *NYTimes.com*. New York Times, 7 Jan. 2015. Web (https://www.nytimes.com/2015/01/08/world/europe/charlie-hebdo-editor-made-provocation-his-mission.html).

[22] "A Man Called to Behead the Director of 'Charlie Hebdo' Arrested." *20minutes.fr*. 20 Minutes, 22 Sept. 2012; updated 29 Jan. 2014. Web (http://www.20minutes.fr/societe/1008383-20120922-homme-appele-decapiter-directeur-charlie-hebdo-interpelle).

Flemming Rose

In 2005, Rose was the cultural editor of *Jyllands-Posten* and the primary person responsible for commissioning the group of drawings of Muḥammad that ignited the worldwide controversy and resulting protests and violence in the Muslim world. He was concerned that many European creative artists were being forced to censor their work out of fear of Muslim violence and invited Danish illustrators to depict Muḥammad as they saw him.[23] He too has bodyguard protection, and the Federal Bureau of Investigation (FBI) foiled one attempt to assassinate him and Westergaard in 2009.[24] (See **Kurt Westergaard**.)

Morris Sadek

This Egyptian-American Coptic Christian was the promoter of the highly controversial 2012 film *Innocence of Muslims*,[25] which was created by another Egyptian-born Coptic Christian, Mark Basseley Youssef (formerly known as Nakoula Basseley Nakoula), now a US resident. This amateurishly made anti-Islam video was roundly criticized as inaccurate and offensive and ignited mass demonstrations protesting its circulation in Muslim countries.[26] At one point, angry protests triggered by the film were initially blamed as the catalyst for the deadly attack September 11, 2012, on the US embassy in Benghazi, Libya, where four Americans, including US Ambassador to Libya, J. Christopher Stevens, were killed. This accusation was later discredited.[27] (For more information about Nakoula and the Benghazi attack, see Chapter 1, page 32.)

---

[23] See Cottee, Simon. "Flemming Rose: The Reluctant Fundamentalist." *TheAtlantic.com*. Atlantic Media, 15 Mar. 2016. Web (https://www.theatlantic.com/international/archive/2016/03/flemming-rose-danish-cartoons/473670/).

[24] Freeze, Colin, and Tu Thankh Ha. "The 'Mickey Mouse' Mastermind: Canadian Charged in Plot against Danish Newspaper." *TheGlobeandMail.com*. The Globe and Mail, 28 Oct. 2009. Web (https://theglobeandmail.com/news/world/the-mickey-mouse-mastermind-canadian-charged-in-plot-against-danish-newspaper/article1205029).

[25] *Innocence of Muslims*. By Nakoula Basseley Nakoula. 2012. Film. (To view film, see URL: https://archive.org/details/Muḥammadfullmovie)

[26] Spillius, Alex, Adrian Blomfield, Rob Crilly, and Ben Farmer. "Protests Spread against Anti-Islam Film." *Telegraph.co.uk*. Telegraph Media Group, 17 Sept. 2012. Web (https://www.telegraph.co.uk/news/worldnews/middleeast/9548665/Protests-spread-against-anti-Islam-film.html). See Coscarelli, Joe. "This Is the Absurd, Islamophobic Video That Sparked Violent Protests in Libya and Egypt." *NYMag.com*. New York Magazine, 12 Sept. 2012 (updated). Web (http://nymag.com/daily/intelligencer/2012/09/innocence-of-muslims-terry-jones-video-sparked-protests-libya-egypt.html).

[27] Myre, Greg. "From Threats against Salman Rushdie to Attacks on 'Charlie Hebdo.'" *NPR.org*. National Public Radio, 8 Jan. 2015. Web (http://www.npr.org/sections/parallels/2015/01/08/375662895/from-threats-against-salman-rushdie-to-attacks-on-charlie-hebdo).

Salman Rushdie

Probably the most well-known person on this list is British Indian novelist Salman Rushdie, who incurred a fatwa in February 1989 calling for his assassination on Iranian radio by Ayatollah Ruhollah Khomeini, the Supreme Leader of Iran, after the publication of his fourth novel, *The Satanic Verses*. Iranian officials followed this fatwa days later with a bounty of US$6 million for killing him. Muslims claimed that the book blasphemed and insulted their faith, because it includes references to the "satanic verses" of the Qur'ān and allusions to Muḥammad and his life in a series of dream vision narratives. With the highly publicized fatwa, the British government placed the author under police protection, and he spent ten years on the run living in over twenty different "safe houses." He published the book *Joseph Anton* in 2012 to give a full account of those years.[28] (Since 2000, he has lived in the United States.) Though the many assassination attempts against him over the years have been foiled or failed, one of the translators, Hitoshi Igarashi, of *The Satanic Verses*, was found stabbed to death in his office in 1991. No one has ever been charged with his murder, though some suspect the attack was connected to his Japanese translation of the novel.[29]

Ayaan Hirsi Ali

This Somali-born Dutch-American activist, feminist, author, film producer, and former politician collaborated with Dutch film director Theo van Gogh in 2004 to create and produce the short television film *Submission*,[30] which describes and criticizes the treatment and oppression of women under Islam. Outrage from the Dutch Muslim community regarding this film culminated in the assassination of its director by Mohammad Bouyeri (a Dutch-Moroccan Muslim with a

---

[28] Suroor, Hasan. "Salman Rushdie's New Book Tells of Life in Hiding." *TheHindu.com*. The Hindu, 9 Sept. 2012; last updated 25 July 2016. Web (http://www.thehindu.com/books/salman-rushdies-new-book-tells-of-life-in-hiding/article3878175.ece).

[29] Helm, Leslie. "Translator of 'Satanic Verses' Slain: Japan: The Stabbing of a Scholar at a Campus near Tokyo May Be Related to Salman Rushdie's Controversial Novel." *LATimes.com*. Los Angeles Times, 13 July 1991. Web (http://articles.latimes.com/1991-07-13/news/mn-1822_1_satanic-verses).

[30] *Submission*. Script by Ayaan Hirsi Ali. Dir. Theo van Gogh. VPRO, 29 Aug. 2004. Television. (To read about this film, see URL: http://www.imdb.com/title/tt0432109/?ref_=nm_flmg_prd_2; to view film, see URL: https://www.youtube.com/watch?v=oPZEy7_6etI) **Note:** English voice-over in the film begins approximately 1:25.

Dutch passport) about two months after the film's broadcast.[31] Ali's involvement with this film as well as her published books and public views critical of Islam have resulted in numerous death threats since the early 2000s.

Molly Norris

Inspired by the uproar when Comedy Central "edited" (censored) part of an episode (which depicted Muḥammad dressed as a bear) of the highly irreverent *South Park* television program, *Seattle Weekly* cartoonist and journalist Molly Norris decided to stand up for free speech by publishing an online cartoon about an imaginary group called "Citizens Against Citizens Against Humor" that proposed an "Everybody Draw Mohammad Day."[32] In turn, her cartoon stimulated others to start a campaign to create pictures of Muḥammad across the Internet with more than 100,000 people signed up on a Facebook page. She "distanced herself immediately" from this Facebook page, which included some of the "most vulgar cartoons" imaginable.[33] She apologized but continued to receive death threats. The FBI moved to offer her protection, and she went into hiding. Since 2010, Norris has virtually disappeared from view, her whereabouts unknown by family and friends.[34] (Incidentally, she and Terry Jones are the only Americans on this hit list.)

What is the common thread among all these people? Why are they wanted dead? Why do Muslims from different backgrounds—and even a Muslim government like Iran—try to kill them? If Al Qaeda and Islamic groups are only exceptions or aberrations in the Muslim world, why are there massive demonstrations in the entire Muslim world protesting caricatures of Muḥammad? Why do Muslims burn embassies and demand the immediate execution of these cartoonists and writers?

---

[31] Simons, Marlise. "Dutch Filmmaker, an Islam Critic, Is Killed." *NYTimes.com*. New York Times, 3 Nov. 2004. Web (http://www.nytimes.com/2004/11/03/world/europe/dutch-filmmaker-an-islam-critic-is-killed.html).

[32] Almasy, Steve. "After Four Years, American Cartoonist Molly Norris Still in Hiding after Drawing Prophet Mohammad." *CNN.com*. Cable Network News, 14 Jan. 2015. Web (http://edition.cnn.com/2015/01/13/us/cartoonist-still-in-hiding/index.html).

[33] Ibid.

[34] Ripley, Brie. "The Vanishing of Molly Norris." *SeattleGlobalist.com*. Seattle Globalist, 9 Feb. 2015. Web (http://www.seattleglobalist.com/2015/02/09/molly-norris-draw-mohammed-cartoon-charlie-hebdo-seattle/32674).

Criticism of the Prophet

The common denominator among all the people on this hit list is that they are accused of insulting or cursing Prophet Muḥammad in some way. In Islam, insulting Muḥammad is a sin that deserves the punishment of death. The Kouachi brothers carried out their deadly attack on the journalists of *Charlie Hebdo* because of this religious doctrine. Their motive did not suddenly develop from reading Al Qaeda's magazine *Inspire* or listening to the online inflammatory oratory of Yemeni Muslim sheikh Anwar al-Awlaki but from the Islamic texts that teach Muslims from childhood on that whoever curses the prophet must be killed. The Prophet himself killed those who cursed or mocked him, and his Companions did the same.

This familiar Islamic rule is easy and simple: Whoever insults the prophet must be killed. Thus, Moroccan Dutchman Mohammed Bouyeri, the man who shot and then slashed the throat of television host and film provocateur Theo van Gogh, is Dutch by nationality but had completely adopted the Islamic identity that was established within him. This total Islamic identification was evident during his trial when he addressed the judges:[35]

> [Bouyeri entered the court clutching a Qur'ān.] "I did what I did purely out of my beliefs.... I want you to know that I acted out of conviction and not that I took his life because he was Dutch or because I was Moroccan and felt insulted.... If I ever get free, I would do it again."

In line with these remarks, he offered no apology to van Gogh's mother and told her he did not sympathize with her loss: "I have to admit I do not feel for you, I do not feel your pain, I cannot—I don't know what it is like to lose a child.... I cannot feel for you...because I believe you are a nonbeliever [infidel]...."[36]

---

[35] "Van Gogh Murder Suspect Confesses to Killing." *NBCNews.com*. National Broadcasting Corporation, 12 July 2005. Web (http://www.nbcnews.com/id/8551653/ns/world_news/t/van-gogh-murder-suspect-confesses-killing/#.WfuRVbpFyUk).

[36] "Suspected Killer of Van Gogh Confesses." *DW.com/en*. Deutsche Welle (English), 12 July 2005. Web (http://www.dw.com/en/suspected-killer-of-van-gogh-confesses/a-1647199); "Van Gogh Murder Suspect Confesses to Killing." *NBCNews.com*. National Broadcasting Corporation, 12 July 2005. Web (http://www.nbcnews.com/id/8551653/ns/world_news/t/van-gogh-murder-suspect-confesses-killing/#.WfuRVbpFyUk).

He later stated at his sentencing that "the [Islamic] law compels me to chop off the head of anyone who insults Allah and the prophet."[37]

What is the source of these religious teachings that preach the killing of those who insult the prophet Muḥammad? One incident from Muḥammad's time, which has been repeatedly mentioned throughout the Hadith literature and Muḥammad's biography, provides an illuminating response to this question. This particular incident concerns a Medinan Jewish leader and poet, Ka'b Ibn al-Ashraf, who became alarmed and angry when he learned that Muḥammad and his Muslims had killed so many Quraysh noblemen during the Battle of Badr. According to Islamic sources, he left Medina for Mecca, where he began to "inveigh against the apostle and to recite verses in which he bewailed the Quraysh who were thrown into the pit" after their slaughter at the hands of the Muslims.[38] His verses riled up the Meccans' desire for revenge.[39] When he returned to Medina, "he composed amatory verses [satirical poems related to sexual love] of an insulting nature about the Muslim women."[40]

At this point, Muḥammad asked his Companions, "Who is willing to kill Ka'b Ibn al-Ashraf who has insulted Allah and His apostle?"[41] Muḥammad Ibn Maslama offered to assassinate Ka'b, exclaiming, "O Allah's messenger! Would you like that I kill him?" And the prophet "replied in the affirmative."[42] So Maslama, with a few accomplices, lured Ka'b outside and alone for a phony private late-night business meeting. They overpowered and killed him, "and his head [was] carried off and flung at Muḥammad's feet."[43]

Almost fourteen centuries later, the Kouachi brothers implemented the same retaliation—assassination—for perceived insults to Prophet Muḥammad as if they had received the command, like Maslama, from Muḥammad himself: "Who is willing to kill the journalists of *Charlie Hebdo* for insulting Allah and His apostle?" In their minds, as true

---

[37] "Van Gogh Killer Jailed for Life." *BBC.co.uk*. British Broadcasting Corporation, 26 July 2005. Web (http://news.bbc.co.uk/2/hi/europe/4716909.stm).

[38] Ibn Hishām (Ibn Isḥāq), *The Life of Muḥammad* 364-365; Ibn Hishām (Ibn Isḥāq), *Al-Sīra al-Nabawīya* 3: 230-231.

[39] Watt, *Muḥammad at Medina* 18.

[40] Ibn Hishām (Ibn Isḥāq), *The Life of Muḥammad* 366-367; Ibn Hishām (Ibn Isḥāq), *Al-Sīra al-Nabawīya* 3: 233; Ibn Kathīr, *Al-Bidāya* 4: 6.

[41] *Sahih Bukhari*, Book of Fighting for the Cause of Allah (p. 697); *Ṣaḥīḥ al-Bukhārī*, Kītāb al-Jihād wa al-Sīyar 3: 1103.

[42] *Sahih Bukhari*, Book of Fighting for the Cause of Allah (p. 697); *Ṣaḥīḥ al-Bukhārī*, Kītāb al-Jihād wa al-Sīyar 3: 1103.

[43] Watt, *Muḥammad at Medina* 18-19.

followers of Islam, Said and Chérif Kouachi can only reflexively respond, "O Allah's messenger! Would you like that we kill them?"

The story of Ka'b Ibn al-Ashraf's killing is a precedent that Muslim scholars often cite to determine rulings on those persons who "insult the Prophet." The insult can be criticism or ridicule in some form of written text, oratory, or drawing. Ka'b Ibn al-Ashraf used his verbal poetry to criticize and ridicule the prophet, while the journalists and cartoonists used their written essays and drawings. And thanks to the teachings and actions of Prophet Muḥammad, Ka'b and the *Charlie Hebdo* staff sacrificed their lives for their freedom of expression.

In his explanation of this *ḥadīth* concerning the killing of Ka'b Ibn al-Ashraf, revered Egyptian Muslim scholar Ibn Ḥajar al-'Asqalānī relates the opinions of earlier Muslim scholars: "The words 'Who is willing to kill Ka'b Ibn al-Ashraf?' contain the permissibility to kill whoever insults the prophet Muḥammad."[44] Other Muslim scholars have reached the same conclusion—that it is permissible to kill those who insult the Prophet—because Muḥammad himself did so (or issued the command for the killing). This permissibility is very clear; there is no dilemma here except for those who want to exonerate Islam by any means, even if they must separate themselves from the Islam of Muḥammad's time. But in this case, Islam wouldn't be "the real Islam of Muḥammad" anymore. Yet the ruling and precedent are clear: Criticism of the prophet is considered an insult that deserves the punishment of death.

The Hadith literature also includes the following incident, which exemplifies the supersensitivity of the early Muslims regarding any perceived criticism of their prophet. In this *ḥadīth*,[45] Muḥammad went to visit 'Abd Allah Ibn Ubayy.[46] The Prophet traveled to 'Abd Allah Ibn Ubayy and his tribe riding on a donkey while his small Muslim entourage walked on foot. When they reached 'Abd Allah Ibn Ubayy, the tribal leader exclaimed, "Keep away from me! By Allah, the bad smell of your donkey has harmed me." One of Muḥammad's Companions retorted,

[44] al-'Asqalānī, *Fatḥ al-Bārī* 5: 442.

[45] *Sahih Bukhari*, Book of Peacemaking (p. 615); *Ṣaḥīḥ al-Bukhārī*, Kītāb al-Ṣulḥ 2: 958.

[46] **Note:** 'Abd Allah Ibn Ubayy, also known as Ibn Salūl, was a high-ranking Arab leader in pre-Islamic Medina and one of the Khazraj chiefs. He converted to Islam after Muḥammad came to Medina, but Islamic sources characterize him as an insincere convert who was jealous of Muḥammad for usurping his status and leadership in Medina. Because of his frequent conflicts with Muḥammad, Islamic tradition has labelled 'Abd Allah Ibn Ubayy as the "leader of the Munāfiqīn (Hypocrites)," a term used to define Muslims who demonstrate outwardly their devotion to and belief in Islam but are secretly unsympathetic to the Muslim cause and actively try to subvert or destroy it.

"By Allah! The smell of the donkey of Allah's Apostle is better than your smell." This hostile interaction soon developed into a brawl between the two groups, with both sides fighting each other with sticks, shoes, and hands. According to this *ḥadīth*, Q 49.9 (Palmer trans.) was revealed to Muḥammad regarding this altercation: *"And if the two parties of the believers quarrel, then make peace between them; and if one of the twain outrages the other, then fight the party that has committed the outrage until it return to God's bidding. . . ."*

If the early Muslims could not tolerate criticism directed toward the donkey of their prophet, how much greater the intolerance then (and now) for any perceived criticism directed toward Muḥammad himself? Notice that these volatile reactions to perceived criticism of one's religion or religious leaders in today's world disproportionately come from Muslims who express their outrage through rioting, vandalism, and calls for execution of the perpetrator(s). Even though the journalists of the *Charlie Hebdo* magazine criticized other religions, including Christian and Jewish religious figures, no one from those religions physically attacked them or called for their heads. Yet Muslims maintained their desire for revenge and continued their threats against the magazine staff, until the Muslim Kouachi brothers were finally able to fulfill this revenge by carrying out one of the most heinous crimes against freedom of expression in modern times.

Religious and political hypocrisy in Muslim countries

According to Muslim scholars, the religious ruling concerning anyone who insults, mocks, or speaks ill of the Prophet is death. For example, on Saudi Arabia's official Web site (*General Presidency of Scholarly Research and Iftā'*) Sheikh 'Abd al-'Azīz Ibn Bāz, the former Grand Mufti of Saudi Arabia, weighs in on this ruling:[47]

[47] Ibn Bāz, 'Abd al-'Azīz. [Fatwa:] "Ruling Concerning One Who Mocks the Great Prophet." *Alifta.net*. General Presidency for Scientific Research and Iftā' (Saudi Arabia), n.d. Vol. 6, p. 254. Web (http://www.alifta.net/Fatawa/fatawaChapters.aspx?languagename=ar&View=Page&PageID=721&PageNo=1&BookID=4).

> More than one scholar conveyed the unanimous agreement of Muslim scholars that whoever insults or degrades the Messenger of Allah is a *kāfir* (an infidel) who must be killed.... All scholars unanimously agreed that the Ḥadd (ordained punishment for violating Allah's Law) of whoever insults the Prophet, is death.... Undoubtedly, there are many forms of insult; however, mocking the Prophet, degrading him, or likening him to a base animal is one of the worst kinds of insult and degradation. Whoever does so is a *kāfir* and his soul and wealth are lawful [to be taken by Muslims].

So Saudi Arabia teaches that it is lawful to take the life and property of whoever insults or degrades the Messenger but at the same time contradictorily condemns the bloody attack on the journalists of *Charlie Hebdo*.[48]

I wonder what would happen if the journalists of *Charlie Hebdo* had been living and working in Saudi Arabia. Would they have stood a better chance to freely express their viewpoints? I am also perplexed by this statement from Saudi Arabia by one of its officials: "...The kingdom therefore strongly condemns and denounces this cowardly terrorist act that is rejected by true Islamic religion as well as the rest of religions and beliefs."[49] Does the Islamic religion really reject the killing of those who insult the prophet Muḥammad? It seems hypocritical to me for Saudi Arabia to join the international condemnation of this terrorist act and send its diplomats to offer condolences to the French government while simultaneously claim on its official Web site that it is lawful to take the lives of those who criticize the Prophet.

Saudi Arabia is not alone in this dual-but-hypocritical political strategy. Similarly, Qatar (and other Arab states, e.g., Iran, Jordan, Bahrain, Morocco, Algeria) also strongly condemned the attack on the staff of *Charlie Hebdo*[50] but its official Web site includes a fatwa entitled, "The Islamic Ruling on the One Who Insults the Prophet [Muḥammad]":

[48] "Saudi Arabia Condemns Deadly Attack on Paris Satirical Magazine." *Reuters.com*. Reuters, 7 Jan. 2015. Web (http://www.reuters.com/article/us-france-shooting-saudi/saudi-arabia-condemns-deadly-attack-on-paris-satirical-magazine-idUSKBN0KG1OM20150107).

[49] Ibid.

[50] Black, Ian. "Charlie Hebdo Killings Condemned by Arab States—but Hailed Online by Extremists." *TheGuardian.com*. The Guardian, 7 Jan. 2015. Web (https://www.theguardian.com/world/2015/jan/07/charlie-hebdo-killings-arab-states-jihadi-extremist-sympathisers-isis).

"...anyone who insults the prophet must be killed, a Muslim or an infidel."[51] And the West either denies or refuses to call out this hypocrisy.

The Muslim world suffers from this religio-political schizophrenia, where governments of Muslim countries teach Muslim children to hate the West through many and various means, like mosques, schools, newspapers and Web sites, yet, at the same time, maintain alliances with Western nations and claim to be their friends. Unfortunately, this subterfuge has fooled Western countries for decades, and they still do not grasp or understand this duplicity.

It is long overdue for these Muslim countries to be responsible and transparent by either declaring their hostility openly and explicitly or suspending two contradictory policies—one policy for interior affairs and a different one for exterior affairs—in an effort to satisfy and please citizens while confuse or hoodwink outside observers.

The widespread participation of Muslim countries in condemning the *Charlie Hebdo* massacre on January 7, 2015, was only a diplomatic maneuver and not religious conviction. In fact, government representatives of Morocco declined to attend an anti-terrorism solidarity march about a week after the deadly attack after the Moroccan government viewed the next cover of the magazine (issued on January 13) and declared it "blasphemous."[52] Egypt, Jordan, and other Muslim communities joined Morocco in declaring this issue cover as "offensive" and "unjustifiably provocative."[53]

What irony! This swift "about-face" support for the staff of *Charlie Hebdo* shows clearly that these Muslim governments might initially condemn vehemently the use of bullets to brutally silence those who would dare to exercise their right to freely express themselves—even offering condolences to the grieving families of the victims—only to later condemn expressions of this freedom they find unacceptable or offensive. Where, then, is the "freedom" in "freedom of expression" in this response?

---

[51] [Originally Fatwa no. 268741, but this fatwa is now listed as an article and not a separate fatwa.] "Islamic Ruling on the One Who Insults the Prophet." *Islamweb.net.* Ministry of Endowments and Islamic Affairs of Qatar, 25 Jan. 2006. Web (http://articles.islamweb.net/media/index.php?page=article&lang=A&id=111861).

[52] Atef, Ghada. "Muslim Countries React to New Charlie Hebdo Cartoon." *English.Ahram.org.eg.* Ahram Online (English), 14 Jan. 2015. Web (http://english.ahram.org.eg/NewsContent/2/8/120310/World/Region/Muslim-countries-react-to-new-Charlie-Hebdo-cartoo.aspx). The cover of the January 13, 2015 issue depicts a caricature of Muḥammad, dressed in a white *galabeya*, crying and holding a large placard that reads, "*Je Suis Charlie*" ["I Am Charlie"]. Above his head, the headline reads, "*Tout Est Pardonné*" ["All Is Forgiven]." (For more information about this cover, see URL: https://www.theguardian.com/media/2015/jan/13/charlie-hebdo-cover-magazine-prophet-Muḥammad)

[53] Ibid.

On the extremely popular Web site, *IslamQA*, Saudi sheikh Muḥammad Ṣāliḥ al-Munajjid issued Fatwa no. 22809 regarding "the ruling on one who insults the prophet":

> The scholars are unanimously agreed that a Muslim who insults the Prophet becomes an infidel and an apostate who is to be executed.... It may be noted from this that the Prophet had the right to kill whoever insulted him and spoke harshly to him, and that included both Muslims and infidels.

This fatwa was deleted (January 13, 2015) after I mentioned it on Twitter and people circulated it. Fortunately, I retained a copy, just in case.

Criticism of Muḥammad worthy of death

This constant state of danger that threatens anyone who would presume to criticize Islam or criticize, mock, or ridicule Muḥammad is the best evidence that the entire Muslim world does not tolerate criticism of their religion and its prophet. This intolerance is manifested in Islam's religious texts, which contain this doctrine requiring Muslims to kill those who criticize their prophet, as exemplified in Q 9.12 (Palmer trans.): *"But if they break faith with you after their treaty, and taunt your religion, then fight the leaders of misbelief; verily, they have no faith, haply they may desist."* In this verse, those who would challenge or insult Islam have thus broken their relationship with the believers and must be fought until they are stopped. The respected Muslim commentator al-Qurṭubī states that "some scholars extracted from this verse that it is a must to kill whoever speaks ill of religion [Islam], for such a person is an infidel."[54] In other words, to taunt the Islamic religion is worthy of death. The executioners of this doctrine, like the Kouachi brothers who attacked the *Charlie Hebdo* staff members, are victims of these teachings. They are, of course, responsible for their actions, but these teachings also bear responsibility, perhaps an even greater responsibility than the executioners.

If little Muslim children learn from an early age—at home, in their school, and in their mosque—that anyone who insults the prophet is to be killed, imagine their reaction when they see a cartoon of Muḥammad bearing a bomb on his head? Their first reaction would be to recall what they have been taught and stored in their minds and memories all these

[54] See the commentary on Q 9.12, *Tafsīr al-Qurṭubī* 8: 86.

years. It is this continual exposure to and inculcation of these teachings in the minds of Muslims that make these teachings primarily responsible. What other explanation can we offer when millions of angry Muslims rush out into the streets to demonstrate, targeting cars and buildings for looting, vandalizing, and burning, because of some cartoon?

Shortly before dying during a police shootout, Chérif Kouachi talked by phone to a reporter from French television station BFM-TV about the attack two days earlier on *Charlie Hebdo*: "I, Cherīf Kouachi, was sent by Al Qaeda of Yemen. I went there and it was Sheikh Anwar al-Awlaki… who sponsored me."[55]

An Al Qaeda affiliate in Yemen upheld Kouachi's final public remarks soon after the three-day manhunt ended with the deaths of the two Kouachi brothers. According to a statement given to the Associated Press from Al Qaeda in the Arabian Peninsula (AQAP), Al Qaeda "directed the operations" and "[chose] their target carefully."[56] One of Al Qaeda's top *sharīʿa* clerics in Yemen, Ḥārith Ibn Ghāzī al-Nadhārī (who was killed soon after in a US-led drone strike on January 31)[57] posted this comment about the *Charlie Hebdo* journalists and the deadly attack by the Kouachi brothers: "Some of the sons of France were disrespectful to the prophets of Allah. So a group from among the believing soldiers of Allah marched unto them, then they taught them respect and the limit of the freedom of expression."[58]

Al Qaeda reaffirms its responsibility for the Paris attacks in a video posted by one of its media outlets on January 13, 2015, entitled *Vengeance for the Messenger of God: A Message Regarding the Blessed Battle of Paris.*[59] This title suggests that the assault operation was an act of revenge for

---

[55] "Before Dying, French Suspects Speak." BFM Television (BFM TV). 9 Jan. 2015. Television. (To hear audio recording, see URL: https://www.nytimes.com/video/world/europe/100000003440575/before-dying-french-suspects-speak-out.html?action=click&contentCollection=world&module=embedded&region=caption&pgtype=article). See Higgins, Andrew, and Dan Bilefsky. "French Police Storm Hostage Sites, Killing Gunmen." *NYTimes.com*. New York Times, 9 Jan. 2015. Web (https://www.nytimes.com/2015/01/10/world/europe/charlie-hebdo-paris-shooting.html).

[56] Vick, Karl. "Al-Qaeda Group Claims Responsibility for Paris Terror Attack." *Time.com*. Time Inc., 9 Jan. 2015. Web (http://time.com/3661650/charlie-hebdo-paris-terror-attack-al-qaeda).

[57] Almasmari, Hakim, Jason Hanna, and Margot Haddad. "Senior Al Qaeda Cleric Killed in Yemen Drone Strike, AQAP Says." *Edition.CNN.com*. Cable Network News, 5 Feb. 2015. Web (http://edition.cnn.com/2015/02/05/world/yemen-violence/index.html).

[58] Edwards, Steven. "Bloody Rivals: Paris Attack Helps Al Qaeda Gain Edge on ISIS." *FoxNews.com*. Fox Entertainment Group, 11 Jan. 2015. Web (http://www.foxnews.com/world/2015/01/11/paris-attacks-may-reveal-hidden-fight-for-recognition-between-al-qaeda-and.html).

[59] Al Qaeda in the Arabian Peninsula (AQAP). *Vengeance for the Messenger of God: A Message Regarding the Blessed Battle of Paris. Jihadolody.net*. Al-Malāhim Media, 13 Jan. 2015. Video. (To view video, see URL: http://preview.tinyurl.com/yb82elye)

Muḥammad. Naming the operation "the blessed Battle of Paris" seems like a deliberate effort to evoke and remind Muslim viewers of the celebrated military campaigns of Muḥammad and the early Muslims, e.g., Battle of Badr, Battle of the Trench, etc.

The video begins with a Qur'ānic verse (Q 15.95-96; Palmer trans.): *"Verily, we are enough for thee against the scoffers. / Who place with God other gods; but they at length shall know!"* Following this introduction is an audio recording by the late chief of Al Qaeda, Osama Bin Laden: "If there is no check on the freedom of your words, then let your hearts be open to the freedom of our actions." The rest of the video is primarily a speech presented by a senior leader of AQAP based in Yemen, Sheikh Nāṣir Ibn 'Alī al-Ānsī:[60]

> "As for the blessed Battle of Paris: We in the Jihadi Organization of Al Qaeda in the Arabian Peninsula [AQAP], claim responsibility for this operation as a vengeance for the Messenger of Allah. We clarify to the ummah that the one who chose the target, laid the plan, financed the operation, and appointed its emir, is the leadership of the organization. We did it in compliance with the Command of Allah and supporting His Messenger...then the order of our general amir, the generous Sheikh Aiman bin Moḥammad Adhawāhirī [Ayman Ibn Muḥammad al-Zawahirī]...and following the will of [the late] Sheikh Usama bin Laden [Osama Bin Laden].... The arrangement with the amir of the operation were made by Sheikh Anwar al-'Awlakī..., who threatens the West both in his life and after his martyrdom.... This blessed battle was carried out by two heroes of Islam, the Kouachi brothers Sharrīf and Sa'īd, may Allah have mercy on their souls...."

Although Islamic State was not behind or directly involved in the *Charlie Hebdo* massacre, having already split from Al Qaeda and then clashing with Al Nuṣra Front (once known as Al Qaeda in Syria/Levant)—even on the battlefield—it blessed and praised the Paris operation and attacks. Islamic State posted its own video, entitled *Meetings on the Blessed French Operations.*[61] The video consists of three French Islamic State militants, each giving his opinion and comments on the *Charlie Hebdo* attack:[62]

---

[60] Al Qaeda in the Arabian Peninsula (AQAP). *Vengeance for the Messenger of God: A Message Regarding the Blessed Battle of Paris. Jihadolody.net.* Al-Malāhim Media, 13 Jan. 2015. Video. (To view video, see URL: http://preview.tinyurl.com/yb82elye). **Note:** Nāṣir Ibn 'Alī al-Ānsī was killed in a US drone strike on May 7, 2015.

[61] The Islamic State. *Meetings on the Blessed French Operations. Jihadology.net.* Wilāyat al-Raqqah, 14 Jan. 2015. Video. (To view video, see URL: http://preview.tinyurl.com/y9d7dhby)

[62] Ibid.

> [IS militant #1] "It should have been done [meaning the *Charlie Hebdo* attack] for a long time, because the evil ones in France and all over Europe wish to destroy the true Islam.... Operations like this will continue all over Europe...in France, Belgium, Germany, Switzerland, and everywhere in Europe and everywhere in America with the will of Allah Almighty.... I would say to those brothers, who have not been able to emigrate towards the Islamic caliphate, I'd tell them: 'Do your best, do all you can. Kill them, slaughter them, burn their cars, burn their homes. Do all you can.'"

> [IS militant #2] "If you have not been able to emigrate, then work for Islam from wherever you are. We have received some good news that the brothers have defended Islam and have sent whoever mocked the prophet straight to hell. And so you [must] also continue sending them to hell."

> [IS militant #3] "If you see a policeman, kill him, kill them all, kill every *kāfir* [infidel] that you see in the street, so that they are terrorized.... This is the true path to dignity: the path of pride is jihad for the sake of Allah."

Islamic State released this video for two reasons: (1) propaganda tool to encourage "lone wolves" (attackers working alone) to do similar operations and (2) clarification of its position on such operations, even if they were to be carried out by other Islamic groups. Despite their differences, it seems that Al Qaeda and Islamic State agree on many goals and the means to accomplish them. Most importantly, they agree on the killing of people who criticize Muḥammad or Islam. Islamic State has executed numerous people accused of apostasy or insulting the Prophet. These executions have often been carried out in public squares where Muslim crowds watched as these accused people were shot in the head or beheaded with a sword.

Muslim scholarly consensus on killing those who "insult the prophet"

The Hadith literature includes accounts where Muḥammad waived punishment or "blood money" compensation in the wrongful deaths of people who were critical of him. Companion and cousin 'Alī Ibn Abū Ṭālib narrates in one *ḥadīth* that a Jewish woman who "used to revile and disparage the Prophet" was strangled by a man until she died, but "the Messenger of Allah...declared that no recompense was payable for her blood."[63] In other words, Muḥammad considered her life worthless, which means her murderer was not punished or required to pay any compensation to her family.

Muḥammad even encouraged the killing of those who insulted or criticized him by disregarding their rights or fair treatment. For example, the Prophet seemed willing to pardon murderers if they claimed they had killed because the victim was insulting Muḥammad, as reported in this *ḥadīth* narrated by Muḥammad's cousin and early Qur'ānic scholar Ibn Abbas:[64]

> A blind man had a female slave[65] who had borne him a child [and she] reviled the Prophet and disparaged him, and he told her not to do that, but she did not stop.... One night, she started to disparage and revile the Prophet, so he took a dagger and put it on her stomach and pressed on it and killed her. There fell between her legs a child who was smeared with the blood that was there. The next morning mention of that was made to the Prophet...and he assembled the people and said: "By Allah, I adjure [command] the man who did this, to stand up." The blind man stood up...and said: "O Messenger of Allah, I am the one who did it. She used to revile you and disparage you...and I rebuked her, but she paid no heed. I have two sons from her who are like two pearls, and she was good to me. Last night she started to revile you...and I took a dagger and placed it on her stomach and I pressed on it until I killed her." The Prophet said: "Bear witness that no retaliation is due for her blood."

Was Muḥammad concerned about the two children whose blind father now had made them motherless? Did Muḥammad rebuke the blind man for killing his wife, especially as she had taken care of him because of his blindness, attending to his and their children's many needs? The man himself confessed that "she was good" to him. However, all that seemed to matter to Muḥammad in his ruling was that the man killed the woman for supposedly insulting Muḥammad (but we only have the man's word on this matter). Despite such a grievous assault on this young wife and mother, her killer received neither censure nor punishment, and so her life (like the life of the murdered Jewish woman) apparently had no value.

[63] *Sunan Abū Dawūd,* Book of Legal Punishments (Ḥudūd) 5: 21.

[64] Ibid. 5: 20-21.

[65] **Note:** The original Arabic text characterizes her status as *ūm walad,* which means she is a mother of a child. In Islam, if a slave girl gives birth to a child she becomes *ūm walad.* She becomes a free person when her owner (father of the child) dies. He cannot sell her as she has become his wife now.

What must go on in the mind of a Muslim who reads this story? The blind man killed his female slave, the mother of his children, who in all respects was his wife, over an argument concerning her criticism of someone claiming to be a prophet. However, Islamic sources consider this blind man a hero who should be eulogized in the religious texts and not denounced as a criminal who must be rebuked and punished for what he did. If this man's case is held up for adulation, how will similar stories encourage Muslims to peacefully accept or at least tolerate criticism? Will they encourage Muslims to respond to criticism with rational debate or with the sword? All over the Muslim world children are learning these kinds of stories from their textbooks and deriving spiritual and moral values from them. So if they do end up killing a person for alleged slander or ridicule of Muḥammad or Islam, these stories must bear the brunt of the blame.

Muslim scholars have written texts that specifically deal with the appropriate punishment for those who criticize the Prophet, such as *Al-Sayf al-Maslūl 'ala man Sabb al-Rasūl* (*The Unsheathed Sword Upon the One Who Curses the Messenger*) by medieval Egyptian Muslim scholar Taqīy al-Dīn al-Subkī (c. AD 1275-1355). During this same era, famous sheikh Ibn Taymīya wrote a similar text entitled *Al-Sārim al-Maslūl ala-Shātim al-Rasūl* (*Raising the Sharp Sword Against Those Who Insult the Messenger*). These books are still published in different editions and sold throughout the Arab Muslim world and even sold in Western countries. These books are not only sold in bookshops and book fairs but are also taught in Muslim universities and schools, especially religious schools, and considered reliable references. In fact, research on one of the editions has been the subject of masters' theses in Saudi Arabia.[66] The covers of these books usually include an illustration of a sword—the sword of Muḥammad, which is placed on the necks of anyone who criticizes him or his religion.

These books blatantly urge Muslims to kill anyone who curses or insults Muḥammad. In these books, *insulting* or *cursing* is defined as deprecating Muḥammad's character. Thus, anyone who denies

[66] For an example, see this document: Al-Magish, Salih Ibn Saud. "Presentation and Study of Ibn Taymiya's Curriculum in Proving the Rulings on Insulting through His Book *Al-Sārim al-Maslūl ala-Shātim al-Rasūl*." MA Thesis. U of King Saud, 2004. Print.

Muḥammad's prophethood is worthy of death. In his book, Ibn Taymīya summarizes his opinion in four points:[67]

1. Whoever curses the Prophet, whether a Muslim or a *kāfir* (infidel), must be killed.
2. The guilty curser must be killed, even if he is of the People of the Book [Jew or Christian], and he cannot be pardoned or ransomed.
3. The guilty curser must be killed without being given the opportunity to repent.
4. The term *insulting* is clarified and the difference between insulting and misbelieving is discussed in detail.

Ibn Taymīya's book reviews the words and actions of Muḥammad concerning those who insulted or disparaged him and includes statements and actions by the Companions toward Muḥammad's critics, as well as the sayings and rulings of notable Muslim scholars. The conclusion of the book is essentially a restatement of its title: Whoever insults the prophet deserves to be killed by the sword.

One of today's leading Saudi Muslim scholars, the head of the International Islamic Fiqh Academy and a member of the Supreme Council of Scholars in Saudi Arabia, Bakr Ibn 'Abd Allah Abū Zayd, wrote the following text in the introduction of the 1997 edition of this book:[68]

> The Muslims have unanimously agreed that whoever insults the Prophet is certainly a disbeliever, seeking corruption in the land. It is a must to take revenge for him [the Prophet] by killing the one who insults him, and no one in the Ummah has the right to pardon this person. This is for purifying the land and for demonstrating Islam in its perfect picture.

Some of the evidence that Ibn Taymīya cites to support his opinion include commentary of Muslim scholar Ḥamd Ibn Muḥammad al-Khaṭṭābī (c. AD 931-998), who states, "I do not know of any Muslim who disagrees about the necessity of killing such a person [referring to the one who insults the prophet]."[69] Ibn Taymīya also refers to one of the most important early Muslim scholars of Islam, Aḥmad Ibn Ḥanbal, who founded an entire Islamic school of jurisprudence, the Ḥanbalī

---

[67] Ibn Taymīya, *Al-Sārim* 1: 166.
[68] Ibid. 1: 8.
[69] Ibid. 2: 15.

school. This Faqīh of Baghdad stated that "whoever insults the Prophet or detracts from him, whether a Muslim or a Kāfir, should be killed, and I think that he should be killed and not be given the chance to repent."[70] Similar statements have been expressed by Mālik Ibn Anas (AD 711-795), founder of the Mālikī school: "Whoever insults, curses, mocks or detracts from the Prophet, whether a Muslim or a *kāfir,* should be killed, without being given the chance to repent."[71]

According to these Muslim scholars, a comment where a person points out that the clothes of Muḥammad are dirty with the intent of belittling him would be counted an insult.[72] Ibn Taymīya recounts that someone was killed for insulting Muḥammad for saying that the prophet was "black."[73] Another man was killed because he likened the looks of the prophet to an ugly man, saying, "You want to know what he looked like? He looked like this [ugly] passerby in physique and beard."[74] Ibn Taymīya reports another narrative where a Jewish man was passing by a mosque prayer leader who said, "I bear witness that there is no god but Allah, and I bear witness that Muḥammad is the Messenger of Allah." The Jewish man told him, "You lie." For this comment, the Jewish man was killed, as commanded by Imām Aḥmad Ibn Ḥanbal.[75]

A particularly grisly story concerns a Christian man, who said that God preferred Christ over Muḥammad. To punish the Christian for this horrible insult to Muḥammad, the great Muslim jurist, Abū Muṣʿab al-Hilālī (a nephew of Mālik Ibn Anas), commanded that the Christian be beaten and then killed, dragged by his feet and afterward thrown into a garbage dump where the dogs could eat him.[76]

The documentation and justification for the killing of people for insulting the Prophet is easily found in the Islamic sources. References mentioned here include founders of two of the five major Sunni Islamic schools of doctrine (Ḥanbal and Malīkī). Yet people still insist that Islamic State, Al Qaeda, and the Kouachi brothers have nothing to do with Islam—even as they themselves refer to these early Muslim scholars. So do Aḥmad Ibn Hanbal, Mālik Ibn Anas, and Ibn Taymīya all have

[70] Ibn Taymīya, *Al-Sārim* 2: 16.
[71] Ibid. 3: 979.
[72] Ibid. Mālik Ibn Anas states that "anyone who says that the Prophet's cloak was dirty, thereby intending to find fault with him, should be killed."
[73] Ibid. 3: 980.
[74] Ibid.
[75] Ibid. 3: 996.
[76] Ibid. 3: 997.

nothing to do with Islam? Who has anything to do with Islam if the founders of the major schools of Islam are not Muslims?

Muslims have been raised since childhood not to accept any criticism of Islam, its prophet Muḥammad, or the Qur'ān. Muslims are to consider anyone who dares to do so as someone who has committed a major crime. That is why we Muslims have not gained much ground concerning the freedom of expression in Muslim countries; freedom of expression is still in its infancy stage. Writers are still being denounced as infidels and threatened with imprisonment, punishment, and even death. Many are silenced through self-censorship, intimidated by threats to themselves (or for their loved ones) or even physically persecuted.

The catastrophe is that this ruthless suppression of free speech is also reaching Western countries. Many Westerners are now afraid to publicly speak about or criticize Islam because of potentially violent Muslim repercussions, like rioting in the streets, burning of embassies, or death threats. Those that do speak out are often publicly upbraided and charged with Islamophobia or being insensitive or offensive. Examples of this Muslim resistance toward and intolerance of free expression are easily seen in the worldwide Muslim outrage over the "Muḥammad cartoons" in Danish newspapers and remarks given in a lecture by Pope Benedict XVI in September 2016 concerning a Byzantine emperor's assessment of Muḥammad's teachings.[77]

Criticism of Muḥammad "unlawful"

Many Muslim countries have enacted laws that prohibit criticism of the Islam religion, but they camouflage it by categorizing such criticism as "defamation of religions." Criticism of Muḥammad is legally prohibited under statutes forbidding the "insulting of prophets." Curiously, I have never seen the Muslim world protest those who criticize Christ, who is considered a prophet in Islam. If Muslims are prohibited from criticizing any of the prophets, why do we find anti-Christ stories, e.g., *The Da Vinci Code*, translated into Arabic and openly sold in Muslim countries, but no books critical of Muḥammad? In 2015 the United Arab Emirates (UAE) issued a legal decree prohibiting the criticism of Islam and the prophet Muḥammad under the category concerned with the "defamation of

[77] Shadid, Anthony. "Remarks by Pope Prompt Muslim Outrage, Protests." *WashingtonPost.com*. The Washington Post, 16 Sept. 2006. Web (http://www.washingtonpost.com/wp-dyn/content/article/2006/09/15/AR2006091500800.html).

religions." Penalties include imprisonment from "six months to over ten years and fines…from AED50,000 to AED2million (about US$13,600-544,500)"[78] for people convicted of an act "that would be considered as insulting God, his prophets or apostles or holy books or houses of worship or graveyards."[79] Of course, the real purpose of this decree is to safeguard the prophet Muḥammad from criticism; the plural use of "prophets" is only a deceptive ploy to appear fair and nothing else.

In the same context, Morocco recently passed legislation criminalizing anyone who "insults the Islamic religion or the royal regime," sentencing convicted offenders with imprisonment ranging from six months to two years and fines of MA$20,000 to $200,000 (~US$2000 to $20,000).[80] If the offensive insult is widely and publicly circulated through speech, media outlets, printed materials, etc., the punishment greatly increases, with imprisonment ranging from two to five years and fines of MA$50,000 up to $500,000 (~US$5000 up to $50,000).[81]

In 2012, the Kuwaiti National Assembly passed an amendment that could make cursing God, the Qur'ān, all prophets, and wives of Prophet Muḥammad punishable by death. The amendment was approved by forty-six votes. Four opposed it and several abstained. However, all fifteen members of the cabinet voted in favor of the amendment.[82]

The prince of Kuwait did not sign this bill—not because he rejected this penalty, but because he knows that its passage could intensify conflict between Sunnis and Shiites in the country, for Shiites do not sanctify 'Ā'isha or Muḥammad's Companions. In fact, they generally have a very unfavorable view of her. Consequently, if this proposed amendment was to become law, it could be used as a political tool to kill Shiites and get rid of them from the country. The prince's rejection signaled his unwillingness to jeopardize the political and social stability of his country. Perhaps he

---

[78] Johnson, Constance. "United Arab Emirates: New Law Banning Discrimination." *LOC.gov*. Library of Congress, 22 July 2015. Web (http://www.loc.gov/law/foreign-news/article/united-arab-emirates-new-law-banning-discrimination).

[79] WAM. "UAE Anti-Discriminatory Law Bans Hate Speech, Promotion of Violence." *Emirates247.com*. Dubai Media Inc., 22 July 2015. Web (http://www.emirates247.com/news/government/uae-anti-discriminatory-law-bans-hate-speech-promotion-of-violence-2015-07-22-1.597389).

[80] *Moroccan Penal Code*. 12 Mar. 2018: bk. 3 (Various Crimes and Penalties), vol. 1, ch. 4, art. 267-5. *Justice.gov.ma*. Morocco Ministry of Justice. Page 91. Print and Web (To download document PDF, see URL: https://preview.tinyurl.com/ybbstr2b).

[81] Ibid.

[82] Harbi, Mahmoud, et al. "Kuwait Mulls Death Penalty for Insulting God, Prophet." *Reuters.com*. Reuters, 12 Apr. 2012. Web (http://www.reuters.com/article/us-kuwait-prophet/kuwait-mulls-death-penalty-for-insulting-god-prophet-idUSBRE83B0TN20120412).

was also influenced by the extremely controversial case of Shiite blogger and tweeter Hamad al-Naqi, who had been convicted by a Kuwaiti court for posting tweets that "denigrated Islam as a religion, ridiculed its beliefs and teachings and scorned its iconic figures."[83] For this religious offense, he received ten years' imprisonment.[84]

From 1999 to 2010 the Organization of Islamic Cooperation (OIC) delivered a defamation of religions resolution to the United Nations Commission on Human Rights (UNCHR).[85] Even though any resolution passed by this committee has no binding effect on the international community, continual passage may result in its inclusion in international legal norms. The OIC submitted their defamation of religions resolution repeatedly, hoping to achieve this goal. To gain more support, the resolution's language was expanded to include all religions. After a decade of submissions, however, the US and most other Western democratic countries had reached an impasse with the OIC and its resolution. These governments felt that blasphemy laws were really vehicles for repressive governments to restrict free speech and imprison or execute religious minorities and political rivals.[86]

At this point (2011), the language of this resolution was changed to emphasize protection of persons rather than religions: "...any advocacy of national, racial, or religious hatred that constitutes incitement to discrimination, hostility, or violence" is condemned.[87] This modification eventually led to UN Resolution 16/18,[88] which was adopted in 2011 by the UNHRC and condemns "stereotyping, negative profiling

[83] Toumi, Habib. "Blogger Sentenced to 10 Years for Abusive Posts." *GulfNews.com.* Al Nisr Publishing, 4 June 2012. Web (http://gulfnews.com/news/gulf/kuwait/blogger-sentenced-to-10-years-for-abusive-posts-1.1031690).

[84] Ibid.

[85] Holzaepel, Caleb. "Can I Say That?: How an International Blasphemy Law Pits the Freedom of Religion against the Freedom of Speech." *Emory International Law Review* 28.1 (2014): 597-648; see page 616. Print and Web (http://law.emory.edu/eilr/content/volume-28/issue-1/comments/can-i-say-that-blasphemy-law.html). **Note:** Its real purpose was revealed with the name of its first resolution submission, "Defamation of Islam."

[86] Ibid.; see page 620.

[87] Ibid.; see page 621.

[88] UN Human Rights Council, 46th Meeting. "Resolution 16/18: Combating intolerance, negative stereotyping and stigmatization of, and discrimination, incitement to violence and violence against, persons based on religion or belief." (A/HRC/RES/16/18). 24 Mar. 2011. Web (http://www2.ohchr.org/english/bodies/hrcouncil/docs/16session/A.HRC.RES.16.18_en.pdf).

and stigmatization of persons based on their religion."[89] Even though this resolution was accompanied by Comment 34, which states that defamation laws should not be used to "stifle freedom of expression," its text is too general for a clear statement for and protection of free speech.[90] As a result, Muslim nations continue to enjoy international protection against criticism or insulting speech (albeit in protection of persons rather than the religion of Islam), and they can still convict and punish their citizens for blasphemy by claiming the offenses were made against individual Muslims instead of against Islam. No matter the target—people or religions—laws against blasphemy threaten freedom of expression.

Western countries, the Internet, and satellite channels are the only outlets for young people who live in Muslim countries to find freedom of expression and opinions that challenge the government-controlled information they receive. The governments of Saudi Arabia and other Muslim countries are well aware of this outside access to "free" information and opinions. Therefore, they want to take advantage of any opportunity to impose a global law that prohibits the defamation of religions in all countries and thus eliminate lawful criticism of Islam. This desire to protect Islam and its prophet Muḥammad from any criticism is especially keen in Muslim governments that derive their legitimacy from Islam. Any threat to Islam is a threat to the legitimacy of their rule.

Prophet of Islam and terrorism

In 2014 I asked one of my friends to buy me school textbooks used in Moroccan elementary schools, so I could review the subjects that are being taught, especially those related to religion. As I began browsing the Islamic studies for the first grade, I noticed each lesson concluded with a sentence summary for the student to memorize or write as a slogan. One of the lessons was summarized with the following sentence: "I love those who love the Prophet and consider those who oppose him my enemies."[91] When a six-year-old kid learns to become an enemy of anyone who criticizes Muḥammad, then this is an educational system

[89] Holzaepel, Caleb. "Can I Say That?: How an International Blasphemy Law Pits the Freedom of Religion against the Freedom of Speech." *Emory International Law Review* 28.1 (2014): 597-648; see page 623. Print and Web (http://law.emory.edu/eilr/content/volume-28/issue-1/comments/can-i-say-that-blasphemy-law.html).

[90] Ibid.

[91] *Al-Mufīd fī al-Tarbīya al-Islāmiya* 26.

that manufactures terrorists. When indoctrinated with this kind of instruction and memorization, it is inevitable that many of these children will end up intolerant of any criticism of Islam and Muḥammad and intolerant of non-Muslims. Is it really too far a leap to think that a child, taught intolerance of others, might turn to hatred of and violence toward those who would criticize Muḥammad or the religion of Islam? Apparently, I am not the only one who foresees such a likely outcome. In 2016, Morocco's King Mohammed VI ordered a review of his country's religious education, reforming the curriculum so that it would "highlight tolerance and moderation, following the spread of extremist religious culture."[92]

I have been personally affected by this Islamic education of intolerance toward others. I am personally threatened by Islamic extremists on a daily basis, and I cannot enter any Arab Muslim country. I maintain a low public profile and frequently change my place of residence. I limit access to my person and information about my movements. I must restrict my life just because I have the audacity to publicly criticize Islam and openly discuss its problems and taboos.

Many young people sympathize with me because they have the same questions and doubts. Yet many others wish to tear me apart or burn me alive like the Jordanian pilot or shoot me like the *Charlie Hebdo* journalists. Why so much rage? Why this hatred? It is the result of the teachings that we learned from our families, from our schools, from our mosques, and from our own society. Unfortunately, we have never learned to tolerate criticism in a civilized manner. The mentality of the Arab desert tribes of seventh century AD continues to control us. The Islamic religion transformed ancient Arab tribal customs into something sacred, and therefore it is difficult even now for the Muslim world to get rid of them and enter the modern world of the twenty-first century.

Moroccan Amazigh activist Aḥmad 'Aṣṣīd[93] has pointed out the problems embedded in Muslim school curriculums and the contradictions that exist in them. For example, school textbooks that include letters

[92] Waked, Ali. "Moroccan King Orders Overhaul of Religious Education in Bid to Counter Terrorism." *Breitbart.com*. Breitbart News Network, 8 Feb. 2016. Web (http://www.breitbart.com/middle-east/2016/02/08/moroccan-king-orders-overhaul-of-religious-education-in-bid-to-counter-terrorism).

[93] See "Moroccan Amazigh Activist Ahmad Assid on the Need for Secularism in Morocco: The Rise of the Islamists Poses a Danger to Democracy." *MEMRI.org*. Middle East Media Research Institute (MEMRI), 4 Apr. 2012. Transcript excerpts from television interview on Al-Arabiya TV. Web (https://www.memri.org/tv/moroccan-amazigh-activist-ahmad-assid-need-secularism-morocco-rise-islamists-poses-danger/transcript).

Prophet Muḥammad sent to kings, "inviting" them to accept Islam are, in fact, threatening messages. One sample letter from Muḥammad to Heraclius (c. 575-641), Emperor of the Byzantine Empire, is described in Islamic books as Muḥammad's merciful attempt to save Heraclius and his people from the wars of the prophet:[94]

> In the name of Allah, the most Beneficent, the most Merciful. (This letter is) from Muḥammad, the slave of Allah, and His Apostle, to Heraclius, the Ruler of the Byzantine. Peace be upon the followers of guidance. Now then, I invite you to Islam (i.e., surrender to Allah), embrace Islam and you will be safe; embrace Islam and Allah will bestow on you a double reward. But if you reject this invitation of Islam you shall be responsible for misguiding the peasants (i.e., your nation)....

This fourteen-century-old letter of "invitation" to embrace Islam is still treated like an aspirational template regarding foreign policy, even for modern Muslim governments and rulers. If a modern Muslim government or ruler is to emulate Muḥammad, then it/he should "invite" the foreign government to accept Islam. If this "invitation" is rejected, then the Muslim government or ruler should offer the foreign government—if primarily Christian or Jewish—the alternative of "paying the tribute," i.e., head tax. If the foreign government also refuses to pay this tax, then the Muslim government (or ruler) has the religious authority to invade the foreign government.

Aḥmad 'Aṣṣīd discusses this early Islamic foreign policy, where rejection by foreign nations to accept Islam led to threats of forced taxation and even war by Muslim invaders, and its inclusion and treatment in the elementary curriculum:[95]

---

[94] *Sahih Bukhari*, Book of Fighting for the Cause of Allah (p. 678); *Ṣaḥīḥ al-Bukhārī*, Kītāb al-Jihād wa al-Sīyar 3: 1073.

[95] Baidoun, Ibrahim. "Messages of the Prophet...Sent to the Kings and 'Assīd." *Hespress.com*. Hespress, 2 May 2013. Web (https://www.hespress.com/opinions/78247.html).

> The need to reconsider this ideology of the educational system [is] now: students in the existing curricula are studying things that completely contradict with what we are talking about the values of human rights, when taught to the student of the common core [classes]. The message that is taught in the curriculum to our students at the age of sixteen is in fact a terrorist message because it is related to the context of the Prophet Muḥammad, which is a threatening message "*Aslim Taslam*" [Accept Islam and you will be saved from slaughter], and then come later and [contradictorily] talk about [interfaith] dialogue and freedoms.... When today religion is a personal free choice for individuals, students cannot study a message that says ["]accept Islam and you will be saved, or else you will die["] and...taught [it] as the supreme values of Islam....

'Aṣṣīd asserts in his comments that Prophet Muḥammad's letter to the foreign kings was a terrorist message that has no place in today's world, which emphasizes human rights and recognizes the freedom to choose one's religion. No king or leader of any Muslim country should be sending a letter to the president of any foreign, non-Muslim country, inviting him or her to embrace Islam or to pay the tribute (*jizya*) and then resort to war against this country if the first two options are rejected. Why then, 'Aṣṣīd asks, do we require our students to study these early letters, teaching them that they are the ideal model for inviting others to Islam?

'Aṣṣīd's statements have brought him misery. Many Moroccans have derided and even threatened him, especially Muslim sheikhs.[96] They consider his statements insulting to the prophet Muḥammad himself, because stating that Muḥammad's letters are terrorist messages according to modern day standards is stating by extrapolation that the prophet himself is a terrorist. One incensed Moroccan Salafist sheikh even declared that Aḥmad 'Aṣṣīd is an infidel and called for his immediate death (killing):[97]

> ...'Aṣṣīd challenged the nation, feelings, history and civilization, and tore...hearts.... The imāms of the Sunnah and the Jamā'ah, gathered together with all their sects, [have unanimously agreed] that whoever came in the same way [said the same things] that the one who brought it ['Aṣṣīd] was a *kafir* [an infidel and apostate and must be executed].

---

[96] Gabbay, Tiffany. "Morocco's Islamist PM [Prime Minister]: Criticizing Prophet Muḥammad Is Unacceptable." *TheBlaze.com*. Mercury Radio Arts, 29 Apr. 2013. Web (http://www.theblaze.com/news/2013/04/29/moroccos-islamist-pm-criticizing-prophet-Muḥammad-is-unacceptable).

[97] "Abū al-Na'īm Declares 'Aṣṣīd As Infidel and Calls for His Death." *Menara.ma*. Lighthouse Magazine, 16 July 2014. Web (https://preview.tinyurl.com/z53ujzq). See "Moroccan Cleric Abu Naim Accuses Again Driss Lachgar of Apostasy." *The MoroccanTimes.com*. The Moroccan Times, 27 July 2014. Web (http://themoroccantimes.com/2014/07/7459/moroccan-cleric-abu-naim-accuses-driss-lachgar-apostasy).

A year later, members of a Moroccan-based Islamic terrorist cell were arrested before carrying out plans to kill public figures, including Aḥmad ʿAṣṣīd.[98] By some Islamic groups he is to be counted as an infidel who has cursed the Prophet and thus deserves to be killed, like the journalists of *Charlie Hebdo*. If this happens in Morocco, which is one of the more open-minded Muslim countries, how much more so in the closed-minded Muslim countries?

This belief in the death punishment for those judged as insulters of Prophet Muḥammad is a doctrine that motivated ISIS (and later, Islamic State) to execute convicted "insulters" in public squares, propelled Al Qaeda supporters to carry out the massacre of the *Charlie Hebdo* journalists, and activated massive violent demonstrations and riots in Muslim countries in protest of the Muḥammad caricatures in Danish newspapers and Pope Benedict XVI's remarks in 2006. In 2012, this very same doctrine fueled a series of violent attacks protesting the anti-Muslim film *Innocence of Muslims*. It continues to threaten the lives of Salman Rushdie, Aḥmad ʿAṣṣīd, and thousands of others around the world who would dare critique Muḥammad's words and actions.

Among the numerous attacks associated with alleged insults of the prophet Muḥammad is the May 3, 2015, attempted attack at the Curtis Culwell Center in Garland, Texas. The center was the site that day for a Muḥammad cartoon contest, organized by the American Freedom Defense Initiative, with right-wing Dutch politician Geert Wilders (listed on Al Qaeda's Most Wanted List in 2013) speaking that night. Roommates Elton Simpson and Nādir Ṣūfī (the former a Muslim convert, the latter a Muslim Pakistani-American) attempted to enter the center and kill the participants with assault rifles. The two men were both shot and killed by security forces hired to protect the event.[99]

Two days after the failed attack, Islamic State claimed responsibility, calling the two attackers "soldiers of the Caliphate" and warning the US that "future attacks are going to be harsher and worse. The Islamic State

---

[98] "Moroccan Aḥmad ʿAṣīd: I Will Not Change My Secular Approach Because of the Threat 'Urging' to Kill Me." *Arabic.CNN.com*. Cable News Network (Arabic), 4 Apr. 2015. Web (https://arabic.cnn.com/middleeast/2015/04/04/ahmad-aseed-morocco).

[99] Shoichet, Catherine, and Michael Pearson. "Garland, Texas, Shooting Suspect Linked Himself to ISIS in Tweets." *CNN.com*. Cable News Network, 4 May 2015. Web (http://www.cnn.com/2015/05/04/us/garland-mohammed-drawing-contest-shooting/index.html); Martin, Naomi, and Ray Leszcynski. "Garland Police Say They Had No Tip about Attack at Culwell Center." *DallasNews.com*. Dallas Morning News, 11 May 2015. Web (https://www.dallasnews.com/news/crime/2015/05/11/garland-police-say-they-had-no-tip-about-attack-at-culwell-center).

soldiers will inflict harm on you with the grace of God. The future is just around the corner."[100] (The Curtis Culwell Center attack is the first time Islamic State claimed responsibility (true or not) for an attack in the United States. Though there is evidence that the two attackers were sympathetic to Islamic State, US officials have been unable to verify direct links between them and the terrorist organization.)

All the public outrage, mass demonstrations, murderous attacks, and violent killings connected to perceived insults of Prophet Muḥammad stem from a religious conviction based on the Islamic texts and Islam's history; they are not mere coincidences or terrorist tendencies. Islamic doctrine is the primary factor that motivates these Muslims to risk their lives in order to defend Muḥammad, because the Hadith literature promises that those who die in defense of the Prophet are guaranteed entrance into Paradise.[101] Their love for the person of Muḥammad is a blind and obedient devotion that does not stem from any place other than religion. This extreme veneration of Muḥammad is promoted by the prophet himself, according to this *ḥadīth*: "...none of you will have faith till he loves me more than his father, his children and all mankind."[102] As if to prove this point, no marches were organized in the Muslim world to support the *Charlie Hebdo* victims, but thousands of Muslims demonstrated to protest the first *Charlie Hebdo* magazine issued after the massacre, because it dared to publish yet another satirical cartoon of Muḥammad.[103] People came out saying, "*Je suis* Muḥammad" ("I am Muḥammad") instead of "*Je suis* Charlie" ("I am Charlie").[104] Some protesters were even more pointedly opposed, carrying placards that read, "If You Are Charlie Then I am Kouchi [Kouachi brothers who carried out the massacre]."[105] Defending Muḥammad supersedes any

[100] Yan, Holly. "ISIS Claims Responsibility but Offers No Proof." *CNN.com*. Cable News Network, 6 May 2015. Web (http://edition.cnn.com/2015/05/05/us/garland-texas-prophet-mohammed-contest-shooting/index.html).

[101] *Sahih Muslim*, Book of Jihad and Expedition: The battle of Uhud (p. 1109); *Ṣaḥīḥ Muslim*, Kītāb al-Jihād wa al-Sīyar. 2: 861. According to this *ḥadīth*, Muḥammad told nine companions (seven Anṣār and two Quraysh) who were with him during the battle that any of them who could turn away the advancing enemy from him "will attain Paradise." He repeated this promise after each of the seven Anṣār died protecting him until all seven were killed.

[102] *Sahih Bukhari*, Book of Belief (p. 14); *Ṣaḥīḥ al-Bukhārī*, Kītāb al-Imān 1: 14.

[103] Barnard, Anne. "New Charlie Hebdo Muḥammad Cartoon Stirs Muslim Anger in Mideast." *NYTimes.com*. New York Times, 14 Jan. 2015. Web (https://www.nytimes.com/2015/01/15/world/middleeast/new-charlie-hebdo-Muḥammad-cartoon-stirs-muslim-anger-in-mideast.html).

[104] "Marches against 'Charlie Hebdo' in Arab and Islamic Countries." *Arabic.RT.com*. Arabic RT (formerly Rusiya Al-Yaum), 16 Jan. 2015; updated 28 Jan. 2015. Web (https://preview.tinyurl.com/zmukkw9).

[105] Ibid.

compassion or sympathy for victims killed in his name. In the eyes of Muslims, the name of Muḥammad is holier than the blood of human beings—especially if these human beings are infidels who dare to draw cartoons of the Prophet.

FIFTEEN

Dābiq is our appointed destination at the end of time

We Muslims have been taught since childhood that Islam is a triumphant religion, and our battle with disbelief will continue until the Day of Judgment. We learn that in the Last Days there will be a great battle between the people of belief and the people of disbelief, the Muslims and the infidels. Of course, the final victory will belong to the Muslims. The Hadith literature and Islamic religious texts attest to this belief. Muslim sheikhs stand in their mosque's *minbar* (pulpit) boasting about Islam's future, claiming that we are now living in the Last Days. They point out situations and sites in the world that they assert are examples of fulfilled Islamic prophesies. For example, Islam doctrine states that at the end of times there will be tall buildings. When Muḥammad himself was asked about the signs of the Final Hour, he mentioned such signs as "barefooted destitute goat-herds vying with one another in the construction of magnificent buildings."[1] Although

[1] *Sahih Muslim*, Book of Faith (pp. 60-61); *Ṣaḥīḥ Muslim*, Kītāb al-Imān 1: 23-24.

tall, impressive structures existed before Islam (e.g., Egypt's Lighthouse of Alexandria, Greece's Parthenon, Rome's Colosseum, Constantinople's Hagia Sophia, and assorted monasteries, churches, walls, fortresses, etc.), Muslims consider the vast multitude of tall, imposing buildings around the world today as evidence of this prophecy fulfilled.

Islamic prophecies regarding the end of times dominate the religious mind-set of every Muslim. Most of these prophecies describe a decisive confrontation between Muslims and infidels, but particularly the infidel Christians and Jews. According to Islam, Jesus will return in the Last Days to "break the cross" (symbol of Christian belief) and "kill the swine," (symbolic removal of the corruption of the religion by Christians).[2] The conflict between Muslims and Jews will last until the stones and trees stand in solidarity with the Muslims against the Jews; the stones will betray any Jew hiding behind them and urge the Muslim to kill the Jew.[3] The Islamic prophesies also highlight "The Great Battle" where the final confrontation between Muslims and infidels will take place, and Constantinople will be conquered, the symbol of Christianity during Muḥammad's time.[4]

Muslims are charmed by these prophecies, which hold them spellbound in eager anticipation of the great final confrontation between Muslims in the East and infidels in the West, especially with representatives of the Judeo-Christian world.

[2] *Sahih Bukhari*, Book of Oppressions (p. 564); *Ṣaḥīḥ al-Bukhārī,* Kītāb al-Maẓālim 2: 876. According to this *ḥadīth*, the "Hour will not be established until the son of Mary (i.e., Jesus) descends amongst you as a just judge. He will break the cross, kill the pigs, and abolish the Jizya tax. Money will be in abundance so that nobody will accept it (as charitable gifts)."

[3] *Sahih Bukhari*, Book of Fighting for the Cause of Allah (p. 674); *Ṣaḥīḥ al-Bukhārī,* Kītāb al-Jihād wa al-Sīyar. 3: 1070. According to this *ḥadīth*, the "Hour will not be established until you fight with the Jews, and the stone behind which a Jew will be hiding will say, 'O Muslim! There is a Jew hiding behind me, so kill him.'"

[4] *Sunan Abū Dawūd*, Book of The Great Battles 4: 514-515. According to this *ḥadīth*, "The Messenger of Allah...said: The Great Battle, the conquest of Constantinople and the emergence of the Dajjāl [Anti-Christ] will all happen within seven months."

During Operation Desert Storm[5] in 1991 I was attending secondary school in Morocco. Young people were enthusiastic about Saddam Hussein because he stood against America (although he invaded Kuwait, which is a Muslim country). Public prayers were held and young people prayed for victory for Saddam Hussein. They deemed the Persian Gulf states as corrupt countries and that Saddam Hussein was the promised "savior" who would restore glory to Islam. A renewed wave of religiosity suddenly dominated the region as if the end of time was fast approaching. *Ḥadīths* (that I had not heard before) started appearing in print and other media to justify the prevailing mood, such as "Astonishment and all astonishment is between the month of Jumāda and the month of Rajab,"[6] especially during the launch of Operation Desert Storm, which occurred the end of Jumāda II, the sixth month of the Islamic year.

Saddam Hussein himself exploited Muslims' religious sensitivities, promoting his military aggression as a holy war between Muslims and infidels—that is, between good and evil. On January 13, 1991, he added the phrase "*Allahu akbar*" ("God is great") to the Iraqi flag, a change he might have instituted as a bid to win support from Muslim religious leaders, reduce disrespect for the Iraqi flag in Iraqi-controlled Kuwait, or improve Iraq's credibility as an Islamic state with other Arab Muslim countries.[7] Certain *ḥadīths* with prophetic messages were cited and interpreted as evidence that Saddam was the Eastern knight who would defeat the Western infidels, such as this *ḥadīth*, which was published in Muslim and secular newspapers:[8]

---

[5] In August 1990, Iraq's Saddam Hussein ordered his army to invade Kuwait, a major oil supplier to the US. The Iraqi takeover of Kuwait threatened neighboring Saudi Arabia, another major oil exporter. To prevent Iraq's potential control of one-fifth of the world's oil supply, the US and others came to the defense of Saudi Arabia in a deployment known as Operation Desert Shield in the final months of 1990. After the United Nations condemned Iraq and formed a military multinational coalition to fight Saddam, the US issued an ultimatum for Iraq to leave Kuwait by January 15, 1991, or face attack by the coalition. When the deadline passed with no response by Iraq, Operation Desert Shield became Operation Desert Storm. For the first few weeks, Iraqi military targets were bombed. On February 24, 1991, the multinational coalition began a ground war, liberating Kuwait and advancing into southern Iraq within four days. Fearing civil war and lack of allied support if the coalition forces moved to occupy Baghdad or try to forcibly remove Saddam, the coalition leaders negotiated successfully with Iraq to reach terms for a ceasefire and an end to the conflict.

[6] al-Nīsābūrī, *Al-Mustadrak* 4: 563.

[7] To this day, the Iraqi government has not removed the phrase "*Allahu akbar*" from the country's flag because it might provoke the people, who would view this act as anti-Islam.

[8] "Read the Prophesies (the Anti-Christ)." *Alrased.net*. Al Rased, 11 Sept. 2006. Web (http://www.alrased.net/main/articles.aspx?selected_article_no=5254).

> The Banū al-Aṣfar [blond-haired people, or foreigners[9]] and the Franks[10] will gather together in the wasteland with Egypt against a man whose name is Ṣādim [similar to the name *Saddam*], none of them will return. They said: "When, O Messenger of God?" He said: "Between the months of Jumāda and Rajab, and you will see an amazing thing come of it."

The Arab peoples supported Saddam Hussein despite their governments' backing of the multinational coalition forces—evidence that Muslims are motivated by religious fervor rather than political or economic interests. In fact, any review of Islamic history will quickly reveal that Muslims' emotions can be easily whipped up with *ḥadīth* "prophecies" and the visualization of Muslims triumphing over infidels in a jihadist war.

When the multinational coalition attacked the Iraqi army in January 1991, Morocco's schools and universities were temporarily closed because King Hassan II was afraid that pro-Saddam demonstrations would erupt and become uncontrollable or violent. The Moroccan army was ordered to guard the streets and prevent gatherings. Yet when Saddam Hussein's forces fired rockets into Israel, Moroccan women were ululating for joy in the alleys and popular neighborhoods of Casablanca. Many Moroccan newborns were named *Saddam*, because people were proud that he stood against the infidel West. All these reactions prove that our people are obsessed with the prophesies concerning the Last Days, eagerly contending that certain similarities or coincidences to events or text in the apocalyptic *ḥadīths* are indeed signs that the end is near.

Dābiq and the Great Battle

The leaders of Islamic State and other Islamic movements like Al Qaeda and Al-Shabaab are well acquainted with and believers of these "prophetic" *ḥadīths*. They know that their militants have been brought up learning these *ḥadīths*, and they know they can affect the emotions of these fighters most powerfully by using these *ḥadīths* and other religious texts rather than by appeals to logic or rational thinking. Muslims are a religious people and their religiosity predominates rationality. Therefore, if the Prophet Muḥammad says that there will be a confrontation between Muslims and infidels, then it is taken for granted that this event will

9 **Note:** Islamic sources often refer to the Byzantines as "the yellow-haired people."

10 **Note:** In Islamic literature, the term *Franks* generally refers to Europeans.

certainly happen. No one will debate the validity of these prophecies, because Muslims and Islamic institutions (like Al Azhar) will judge that person an infidel.

Abū Muṣ'ab al-Zarqāwī, the original founder of ISIL, once said, "The spark has been lit here in Iraq, and its heat will continue to intensify—by Allah's permission—until it burns the crusader armies in Dābiq."[11] This statement, which is quoted on the opening pages of every issue of the Islamic State magazine *Dabiq*, is considered an apocalyptic prophecy by believing jihadists. Islamic State widely promotes it as a cornerstone of its beliefs concerning the last events at the end of time, when the Caliphate will finally be restored after the most important and final battle is fought and won in Dābiq by Muslims against the infidels.

Choosing the word *Dābiq* as the official name for the Islamic State magazine was not decided arbitrarily. Indeed, it is the product of all these apocalyptic prophecies we Muslims have heard and learned all our lives. The land of Syria plays a major role in these prophesies, especially the Syrian cities of Damascus and Dābiq. Damascus supplanted Medina (the power base of Muḥammad) as the seat of Muslim power with the establishment of the Umayyad caliphate (AD 661-750). The Umayyad caliphate greatly extended its borders through military conquest, eventually making it one the largest empires in history in size and population. During this expansion, the Umayyad rulers attempted several times to conquer Constantinople, at that time the Eastern Roman (Byzantine) capital and potent symbol and bastion of Christendom. Given this heady, rapid expansion of the Umayyad caliphate with Christian Constantinople, its most powerful rival, it is easy to understand the materialization of these apocalyptic *ḥadīths* about Damascus and a final power struggle between Muslims and "infidels" (i.e., Christians) during the Last Days.

According to some of these *ḥadīths*, "Christ, the son of Mary," will descend into Damascus, where he will search for and kill the false Messiah, or Dajjāl.[12] This Al-Masīḥ al-Dajjāl is a one-eyed liar with the letters *k*, *f*, and *r* (which represents the word *kāfir*, or disbeliever) written

[11] *Dabiq*. Issue 2 (July 2014): 2. Web (http://www.ieproject.org/projects/dabiq2.pdf).

[12] *Sahih Muslim*, Book Pertaining to the Turmoil and Portents of the Last Hour: Account of the Dajjal and his features and what would be along with him (pp. 1747-1748); *Ṣaḥīḥ Muslim*, Kītāb al-Fitan wa Ashrāṭ al-Sā'a 2: 1341-1342. According to this *ḥadīth*, "...Allah would send Christ, son of Mary, and he will descend at the white minaret in the eastern side of Damascus wearing two garments lightly dyed with saffron and placing his hands on the wings of two Angels.... He [Jesus] would then search for him [Dajjāl] until he would catch hold of him at the gate of Ludd and...kill him...."

"between his eyes" or "on his forehead."[13] The Dajjāl will appear "on the way between Syria and Iraq," and the true Christ will kill him "at the gate of Ludd," which is located in Palestine.[14]

The many centuries-old town of Dābiq, located in northern Syria, is about twenty-five miles (40 kilometers) northeast of Aleppo, the largest Syrian city before the Syrian war (AD 2011 to present). The Hadith literature mentions it as a possible site for the final confrontation between Muslims and the infidel Christians:[15]

> The Last Hour would not come until the Romans would land at al-A'māq or in Dābiq. An army consisting of the best (soldiers) of the people of the earth at that time will come from Medina (to counteract them).... They [Muslims] will then fight them [Romans]...and they [Muslims] would be conquerors of Constantinople....

Some Muslim scholars place the town of Dābiq and the valleys of al-A'māq near Aleppo in northern Syria.[16] Others place al-A'māq on the Turkish side close to the city of Antioch.[17] In keeping with its dream and efforts to fulfill these apocalyptic *ḥadīths*, Islamic State named its magazine *Dabiq* and its news agency Al-A'maq.

In the Islamic State video entitled *Even Though the Infidels Abhor It,* masked executioner "Jihadi John" is shown standing on a hillock on the outskirts of Dābiq with the severed head of American Peter Kassig at his feet. He repeats Abū Muṣ'ab al-Zarqāwī's words that are always quoted in every *Dabiq* issue ("The spark that was lit in Iraq...") before adding,

---

[13] *Sahih Muslim*, Book Pertaining to the Turmoil and Portents of the Last Hour: Account of the Dajjal and his features and what would be along with him (pp. 1745, 1746); *Ṣaḥīḥ Muslim*, Kītāb al-Fitan wa Ashrāṭ al-Sā'a 2: 1340.

[14] *Sahih Muslim*, Book Pertaining to the Turmoil and Portents of the Last Hour: Account of the Dajjal and his features and what would be along with him (pp. 1747-1748); *Ṣaḥīḥ Muslim*, Kītāb al-Fitan wa Ashrāṭ al-Sā'a 2: 1341-1342.

[15] *Sahih Muslim*, Book Pertaining to the Turmoil and Portents of the Last Hour: Account of the Dajjal and his features and what would be along with him (pp. 1727); *Ṣaḥīḥ Muslim*, Kītāb al-Fitan wa Ashrāṭ al-Sā'a 2: 1324.

[16] al-Nawawī, *Sharḥ* 18: 18.

[17] See BBC Monitoring. "Dabiq: Why Is Syrian Town So Important for IS?" *BBC.com*. British Broadcasting Corporation, 4 Oct. 2016. Web (http://www.bbc.com/news/world-middle-east-30083303); Mortada, Radwan. "The Islamic State Gearing Up for the 'War of the Cross.'" *English.Al-akhbar.com*. Al Akhbar (English), 16 Sept. 2014. Web (http://english.al-akhbar.com/node/21543).

"Here we are, burying the first American crusader in Dābiq, eagerly waiting for the remainder of your armies to arrive."[18]

Dābiq is mentioned again in another Islamic State video released three months later (February 2015) entitled *Message Signed with BLOOD to the Nation of the Cross*, where twenty-one kidnapped Coptic Christians are beheaded by Islamic State fighters along a beach near Tripoli, Libya. The unidentified lead executioner, speaking in fluent English and looking directly into the camera, delivers the following text before the executions begin:[19]

> "O people, recently you've seen us on the hills of al-Sham [Syria] and on Dābiq's plain, chopping off the heads that had been carrying the cross delusion for a long time, filled with spite against Islam and Muslims. And today, we are in the south of Rome, on the land of Islam, Libya, sending another message: 'Oh Crusaders, safety for you will only be wishes, especially when you're fighting us all together. Therefore, we will fight you all together, until the war lays down its burdens and Jesus, peace be upon him, will descend, breaking the cross, killing the swine and abolishing jizya....'"

After all the captive men are beheaded, the video concludes with the lead executioner's final remarks: "And we will conquer Rome, by Allah's permission, the promise of our Prophet, peace be upon him."[20]

Islamic State did not come up on its own the phrases "Dābiq's plain," "nation of the cross," and "fight you all together" or references to Jesus descending to earth, "breaking the cross," "killing the swine," and "abolishing *jizya*." These phrases and references can be found in the Qur'ān and Hadith literature and are considered integral beliefs of Islam. Generations of Muslims have been brought up learning and memorizing them, Islamic schools and universities teach them, and Muslim scholars have written volumes about them. How can Islamic State and similar jihadist movements not represent Islam if they are trying to implement these teachings, teachings that have been taught for centuries?

---

[18] Brown, Stephen Rex. "Peter Kassig, American Aid Worker and ISIS Hostage Beheaded by Terrorist Group." *NYDailyNews.com*. Daily News, 16 Nov. 2014. Web (http://www.nydailynews.com/news/world/isis-hostage-peter-kassig-beheaded-new-video-claims-article-1.2012598; for video clip, see URL: https://leaksource.wordpress.com/2014/11/16/graphic-video-islamic-state-claims-beheading-of-former-u-s-army-rangeraid-worker-peter-kassig).

[19] Durie, Mark. "A Message Signed with Blood to the Nation of the Cross." *MyIslam.dk*. Jens Bombadillo Hansen, 4 Mar. 2015. Web (https://myislam.dk/articles/en/durie%20a-message-signed-with-blood-to-the-nation-of-the-cross.php; to view video, see URL: http://schnellmann.org/message-signed-with-blood.html).

[20] Ibid.

Dābiq and the dream to invade the West

It was a priority for the Umayyad caliphate to conquer Constantinople, the stronghold of Christianity. Muslim animosity towards Christianity and its symbols has been very clear from the beginning of Islam. As leader and prophet of the early Muslims, Muḥammad forced the exile of many Jewish tribes, and, later, advocated for the expulsion of the Christians and any remaining Jewish tribes from the Arabian Peninsula. His Companions who became caliphs after his death undertook invasions of Iraq, Syria, Egypt, and North Africa, bringing the peoples and territories of these regions under Muslim domination. Even Andalusia in the Iberian Peninsula could not withstand the Muslim armies and was subjected to Muslim rule for nearly eight centuries (AD 711-1492). All these successful campaigns only strengthened the resolve of the Umayyad caliphs to capture and conquer Constantinople, the capital and richest city during the Middle Ages of the Christian Byzantine Empire.

But Constantinople was a formidable target. Protected on two sides by water and fortified over several centuries with a complex system of double walls and a moat, Constantinople had successfully defended itself from numerous sieges by different peoples since AD 330, when Roman emperor Constantine I renamed the city (formerly Byzantium) after himself and made it the capital, the "new Rome," of the empire.

Mu'āwiya Ibn Abū Sufyān, or Mu'āwiya I (AD 602-680), who established the Umayyad dynasty and was the first caliph of the Umayyad caliphate, was the first Muslim leader to attempt a serious siege of Constantinople. According to one historical source, Mu'āwiya used the plains of Dābiq as his base for planning and staging military campaigns.[21] In AD 674, Umayyad naval and military forces under the leadership of Mu'āwiya's son, Yazīd Ibn Mu'āwiya, laid siege to Constantinople but were soundly defeated by "Greek fire," a newly developed incendiary weapon the Byzantines used to destroy enemy ships.[22]

Another Umayyad caliph, Sulaymān Ibn 'Abd al-Malik Ibn Marwān (AD 674-717), pledged to lay siege to Constantinople, swearing he

---

[21] Ibn 'Asākir, *Tārīkh Dimashq* 2: 230. The author reports that "the establishment of the [Muslim] military missions was in the land of Damascus, in the time of 'Umar and 'Uthmān, until Mu'āwiya Ibn Abū Sufyān moved them to the camp of Dābiq due to its location near water."

[22] Wasson, Daniel L. "Constantinople." *Ancient.eu*. Ancient History Encyclopedia, 9 Apr. 2013. Web (https://www.ancient.eu/Constantinople/). See Ibn Kathīr, *Al-Bidāya* 11: 435.

would not return until his forces conquered it.[23] He camped in Dābiq for a long time, but instead of opening Constantinople he died there and was buried in Dābiq.[24] The Muslim siege then continued under the leadership of Sulaymān's brother, Maslama, but was ultimately unsuccessful.

These apocalyptic *ḥadīths*, which were collected during the time of the Umayyad caliphate, appear as manipulative instruments by the Umayyad rulers to drum up support for their annual campaigns to beleaguer the Byzantine armies and periodically mount large-scale attacks on Constantinople. What better way to fire up the enthusiasm and zeal in the Muslim soldiers to conquer Constantinople than by having Muslim scholars and sheikhs present texts with promises of victory embedded with details and a context reflecting their current world? And, of course, nothing is more inspiring and persuasive than a *ḥadīth* allegedly attributed to the prophet Muḥammad himself.

Despite their best efforts (reinforced by a religious mind-set that it was an Islamic duty to take Constantinople and overthrow the Byzantine empire), the Umayyad caliphs were unable to obtain their long sought-after prize. For another seven centuries, Constantinople remained unattainable for the Muslims until it was besieged and conquered by the Ottoman Empire under Sultan Mehmed II (AD 1432-1481). With Constantinople's surrender to the Muslims in AD 1453, the Byzantine Empire soon crumbled. The Ottomans transformed Constantinople from a bastion of Christianity to a symbol of Islamic culture. (Today Constantinople, now called Istanbul, is Turkey's most populous city and its economic, cultural, and historic center. Today Christianity in Turkey is less than 0.2% of the population.)[25]

Yet Muslims still believe today that Muḥammad was prophesizing about the Muslims' final showdown with the infidel armies in Dābiq, even if this plain no longer has any military importance as it did during the Umayyad caliphate, and Constantinople (Istanbul) has been in Muslim control for centuries. It is strange that even in the era of satellites, missiles, and fighter jets, Muslims still dream of combat with swords in Dābiq, like the kinds of fighting in the era of the early Islamic caliphates,

[23] Ibn 'Asākir, *Tārīkh Dimashq* 24: 74. The author reports that "Sulaymān stayed in Dābiq, and said that he would not leave from Dābiq until he conquers Constantinople."

[24] al-Ḥamawī, *Mu'jam al-Buldān* 2: 416.

[25] Chastain, Mary. "'Endangered Species': Christianity at the Brink of Extinction in Turkey." *Breitbart.com.* Breitbart News Network, 21 Apr. 2015. Web (http://www.breitbart.com/national-security/2015/04/21/endangered-species-christianity-at-the-brink-of-extinction-in-turkey).

because they are still controlled by the doctrinal texts, the same texts that guide and control the policies and actions of Islamic State.

Then and now, Muslims were and are enthralled by the *ḥadīths* that prophesy the final battle between Muslims and infidels and the victory of Islam during the Last Days. The Umayyad caliphs not only used these *ḥadīths* to exploit this intense Muslim desire to fulfill the prophesies concerning the conquest of Constantinople, but the *ḥadīths* undoubtedly reassured them that their military agenda was righteous and their Islamic destiny. According to Islamic sources, Muḥammad stated that "Constantinople will be conquered, the best prince is its prince and the best army is that army" in a *ḥadīth* narrated by 'Abd Allah Ibn Bishr, an extremely pious Companion of Muḥammad. 'Abd Allah Ibn Bishr states that his father heard Muḥammad say these words and that Maslama Ibn 'Abd al-Malik besieged Constantinople after he too learned about Muḥammad's words from him.[26]

In the same vein, many of these same prophetic *ḥadīths* also foretell the conquest of Rome after the conquest of Constantinople. For example, in one such *ḥadīth*, Muḥammad is asked, "Which of the two cities will be conquered first—Constantinople or Rome?" The Prophet reportedly answers, "The city of Heraclius will be opened first!"[27] Since Muslims believe Muḥammad's words are always true, they seek to connect events to his prophecies to prove their fulfillment and the veracity of his words. Today Islamic State refers to these same *ḥadīths* to endorse its threat to conquer Rome (and fulfill the prophesied Muslim victory)—sooner or later.

However, these alleged prophecies are self-fulfilling prophecies, not unlike the person who moves the target to ensure that the arrow will hit it. The Muslims who create the text will then seek ways to fulfill it so it will be considered proof of the validity of the prophecy. Described in another way, it is as if Person A prophesizes the death of Person B, sends an assassin to kill him, and then claims that Person B's death is proof that Person A is a prophet. Islamic State follows the same pattern because it keenly understands that its fighters firmly believe in the authenticity of these prophecies. It strives to carefully orchestrate the choice of battle

[26] *Musnad Aḥmād* 5: 44.
[27] Ibid. 2: 369.

fields, tactics, and policies to make it appear that these prophesies are being "fulfilled."

Among the prophetic *ḥadīths* that particularly interest Islamic State is one where Muḥammad reportedly mentions "six signs" that will indicate "the approach of the [Final] Hour," and one sign is "a truce between you [Muslims] and Banū Al-Asfar (i.e., the Byzantines) who will betray you and attack you under eighty flags. Under each flag will be twelve thousand soldiers."[28] Because of the specific details in this *ḥadīth*, Islamic State attentively tracks the number of countries participating in the multinational coalition united against it, in the hope it will see this prophesy fulfilled. In 2015, about sixty countries were part of this coalition.[29] The Islamic State leadership was heartened by the growing number of coalition members, because in its eyes only twenty more coalition members meant the prophecy was heading toward fulfillment. It also meant that Islamic State was moving closer to the prophesied confrontation with the infidels and its inevitable, destined occupation of Rome, the IS black banners flying above the Vatican.

Islamic State's aspirations are readily apparent in the fourth issue of its magazine *Dabiq*. On its front cover is the black Islamic State flag superimposed over the cross on top of the Egyptian obelisk in Vatican Square.[30] Inside the magazine, an entire article entitled "Reflections on the Final Crusade" contains most of the *ḥadīths* already discussed in this chapter.[31] All these *ḥadīths* describe the final events of the Last Hour, and that they are being fulfilled now. Islamic State also believes that the battle with the Christian West precedes the battle with the Jews. And this battle with the Jews is the end that Muslims are waiting for....

Islamic apocalyptic texts and Islamic State propaganda

Islam's apocalyptic texts have been another reason that has driven Muslim youth to join the fighting ranks of Islamic State. In their opinion, no army now—except the army of Islamic State—is fighting the infidels; the Hadith literature describes this conflict with infidels as a continuous

[28] *Sahih Bukhari*, Book of One-Fifth Booty to the Cause of Allah (p. 737); *Ṣaḥīḥ al-Bukhārī*, Kītāb al-Jizya wa al-Muwāda'a 3: 1159.

[29] Fantz, Ashley, and Michael Pearson. "Who's Doing What in the Coalition against ISIS." *Edition.CNN.com.* Cable News Network, 28 Feb. 2015. Web (http://edition.cnn.com/2014/10/06/world/meast/isis-coalition-nations/index.html).

[30] *Dabiq*. Issue 4 (Sept. 2014): 1. Web (http://www.ieproject.org/projects/dabiq4.pdf).

[31] Ibid. 32-44.

war. In their mind, the governments of Muslim countries are betraying Islam because they do not apply these religious texts, especially those that call for a comprehensive war against Christians and Jews, in their foreign policies. Even the destination of many Muslim fighters from European countries, America, Australia, and Canada to the territories controlled by Islamic State was partly due to the many prophecies that talk about the land of "the Levant" (historical region of Syria).

The Levant is considered a blessed land in Islam, as noted in Hadith literature. In one *ḥadīth*, Muḥammad remarks, "Blessings for the Levant." When asked why the Levant has been singled out for special favor, he replies, "The angels of Allah have rested their wings upon the Levant."[32] In another *ḥadīth*, Muḥammad advises Muslims to travel to the Levant in the end times: "Go to Syria [the Levant] as it is the land Allah has chosen on this earth. Allah sends to it the best of his people.... Indeed, Allah has promised me to look after Sham (ancient Syria) and its people."[33] And the best cities that Muslims must join to help fight the infidels are located in the land of the Levant: "[Muḥammad states that] on the day of the Great Battle, there will be an assembly of Muslims in a land called al-Ghūṭa near a city called Damascus. This would be one of the best cities in the Levant that day."[34]

Islamic State refers to and quotes from these *ḥadīths* extensively in its propaganda. Their use in its publications is extremely seductive as a communication tool because the Muslim reader can easily discover that these *ḥadīths* actually exist in the Islamic religious texts. This discovery only elevates the credibility (and authenticity) of Islamic State and similar jihadist groups for its readers. Now, the Muslim reader is faced with a soul-searching dilemma: Reject Islam or accept it completely by applying it literally and joining the Muslim fighting in the land of the Levant, just as Muḥammad foretold.

One British Muslim man, Nāṣir Ahmed al-Mathana (a.k.a. Abu Muthanna al-Yemeni), is a representative example showing how these texts can possess the minds of young Muslims, even in the West. Al-Mathanī, of Yemeni background, appears in the ISIL (ISIS) recruitment video, *There Is No Life without Jihad*, telling viewers that jihadi fighters come from all parts of the world ("Bangladesh, Iraq, Cambodia, Australia,

[32] *Musnad Aḥmad* 6: 236.
[33] al-Bayhaqī, *Al-Sunan al-Kubra* 13: 579.
[34] al-Nīsābūrī, *Al-Mustadrak* 4: 532-533.

UK") and urges his "brothers and sisters" to join them in the land of the Levant:[35]

> "O you who believe, answer the call of Allah and His Messenger. When He calls you to what gives you life...what gives you life is jihad.... [M]y brothers and sisters, you need to look to the Ḥadīth of the Prophet Muḥammad...[who] said the land of Sham [another name for the Levant] is the best of lands from Allah...He has made this the best of His lands...and He chooses the best of people to come here.... This is the biggest evidence that they are upon the *haq* [truth]...."

Muslims who believe in these *ḥadīths* will feel pressured, even divinely commanded, to travel to Syria to be in the "best land" for Muslims. Those who obey this call and are there in the Levant when the day of the Great Battle arrives will be filled with joy, because they will be with other Muslims, all fighting the infidels and applying the Prophet's commands and fulfilling his prophecies.

Islamic State (and precursors, ISIL and ISIS) has even linked its slaughter of people it considers religious hypocrites (Muslims externally but infidels internally) to *ḥadīth* prophesies about the Last Days. As evidence, Islamic State has referred to *ḥadīths*, such as the following one, where Muḥammad allegedly speaks these words to his close Companion and son-in-law, 'Alī:[36]

> "There would arise at the end of the age a people who would be young in age and immature in thought, but they would talk (in such a manner) as if their words are the best among the creatures. They would recite the Qur'an, but it would not go beyond their throats, and they would pass through the religion as an arrow goes through the prey. So when you meet them, kill them, for in their killing you would get a reward with Allah on the Day of judgment."

If critics point to the killing of Muslims as proof that Islamic State is not related to Islam, then it must be emphasized that Islam's prophet Muḥammad himself commanded the killing of Muslims—in this case,

---

[35] Islamic State of Iraq and al-Shām (Al-Hayat Media Center). *There Is No Life without Jihad. Jihadology.net.* Al-I'tisām Media, 19 June 2014. Web (http://jihadology.net/2014/06/19/al-%E1%B8%A5ayat-media-center-presents-a-new-video-message-from-the-islamic-state-of-iraq-and-al-sham-there-is-no-life-without-jihad). **Note:** Video available on this Web site. Message from Abu Muthanna al-Yemeni follows the one-minute introduction.

[36] *Sahih Muslim,* Book of Zakat: Exhortation to kill the Khwarij (p. 590); *Ṣaḥīḥ Muslim,* Kitāb al-Zakāt 1: 474.

the killing of Muslims who are not "authentic" Muslims. Unfortunately, Muslim leaders and caliphs throughout Islamic history have used this *ḥadīth* to justify their killing of entire Muslim sects, like the Kharijites, a sect that was eliminated because of such texts.

Muslims who do not apply these *ḥadīths* in their life either do not know about their existence, choose to ignore them, or pick the Islamic doctrines or teachings that do suit them. Islamic State fighters, however, take these texts very seriously and promote the sanctity of these texts to convince young people to join them and die as martyrs for Allah. They remind Muslims that the Prophet has condoned the killing of "false" Muslims and even promised that those who do this killing will be rewarded by Allah. Of course, the words and the promises of the Prophet are true. Whoever opposes the Prophet's words is a liar.

Caliphate "cubs" and jihad

I do not want to end this chapter without talking about the "cubs of the caliphate," because they are viewed by Islamic State as an integral, even inseparable, part of the future, which will culminate in the Great Battle. These "cubs of the caliphate" are an army of young boys who have been recruited and "nurtured meticulously by the Islamic State to comprise the next generation of jihadists."[37]

Boys between the ages of eight and eighteen who have entered Islamic State youth training camps begin jihadi training by learning and memorizing the Qur'ān. During their training, they have limited contact with the outside world, their families, and local communities. Later, they complete rigorous physical training and education in the use of firearms and assault weapons. They may also learn how to build explosive devices and how to be a suicide bomber.[38] A series of Islamic State videos tracked the progress of one Kazakh "cub" named Abdullah who started as an innocent youngster but developed into a cold-blooded killer in less than eighteen months, when he calmly and unemotionally raised his pistol to execute an alleged captive Russian spy.[39]

---

[37] Yeung, Isobel. "Cubs of the Caliphate." *News.Vice.com*. Vice Media, Inc. 13 Oct. 2017. Web (https://news.vice.com/story/cubs-of-the-caliphate).

[38] Ibid.

[39] "'Cubs of the Caliphate': Role of Kids in ISIS" (Part 6 of an MSNBC report, "ISIS and the Internet"). *NBCNews.com*. National Broadcasting Corporation, 1 Apr. 2016. Web (https://www.nbcnews.com/meet-the-press/video/cubs-of-the-caliphate-role-of-kids-in-isis-657411651738).

To better understand this phenomenon of Islamic State's war strategy, one must examine Islamic teachings and history. Islam teaches that the strength of the Islamic state is in its large number of followers. In one *ḥadīth*, Muḥammad reportedly states, "Marry the one who is loving and fertile, for I will be proud of your great numbers."[40] Islamic State obeys this directive by encouraging its members to get married and have lots of children. But this objective is not just a policy of Islamic State; all Islamic organizations highlight the fact that the world population of Muslims is growing, a trend that can only strengthen and propel jihad, and contrast this growth with the declining birth rate of "infidel" countries, which can only weaken them as adversaries.

In 2006, then Libyan dictator Muammar el-Qaddafi gave a speech on Al Jazeera TV, where he reinforced this belief that Islam can win over the world through population growth:[41]

> We have fifty million Muslims in Europe. There are signs that Allah will grant Islam victory in Europe—without swords, without guns, without conquests. The fifty million Muslims of Europe will turn it into a Muslim continent within a few decades.
>
> Allah mobilizes the Muslim nation of Turkey, and adds it to the European Union. That's another fifty million Muslims. There will be a hundred million Muslims in Europe. Albania, which is a Muslim country, has already entered the EU. Bosnia, which is a Muslim country, has already entered the EU. Fifty percent of its citizens are Muslims....

When I was studying at the University of Hassan II in Casablanca, the students of the Moroccan Islamic group Al-'Adl wal Iḥsān (Justice and Charity) invited the Moroccan sheikh, Abū Zayd al-Muqri' al-Idrīsī, to give a lecture there. During the lecture, he encouraged young women to make more children, because the large number of Muslims will free Palestine, and the audience applauded to confirm his words. His position is also supported in the Hadith literature. In fact, one *ḥadīth* reports

---

[40] al-Bayhaqī, *Al-Sunan al-Kubra* 10: 243.

[41] "Libyan Leader Mu'ammar Al-Qadhafi: Europe and the U.S. Should Agree to Become Islamic or Declare War on the Muslims." *MEMRI.org*. Middle East Media Research Institute (MEMRI), 10 Apr. 2006. Clip no. 1121. Web (https://www.memri.org/tv/libyan-leader-muammar-al-qadhafi-europe-and-us-should-agree-become-islamic-or-declare-war-muslims/transcript).

that Muḥammad prohibited one of his followers from marrying a barren woman.[42]

In Islam, a neverending supply of children provides the necessary strength for wars and jihad; this obviously pragmatic consideration explains Islamic State's priority in recruiting, educating, and training new generations of young warriors for the caliphate, who will carry the banner of jihad in the future. Even supporters and leaders of Al Qaeda, a forerunner of Islamic State, have expressed similar thinking. One of the wives of Al Qaeda leader al-Ẓawāhirī advised her Muslim sisters in a publicized written statement "to bring up your children in the cult of jihad and martyrdom and to instill in them a love for religion and death."[43] In other words, these jihadist organizations are urging Muslims to teach and train their children from an early age to die for the sake of Allah, and, upon their death, they are promised paradise and fellowship with the martyrs who died before them. How is this ideology not unlike the way Hitler indoctrinated and trained Germany's children through his Hitler Youth programs? Are not both examples of state-imposed brainwashing?

In July 2015, Islamic State posted a video showing twenty-five of its trained teenagers, lined up and dressed in matching camouflage clothing, ready to execute twenty-five captured Syrian soldiers kneeling in front of them on the stone center stage of the ancient Roman amphitheater in Palmyra, Syria.[44] (The actual shootings were not included in the video.) In another Islamic State video posted later that month, another trained boy, perhaps as young as ten years old, slits the throat of and beheads a

---

[42] *Sunan Abū Dawūd* 2: 501-502. This *ḥadīth* reports that a man asked Muḥammad if he should marry a woman "of nobility and beauty" but could not bear children. Muḥammad told him not to marry this woman. The man asked him a second, and then a third time. After telling him "no" the third and final time, Muḥammad said to him, "Marry loving women who give birth, for I will compete with you against other nations."

[43] Henderson, Barney. "Al-Qaeda Statement by Ayman al-Zawahiri's Wife Released." *Telegraph.co.uk*. Telegraph Media Group, 8 June 2012. Web (http://www.telegraph.co.uk/news/worldnews/al-qaeda/9320323/Al-Qaeda-statement-by-Ayman-al-Zawahiris-wife-released.html).

[44] Calderwood, Imogen. "Slaughter in the Roman Amphitheatre: Horrific Moment ISIS Child Executioners Brutally Shoot Dead 25 Syrian Regime Soldiers in front of Bloodthirsty Crowds at Ancient Palmyra Ruin." *Daily.Mail.co.uk*. Telegraph Media Group, 4 July 2015; updated 5 July 2015. Web (http://www.dailymail.co.uk/news/article-3149469/Slaughter-amphitheatre-ISIS-executioners-brutally-shoot-dead-25-Syrian-regime-soldiers-bloodthirsty-crowds-ancient-Palmyra-ruin.html). See Winter, Charlie. "Shocked by the 'Cubs of the Caliphate'? Of Course You Are—That's ISIS's Plan." *TheGuardian.com*. The Guardian, 5 Jan. 2016. Web (https://www.theguardian.com/commentisfree/2016/jan/05/cubs-of-caliphate-isis-children-videos-propaganda).

Syrian army officer.[45] One extremely disturbing photograph of a seven-year-old holding a man's severed head was taken by the boy's father and posted on his Twitter account (which has since been removed). The father, Khaled Sharrouf, an Islamic State militant from Australia, boastfully wrote "That's my boy" next to the photograph.[46] If a child becomes inured to such violently brutal scenes, even forced or coached to participate in them, what will be the future for this child?

This programmed desensitization of children toward violence reminds me of the zealous songs I learned at school as we chanted for Palestine during holidays and special occasions. Consider this verse composed by Egyptian poet 'Alī Maḥmūd Ṭāha (AD 1901-1949) and included in my school textbook. I was forced to memorize it (along with other similar poems), and its words still remain firmly embedded in my mind:

Brother, the tyrants have exceeded their atrocities.
Let us embark on jihad and martyrdom.
Pull out your sword
And do not put it back in its sheath.

We were also taught to chant and recite songs calling for using the sword against the Jews to liberate Palestine—and we were still in the second and third grades of primary school! At that young age, we knew little of the outside world or about life in general; our education came primarily from the grownups around us. Essentially, we too were "cubs of the caliphate" without even knowing it, even though Morocco, comparative speaking, is one of the least radical Muslim countries in the world.

Muslim sheikhs also participate in establishing this culture of training children for jihad. Some Muslim television channels particularly target children, like Canary TV and Toyor Al Janah (Birds of Paradise) TV. These channels serve no other purpose but to shape the religious beliefs of children. The most important Islamic songs taught to these very young viewers are jihadist songs, particularly songs promoting hatred and jihad

[45] Hall, John. "ISIS Film a Child Carrying Out a Beheading for the First Time: 'Cub of the Caliphate' Is the First Seen Executing a Prisoner by Decapitation as the Terror Group Increasingly Uses Boys to Kill." *DailyMail.co.uk*. Telegraph Media Group, 17 July 2015. Web (http://www.dailymail.co.uk/news/article-3164999/ISIS-film-CHILD-carrying-beheading-time-Cub-Caliphate-seen-executing-prisoner-decapitation-terror-group-increasingly-use-boys-kill.html).

[46] Mazza, Ed. "Australian Boy, 7, Poses for Photo with Severed Head in Syria." *HuffingtonPost.com*. The Huffington Post, 12 Aug. 2014. Web (https://www.huffingtonpost.com/2014/08/12/australian-boy-severed-head_n_5670673.html).

against Islam's traditional enemies. For example, Saudi sheikh Salmān al-Ouda[47] (AD 1956-present) has created lessons in Islamic education for children, ready to download online. The following excerpts about "Jihadi Education" are taken from transcripts of audio recorded lectures he has given on this subject. In this excerpt, he maintains that "youth and children" should be raised on jihad:[48]

> Jihadi education...is a totalitarian education in several aspects: it is comprehensive [and] means male and female, large and small.
>
> There is no doubt that the young man is the goal of this basic education, and young people are the fuel of wars and battles, like firewood, so care for them more than the care for others. However, the elderly, children and women are the goal of this education too. Therefore, see that young children are targeted for jihadi education, which teaches them about piety, obedience, and discipline by performing prayers, and raises them to be patient, accustoms them to fasting, and educates them to sacrifice for the sake of Allah...[which], by definition, means the Hereafter.... A man may lose [himself] in this world yet find him[self] in the Hereafter....

On the topic, "How to Raise a Girl," al-Ouda writes that girls must be prepared to be good Muslim mothers: "...feed their souls on the love of procreation, raise children in obedience to Allah, and fill their souls with the meanings of jihad."[49] In a related subtopic about instilling the doctrine of Allah and fate in children, he points to the example of jihadi education in Palestine:[50]

> A mother is a school [and] if you prepare it, you have prepared a good people. Consider the mother who raises her son to jihad and fills his heart with the spirit of martyrdom and the love of killing for the sake of God Almighty.... [W]e have a real live example...in the so-called children of the stones, who are fighting in Palestine, some the age of six. [If not their mothers]...then tell me, "Who planted hatred in the hearts of these children toward Jews? Who instilled in these children the love of jihad for the sake of Allah? And who made the little child recognize that this Jew is your enemy, and you must get him out of your land, and Islam must rule your country?"

---

[47] This Saudi sheikh is a Muslim scholar, a member of the IUMS, and currently the director of the *Islam Today* Web site (Arabic edition). He has published over fifty books. He was imprisoned for five years (1994-1999) for anti-government activities, though today he professes that he supports coexistence with other religions. Despite these claims, the Danish government banned his entry into Denmark in May 2017.

[48] al-Ouda, Salmān. "Jihadi Education." *Audio.IslamWeb.net*. Ministry of Endowments and Islamic Affairs of Qatar, 1998. Web (http://audio.islamweb.net/audio/index.php?page=FullContent&audioid=13795).

[49] Ibid.

[50] Ibid.

The constant conflict in Palestine is a real-life example of the effects of formal radicalization of Palestinian children who are indoctrinated to hate non-Muslims, especially Jews and Christians, and trained to fight Islam's enemies as young as six years old. Generation after generation, they grow up, surrounded by hatred and violence toward "the infidels" and taught to desire jihad above all earthly pursuits. Their hostility, manifested first as belief and attitude and then physical acts, infects Muslims in other countries, from Morocco to Indonesia.

Yet people miss or ignore this deadly educational paradigm and still wonder: Where did Islamic State (and precursors, ISIL and ISIS) come from? Is it some aberrant seed that fell down from the sky and planted itself in a foreign land?

Have we not already planted its seeds all these years?

The Hadith literature includes narrations of young boys who killed enemies of Muḥammad and were rewarded. For example, during the Battle of Badr, Quraysh leader and Muḥammad's archenemy Abū al-Ḥakam (but called Abū Jahl by the early Muslims), was mortally wounded at the hands of two young boys, Muadh Ibn 'Afra and Muadh Ibn Amr Ibn al-Jamuh:[51]

> So, both ["two young Anṣāri boys"] attacked him [Abū al-Ḥakam] with their swords and struck him to death and returned to Allah's Apostle to inform him of that. Allah's Apostle asked, "Which of you has killed him?" Each of them said, "I have killed him." Allah's Apostle asked, "Have you cleaned your swords?" They said, "No." He then looked at their swords and said, "No doubt, you both have killed him and the spoils of the deceased will be given to Muadh bin Amr bin al-Jamuh [Muadh Ibn Amr Ibn al-Jamuh]."[52]

This story is a source of pride in Islam: two young boys who risked their lives to kill an important enemy of their prophet Muḥammad. Their story provides a template for how Islamic State should raise their "cubs of the caliphate." They should be trained for slaughter and be harsh with enemies, as instructed by Q 48.29 (Palmer trans.): *"Mohammed is*

[51] *Sahih Bukhari*, Book of One-Fifth of Booty to the Cause of Allah (p. 727); *Ṣaḥīḥ al-Bukhārī*, Abwāb al-Khums 3: 1144.

[52] **Note:** Though the two boys mortally wounded Abū al-Ḥakam, Muḥammad wanted conclusive proof that his enemy was dead. Companion Ibn Mas'ūd searched among the slain and discovered the dying man "at his last gasp." A few final words were spoken between the two men before Ibn Mas'ūd "cut off his head and brought it to the apostle...." See Ibn Hishām (Ibn Isḥāq), *The Life of Muḥammad* 304; Ibn Hishām (Ibn Isḥāq), *Al-Sīra al-Nabawīya* 3: 169.

the Apostle of God and those who are with Him are vehement against the misbelievers...."

Islamic State applies these teachings and is intent in making sure these same teachings are taught to the next generation of Muslims. Therefore, it is imperative that these teachings—these evil seeds—are not planted, generation after generation, in the young fertile minds of our children. Otherwise, the eventual destruction of one crop will only be replaced by another, and perhaps an even more invasive or virulent, crop of greater yield.

SIXTEEN

Is it lawful (*ḥalāl*) to carry out suicide attack operations?

Before I finished writing this book in its original Arabic version, terrorism once again struck the City of Lights, where Islamic State carried out one of its biggest terrorist operations in Europe after the Madrid train bombings in 2004. On Friday, November 13, 2015, Paris experienced its worst night of this century: suicide bombings, random mass shootings, hostage-taking...and dead bodies everywhere. The terrorists carried out their deadly attacks as if engaged in a war. But in reality, these attacks were war crimes committed against innocent civilians—not combatants—who were just attending a music concert, watching an outdoor football match, or enjoying a meal at a restaurant.

The coordinated operation was carefully orchestrated to kill as many people as possible. And the selection of Paris as the primary target was also deliberate. Terrorist organizations, especially Islamic State (and precursors, ISIL and ISIS), do not choose their targets randomly; rather, they choose them to achieve specific goals or deliver a particular message to their enemies: "they strike them in their values and in their symbols." For example, Al Qaeda leaders targeted New York City for attack in 2001 because it is America's center of financial power and represented to them American arrogance and economic success. The September 2001 attacks were designed to disrupt America's financial institutions and humiliate the US government. Similarly, Paris represented to Islamic State European freedom and Western democracy and epitomized France's strong pride in its culture, language, and republican ideals. In directly terrorizing Paris, one of the most important and influential cities of Europe, Islamic State hoped to indirectly strike fear in all of Europe and challenge Europe's belief in the supremacy and righteousness of its most precious commodity: freedom. Thus, the selection of Paris as the assault target was more than just picking some capital and most populous city of an important European country; Paris became the symbol or proxy for all European cities and the European countries that govern them with laws based on democratic ideals and the protection of individual freedoms. Through its attack on Paris, Islamic State wanted Europe to become a living hell for its peoples, instilling in them such acute insecurity about their personal safety that they would not resume normal daily lives but feel forever fearful going to small or local destinations, such as work, school, grocery stores, cafes, and restaurants, as well as larger and more public theaters and stadiums.

During these Paris attacks, as in the Madrid train bombings, the Islamic State terrorists who carried out these operations expressed their hatred towards the West as brutally as they could by resorting to "wide slaughter" (to borrow the language of the Qur'ān).[1] As usual, Western politicians and government leaders exonerated and defended Islam

[1] See Q 8.67 (Arberry trans.): *"It is not for any Prophet to have prisoners until he make wide slaughter in the land...."* See also Q 47.4 (Arberry trans.): *"When you meet the unbelievers, smite their necks, then, when you have made wide slaughter among them, tie fast the bonds...."*

instead of examining the relationship between these operations and the Islamic faith.[2]

The day after the Paris terrorist attacks (November 14, 2015), Islamic State issued a text and audio statement claiming responsibility.[3] The message was entitled *A Statement on the Blessed Onslaught in Paris against the Crusader Nation of France* and issued in several languages, including Arabic and French. The title alone should arouse the religious feelings of any ordinary Muslim, for the word *onslaught* refers to the military campaigns of Prophet Muḥammad and hints at the dreamed-for revival of the era of the Caliphate. The phrase "Crusader Nation of France" is a general reference to Christianity with France singled out not only as one of the medieval European participants of the Crusades but also as a historical occupier and colonizer in parts of the Middle East and North Africa.[4]

So, this Islamic State pronouncement is a proclamation of war, a war between Muslims and infidels, just like the military campaigns of Muḥammad, who attacked and conquered neighboring Jewish tribes, and his successors, who invaded and conquered Christian cities and territories and repelled the Crusaders. Those Islamic organizations and supporters who implement these horrific operations wholeheartedly believe in this holy war, and this mind-set underlies the thinking of a large segment of Muslims, despite the different degrees of their faith.

Islamic State pronouncement about the 2015 Paris attacks

Its formal statement begins with the Basmala ("In the Name of Allah, the Most Merciful, the Most Beneficent"), followed by a relevant

---

[2] See President Barack Obama. *Press Conference by President Obama—Antalya, Turkey*. 16 Nov. 2015. Print and Web (https://obamawhitehouse.archives.gov/the-press-office/2015/11/16/press-conference-president-obama-antalya-turkey). Excerpt: "The overwhelming majority of victims of terrorism over the last several years, and certainly the overwhelming majority of victims of ISIL, are themselves Muslims. ISIL does not represent Islam. It is not representative in any way of the attitudes of the overwhelming majority of Muslims.... And so to the degree that anyone would equate the terrible actions that took place in Paris with the views of Islam, those kinds of stereotypes are counterproductive. They're wrong. They will lead, I think, to greater recruitment into terrorist organizations over time if this becomes somehow defined as a Muslim problem as opposed to a terrorist problem." **Note:** The Obama administration generally referred to this terrorist organization as ISIL, rather than ISIS or Islamic State.

[3] "The Islamic State Claims Responsibility for Paris Attacks." *CounterJihadReport.com*. Counter Jihad Report, 14 Nov. 2015. Web (https://counterjihadreport.com/2015/11/14/the-islamic-state-claims-responsibility-for-paris-attacks/).

[4] **Note:** The Crusades were actually sanctioned and managed by the Latin Church and not by countries, separately or collectively. Crusade volunteers came from all parts of Europe. Nation states did not emerge in Europe until sixteenth century AD. The eight major Crusade expeditions occurred AD 1096 and 1291.

Qur'ānic verse for the event. In quoting Q 59.2 (Palmer trans.), Islamic State selected a particularly satisfying verse that exults over the defeat and banishment of the Jewish tribe of Banū al-Naḍīr after a long harsh siege by Muḥammad and his forces. The Jews of Banū al-Naḍīr tried to withstand the siege within their fortresses but were forced to capitulate when Muḥammad ordered the burning of their palm trees, which were critical to their livelihood and wealth:

> *...and they thought that their fortresses would defend them against God; but God came upon them from whence they did not reckon, and cast dread into their hearts! They ruined their houses with their own hands and the hands of the believers; wherefore take example, O ye who are endowed with sight!*

Obviously, Islamic State was drawing a parallel between its attacks in Paris to Muḥammad's siege of Banū al-Naḍīr.

According to Islamic sources, the terms of surrender for the Jews of Banū al-Naḍīr were their lives and their exile from Medina in exchange for their lands, armor, and any possessions they could not carry away on their camels. Before they left, many of the Jewish men, with help from some Muslims, destroyed their homes but took the lintel above the door and placed it on their camels.[5]

I have mentioned these verses when I earlier discussed the Battle of Banū al-Naḍīr. (See Chapter 5, page 103.) The interesting point here is that Islamic State wanted this "onslaught" to begin with the destruction of France, where the French people themselves would demolish their homes and the *mujahīdīn* would help them to accelerate the pace of this destruction. Perhaps, Islamic State meant that France had been helping the *mujahīdīn* indirectly, because the government of France had eased restrictions on extremists and allowed the presence of Salafist mosques, even protecting them and their practices by French laws. In other words, did Islamic State mean that it would exploit the laws of France against France itself and thereby destroy the country through the hands of its own people and its own laws?

What about the phrase, *"but God came upon them from whence they did not reckon..."*? (See Q 59.2). Did Islamic State take this phrase to mean the infiltration of their fighters into France through the same routes

[5] See the commentary on Q 59.2-4, *Tafsīr al-Tabarī* 28: 30. See also Ibn Hishām (Ibn Isḥāq), *The Life of Muḥammad* 437; Ibn Hishām (Ibn Isḥāq), *Al-Sīra al-Nabawīya* 3: 390.

travelled by the refugees, where "the fortresses" (i.e., the border security forces) could not prevent their entrance into France? These are questions that need definitive answers, but it is certain that Islamic State believed its actions conform with Muḥammad and his military operations in the seventh century AD.

The November 14 Islamic State proclamation addressing the Paris terrorist attacks refers to Paris as "the capital of prostitution and vice" and "the lead carrier of the cross in Europe." These derogatory descriptions are just some of the epithets we Muslims learned about infidels since our childhood. We are educated, generation after generation, to believe that we are the best and the highest of all peoples, while those who are not Muslims are the worst of peoples and the source of all vices. We learn that the infidel West means alcohol, corruption, adultery and fornication, and its capitals represent "prostitution and vice." Islamic State here is only repeating phrases common to both old and young Muslims; they are only restatements of similar phrases we have all been brought up to learn and believe. Islamic State was trying to capitalize upon this highly familiar, "shared-in-common" Islamic heritage by appealing to Muslims' religious sensibilities and their ingrained belief in their superiority.

Though Islamic State did not announce in its statement the actual names of the attackers,[6] it did describe their role and mission:[7]

> ...a group of believers from the soldiers of the Caliphate (may Allah strengthen and and support it) set out targeting...Paris. This group of believers were youth who divorced the worldly life and advanced towards their enemy hoping to be killed for Allah's sake, doing so in support of His religion, His Prophet...and His allies. They did so in spite of His enemies....

This excerpt summarizes what the world must understand about these terrorist attackers. These young men have really detached themselves from the world and earthly pursuits. Political leaders and news commentators cannot justify that the atrocities these attackers committed were based

[6] **Note:** The names and footage of nine of the Paris attackers are included later in an Islamic State video entitled *Kill Them Wherever You Find Them*. (To view video, see URL: https://www.jihadwatch.org/2016/01/new-islamic-state-beheading-video-celebrates-jihad-murders-promises-more) See Jalabi, Raya. "ISIS Video Threatening UK Claims to Show Paris Attackers in Syria and Iraq." *TheGuardian.com*. The Guardian, 25 Jan. 2016. Web (https://www.theguardian.com/world/2016/jan/24/isis-video-paris-attackers-iraq-syria-david-cameron).

[7] "The Islamic State Claims Responsibility for Paris Attacks." *CounterJihadReport.com*. Counter Jihad Report, 14 Nov. 2015. Web (https://counterjihadreport.com/2015/11/14/the-islamic-state-claims-responsibility-for-paris-attacks/).

on the attackers' desire for financial gain, for they desired no tangible rewards for themselves. They came to blow themselves up and take with them as many infidels as possible. They did not come to Paris to earn money but only to slaughter and "to be killed for Allah's sake." In short, they came to serve their religion and its beliefs. They openly declared that they are dying for the sake of their religion. Yet Western politicians continue to debate and deny these public declarations: "No, you are not dying for the sake of your religion. We know your goals better than you do."

We must stop this kind of response and instead take their statements seriously. We must believe these terrorists at their word—that they do seek to die for their religion—otherwise, why else are they strapping bombs to themselves and committing suicide in public places?

Paris before Rome

After the Paris terrorist operation, Islamic State members and their supporters who are active on social media attempted to raise Muslims with the slogan: "Paris before Rome." For Islamic State, Rome is the ultimate goal. Its submission and defeat will announce the final victory of Islam over Christianity. However, to achieve the overthrow of Rome, Islamic State must subdue other cities in its quest to finally conquer Rome. By repeating the slogan "Paris before Rome," Islamic State leaders were sending the message that its fighters are on a planned, orderly—some may even say divine—mission to subdue and conquer certain targeted cities and regions in its quest to reach and conquer Rome. An official spokesman for Islamic State, Abū Muḥammad al-'Adnānī (AD 1977-2016), spoke in an audio recording about the planned destruction of Paris and other places and institutions before the caliphate's victory in Rome:[8]

[8] al-'Adnānī, Abū Muḥammad. *Say to Those Who Disbelieve.* Al Furqan Media Productions, 13 Oct. 2015. Audio file. (To hear audio file, see URL: http://jihadology.net/category/al-furqan-media/page/2/) **Note:** Title of audio recording refers to Q 3.12 (Palmer trans.): *"Say to those who misbelieve, 'Ye shall be overcome and driven together to hell....'"*

> "O Crusaders, if you are betting on Salāḥuddīn, hoping for Mosul, dreaming of Sinjar, al-Hawl, Tikrit, or al-Hawijah, or dreaming of Mayadin, Jarabulus, al-Karmah, Tal Abyad, al-Qa'im, or Darnah, or dreaming of capturing a forest in the jungles of Nigeria or capturing nests of wild plants in the desert of Sinai, then know that we want Paris (by Allah's permission) before Rome and before Spain, after we blacken your lives and destroy your White House, the Big Ben, and the Eiffel Tower (by Allah's permission), just as we destroyed the palace of [Persian king] Khosrow [II] before. We want Kabul, Karachi, the Caucasus, Qom, Riyadh, and Tehran. We want Baghdad, Damascus, Jerusalem, Cairo, San'ā', Doha, Abū Dhabi, and Amman. The Muslims will return to rule and leadership in every place. Here is Dābiq, Ghūṭa, and Jerusalem. There is Rome. We will enter it and this is not a lie. It is the [Prophet's] promise of the truthful and trustworthy."

Al-'Adnānī clearly spells out a series of "infidel" cities, places, and institutions that Islamic State wants to destroy or capture before the onslaught on Rome. They will remain tempting targets for the *mujāhidīn* of Islamic State, wherever they are, if they can manage to reach them. Islamic State's primary goal is to fulfill the dream of Islam's leadership and the rule of Muslims over the whole world. In achieving this goal, Islamic State will be fulfilling the prophecy of Prophet Muḥammad. It is convinced it can fulfill its prophesized goal, certain of its takeover of Rome and the recovery of Andalusia. But, before those prizes, its militants must reach and conquer Paris, Washington DC, and London.

Given the statements and literature of Islamic State, I was not surprised to read about the terrorist attacks in Paris, and I will not be surprised if there are attacks in the future in other capitals of the Western world. I noticed that even some "ordinary" Muslims on Twitter were delighted about the use of the slogan, "Paris before Rome," because they began to circulate it after the attacks to show that al-'Adnānī was truthful about his threats. He, as official spokesman of Islamic State, threatened to strike Paris, and he fulfilled his threat.

Muslim reactions to Paris attacks

After reading comments regarding the Paris attacks on various—especially Arabic—Web sites as well as comments of many Muslims whom I debate on my Facebook page or Twitter, I was not surprised by the high level of justification. Some justified the attacks on the basis that France had colonized Muslim countries at one time in its history, and so they would say, "Let France taste some of what these countries have once tasted." The joy of vengeance was evident in these online comments. Some Muslims strongly criticized or insulted fellow Muslims expressing solidarity with France by shaming them for posting the image of the French flag; in fact, they were surprised that any Muslim would show solidarity with a country that has killed Muslims in Algeria, Mali, Morocco, and other countries. Some Muslims brought up the 2010 French law banning the public wearing of the *niqāb* and *burqa* as a pretext to prove that France is a state hostile to Islam and Muslims. To them, France's "hostility" to such Islamic traditions means that France was deserving of such an attack by Islamic State fighters.

More worrisome was that even some of the enlightened Muslims who had denounced the attacks also resorted to justifying them. For example, some of them said, "Yes, I am against those bombings, but France has to stop provoking Muslims." Some insisted that the "attacks" were part of a Western conspiracy to discredit Islam. One reader on my Web page even asked, "Where are the pictures of the victims?" In his view and others like him, this "attack" was fabricated by the French intelligence service as a pretext to strike Islam.

As I monitored the reactions in the Muslim world, I found that most voices were trying to exonerate Islam more than sympathize with the Paris victims. Egypt's Al Azhar University did issue a brief statement condemning the terrorist attacks in Paris, but on several occasions the Grand Imam of Al Azhar, Ahmed Al Tayeb, sternly criticized the West and warned it about any transgression against Muslims and their sacred things; he placed such disrespectful transgression at the same level as the very terrorism that rocked Paris. In fact, three days after the attacks, Al Azhar called on "Western governments to protect the Muslims and prevent attacks on their mosques and respect its sanctity."[9] Such declarations seem to paint the Europeans as terrorists and the Muslims as victims who need be protected by the world—at a time when France was still reeling under the shock of the Paris attacks and still desperately

[9] "Al-Azhar Condemns the Burning of Mosques in the West." *Azhar.eg*. Al Azhar Observatory for Combating Extremism, 16 Nov. 2015. Web (http://preview.tinyurl.com/zvsgyz7).

hunting fugitive attackers. Yet even the next day (November 17), Al Azhar renewed its demand that Western governments protect Muslims:[10]

> Al-Azhar Al-Sharif affirms its strong condemnation of these racial acts which run counter to all that heavenly divine religions and international conventions have called for regarding the necessity of respecting others' beliefs and protecting their sacred sites, houses of worship and properties—calling the Western governments to take all necessary measures and precautions to protect all Muslims living in their countries from any possible attacks and not to link the terrorist acts of that little deviated group of Muslims...and the teachings of the upright Islamic religion, which calls for peace, tolerance and peaceful coexistence with the other....

Obviously, the goal of these declarations was to protect the sanctity of all things Islamic from any criticism, lest Islam receive any blame for any of these violent terrorist operations. These declarations insisted that Western countries must never confuse this kind of violence with Islam. And here I ask: How many people died as a result of this confusion? How many people died in France after the terrorist attacks because of hatred towards Muslims? The terrorists shouted "*Allahu Akbar!*" before they ended the lives of 130 innocent people, the battle cry first used by Islam's prophet Muḥammad before he slaughtered people.[11] However, most of the statements Al Azhar directed toward Western governments after the Paris attacks concern admonitions to target and suppress hatred towards Islam and Muslims. The clerics of Al Azhar believe that the West should never point an accusatory finger at Islam even if hundreds of Western citizens lose their lives because of Islamic beliefs.

Why don't the clerics of Al Azhar spend more time and energy addressing Muslims about doctrinal distortions and how to correct them? Why don't they undertake a comprehensive review of the Islamic

---

[10] "Al-Azhar Condemns the Escalating Acts of Violence against Muslims in the West." *Azhar.eg*. Al Azhar Observatory for Combating Extremism, 18 Nov. 2015. Web (http://www.azhar.eg/observer-en/al-azhar-condemns-the-escalating-acts-of-violence-against-muslims-in-the-west). For original Arabic publication of this article, see "Al-Azhar Condemns the Scenes of Escalating Violence against Muslims in the West: And Confirms Incitement to Muslims Serves Terrorism." *Azhar.eg*. Al Azhar Observatory for Combating Extremism, 17 Nov. 2015. Web (https://preview.tinyurl.com/y9cebyqu).

[11] *Sahih Bukhari*, Book of Fighting for the Cause of Allah (p. 679); *Ṣaḥīḥ al-Bukhari*, Kītāb al-Jihād wa al-Sīyar 3: 1090-1091. See *Sahih Muslim*, Book of Jihad and Expedition: The battle of Khaibar (p. 1116); *Ṣaḥīḥ Muslim*, Kītāb al-Jihād wa al-Sīyar 2: 868. When Muḥammad and his army entered the outskirts of Khaybar, he said, "*Allahu Akbar* [God is great]. Khaybar shall face destruction.... It will be a bad day for them who have been warned (and not taken heed)." The *ḥadīths* also mention that he said these words "thrice."

teachings and beliefs rather than devote the majority of their time criticizing the West? A week after the terrorist attacks, the Grand Imam of Al Azhar gave a speech to the Muslim Council of Elders (MCE), which he himself chairs. His speech was a defense of Islam, asserting that terrorism should not be linked to any religion because it is an intellectual and psychological disease: "What triggers terrorism is not always religious extremism. In many cases, terrorism emerged as a product of social, economic and political doctrines."[12]

The Grand Imam's assessment of these violent attacks uses faulty, blinkered reasoning. He is suggesting that social, economic, or political factors are behind this violence because historically such factors have contributed to similar violence by other (non-Muslim) groups. However, the exclusion of religious factors (which would then uncritically absolve Islam) does not agree with history and is just another attempt to insulate Islam from objective scrutiny.

The Grand Imam of Al Azhar also sought to cast Muslims as victims of this violence, who should be deserving of Western sympathy: "We Muslims have suffered many such attacks by the gangs that hide behind religion. As I speak to you now, blood is shed profusely, but it has never occurred to us that there is a link between such crimes and the religion in whose name they were committed."[13]

Again, the Grand Imam denounced Westerners who burn copies of the Qur'ān and attack mosques, qualifying these actions as acts of "terrorism."[14] He then blamed this Western intolerance of Islam and its symbols, claiming it is the catalyst for these terrorist attacks: "In fact, they are the fuel for the terrorist thought from which we are currently suffering."[15]

The Grand Imam's words thus insinuated that whoever burns a Qur'ān is as much as a terrorist as any one of the Islamic State militants who gunned down the innocent people in Paris. For him, both types of activists are terrorists, because sacrilege is equal to terrorism.

I personally consider burning mosques a crime, and I know that Western laws will punish those who are convicted of deliberately

---

[12] "Grand Imam of Al Azhar Condemns Terrorist Acts in Lebanon, France, and Mali." *WAM.ae/en*. Emirates News Agency (WAM), 22 Nov. 2015. Web (http://wam.ae/en/details/1395288293349).

[13] Ibid.

[14] Ibid.

[15] Ibid.

vandalizing or destroying any house of worship. I also know that these malicious acts of arson are few, barely mentioned in the media, and never result in victims. I am also against burning copies of the Qur'ān, but I cannot say that burning a Qur'ān is a terrorist act. Yet the Grand Imam of Al Azhar wants to generalize the term *terrorism* to include the destruction of sacred objects. His main purpose in his speech was to exonerate Islam, an objective crystallized in this summary statement:[16]

> The lesson here is that terrorism has no religion, no identity. It is totally unfair to be biased and to link these crimes of destruction and bombing spreading everywhere to Islam just because those who commit them shout "*Allahu Akbar*" while indulging in their heinous acts.

I might have been persuaded by the Grand Imam's assertion that those terrorists who shouted "*Allahu Akbar*" were perverting or falsifying the teachings of Islam had I not read that the first one who shouted "*Allahu Akbar*" was none other than Prophet Muḥammad before he attacked and killed people who resisted him and his religion. The terrorists were only following Muḥammad's example. The acts and policies carried out by Islamic State in this event are identical to Muḥammad's actions and policies throughout his prophethood. Any condemnation against Islamic State is then a condemnation against Muḥammad, whose actions, attitudes, and sayings are heavily documented in his biography, which was written by the early Muslims.

Terrorist operations and the spread of Islam

One phenomenon associated with terrorist attacks, according to the media in the Muslim world, is the supposed spread of Islam after each operation. The Muslim media suggests that there is a Western conspiracy behind these terrorist attacks so that the West can justify a retaliatory strike against Islam; but—thank Allah!—after this incident, Islam has spread even more. One follower of my Facebook page once commented, "Praise be to Allah, because after every act of terrorism, Americans and Europeans tend to buy more copies of the Qur'ān and the number of converts to Islam increases." I could not control myself after this simplistic analysis (which has been deceptively publicized by Muslim media), so

[16] "Grand Imam of Al Azhar Condemns Terrorist Acts in Lebanon, France, and Mali." *WAM.ae/en*. Emirates News Agency (WAM), 22 Nov. 2015. Web (http://wam.ae/en/details/1395288293349).

I responded to his comment: "Do I understand from your words that terrorists should increase their terrorist acts in order for Islam to spread more?"

Is Islam spreading more because of these terrorist attacks? *Hespress*, the first electronic newspaper in Morocco, headlined one article in early 2015 "A Large Demand for the Qur'ān after the Attack on Charlie Hebdo" and reported increased sales of books in France on Arab and Islamic culture, jihad, and racism. The "French RTL rating of the top 20 bestsellers in France, after the events of Charlie Hebdo, revealed that books on Islam and Jihad were in the lead...."[17] One of the largest Egyptian newspapers in the Arab world, *Al-Yawm al-Sābi'* (Youm 7), reported in February 2015 that sales of the Qur'ān translated into French by Jacques Perc increased "fivefold" after the attack (January 12-18) on the *Charlie Hebdo* magazine offices.[18]

(Though many Arabic newspapers directly or indirectly concluded that this uptick in sales indicated a growing interest in Islam for potential conversion, other newspapers attributed the increased sales in France to citizens wanting "a better understanding of the religion that the extremist group ISIL claims to represent, so that they can make up their own minds."[19] According to Fabrice Gerschel, director of *Philosophie* magazine, which published a highly popular special supplement on the Qur'ān, "The French are asking more and more questions, and they feel less satisfied than ever by the answers they're getting from the media."[20])

Arabic (Muslim) news media made the same connection—that jihadist terrorism prompted conversion—after the events of 9/11, as exemplified by one article ("Conversion to Islam Has Increased in America after

---

[17] al-Raymi, Ayoub. "A Large Demand for the Qur'ān after the Attack on Charlie Hebdo." *Hespress.com*. Hespress, 30 Jan. 2015. Web (http://www.hespress.com/art-et-culture/253603.html). **Note:** The acronym RTL stands for *Radio Télévision Luxembourg*, a French commercial radio network.

[18] "Sales of Qur'ān Translated into French Increased Five-Fold after the Events of Charlie Hebdo." *Youm7.com*. Youm 7 [The Seventh Day], 14 Feb. 2015. Web (http://preview.tinyurl.com/jsa2b2f).

[19] "Sales of Books on Islam Rocket in France after Terror Attacks." *TheNational.ae*. The National, 4 Apr. 2015. Web (https://www.thenational.ae/world/sales-of-books-on-islam-rocket-in-france-after-terror-attacks-1.3771). See Newton, Jennifer. "Books about Islam Selling Out in France after Charlie Hebdo Terror Attack Raised Questions about the Religion." *DailyMail.co.uk*. Telegraph Media Group, 4 Apr. 2015. Web (http://www.dailymail.co.uk/news/article-3025520/Books-Islam-selling-France-Charlie-Hebdo-terror-attack-raised-questions-religion.html).

[20] "Sales of Books on Islam Rocket in France after Terror Attacks." *TheNational.ae*. The National, 4 Apr. 2015. Web (https://www.thenational.ae/world/sales-of-books-on-islam-rocket-in-france-after-terror-attacks-1.3771).

9/11"), which was published on a Qatar Web site.[21] One of Egypt's leading online newspapers, *Veto Gate*, reported that the "Washington-based Council of American-Islamic Relations (CAIR) said that the number of converts to Islam in the United States has increased four times since the attacks on New York and Washington last month...."[22] The article also included debatable findings from so-called studies and from articles from Western newspapers stating that Islamic conversion has greatly increased in Spain, Russia, Belgium, France, UK, Sweden, and Brazil. The sources (if given at all) for most of these claims were attributed to "Muslim scholars" and Muslim organizations and centers—hardly objective references.[23] One dubious and undocumented statistic states that "some American experts estimate the number of Americans converting to Islam every year at 25,000."[24]

These news organizations are not concerned about preventing or understanding terrorist operations but rather defending Islam, maintaining its prestige and promoting it as a fast-spreading religion, even when terrorist operations occur; in fact, its spread accelerates (according to these articles) whenever there is a certain terrorist act. Many simple people believe this media propaganda, even though so much of it makes assumptions or relationships without objective examination or hard evidence.

Unfortunately, this propaganda will never end until Muslim readers and institutions confront it and expose its shallow reporting and falsehoods. In a perverse way, this kind of shoddy, overreaching journalism may actually encourage more terrorist operations. According to these biased news sources, if terrorism increases the spread of Islam, then Muslims

---

[21] "Conversion to Islam Has Increased in America after 9/11." *Islamweb.net*. Ministry of Endowments and Islamic Affairs of Qatar, 23 Oct. 2001. Web (http://articles.islamweb.net/media/index.php?page=article&lang=A&id=6173).

[22] Muftah, Shaimā'. "Islam after the Events of 'September 11'...." *Vetogate.com*. Vetogate, 11 Sept. 2014. Web (http://www.vetogate.com/1217113).

[23] Ibid.

[24] Ibid. **Note:** Although a *New York Times* article dated October 22, 2001, does state that "Islam is said to be the nation's fastest-growing religion, fueled by immigration, high birth rates and widespread conversion" and that "[o]ne expert estimates that 25,000 people a year become Muslims in this country," the reputable Pew Research Center (a nonpartisan American "think tank" based in Washington, DC, that provides information on social issues, public opinion, and demographic trends) estimates that 3.45 million Muslims of all ages were living in the US in 2017 and made up about 1.1% of the total US population. Even if Muslims are projected to become the second largest religion in the US by 2040, it will still only reach 2.1% of the nation's total population. To date, the growth is attributed to higher fertility rates and continued migration to the US from outside the country—not conversion within the country. (See related URLs: http://www.nytimes.com/2001/10/22/us/nation-challenged-american-muslims-islam-attracts-converts-thousand-drawn-before.html; http://www.pewresearch.org/fact-tank/2018/01/03/new-estimates-show-u-s-muslim-population-continues-to-grow/).

should thank the Al Qaeda terrorists of 9/11 and thank the Paris Islamic State terrorists because they were able to spread Islam more quickly and convert more Westerners than through traditional advocacy.

Doctrinal questions about suicide operations

Three questions related to the Paris terrorist operations must be answered to understand the mentality of the suicide bombers and the suicidal attacks. I personally do not think that these kinds of acts will stop any time soon. If we truly want to eliminate them, we must confront the ideology—the doctrinal and intellectual origins of this thinking and behavior—behind them.

Question 1: Does Islam permit suicide bombings?

Yes! Islam permits the jihadist (*mujāhid*) Muslim to enter among his enemies and cause as much death as possible, even if he himself dies during the execution of this slaughter. These attacks are called suicide attacks, because the person who implements them deliberately plans not to survive. Muslim scholars and clerics have not prohibited suicide bombings—but under certain conditions. This opinion is based on the Hadith literature and the Qur'ān, such as Q 9.111 (Palmer trans.): *"Verily, God hath bought of the believers their persons and their wealth, for the paradise they are to have; they shall fight in the way of God, and they shall slay and be slain...."* The verse clearly states that Muslims shall kill and be killed. Their life and wealth belong to Allah, who will reward them with paradise should they fight and die for his sake.

Some of the conditional terms Muslim scholars have prescribed for suicide operations center on motive and purpose. One of the most respected modern scholars in the Muslim world, Sheikh Muḥammad Nāṣir al-Dīn al-Albānī (AD 1914-1999), includes this comment about permissible suicide operations in a footnote in one of his writings:[25]

> The Ḥadīth indicates the permissibility of what is known today as the suicide operations carried out by some Muslim youth against the enemies of Allah. But there are conditions for that, the most important of which is that the intended purpose is for the sake of Allah, and for the victory of the religion of Allah.

[25] al-Albanī, *Ṣaḥīḥ Mawārid* 2: 119; see footnote 2.

This opinion is not unique to the contemporary Muslim commentator al-Albānī, lest critics counter that this opinion is an outlier or an aberration. Al-Qurṭubī, one of the Muslim world's most respected commentators, states a similar opinion:[26]

> If one man [Muslim] advances alone on a thousand men [infidels], there is no harm at all if he thinks that he could be saved or that he could inflict harm on the enemy. If it was not so, then this would be hated, because he is exposing himself to harm without benefiting the Muslims...and if he intends to terrorize the enemy, and to show the strength of the Muslims in their religion, then it is also allowed. And if there is a benefit for the Muslims, if he inflicts damage to himself in order to exalt the religion of Allah, and to cause a reduction of the disbelief, then this is the honorable place which Allah had promised the believers.

This principle, called in jihad "plunging into the enemy," is well known to Muslim scholars. However, many Western scholars of Islam and researchers who follow and analyze jihadist movements appear unfamiliar, ignorant, or reserved about this principle. Many Muslim scholars have written about this principle, including Ibn Taymīya, the prominent Sunni theologian and scholar, who titled one of his books especially on this topic: *Qāʿidat al-Inghimās fī al-ʿAdūw wa-hal Yubāḥ?* (*The Principle of Plunging into the Enemy and Is It Permitted?*). This book has been available and familiar to Muslim scholars for seven centuries so far, which means that this principle did not newly appear with the rise of Islamic State and other jihadist movements. In his book, Ibn Taymīya defines this "principle ofplunging":[27]

> An individual or a group can fight an enemy more than double their number on condition there is some benefit to Islam in fighting, even if they are likely to be killed! Like a man who storms the ranks of the infidels and penetrates them. Scholars call this "plunging into the enemy," since the man is swallowed up in them like a thing that gets submersed in something that engulfs it.

According to this definition, the perpetrators of the attacks of September 11, 2001, who "plunged" into America intent to cause great harm to its citizens, were applying this principle. The goal of these suicidal attacks was to advance the victory of Islam and Muslims and to inflict maximum

---

[26] See the commentary on Q 2.195, *Tafsīr al-Qurṭubī* 2: 365.
[27] Ibn Taymīya, *Qāʿidat al-Inghimās* 23.

damage on the enemy. They expected to die during the commission of these attacks. Most certainly they were holding fast to the verses of the Qur'ān, which promises them paradise if they kill for the sake of Allah and die in the killing of infidels, Allah's enemies.

Similarly, the Islamic State perpetrators of the 2015 Paris attacks applied the same principle when they blew themselves up with their explosive belts—not to commit suicide per se but to retaliate against the enemy (France), because its governmental forces had attacked Islamic State and was participating in the multinational coalition, which was bombing Islamic State strongholds in Syria and Iraq. In other words, the perpetrators during both of these terrorist operations were not committing "suicide" but offering themselves as a sacrifice for the good of their religion and fellow Muslims. Consequently, these and similarly executed terrorist operations are considered religiously lawful because they do not violate the conditions laid down by Islamic jurists.

Suicidal operations undertaken to "plunge" into enemy forces or strongholds to further Islam and destroy infidels is not a new battle strategy in Islam's history. Since Muḥammad's time, these kinds of operations have been employed—repeatedly—for more than fourteen hundred years. Prophet Muḥammad himself would bless these operations and rejoice in them, considering them as divine victories. Ibn Taymīya mentions their prevalence in his book:[28]

> ...at the time of the Prophet, one man alone would advance on the enemy within the sight of the Prophet and he would plunge into them, and fight them until he got killed. This was known among the Muslims in the era of the prophet and his successors.

Therefore, the suicide bombers of the twenty-first century AD are only following the example of the suicide "bombers" of seventh century AD and the centuries in between. The only difference are the tools, where yesterday's *mujāhidīn* carried out their suicide operations with swords and conventional fighting tools, and today's *mujāhidīn* carry Kalashnikovs and explosive belts.

This principle is not an extremist Islamic opinion or limited to one Islamic school, i.e., Wahhabism. Rather it is the opinion of the four major Islamic schools of jurisprudence (which guide the majority of Muslims

---

[28] Ibn Taymīya, *Qā'idat al-Inghimās* 46.

today). Even Ibn Taymīya recognizes this concurrence: "For this reason the four imams have permitted a Muslim to plunge into the ranks of the unbelievers, even if he thinks they will kill him, on condition that this act is in the interest of Muslims."[29]

The condition of interest here is relative. Anyone can see an "interest" in blowing up an explosive belt among infidels, the enemies of Islam. Islamic State believed that bombing French people would scare the French government and persuade it from entering further military operations against its organizations then in Raqqa, Basra, and other areas. The bombings were also intended to raise the morale of the fighters and jihadists in its ranks, weaken the economy and challenge the security of France, and create endless problems for the European Union and other countries participating in the international coalition against it and other jihadist organizations. Are not these aims a major interest for Islam and the Muslims in the eyes of Islamic State?

Al Qaeda saw the suicidal plane crashes into the twin towers of the World Trade Center as a major "interest" for Al Qaeda and Muslims, because the planned attacks were meant to weaken America by terrorizing Americans and disrupting the US economy. The condition of "interest" is therefore available in all these attacks because each organization sees the interest in its own way.

Saudi Arabia condemned the suicide bombings in Paris, declaring that they had nothing to do with Islam. However, at the same time, Saudi scholars who are honored by the Royal Family and valued by the Saudi people, discussed the suicide bombings and clearly supported them. These public but contrasting declarations are just another demonstration of Saudi Arabia's practice of political hypocrisy, where the monarchy or its representative issues a global statement that aligns or sympathizes with the West but then allows or overlooks a contradictory sermon for domestic consumption among its people and among all Muslims. Make no mistake: Saudi Arabia's top scholars and clerics accept the religious lawfulness of suicide bombings against the enemies of Allah and the enemies of Islam. Sheikh Sulaymān al-Manī', a member of the Saudi Supreme Council of Scholars and a royal adviser, makes this position very plain:[30]

[29] Ibn Taymīya, *Majmū' Fatāwā* 28: 540.

[30] al-Manī', Sulaymān. "The Book of Fatāwa in Martyrdom Operations." *Islamport.com*. The Comprehensive Encyclopedia, 25 Apr. 2001. Web (http://islamport.com/w/aqd/Web/4375/12.htm); see page 12.

> There is no doubt that the suicide operations in the cause of Allah against the enemies of Allah and His Messenger and the enemies of Muslims is an honorable nearness that draws the Muslim closer to his Lord. It is undoubtedly one of the best doors of jihad for the sake of Allah....

Saudi sheikh Salmān al-Ouda provides a lengthy response on his Web site, *Islam Today*, to questions about Palestinians who blow themselves up. His summary statement includes the following text:[31]

> The person who carries out these operations according to the conditions that are considered legitimate is, in the name of Allah, a martyr, if his intention is correct[:] "For acts are judged by the intention." Narrated by al-Bukhari...and Muslim.... Such a person is to be prayed to Allah to have mercy on his soul. It is permissible to pay the expenses of these operations from the house of money, or from *zakat*, because it is from the path of Allah....

Ḥamūd Ibn 'Uqlā al-Shu'aybī (AD 1925-2002) was an influential sheikh representative of a conservative body of Saudi Muslim scholars, the *Shu'aybi 'ulamā'*, and influenced the men who committed the September 11 attacks in the United States in 2001. The works of this movement have "galvanized *jihādī* tendencies," "encouraged recruitments of *jihādīs* in Saudi Arabia," and "provided a religious legitimacy for *jihādī* operations."[32] In one of his fatāwa, he states that martyrdom operations against the enemies of Muslims are religiously lawful:[33]

> The martyrdom operations mentioned are a legitimate act of jihad for the sake of Allah, if the intention of the owner is sincere, and is one of the most successful means of jihad and effective means against the enemies of this religion because of its potential to cause their suffering and injuries from killing or wounding and because of the spread of terror and anxiety and panic in them and because of Muslims [to] strengthen their hearts and break the hearts of enemies.... [E]vidence from the Holy Qur'ān and Sunnah...confirm the validity of martyrdom operations....

---

[31] al-Ouda, Salmān. "Fatwa in Response to the Question about the Palestinian Suicide Attackers and If They Are Terrorists...." *IslamToday.net.* Islam Today, 21 Apr. 2002. Web (http://www.islamtoday.net/fatawa/quesshow-60-6964.htm).

[32] Ismail, Raihan. *Saudi Clerics and Shī'a Islam* 30.

[33] "Saudi Scholar: Martyrdom Operations Is a Jihad in the Cause of Allah." *Islamweb.net.* Ministry of Endowments and Islamic Affairs of Qatar, 30 Apr. 2001. Web (http://articles.islamweb.net/media/index.php?page=article&lang=A&id=2041).

The chairman of the IUMS, Sheikh Yūsuf al-Qaraḍāwī,[34] who is considered one of the most influential Muslim scholars living today, has stated publicly that bombing by the *mujāhidīn* against "occupiers" (referring to Palestinian suicide bombers in Israeli-held territory) is legitimate resistance and one of the greatest types of jihad in the cause of Allah:[35]

> The martyr operation is the greatest of all sorts of jihad in the cause of Allah. A martyr operation is carried out by a person who sacrifices himself, deeming his life [of] less value than striving in the cause of Allah, in the cause of restoring the land and preserving the dignity. To such a valorous attitude applies the following Qur'ānic verse: *"And of mankind is he who would sell himself, seeking the pleasure of Allah; and Allah hath compassion on (His) bondmen"* [Q 2.207; Pickthall trans.].

Suicide attacks, therefore, are not called or considered "suicidal" actions in Muslim countries; rather, they are called "martyrdom operations," because in the eyes of Allah the perpetrator who dies is counted as a martyr who died for the sake and supremacy of Islam and for the victory of the religion and Muslims. Thus, his reward for his "sacrifice" will be Paradise and the beautiful wide-eyed virgins.

Those who try to separate the religion of Islam from these suicide attacks will face the fatāwa of the sheikhs, who base their opinions on the texts of the Qur'ān and Muḥammad's examples reported in the Sunna.

Question 2: What if innocent people are among those who are killed?

To answer this question, one must first define the word *innocent*. The definition of this term is not universal—at least in the eyes of jihadists—and hence the term *innocent* is a relative term: innocent to whom? Those who disbelieve in the one true religion, i.e., Islam, are enemies—enemies of Allah and enemies of Muslims simply because they are infidels: *"O ye who believe! take not my enemy and your enemy for patrons, encountering them with love for they misbelieve in the truth that is to come to you..."* (Q 60.1; Palmer trans.). And if these disbelievers, these enemies, are warriors, then they are not just any enemy—they are the greatest enemy. So, in the

[34] Sheikh Yūsuf al-Qaraḍāwī posts texts of nearly 150 of his fatāwa on a highly visited Web site, *IslamOnline.com*, and hosts an extremely popular television show on Al Jazeera TV, *Al-Sharī'a wa al-Ḥayāh* (*Sharī'a and Life*).

[35] "Qaradawi Fatwas." *The Middle East Quarterly* 11.3 (Summer 2004): 78-80. Print and Web (http://www.meforum.org/646/the-qaradawi-fatwas).

eyes of Al Qaeda, Islamic State, and other Islamic jihadist groups, America is an enemy because of (1) its disbelief in Islam and (2) its use of military force against Muslims. America, in fact, is a doubly dangerous enemy of Islam.

The same jihadist view applies to France. It is also a twofold dangerous enemy because it is a stronghold of disbelief and is participating in a multinational coalition against Islamic State. Therefore, fighting France (or America) is considered lawful to Islamic State, which considers both the French government and its citizens enemies of Islam. Because France is a representative democracy, where its citizens elect the country's leaders (who supposedly carry out the wishes of its citizens) and fund their government's programs with their taxes, Islamic State will not hold the French people blameless. The French pilots who carry out raids are also responsible because by extension they are carrying out their government's policies. Therefore, killing French people randomly in any attack is not considered a killing of innocents. According to this viewpoint, the French people (civilians) who were killed in the theater, stadium, restaurants, and cafes during the Paris attacks were not considered "innocent" by the Muslim attackers.

Similarly, Al Qaeda does not consider the American citizens who were killed during the September 11 attacks as innocent victims. To Al Qaeda, these people were involved, directly or indirectly, in America's war against Islam. It holds the American people accountable for its support of Israel and its support of the US military in its wars by sending their sons and daughters to participate in them. Therefore, the typical *mujāhid* does not feel sorry for the death of any one of the ordinary citizens who was working in his or her office on September 11, 2001 and was killed in those operations. These ordinary citizens are just disbelievers, which means they are enemies of Islam.

But even if some of the victims are "innocent" in the eyes of these jihadists, these deaths are still considered justifiable, even if these "innocent" victims may be individuals who reject their country's politics or secretly support jihad. It does not matter to jihadists because the great interest of the goal—victory of Islam and all Muslims—trumps the harm of these unintended "innocent" deaths. The victory of Islamic State and its efforts to maximize the damage to and number of deaths among its enemies is more important than the security and salvation of a few "innocent" lives.

Are there Islamic texts that support this definition and view? Of course. Jihadists do not adopt a single idea that has no religiously lawful basis. According to Islamic doctrine and scholarly interpretation, the killing of "innocents" is permissible if it is a way to kill the leaders or the heads of disbelief, further the victory of Islam, and inflict the greatest harm on the enemies of Islam. Islamic texts speak of how the early Muslims, who would carry out their attack raids (primarily at night) on the "infidel" tribes, had killed women and children not actively engaged in the fighting. During these night attacks, when visibility was poor, there were naturally many casualties among the "civilian" population, i.e., children, women, and the elderly. When Muḥammad's followers came to him, asking about the lawfulness of inadvertently killing the women and children when targeting the infidel men, he answered that it was permissible to kill the women and children.[36] Muḥammad permitted the killing of children and women, as long as it serves the interest of killing the adult male infidels—a permissible tactic that caused them and their tribes psychological and physical damage. Though children and women are generally considered "innocent" in times of war, Muḥammad allowed their unintentional injury or killing during the pursuit of killing all the adult male infidels. Accordingly, today's *mujāhidīn* can kill "the innocent" if the intention is to kill the adults and "the non-innocent" infidels.

In a related *hadith*, Muḥammad stated that Allah will cause the earth to swallow many people because of an army that will raid the Ka'ba (most sacred site in Islam) in the Last Days. 'Ā'isha, his favorite wife, objected because innocent people would be among those who would be swallowed by the earth. But Muḥammad replied that even though they would all be swallowed up, they would be treated differently at the Day of Resurrection and would be resurrected for judgment according to their belief at the time of their death.[37]

[36] *Sahih Muslim*, Book of Jihad and Expedition: Permissibility of killing women and children in the night raids, provided it is not deliberate (p. 1076); *Ṣaḥīḥ Muslim*, Kītāb al-Jihād wa al-Sīyar 2: 832-833. According to these *ḥadīths*, Muḥammad was asked about women and children of the polytheists who were being killed during night raids. He responded, "They are the same," or, in different narrations, "They are following their fathers. "In other words, their disbelief (infidelity) does not merit mercy. See *Sahih Bukhari*, Book of Fighting for the Cause of Allah (pp. 693-694).

[37] *Sahih Bukhari*, Book of Sales and Trade (p. 479); *Ṣaḥīḥ al-Bukhārī*, Kītāb al-Biyū' 2: 746. According to a *ḥadīth* narrated by Muḥammad's favorite wife, 'Ā'isha, Muḥammad prophesied that an army will try to invade the Ka'ba but when it reaches the desert Al-Baida', "all the ground will sink and swallow the whole army." When 'Ā'isha protested that some innocent merchants and other people not part of this army would also perish, Muḥammad replied that even though they would all be swallowed up, the innocent people "will be resurrected and judged according to their intentions."

If Allah does not distinguish between the oppressor and the innocent and will cause the earth to swallow all the people until he separates them on the Day of Judgment, then why wouldn't the *mujāhidīn* imitate Allah's actions and cause the earth to swallow all the people (or its modern equivalent)—especially when they are certain there are more infidels than Muslims—and then leave the matter of their eternal judgment concerning their belief to Allah on the Day of Resurrection?

Question 3: What if Muslims are among those who are killed?

Muslims have been victims in the Paris attacks, the attacks in the United States on September 11, and numerous suicide attacks in Iraq, Syria, and other countries. So, what is their status to these jihadist terrorist organizations? Is it permissible to kill Muslims?

In Islam, Muslims may be killed if the enemy is hiding among them for protection and there is no way to reach and kill the enemy except by killing these Muslims. For jihadists, this condition is a well-known permissibility often called the principle of *al-tatarrus* (the shield), which means, "to seek cover." In other words, when the enemy protects itself, using Muslims (or others who are not the target of the *mujāhidīn*) as shields, the *mujāhid* is not prohibited from killing the person being used as a shield as well as the person hiding behind this human shield. In fact, Muslims who are accidentally killed in this situation become martyrs who will go to Allah and will be resurrected as a believer on the Day of Resurrection, according to Muslim scholars and commentators.

Ibn Taymīya discusses this situation in his writings:[38]

> The scholars of Islam have agreed that if the army of infidels used their Muslim captives as shields, and those Muslims were in danger of harm if they didn't fight, then they should be fought, even if the result was killing the Muslims who were used as shields.... If these Muslims were killed, they would be considered martyrs, and did the obligatory jihad should not be abandoned for those who are killed as martyrs. And when Muslims fight the infidels, the Muslims who are killed would be martyrs, and whoever was killed but does not deserve to be killed for the sake of Islam is also considered a martyr.

This doctrine is not a unique invention of Ibn Taymīya but is confirmed by many other Muslim jurists and scholars. Unfortunately, jihadists are

[38] Ibn Taymīya, *Majmū' Fatāwā* 28: 546, 547.

vastly more familiar with the jurisprudence of jihad than ordinary Muslims, because they are trying to practically apply jihad. They studiously examine everything in the Qur'ān and other Islamic literature related to jihad to obtain the most accurate details of its meaning, purpose, and application. Undoubtedly, jihadists have studied the opinion of the highly renowned al-Qurṭubī on the same subject:[39]

> It is permissible to kill the [Muslim] person who is used as a shield, and there is no disagreement about that if Allah wills it, and that is if the interest is absolutely and entirely necessary. And by necessary it means: that reaching the infidels can only be achieved by killing the person who is used as a shield. And by entirely it means that it applies to all the nation, so that the interest of all Muslims is achieved by killing this person who is being used as a shield.

The conclusion is that the objection regarding the killing of infidels because of the presence of Muslims, forced or otherwise, among them is not strongly supported in Islamic religious texts. These texts clearly permit the killing of Muslims used as shields in order to reach the enemy infidels, according to many Muslim scholars and commentators, including Muḥammad Anwar al-Kashmīrī (AD 1875-1933):[40]

> If the infidels use Muslims as shields, the rule is to fight them, targeting the infidels, because we either quit the fight and be defeated or continue fighting and kill the Muslims along with the infidels. We are left with only one of the two choices, and we have chosen the easiest, targeting the infidels lest we kill the Muslims intentionally.

Thus, it is permissible for Muslims to kill other Muslims, if that is the solution to kill the infidels and cause them severe damage for the victory of Islam and Muslims.

This religiously-based rationale was certainly behind the Islamic State bombing of Russian Metrojet Flight 9268, which completely broke apart midair after an onboard explosive device detonated twenty-two minutes after takeoff from Egypt headed for St. Petersburg, Russia, on October

---

[39] See the commentary on Q 48.25, *Tafsīr al-Qurṭubī* 16: 288.
[40] al-Kashmīrī, *Fayḍ al-Bārī* 4: 225.

31, 2015. All 224 passengers and crew members perished.[41] An Islamic State local affiliate claimed responsibility for the crash, justifying the downing of the jet "in response to Russian airstrikes that killed hundreds of Muslims on Syrian land."[42] It did not matter that the majority of the plane's innocent victims were women and included seventeen children.[43] It did not matter if the victims were infidels or Muslims. To these jihadists, the gains are more than the losses, and defeating the enemies of Islamic State is more important than the death of a few Muslims.

Airplanes will continue to be the preferred target for maximum damage and dramatic effect for terrorists, especially after Al Qaeda's magazine *Inspire* published in 2014 an extensive section, an Open Source Jihad[44] feature, entitled "The Hidden Bomb," which details how to breach airport security with homemade weapons and bombs, make bombs using materials and tools found in a kitchen, and identify and destroy targets.[45] Open Source Jihad not only provides information globally to all Muslims for carrying out jihadist operations, it also pairs this information with articles, photographs, interviews, and other literature praising and extolling the jihadist path and inciting readers to seek out and destroy the enemies of Allah, his prophet, and all Muslims.

Regrettably, I believe these kinds of teachings and propaganda will continue to inspire and incite jihadist terrorist groups to down more passenger planes or a "lone wolf" attacker in a stolen vehicle to mow down pedestrians if Western nations do not take proactive steps.

---

[41] "Russian Plane Crash: What We Know." *BBC.com*. British Broadcasting Corporation, 17 Nov. 2015. Web (http://www.bbc.com/news/world-middle-east-34687990); Stewart, Will. "ISIS Bomb Blast: Russian Plane Crash Victims 'Died from Decompression and Bodies Were Left Unrecognisable as Human Beings' Following Sinai Terror Attack." *TheSun.co.uk*. The Sun, 14 Sept. 2016. Web (https://www.thesun.co.uk/news/1781629/sinai-isis-plane-attack-victims-died-from-decompression-and-bodies-were-left-unrecognisable-as-human-beings-following-attack-on-russian-tourists/).

[42] Dearden, Lizzie. "Russian Plane Crash: 16 Passengers Cancelled Flight Tickets on Day before Disaster Killed 224 People." *Independent.co.uk*. The Independent, 2 Nov. 2015. Web (http://www.independent.co.uk/news/world/europe/egypt-plane-crash-16-passengers-cancelled-flight-tickets-on-day-before-disaster-killed-224-people-a6717851.html).

[43] Abrams, Abigail. "Russian Plane Crash Victims Identified? Everything We Know about Passengers of Metrojet Flight 7K9268 As Families Await Official News." *IBTimes.com*. International Business Times, 31 Oct. 2015. Web (http://www.ibtimes.com/russian-plane-crash-victims-identified-everything-we-know-about-passengers-metrojet-2163848).

[44] The magazine defines Open Source Jihad (OSJ) as a "resource manual for those who loath the tyrants; includes bomb making techniques, security measures, guerrilla tactics, weapons training and all other jihād related activities.... The open source jihād is America's worst nightmare. It allows Muslims to train at home instead of risking a dangerous travel abroad...."

[45] "The Hidden Bomb: What America Does Not Expect." *Inspire*. Issue 13 (Winter 2014): 66-111. Web (https://azelin.files.wordpress.com/2015/09/inspire-magazine-issue-13.pdf).

Religious identity and the Paris attackers

All the jihadist terrorists, including the suspected leader Abdelhamid Abaaoud, who planned and carried out the Paris attacks in November 2015 had ethnic roots from North Africa, primarily Morocco and Algeria. Though many of these attackers were born in Europe, in Belgium and France, their minds and attitudes were immersed and shaped by Islamic doctrine, similar to my upbringing where I was taught the religious separation, judgment, and value of "we are/they are"—which is to say, "Muslims versus infidels." Many of them (and others of their generation born in a Western country) grew up under this same influence, as their Muslim families urge their children not to imitate the infidels, hold their distance from them, and maintain and practice their Muslim identity. Our religious beliefs continuously affirm that we are Muslims and "they" (non-Muslims) are infidels; for this reason, we Muslims are better than "them," and we will rule "them" one day.

These orthodox and even traditional Muslim families contribute greatly in forming the character of terrorists. Many such families do not try to adapt to or assimilate with the European culture of their surroundings, thus isolating themselves and their children within it by living in self-segregated communities. In this way, these families are not only disconnected physically from Europeans, they are also separated from Europe culturally as they try to maintain centuries-old traditional ways of living. This isolation and separateness creates tension in young people who are trying to find their own identity in this situation.

Unfortunately, Islam teaches that our identity is only Islam; there is no need or value to include our homelands or other components of our lives as part of our identity. There is no pride for a Muslim except in his Islam. He is to despise any other components. The prophet Muḥammad commanded his followers to revile people who were proud of their riches or family background or any component of identity other than Islam.[46] The Paris terrorists, such as Salah Abdeslam, Brahmin Abdeslam, and Abdelhamid Abaaoud, are victims of this kind of Muslim upbringing

---

[46] *Sunan al-Nisā'ī al-Kubra* 5: 272. This *ḥadīth* reports that anyone who is proud of personal riches, family background, or any component of identity related to the pre-Islamic era other than Islam should be reminded to remember the memory of one's father, though stated in less polite terms: One should tell him verbally, "Suck the **** of your father! To remind him of his origins!" (يقول الحديث إن من افتخر بي من جاهليته مثل نسبه أو حسبه أو أي شيء يمت للجاهلية بصلة علينا أن نقول له اعضض ذكر أبيك، «من تعزَّ بعزاء الجاهلية فاعضوه بهن أبيه ولا تكنوا»).

perpetrated by their families, the mosques and their insulated, isolated surroundings.

The self-imposed isolation and insulation of Muslims living in European countries derive from the teachings of Islam, Islamic arrogance, adulation of Islam's past, and the dream of an Islamic government governed by Islamic law, as well as the hatred of infidels and anything produced by or connected with infidels. This isolation and segregation have also contributed to the creation of young Muslims living in conflict with the European society in which they were born, a country that received their parents and provided them and their family with financial help, courtesy of taxes (paid for by the infidel citizens) and open markets for goods, services, and education. Yet Muslim thinking considers Western society a disbelieving, wrong, and corrupted society, one that Muslims must correct and subject to the law of Allah. These Muslims believe they must strive to ensure that right (Islam) overcomes the wrong (infidels).

Despite the advantages and assistance Muslims receive from their Western host countries, many joined Moroccan and Algerian Muslims in feeling and expressing sympathy over the killing of Abdelhamid Abaaoud and supported the escape of Salah Abdeslam. It took the help of the Moroccan government's intelligence—and not Muslims living in France—for French authorities to learn that the key planner of the attack, Abdelhamid Abaaoud, was in France (and not Syria as they had believed).[47] Apparently, none of the French Muslim residents (most were immigrants from North Africa) living in the Saint-Denis area reported the presence of Abdelhamid Abaaoud to the French security authorities. Presumably, their failure to report him to the French authorities stems from their loyalty to and solidarity with a brother in Islam, because their religious relationship to fellow Muslims is stronger than any national tie to France or moral obligation to defend fellow French citizens. In fact, Salah Abdeslam was helped by Belgian-Moroccans to flee from Paris

[47] MacCormaic, Ruadhan. "Moroccan Intelligence Led French Police to Suspected Architect of Paris Attacks." *IrishTimes.com*. The Irish Times, 21 Nov. 2015. Web (https://www.irishtimes.com/news/world/europe/moroccan-intelligence-led-french-police-to-suspected-architect-of-paris-attacks-1.2438652).

to Brussels, and others helped him to hide from the authorities.[48] This protection and assistance is the result of a religious brotherhood that calls for the victory of Muslims against the enemies of Islam.

Soon after the Paris attacks (November 13, 2015), France declared that it would shut down extremists' mosques in France and expel extremist imams.[49] This new policy is a positive step, but it comes very late, and, at the same time, it is not enough. Many families among these Muslim communities continue to believe in and apply these teachings, which foster and encourage this hatred towards the West. They are passing on to their children the same religious (and intolerant) teachings that were instilled in them.

What we Muslims really need to do is to nurture, highlight, and promote the values of tolerance, brotherhood, and cooperation among all people. Unfortunately, Islam does not advance this ideology. It is a religion that classifies people into believers and disbelievers, into "us" and "them," whom we will defeat one day. This is the religious education that I have learned, the same kind of upbringing and education many other Muslim youth have been taught. Islam needs a comprehensive review and radical change. Muslims must face up to their heritage, because shutting down a few mosques is only like giving a pain killer to someone who suffers from cancer that has been spreading through his entire body for years.

Terrorist operation in San Bernardino (California)

On December 2, 2015, Syed Rizwan Farook and his wife, Tashfeen Malik, both committed Muslims, carried out a terrorist operation that killed fourteen people and left twenty-two wounded. The mass shooting at a holiday party at the Inland Regional Center was not planned by Islamic

[48] Bishop, MacWilliam, Cassandra Vinograd, and Nancy Ing. "Paris Attacks: Salah Abdeslam's Alleged Getaway Drivers Charged." *NBCNews.com*. National Broadcasting Corporation, 17 Nov. 2015. Web (https://www.nbcnews.com/storyline/paris-terror-attacks/paris-attacks-salah-abdeslams-alleged-getaway-drivers-charged-n464666); Chazan, David. "Belgian Terror Suspect 'May have Missing Attacker Stay as His Flat.'" *Telegraph.co.uk*. Telegraph Media Group, 1 Jan. 2016. Web (http://www.telegraph.co.uk/news/worldnews/europe/france/12077522/Belgian-terror-suspect-may-have-let-missing-attacker-stay-at-his-flat.html).

[49] "France Threatens to Close Mosques 'Inciting Hatred.'" *Aljazeera.net*. Al Jazeera Media Network, 16 Nov. 2015. Web (http://preview.tinyurl.com/owx3ce4).

State, but the so-called self-radicalized couple had pledged allegiance to the organization on Facebook.[50]

This type of terrorist operation, planned and undertaken by one or several individuals, is the kind of violent action Islamic State encourages its supporters throughout the world to do. These two carried out a mass murder against those whom they regarded as American infidels. The occasion they chose for their attack was a department holiday luncheon, which was preceded by a semiannual all-staff meeting and training event.[51] Being December, the "holiday" obviously refers to Christmas, a Christian holiday. This detail is important because Muslim preachers and clerics warn Muslims not to engage in Christian feasts or celebrations, such as Christmas or Easter.

In 2009 would-be suicide bomber Umar Farouk Abdulmuṭṭalib tried to detonate an explosive device sewn into his underwear in a plan to blow up international Northwest Flight 253—Netherlands to Michigan—on Christmas Day, December 25. Fortunately, the ignited bomb only succeeded in setting Abdulmuṭṭalib's pants, leg, and the plane's interior wall on fire and not destroying the entire plane and its passengers.[52] Abdulmuṭṭalib, a Nigerian Al Qaeda recruit, was arrested and later convicted.

Both events exemplify one of the strategies used by the Islamic terrorist organizations, which is to kill "the infidels" during or on their holy feast days because it gives them a sense of victory over the Crusader West by turning their Christian religious celebrations into events of deep grief and sorrow. They want to turn these times of joy, hope, and positive uplift in the West into fear, sadness and destruction.

---

[50] "San Bernardino Updates." *LATimes.com*. Los Angeles Times, 9 Dec. 2015. Web (http://www.latimes.com/local/lanow/la-me-ln-san-bernardino-shooting-live-updates-htmlstory.html); Serrano, Richard A. "Tashfeen Malik Messaged Facebook Friends about Her Support for Jihad." *LATimes.com*. Los Angeles Times, 14 Dec. 2015. Web (http://www.latimes.com/local/lanow/la-me-ln-malik-facebook-messages-jihad-20151214-story.html).

[51] Berman, Mark. "One Year after the San Bernardino Attack, Police Offer a Possible Motive as Questions Still Linger." *WashingtonPost.com*. The Washington Post, 2 Dec. 2016. Web (https://www.washingtonpost.com/news/post-nation/wp/2016/12/02/one-year-after-san-bernardino-police-offer-a-possible-motive-as-questions-still-linger/?utm_term=.3bf12ddf43de). According to this article, "Malik had said online 'that she didn't think that a Muslim should have to participate in a non-Muslim holiday or event,' [Chief of Police] Burguan told ABC News."

[52] Daragahi, Borzou. "Bin Laden Takes Responsibility for Christmas Day Bombing Attempt." *Articles.LATimes.com*. Los Angeles Times, 24 Jan. 2010. Web (http://articles.latimes.com/2010/jan/24/world/la-fgw-bin-laden25-2010jan25); Shane, Scott, and Eric Lipton. "Passengers' Quick Action Halted Attack." *NYTimes.com*. New York Times, 26 Dec. 2009. Web (http://www.nytimes.com/2009/12/27/us/27plane.html).

Other details to note in the San Bernardino attack besides the timing are the names chosen by the couple who planned and carried it out. For instance, the surname of the husband is "Farook," which most likely refers to the second caliph of early Islam, 'Umar Ibn al-Khaṭṭāb, who was known as "Al-Fārūq" (the one who distinguishes truth from falsehood). 'Umar was also known for expelling the Christians and Jews from the Arabian Peninsula, conquering the then Christian-dominated city of Jerusalem and purportedly imposing the (in)famous covenant between Muslims and Christians called the Pact of 'Umar, which specifies a set of restrictive regulations limiting Christians' religious and social practices.

The family name of the wife, Tashfeen Malik, is *Tāshfīn*, which is the family name of the famous Moroccan Muslim commander, Yūsuf Ibn Tāshfīn (AD 1009-1106), leader of the Berber Muslim Almoravid empire, who cofounded the city of Marrakesh. After uniting all the Muslim dominions (except Zaragova) of the Iberian Peninsula (al-Andalus) with the Kingdom of Morocco, he took the title, "Prince of the Muslims." In AD 1086, he led his Almoravid forces against King Alfonso VI in the Battle of Sagrajas (Zallāqa) after he offered the Castilian Christian king three choices: convert to Islam, pay the *jizya* (tribute), or war. (The Muslims won.)

The names of both the husband and the wife indicate that they were brought up in conservative Muslim families who venerate Islam's history and heroes. Naming a child after an early Muslim leader expresses this honor and the hope that the child will one day emulate his or her namesake. Interestingly, both names refer to past Muslim leaders who pursued aggressive enmity toward Christians.

Religious motivation of terrorist operations and political correctness

The purpose of the San Bernardino operation is the same as the Paris attacks (which occurred less than three weeks earlier): terrorize Islam's enemies and kill as many "infidels" as possible. During their collection and inspection of the evidence left behind by the San Bernardino shooters, investigators found "an explosive at the [Inland] center that did not detonate, made of three pipe bombs" and "more than 2500 rounds for the assault rifles, more than 2000 for the pistols, several hundred for a .22 caliber rifle, and twelve pipe bombs [and]…supplies for making more bombs."[53] These small, portable yet powerful bombs are the very same explosive devices that Al Qaeda magazine *Inspire* discusses in extreme detail over forty-six pages of instructions and photographs to educate and encourage "lone wolves" to carry out their own terrorist operation or suicide mission. The use of bombs, mass shootings, and assassinations are among the military tactics used by Al Qaeda, which it, in turn, is now teaching would-be terrorists who have pledged allegiance to the organization.

While Al Qaeda may be the initial teacher as Islamic State reaps the fruits of this online education, in the end the two organizations share the same goal and target, despite their differences in ideology and political hostilities. In the coming days, the West will continue to face (and suffer from) more of these types of terrorist operations: downed aircraft destroyed with homemade explosive devices, groups of civilians blown up with pipe bombs or mown down by stolen vehicles, and influential individuals assassinated in drive-by shootings or knife attacks. The goal, of course, is to torment, exhaust, and terrorize the West.

It is strange that even a year after the incident, the American media is still wondering about the objectives of the San Bernardino operation, as if killing through terrorism is not the purpose of Islamic groups. Western analysts only seek tangible reasons; they do not seem to understand or accept that the killing itself is the aim of Islamic terrorists—in fact, causing the greatest physical and mental damage possible to its enemies and terrorizing the West to raise the morale of Muslims across the world is the ultimate goal.

Muḥammad responded with evil to the kindness of the Abyssinian Christians, who offered hospitality, freedom of religion, and protection to his followers when they fled the persecution of the ruling Quraysh tribe of Mecca (c. AD 613-615). Once he had a large army, he responded to their kindness by expelling them from the Arabian Peninsula so that only Muslims would remain. Similarly, Syed Rizwan Farook, who was born and raised in America, studied at its expense and enjoyed its services and opportunities, responded by killing his country's citizens, including his colleagues who had months earlier held a baby shower for his newborn

[53] Medina, Jennifer, Richard Pérez-Peña, Michael S. Schmidt, and Laurie Goodstein. "San Bernardino Suspects Left Trail of Clues, but No Clear Motive." *NYTimes.com*. New York Times, 3 Dec. 2015. Web (https://www.nytimes.com/2015/12/04/us/san-bernardino-shooting.html).

daughter.[54] In his mind, these people, his country's citizens, will always be considered infidels and therefore their actions hold no value no matter what they do; whatever they do is only by grace from Allah, because Allah has subjugated them to serve him.

This way of thinking is the mind-set of Farook and others like him and applies even to his wife, Tashfeen Malik, who was born in Pakistan but lived in Saudi Arabia when she became a young adult. Though she hated America, she came to the country in July 2014 on a fiancée visa (K-1) before becoming a permanent resident after her marriage to Farook in August 2014. However, she came to America not because she loved it but to do it harm. She and her then future husband, Farook, "used private online messages to express their commitment to jihad and martyrdom in the years before the attack."[55]

Many Muslims are brought up to hate the Western countries in which they live because of Islamic doctrines. They may receive these teachings from their families, their mosques, Muslim school curriculums, and religious books, where they memorize these doctrines by heart. The Islamic texts are the source of all these teachings regardless of the teaching environment.

Western governments must take some responsibility for these terrorist operations, because they still seem unable or unwilling to identify and understand this enemy and fail to recognize its true thoughts and objectives. America, for example, tries not to target Muslims by monitoring them without monitoring others, lest it be considered a "racist" policy. However, there is not a more efficient method in all types of fields, e.g., law enforcement, epidemiology, etc., than looking for patterns and eliminating variables that never appear in order to efficiently and quickly solve a problem, such as these two examples: (1) detectives trying to identify and find a serial killer through similarities shared among the victims, murder locations, or murder methods or (2) medical researchers trying to determine the transmission of a new, unknown disease through similarities shared among the victims, timing of outbreak, and actions of the victims, etc. Despite the known effectiveness of this process,

---

[54] McKay, Holly. "Picture of Innocence: Baby Orphaned by Terrorists at Center of Custody Battle." *FoxNews.com.* Fox Entertainment Group, 8 Dec. 2015. Web (http://www.foxnews.com/us/2015/12/08/picture-innocence-baby-orphaned-by-terrorists-at-center-custody-battle.html).

[55] Baker, Al, and Marc Santora. "San Bernardino Attackers Discussed Jihad in Private Messages, FBI Says." *NYTimes.com.* New York Times, 16 Dec. 2015. Web (https://www.nytimes.com/2015/12/17/us/san-bernardino-attackers-discussed-jihad-in-private-messages-fbi-says.html).

Western governments seem intent to monitor all categories of people without eliminating those of extremely low or nonexistent risk. Why heavily monitor or restrict Syrian Christians, for instance, when terrorist operations from that country have all been organized by Syrian Muslims? Not only is blanket monitoring time-consuming and expensive, it dilutes resources in monitoring the most likely targets. Political correctness will destroy the security of the West.

A committed jihadist Muslim like Syed Rizwan Farook, who knows the Qur'ān by heart, can freely purchase weapons and practice target shooting. Yet no one monitors him. This laxity is unlimited stupidity. The gun store owner who sold him the weapons should have been suspicious and reported him to the proper authorities. The owner of the shooting range where he was trained should have had doubts and reported him, not to mention the authorities who were supposed to be aware of his extremism and his possession of weapons. Extremism and weapons are a ready recipe for terrorism, but Americans are still too naïve about Islam. Sadly, they will pay dearly if they do not wake up and correctly and adequately address this peril.

SEVENTEEN

Islam is at a crossroads in Muslim countries

Since the day that my family learned about me leaving Islam, I've been living in conflict with them. Things have not been the same again. Some of my family members have disowned me, and some of them avoid or despise me. Others have severed all relations with me; they wish that I had never been a member of their family.

After I made the decision to leave Islam, my father had heated verbal exchanges with me. As imam of the village mosque, he now faced the rebuke and ridicule of his people—followers who once so highly respected him they would kiss his hand upon greeting him—because of me. Now, his people used me to insult him: I had become a source of shame, disgrace, and humiliation for him. How can he teach them about religion when his own son abandoned Islam to join Christians—the "infidels"—in their religion? One particular time he angrily confronted me, sparks in his eyes: "Why did you leave Islam? Why did you do this to us? Don't you see that you have brought shame to me? What have I done to you to deserve this?"

I too was very emotional and deeply grieved my situation. I had left Islam because of my convictions, but my decision caused my family, whom I love, extreme pain. So what should I do now? Should I reject my convictions to satisfy my family, or should I hold fast to my convictions but see my family suffer? I could hardly bear to see my father in such a miserable state, and I felt deeply sorry for him and for myself. My poor mother, who did not know what to do, cried continuously because I had become the talk of the town. Parents want to be proud of their children, but I was no longer a source of pride but scorn and ridicule for my family.

Of course, my father questioned my reasoning and peppered me with questions. I did not know how to respond, so I asked him, "What does your religion tell you to do?" He didn't answer and looked at me with fear. Then he said, "What do you mean?" So I asked him again: "What does Islam require you to do with someone like me?" He replied, "You know the answer. Why do you ask?" I persisted, saying, "Because I want to hear it from you." Then he reluctantly said, "Yes, Islam commands me to kill you because you are an apostate,[1] but I will not do it, and you know that very well." I then told him, "Please kill me so I can rest! Kill me because I'm sick of this life, and I'm sick of this situation. I do not wish to live!" It was a very difficult and tense moment for him and for me. Then he started to cry, telling me, "You know that I can never kill you, my son! How could I kill my own son?" I told him, "See, you have a heart, but the god that you worship has no heart."

I mention my personal story because it illustrates the tragedy facing all Muslim families living in the Muslim world when family members want to leave Islam. Many Muslims, like my father and my mother, are kind and friendly. They love people and love goodness. However, they follow a doctrine that sometimes commands them to submerge their tender, sympathetic feelings for others for the sake of Allah. They have a heart, but their god asks them to remove it.

---

[1] The four major Islamic schools permit the killing of a Muslim for apostasy. Morocco follows al-Mālikī doctrine, which commands that apostates be killed. See *Sahih Bukhari*, Book of Fighting for the Cause of Allah (p. 694); *Ṣaḥīḥ al-Bukhari*, Kītāb al-Jihād wa al-Sīyar 3: 1098. According to this *ḥadīth*, the prophet Muḥammad said, "If somebody (a Muslim) discards his religion, kill him." See *Sunnah.com*: *Sahih al-Bukhari*, *Sahih Muslim*, and other Hadith literature; Web (https://preview.tinyurl.com/y7bydq49). All these sources report that Prophet Muḥammad said it was not permissible to kill a Muslim except for three cases: murder, adultery, and apostasy.

When someone approaches me, asking, "How can there be good Muslims who are kind and friendly when Islam can be so violent?" I simply answer that the good Muslims have allowed their humanity to overcome their religion. Fortunately, the majority of Muslims do so, otherwise we would be facing a global crisis on every possible scale. Many Muslims choose to adopt and follow only some rituals or teachings from their religion. They may be ignorant of the more violence-promoting teachings (or choose to dismiss these kinds of teachings).

My mother is selective in what she chooses to adopt and follow from Islam: praying, fasting, wearing the head cover (*hijāb*), and some minor things. She ignores the rest. For example, whenever she saw or read any news about the slaughtering of people by Islamic militants, she would say, "This is not from Islam. Islam does not order its followers to kill." As my mother has not rigorously studied Islamic doctrine to reach that definitive kind of conclusion, her statement really reflects her own abhorrence of killing and violence. She thinks that her view is how Islam should be. In other words, she applies her own humanity to the religion that she loves, and she thinks that every good thing she loves exists in Islam. Yet, she never searches for direct confirmation of her views because she assumes that it exists in the Islamic sources and Hadith literature.

Conversely, my father knows that fighting is "a duty" and that the killing of the apostate is also obligatory, but he admits that he cannot do it and quotes from Q 2.286: *"God will not require of the soul save its capacity…"* (Palmer trans.). By quoting these kinds of Qur'ānic verses, he tries to find a religious way to exempt himself from committing acts against his instincts and moral conscience as a father and a human being.

Millions of Muslims are like my father and mother. Kind Muslims are found everywhere in the world. But does their kindness mean that Islam does not enjoin them to hate Jews and Christians and to fight them? No, never. Therefore, I always differentiate between Islam and Muslims. But every person should have the right to criticize a doctrine without being vilified. Criticism—even hatred—of any idea does not mean hatred of the people who created or follow a given idea. Consequently, I do not hate my Muslim father and Muslim mother. However, I do reject this doctrine, which they both believe, that can turn a compassionate father into a cruel monster who would kill his own son to satisfy his god. (My father is now deceased. He died in April 2016.)

Kind Muslims and Islam

Muslims who do not fight jihad do not represent evidence that Islam does not teach jihad. Similarly, Muslim men who do not have multiple wives are not proof that Islam does not teach or permit polygamy. (See Q 4.3.) Unlike his brothers and other friends, my father only married one woman, my mother, but his monogamy does not mean that this doctrine does not exist in Islam. It only means that my father's love for and devotion to my mother is greater than his religion's teachings on this issue or that his financial circumstances did not allow him to marry more than one woman.

Even if there are Muslim countries that do not punish thieves with hand amputation or punish adulterers with death by stoning, it does not mean that such doctrines do not exist in Islam. It just means that Muslims in those countries do not apply these doctrines for other reasons, such as international pressure. Some Muslims may also reject the application of such severe punishments because they have allowed their own humanity to override their religion's more draconian sentences. But these punishments do exist in the Islamic religion, and therefore we cannot consider the large percentage of the Muslims who do not carry out terrorist acts as an argument to say that these teachings don't exist in Islam. For example, if a large percentage of Muslims do not daily pray the five prayers, would that mean that Islam does not have this teaching? Islam isn't what Muslims do or not do. Islam should be based and judged on its own texts, which includes the Qur'ān, Ḥadith literature and the Prophet's biography, in addition to the interpretation (commentary) of these texts and their application in the early days of Islam's history. Islam must be held accountable if its sacred texts teach its followers to think and do evil things. And any Muslim who thinks or behaves according to these teachings must be judged in conjunction with his religion.

Representation of Islamic State

Defenders of Islam will argue that Islamic State does not represent Islam because a billion and a half Muslims cannot be fairly represented by only tens of thousands of terrorists. Is it reasonable to blame all Muslims for the barbaric actions committed by a small percentage of them? But this argument is a logical fallacy, because the question itself is wrong. The correct question is not "Who represents Muslims?" but rather "Who represents Islam?"

Muslims have never agreed during any time in Islamic history regarding which person or group correctly represents them. For example, Shiites do not accept representation by Sunnis, and Sunnis do not accept representation by Shiites. Within these two major sects are subsects, which, in turn, do not accept representation by others outside their own sect, i.e., Salafists do not accept representation by Sufis and vice versa, etc. Consequently, Islamic State (or Al Qaeda, or the Taliban, etc.) cannot represent all Muslims because Muslims have grouped themselves into separate sects, which do not accept representation or authority from other sects. So we are then left with the correct question, "Who represents Islam," by empirically examining Islamic State and asking, "Does Islamic State apply Islam?"

By studying its online and printed literature and observing its practices, we know that faithful Islamic State militants fast and pray the five daily prayers and apply certain punishments as specified in Islamic sources to those who commit a criminal or moral offense, e.g., hand amputation for thievery, stoning for adultery, execution of homosexuals, apostates, and critics of Muḥammad, etc. The majority of Muslim countries may observe and support some Islamic rituals, such as fasting and praying, but they do not apply wholesale these extremely cruel punishments—which means that Islamic State's practices and application adhere more closely to Islamic doctrine than such Muslim countries as Morocco, Tunisia, Algeria, Kuwait, United Arab Emirates (UAE), etc. The UAE, for example, does not amputate the hand of a convicted thief, even though this crime and its punishment are clearly mentioned in the Qur'ān: *"The man thief and the woman thief, cut off the hands of both as a punishment, for that they have erred;—an example from God, for God is mighty, wise"* (Q 5.38; Palmer trans.). So, in this case, which state more closely applies this Qur'ānic text: UAE or Islamic State? And in the same vein, which of these states applies the caliphate form of government established by Muḥammad's Companions? Which state presents Christians with the Islamic text-based ultimatum to pay the tribute, convert to Islam, or fight? (See Q 9.29.) Which state fully embraces the Qur'ān's advice to marry multiple wives or have sex slaves to encourage just behavior? (See Q 4.3.) Muslim countries seem to ignore or disregard these Qur'ānic texts because they do not fully apply them. The omission of these applications in these Muslim countries does not mean they do not exist in Islam; it only means that these countries are embarrassed to apply (or pressured by the international community not to apply) them. Therefore, Islamic State is more sincere in applying these Islamic texts.

So, enough of this misplaced justification, because it just prolongs the tragedy. It is long time to seek solutions.

A correct diagnosis

Before any treatment, an accurate diagnosis is necessary because an incorrect diagnosis will lead to improper treatment and possibly create catastrophe, even death. So we must carefully examine the symptoms to determine the true cause of the phenomenon.

Regrettably, the West has not been aware until recently the dangerous degree the Islamic doctrine influences what is happening in the Middle East. Although the West has set boundaries concerning religion and the state, the social and governmental affairs of the Eastern world are still dictated by religion. Whatever happens in Egypt, Iraq, Syria, Yemen, and Libya cannot be divorced from Islamic doctrine because our feelings are controlled by doctrine and so are our peoples. Any political party can win an election simply by using phrases such as "Allah says" and "the Prophet says" in an election campaign. Thousands of Muslims will immediately take to the streets in protest demonstrations, incited by perceived threats (honest or false) to their religion. Imams' sermons and their fatāwa are instantly and widely accessible to everyone through satellite TV channels and the Internet. Islamic satellite channels, such as Ṭuyur al-Jannah (The Birds of Paradise),[2] are targeting and shaping the minds of rising generations, the very young children, who are being taught songs and behavior promoting religious hatred, jihad, and martyrdom.[3] In this insidious way, little children learn to parrot jihadist songs and practice jihadist behavior without even understanding what they really mean. Religion, therefore, is not just one of many factors—it is the most important factor. Consequently, the ideology of Islamic State

---

[2] Ṭuyur al Jannah, founded in 2008 and based in Jordan, is a popular and widely watched satellite channel for children in the Arab world.

[3] "'Birds of Paradise': Martyrdom Recruitment as Children's Entertainment." *InvestigativeProject.org*. The Investigative Project on Terrorism News, 19 June 2009. Web (https://www.investigativeproject.org/1072/birds-of-paradise-martyrdom-recruitment-as); Al-Naīm, Fawzia Nasīr. "Birds of Paradise: Time Bomb in Every House." *Al-Jazirah.com*. Al Jazirah Corporation, 26 Apr. 2009. Web (http://www.al-jazirah.com/2009/20090426/at4.htm). In both articles, Saudi journalist Fawzia Nasīr al-Naīm expresses her concerns about one of the hits, "When We Seek Martyrdom," on the Ṭuyur al-Jannah channel: "It encourages the use of arms, killing, explosives, shedding blood and terrorism.... Our children parrot what they hear, and it enters their minds. This data is filed away, and over time it ripens into beliefs and principles which they believe in... so that when the dream is achieved, an explosive belt is put on, and he begins to proclaim the Jihad...."

and similar groups cannot be defeated or overthrown by force alone. But we must find and pursue the appropriate solution after we make the correct diagnosis.

Terrorism and rational choice theory

Many people have presented a variety of theories to explain the phenomenon of terrorism in general and Islamic terrorism in particular. One of these theories, the rational choice or rational action theory, assumes that rational individuals "choose a course of action that is most in line with their personal preferences"[4] and "are…motivated by the wants or goals that express their 'preferences.' They act within specific, given constraints and on the basis of information that they have about the conditions under which they are acting."[5] In other words, a rational person will calculate the costs and rewards of a particular action and only proceed if the gains exceed the losses; otherwise, he or she is not motivated to do the action. (These "gains" can be material or moral in nature or both.) Each person has his or her own way of calculating the rewards.

This theory of rational choice can be applied to Islamic terrorists as a useful tool to help explain their actions, for they cannot all be dismissed as mentally ill, foolish, or ignorant. For the most part, they are rational people who have weighed the potential gains and losses before choosing their course of action and have concluded that they will lose much less than what they will win.

The person who blows himself up—believing he will immediately enter eternal bliss and, at the same time, remove his earthly sufferings—considers his suicide act rational, according to his own calculations. Although his act will cost him his own life, he sees many rewards for his sacrifice: (1) He will live eternally in paradise and enjoy the bliss and (sexual) pleasures that come with it; (2) he will no longer endure the pain and suffering from living in this world; (3) he will have injured and hopefully killed some of his religion's enemies and damaged or destroyed their equipment and buildings; (4) he will have contributed to the eventual victory of the true religion; and (5) he will be considered a martyr in the

---

[4] Amadae, S. M. "Rational choice theory." *Brittanica.com*. Encyclopædia Brittanica, Inc., 17 Nov. 2017. Web (https://www.britannica.com/topic/rational-choice-theory).

[5] Scott 127-128.

sight of his friends, his name immortalized.[6] Religious rewards play a key role as the would-be suicide bomber considers potential gains and losses. Material gain is not enough to motivate a rational person to kill himself.

Mental illness cannot be ascribed to the many suicide bombers who were sent by Islamic State (and precursors, ISIL and ISIS) to blow up the Iraqi army's bulldozers (and their occupants) in order to open an area for invasion and control. For these willing suicide recruits, their act is a rational choice based on rewards and losses. Islamic State may have enticed potential recruits with material goods (money, land, house, appliances, etc.) and women (wives and sex slaves), but the recruits who are eventually selected to become part of the organization receive continuous Islamic instruction and jihad training. The men pray daily with their brothers, eat kebabs together, and sing religious songs—and prepare themselves for the day they will sacrifice themselves for their religion. If these fighters truly were motivated by the worldly possessions, why would they willingly give them up to commit suicide? Therefore, the crucial consideration in this life-ending decision is religious motivation. This same motivation applies to those who leave their homes, families and close relatives, whether in the West or the East, to join Islamic State (ISIS). There is no other explanation for their decision except religious motivation.

There should be no doubt that jihadists are religiously driven; they have either been so for a long time or some profound religious change occurred at a critical stage in their lives. Marc Sageman, a former foreign service officer and currently a forensic psychiatrist, published in 2004 the results of his intensive study on 172 jihadists. He notes that of the 155 *muhājidīn* he could find relevant biographical information, "99 percent were very religious" at the time of their jihad and "all but one were considerably more devout right before joining the jihad than they had been as children."[7]

It is not possible to understand Islamic jihadist groups without religion. Therefore, the solution must address Islam's religious texts and this ideology that has promoted and will continue to promote the death and destruction of millions of people. Of course, I do not exclude the

---

[6] Scott 127, 129. This author mentions that George Homans, "a pioneering figure in establishing rational choice theory in sociology," maintained "that *approval* is the most fundamental human goal. Approval is a 'generalized reinforcer' that can reinforce a wide variety of specialized activities."

[7] Sageman 93.

military solution of eliminating the physical presence of these groups on the ground. However, Islamic State is just one strain of this disease, just like Al Qaeda, Boko Haram, Al Shabaab, and the Taliban are all different strains of this same disease. Military combat, technology, and human intelligence are the necessary means to eradicate terrorism, but we need more effective solutions to eradicate the disease and not just eliminate its symptoms: We need a cure and not just a few doses of painkillers.

Universal respect for human rights

The West should use its military, economic, and political capabilities to force Muslim countries through diplomatic efforts to fully respect human rights, including the freedoms of religion and speech. The deafening silence of the West towards the repeated attacks against the freedom of speech and human rights violations is part of the problem. How long will Western countries deal with Saudi Arabia, for example, by selling their silence in exchange for mutually beneficial diplomatic relations or economic interests? It is disgraceful how the Western countries shamefully keep silent when this country can legally and severely punish its citizens for criticizing the ruling family or changing or rejecting their religion. Saudi women do not receive equal rights or protections under its laws; in fact, Saudi women have only been given the mundane legal right in 2018 to drive a car.

Saudi Arabia is but one of a long list of Muslim countries that do not provide or protect human rights for all citizens, e.g., Rā'if Badawī, Moḥammad Cheikh Ould M'khaitir, etc. (See Chapter 7, page 183). If the leading Western countries openly and aggressively encouraged and defended the freedoms of religion and expression by pressuring the United Nations to compel all countries to abide by international human rights instruments, we would have then taken the first and most important step towards reaching a lasting solution. The international community must also press for the inclusion of minority groups—the voices of young people, secularists, atheists, and scholars of our people—to openly and objectively examine and discuss Islamic matters in rational debates without government suppression or imprisonment. Defamation of religion laws should also be resisted and removed because these kinds of laws are some of the most important weapons used to suppress the freedoms of religion, opinion, and expression.

It is the silence of Western countries that has prompted countries like the UAE, Morocco, and Kuwait to propose the re-adoption of these defamation of religion laws after they were once absent from their legal arsenal. Silence is a sign of consent in our Arab world.

Changes in educational curricula and environment

Muslim countries must revise their state educational curriculums so that logic and critical thinking are taught, emphasized, and valued over rote memorization. Unfortunately, religious authorities do not want to encourage students to seek creativity or allow them intellectual freedom and instead insist on control of content and style of learning. Therefore, more scientific materials promoting experimentation and creativity as well as respecting diversity of thought should be introduced to replace narrowly prescribed systems for study, discussion, and application. Scientific subjects that encourage experimentation and innovation, adopt modern theories in physics and natural sciences, and encourage the study of philosophy and logic should take precedence and more time than religion-based subjects.

Still, these educational programs will not be successful if they do not open up the outside world through the inclusion of world literature and the history and culture of civilizations and nations other than their own. Educational and cultural exchanges should be permitted to help nurture understanding, tolerance, and respect for others, regardless of their beliefs, nationalities, or backgrounds.

Religious hate speech should also be prohibited from school curriculums, and a new culture of accepting and respecting everyone should be instituted, promoted, and protected. On this educational front, Morocco's recent action (2016) to reform its school curricula provides a glimmer of hope and a model.[8] However, the new revised textbooks that were distributed in late 2016 are being challenged by some educators, particularly over chapters related to Islam's teachings.[9]

Without reforming the educational systems of Muslim countries, the same regressive, divisive, inadequate, and intolerant educational

---

[8] al-Rashed, Abdulrahman. "Morocco's Attempt to Reform Islamic Teachings Could Impact the World." *English.Arabiya.net.* Al Arabiya Network (English), 8 Feb. 2016. Web (https://english.alarabiya.net/en/views/2016/02/08/Morocco-s-attempt-to-reform-Islamic-teachings-could-impact-the-world.html).

[9] Lahsini, Chaima. "Moroccan Islamic Education: An Unsuccessful Reform?" *MoroccoWorldNews.com.* Morocco World News, 4 Jan. 2017. Web (https://www.moroccoworldnews.com/2017/01/205229/moroccan-islamic-education-unsuccessful-reform/).

curriculums will continue to be recycled, educating and prejudicing new generations of students to hate and discriminate those who are different from themselves. And the more Muslim children who receive this kind of "education," the more the world will see the rise of hundreds of jihadist organizations, whose members have been methodically indoctrinated from the same monolithic educational source.

One consistent public policy

Muslim countries must dispense with their current "two-faced" policy in their dealings with their allies; their domestic policies must openly align with their international policies. Saudi Arabia cannot claim to be an official and genuine ally of Western countries when it simultaneously and hypocritically allows its sheikhs, educational system, and official government Web sites to spread Wahhabism and the culture of hatred towards the "infidel" West. It is not enough for Muslim countries to condemn the murderous crimes committed against the journalists of *Charlie Hebdo*; they must also forbid the internal propaganda and education that incites people to terrorize others.

This political ambivalence can be eliminated if these countries are pressured to reflect upon and revise their domestic policies so that they align with their foreign policies and actions. How can Qatar, for example, be a true ally of America and, at the same time, broadcast a TV channel funded by its prince, to urge the Arab world to hate America and the West, or all that is Christian or Jewish? How is it not disconcerting when the ministries of endowments and Islamic affairs of Muslim countries hear prayers offered up against America (considered the devil's head) at Friday sermons inside mosques in Riyadh or Casablanca while their kings happily pose for pictures with the President of the United States in the White House?

Similar duplicitous governmental policies are evident in recent diplomacy. In June 2017, Saudi Arabia and its allies (which include Persian Gulf countries Bahrain, Egypt, and the UAE) issued an onerous thirteen-point ultimatum to Qatar in exchange for ending a two-week trade and diplomatic embargo. The ultimatum (and the embargo) reflect long-held allegations that Qatar has been supporting and funding Islamic terrorists and cultivating increasingly closer ties with Iran.[10] Though other nations, including the US, share these same concerns about Qatar, Saudi Arabia's newly aggressive political stance to combat Islamic terrorism by singling out Qatar has drawn criticism and skepticism. Most of the nineteen aircraft hijackers on 9/11 were Saudi citizens, and Saudi Arabia has used its oil wealth "to propagate its fundamentalist Wahhabi strain of Islam via schools and mosques around the world," which have contributed to the same kinds of Islamic extremism and terrorism.[11]

Despite the obvious complicity of all these Persian Gulf countries in breeding and nurturing Islamic terrorism, Qatar has become the latest scapegoat when its actions have apparently hurt the interests of its Muslim neighbors. Western nations need to apply pressure on all these countries to formulate uniform domestic and international policies and not be distracted by these hypocritical political ploys or take sides. This political schizophrenia must stop.

Religious reform

Muslim countries must have the courage and audacity to get rid of their religious arrogance. They do not need to sanctify the past at the expense of the present. Christianity has acknowledged its sins when it strayed from its biblical teachings and purpose—its corruption, abuses, inquisitions, injustices, religious intolerance, and wars during the Middle Ages (exercising its power as a formal political state, the Byzantine Empire, and later, the Holy Roman Empire) and other dark periods of its past. But in admitting guilt, it has moved on to reform itself and now recognizes the individual's freedom to choose (or reject) religion and the separation of church and state. Christian leaders and theologians continue to review, re-examine, and reflect on Christianity's beliefs and practices, always striving to align doctrine and application with biblical teachings and make it relevant to each new generation of believers.

Conversely, the Islamic world still extols the early Muslim raids, military campaigns and caliphates, the plundered riches, the enslaved

[10] Wintour, Patrick. "Qatar Given 10 Days to Meet 13 Sweeping Demands by Saudi Arabia." *TheGuardian.com*. The Guardian, 23 June 2017. Web (https://www.theguardian.com/world/2017/jun/23/close-al-jazeera-saudi-arabia-issues-qatar-with-13-demands-to-end-blockade). **Note:** The ultimatum demands are so severe that Qatar's acceptance would force it to align with the Persian Gulf countries militarily, politically, socially, and economically and end its independence in these areas. As of June 2018, the embargo is still in force and the Qatar-Gulf crisis continues.

[11] Keatinge, Tom. "Why Qatar Is the Focus of Terrorism Claims." *BBC.com*. British Broadcasting Corporation, 13 June 2017. Web (http://www.bbc.com/news/world-middle-east-40246734).

or slaughtered peoples, and the expropriated palaces, temples, churches and conquered territory—or, in Muslim parlance, "Islamic expeditions and conquests." Muslims do not want to admit that these actions were mainly intolerant, violent, and cruel, bringing untold misery to millions. (Remember, Islam is "a religion of peace.") They prefer to glorify Islam's past to such a degree that few dare to discuss and divulge its iniquities.

While it is true that Egyptian President Abdel Fattah El-Sisi called for religious reform in 2015 "to confront the misleading ideologies harming Islam and Muslims worldwide,"[12] he has been stymied ever since by Muslim clerics of Al Azhar University (oldest educational institute of the Sunni Muslim world), who "have largely resisted" his appeals for reform.[13] On July 26, 2017, El-Sisi decreed the establishment of the National Council for Combating Terrorism and Extremism (NCCTE). Part of its mission is "to take charge of reforming religious discourse and fighting extremist ideas in a systematic way" and that the war against terrorism "must include an intellectual and cultural dimension to help correct distorted interpretations of Islam."[14] Some political analysts believe his decision to form this new council was motivated by the unwillingness or inability of Al Azhar after two years to take the lead on reforming religious discourse.[15]

President El-Sisi is not alone in facing strong opposition to his efforts to push forward religious reform. In 2015, Islam al-Behairy, an Egyptian Muslim writer and host of *With Islam* on TV satellite news channel Al Kahera wal Nas, called for religious reform on his program and dared to discuss and question some of the ancient Islamic *hadīths*. His program was subsequently suspended by Al Kahera after Al Azhar condemned his action as an insult to Islam. He was then sentenced to five years in

[12] "Egypt's President Calls for 'Religious Revolution' in Islam." *CBSNews.com*. CBS (Columbia Broadcasting System) Corporation, 5 Jan. 2015. Web (https://www.cbsnews.com/news/egypts-president-calls-for-religious-revolution-in-islam/); "Sisi Calls for a Religious Revolution against Texts That Have Been Sanctified for Centuries." *Aljazeera.net*. Al Jazeera Media Network, 2 Jan. 2015. Web (http://preview.tinyurl.com/z882hs6).

[13] "Reforming Islam in Egypt." *Economist.com*. Economist Group, 18 Feb. 2017. Web (https://www.economist.com/news/middle-east-and-africa/21717081-sisi-versus-sheikhs-reforming-islam-egypt).

[14] El-Din, Gamal Essam. "Egypt's New Anti-Terrorism Council to Reform Religious Discourse and Target Political Islam: Sisi." *English.Ahram.org.eg*. Ahram Online (English), 29 July 2017. Web (http://english.ahram.org.eg/NewsContent/1/64/274432/Egypt/Politics-/Egypts-new-antiterrorism-council-to-reform-religio.aspx).

[15] Ibid.

prison, which was later reduced to one year. President El-Sisi pardoned him, along with others, in late 2016.[16]

The powerful clout of Al Azhar and the high rate of illiteracy in Egypt are major factors behind Egypt's delay of any religious reform process, despite support for such a reform by some political leaders, writers, and media journalists. If Egypt, which currently has a more secular but somewhat authoritarian style of republican government, cannot effectively proceed with religious reform, how can Saudi Arabia with its conservative ruling monarchy and the other Muslim countries with their governments and laws dominated by the Islamic religion ever initiate a similar reform process?

Western countries must push Muslim countries to accelerate the process of religious reform. Any delay will only complicate matters. Lessons can be learned and applied from Western theologians who have already established different scientific fields and centers of study to examine, research, and interpret ancient sacred writings, including Christianity's Bible. Universities in Muslim countries should apply new theories and the latest scientific and technological advances in understanding and interpreting religious texts. Muslim researchers and scholars must accept these Islamic writings as human productions and acknowledge that all religious texts, including Islamic, are affected by the circumstances surrounding their creation. We cannot persist in using texts written for tribal peoples of seventh century AD to regulate modern life of twenty-first century AD. If we continue to insist and mandate this unilateral position, that these texts are valid and appropriate for all times and places, we will threaten and perhaps irrevocably destroy the lives and futures of millions of young people.

Al Azhar and the other Saudi universities need to be more transparent and include religious criticism and study in their curriculums in a meaningful, expansive manner, because religious reform cannot be achieved if universities teach only one point of view. Even the study of comparative religions is not objectively or comprehensively taught because such studies always favor and exalt Islam. True reform begins

---

[16] "Egypt Jails Muslim Scholar for Insulting Islam." *Tribune.com.pk*. The Express Tribune, 29 Dec. 2015. Web (https://tribune.com.pk/story/1018296/egypt-jails-muslim-scholar-for-insulting-islam); "Egypt's Sisi Pardons 82 Jailed 'Youths.'" *Al-Monitor.com*. Al-Monitor, 17 Nov. 2016. Web (https://www.al-monitor.com/pulse/afp/2016/11/egypt-sisi-politics-pardon.html).

by encouraging a wide array of ideas and serious scientific research and learning from the experiences of others who preceded us.

Both Muslim and Western countries should monitor sermons and lessons presented in the mosques and urge religious leaders to focus their teachings on the love of life, charity, and all people and strongly curtail the diatribes promoting discrimination and hatred and glorifying the sacrifice of earthly life for life in the hereafter. Imams and clerics must teach people not to die but to live for the cause of Allah.

Media reform

The news media must be responsible, truthful, and accountable. It should not publicize unverified conspiracy theories or unfairly demonize America and the West by manipulating people's emotions rather than presenting facts. Unfortunately, the media in Muslim countries do not abide by the strict professional standards that exist in Western countries or are held accountable for printing misleading—let alone, downright false—news. In general, Muslim governments do not investigate the accuracy of the news or prosecute news organizations for publishing deliberately false or slanderous content (especially if it is anti-West content). In Arab countries particularly, the media most value and prioritize "precedence," or being the first among rivals to break the news, even if the information is not accurate.

Examples of this sloppy or doctored journalism include published statements supposedly given by Hillary Clinton, US President Obama, and other Western leaders without any credible documentation. The media is only concerned that these "statements" can be used as propaganda to condemn America and the West. This is the same media that claims ISIS is a creation of America (without providing any genuine evidence) to use as an instrument to make Muslim countries regress.[17] Even Web sites and TV channels more familiar to Westerners (e.g., Al Jazeera and Al Arabiya) and Western media with Arab or Middle East departments have often become trumpets for Islam because most of these Arabic departments are managed by Muslims, as they are the majority group in these Arabic-speaking communities. Sky News, a 24-hour international multimedia news organization based in the UK, reveals a lack of neutrality on its

[17] "With Evidence America Made ISIS." *Alarabiya.net*. Al Arabiya Network, 2 Aug. 2015. Web (https://preview.tinyurl.com/y7efsx25).

Arabic site, which is supportive of (Sunni) Saudi Arabia's aggressive use of its air force to combat the (Shiite) Houthi insurgency in Yemen.[18] The content on Sky News Arabia is so biased in favor of Saudi Arabia that it looks like a duplication of the Saudi Web site, Al Arabiya.

A related example about biased, shallow, and weak news reporting in the Arab world is Alhurra, a US-based public Arabic language satellite television network. Alhurra ("The Free One") was launched in 2004 with the specific purpose to counter misinformation about America, improve understanding of American culture and democratic values, and raise standards of journalism not generally presented in the Arab media, with its lack of independence from government oversight and emphasis on sensationalism and mediocre coverage. Its inception was planned to be the biggest news media project aimed at the Middle East since the launch of Voice of America in 1942. Yet, in 2006, two years after its launch, Alhurra has received scathing criticism for its utter failure to achieve any of its goals. Among some of the reasons for its inability to fulfill its promises were incompetent Arab employees, cronyism (discriminating "in the hiring of...experienced Arabic radio broadcasters—all US citizens—in favor of inexperienced young workers, many of whom were Lebanese...."), possible infiltration by Arab intelligence services, corruption, mismanagement, and the absence of an American role.[19] Magdi Khalil, a writer and political analyst, summarized the fiasco in a study:[20]

> Alhurra is supposed to "explain" America to the Arabs, and bridge the gap that exists between the two; if it mostly acts like a mirror for the Arab viewer to see the reflection of his own image, then it has lost its purpose. Unfortunately that's what Alhurra has been doing, joining the same league as the Arab news channels.

---

[18] **Note:** The Houthis are members of an Islamic political movement that originated in northern Yemen in the 1990s. This group started a rebellion in 2004 against Yemeni President Ali Abdullah Saleh, condemning his government for corruption and marginalization. Over time, the Houthis have gained control over parts of Yemen. Although the Houthis are considered a terrorist organization by Saudi Arabia, the UAE, and other nations, the Houthis have never been linked to any terrorist movements. On December 4, 2017, Houthis assailed Saleh's house and then later brutally killed him. To date, Yemen, one of the Arab world's poorest countries, is still embroiled in a bitter civil war, which has killed thousands and left 20 million people in dire need of humanitarian assistance.

[19] Khalil, Magdi. "Why Did Alhurra Fail?" *Metransparent.com*. Middle East Transparent, 19 Apr. 2006. Print and Web (https://www.metransparent.com/old/texts/magdi_khalil/magdi_khalil_why_al_hurra_failed_english.htm).

[20] Ibid.

In August 2017, Alberto Fernandez (who follows three predecessors) was installed as the new president of US government-funded Middle East Broadcasting Networks (MBN), which owns and operates Alhurra. The new president claims that he wants the station to be "an oasis for Arab liberals...who are confronted by censorship or drowned by Islamists calling them infidels [on TV screens] in the region."[21]

Even if Alhurra, under new leadership, can improve its operations and journalism, it still faces a bigger and possibly insurmountable problem. According to Claudia Kozman, a visiting assistant professor of multimedia journalism at Beirut's Lebanese American University, the bigger uncertainty than one media outlet's need to achieve success is "finding an [Arab] audience who is sympathetic to US policy."[22] America is "the great Satan" in the eyes of Muslims, especially in the Arab world.

To counter this negative propaganda, misinformation, and demonization of the West disseminated by religious Islamic channels funded by Persian Gulf money over the past decade, the West should help establish and effectively maintain independent, alternate satellite channels that employ critical and scientific thinking and balanced, accurate reporting. At the same time, we must help open-minded young people find alternative platforms and satellite channels to express themselves freely without intimidation.

Decriminalization of *takfir*

The classification of people as infidels must be outlawed and decriminalized, as this classification can lead to their legal killing (*takfir*) in some Muslim countries. Current laws protecting this act to classify others cannot be justified as a right of free expression because it incites hatred and leads, at best, to discrimination and, at worst, to the killing of people given this designation. Religious and other kinds of minorities—e.g., Christians, atheists, homosexuals, secularists, Yazidis, and Druze—in Muslim countries especially require protection because they are routinely classified as infidels and treated with discrimination and often persecution in the Middle East and Africa. This classification,

[21] Karam, Joyce. "Arabic TV Station Al Hurra Should Have Rivalled Al Jazeera, but Has Yet to Find Its Voice." *TheNational.ae*. The National, 5 Aug. 2017. Web (https://www.thenational.ae/world/the-americas/arabic-tv-station-al-hurra-should-have-rivalled-al-jazeera-but-has-yet-to-find-its-voice-1.617037).

[22] Ibid.

discrimination, and persecution even follows people who convert from Islam to another religion. Often, these converts are tried in court, accused of vilifying Islam or apostasy. If convicted, they are sentenced to imprisonment, physical punishment, or death.

The international community must take responsibility and force Muslim countries to protect their minorities. It is unconscionable for any country to classify its citizens for the purpose of diminishing or removing their rights, even permitting their persecution, just because the majority of its citizens are Muslims.

The use of *takfir* is one of Islamic terrorism's most potent tools in subjugating and eliminating its critics and enemies. We must eradicate it with a legal arsenal that protects all citizens, regardless of their religious (or non-religious) persuasion.

Zero tolerance for all terrorists

Muslim countries must stop colluding with, funding, assisting, or turning a blind eye to Islamic terrorists who harm the West more than harming the Muslim countries. For example, Saudi Arabia placed detainees released to it from the Guantánamo Bay detention camp in Cuba into deradicalization programs (where they were eventually pardoned and released after completion) instead of facing any condemnation or imposing any punishment for their terrorist acts. Why were these terrorists, these assassins and criminals, given this special treatment when other Saudi citizens suffer severe punishment just for expressing their (non-lethal) opinions, such as blogger Rā'if Badawī, who is serving ten years in prison plus floggings? Yet the Islamic terrorist, who had adopted and brutally applied the ideology of slaughtering and terrorism, is counseled and then reintegrated into society. This difference in the treatment and sentencing of these Guantánamo detainees indicates that Saudi Arabia does not believe that these men are terrorists or their acts heinous enough to deserve harsher treatment or sentencing.

Saudi Arabia's leniency with the discharged Guantánamo prisoners is neither just, appropriate, or even effective. Many of those who returned and completed the deradicalization program soon returned to terrorism and terrorist organizations and even became leaders, such as Sa'īd al-Shahrī, who became the deputy commander of Al Qaeda in the Arabian

Peninsula.[23] Five years after the introduction of its deradicalization program in 2004, Saudi experts admit that the recidivism rate of this unique program may be ten to twenty percent.[24] The US Defense Department reported in 2009 that at least seventy-four Guantánamo detainees (20%) "returned to terrorist activity after release" and eleven of these men were graduates of the Saudi deradicalization program.[25] Though Saudi authorities stress the "success" of the eighty percent who have completed the program and resumed normal lives, critics note the return to terrorism by at least fifty-nine graduates (as of 2014)[26] and argue that the current recidivism rate is not acceptable, especially when the "most hardened ideologues," the main target group, "do not respond to rehabilitation."[27]

Turkey is another Muslim country that has accommodated terrorist organizations by allowing weapons transfers to Islamic terrorist groups linked to Al Qaeda or Islamic State from its territory, unchecked flight passage of thousands of foreign fighters to Syria from countries around the world, and the establishment of radical Islamic networks within its borders.[28] Turkey eventually changed its position of political "passivity" and participated more directly with its NATO allies in 2015 against Islamic State after one of its suicide bombers killed Turkish citizens, terrorist groups increased their efforts to recruit Turks, and the international community intensified its demands for Turkish cooperation.[29]

---

[23] "Saudi Arabia's Most Wanted Qaeda Man Killed in Yemen: Correspondent." *English.Alarabiya.net.* Al Arabiya News (English), 22 Jan. 2013. Web (https://english.alarabiya.net/en/News/2013/01/22/Saudi-Arabias-most-wanted-Qaeda-man-killed-in-Yemen-Correspondent.html); "Saeed Al-Shihri." *Aljazeera.net.* Al Jazeera Media Network (Al Jazeera Encyclopedia), 2018.Web (http://preview.tinyurl.com/hdof4rj).

[24] Porges, Marisa. "The Saudi Deradicalization Experiment." *CFR.org.* Council on Foreign Relations, 22 Jan. 2010. Web (https://www.cfr.org/expert-brief/saudi-deradicalization-experiment).

[25] Ibid.

[26] al-Shamrani, Saud. "The Return of 59 People to the Deviant Ideas after the Counseling Does Not Indicate the Program's Failure." *Okaz.com.sa.* Okaz, 4 Sept. 2014. Web (http://preview.tinyurl.com/hu9hbel).

[27] Porges, Marisa. "The Saudi Deradicalization Experiment." *CFR.org.* Council on Foreign Relations, 22 Jan. 2010. Web (https://www.cfr.org/expert-brief/saudi-deradicalization-experiment). See al-Balawi, Saud. "Has the Advice Failed?" *Alarabiya.net.* Al Arabiya Network, 13 Feb. 2009. Web (http://preview.tinyurl.com/hpz4xym).

[28] Tol, Gönül. "Turkey's Syria and Iraq Policy Hostage to Islamic State." *MEI.edu.* Middle East Institute, 1 Sept. 2014. Web (http://www.mei.edu/content/at/turkeys-syria-and-iraq-policy-hostage-islamic-state).

[29] Tuysuz, Gul, and Zeynep Bilginsoy. "Ministry: Turkey Joins Coalition against ISIS in Syria." *Edition.CNN.com.* Cable News Network, 29 Aug. 2015. Web (http://edition.cnn.com/2015/08/29/europe/turkey-airstrikes/index.html); Melvin, Don. "U.S. Using Turkish Base—But Why Turkey's Turnabout on ISIS?" *CNN.com.* Cable News Network, 12 Aug. 2015. Web (http://www.cnn.com/2015/08/12/middleeast/turkey-isis-q--a/index.html); 'Abd al-Fattah, Bashir. "Turkish Considerations Regarding the War on ISIS." *Aljazeera.net.* Al Jazeera Media Network, 15 Sept. 2014 (updated). Web (http://preview.tinyurl.com/hj49kxz).

Time and again Muslim countries will ignore or keep silent about any hostilities or violence committed by Islamic terrorists against the "infidel" West, as if they cannot condemn these "brothers" of Islam. In recent history, this policy pattern occurred in Saudi Arabia with Al Qaeda, in Morocco in the 1980s when *mujāhidīn* went to Afghanistan to fight the Soviet Army and the Soviet-backed Afghanistan government, and Sudan with Osama Bin Laden. All these examples illustrate the extent of sympathy for the "sons of the Caliphate" in their enmity against the infidels.

Government positions only change when this Islamic terrorism strikes within a "sympathetic" Muslim country.

Monetary oversight of Islamic associations

One of the most important possible short-term solutions is to monitor the funds of the Persian Gulf states, which are used for the propagation of Islam. Much of this funding, supposedly used for religious purposes or humanitarian aid, is actually supporting terrorism, whether by spreading its ideology, expanding its focus, or directly paying expenses. Mosques in Western countries (which have been primarily financed from abroad, specifically from the oil-rich Persian Gulf countries) have played a major role in instilling and nurturing the establishment of such Islamic doctrines as *takfīr* and *al-walā' wa-l-barā* (loyalty and disavowal). Islamic State itself has also been funded and supported by wealthy sympathizers from the Persian Gulf states.[30]

It is most certain that some of these financial supporters have still managed to escape detection by US intelligence agencies even to this day. It would be even better if scrutiny into these activities and laws prohibiting the funding of terrorism came directly from Muslim countries themselves, but their sympathy toward the *mujāhidīn* weakens their resolve in identifying and prosecuting these financiers. In fact, countries such as Qatar and Saudi Arabia as well as individuals have blatantly provided financial support to various Islamic movements in Syria that are trying to overthrow Syrian President Bashar Assad.

[30] "Kuwait Vows to Fight Terror after US Sanctions over Funding." *TheNational.ae*. The National, 8 Aug. 2014. Web (https://www.thenational.ae/world/kuwait-vows-to-fight-terror-after-us-sanctions-over-funding-1.351836); "US Sanctions on Three Kuwaitis Accused of Helping Militants." *Alhurra.com*. Alhurra, 6 Aug. 2014. Web (https://www.alhurra.com/a/kuwait-usa-sanction-terrorism-/254773.html).

Why doesn't Saudi Arabia invest its money in its own people or use its wealth to help the Syrian refugees, instead of financing Islamic groups, supporting Wahhabism ideology, and establishing Islamic centers throughout the world? Why do Western countries allow clerics from Saudi Arabia to preach in their mosques, knowing that their sermons are full of hatred and *takfir* towards others? Western countries should be wary of oil money that could be used to destroy Western civilization, Islam's enemy.

Informed critique of Islam by the West

Political leaders in Western countries should stop blindly exonerating Islam. By always praising or excusing Islam and appeasing or indulging Muslim political leaders, they do not really help Muslims. Instead, they only reinforce Islam's culture of intolerance toward any criticism and impede or undermine efforts to initiate religious reform. These politicians should direct their pronouncements and policies only toward the terrorist operations and not include disclaimers concerning Islam and terrorism. They may think their public declarations defending Islam will change the Islamic world's view towards them, but in reality the Islamic world will still consider them as enemies of Islam. In addition, their comments interfere with Muslims who are trying to reform the religion by encouraging open objective discussion and debate.

When a terrorist attack or atrocity occurs, Western political leaders should let Islam speak for itself. The citizens of Western countries did not elect their leaders to serve as preachers or as religious reformers; they have elected their representatives to carry out political responsibilities and protect citizens from any danger they might face. Any public political defense of Islam not only does not serve the citizenry—even if some are Muslims—but it also pointedly serves only the Islamic faith. In a democratic society, all religions are to be treated neutrally. Unfortunately, presidents and other political leaders of Western countries act like Muslim clerics, speaking only of the "goodness," "beauty," and "peace" of Islam, rather than focusing on the horrific crimes committed in its name. Whether we like it or not, the Islamic texts are behind this violence.

Smart immigration policies

Western countries should carefully investigate the people who desire to visit or emigrate to their countries before they are allowed entrance.

Governments cannot naïvely permit wholesale emigration, or even visits, to those who hate Europe and America, while simultaneously deny visas to many Christians, atheists, and secularists from the Middle East and North Africa. The files of this latter group are rejected in many Western consulates, even though these people seek to emigrate because of (often legalized) discrimination, persecution, and personal threats in their homeland.

Despite these common-sense suggestions, advocates of hatred, such as Islamic clerics and other extremists, have been granted visas. They enter these Western countries, considered Islam's enemies, and preach sermons in mosques to incite the youth against "infidels" and attack Western values and democratic principles.

It is not racial discrimination to select those who love Europe and America to enter as visitors and perhaps later residents and even citizens of Europe and America. It is utterly not racist or discriminatory to deny a visa to anyone who promotes or supports violence against America and the West. For example, Moroccan sheikh Muḥammad al-Fizāzī was allowed to travel extensively throughout Europe, where he frequently gave sermons at Germany's Hamburg mosque—even though he had been identified since 2001 as a preacher with radical Islamic views. (In fact, Morocco temporarily barred him from preaching in his own country during the 1990s.) In 2005, he was imprisoned again in Morocco for "inspiring deadly bombings in Casablanca" (which killed 45 people).[31] He has subsequently been implicated in the 2004 Madrid train bombings (which killed 191 people) and is linked to the September 9/11 attacks because of his frequent contact and private meetings with the future pilots, including Mohamed Atta, during his stays in Germany.[32]

In 2005 another Moroccan sheikh, Abdallah al-Nhārī, gave a hate-filled speech in his homeland against Jews and the West. During this speech (which was subsequently posted online and thus publicly heard by an even larger audience), he prayed aloud to Allah to "disperse the accursed Zionists [Jews], defeat the tyrannical and oppressive soldiers of America and allies" and "please turn Iraq into a launching pad for the

---

[31] McDermott, Terry. "Moroccan Preacher Said to Have Met with 9/11 Plotters." *Articles.LATimes.com.* Los Angeles Times, 6 July 2005. Web (http://articles.latimes.com/2005/jul/06/world/fg-fizazi6).

[32] Ibid.

revival of awareness in the Islamic nation."[33] In another video clip posted online on June 28, 2012, the sheikh sanctioned the killing of a Moroccan journalist who had publicly supported the right for people to engage in sexual relations before marriage in a televised interview several days earlier. Al-Nhari mocks this position in the video, stating, "Whoever has no zeal—kill him. A *dayouth* [one who is not jealous for his womenfolk] is denied entrance to Paradise."[34] Yet this sheikh, who called for violence against America, Israel, and other Western countries and encouraged the execution of journalists for opinions contrary to his own, was allowed into the United States as an invited guest speaker during Ramadan in July 2012 at the American Muslim Center in Everett, Massachusetts (which is near Boston).[35]

These clerics should be banned from entering any Western country when their purpose is to freely preach hatred and violence toward others. How is permitting them this venue any different than graciously arming an enemy with a rock so he can knock us right in our own home?

Western countries should also scrutinize all applications for political asylum. Even today, there are Islamic clerics who openly profess hatred of the West yet enjoy asylum and state financial aid, such as Sheikh Hānī al-Sībā'ī, an Egyptian who lives in London supporting and defending Islamic terrorists.[36] In fact, a representative of Anṣār al-Sharia (Tunisia), a radical Islamic group, named Hānī al-Sībā'ī as one of five key thinkers

---

[33] "Moroccan Cleric Abdallah Al-Nhari in 2005: May Allah Turn Iraq into a Nail in the Coffin of American Tyranny." *MEMRI.org*. Middle East Media Research Institute (MEMRI), 2 Sept. 2005. Web (https://www.memri.org/tv/moroccan-cleric-abdallah-al-nhari-2005-may-allah-turn-iraq-nail-coffin-american-tyranny/transcript; to view MEMRI video clip of September 2005 Internet post, see URL: http://www.memri.org/legacy/clip/3502).

[34] "Moroccan Cleric and Ramadan Guest Speaker at Massachusetts-Based American Muslim Center, Who Has Attacked US in the Past, Sanctions Killing of Liberal Moroccan Journalist." *MEMRI.org*. Middle East Media Research Institute (MEMRI), 24 July 2012. Web (https://www.memri.org/reports/moroccan-cleric-and-ramadan-guest-speaker-massachusetts-based-american-muslim-center-who-has; to view MEMRI video clip of the TV interview with Laghzioui and al-Nhari's Internet response, see URL: http://www.memri.org/legacy/clip/3503).

[35] In anticipation of Ramadan 2012, Imam Abdellah Marhoum of the American Muslim Center publicizes online the arrival and lecture series of invited AMC guest, Sheikh al-Nhārī. (To view a segment of the first lecture given by Sheikh al-Nhārī at the center, see URL: https://www.youtube.com/watch?v=vZhbuPoDGRU)

[36] Bentley, Paul. "Living Here on £50,000 Benefits, the Hate Preacher Who Inspired Tunisian Beach Killer: Cleric Lives in Five-Bedroom Home with Wife and Five Children after Thwarting Deportation Attempts for 15 Years." *DailyMail.co.uk*. Telegraph Media Group, 5 July 2015. Web (http://www.dailymail.co.uk/news/article-3150348/Living-50-000-benefits-hate-preacher-inspired-beach-killer-Cleric-lives-five-bedroom-home-wife-five-children-thwarting-deportation-attempts-15-years.html). **Note:** The infamous ISIS militant "Jihadi John" who beheaded several captured Westerners, including journalist James Foley, was influenced and impressed by Hānī al-Sībā'ī. (See URL: https://www.theguardian.com/uk-news/2015/mar/02/who-is-mohammed-emwazi-from-lovely-boy-to-islamic-state-executioner)

who most influence Tunisian terrorists.[37] Why then is he still granted residency and asylum in the West? His situation is but one of several that illustrate the critical need to reassess current procedures and adopt and enforce stricter standards for processing asylum applications by Western consulates.

A tremendous flood of refugees, especially from Syria, Iraq, and Afghanistan, applied for asylum in the European Union in 2015. The biggest driver was the conflict in Syria, but ongoing violence and abuses in other countries contributed to the mass exodus of people looking to start new lives in more stable parts of the world. Germany received the highest number—more than 476,000—of new asylum applications that year.[38] However, according to German officials "more than a million refugees had been counted in Germany's 'EASY' [initial registration of asylum candidates] system for counting and distribution people before they make asylum claims."[39]

While it is true that thousands of these refugees were fleeing horrific war zones, brutal terrorism, and other human rights abuses in their homelands, not all of them were peace-minded, terrified refugees. As predicted and later confirmed, some of these "refugees" have turned out to be Islamic terrorists intent to exploit the rather chaotic and loosely regulated situation and illegally entered Western countries undetected to plan and carry out destructive operations.[40] Therefore, Western countries must be vigilant and careful in screening all refugees, even in the face of a dire humanitarian crisis, because terrorist groups will not waste any "open-door" opportunities for their members to infiltrate welcoming countries and form sleeper cells capable of carrying out terrorist acts in the future.

Critics of enhanced and stricter refugee application policies might argue that the number of these undetected terrorists is miniscule compared to the many thousands of refugees seeking new homelands,

---

[37] Gartenstein-Ross, Daveed. *Ansar al-Sharia Tunisia's Long Game:* Dawa, Hisba, *and* Jihad. ICCT Research Paper. International Centre for Counter-Terrorism. Netherlands: The Hague, May 2013. Page 6. (To view or download document, see URL: https://www.icct.nl/download/file/Gartenstein-Ross-Ansar-al-Sharia-Tunisia›s-Long-Game-May-2013.pdf)

[38] "Migrant Crisis: Migration to Europe Explained in Seven Charts." *BBC.com*. British Broadcasting Corporation, 4 Mar. 2016. Web (http://www.bbc.com/news/world-europe-34131911).

[39] Ibid.

[40] Gutteridge, Nick. "Rise of European Jihadis: EU Admits ISIS Is Exploiting Refugee Crisis to Infiltrate Europe." *Express.co.uk*. Daily Express, 6 Apr. 2016. Web (https://www.express.co.uk/news/world/658508/EU-migrant-crisis-Islamic-State-ISIS-refugees-Syria-Greece-Italy-terror-Paris-attacks).

implying that small numbers reduce risk and danger. This argument is weak. Do not forget that the life-altering events of September 11 were carried out by only nineteen terrorists. Only nine Islamic State militants were involved in the November 2015 Paris terrorist attacks, killing 130 people and injuring 413, and subjecting the whole country to a higher level of fear and insecurity.

We cannot allow for the real potentiality of unchecked destruction of an entire country and the terrorism of its citizens by admitting refugees—even for the best of human rights reasons—before a rigorous review of their applications is completed. To be sure, the desire to help relieve the suffering and hardship of others is noble and should be encouraged, but any country that perceives potential danger to its citizens as it commits to accepting refugees owes those citizens a meticulous emigration process to ensure peace and security. Every country must prioritize its citizens' security over altruistic motivations. Since Europe has received the brunt of this migration crisis (and subsequent terrorist attacks), it should strongly protect its security before receiving refugees, especially as some individuals have used forged identification papers—or none at all.

Germany's current system for processing refugees, while magnanimous and compassionate, lacks an orderly, thorough examination of these refugees' applications. People only need to view YouTube videos to learn how to buy passports, receive discounts from smugglers, change data on their papers, and lie to investigators without detection. In its haste to provide help to refugees, Germany's less-than-optimal system makes it easier for applicants to exploit its weaknesses in accurately and completely assessing background history and asylum requests. Consequently, "refugees" with questionable intentions can slip through and not only become a problem for Germany in the future but can also cause problems in neighboring countries.

Advice for Muslim readers

To the Muslim who asks me, "What is the solution? What should I do?" I reply that we become responsible when our ignorance is replaced with enlightenment. However, every Muslim must find his or her own solution. The world is vast with many and diverse views of the universe. Search and examine these alternatives, and do not allow society's restrictions and limitations and the Islamic religion imprison you to just one narrow corner.

For me, the solution was abandoning Islam. I could not remain in it when I realized that it was a religion that stripped me of my humanity: a religion that commanded me to honor a doctrine that sanctifies killing at the expense of human life, a religion that required me to blindly obey its decrees without question, a religion that took away my brain and my heart and replaced them with rote-memorized beliefs and actions propelling me toward killing and destruction.

When I chose to leave Islam, I had to face my father, an imam, and my Muslim community, and I have paid dearly for my decision. As of this moment, I still cannot enter my own native country of Morocco, the birthplace I still love. In fact, I cannot set foot in any Arab country without the risk of imprisonment or possible death—because I dare to speak about "sacred" Islamic matters and dare to say "No!" I eventually decided to become a Christian because I saw in the message of Christ, especially in his famous Sermon on the Mount, a definition of what it means to love others and a template of how to love others unconditionally—even sacrificing one's life to express this unconditional love.

My family reacted in disbelief to my decision to leave Islam and become a Christian. To leave Islam is unthinkable; I would be committing apostasy. How dare I join the "infidels," Islam's enemies! Why would I leave the religion of Islam to embrace the religion of disbelief? For this decision, I was insulted, abused, and vilified. I was labeled a spy and a traitor: a person who had disowned his religion. I was forced out from their homes to live on the streets as a homeless person. After persecution by the Moroccan intelligence forces, I had to leave my country.

Today I live in disguise. I cannot live a normal life like other people. Why? Because I reject Islam and speak publicly against it. Yet I am not the only one who is facing abuse, harassment, and persecution. Thousands of other Muslims in Morocco, Algeria, Tunisia, Egypt, and even in Saudi Arabia, where Muḥammad's tomb and the holiest of the holy symbols of Islam are located, face similar maltreatment for their decision to leave Islam. Some chose Christianity, some atheism, some secularism, and so on. But each one of them is now free because *they* made their own choices. They finally freed themselves from all the soulless religious restrictions and conditions and became the master of their own decisions, choosing what they want out of personal conviction—not out of imitation or coercion.

Final word

I hope that all readers, Muslims and non-Muslims, realize that the real reason for writing this book is my love for my family, my friends, and for all Muslims. I know firsthand that most of them are good people who deserve better than what Islam offers them. It grieves me to see the status and plight of Muslims today. Islam has offered my family and my people only destruction and backwardness.

My family, my friends, and all other good Muslims believe with all their hearts that they are serving Allah and serving a great cause. But in truth, they serve only a rusty culture from 1,400 years ago that will not advance them and will only pull them backward. Instead of peacefully competing with the world's great powers on equal footing in all the scientific and artistic fields, we have become the most prolific "state" for terrorism in all its forms.

The "infidels" pool their ingenuity, resources, and efforts to invent new and better aircraft...and we blow them up! They invent or elevate many forms of transportation to improve travel—cars, ships, helicopters, trains, etc.—and we blow them up! They build skyscrapers and other architectural marvels...and we blow them up. They sent men to the moon while we still dream of meeting the wide-eyed virgins of paradise. They launch robots into space and to distant planets to collect information and discard the myths of the unknown, while we continue to classify people into "infidels" and "believers," limiting their humanity and their potential, and endlessly wander in the unknown.

I fear that Muslims will continue to wander endlessly in the unknown unless they critically look at their religion with an objective and honest eye. This change in view and mind-set requires that they chart a new—and yes, difficult—path, which they must face with responsibility and act with boldness. For there is no doubt that the ideology behind Islamic terrorism is in Islam itself.

Works Cited

In general, all online sources (such as Web sites, periodicals, and newspapers) are cited and listed only in the footnotes; printed sources (such as books) are listed in the Works Cited. Unless otherwise noted, all footnoted online sources were revisited for viability between January through April 2018.

Arabic

al-ʿAdnānī, Abū Muḥammad. *This is the Promise of Allah. Jihadology.net.* Al-Hayat Media Center, 19 June 2014. Audio file. <http://www.dailymotion.com/video/x3u3io>. (To read English transcript of the entire proclamation, see URL: https://scholarship.tricolib.brynmawr.edu/bitstream/handle/10066/14242/ADN20140629.pdf?sequence=1)

al-Albanī, Muhammad Nāṣir al-Dīn. *Ṣaḥīḥ Mawārid al-Ẓamʾān Ila Zawāʾid Ibn Ḥabbān.* 2 vols. Riyadh: Dār al-Ṣumayʿī, 2002. Print.

---. *Silsilat al-Aḥādīth al-Ṣaḥīḥa: Wa Shaīʾ min Fiqhahā wa Fawʾidihā.* 7 vols. Riyadh: al-Maʿārīf, 1995-2002. Print.

ʿAlī, Jawād. *Al-Mufaṣṣal fī Tārīkh al-ʿArab Qabl al-Islām.* 10 vols. Riyadh: Jarīr, 2006. Print.

al-ʿAsqalānī, Ibn Ḥajar. *Fatḥ al-Bārī fī Sharḥ Ṣaḥīḥ Bukhārī.* Eds. ʿAbd al-ʿAzīz Ibn ʿAbd Allah Ibn Bāz and Muḥib al-Khaṭīb. 15 vols. Beirut: Dār al-Fikr, 1993. Print.

al-Balādhurī, Aḥmad Ibn Yaḥya Ibn Gabir Ibn Dawūd. *Kitāb Futūḥ al-Buldān*. Ed. 'Abd al-Qādir Muhammad 'Alī. 2 vols. Beirut: Dār Kutub al-'Ilmīya, 2000. Print.

al-Bayhaqī, Aḥmad Ibn al-Husaīyn Ibn 'Alī. *Al-Sunan al-Kubra*.17 vols. Beirut: Dār al-Fikr, 1996. Print.

Daniel, Robin. *Al-Turāth al-Masīhī fi Shamāl Ifrīqīyā: Dirāsa Tārīkhīya min al-Qarn al-'Awal ila al-Qurūn al-Wusta* [*The Christian Heritage of North Africa: A Historical Study from the First Century to the Middle Ages*]. Trans. Samīr Mālik. Beirut: Dār Manhal al-Ḥayāt, 1999. Print.

al-Dhahabī, Muḥammad Ibn Aḥmad Ibn 'Uthmān. *Sīyar A'lām al-Nubalā'*. Ed. 'Umar Ibn Ghulāma al-'Amrawī. 18 vols. Beirut: Dār al-Fikr, 1997. Print.

al-Ḥalabī, 'Alī Ibn Burhān al-Dīn. *Al-Sīra al-Halabīya fi Sīrat al-'Amīn al-Ma'mūn*. 3 vols. Beirut: Dār al-Ma'rifa, 1980. Print.

al-Hamawī, Yaqūt. *Mu'jam al-Buldān*. 5 vols. Beirut: Dār Ṣādir, 1977. Print.

Ibn 'Abd al-Bar, Yūsuf. *Al-Istidhkār*. Ed. Sālim 'Aṭa and Muḥammad Mu'awaḍ. 9 vols. Beirut: Dār al-Kutub al-'Ilmīya, 2000. Print.

Ibn Abū Shayba, 'Abd Allah Ibn Muḥammad. *Al-Musannaf fi al-Aḥādīth wa al-Athar*. 9 vols. Beirut: Dār Al-Fikr, 1994. Print.

Ibn 'Asākir, *Tārīkh Dimashq* [*History of Damascus*]. Ed. 'Alī Ibn al-Ḥasan Ibn Hibat-Allah. 70 vols. Beirut: Dār Iḥyā' al-Turāth al-'Arabī, 2003. Print.

Ibn 'Āshūr, Muḥammad al-Ṭāhir. *Tafsīr al-Taḥrīr wa al-Tanwīr*. 30 vols. Tunis: Al-Dār al-Tunisīya, 1984. Print.

Ibn Baz, 'Abd al-'Azīz. *Subbul al-Salām: Sharḥ Nawāqiḍ al-Islām*. Ed. Abū 'Abd Allah Muḥammad Ibn Nāṣīr al-Fahrī. N.p.: N.p., 2011. Print.

Ibn Duwaiyan, Ibrahim Ibn Muḥammad Ibn Salim. *Manār al-Sabīl fi Sharḥ al-Dalil*. Ed. Zuhayr al-Shawish. 2 vols. Beirut: al-Maktab al-Islami, 1989. Print.

Ibn Ḥabbān, Muḥammad Ibn Ahmad. *Al-'Iḥsān bi-Tartīb Ṣaḥīḥ Ibn Ḥabbān* [a.k.a. *Ṣaḥīḥ Ibn Ḥabbān*]. Ed. Kamal Yūsuf al-Hūt. 6 vols. Beirut: Dār al-Fikr, 1996. Print.

Ibn Hishām, Abd al-Malik al-Ma'āfrī. *Al-Sira al-Nabawīya*. Ed. Taha 'Abd al-Ra'ūf Sa'd. 4 vols. Beirut: Dār al-Jil, 1990. Print.

Ibn al-Jawzī, Abū al-Faraj 'Abd al-Raḥman. *Nawāsikh al-Qur'ān*. Ed. Muḥammad Ashraf 'Alī al-Milbārī. Medina: al-Majlis al-'Ilmī, 1984. Print.

Ibn Kathīr, Ismail. *Al-Bidāya wa al-Nihāya*. Ed. 'Abd Allah al-Turkī. 21 vols. Cairo: Hajr, 1997-1999. Print.

---. *Tafsīr al-Qur'ān al-'Aẓīm* [a.k.a. *Tafsīr Ibn Kathīr*]. Ed. Muṣṭafā al-Sayīd Muḥammad, et al. 14 vols. plus index. Giza: Qurṭuba Est., 2000. Print.

Ibn Khaldūn, 'Abd al-Raḥman Ibn Muḥammad Ibn Muḥammad. *Tarīkh Ibn Khaldūn*. 8 vols. Beirut: Dār Kutub al-'Ilmīya, 2002. Print.

Ibn Khalkān, Ahmad Ibn Muḥammad Ibn Abī Bakr. *Wafiyāt al-A'yān wa 'Anbā' 'Abnā' al-Zamān*. Ed. Muḥammad 'Abd al-Rahmān al-Mar'ashlī. 3 vols. Beirut: Dār Ihiya' al-Turath al-'Arabī, 1997. Print.

Ibn Māja, Muḥammad Ibn Yazīd al-Rāb'ī. *Sunan Ibn Māja*. Ed. Muḥammad Fou'ād 'Abd al-Bāqī. 2 vols. Beirut: Dār Ihiā' al-Turāth al-'Arabī, 1975. Print.

Ibn Manẓūr. *Lisān al-'Arab*. Ed. Dār al-Ma'ārif. Cairo: Dār al-Ma'ārif, n.d. Print.

Ibn Mufliḥ, Shams al-Din Muḥammad. *Kitāb al-Furū'*. Ed. 'Abd al-Sattar Ahmad Farrag. 4th ed. 6 vols. Beirut: 'Alam al-Kutub, 1985.

Ibn Qayyīm al-Jawzīya, Muḥammad Ibn Abū Bakr. *Aḥkām Ahl al-Dhimma* [*The Rules Governing Dhimmi*]. Eds. Yūsuf Aḥmad al-Bakrī and Shākir Tawfīq al-'Ārūrī. 3 vols. Beirut: Dār Ibn Ḥazm, 1997. Print.

---. *Al-Qaṣida al-Nūniya*. [a.k.a. *Al-Kafia al-Shafia fi al-Intisar lil-al-Firqa al-Najia*]. Cairo: Al-Taddum al-'Ilmīya, 1926. Print.

---. *Zādu al-Ma'ād fi Hadī Khayr al-'Ibād*. Eds. Shu'ayb al-'Arnā'ūt and 'Abd al-Qādir al-'Arna'uṭ. 6 vols. Beirut: al-Risāla, 1996. Print.

Ibn Qudāma, 'Abd Allāh Ibn Aḥmad al-Maqdisī. *Al-Kāfi fi Fiqhi Aḥmad Ibn Ḥambal*. Eds. Muḥammad Fāris and Mus'ad 'Abd al-Ḥamīd al-Sa'danī. 4 vols. Beirut: Dār al-Kutub al-'Ilmiya, 1994. Print.

---. *Al-Mughnī 'Ala Mukhtaṣar al-Kharaqī*. Eds. 'Abd Allāh Ibn 'Abd al-Muḥsin al-Turkī and 'Abd al-Fattāḥ Muḥammad al-Ḥilū. 3rd ed. 15 vols. Riyadh: Dār 'Ālam al-Kutub, 1997. Print.

---. *Al-Sharḥ al-Kabīr*. 6 vols. Beirut: Dār al-Fikr, 1993. Print.

Ibn Sa'd, Muḥammad Ibn Sa'd Ibn Manī'. *Al-Ṭabaqāt al-Kubra*. Ed. Iḥsān 'Abbās. 8 vols. Beirut: Dār Ṣādir, 1968. Print.

Ibn Taymīya, Aḥmad Ibn 'Abd al-Ḥalīm Ibn 'Abd al-Salām. *Iqtiḍā' al-Ṣirāt al-Mustaqīm li-Mukhālafat Asḥāb al-Jaḥīm*. Ed. Naṣir Ibn 'Abd al-Karīm al-'Aql. 2 vols. Riyadh: Dār Ashbilīa, 1998. Print.

---. *Majmū' Fatāwā Sheik al-Islām Aḥmad Ibn Taymīya*. Ed. 'Abd al-Raḥmān Muḥammad Ibn Qāsim. 37 vols. Medina: King Fahd Printing Complex, 2003-2004. Print.

---. *Minhāj al-Sunnati al-Nabawīya fi Naqḍ Kalām al-Shī'a al-Qadarīya*. Ed. Muḥammad Rashād Sālim. 9 vols. Riyadh: Al-Imam Muḥammad Ibn Saud Islamic U, 1986. Print.

---. *Qā'idat al-Inghimās fi al-'Adūw wa-hal Yubāḥ*. Ed. Ashraf Ibn 'Abdel-Maqṣūd. Riyadh: Aḍwā' al-Salaf, 2002. Print.

---. *Al-Sārim al-Maslūl ala-Shātim al-Rasūl*. Eds. Muḥammad al-Halawani, Muḥammad Shudari. 3 vols. Dammam: Ramadi, 1997. Print.

'Imāra, Muḥammad. *Izālat al-Shubuhāt 'an Ma'ānī al-Muṣṭalaḥāt*. Cairo: Dār al-Salām, 2010. Print.

al-Jazīrī, 'Abd al-Raḥmān. *Kitāb al-Fiqh 'ala al-Madhāhib al-Arba'a* [*Jurisprudence According to the Four Schools*]. 5 vols. Beirut: Dār al-Kutub al-'Ilmīya, 2002. Print.

al-Kashmīrī, Muḥammad Anwar. *Fayḍ al-Bārī 'ala Ṣaḥīḥ al-Bukhārī*. Ed. Muḥammad Badr 'Ālim al-Mirtahī. 6 vols. Beirut: Dār al-Kutub al-'Ālamīya, 2005. Print.

Mālik Ibn Anas. *Muwatta' al-Imām Mālik*. 4 vols. Beirut: Dār al-Kitāb al-'Arabī, 1988. Print.

al-Mālikī, Abū Bakr 'Abd Allah Muḥammad. *Kitāb Riyāḍ al-Nufūs*. Ed. Bashīr al-Bakkūsh. 2nd ed. 2 vols. Beirut: Dār al-Gharb al-Islamī, 1994. Print.

al-Manāwī, Muḥammad 'Abd al-Ra'ūf. *Fayḍ al-Qadīr: Sharḥ al-Jāmi' al-Saghīr*. Ed. Ahmad 'Abd al-Salām. 6 vols. Beirut: Dār al-Kutub al-'Ilmīya, 1994. Print.

al-Maqrīzī, Aḥmad Ibn 'Alī Ibn 'Abd al-Qadīr. *Al-Mawā'iẓ wa al-'I'tibār*. Ed. Khalil Mansūr. 4 vols. Beirut: Dār al-Kutub al-'Ilmīya, 1998. Print.

al-Mubarakfurī, Muḥammad 'Abd al-Raḥman. *Tuḥfat al-Aḥwadhī fī Sharḥ Sunan al-Tirmidhī*. Ed. Sidqī al-'Aṭṭār. 11 vols. Beirut: Dār al-Fikr, 1995. Print.

al-Mubarakpūrī, Ṣafiyy al-Raḥmān. *Al-Raḥīq al-Makhtūm: Baḥth fī al-Sīra al-Nabawīya 'Ala Ṣāḥibihā Afḍal al-Ṣalāt wa-al-Salām*. 19th ed. Beirut: Dār al-Wafā', 2007. Print.

Al-Mufīd fī al-Tarbīya al-Islāmīya [*The Beneficial in Islamic Education*]. Casablanca: Dār al-Thaqāfa, 2014. Print.

Musnad al-Dārmī [a.k.a *Sunan al-Dārmī*]. Comp. 'Abd Allah Ibn 'Abd al-Raḥman al-Dārmī. Ed. Husayn Salīm al-Dārnī. 4 vols. Riyadh: Al-Mughnī, 2000. Print.

Musnad al-Imām Aḥmad [a.k.a. *Musnad Aḥmad*]. Comp. Aḥmad Ibn Muḥammad Ibn Hanbal. 7 vols. Beirut: Dār Ihīyā' al-Turāth al-'Arabī, 1993. Print.

Nājī, Abū Bakr. *Idārat al-Tawaḥḥush: Akhṭar Marḥala sa-Tamur bi-ha al-Umma*. 2004. Web. <https://archive.org/details/edatalt>.

al-Nawawī, Yeḥīa Ibn Sharaf. *Sharḥ al-Nawawī 'ala Ṣaḥīḥ Muslim*. 18 vols. Cairo: Al-Tawfiqīya, 1995. Print.

al-Nīsābūrī, Muḥammad Ibn 'Abd Allah al-Ḥākim. *Al-Mustadrak 'alā al-Ṣaḥīḥayn*. Ed. Musṭafa 'Abd al-Qādir 'Aṭā. 5 vols. Beirut: Dār al-Kutub al-'Ilmīya, 2002. Print.

al-Nisā'ī, Aḥmad Ibn Alī. *Sunan al-Nisā'ī al-Ṣughra wa Ḥāshīyat al-Sanadī*. Ed. Jalal al-Din al-Suyutī. 8 vols. Beirut: Dār al-Ma'rifa, 1994. Print.

al-Quranī, 'Ā'id. *'Ālam al-Siḥr* [*World of Sorcery*]. Riyadh: al-'Ubaykan, 2008. Print.

al-Qurṭubī, Muḥammad Ibn Aḥmad. *Al-Jāmi' li-Aḥkām al-Qur'ān: wa al-Mubayin li-mā Taḍammanahu min al-Sunna wa Āay al-Furqān* [a.k.a. *Tafsīr al-Qurṭubī*]. 20 vols. Beirut: Dār Ihīyā' al-Turāth al-'Arabī, 1985. Print.

al-Rājhī, 'Abdul Azīz. *Tabṣīr al-'Anām Bisharḥ Nawāqiḍ al-Islām*. Cairo: Dār al-Athariya, 2010. Print.

Ṣaḥīḥ al-Bukhārī. Comp. Abū 'Abd Allah Muḥammad Ibn Ismā'īl al-Bukhārī. Ed. Mustafa Dīb al-Bughā. 6 vols. plus index. Damascus and Beirut: Dār Ibn Kathīr, 1993. Print.

Ṣaḥīḥ Muslim. Comp. Muslim Ibn al-Hajjāj al-Naysaburī. Ed. Abū Qutayba Naẓar Muḥammad al-Fārīābī. 2 vols. Riyadh: Dār Ṭība, 2006. Print.

al-Shāfi'ī, Muḥammad Ibn Idrīs. *Kītāb al-Umm*. 9 vols. Beirut: Dār al-Kutub al-'Ilmiyya, 2002. Print.

Sharḥ Diwan Abū Tammām. Ed. Rāgī al-Asmar. 2nd ed. 2 vols. Beirut: Dār al-Kitāb al-'Arabī, 1994. Print.

al-Subki, Taqīy al-Dīn 'Alī Ibn 'Abd al-Kāfī. *Al-Sayf al-Maslūl 'ala man Sabb al-Rasūl*. Ed. Iyad Ahmad al-Ghuj. Amman: Dār al-Fath, 2000. Print.

Sunan Abū Dawūd. Comp. Abū Dawūd. Ed. Hāfiz Abū Tāhir Zubair 'Alī Za'ī. Trans. Yaser Qadhi and Nasiruddin al-Khattab. 5 vols. Riyadh: Darussalam, 2008. Print.

Sunan al-Nisā'ī al-Kubra. Eds. Abdul Ghaffār Sulaymān al-Bindārī and Sayid Kasrawī Ḥassan. 6 vols. Beirut: Dār al-Kutub al-'Ilmiyya, 1991. Print.

Sunan al-Tirmidhī. Comp. Muḥammad Ibn 'Issa Ibn Sawra al-Tirmidhī. Ed. Ahmad Shakīr and 'Abd al-Baqī Fū'ād. 10 vols. Beirut: Dār al-Fikr. 1994. Print.

al-Suyūtī, Jalāl al-Dīn 'Abd al-Raḥman. *Asbāb al-Nuzūl* [a.k.a. *Lubāb al-Nuqūl fī Asbāb al-Nuzūl*]. Beirut: Al-Kutub al-Thaqāfiya, 2002. Print.

al-Ṭabarī, Abū Ja'far Muḥammad Ibn Jarīr. *Jāmi' al-Bayān 'an Tā'wīl Āay al-Qur'ān* [a.k.a. *Tafsīr al-Ṭabarī*]. Ed. 'Abd Allah Ibn 'Abd al-Muḥsin al-Turkī. 30 vols. Beirut: Dār al-Ma'rifa, 1992. Print.

al-Ṭarīfī, 'Abd al-Azīz Ibn Marzouk. *Al-I'lām: Bitawdih Nawāqid al-Islām li-Sheikh al-Islām Muḥammad Ibn 'Abd al-Wahhāb*. Riyadh: Al-Rushd, 2004. Print.

al-Waḥidī, Abū al-Hassan 'Alī Ibn Ahmad. *Asbāb Nuzūl al-Qur'ān*. Ed. Kamāl Basyūnī Zaghlūl. Beirut: Dār al-Kutub al-'Ilmīya, 1991. Print.

al-Wāqidī, Muḥammad Ibn Umar. *Kitāb al-Maghāzī*. Ed. Marsden Jones. 3rd ed. London: Oxford UP, 1966. Print.

---. *Kitāb al-Ridda ma' Nabdha min Fotūḥ al-'Iraq wa Dhikr al-Muthanna Ibn Haritha al-Shaybanī*. Ed. Yehiya al-Jabburi. Beirut: Dār al-Gharb al-Islami, 1990. Print.

English

al-ʿAdnānī, Abū Muḥammad. *This is the Promise of Allah* [English translation]. *Jihadology.net*. Al-Hayat Media Center, 19 June 2014. Print and Web. <https://scholarship.tricolib.brynmawr.edu/bitstream/handle/10066/14242/ADN20140629.pdf?sequence=1>.

Akram, Agha Ibrahim. *The Sword of Allah: Khalid bin al-Waleed—His Life and Campaigns*. Oxford: Oxford UP, 2004. Print.

Arberry, Arthur J., trans. *The Koran Interpreted.* New York: MacMillan, 1955. Print.

Note: This translation does not assign a verse number to the opening line (*Alim. Lam. Mim.*) of each sura, or chapter, unlike most other English translations. For ease of comparison, the verse number(s) for any translated verse(s) attributed to Arberry in this book will reflect the more customary verse numbering system used in other notable English translations of the Qur'ān.

Berg, Herbert. *The Development of Exegesis in Early Islam: The Authenticity of Muslim Literature from the Formative Period.* New York: Routledge, 2000. Print. Routledge Studies in the Qur'an.

Bewley, Aisha, trans. *Tafsir al-Qurtubi: Classical Commentary of the Holy Qur'an*. Ed. Abdalhaqq Bewley. Vol. 1. London: Dar Al Taqwa, 2003. Print.

Crawford, Peter. *The War of the Three Gods: Romans, Persians, and the Rise of Islam*. New York: Skyhorse, 2013. Print.

Daniel, Robin. *This Holy Seed.* 2nd ed. Chester: Tamarisk, 2010. Print.

Goldziher, Ignaz. *Muslim Studies*. Trans. C. R. Barber and S. M. Stern. Ed. S. M. Stern. Vol 2. Albany: State U of New York P, 1966. Print.

al-Hilâlî, Muḥammad Taqî-ud-Dîn and Muḥammad Muḥsin Khân, trans. *The Noble Qur'ān*. 4th ed. Riyadh: Dar-us-Salam, 1993. Print.

The History of al-Tabarī: An Annotated Translation. Gen. ed. Ehsan Yar-Shater. Trans. Franz Rosenthal et al. 39 vols. plus index. Albany: State UNY Press, 1989. Print. SUNY Series in Near Eastern Studies.

Ibn Hishām, ʿAbd al-Malik. *The Life of Muhammad: A Translation* [from Ibn Hishām's adaptation] *of* [Ibn] *Isḥāq's* Sīrat Rasūl Allāh. Trans. Alfred Guillaume. 1955. London: Oxford UP. Print.

Ismail, Raihan. *Saudi Clerics and Shīʿa Islam*. New York: Oxford UP, 2016. Print.

Khalifa, Rashid, trans. *Quran: The Final Testament, Authorized English Version with Arabic Text*. Rev. 4th ed. Capistrano Beach: Islamic Productions, 2005. Print.

Mandaville, Peter. "Sufis and Salafis: The Political Discourse of Transnational Islam." *Remaking Muslim Politics: Pluralism, Contestation, Democratization*. Ed. Robert W. Hefner. Princeton: Princeton UP, 2005. Print. Princeton Studies in Muslim Politics.

al-Maqqari, [Ahmad Muhammad]. "Al Maggari's 'Breath of Perfumes.'" *The Sacred Books and Early Literature of the East.* Ed. Charles F. Horne. Vol. 6. New York: Parke, 1917. 241-242. Print. See "Tarik's Address to His Soldiers."

Meselmani, Malek. *The Sword Verse: Qur'ānic Weapon Against Peace?* Seattle: Waterlife Publishing, 2015. Print.

Miller, Judith. *God Has Ninety-Nine Names: Reporting from a Militant Middle East.* New York: Touchstone, 1996. Print.

al-Mubarakpuri, Safiur-Rahman. *The Sealed Nectar: Biography of the Noble Prophet.* Ed. Abdul Malik Mujahid. Rev. ed. Riyadh: Darussalam, 2015. Print.

Naji, Abu Bakr. *The Management of Savagery: The Most Critical State Through Which the Umma Will Pass.* Trans. William McCants. John M. Olin Institute for Strategic Studies at Harvard University. 23 May 2006. Print and Web. <https://archive.org/stream/TheManagementOfBarbarismAbuBakrNaji/The%20Management%20of%20Barbarism%20-%20Abu%20Bakr%20Naji#page/n1/mode/2up>.

The NIV Study Bible: New International Version. Eds. Kenneth Barker, et al. Grand Rapids: Zondervan, 1985. Print.

Nöldeke, Theodor, et al. *The History of the Qur'ān.* Ed. and trans. Wolfgang H. Behn. Leiden: Brill, 2013. Print. Texts and Studies on the Qur'ān Vol. 8.

Organisation of the Islamic Conference (OIC)/Statistical Economic and Social Research and Training Centre for Islamic Countries (SESRIC). "Education and Scientific Development in OIC Member Countries." Ankara: SESRIC, 2010. Print and Web. <http://www.sesric.org/files/article/416.pdf>.

Palmer, E[dward] H[enry], trans. "The Qur'an." *Sacred Books of the East.* Ed. F. Max Müller. Vol. 6. Oxford: Clarendon, 1880. *Internet Archive.* Web. <http://www.archive.org/details/qurn00palmgoog>.

Pickthall, Marmaduke William, trans. *The Meaning of the Glorious Quran: Text and Explanatory Translation.* Beirut: Dār al-Kitāb al-Lubnani, 1971. Print.

The Qur'an: An Encyclopedia. Ed. Oliver Leaman. London: Routledge, 2006. Print.

Roberts, J. M., and Odd Arne Westad. *The History of the World.* 6th ed. Oxford: University P, 2013. Print.

Rodwell, J[ohn] M[edows], trans. *The Koran.* London: J. M. Dent, 1909. Web (Internet Archive). <https://archive.org/stream/TheKoranTranslatedByRodwell/Quran-Rodwell#page/n63/mode/2up>.

Sageman, Marc. *Understanding Terror Networks.* Philadelphia: U Pennsylvania P, 2004. Print.

Sahih Bukhari. Trans. M. Muhsin Khan. Ed. Mika'il al-Amany. 1st ed. 9 vols. 2 Oct. 2009. *IslamHouse.com.* N.p. Web. <http://www.islamhouse.com/en/books/70510>.

Sahih Muslim. Trans. 'Abd al-Hamid Siddiqui. Ed. Mika'il al-Almany. 1st ed. 2 Oct. 2009. *IslamHouse.com.* N.p. Web. <http://www.islamhouse.com/en/books/70896>.

Sale, George, trans. *The Koran: Commonly Called the Alcoran of Mohammed.* 5th ed. Philadelphia: J. W. Moore, 1856. *Google Books.* Web. <https://preview.tinyurl.com/y943kbnt>.

Scott, John. "Rational Choice Theory." *Understanding Contemporary Society: Theories of the Present.* Eds. Gary Browning, Abigail Halcli, and Frank Webster. London: SAGE, 2000. 126-139. Print.

Shahîd, Irfan. *Byzantium and the Arabs in the Sixth Century.* 2 vols. Cambridge: Harvard UP, 2010. Print.

Shakir, M. H. trans. *The Qur'an.* Elmhurst: Tahrike Tarsile Qur'an, 1985. Print.

Sher 'Alī, Maulawī, trans. *The Holy Qur'ān: Arabic Text and English Translation.* Tilford: Islam International, 2004. Print.

Sunan Abū Dawūd. Comp. Abū Dawūd. Ed. Hāfiz Abū Tāhir Zubair 'Alī Za'ī. Trans. Yaser Qadhi and Nasiruddin al-Khattab. 5 vols. Riyadh: Darussalam, 2008. Print.

Tafsir Ibn Kathir (Abridged). Comm. Ibn Kathīr. Supervisor Safiur-Rahman al-Mubarakpuri. 2nd. ed. 10 vols. Riyadh: Darussalem, 2003. Print.

Tertullian of Carthage. *The Apology of Tertullian* [*Apologeticus*]. Trans. S. Thelwall. Philadelphia: Dalcassian, 2017. Print.

Watt, W. Montgomery. *Muhammad at Mecca.* Oxford: Clarendon P, 1952. Print.

---. *Muhammad at Medina.* Oxford: Clarendon P, 1956. Print.

Wherry, E[lwood] M[orris]. *A Comprehensive Commentary of The Qur'an: Comprising Sale's Translation and Preliminary Discourse with Additional Notes and Emendation.* 4 vols. London: Paul, Trench, Trübner, 1898. Print.

Zarra-Nezhad, Mansour. "A Brief History of Money in Islam and Estimating the Value of Dirham and Dīnār." *Review of Islamic Economics* 8.2 (Jan. 2004): 51-65. Print and Web. <https://www.researchgate.net/publication/235761489_A_Brief_History_of_Money _in_Islam_and_Estimating_the_Value_of_Dirham_and_Dinar>.

Name Index

Abaaoud, Abdelhamid 499, 500
al-'Abādī, Ḥaydar (former Prime Minister of Iraq) 217
al-'Abbas Ibn 'Abd al-Muṭṭalib 44, 89, 239, 254, 352
'Abd Allāh Ibn 'Abd al-'Azīz al-Sa'ud (former King of Saudi Arabia) 77
'Abd Allah Ibn Bishr 464
'Abd Allāh Ibn Jahsh 240, 242, 243, 247
'Abd Allāh Ibn Mas'ūd 260, 384, 386, 473
'Abd Allah Ibn Ubayy 433
'Abd Allāh Ibn al-Zubayr 366, 371, 408, 417
'Abd Allah Ubayy Ibn Salūl 281, 433
'Abd al-Ḥayy Yūsuf 146
'Abd al-Malik Ibn Marwān 366, 367
'Abd al-Raḥmān Ibn Maljam 352
Abdel-Raḥmān, 'Umar 158
Abdeslam, Brahmin 499
Abdeslam, Salah 499-501

'Abdrabu, Muḥammad Abū El'Ela 159

'Abdul 'Azīz—SEE **Ibn Saud**

Abdul Nasir, Gamal (former President of Egypt) 376

'Abdul Raḥmān 43

'Abdul Raḥmān Ibn Auf 205

'Abdullah II (King of Jordan) 374

Abdulmuṭṭalib, Umar Farouk 502

Abraham 173, 177, 280, 384, 385, 405

Abū al-'Abbās 352, 353

"Abū 'Ā'isha al-Gharīb" 383

Abu Azrael—SEE **al-Rabaie, Ayyub**

Abū Bakr (first Rashidun caliph) 43, 151-153, 204, 212, 246, 251, 255, 283, 318-319, 324, 339, 347-350, 354, 361, 364-368, 370-371, 373, 389, 394, 405, 407-408, 416-417, 420-421

caliphate 151-153, 319, 324, 339, 347-349, 354, 361, 364, 365, 366, 367-368, 370-371, 373, 389, 394, 405, 407-408, 416-417, 420-421

Muḥammad's Companion 43, 204, 212, 251, 255, 283, 318-319, 364

Abū Baṣīr 266-268

Abū Dharr al-Ghifārī 264-265

Abū al-Fadl 'Ayyāḍ 146

Abū al-Ḥakam—SEE **'Amr Ibn Hishām**

Abū Harīth Ibn 'Alqamā 113

Abū al-Hayyāj al-Asadī 170

Abū Ḥudhayfa 253-254

Abū Hurayra 15, 54, 61, 64, 78, 166, 206, 307, 315, 320

Abū Jahl—SEE **'Amr Ibn Hishām**

Abu Khattala, Ahmad 33

Abū Labāba 290

Abū Mūsa 190

Abū Muṣ'ab al-Hilālī 444

Abū Sa'īd al-Khudrī 86

Abū Sufyān (a.k.a. Sakhr Ibn Harb) 243-245, 286, 287, 308, 311

Abū Tammām 317

Abū 'Ubayda 43, 255

al-'Adnānī, Abū Muḥammad 222, 223, 357-364, 366, 480, 481

Ahmad Ibn Hanbal (Imām Aḥmad) 366, 444

'Ā'isha ('Ā'isha Bint Abī Bakr) 54, 55, 66, 175, 189, 190, 318, 351, 354, 370, 371, 388, 390, 394, 446, 495

al-'Alāwī, Muḥammad Ibn Bakr Ibn Ṣāliḥ 187

al-Albānī, Muhammad Nāṣir al-Dīn 54, 488, 489

Alfonso VI 503

'Alī Ibn Abī Ṭālib (fourth Rashidun caliph) 44, 156-157, 170, 173, 204, 212, 240, 249, 254, 255, 283, 290, 347-348, 349-352, 354, 357, 365, 366, 370-373, 380, 401, 408, 415-417, 420, 440, 467

- caliphate 156-157, 170, 350-351, 352, 354, 357, 365, 370-372, 401, 408, 416-417
- Muḥammad's Companion 44, 173, 204, 212, 240, 249, 254, 255, 283, 290, 347-348, 350, 372, 380, 415, 420, 440, 467

'Alī, Jawād 264, 274

'Alī Maḥmūd Ṭāha 471

Allah *See also* **God** 15-17, 19, 21-24, 26, 29-31, 39-47, 51-52, 54, 56-59, 64-65, 67, 71, 72, 77-80, 85, 88-89, 99, 105-107, 111, 114-115, 121, 123, 139-141, 144, 147-149, 150, 151-153, 155, 156, 160-162, 164-165, 168-169, 173, 175-178, 180, 182-184, 186, 189, 190, 194-197, 200, 204, 207, 208, 210-214, 220, 223, 232, 233, 242-246, 249, 251, 255-257, 259, 260, 262, 263, 265, 273-275, 282-285, 290-291, 294, 297, 300, 303, 304, 306, 308, 314, 318-324, 326, 328-338, 340, 342, 344, 348, 350-351, 357-358, 362, 363, 364, 366, 371-372, 383-385, 388, 390, 391, 398, 400, 401, 403, 406-408, 415, 418, 422, 432, 435, 438, 439-440, 444, 450, 459, 461, 466-470, 472, 488-493, 495-498, 500, 505, 508, 512, 521, 533

- characteristics of 15, 22, 23, 30, 88, 107, 147, 152, 156, 165, 168, 173, 178, 246, 350-351, 415, 418
- commands 39-40, 140, 144-145, 161-162, 211, 326, 383
- cursing of infidels, misbelievers 16, 26, 41-42, 52, 57-58, 138-139
- enemies of 40, 140, 263, 490, 491-492, 493, 498
- law of 85, 107, 161, 178, 182, 208, 223, 210, 297, 304, 358, 364, 371, 388, 435, 500

Alwardi, 'Alī 49

'Amr Ibn al-'Āṣ 120, 121, 126

'Amr Ibn al-Ḥaḍramī 240-241, 245, 247, 254

'Amr Ibn Hishām 239, 260, 384, 386, 473

al-Ānsī, Nāṣir Ibn 'Alī 439

Anti-Christ 61, 445, 456, 457
al-ʻArifī, Muḥammad 356
al-ʻAsqalānī, Ibn Ḥajar 141, 142, 416-418, 433
al-Assad, Bashar (President of Syria) 227, 356
ʻAṣṣīd, Aḥmad 449-452
ʻAtaba 44
al-ʻAwā, Muḥammad Salīm 131
al-ʻAwaḍī, Nabīl 382
al-Awlaki, Anwar 431, 438
ʻAzīz, ʻAbdul Ghaffār 159
ʻAzzām, ʻAbd Allāh 222
Badawī, Rā'if 179-184, 186, 395-396, 515, 524
al-Baghdādī, Abū Bakr (Islamic State caliph) 12, 14, 91, 96, 109, 122, 231, 256, 258, 269, 271, 273, 345, 357, 361, 364-368, 416
al-Balādhurī 120
Barfi, Barak 256-259
Belaid, Chokri 161, 268
Berg, Nicholas 260, 381
al-Bilāwī, Abū ʻAbdul-Raḥmān 274
Bilʻūdī, Dhū al-Fiqār 31
Bouyeri, Mohammed 429, 431
Brahmi, Mohamed 161, 268
Brother Rachid 6-8, 11, 15-19, 23, 25-28, 30, 32, 34-35, 37-38, 41, 48, 53, 78, 85, 90, 92, 97-98, 105-106, 122, 128, 129, 132, 148, 149, 165, 174-175, 179, 186, 197, 219-220, 253, 259, 279, 285-286, 292, 297, 323, 326-328, 329, 344, 369, 371, 387-388, 390, 393-394, 417, 423, 435, 448-449, 457, 468, 469-470, 471, 475, 478, 481-483, 485-486, 488, 498, 499, 501, 507-508, 509, 531-533
  apostasy and 148, 186, 507-509
  indoctrination (religious) of 6, 15-19, 26-27, 53, 90, 92, 105-106, 122, 132, 174-175, 197, 219-220, 259, 279, 323, 328, 329, 344, 449, 471, 499, 501
  interviews by 23, 97-98, 128, 129, 179, 186, 285-286, 485-486
Bush, George W. (former President of United States) 12, 269
Buzān, Adnan 167
Charbonnier, Stéphane 424, 427

Christ *See also* **Jesus**
Clinton, Hillary 13, 188, 521
Constantine, Wafa' 124, 127-130
Coulibaly, Amedy 69
Dajjāl 456, 459, 460
al-Dhahabī, Muḥammad Ibn Aḥmad Ibn 'Uthmān 264, 265, 421
Disney, Walt 175, 176
Dunleavy, Patrick 272
El-Ḥussein, Omar Abdel Hamid 69
El-Naggār, Zaghlūl 130
El-Sisi, Abdel Fattah (President of Egypt) 519, 520
Emil Shimoun Nona 97
Emwazi, Muhammad Jassim—SEE **"Jihadi John"**
Fahd Ibn 'Abd al-'Azīz al-Sa'ud (former King of Saudi Arabia) 375
Faisal II (former King of Iraq) 374
Al-Fajā'a 416-418
Fajāl, Muḥammad Ibn Yūsuf 92
Farook, Syed Rizwan 501, 503-506
Fatima 15, 350, 373
Fernandez, Alberto 523
al-Fizāzī, Muḥammad 382, 528
Foley, James 224, 253, 386, 529
Fouda, Farag 157-160
al-Fūzān, Ṣāliḥ 303
Gabriel 290
Gerschel, Fabrice 486
al-Ghazālī, Muḥammad 158, 159
al-Ghazawī, Zaynab 423

God *See also* **Allah** 15, 16, 19, 22, 39-41, 43, 44, 52, 58, 63, 75, 76, 80, 88, 103, 104, 111, 114, 130, 136-140, 144, 146, 147, 152-153, 164-166, 168, 170, 172, 177, 178, 180, 182, 183, 189, 192, 199, 206, 207, 213-215, 233, 242, 245-246, 250, 251, 255-258, 260, 263, 267, 281, 284, 285, 290, 300, 310, 315, 317, 318, 321-324, 326, 329, 331, 332, 334, 344, 348, 355, 337-358, 363, 368-371, 385, 388, 391, 394, 405, 406, 410, 413, 417, 419, 421, 434, 439, 444, 446, 453, 457, 472, 474, 478, 488, 508, 509, 511

oneness of 15, 104, 136-137, 138, 147, 152-153, 246, 348, 444

worship of other gods 64, 164-166, 168, 177, 370, 439

Gom'a, 'Alī (Grand Mufti of Egypt) 136

Goto, Kenji 224

al-Ḥāfiz Ibn Hajar 413

al-Ḥāfiz al-Mundhirī 408, 417

Haines, David 224, 386

al-Ḥajjāj Ibn Yūsuf 366-367

al-Hakim, Boubakr 161

Ḥamza Ibn 'Abd al-Muṭṭalib 44, 239, 255, 282

Haniya, Ismail 325

Hārūn al-Rashīd 353

al-Ḥasan al-Baṣrī 64

Ḥasan Ibn 'Alī 15

Ḥassān Ibn Thābit 394

Ḥassān, Muḥammad 131

al-Ḥawālī, Safar 30-31

Henning, Alan 224, 386

Heraclius 311, 450, 464

Heyns, Christof 168

Hilāl Ibn Umayyah 142

Hirsi Ali, Ayaan 429

Hishām Ibn 'Abd al-Malik 408, 417

Hormuzan 81

Ḥusayn Ibn 'Alī 373-375

Hussein, Saddam (former President of Iraq) 22, 269, 273, 278, 457, 458

Ḥuyayy Ibn Akhṭab 288, 290-291, 296

Iblīs (Satan) 62, 168, 523
Ibn 'Abbās 407-408
Ibn Bāz, 'Abd al-Azīz 24, 43, 109-110, 164, 434
Ibn Isḥāq 355
Ibn Kathīr, Ismail 21, 25, 26, 40, 43, 57, 69, 121, 204, 216, 251, 255, 257, 274, 326
Ibn Khaldūn 119-121
Ibn Khalkān 121
Ibn al-Mundhir al-Nisāburī 147
Ibn Qayyīm al-Jawzīya 147, 148, 227, 303, 341, 380, 381
Ibn Qudāma 144, 402- 403
Ibn Saud (founder and first King of Saudi Arabia, third Saudi state) 198
Ibn Taymīya 25, 90, 92, 188, 316, 371, 372, 385, 407, 412-413, 418, 442-444, 489-491, 496
Ibn 'Umar 190, 400
Ibrahim, Adnan 66
Ibrāhīm, Muḥammad Abū Bakkār 399
al-Idrīsī, Abū Zayd al-Muqrī' 469
'Imāra, Muḥammad 158
Iyās Ibn 'Abd Yalīl—SEE **Al-Fajā'a**
Jābir Ibn 'Abd Allah 304
al-Ja'd Ibn Dirham 384-385
Jesus *See also* **Christ** 16, 34, 61, 114, 118, 126, 133, 137, 165, 280, 456, 459, 461
"Jihadi John" 223-225, 386, 460, 529
Jonah *See also* **Yūnus** 170, 171
Jones, Terry 424, 425, 430
Joshua 112
Juste, Carsten 425, 426
Jūwayriyya Bint al-Ḥārith 293
Ka'b Ibn Asad al-Qurazī 288
Ka'b Ibn al-Ashraf 150, 384, 386, 432-433
Kamil Ishak 106
Kamleh, Tareq 333
al-Kasāsbeh, Mu'āth 410-411, 414, 416

al-Kashmīrī, Muḥammad Anwar 497
Kassig, Peter 224, 386, 460, 461
Khadīja (Khadīja Bint al-Khūwaylid) 19, 89, 204, 318
Khālid Ibn 'Abd Allāh al-Qasrī 384-385
Khālid Ibn al-Walīd 324-326, 328, 349, 401, 408, 417, 420-422
Khalil, Magdi 522
al-Khaṭṭābī, Ḥamd Ibn Muḥammad 443
Khurto Hajji Ismail 316
Kināna Ibn al-Rabī' 296, 420
Kouachi, Chérif 424, 431-434, 437-439, 444, 453
Kouachi, Said 424, 431-434, 437-439, 444, 453
Kozman, Claudia 523
Labīd Ibn al-A'ṣam 55, 189
Lot 405-407
Louis Raphaël I Sako (Patriarch of Chaldean Catholic Church) 96
Lutnick, Edith 327
Mahdī 61
Mā'iz Ibn Mālik 400
Mālik Ibn Anas 444
Mālik Ibn Nuwayra 349, 420-421
Malik, Tashfeen 501-503, 505
al-Maliki, Nouri (former Prime Minister of Iraq) 234
Ma'mūn al-Huḍaybī 158, 159
al-Manī', Sulaymān 491
Mansour, Ahmed 13, 131
al-Maqdisī, Abū Muḥammad 164, 260, 261
Maria al-Qibṭiya 299
Marwan I 366
Marwan II 352, 366
Maslama Ibn 'Abd al-Malik 464
Mauro, Ryan 273
Mazrū'a, Maḥmūd 159

McCain, Douglas McAuthur 270
Mehmed II 463
Melek Taus (Peacock Angel) 168
M'khaitir, Mohamed Cheikh Ould 184-186, 515
Mohammed VI (King of Morocco) 70, 373, 449
Morsi, Mohamed 159, 358, 368
Muadh Ibn 'Afra 473
Muadh Ibn Amr Ibn al-Jamuh 473
Mu'āwiya Ibn Abū Sufyān (Mu'āwiya I) 156, 350, 352, 355, 357, 371, 462
Mubarak, Hosni (former President of Egypt) 128, 356
Mueller, Robert 272
MUḤAMMAD, Prophet 11, 14-16, 18-23, 25-28, 33, 43-48, 51, 52, 54, 55, 57-61, 63-69, 72, 78-80, 85-93, 95, 97, 98, 101, 102, 104-105, 108-112, 113-116, 123, 124, 126, 129, 133, 136, 137, 139, 141-144, 147, 149-155, 160, 165-166, 168-170, 173-175, 177, 182-186, 189-190, 195-197, 201-202, 203-204, 205-207, 208-209, 211-215, 217, 220, 226-228, 230-233, 235, 237-242, 243-249, 250-251, 252-256, 259-261, 263-268, 270, 273-276, 279-312, 313-324, 326, 329-330, 333-340, 343, 346-350, 354-355, 356-357, 363, 364, 367-368, 370, 372-373, 379-390, 393-395, 400-403, 407-408, 410, 413-422, 424-437, 439-446, 448-454, 455, 458, 459, 461-468, 469-470, 473-474, 476-479, 481, 483, 485, 490, 493, 495, 498, 499, 504, 508, 511-512, 532
  call of 19, 136, 266, 317, 380
  criticism/mockery/ridicule of 14, 63, 48, 104, 149, 150, 182, 183, 184-186, 249, 317, 425-430, 431-441, 442-446, 447-448, 449-452, 453-454, 511
  Islam's supreme role model 52, 85, 87, 89-90, 92, 110, 112-113, 169, 177, 203-204, 211, 253, 261, 319-320, 386, 453-454
  livelihood of 237-239, 249, 273, 274, 286, 310-311, 317-318, 329-330, 380-381
  rejection of his prophethood 14, 19, 20-21, 22-23, 136, 139, 195, 317
Muḥammad Ibn 'Abd al-Wahhāb 164, 165, 169, 176, 177, 187, 192, 375
Muḥammad bin [Ibn] Maslama 150, 420, 432
Muḥammad Ibn Sa'ūd (founder of first Saudi state and Saud dynastry) 164, 374-375
al-Munajjid, Muḥammad Ṣāliḥ 109, 209, 408, 437
Mūsā Ibn Nuṣayr 120-121, 126
Muṣ'ab Ibn 'Umayr 43, 255, 367
Mutawakkil, Wakīl Aḥmad 172
Muthana, Ahmed 47

Muthana, Nasser (a.k.a. Abu Muthanna al-Yemeni) 47, 466
al-Nadhārī, Ḥārith Ibn Ghāzī 438
al-Naḍr Ibn al-Ḥārith 249
Nahas, Subhi 405
Nājī, Abū Bakr 228-230
Nakoula Basseley Nakoula ("Sam Bacile") 33, 428
al-Naqi, Hamad 447
al-Nawawī, Yehīa Ibn Sharaf 107
Negus 19, 126
al-Nhārī, Abdallah 528-529
Nolen, Alton 272, 273
Norris, Molly 430
Nu'aym Ibn Mas'ūd 289
Obama, Barack (former President of the United States) 33, 77-78, 188, 223, 477, 521
Origen 118, 119
Osama Bin Laden 61, 205, 219, 221, 222, 321, 325, 439, 502, 526
al-Ouda, Salmān 472, 492
Owers, Dame Anne 270
Perry, Rick 272
Pope Benedict XVI (former Catholic Pope) 445, 452
Ptolemy I 118
el-Qaddafi, Muammar (former dictator of Libya) 22, 33, 34, 67, 229, 469
al-Qaraḍāwī, Yūsuf 196, 345-346, 365, 493
Qays Ibn Sa'd 190
al-Qurṭubī, Abū 'Abd Allah 58, 112, 262, 359-360, 382, 437, 489, 497
al-Rabaie, Ayyub 414
Rabi' Ibn Sabra 339
al-Rājḥī, 'Abdul 'Azīz 192, 195
Rayḥāna 293
Rose, Flemming 428
Rushdie, Salman 428, 429, 452
al-Ruwaysī, Aḥmad (a.k.a. Abū Zakaryā al-Tūnisī) 268

Sa'd Ibn Abū Waqqās 239
Sa'd Ibn Mu'ādh 57, 288-291
Sa'd Ibn al-Rabī' 205
Sa'd Ibn 'Ubāda 288
Sadek, Morris 428
Ṣafīya Bint Ḥuyayy Ibn al-Akhṭab 296-297, 299
Sageman, Marc 514
al-Ṣaḥḥāf, Muḥammad Sa'īd (former Prime Minister of Iraq) 90
Saint Augustine 117, 119
Saint Felix of Nola 213
Saint Mark 118
Salmān the Persian 288
Saul 112
Schulz, Martin 396
Sennacherib 171
al-Shāfi'ī, Abū 'Abd Allāh Muḥammad Ibn Idrīs 148, 196, 304
al-Shahrī, Sa'īd 524
Sharrouf, Khaled 471
al-Shaṭlī, 'Abdul Qādir 71
al-Shawwālī, 'Azzūz 162
al-Sheikh, 'Abdul-'Azīz Ibn 'Abdullah 12, 24, 155
Shība 44
Shiḥāda, Rabī' 324
al-Shīshānī, Abū 'Umar (a.k.a. Abū Omar the Chechen) 222, 363
al-Shu'aybī, Ḥamūd Ibn 'Uqlā 492
al-Shwaī'ir, Muḥammad Ibn Sa'd 24
al-Sibā'ī, Hānī 223, 381
Simon of Cyrene 118
Simpson, Elton 452
Ṣiyām, Riḍā 330
al-Smī'ī, Ahmed 161
Smith, Anita 34

Smith, Ronnie 34

Sotloff, Steven 224, 253, 255-256, 258, 386

Stern, Jessica 405

Stevens, Christopher (former US Ambassador to Libya) 33, 34, 428

al-Subkī, Taqīy al-Dīn 442

Ṣūfī, Nādir 452

Sulaymān Ibn 'Abd al-Malik Ibn Marwān 462-463

al-Ṭabarī, Abū Ja'far Muḥammad Ibn Jarīr 21, 29-30, 39-40, 45, 76, 100, 139, 215, 250, 336, 383, 410

Talha Ibn 'Ubayd Allah 349, 351

al-Tarīfī, 'Abd al-Azīz Ibn Marzouk 165

Tāriq Ibn Ziyād 343-344

al-Tayeb, Ahmed (Grand Imam of Al Azhar) 136

Tertullian 117, 119

Trump, Donald (President of the United States) 6, 333

al-Turkmānī, Abū Muslim 274

'Ubayd Ibn 'Umayr 44

'Ubayda Ibn al-Ḥārith 44, 239

'Umar Ibn 'Abd al-'Azīz 64, 190

'Umar Ibn al-Khaṭṭāb (second Rashidun caliph) 44, 79, 100, 101, 108-109, 110, 115-116, 120, 121, 190, 319, 339, 347, 349, 373, 399-401, 503

caliphate 79, 100-101, 108-109, 110, 115-116, 120, 121, 190, 319, 339, 349, 373, 399-400, 503

Saqīfa 347

Um John 129

Umm Sumayyah al-Muhājirah 216-217

'Uqba Ibn Abū Mu'ayṭ 250

'Uqba Ibn Nāfi' 344

Usāma Ibn Zayd Ibn Ḥāritha 310, 313

'Utba Ibn Rabī'a 247, 253, 254

al-'Uthaymīn, Muḥammad Ibn Ṣāliḥ 43, 209

'Uthmān Ibn 'Affān (third Rashidun caliph) 156, 190, 349-352, 357, 365, 370, 462

'Uyaynah Ibn Ḥisn 287

van Gogh, Theo 426, 429, 431, 432
Vilks, Lars 69, 427
al-Walīd Ibn 'Abd al-Malik 120-121, 344
al-Walīd Ibn 'Ataba 44
Walīd Ibn 'Utba 253
Waraqa Ibn Nawfal 19
Westergaard, Kurt 425, 426, 428
Wilders, Geert 426, 452
Yassine, Abdesslam 219
Yazīd Ibn Mu'āwiya (son of Mu'awiya) 352, 462
Ye, Hussein 17
Yukawa, Haruna 224
Yūnus *See also* **Jonah** 170, 171
Yūsuf Ibn Tāshfīn 503
Zakher, Kamilia Shehata 124, 127-130
al-Zarqāwī, Abū Muṣ'ab 164, 204, 221, 260, 367, 459, 460
al-Ẓawāhirī, Ayman 61, 123, 221, 223, 381, 470
Zubayr Ibn al-'Awam 349, 351

Subject Index

'Abbāsid(s) 87, 314, 352-355

Abyssinia(n) 19, 126, 504

adultery 77, 81, 127, 148, 156, 164, 178, 182, 303, 338, 394, 397-404, 407, 409, 479, 508, 510, 511

Al Azhar *See also* **university, universities** 18, 24, 60, 96-97, 107, 112, 129, 136, 138, 141, 158-159, 459, 482-485, 519-520

Al Qaeda 5, 7, 12, 47, 56, 61-62, 69, 73, 80, 102, 134, 155-157, 161, 205, 219-223, 228, 246, 268, 311, 321, 345, 371, 381, 382, 399, 424, 427, 430, 431, 438-440, 444, 452, 458, 470, 476, 488, 491, 494, 498, 502, 504, 511, 515, 524-526

9/11 attacks 5, 12, 476, 488, 491, 493-494

Inspire magazine 424, 427, 431, 452, 498, 504

Al Qaeda in Iraq (AQI) 129-130, 157, 164, 233-234, 260

"*Allahu Akbar*" 14, 99, 122, 129, 180, 259, 295, 424, 457, 483, 485

alliance 22, 39-40, 45, 193, 206-207, 211, 221, 225, 227, 228, 230-234, 264-266, 268, 269, 280, 287, 288, 295, 347-348, 350, 356, 357, 360-361, 364-366, 368, 374, 376, 502, 504, 517, 525

Muḥammad and Anṣār 206-207, 230-233

Muḥammad Ibn Sa'ūd and Ibn 'Abd al-Wahhāb 164, 374-375

Amazigh 117, 119-121, 343, 449, 503

Amnesty International (AI) 180, 298-299, 402

amputation(s) 50, 88, 104, 178, 182, 383, 388-393, 415, 510, 511

Anbar Awakening 233-234

al-Andalus 80, 503

Anṣār (Helpers) 193, 204-207, 230-233, 237, 239, 243-245, 248-249, 254, 281-282, 288, 293, 307, 318, 347, 350, 365, 401, 453, 473

al-'Aqaba 230, 232, 233, 280

apostates, apostasy 6, 11, 135, 137, 147-154, 158-160, 163-164, 179-181, 183-186, 192, 194-197, 201, 319, 334, 348-349, 361, 370, 371, 383-384, 388, 389, 391, 396, 411, 416-417, 421, 437, 440, 451, 508-509, 511, 524, 532

burning of 411, 416-417, 421

rulings on 147-154, 159-160, 163, 192, 196, 383-384, 437, 451

Arabian Peninsula 64, 97, 103, 108-110, 113, 115, 116, 120, 124, 126, 203, 279, 313, 322, 324, 374, 438, 439, 462, 503, 504

Arab League 390, 393, 397, 404

Arab Spring 67, 80

Arab-Israeli conflict—SEE **Israeli-Palestinian conflict/hostilities**

Arabs 49, 54, 62, 49, 88-93, 109-110, 120, 126, 138, 145, 152, 232, 240, 247, 254, 264, 269, 311, 322, 334, 342, 348-349, 362, 522

art 119, 171-173, 175-176, 275, 425-430, 446

Asia 42, 120, 172, 197, 203, 425

aslim taslam *See also* **"invitation"** 311, 314, 324, 451

assassination(s) 67, 102, 158-159, 161, 268, 287, 349, 353, 374, 425-427, 429, 432-433, 504

assimilation 42, 45, 86, 123, 373, 499

attack(s) (recent Muslim/Islamic) 5, 12, 32, 33, 67-71, 96, 102-103, 128-131, 133, 167, 193, 204, 218, 225-227, 229, 259, 268, 271-273, 327, 328, 330, 372, 405, 423-429, 431, 435-436, 438-440, 452, 453, 475-496, 498-505, 531

bandits (*al-sa'ālīk*) 242, 264-268, 270, 273, 274

banishment—SEE **expulsions**

Banū Hāshim (Muhammad's clan) 89-90, 92-93, 168, 232, 350, 352

battles (early Muslim) 20, 43, 59, 60, 79, 110, 111, 152, 156-157, 170, 207, 215, 217, 220, 227, 243-251, 253-255, 256, 260, 261, 279, 281-283, 286-288, 289-292, 294-297, 298, 302, 306, 307-308, 309-311, 317-320, 322, 324, 326, 343, 348, 350-352, 354, 367, 370, 384, 421, 432, 453, 478, 503

Battle of Badr 110-111, 217, 243-251, 253-255, 256, 260, 279, 281, 432

Battle of the Camel 350-352, 354, 370

Battle of the Trench 289-292

Battle of 'Uḥud 282-283, 367, 453,

Conquest of Mecca 307-309

Bayt al-Anṣār (House of Comrades)—SEE **guest houses**

beheading—SEE **decapitation**

"best nation" 18, 75-76, 78-82, 84-85, 90-91, 171-172, 479

Bible 18, 21, 63, 111-112, 118, 322, 332, 385, 405, 520

"blood money" *See also* **indemnity** 142, 143, 264, 283, 440

bomb(s), bombings 38, 56, 68, 102, 170, 192-193, 226-227, 259, 271, 327, 341, 412, 414, 425, 426, 427, 437, 457, 468, 475-477, 480, 482, 485, 488-493, 497-498, 502-504, 525, 528

book(s) 14, 19, 20, 27, 30, 38, 46, 60, 63, 118-119, 131, 132, 154, 158, 159, 164, 169, 184, 186, 222, 228-230, 253, 256, 272, 304, 314, 317, 335, 336, 344, 355, 380, 417, 418, 420, 426, 429, 430, 442-443, 445, 446, 448, 449, 450, 471, 472, 486, 489-490, 505, 516

holy texts (Christian) 63, 118

holy texts (Muslim) 118-119, 442, 448, 449, 471, 516

booty 105, 111, 239, 241, 242, 247-249, 251, 274, 275, 281-284, 292, 293, 297, 300, 305, 309, 317-319, 321, 322, 344, 465, 473

boy(s) (Muslim) 48, 292, 316, 342, 369, 375, 468-474

British Commonwealth War Graves Commission cemetery 67-68

Buddhists, Buddhism 17, 110

Byzantine empire—SEE **Eastern Roman Empire**

caliph(s) 3, 64, 79, 81, 85, 91, 93, 95, 96, 101, 102, 108-110, 115, 116, 120-122, 151-153, 156, 170, 190, 246, 248, 254, 258, 269, 273, 285, 319, 324, 340, 344, 345, 347-350, 352, 353, 356, 357, 360, 361, 364-368, 370-374, 377, 380, 389, 394, 399, 401, 402, 405, 407, 408, 416-418, 420-422, 462-464, 468, 503

qualifications of 364-367

Rashidun caliphs 79, 81, 101, 108-109, 110, 115, 121, 151-153, 156, 190, 246, 248, 285, 319, 324, 348-350, 352, 357, 365, 368, 373, 389, 394, 399, 401-402, 405, 407, 408, 416-418, 420-422, 503

Umayyad dynasty 64, 344, 366, 367, 462-464

caliphate 85, 91, 96-97, 100, 105, 120, 122, 125-126, 156, 157, 160, 182, 208, 209, 211, 215, 219, 223-224, 231, 234, 314, 324, 339, 343, 367, 369, 371-377, 385, 387, 391, 394, 396, 419-422, 440, 452, 459, 462, 463, 468, 470, 471, 473, 477, 479, 480, 511, 526

camel(s) 59, 104, 115, 121, 152, 238, 241, 250, 284, 304, 307, 318, 348, 351, 393, 415, 478

Camp Bucca 269, 271, 272

Camp Speicher 277-279, 292, 372

captive(s) 121, 124, 224, 241-243, 247-253, 258, 259, 262, 275, 281, 291-294, 296-301, 304-306, 315, 319, 322, 370, 376, 386, 393, 410, 419, 461, 468, 496

early Islam 121, 241-243, 247-251, 281, 291-294, 295-296, 297-300, 304-306, 315, 319, 322, 393

recent history 124, 252, 258, 259, 275, 292, 296, 297-299, 301, 304-306, 370, 376, 386, 410, 419, 461, 468

caravan(s) 110-111, 113, 238-245, 247, 254, 256, 265, 267, 286, 318

cartoons, caricatures (of Muhammad) 63, 69, 425, 430, 437-438, 445, 452-454

censorship 427, 428, 430, 445, 523

Charlie Hebdo 14, 69, 271, 423, 424, 427, 431-440, 449, 452, 453, 486, 517

children, childhood 14-19, 23, 24, 26, 34, 42, 47, 50, 51, 57, 59, 77, 88, 100, 101, 104, 105, 115, 120, 148, 151, 179, 184, 193, 196, 197, 212, 219, 250, 257, 258, 260, 291-295, 298, 301, 303-305, 309, 310, 311, 316, 323, 328, 329, 331, 340, 342, 350, 359, 361, 363, 384, 387, 396, 401, 412, 431, 436, 437, 441-442, 445, 449, 453, 455, 469-474, 479, 495, 498, 499, 501, 503, 508, 512, 514, 517

Christianity 15, 18, 23, 28, 115-118, 121, 126, 128-129, 132, 133, 136, 168, 171, 456, 462, 463, 477, 480, 518, 520, 532

Christians 6, 11-32, 34, 37-42, 44-47, 52, 57, 58, 61, 62, 64-68, 70-72, 76, 80, 86, 87, 95-103, 105-119, 121-134, 136-138, 140-145, 147, 149, 157, 163, 165, 166, 168, 176, 192, 194, 213, 253, 259, 270, 272, 274, 285, 299, 301, 305, 315, 324, 372, 385, 425, 428, 434, 443, 444, 456, 459-462, 465, 466, 473, 477, 502, 503, 504, 506, 507, 509, 511, 517, 518, 523, 528, 532

enemies of Islam 11-14, 18-19, 20, 21-23, 29-30, 31, 37, 40-41, 45-47, 57, 62, 70, 71, 72, 98, 106, 110, 124, 130, 133, 456, 459-460, 465-466, 509, 517

persecution of 6, 20, 42, 52, 58, 61, 64-65, 67, 68, 70, 71, 95-103, 105, 107-108, 109, 110, 114-115, 116-117, 119, 121, 124-126, 128, 129-130, 131, 132, 133, 140, 141, 142, 144, 145, 149, 157, 166, 168, 259, 274, 285, 315, 324, 443, 444, 461, 462, 473, 477, 503, 504, 511, 523,

church(es) 34, 42, 52, 58, 63, 67, 96, 102, 106, 108, 109, 115, 117-119, 122, 124-131, 133, 134, 178, 272, 425, 456, 477, 518, 519

city, cities (Muslim) 32, 34, 38, 46, 47, 65, 67, 90, 95-98, 100, 102, 105, 107, 117-119, 121, 124, 125, 128-129, 131, 157, 167, 170-171, 188, 193, 194, 200, 204, 214, 218, 219, 230, 231, 233, 252, 258, 259, 262-263, 266, 269, 274, 275, 277-279, 285, 288, 298, 305, 307, 314, 315, 319, 330, 351-352, 356, 366, 368, 399, 406-407, 425, 428, 444, 457-463, 466, 469, 480, 481, 491, 503, 517, 528

Baghdad 90, 100, 124, 129, 157, 204, 258, 314, 352, 481

Benghazi 33, 34, 67, 428

Cairo 33, 46, 128, 131, 356

Casablanca 32, 68, 46, 219, 458, 469, 517, 528

Dābiq 459-463

Mosul 95-98, 100, 105, 107, 125, 170, 171, 252, 262-263, 275, 298, 315, 330, 368,

Raqqa 47, 188, 214, 218, 230, 279, 399, 491

city, cities (Western or non-Muslim) 14, 47, 60, 65, 66, 69, 112, 214, 223, 326-327, 438-439, 456, 461, 462-464, 465, 475-482, 484, 487, 488, 490, 491, 494, 496, 499-504, 528, 529, 531

NYC 326-327, 476, 487, 488, 491

Paris 14, 69, 438-439, 475-484, 481, 484, 488, 490, 491, 494, 496, 499-501, 531

Rome 65, 456, 461, 464, 465, 480, 481

Committee for the Promotion of Virtue and the Prevention of Vice (CPVPV) 179, 187, 198-199, 395

compact(s)—SEE **treaty**

Companion(s) 43, 44, 64, 78, 79, 86, 97, 98, 104, 108, 109, 113, 123, 124, 150, 154, 155, 157, 165, 170, 190, 204, 211, 212, 228, 230, 239-241, 243, 244, 247, 248, 250, 251, 255, 260, 263, 283-284, 292, 297, 300, 301, 304, 306-308, 311, 313, 315, 318, 319, 325, 336, 339, 343, 347-349, 351, 355, 360, 364, 366, 367, 371-372, 380, 383-385, 387, 400-403, 407, 408, 410, 413-418, 420, 422, 431-433, 440, 443, 446, 453, 462, 464, 467, 473, 511

Abū Bakr 43, 212, 251, 255, 283, 319, 347, 348, 364, 408, 416-417

'Alī Ibn Abī Ṭālib 44, 157, 240, 255, 283, 347, 348, 371-372, 401, 408, 415-416, 440, 467

'Umar Ibn al-Khaṭṭāb 79, 190, 251, 283, 308, 319, 347, 348, 349, 401

conquest(s) *See also* **Mecca** 43, 79, 80, 121, 125, 126, 168, 203, 212, 220, 249, 276, 279, 307-309, 314, 315, 319, 324, 338, 343, 352, 413, 422, 456, 459, 464, 469, 519

conspiracy theory 13, 19, 20, 32, 37, 223, 482, 485, 521

Constantinople 456, 459, 460, 462-464

conversion (religious) 15, 18, 20, 28, 48, 49, 70, 72, 95, 96, 98, 99, 102, 105, 109, 116, 118-120, 122, 124, 125, 127-129, 133, 134, 145, 149, 152, 166-168, 194, 223, 230, 265, 266, 267, 270, 271, 272, 273, 280, 289, 290, 292, 299, 308, 314-316, 318, 324, 333, 348, 433, 452, 485-488, 503, 511, 524

Coptic Church, Coptic Christians 87, 117, 124, 127-129, 130-131, 132

countries (Muslim) *See also* **Muslim world** 7, 12-14, 17-19, 21, 22, 24, 26, 27, 30-35, 38, 42, 46-52, 54, 57, 61, 64, 67-71, 77, 79-82, 83-84, 91, 92, 96, 101, 107, 109-110, 112, 116-122, 127-135, 140, 142, 145-147, 149, 157-161, 164, 169-172, 174, 176, 178, 179, 181-182, 183, 184-186, 187-188, 190-191, 193, 194, 196-205, 210-212, 214, 215, 217-223, 225-227, 229, 231, 232, 243, 252, 259, 268, 270, 275, 279, 288, 299, 302-304, 310, 313, 314, 325, 326, 333, 334, 342, 344-346, 348, 350, 352, 356, 358, 361-363, 371-376, 382, 387, 389-392, 395-399, 403, 404, 409-412, 416-418, 423, 425, 428, 434-436, 438, 439, 442, 443, 445-449, 451, 452, 456-462, 466, 467, 470-473, 482, 485-487, 490-493, 496, 497, 499, 500, 503, 505, 508, 510-512, 515-530, 532

Egypt 33, 42, 117, 118, 120, 121, 127-129, 130-131, 142, 147, 157-160, 356, 376, 519-520

Iraq 22, 24, 96, 121, 129, 215, 231-232, 275, 279, 398, 457-458, 530

Libya 22, 33, 34, 67, 119

Morocco 24, 32, 38, 50, 68, 70-71, 119, 121, 122, 145, 190-191, 219-220, 373, 409, 446, 457, 499, 532

Saudi Arabia 18, 24, 51, 54, 64, 109-110, 112, 147, 164, 170-179, 181-182, 184, 187-188, 198-200, 302, 374-375, 389-390, 392, 395-396, 404, 434-435, 491, 515, 518, 524-525

Syria 13, 47, 116, 121, 214, 215, 226, 231-232, 268, 270, 275, 459-460, 467, 530

countries (non-Muslim) *See also* **The West, Western countries** 5, 6, 12, 18, 21-24, 30-35, 37-38, 41, 46-52, 58, 69-70, 77, 79, 82-85, 96, 107, 116, 122, 140, 145, 150, 154, 160, 167, 172, 173, 178, 180-182, 190, 193, 206-207, 209-212, 214, 215, 217, 218, 221, 223-226, 229, 234, 252, 267, 269, 270, 271, 272, 273, 298, 302, 304, 312, 313-314, 321, 326, 328-330, 333, 338, 340-346, 362, 363, 374, 376, 386, 389, 391, 396, 403, 409, 414, 424-430, 434, 438-440, 442, 445, 446, 447-449, 452, 453, 457, 458, 461, 465-466, 469, 471, 473, 475-479, 481-487, 490-491, 493, 494, 496-502, 505, 510, 511-512, 515-518, 520-531

France 18, 31, 207, 218, 221, 362, 477-478, 482, 486, 501

UK 31, 32, 34, 47-48, 214, 218, 221, 362

US 5, 6, 12, 21-24, 51-52, 207, 224, 229, 224, 252, 269, 457, 487, 494, 521

criminal law *See also* **penal code** 50, 161, 180, 182-184, 185, 271, 299, 389, 390, 392, 393, 396, 397, 403, 404, 409, 410, 446

cross (Christian) 67, 68, 98, 117, 118, 124, 125, 132-134, 187, 247, 456, 460, 461, 465, 479

crucifixion 118, 126, 379, 391-393

Crusades 57, 61, 67, 119, 124, 459, 461, 465, 477, 481, 502

"cubs of the caliphate" 468, 470-473

culture (Muslim/Arab) 13, 14, 18, 19, 37-39, 41, 53, 55, 56, 62, 67, 68, 71, 72, 78, 98, 106, 132, 258, 263, 274, 449, 463, 471, 486, 517, 527, 533

culture of death 321, 324, 326, 328

culture of life 326

Dabiq (Islamic State publication) 124-125, 215-217, 301-302, 318, 330, 459, 460, 465

Daring Question 6, 97, 106, 128, 285

Day of Judgment 16, 155, 175, 419, 455, 467, 496

Day of Resurrection 22, 26, 40, 59, 65, 66, 123, 175, 211, 265, 294, 403, 495, 496

decapitation 54, 98, 100, 111, 124-127, 133, 163, 179, 182, 183, 188, 197, 224, 249, 251, 252, 253, 256, 258-259, 260-262, 263, 272, 273, 292, 305, 379-386, 387, 388, 389, 391, 392, 396, 406, 420, 425, 427, 432, 451, 467, 470-471

use during early Islam 100, 111, 249, 251, 260-262, 263, 292, 305, 380-385, 386, 387, 420, 432, 451

use by ISIL/ISIS/Islamic State 111, 124-127, 133, 163, 183, 188, 224, 252, 253, 256, 258, 259, 262, 263, 292, 305, 379, 385-387, 391, 396, 406, 467, 470-471

democracy 49, 50, 85, 362, 373, 374, 375, 476, 494, 528

demonstrations 33, 38, 63, 106, 127, 128, 131, 396, 425, 427, 428, 430, 436, 445, 452, 453, 458, 512

deportations—SEE **expulsions**

deradicalization programs 524-525

dhimmi 95, 98-102, 107, 116, 143, 148, 165, 324, 400

diplomacy 156, 174, 266, 311, 389, 409, 435, 436, 515, 517

disbelief (in Islam) 26, 80, 125, 136, 137, 139, 144, 146, 150, 154, 165, 176, 177, 187, 192, 195, 197, 208, 210-212, 215-217, 242, 329, 455, 494, 501, 532

Muslims 136, 137, 139, 154, 176, 187, 192, 195, 197, 215, 455, 501

non-Muslims 26, 80, 125, 136, 137, 139, 150, 154, 165, 242, 329, 455, 501

discrimination 41, 42, 58, 65, 108, 144-146, 316, 373, 486, 517

divorce 127, 178, 186, 205, 479

doll(s) 174-176

drone strike(s) 224, 225, 438, 439

dynasty, dynasties 87, 164, 353-355, 370, 373, 374, 402, 462

Eastern Roman Empire 300, 307, 309-310, 313, 324, 450, 462, 463, 518

education 7, 13, 14, 16-19, 21, 23, 24, 26-30, 46, 47, 53, 59-60, 65, 69, 82-83, 106, 118, 119, 174, 199, 209, 213, 270, 271, 297, 304, 314, 321, 337, 344, 345, 358, 361, 366, 436, 437-438, 443, 444, 445, 448-451, 457, 458, 461, 468, 471, 472, 500, 501, 505, 516-518, 520-521

indoctrination (religious) 14, 16, 17, 18, 21, 24, 26, 30, 46, 47, 59-60, 65, 106, 174, 296-297, 321, 337, 344, 345, 361, 436, 437-438, 442, 448-451, 461, 471, 501, 505

reforms in 28-30, 118-119, 516-517, 520-521

embassy, embassies 33, 34, 122, 425, 428, 430, 445

Emigrants (Muhājirīn) 126, 204-208, 216, 217, 226, 227, 230, 231, 237-241, 243-245, 249, 253, 254, 280, 282, 284, 288, 293, 318, 347, 349, 350, 365

emigrants, emigration *See also* **immigration** 104, 110, 116, 126, 149, 204-209, 210-216, 217, 218, 219, 220, 221-227, 228, 230, 246, 268, 279-280, 285, 317, 346, 347,440, 527, 528, 531

empire(s) 91, 116, 120, 126, 313, 314, 316, 319, 324, 343, 344, 352, 353, 362, 370, 373, 420, 450, 459, 462, 463, 503, 518

Entente Cordiale 31

Ethiopian Church 125, 126

ethnic cleansing/genocide 22, 100, 103, 116, 121, 167, 168, 227, 279

European Union (EU) 77, 84, 218, 325, 396, 469, 491, 530

evil eye 53, 54, 191-192

excommunication—SEE ***takfir***

execution(s) 54, 98, 124, 142-143, 147, 149, 150, 158-160, 163, 166, 167, 168, 176, 183-188, 193, 224, 226, 249, 250, 252, 258-260, 262, 263, 278, 279, 284, 292, 296, 299, 308, 315, 351, 353, 369, 386, 387, 389, 392, 396, 398, 401-408, 410, 411, 417-418, 420, 430, 434, 437, 440, 447, 451, 452, 460, 461, 468, 470, 488, 511, 529

executioner(s) 8, 193,225, 262, 292, 385, 386, 406, 437, 460, 461, 470

exodus 70, 96, 105, 210, 530

exoneration (of Islam) 8, 99, 157, 306, 422, 433, 476, 482, 485, 527

"expeditions" and raids (early Muslim) 243-249, 257, 281, 286-288, 293-295, 296, 298, 300, 306-308, 309-311, 318-319, 321, 324, 338, 339, 400, 495, 518, 519

expulsions 64, 65, 69, 70, 71, 97, 98, 103, 104, 105, 107, 108, 109, 110, 115, 116, 126, 141, 169, 223, 227, 242, 246, 259, 264, 274, 277, 279, 282, 284, 285, 287, 290, 295, 305-307, 309, 315, 318, 319, 381, 391, 462, 478, 501, 503, 504

extermination—SEE **ethnic cleansing/genocide**

fasting, fast(s) 75, 153-155, 182, 183, 197, 472, 509, 511

fatwa, fatāwa 24, 43, 61, 64, 65, 109, 134, 135, 146, 147, 158, 159, 162-164, 172-174, 196, 209, 210, 303, 325, 341, 345, 346, 354, 369, 382, 390, 397, 398, 403, 404, 408, 413, 414, 417, 418, 429, 434-437, 492-493, 512

festivals—SEE **holy days**

Fitna wars 350-351

flag(s) 134, 216, 246, 326, 358, 457, 465, 482

flogging 178-184, 201, 394-397, 401, 403, 404, 409, 524

food(s) 26, 38, 66, 90, 101, 132, 167, 192, 201, 229, 250, 270, 272, 393, 401

foreign fighters *See also* ***mujāhīd, mujāhidīn*** 188, 206, 217-219, 222, 225-227, 231, 233, 234, 252, 270, 525

fort(s) 225, 284, 288, 290, 291, 295, 306

freedom(s) 49, 51, 56, 181, 182, 194, 221, 423, 426, 427, 433, 434, 436, 438, 439, 445, 448, 451, 476, 504, 515, 516, 518

friendship 38-43, 45, 48, 49, 98, 140, 177, 192, 215, 231, 377, 385, 436

girl(s) 54, 77, 88, 129, 131, 186, 192, 199, 207, 214, 293-296, 297-307, 316, 322, 335, 392, 401, 402, 441-442, 472

global rankings 79, 81-85

god(s) (false) 64, 76, 147, 152-153, 164, 178, 246, 348, 419, 439, 444, 446, 508, 509

grave(s) 52, 59, 67-68, 169, 170, 171, 173, 174, 176, 190-191, 211, 278, 328, 350, 353, 372, 416, 446

Great Battle 455, 456, 458, 466-468

Guantanamo Bay detention camp 269, 270, 524, 525

guest houses 205, 222

ḥadīth(s) *See also* **Hadith literature** 15, 16, 26, 54, 55, 60, 64-66, 78, 79, 86, 91, 106-108, 112-113, 123, 126, 133, 139, 141-144, 147-148, 150, 152, 154, 155, 170, 173, 175, 184, 189, 190, 196, 197, 205, 208, 209, 215, 217, 231, 257, 286, 291, 294-297, 300, 303, 304, 308, 311, 315, 318, 320-323, 328-330, 333-334, 335, 336, 339, 354-357, 359, 363, 364, 381, 382, 384, 388, 389, 395, 399-402, 406-408, 416-418, 433, 434, 440-441, 453, 456-460, 463-470, 483, 488, 495, 499, 508

jihad and martyrdom 320, 321-323, 329, 330, 333-334, 336, 381, 382, 384, 463, 467, 488

treatment of non-Muslims 108, 126, 141, 142, 143, 152, 208-209, 257, 300, 311, 315, 328, 381, 382, 384, 440-441, 463, 467, 483

Hadith literature *See also* ***ḥadīth(s)*** 16, 19, 23, 44, 55, 57-59, 61, 64, 66, 72, 86, 91, 98, 101, 108, 109, 111, 123, 141, 143, 147-148, 150, 156, 163, 164-165, 166, 174, 184, 188, 191, 196, 201, 215, 227, 246, 248, 253, 258, 259, 261, 276, 296, 298, 300, 301, 302, 304, 307, 308, 311, 314, 315, 329, 334, 336, 340, 354, 355, 365, 379, 382, 385, 390, 393-395, 401, 406, 407, 413, 416, 420, 432, 433, 440, 453, 455, 460, 461, 465, 466, 469, 473, 488, 508, 509-510

demonization, hatred of non-Muslims 44, 55, 57-58, 72, 86

execution of apostates 147-148, 150, 163, 164-165, 196, 379, 416

Hai'a—SEE **Committee for the Promotion of Virtue and the Prevention of Vice (CPVPV)**

Ḥamās 325, 345

harām (religiously unlawful) 38, 103, 174, 175, 210

hate speech *See also* **mosque(s): hate speech sermons** 57, 221, 446, 516

hell 129, 138, 142, 154, 166-175, 176, 208, 250, 253, 300, 323, 334, 336, 338, 418, 419, 440, 476, 480

Helpers (Anṣār)—SEE Anṣār

hereafter 139, 142, 251, 283, 300, 323, 329, 331, 332, 334, 336-338, 340, 342, 358, 391, 472, 521

hijāb 77, 81, 127, 199, 509

Hijra (Muḥammad's migration, AD 622) 86, 213, 214, 217, 228, 280, 310, 318, 347, 380

al-ḥisba 199-200

Ḥisba 200

holy days *See also* **Ramadan** 47, 110, 182, 183, 197, 256, 259, 384, 423, 529

homosexuals, homosexuality 77, 404-409

hostage(s) 69, 124, 130, 224, 241-243, 247-250, 252, 258-260, 262, 275, 385, 386, 410, 412, 419, 461, 468, 496, 525

houris 300, 323, 334-338, 341, 342, 493, 533

Houthi rebels 187, 522

human trafficking *See also* **slavery** 297, 298, 302, 304

Hypocrites (Munafiqūn) 250, 281, 433

hypocrites 51, 77, 92, 150, 150, 155, 174, 182, 221, 250, 369, 404, 467

Iberia (Spain) 80, 121, 203, 313, 314, 343-344, 352, 462, 503

idols, idolaters, idolatry 25, 29, 31, 58, 63, 64, 103, 110, 112, 125, 133, 136, 137, 138, 144-145, 161, 165, 170-174, 177, 257, 308, 315, 362, 363, 416

Al-Ifk 394

immigrant(s), immigration *See also* **emigrant(s)**, **emigration** 49, 56, 69, 333, 487, 500, 527

immolation 194, 201, 379, 410-419, 420-421

immorality 46, 49, 56, 68, 76, 200, 201, 296, 300, 397, 409

imprisonment 42, 52, 77, 129, 159, 179, 180, 184, 186, 188, 196, 212, 258, 266, 268, 269-270, 271, 272, 273, 299, 353, 390, 392, 395, 397, 403, 409, 445-447, 472, 515, 520, 524, 528, 532

indemnity *See also* **"blood money"** 102, 142, 143, 152, 264, 440, 441

infidel(s) *See also* **non-believers; non-Muslims** 11, 14, 21-23, 28-30, 32, 42-44, 46-51, 55-57, 61, 63, 64, 72, 76, 78, 80, 83, 85-87, 90, 91, 100, 102, 103, 106, 110-111, 122, 129, 131, 135-154, 156-160, 163-166, 169, 176-178, 180-182, 186, 191-195, 197, 204, 208-212, 215, 221, 223, 253-255, 261, 263, 267, 275, 295, 298, 302, 303, 305, 311, 318, 326, 328-330, 346, 347, 357, 362, 371, 372, 379, 383, 391, 410, 413, 424, 426, 431, 435-437, 440, 443, 445, 451, 452, 454, 455-460, 463-467, 469, 473, 477, 479-481, 489-491, 493, 495-500, 502, 503, 505, 507, 517, 523, 526, 528, 532, 533

definition, identification, and classification of 11, 23, 29, 43, 63-64, 85, 91, 106, 122, 135-140, 147-148, 150, 151, 152-153, 154, 155, 160, 163, 164-165, 169, 176-177, 180, 182, 191, 192, 194, 195, 263, 303, 330, 371-372, 435-437, 490, 493, 523

treatment prescribed by Islam, Muslims 42, 46, 47, 50-51, 86, 87, 100, 102, 103, 110-111, 131, 140, 141, 142, 143-146, 148-151, 152-153, 154, 160, 166, 176-177, 186, 191, 192, 194, 208, 209-210, 212, 215, 254, 261, 263, 275, 298, 318, 329, 379, 383, 413, 435-437, 495, 497, 499

inheritance 50, 88, 89, 144

Injīl (Gospel) 16, 332

International Union of Muslim Scholars (IUMS) 96, 131, 196, 346, 365, 472, 493

Internet 14, 24, 30, 31, 32, 48, 84, 130, 136, 147, 160, 163, 164, 179, 224, 228, 256, 272, 305, 324, 327, 341, 342, 354, 393, 395, 398, 224, 228, 256, 272, 305, 324, 448, 472, 482, 487, 504, 505, 511, 512, 528, 529

intolerance/tolerance 25, 41, 107-108, 115, 116, 161, 177, 280, 308, 434, 437, 445, 447, 449, 483, 484, 501, 516, 518, 524, 527

invasion(s) (Muslim/Islamic) 85, 86, 119-120, 121, 126, 167, 168, 203, 229, 238, 252, 274, 305, 313, 343, 359, 374, 380, 450, 457, 462, 477, 495, 514

"invitation" *See also* ***aslim taslam*** 113-115, 125, 207, 311-312, 332, 450, 451

Islam 6-8, 11-16, 18-30, 32, 38-52, 54, 55, 57-59, 62, 64, 66, 69, 71, 72, 76, 78-81, 85-89, 95-97, 99-102, 105, 108-110, 113, 115-117, 119-129, 133-135, 137, 138, 140, 142-143, 145-150, 152, 153, 155, 157, 158, 160, 162-173, 176-177, 180, 182, 183, 186-192, 194-198, 201, 202, 203-205, 207, 209-212, 214-217, 221, 222, 229-231, 233, 237, 239, 240, 250, 253, 254, 258, 261, 265-268, 270-274, 280, 289, 290, 297, 299-306, 311-321, 323-326, 328, 330, 333, 334, 338, 340, 344-350, 353-354, 359, 361, 364, 365, 367-374, 379-383, 385, 386, 388, 390, 391, 394, 395, 398-405, 407, 409-410, 413, 415, 416, 418, 419, 421, 422, 424-427, 429-431, 433, 437, 439-445, 447-451, 453, 455-457, 461, 462, 464-467, 469, 470, 472, 473, 476-477, 480-491, 493-497, 499-501, 503, 506-511, 514, 516, 518-521, 524, 526, 528, 532, 533

early history 20, 87-88, 89-90, 101-102, 109, 110, 116-117, 119-122, 125-126, 152, 166, 190, 203-205, 210, 212, 215, 217, 231, 233, 237, 239, 240, 261, 268, 274, 280, 290, 313, 314, 317, 319, 338, 348, 353-534, 359, 366, 373, 380, 385, 394, 402, 462

forced conversion to 95-96, 98, 99, 102, 105, 109, 121-122, 125, 126, 127, 128, 129, 133, 152, 166, 167-168, 290, 298-299, 314-316, 317, 319, 348, 503, 511

teachings of 11, 14, 15, 16, 18, 21-22, 27, 32, 38-40, 43, 44, 46, 49, 54, 62, 64, 72, 86, 87, 89, 108, 127, 142-143, 162, 165, 172, 189, 215, 300, 304, 333, 386, 431, 451, 499, 500, 510

Islamic State of Iraq and the Levant (ISIL) 7, 12, 13, 62, 110, 111, 124, 150, 157, 171, 183, 200, 206, 222, 223, 227, 253, 273, 274, 277-279, 292, 315, 370-372, 379, 459, 466, 467, 473, 475, 477, 486, 514

Islamic State of Iraq and Syria (ISIS) 6, 7, 12, 13, 47, 48, 62, 91, 95-98, 110, 111, 150, 157, 168, 193, 194, 200-201, 205-207, 214, 215, 221, 229, 234, 252, 253, 256, 261, 262-263, 270, 271, 272, 275, 277, 277, 278, 285, 288, 296-299, 301, 305, 307, 315, 325, 330, 333, 341, 346, 356, 357, 360-367, 370-371, 379, 396, 411, 452, 466, 467, 473, 475, 514, 521

Islamic organizations 7, 40, 50, 61, 67, 71, 72, 80, 81, 85, 93, 100, 103, 113, 124-126, 128, 133, 157, 158, 162, 176, 178, 197, 201, 203, 211, 219, 221, 227, 258, 260, 261, 263, 268, 326, 345, 356, 357, 361, 367-370, 375, 376, 399, 430, 440, 452, 469, 477, 504, 527, 529

Islamic State 5-7, 11-13, 35, 46, 50, 54, 56, 62, 72-73, 80, 91, 93, 95-98, 100-102, 105, 107-112, 122, 124-127, 130, 132-134, 141, 150-157, 160, 163, 166-174, 176, 178-179, 182-184, 188-190, 192-195, 197, 200-203, 205, 206, 208-231, 233, 246, 252-254, 358-359, 261-262, 263, 267-271, 273-276, 277, 279, 285, 288, 299, 301-307, 311-312, 315-316, 318-319, 324, 326, 330, 333, 334, 339-340, 345-346, 349, 356, 358, 360-365, 368-372, 375, 376, 379, 383, 385-394, 396, 398, 399, 404-406, 409-414, 416-420, 422, 439, 440, 444, 452, 453, 458-461, 464-467, 468-471, 473-474, 475-482, 484, 485, 488-491, 494, 497, 498, 502, 504, 510-512, 514, 515, 525, 526, 531

application of Islamic law 80, 97, 101, 107, 109, 110-112, 150, 156-157, 160, 163, 169, 171, 174, 178, 179, 188, 192, 253, 258-259, 261, 301, 302, 303-304, 305-306, 369, 379, 383, 385, 387-388, 391, 392, 398, 409-410, 413-414, 422, 461, 464, 511-512

declaration of caliphate 95, 122, 346, 356, 360-361, 365, 366

rise and spread 13, 35, 46, 50, 72-73, 134, 203, 205-206, 208-209, 210-211, 213, 214, 219, 221, 268, 269, 270-271, 275, 339-340, 369, 526

Islamize, Islamization 49, 122

Islamophobia 41, 42, 445

Israeli-Palestinian hostilities 27, 70, 219

jāhilīya (era of ignorance) 87, 88, 119

Jews 11-27, 29-31, 37-42, 45-47, 52, 55-72, 76, 86, 87, 90, 95, 97, 99, 101, 102, 104-110, 112, 116, 118, 123, 125, 126, 137, 139, 142, 143, 144, 147, 149, 163, 165, 185, 192, 194, 233, 241, 250, 253, 279-281, 283-289, 290-295, 297, 301, 304, 305, 306-307, 315, 322, 324, 372, 384, 385, 400, 419, 432, 434, 440-441, 443, 444, 450, 456, 462, 465-466, 471-473, 477, 478, 503, 509, 517, 528

characterization in Islam 20, 21, 22, 23, 24, 26, 27, 38, 55, 56-59, 62-63, 64, 65-67, 72, 76, 90, 137, 165, 372, 419

enemies of Islam 11-14, 18-19, 21, 24, 25, 29-31, 37-40, 46-47, 56-57, 71, 139, 472

jihad 23, 47, 48, 61, 178, 215, 216, 218-222, 228, 229, 231, 257, 259, 260, 272, 273, 303, 313, 316-317, 320, 321, 323, 326, 329-332, 334, 336-338, 356, 358, 363, 368, 369, 380, 413, 440, 466-473, 486, 489, 492-494, 496-497, 505, 510, 512, 514

jihadist(s), jihadist groups 5, 7, 35, 47, 51, 62, 73, 80, 102, 113, 123, 156, 167, 169, 174, 178, 188, 193, 201, 204, 207, 213, 214, 217, 219-223, 225, 227-229, 231, 234, 246, 252, 262, 264, 269-271, 273, 275, 304, 321, 323, 326, 333, 337-341, 367, 399, 424, 427, 439, 458, 459, 461, 466, 468, 470, 486, 488, 489, 491, 493-499, 506, 512, 514, 517

jizya (head tax) 87, 95, 98, 100-102, 114-116, 133, 141, 168, 301, 310, 315, 319, 324, 450, 451, 456, 461, 503

Judaism 23, 38, 168

Ka'ba 173, 174, 242, 266, 308, 381, 495

kāfir, kuffār—SEE **infidel(s)**

Khawārij, Khārijites 155-157, 350-352

Khaybar *See also* **tribes (seventh century AD)** 26, 66, 110, 285, 287, 294-295, 297, 306-307, 310, 315, 483

kidnapping(s) 102, 124, 127, 128, 129, 132, 461

killing 6, 12, 13, 14, 20, 26, 33, 34, 38, 39, 41, 43, 44, 59, 61, 69-70, 88-89, 99, 100, 103, 108, 111, 115, 116, 120, 121, 124, 125, 128-130, 132, 133, 135, 140-141, 147-149, 150-151, 153-155, 157, 158-167, 176, 183, 184, 190-191, 192-193, 196, 197, 213, 222, 224, 225, 240-243, 245, 247, 249, 251-256, 257-259, 261-263, 264, 267, 268, 272, 273, 276, 277-279, 281, 282, 283-286, 288, 289, 290-293, 295, 296, 298, 305, 307-308, 309, 321, 322, 327, 330, 332, 336-337, 349, 351, 352, 354, 356, 357, 370-372, 380-384, 386, 388, 391, 392, 405-410, 411, 412, 414, 415, 416-418, 420-422, 423-424, 425, 427, 428-433, 435, 436, 437, 438, 439-444, 446, 451, 452, 453-454, 456-461, 464, 467, 468, 471-473, 475, 479, 480, 485, 488, 490-492, 493-495, 496-498, 500, 501-504, 508, 509, 512, 513-514, 522, 523, 525, 528-529, 531, 532

apostate Muslims 100, 135, 147, 150, 153-154, 155-156, 192-193, 196, 371, 372, 416, 437, 442-444, 467-468, 508-509, 523

early Islam 20, 43, 44, 99, 111, 116, 120, 121, 142, 151, 153, 155-156, 190-191, 240-243, 245, 247, 249, 254-256, 257, 281-282, 283, 289, 290-292, 293, 295, 307-308, 309, 349, 351, 352, 354, 366, 370, 372, 380, 381, 385, 386, 393, 415, 416, 420-422, 432-433, 440-442, 444, 467-468, 485

fatwa death sentences 158-160, 417, 429, 451

political assassinations 161, 384, 431, 432-433, 452, 522

Kurdish People's Protection Units (YPG) 194, 226

land of disbelief (*dār al-kufr*) 208, 210, 211-212, 215, 216, 217

land of Islam (*dār al-Islam*) 209, 211, 215-217, 461

language (Arabic) 18, 49, 55, 56, 62, 85, 89, 92, 97, 108, 133, 222, 314, 476, 522

Last Days 455, 456, 458, 459, 464, 467

Last Hour/Final Hour 59-61, 133, 274, 302, 455, 459, 460, 465

law codes (criminal) *See also* **penal code** 50, 161, 180, 182-184, 185, 389, 390, 392, 393, 396-397, 403, 404, 409, 410, 446

laws (secular) 50, 77, 88, 145, 147, 161, 162, 181, 190, 191, 210, 299, 409, 448, 482, 500, 505

League of Arab States—SEE **Arab League**

letter(s) 113, 114, 121, 240, 311, 312, 324, 333, 449-451

Levant (Syria) 86, 96, 105, 109, 110, 116, 121, 211, 215, 217, 221, 225, 231, 232, 275, 288, 304, 326, 334, 363, 371, 413, 439, 460, 462, 466, 467, 479, 490, 496, 530

lineage (Muḥammadan) 89-93, 350, 364, 366

"loyalty and disavowal" (*al-walā' wa al-barā'*) 39, 42, 43, 526

magic—SEE **sorcerer, sorcery**

marriage 54, 77, 89, 127, 129, 144-145, 178, 186, 196, 205, 206, 231, 296, 300, 315, 318, 333, 338-340, 372, 374, 505, 529

Islamic law 127, 129, 144, 145, 178, 186, 189, 196, 300, 340, 529

Muḥammad's marriages 89, 296, 318

"temporary" marriage (*al-mut'a*) 338-339

martyr(s), martyrdom 67, 118, 129, 225-227, 245, 248, 249, 282, 291, 300, 320-323, 325, 333, 334-338, 339, 340, 367, 369, 439, 468, 470-472, 492-493, 496, 505, 512, 513

paradise for 245, 248, 249, 300, 320-323, 333, 334-338, 341, 496

promotion of 367, 369, 468, 470-472, 492-493, 505, 512, 513

massacre(s) 14, 69, 70, 124, 125, 129-130, 157, 167, 193, 261, 277-279, 292, 369, 372, 382, 423, 427, 436, 439, 452-453

Mecca 43, 62, 64-65, 86, 104, 110, 111, 113, 126, 166, 174, 197-199, 204, 212-213, 217, 227, 230, 232, 238, 239, 241-245, 248, 250, 254, 260, 266-267, 279, 280, 282, 283, 286, 287, 294, 307-309, 314, 315, 316, 317, 318, 338-339, 351, 366, 373, 381, 384, 432, 504

Hijra from 86, 104, 126, 212-213, 217, 232, 279, 280, 317, 318, 504

conquest of 43, 166, 174, 314, 315, 338-339

media 7, 12-14, 23, 26, 27, 29, 30, 34, 42, 56, 71, 87, 90, 99, 122, 128, 134, 154, 179, 185, 188, 223, 256, 269, 272, 278, 296, 341, 379, 388, 396, 410, 411, 425, 426, 438, 446, 457, 480, 485-487, 504, 521-523, 526

jihadist groups and social media 163, 278, 341, 396, 480

reporting (biased/false/deceptive) 12-14, 34, 42, 87, 128, 457, 485, 486, 487, 521-523

Western media 30, 71, 154, 179, 223, 256, 269, 272, 298, 379, 425, 426, 485, 486, 504, 521

Medina 20, 69, 86, 104, 110, 111, 113-115, 121, 173, 205, 206, 208, 211, 212, 217, 227, 228, 230, 232, 235, 237-243, 249, 261, 264-268, 279-289, 291, 293-295, 307, 309, 317, 318, 347, 380, 393, 416, 417, 432, 433, 459, 460, 478

beginning of first Islamic state 217, 227, 228, 230, 235, 237-243, 249, 265-268, 279, 280, 281, 286-287, 290-293, 295, 307, 309, 310, 317, 432

confederacy attack on 287-289

Muhammad's migration to 20, 86, 110, 205, 212, 217, 230, 264, 280, 310, 317, 318, 347, 380

Mesopotamia 203, 204, 221, 319, 324, 362

Middle East 7, 12, 19, 21, 70, 82, 84, 97, 98, 116, 117, 128, 149, 158, 160, 197, 198, 334, 362, 380, 425, 477, 512, 521-523, 528

military tactics 225, 227, 233, 262, 310, 504

mind-set (Muslim) 6, 7, 14, 56, 68, 70, 90, 126, 210, 221, 274, 285, 332, 456, 463, 477, 505, 533

money *See also* **oil monies (Middle East)** 13, 24, 49, 60, 81, 100, 102, 105, 144, 148, 149, 151-153, 165, 188, 192, 196, 198, 206, 216, 219, 237-239, 243, 251, 252, 274, 275, 304, 307, 311, 319, 320, 322, 330, 338, 456, 480, 492, 514, 523, 527

revenues of early Muslims and caliphates 100, 148-149, 152, 165, 251, 304, 320, 322,

revenues of today's jihadist groups 13, 60, 102, 105, 188, 219, 148-149, 151, 152, 165, 219, 252, 275, 307, 319, 320, 330, 523, 527

mosque(s) 15, 18, 21, 42, 48-52, 56, 63-67, 95, 103, 105, 128, 134, 162, 169, 180, 182, 197, 200, 208, 213, 220, 221, 242, 259, 290, 326, 337, 344, 350, 352, 356, 366, 368, 375, 384, 395, 436, 437, 444, 449, 455, 478, 482, 484, 500, 501, 505, 507, 517, 518, 521, 526-528

funding of 42, 51, 517, 526

hate speech sermons 42, 48, 50-52, 56, 66-67, 103, 134, 208, 220-221, 436-437, 449, 501, 505, 517-518, 527-528

al-Mubāhala 114-115

Muhājirīn—SEE **Emigrants (Muhājirīn)**

mujahid, mujahidin *See also* **foreign fighters** 228, 260, 325

multinational coalition 457, 458, 465, 490, 494

Muslim(s) 6-8, 11-35, 37-47, 49-52, 54-72, 76-91, 93, 95-117, 119-174, 176-179, 182, 184, 186, 188-202, 204-223, 226, 228, 229, 233, 238-245, 247-251, 253-259, 262-268, 270-274, 279-285, 287-295, 297-311, 313-326, 328-330, 332-377, 379-392, 394-410, 413-418, 420-440, 442-445, 448-474, 477-512, 515-521, 523-527, 529, 531-533

emulation of Prophet Muhammad 110, 112, 113, 169, 254, 261, 299, 313, 320

schism, beginning of 347-352

Muslim Brotherhood 71, 158, 159, 161, 326, 345, 356, 368, 376

Muslim world 6, 16-18, 21, 23, 24, 28, 37, 40, 49, 50, 56, 62, 65, 70, 76-78, 80-82, 85, 132, 134, 140, 159, 160, 176, 220, 259, 301, 314, 336, 348, 353, 359, 362, 367, 381, 382, 384, 397, 417, 428, 430, 436, 437, 442, 445, 449, 453, 482, 485, 488, 489, 508, 519

denigration of Jews, Christians 16-18, 24, 40, 56, 65, 132, 140

demonstrations in 428, 430, 437, 445, 453

nafir 220

Najran Christians 113-116

National September 11 Memorial and Museum 326-328

newspaper(s) 8, 12, 14, 31, 33, 41, 57, 58, 60, 63, 69, 82, 187, 226, 228, 324, 325, 327, 395, 396, 399, 425-427, 436, 445, 452, 457-458, 486, 487

publications (Arabic) 8, 12, 14, 31, 57, 60, 167, 187, 324, 325, 327, 395, 399, 436, 457-458, 486, 487,

publications (Western) 8, 33, 69, 82, 226, 228, 327, 396, 399, 425-427, 445, 452, 457, 487

nonbeliever(s) *See also* **infidel(s); non-Muslims** 39, 43, 62, 111, 123, 140, 143, 256, 416, 431

non-Muslims *See also* **infidel(s); non-believers** 6, 12, 20, 32, 39, 41-46, 48, 49, 51, 57, 62-65, 68, 70-72, 76, 78, 79, 82, 86, 87, 89, 90, 93, 95, 99-102, 109, 122, 123, 127, 137, 140, 141, 143-146, 149, 163, 165, 177, 185, 193, 201, 209-211, 215, 221, 242, 259, 279, 285, 287, 293, 298, 301, 313, 315, 319, 354, 369-371, 391, 449, 451, 473, 484, 499, 502, 533

"inferiority" of 46, 62-65, 68, 72, 76, 78-79, 86, 89, 93, 140, 141, 143-146, 210, 315, 499

Muslim animosity toward 32, 39, 41-46, 49, 57, 63, 71-72, 90, 99, 102, 109, 122, 221, 259, 279, 285, 287, 298, 301, 369, 449, 473

North Africa (Ifriqiya) 19, 86, 116-119, 121, 149, 197, 198, 218, 302, 313, 319, 344, 352, 462, 477, 499, 500, 528

North Atlantic Treaty Organization (NATO) 22, 67, 85, 525

nullification 51, 257, 380

nullifiers (of Islam) 163, 164, 169, 176, 174, 182, 187, 192, 194, 195

nūn (ن) 103, 105-106

oil monies (Middle East) 12, 13, 60, 188, 219, 252, 275, 362, 391, 457, 518, 527

Open Source Jihad 498

Operation Desert Storm 457

Organization of Islamic Cooperation (OIC) 83, 84, 96, 447

"the others" 32, 34, 39, 53, 55, 56, 63, 65, 66, 68, 72, 76, 77, 79, 85, 89, 151

Palestine, Palestinian conflict *See also* **Israeli-Palestinian hostilities** 21, 38, 80, 310, 319, 362, 382, 460, 469, 471-473

paradise (Islamic) 129, 139, 142, 154, 156, 166, 195, 208, 214, 226, 245, 249, 251, 255, 283, 290, 300, 320, 321, 322, 323, 329, 331, 332, 333, 334-338, 340-341, 342, 358, 388, 391, 453, 470, 472, 488, 490, 493, 513, 521, 529, 533

pardon(s) 140, 142, 164, 184, 185, 300, 323, 401, 416, 441, 443, 520, 524

peace 45, 99, 105, 107, 113-116, 122, 140, 148, 149, 230, 233, 239, 241, 256, 280, 307, 310, 311, 362, 379-381, 383, 434, 483, 519, 527, 531

Islam, religion of 97, 99, 113, 256, 379, 383, 483, 519, 527

treaties of 115-116, 148, 233, 239, 280, 307, 310, 351, 362, 434

penal code(s) *See also* **criminal law** 184, 185, 198, 302, 389-390, 392, 393, 396, 397, 402-404, 409, 410, 446

People of the Book *See also* **Jews**; **Christians** 11, 20, 21, 29, 31, 58, 76, 104, 106, 107, 125, 137, 138, 142, 154, 166, 253, 285, 305, 315, 443

Persia, Persians 90, 92, 203, 249, 313, 319, 324

Persian Gulf states 82, 457, 517, 518, 523, 526

Persian Gulf War 22, 219

pilgrims, pilgrimage(s) 88, 153, 170, 190, 197, 240, 265, 266

Pillar(s) of Islam 15, 137, 152, 153, 162, 197, 201

pledge(s) *See also* **al-'Aqaba** 221, 230-233, 244, 265, 268, 280, 347-348, 357, 360, 361, 364-366, 368, 462, 502, 504

"plunging into the enemy" 489-491

poem(s) 106, 341, 363, 432, 471

police *See also* **Committee for the Promotion of Virtue and the Prevention of Vice (CPVPV)**; **Ḥisba** 32, 54, 69, 70, 127, 140, 179, 187, 190, 193, 198-199, 201, 262, 272, 395-396, 425, 427, 429, 438, 440, 452, 500

Muslim countries 32, 127, 140, 179, 187, 190, 193, 198-199, 201, 262, 395-396

Western countries 54, 69, 70, 272, 425, 427, 429, 438, 440, 452, 500

polytheists, polytheism *See also* **infidel(s)** 15, 26, 29, 47, 64, 67, 109, 110, 113, 123, 137, 139, 164-166, 168, 169, 171, 174, 176, 177, 192, 195, 208-210, 212, 216, 248, 259, 266, 302, 304, 305, 308-309, 372, 381, 383, 495

definition of 164-166

Muḥammad's policy toward 308-309

population(s) 12, 70, 71, 77, 82, 84, 87, 96-98, 108, 116-118, 121, 149, 167, 168, 229, 271, 298, 301, 302-303, 306, 365, 396, 459, 463, 469, 487, 495

Muslim peoples 12, 71, 82, 84, 97, 117, 167, 168, 229, 298, 301, 302-303, 305, 365, 396, 459, 463, 469, 487

non-Muslim peoples 70, 84, 87, 96, 98, 108, 116-117, 118, 121, 149, 167, 298, 463, 487

practices (religious) 6, 86, 98, 115, 133, 148, 169, 182, 183, 195, 198, 200, 201, 202, 209, 242, 275, 281, 316, 324, 370, 374, 381, 424, 478, 503, 511, 518

prayer 15-18, 22, 46, 50-51, 52, 62, 63, 75, 80, 81, 86, 95, 103, 104, 113, 114, 140, 147, 152, 153, 155, 179, 182, 183, 189, 195-198, 200-202, 245-246, 250, 259, 265, 269, 270 286, 303, 315, 348, 349, 351, 352, 363, 368, 370, 388, 395, 398, 415, 444, 457, 472, 492, 509, 510, 511, 514, 517, 528

abandonment of prayer 195-198, 415

special types of 15, 16, 17, 51, 104, 140, 153, 265, 286, 363, 398

principle(s) 40, 44, 45, 50, 96, 112, 141, 145, 153, 161, 178-179, 208, 210, 221, 315, 321, 365, 370, 371, 415, 489, 490, 496, 512, 528

prison, prisoners *See also* **imprisonment** 111, 127, 129, 159, 179, 180, 184, 186, 193, 196, 201, 213, 248, 251, 253, 262, 268-273, 293, 309, 395, 418, 419, 476, 520, 524, 525

propaganda 87, 88, 128, 221, 224, 229, 231, 252, 333, 352, 361, 362, 412, 418, 440, 465, 466, 487, 498, 517, 521, 523

prophesy, prophesies 16, 61, 91, 455-459, 463, 464, 465, 467, 481, 495

prophet(s) *See also* **MUḤAMMAD, Prophet** in Name Index 16, 19, 26, 52, 85, 89, 93, 169, 171, 186, 204, 232, 250, 261, 280, 281, 442, 446, 464

prophethood 19, 104, 165, 249, 280, 291, 318, 319, 346, 354-356, 363, 376, 443, 485

prophetic methodology 354-355

punishment(s) (*ḥudūd*) 50, 81, 88, 139, 141, 142, 153, 159, 175, 176, 178, 180, 182-184, 187, 190, 192, 194, 197, 201, 208, 387-418, 421, 431, 433, 435, 442-445, 446, 452, 510, 511, 524

Qur'ān 6, 13, 16-18, 21-23, 25, 27, 28, 30, 41-46, 54, 57, 58, 61-64, 72, 75, 76, 79, 80, 87-89, 97-99, 102-104, 108, 111, 112, 122, 129, 137-140, 143, 144, 148, 151, 155, 156, 163, 165, 166, 170, 171, 173, 176, 177, 180, 183, 184, 187-194, 199, 204, 206-209, 212-214, 216, 248, 253, 255-263, 276, 297, 298, 300-304, 310, 314-317, 320, 326, 329, 331-333, 336, 337, 347, 349, 351, 355, 370, 371, 379, 382, 383, 385, 387, 388, 390, 391, 393, 394, 399, 406, 414, 415, 422, 425, 429, 431, 445, 446, 461, 468, 476, 484-486, 488, 490, 492, 493, 497, 506, 510, 511

burning of 129, 425, 484-485

criticism of 445-446

Muslim view of 21, 23, 89, 102, 165, 301, 394, 422

supremacy of rulings 156, 177-178, 253, 326,

Quraysh 19, 43, 44, 90-92, 110, 111, 113, 126, 156, 166, 170, 185, 212, 213, 217, 227, 230-232, 237-251, 253, 254, 260, 261, 264-267, 273, 277, 278, 280-283, 286, 287, 289, 293, 294, 307-309, 311, 317, 324, 348-351, 364-366, 373, 381, 382, 384, 432, 453, 473, 504

Islam's/Muhammad's view of 90, 91, 92, 170, 273, 364-365, 366, 373

Muslim subjugation and assimilation of 307-309

rejection of Muhammad and his call 19, 237, 241-242, 250, 264, 265, 266, 317

radicalization 174, 223, 271, 272, 473

raid(s)—SEE **"expeditions" and raids (early Muslim)**

Ramadan *See also* **holy days** 110, 182, 183, 197, 256, 259, 368, 423, 529

ransom(s) 248-252, 275, 443

rape 22, 77, 167, 294, 296, 298, 299, 301, 316, 392, 420

rational choice theory, rational action theory 513-514

reforms (religious) 199, 449, 516, 518-521, 527

refugees 223, 381, 405, 479, 527, 530, 531

"regions of savagery" 228-230

religion(s)—SEE **Christianity**; **Islam**; **Judaism**

religiosity 75, 76, 79, 80, 184, 457, 458

repentance 45, 46, 103, 166, 175, 176, 180, 183, 186, 191, 196, 197, 215, 251, 273, 290, 315, 388, 398, 401, 443, 444

residency (unlawful) 209-210, 211-212, 215-217

revelation(s) 19, 28, 102, 114, 195, 204, 241, 242, 251, 256, 318

revolution(s) (Arab) 67, 80, 81, 128, 161, 268, 356, 402

Ridda Wars (Wars of Apostasy) 152-153, 349, 361, 370, 417

sacred month(s) 103, 240-242, 247, 315

Salafism, Salafists 7, 25, 33, 103, 124, 127, 128, 161, 209, 272, 316, 407, 408, 451, 478, 511

schools of jurisprudence (Islamic) 24, 147, 163, 188, 191, 196, 209, 304, 366, 406, 408, 413, 422, 443-445, 461, 490, 508

sculpture 125, 170-174, 176

sects (religious) 45, 154, 155, 168, 183, 302, 325, 369-372, 402, 451, 468, 511

secularism 49, 157, 178, 181, 333, 346, 362, 457, 515, 520, 523, 528, 532

September 11, 2001 (9/11) 5, 12, 32, 33, 326, 327, 425, 428, 489, 492, 494, 496, 531

sharī'a 24, 50, 71, 80, 81, 88, 95, 100, 107, 127, 133, 142, 145-148, 151, 158, 159, 162, 163, 169, 177-179, 182, 192, 194, 200, 201, 219, 258, 301-305, 353, 358, 365-367, 381-383, 387, 391-393, 398, 404, 432, 438, 493, 500

Shiites 45, 150, 153, 157, 227, 234, 259, 278, 338, 348, 365, 369, 370, 371, 372, 372, 402, 414, 415, 446, 447, 511, 522

shrine(s) 169-171, 176, 190, 191

siege(s) 57, 69, 103, 104, 129-130, 167-168, 281, 284, 286, 287, 289-290, 295, 306, 309, 319, 366, 462-463, 464, 478

sin(s) 65, 88, 142, 156, 163-165, 169, 170, 175, 201, 207, 209, 216, 242, 271, 300, 322, 323, 360, 401, 402, 406, 431, 518

- forgiveness of 65, 207, 300, 322, 323, 401
- greatest sin 164-165
- major sins 142, 156, 169, 170, 209, 242, 406, 431

Sinjar 167-168, 298-299, 301, 481

slave(s), slavery 57, 85, 86-87, 121, 167, 206-207, 287, 290, 292, 293, 294, 297, 298, 299, 301-302, 303, 304-306, 310, 315, 316, 322, 329, 340, 349, 359, 441-442, 511, 514, 518

early Islam 57, 87, 121, 287, 290, 292, 293, 297, 302, 303, 304-305, 310, 322, 329, 349, 359, 441-442, 518

Islamic legalization of 303, 304

sex slaves 206-207, 294, 299, 301, 303, 306, 316, 340, 511, 514

sleeper cell(s) 161, 204, 452, 530

slurs 58, 62-63, 68, 90, 138

smoking 81, 200

Sodom and Gomorrah 405-406, 408

sodomy—SEE **homosexuals, homosexuality**

sorcerer(s), sorcery 26, 53-55, 66, 130, 131, 187-192

spoils—SEE **booty**

spy, spies 193-194, 240, 418-419, 468, 532

Statistical Economic and Social Research and Training Centre for Islamic Countries (SESRIC) 83-84

statue(s)—SEE **art**; **sculpture**

stereotype(s), stereotyping 26, 29, 30, 34, 77, 447

stoning 50, 81, 178, 182, 338, 350, 387, 398-404, 406-409, 421, 510, 511

Sufism 169, 191, 195, 511

suicide attacks/operations 225-227, 341, 475, 488, 490, 492, 493, 496, 504, 513

suicide bombers, bombings 68, 193, 226, 227, 259, 468, 475, 488, 490, 491, 493, 502, 504, 514, 525

sunna 16, 52, 184, 260, 301, 363

Sunna 16, 180, 184, 203, 208, 253, 258, 259, 269, 276, 302, 320, 379, 383, 385, 387, 389, 390, 401, 402, 408, 410, 413, 422, 451, 492, 493

Sunnis 18, 21, 24, 45, 90, 102, 107, 151, 188, 193, 206, 222, 227, 230, 231, 233, 234, 269, 277-278, 316, 325, 340, 348, 355, 365, 370-372, 402, 403, 407, 408, 413, 444, 446, 489, 511, 519, 522

collaboration with Islamic State (ISIL, ISIS) 206, 227, 230, 231, 233, 234, 269, 277-278

relations with Shiites 45, 151, 234, 348, 365, 370-372, 446, 511, 522

sword(s) 87, 95, 115, 120, 125, 126, 153, 156, 166-168, 181, 183, 184, 247, 254, 260, 274, 296, 313, 316-318, 320, 322, 324, 326, 344, 348, 352, 363, 366, 367, 369, 380, 381, 383, 388, 408, 420-421, 440, 442, 443, 463, 469, 471, 473, 490

execution/punishment by 153, 184, 408, 440, 443

use to coerce conversion 95, 125, 126, 166-168, 313, 316-318, 348

Sword verse (Q 9.5) 103, 165, 257, 315, 369

Sykes-Picot Agreement 223, 362

Syrian Observatory for Human Rights (SOHR) 387, 398-399, 406

takfīr 150, 151, 153-157, 160-163, 176, 523, 524, 526, 527

Taliban 172, 396, 399, 511, 515

taqīya 45

tax(es), taxation—SEE ***jizya***; ***zakāt***

technology 49, 81, 91, 122, 515, 520

television *See also* ***Daring Question*** 6, 8, 17, 20, 21, 23, 24, 32, 34, 48, 49, 54, 58-60, 66, 97, 103, 106, 111, 128, 131, 136, 161, 271, 285, 327, 340, 344, 381, 382, 429-431, 438, 449, 471, 486, 493, 512, 522, 529

terrorism, terrorists 5-8, 11-14, 32, 46, 47, 69, 110, 113, 129, 130, 132, 134, 157, 187-188, 190, 192, 201, 204, 205, 224, 229, 252, 259, 262-264, 268, 270-273, 311, 313, 328, 342, 349, 365, 371, 376, 381, 387, 411, 418, 420, 422, 424-427, 435-436, 440, 448, 449, 451, 452, 453, 475-477, 479-480, 481, 482-488, 489, 490, 491, 496, 498, 499, 501, 502, 503-506, 510, 512, 513, 515, 517-519, 522, 524-527, 529-531, 533

current status 5

pinnacle of expansion, wealth 7, 275

recent policies and strategies 371, 481, 498, 502, 503, 504

worst enemy of 252-253

tomb(s) 125, 169-170, 174, 326, 532

Torah 21, 59, 63, 104, 332

Treaty of Ḥudaybīya 266-267, 294, 311

treaty, treaties 105, 115-116, 142, 148, 238, 266, 267, 288, 294, 302, 307, 310, 311, 319, 362, 437

tree(s) 59, 60, 81, 104, 105, 206, 257, 284, 322, 327-328, 456, 478

tribes (Arab) *See also* **Banū Hāshim (Muhammad's clan)**; **Quraysh** 57, 75, 89-90, 91, 92, 93, 113-115, 151, 152-153, 156, 168, 203, 204, 205, 227, 228, 230-233, 235, 238, 239, 240-241, 247, 264, 265, 266, 274, 275, 279, 280-281, 286-290, 293-294, 298, 309, 310, 316, 319, 324, 348-349, 350-352, 361, 380, 400, 408, 417, 419-421, 433, 449, 465, 495

Medinan tribes 57, 205, 217, 228, 230, 231-233, 235, 288, 293

Muslim violence toward 152-153, 156, 168, 203, 227, 230, 233, 238, 240-242, 243-247, 275, 286, 287, 293, 298, 307, 308-310, 316-317, 319, 324, 348-349, 350-352, 361, 380, 465, 495

tribes (seventh century AD) *See also* **Khaybar** 26, 55, 57, 69, 103-105, 185, 279, 280, 281-282, 283-286, 287, 290, 293, 294-295, 296, 297, 304, 306-307, 310, 315, 318, 384, 420, 478, 483

Banū al-Naḍīr (Jewish) 26, 69, 103-105, 283-286, 287, 288, 290, 293, 296, 297, 318, 420, 478

Banū Qurayẓa (Jewish) 57, 279, 288-293, 297, 304, 310, 384

Banū Qaynuqāʿ (Jewish) 69, 281-282, 290, 293

Trinity (Christian) 118, 136, 137

Twitter 34, 278, 340, 411, 418, 437, 471, 481

ultimatums 95, 96, 98, 102, 109, 259, 282, 457, 511, 517, 518

Umayyads 64, 87, 120, 352-355, 366, 384, 385, 459, 462-464

umra 266

United Nations (UN) 67, 85, 96, 168, 217, 299, 302, 405, 425, 457, 515

United Nations Commission on Human Rights (UNCHR) 447

United Nations Educational, Scientific, and Cultural Organization (UNESCO) 171

university, universities *See also* **Al Azhar** 18, 23, 24, 28, 60, 71, 82-83, 92, 107, 108, 146, 159, 192, 219-220, 223, 258, 271, 442, 458, 461, 469, 482, 519, 520, 523

institutions (Muslim) 18, 23, 24, 60, 71, 107, 82-83, 92, 146, 159, 192, 219-220, 258, 442, 458, 461, 469, 482, 519, 520

institutions (Western) 28, 82, 92, 108, 223, 523

verse(s) *See also* **Sword verse (Q 9.5)** 16-18, 17, 20-25, 27-31, 39-43, 44, 45, 54, 57-58, 62, 63, 64-65, 71-72, 75, 76, 78, 80, 88, 99, 100, 102, 103, 104-105, 111, 112, 114, 124-125, 136-140, 143, 144, 146, 148, 151, 164-165, 166, 170, 171-172, 173, 174, 176, 177-178, 180, 182, 183, 187, 189, 190, 192, 194, 195, 199, 204-205, 206, 207, 208, 212, 213, 214, 215, 216, 242, 244, 245, 246, 249, 250, 251, 255-258, 261, 263, 266, 273, 274, 283-285, 297, 300-302, 303, 306, 310, 315, 317, 320, 322, 326, 329, 331-332, 334, 335-337, 340, 347, 355, 357, 359, 361, 363, 369, 371, 379, 380, 382-384, 387, 388, 391, 393, 394, 399, 400, 403, 410, 414, 415, 418, 419, 426, 429, 432, 434, 437, 439, 471, 473-474, 478, 488, 490, 493, 509, 511

enemies, fighting and killing 27, 43, 99, 102, 103, 111, 148, 165, 195, 242, 244, 246, 251, 256-258, 261, 263, 283, 310, 320, 326, 334, 380, 382-384, 391, 410, 437, 478

enmity, hatred toward Christians, Jews, nonbelievers 20-21, 24, 25, 29, 31, 39, 41, 44, 57-58, 62, 71-72, 103, 104-105, 111, 124-125, 137-140, 144, 148, 151, 165-166, 177, 192, 195, 215, 242, 250, 255, 256-258, 261, 263, 285, 326, 329, 383, 410, 474, 493

jihad 23, 80, 207, 214, 245, 246, 256-258, 263, 303, 315, 320, 331-332, 488

victim(s) 23, 56, 69, 99, 116, 132, 142, 143, 151, 157, 158, 193, 194, 222, 224, 278, 279, 315, 327, 328, 349, 385, 387, 393, 398, 405, 406, 419, 423, 424, 436, 437, 441, 453, 454, 477, 482, 484, 485, 494, 496, 498, 499, 505

attacks 23, 69, 157, 193, 222, 327-328, 349, 423, 424, 436, 453, 494, 496, 498

brutalities 99, 132, 194, 224, 278, 279, 315, 385, 387, 393, 398, 405-406

video(s) 18, 33, 34, 47-48, 51, 56, 66-67, 68, 78, 97, 106, 124, 125, 128, 129, 133, 134, 136, 160, 161, 166, 167, 170-173, 193, 220, 222-224, 231, 256, 259, 262, 263, 277-278, 285, 303, 316, 321, 324, 325, 333, 341, 356-364, 366, 368, 369, 376, 382, 385-388, 393, 398, 399, 405, 410-414, 417-419, 424, 428, 438-440, 452, 460, 461, 466-468, 470, 479, 529, 531

executions, graphic 124, 125, 133, 160, 193, 223-224, 256, 259, 262, 263, 277-278, 369, 385-386, 387, 388, 398-399, 405, 410-413, 414, 417, 418-419, 460, 461, 470

Innocence of Muslims 33-34, 428, 452

jihadi recruitment 47-48, 220, 222-223, 231, 321, 356, 357-362, 363, 364, 366, 466-467, 468

propaganda against US, "the others" 18, 51, 56, 66-67, 134, 136, 223, 333, 358, 362-363, 412, 438-440

virgins (heavenly)—SEE **houris**

Wahhabism 24, 164, 188, 316, 375, 396, 490, 517, 518, 527

al-walā' wa-l-barā' (loyalty and disavowal) 39, 42-43, 526

war(s) *See also* **Fitna wars; Ridda Wars (Wars of Apostasy)** 22-24, 27, 33-35, 46, 47, 61, 67, 68, 84, 91, 96, 110, 113-115, 131, 149, 152-153, 156-157, 193, 203, 204, 212, 214, 218, 219, 220, 222, 225, 226, 227, 229, 230, 232-234, 238-240, 243, 245, 247, 249, 257, 261, 263, 264, 269, 280-281, 284, 287-290, 293, 295, 299, 305, 307, 310-312, 313, 317, 318, 326, 333, 339, 348-351, 353, 354, 361, 362, 370, 374, 376, 382-383, 386, 391, 417, 418, 450, 451, 457, 458, 460-461, 465-466, 470, 472, 475, 477, 494, 495, 503, 518, 519, 522

faith and misbelief, holy war of 46-47, 114, 220, 326, 465-466, 477

Iraq 24, 96, 204, 219, 229, 234

Islamic/Muslim attitude toward US intervention 22-23, 33-35, 193, 219, 226, 494

Libya 22, 33, 67, 229

Persian Gulf 22, 219

Syria 214, 222, 226, 229, 326, 376, 460

war crime(s) 269, 279, 299, 475

water 15, 111, 167, 246-247, 293, 327-328, 337, 393, 415, 419-420, 462

West, Western countries *See also* **countries (non-Muslim)** 6, 14, 18, 19, 22, 23, 24, 28, 30-32, 35, 37, 40, 41, 42, 45, 47-50, 54, 55-57, 61, 62, 67-68, 72, 76-78, 80, 83-85, 86, 88, 89, 90, 122, 123, 128, 134, 151, 160, 172, 174, 179, 180, 181-182, 184, 187, 190, 198, 209-212, 214, 217, 223, 224, 225, 226, 252, 253, 267, 311, 326, 328, 330, 333-334, 346, 362, 371, 381, 389, 403, 435-436, 439, 442, 445, 447, 448, 456, 457-458, 462, 465, 466, 476-477, 479, 480, 481, 482-486, 488, 491, 498, 499-500, 501, 502, 504-506, 512, 514-516, 517-518, 520-521, 523, 524, 526-530

ignorance of 24, 30, 77-78, 179, 210-211, 214, 253, 326, 333-334, 435-436, 476-477, 480, 504, 505-506, 512, 527

Muslim attitude toward 19, 22, 37, 40, 42, 48, 49, 56-57, 67-68, 72, 77, 85, 86, 89, 90, 134, 179, 267, 330, 362, 482, 500, 505

Muslim perception of 14, 18, 30-32, 35, 37, 48, 49-50, 56-57, 67, 76-78, 85, 89, 90, 123, 182, 209, 330, 346, 457-458, 479, 485-486, 499-500

wife, wives 6, 19, 34, 50, 55, 66, 87, 89, 114, 127-129, 161, 167, 175, 179, 184, 186, 189, 201, 204, 205, 207, 209, 215, 296, 297, 299, 300, 306, 311, 318, 328, 335-336, 339, 340, 351, 388, 394, 401, 404, 420, 421, 441, 442, 446, 470, 495, 501, 503, 505, 510, 511, 514

behavior and dress 87-88, 201

polygamy 297, 510-511

widows 34, 50, 161, 296, 318, 339, 351, 404

witch(es), witchcraft *See also* **sorcerer(s)**, **sorcery** 54, 55, 66, 130, 131, 187-192

woman, women 26, 27, 48, 50, 57, 66, 69, 88, 89, 120, 124, 127-130, 144, 145, 167-168, 186, 189, 192, 198-201, 206, 216, 230, 231, 233, 249, 257-258, 281, 282, 291-298, 300-306, 308, 309, 315, 316, 320, 334-336, 338-339, 359, 384, 387, 388, 394, 397-404, 408, 409, 421, 426, 429, 432, 440-441, 458, 469, 470, 472, 495, 498, 510, 511, 514, 515, 529

enslavement of 57, 167-168, 291-292, 293, 294-296, 297-298, 300, 301-302, 303, 304, 305-306, 309, 316, 514

Jewish Khaybar woman 26, 27, 66, 120

killing of 257-258, 384, 387, 398-399, 400-401, 402, 403, 404, 421, 440-441, 495, 498

World Heritage site(s) 171-172, 406, 470

World Trade Center 12, 32, 326, 327, 381, 398, 481, 491

World War I 91, 353, 362, 374

World War II 67, 376

Yazidi(s) 157, 166-168, 207, 297-299, 301, 303, 315, 316, 523

youth, young people (Muslim) 24, 42, 46-48, 50, 51, 57, 77, 72, 79, 80, 108, 113, 323, 359, 361, 369, 375-377, 465, 479, 488, 528

zakāt 152, 348-349, 420, 492

Printed in France by Amazon
Brétigny-sur-Orge, FR

16541165R00333